APPLIED MULTIVARIATE STATISTICS FOR THE SOCIAL SCIENCES

JAMES STEVENS
University of Cincinnati

LEA LAWRENCE ERLBAUM ASSOCIATES, PUBLISHERS
1986   Hillsdale, New Jersey   London

Lawrence Erlbaum Associates, Inc., Publishers
365 Broadway
Hillsdale, New Jersey 07642

Library of Congress Cataloging in Publication Data

Stevens, James.
  Applied multivariate statistics for the social
sciences.

  Bibliography: p.
  Includes index.
  1. Multivariate analysis.   2. Social sciences—
Statistical methods.   I. Title.
QA278.S74   1986   519.5'35'024301   86-16796
ISBN 0-89859-568-1
ISBN 0-8058-0254-1 pbk.

Printed in the United States of America
10   9   8   7   6   5   4   3

Table of Contents

Preface

This book is directed toward those who will be using, rather than developing, advanced statistical methods. Many of the most popular and useful methods have been included: multiple regression, multivariate analysis of variance (MANOVA), discriminant analysis, analysis of covariance, principal components and repeated measures analysis. For these analyses, a computer is needed for running all but the most trivial data sets. Fortunately, there is high quality software available, and in this book two of the major statistical packages (SPSSX and BMDP) are featured. This was done because in actual practice analyses will *very likely* be run on one or more of these packages due to their quality, wide availability, and ease of use. Interpretation of the printout is crucial, and in this text selected printout is annotated to indicate what the various numbers mean. Because these packages are so easy to use, however, there is the danger of obtaining results which have an aura of sophistication but which indeed may be sample-specific, or which may be misleading. In an attempt to counter this, while still indicating how to use the packages effectively, I have stressed the importance of checking the data, checking for outliers, assessing assumptions and having adequate sample size (by providing guidelines) so that results are generalizable.

The book differs from most other multivariate texts in several ways:

1. There is extensive applied coverage of MANOVA, including thorough discussion of assumptions in MANOVA, multivariate planned comparisons and estimation of power.
2. Complete, annotated control lines are given for every analysis.
3. Selected, annotated printout is presented for every analysis considered. For clarity, the printout has been typeset.
4. There is an emphasis on the assumptions underlying the analyses, and the reader is shown how to effectively use the statistical packages to test those assumptions.
5. Statistical power is given special attention. Power tables, not available in any other textbook as far as I can ascertain, are given for 2 and k group MANOVA.

6. The danger of capitalization on chance, due to the mathematical maximization nature of many of the multivariate procedures, is stressed. The need for large samples for reliable results is emphasized, and sample size guidelines are given for reliable results in multiple regression, discriminant analysis, factor analysis and canonical correlation.
7. Numerous exercises involving a mixture of conceptual, numerical, and computer-related problems are provided for most chapters and answers are given for about half the exercises.

My concern in the book is with conceptual understanding, *not* on proving results. Most social scientists don't have the mathematical background to adequately benefit from a theoretical treatment. Furthermore, even for those who do, it is important to first have a conceptual understanding of what the statistical procedures are accomplishing, and concrete examples of the use of each procedure. Thus, in this book *considerable narrative* discussion is used to enhance understanding. If an instructor, however, wishes to supplement this text with some theoretical material there are several good books available, among which I would highly recommend Bock (1975), Johnson and Wichern (1982) and Morrison (1976).

The background assumed of the reader is two quarter courses in statistics, covering through factorial analysis of variance. The book is written primarily as a text for graduate students, although it should be useful as a reference for applied researchers with little or no training in multivariate methods. The mathematical level of the text has been kept deliberately low. While I do use matrices, since they are the natural way to view multivariate data, I do not assume a knowledge of matrix algebra. A full chapter is devoted to explaining the basic operations with matrices. Also, matrices are not heavily used in the book.

While the range of topics in the text is fairly broad, some choices had to be made, partly because of size considerations. Since a thorough, applied discussion of multivariate analysis of variance didn't exist in social science texts, it was decided to emphasize this topic, along with related topics such as analysis of covariance and repeated measures analysis. Principal components analysis is a useful variable reduction procedure, so it has been included. However, both the scope and mathematical level required to treat factor analysis would have taken us too far afield. Furthermore, there are some good social science texts on this topic (Gorsuch, 1983). Also, although I have included a substantial chapter on multiple regression, obviously all important aspects (e.g., causal modeling) can't be covered in just one chapter. But, again there are good texts on multiple regression which provide the additional coverage (Cohen & Cohen, 1983; Pedhazur, 1982).

A few comments on how a course(s) might be structured from this book. At the University of Cincinnati I have offered a two quarter sequence on multivariate methods for several years, in which I typically have a mixture of graduate students from education, psychology, and from the College of Business. The first quarter course is devoted to regression and correlation, and chapters 1, 2, 3, 11, and 12 are covered. The second quarter course deals with multivariate tests of group differences, and chapters 4 through 7 (dealing with MANOVA and discriminant analysis), along with some material on repeated measures are appropriate. I have found that because of the amount of material on repeated measures and because of the complexity of some of it, that it is better to cover repeated measures along with multivariate analysis of covariance in a separate third quarter seminar.

There are many individuals to thank. I learned a great deal about multivariate statistics from two of my teachers, Paul Lohnes and Jeremy Finn. Darrell Bock, through his writings and textbook, has greatly influenced my thinking. I have had numerous interesting statistical discussions with Robert Barcikowski, with whom I have offered many multivariate workshops throughout the country. I especially wish to thank Scott Maxwell who reviewed the entire manuscript, for a very thorough, thoughtful and detailed critique. I have followed most of his suggestions. Earl Alluisi reviewed several chapters and made many useful suggestions. There are many colleagues at the University of Cincinnati who read one or more chapters, and who improved the clarity of the presentation. Listed alphabetically, they are: Dave Barnett, Ellen Cook, J. Howard Johnston, Glenn Markle, Roger Steubing, Dan Wheeler and Bob Wilson.

I dedicate this book to my mother, who sacrificed much so that I would have the opportunity to write the book, and to my wife, Florence. So finally, after many, many iterations I can say the book is a fait accompli.

James Stevens

1
Introduction

1.1. INTRODUCTION

Studies in the social sciences comparing two or more groups very often measure their subjects on several criterion variables. The following are some examples. A researcher is comparing two methods of teaching second grade reading. On a posttest he measures the subjects on the following basic elements related to reading: syllabication, blending, sound discrimination, reading rate, and comprehension. A social psychologist is testing the relative efficacy of 3 treatments on self concept, and measures the subjects on the academic, emotional, and social aspects of self concept. Two different approaches to stress management are being compared. The investigator employs a couple of paper and pencil measures of anxiety (say the State-Trait Scale and the Subjective Stress Scale) and some physiological measures. Another example would be comparing two types of counseling (Rogerian and Adlerian) on client satisfaction and client self acceptance. A major part of this text involves the statistical analysis of several groups on a set of criterion measures simultaneously, i.e., multivariate analysis of variance, the multivariate referring to the multiple dependent variables.

Cronbach and Snow (1977), writing on aptitude-treatment interaction research, have echoed the need for multiple criterion measures:

Learning is multivariate, however. Within any one task a persons's performance at a point in time can be represented by a set of scores describing aspects of the performance . . . even in laboratory research on rote learning, performance can be assessed by multiple indices: errors, latencies and resistance to extinction, for example. These are only moderately correlated, and do not necessarily develop at

1

the same rate. In the paired associates task, subskills have to be acquired: discriminating among and becoming familiar with the stimulus terms, being able to produce the response terms, and tying response to stimulus. If these attainments were separately measured, each would generate a learning curve, and there is no reason to think that the curves would echo each other. (p. 116)

There are three good reasons why the use of multiple criterion measures in a study comparing treatments (such as teaching methods, counseling methods, types of reinforcement, diets, etc.) is very sensible:

1. Any worthwhile treatment will affect the subjects in more than one way. Hence the problem for the investigator is to determine in which specific ways the subjects will be affected, and then find sensitive measurement techniques for those variables.
2. Through the use of multiple criterion measures we can obtain a more complete and detailed description of the phenomenon under investigation, whether it is teacher method effectiveness, counselor effectiveness, diet effectiveness, stress management technique effectiveness, etc.
3. Treatments can be expensive to implement, while the cost of obtaining data on several dependent variables is relatively small, and maximizes information gain.

Since we define a multivariate study as one with several dependent variables, multiple regression (where there is only one dependent variable) and principal components analysis would not be considered multivariate techniques. However, our distinction is more semantic than substantive. Therefore, since regression and components analysis are so important and frequently used in social science research, we include them in this text.

We have four major objectives for the remainder of this chapter:

1. To review some basic concepts (e.g., type I error and power) and some issues associated with univariate analysis, but that are equally important in multivariate analysis.
2. To discuss the importance of identifying outliers, i.e., points which split off from the rest of the data, and deciding what to do about them. We give some examples to show the considerable impact outliers can have on the results in univariate analysis.
3. To give research examples of some of the multivariate analyses to be covered later in the text, and to indicate how these analyses involve generalizations of what the student has previously learned.
4. To introduce the SPSSX and BMDP statistical packages, whose outputs are discussed throughout the text.

1.2. TYPE I ERROR, TYPE II ERROR AND POWER

Suppose we have randomly assigned 15 subjects to a treatment group and 15 subjects to a control group, and are comparing them on a single measure of task performance (a univariate study, since a single dependent variable). The reader may recall that the t test for independent samples is appropriate here. We wish to determine whether the difference in the sample means is large enough, given sampling error, to suggest that the underlying population means are different. Since the sample means estimate the population means, they will generally be in error (i.e., they will not hit the population values right "on the nose"), and this is called sampling error. We wish to test the null hypothesis (H_0) that the population means are equal:

$$H_0 : \mu_1 = \mu_2$$

It is called the null hypothesis because saying the population means are equal is equivalent to saying that the difference in the means is 0, i.e., $\mu_1 - \mu_2 = 0$, or that the difference is null.

Now, statisticians have determined that if we had populations with equal means and drew samples of size 15 repeatedly and computed a t statistic each time, then 95% of the time we would obtain t values in the range -2.048 to 2.048. The so-called sampling distribution of t under H_0 would look like:

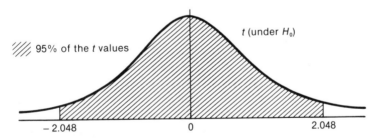

This sampling distribution is extremely important for it gives us a frame of reference for judging what is a large value of t. Thus, if our t value was 2.56 it would be very plausible to reject the H_0, since obtaining such a large t value is *very unlikely* when H_0 is true. Note, however, that if we do so there is a chance we have made an error, since it is possible (although very improbable) to obtain such a large value for t, even when the population means are equal. In practice, one must decide how much of a risk of making the above type of error (called a type I error) they wish to take. Of course, one would want that risk to be small, and many have decided a 5% risk is small. This is formalized in hypothesis testing by saying that we set our level of significance (α) at the .05 level. That is, we are willing to take a 5% chance of making a type I error.

In other words, *type I error (level of significance) is the probability of rejecting the null hypothesis when it is true.*

Recall that the formula for degrees of freedom for the t test is $(n_1 + n_2 - 2)$; hence for this problem $df = 28$. If we had set $\alpha = .05$, then reference to Table B in the Appendix of this book shows that the critical values are -2.048 and 2.048. They are called critical values since they are critical to the decision we will make on H_0. These critical values define critical regions in the sampling distribution. If the value of t falls in the critical region we reject H_0; otherwise we fail to reject:

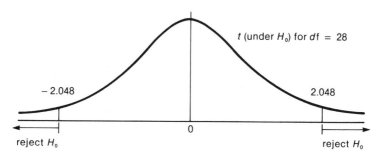

Type I error is equivalent to saying the groups differ when in fact they don't. The α level set by the experimenter is a subjective decision, but is usually set at .05 or .01 by most researchers. There are situations, however, when it makes sense to use α levels other than .05 or .01. For example, if making a type I error will not have serious substantive consequences, or if sample size is small, setting $\alpha = .10$ or .15 is quite reasonable. Why this is reasonable for small sample size will be made clear shortly. On the other hand, suppose we are in a medical situation where the null hypothesis is equivalent to saying a drug is unsafe, and the alternative is that the drug is safe. Here making a type I error could be quite serious, for we would be declaring the drug safe when it is not safe. This could cause some people to be permanently damaged or perhaps even killed. In this case it would make sense to take α very small, perhaps .001.

There is another type of error that can be made in conducting a statistical test, and this is called a type II error. Type II error, denoted by β, is the probability of accepting H_0, when it is false, i.e., saying the groups don't differ when they do. Now, not only can either type of error occur, but in addition they are inversely related. Thus, as we control on type I error, type II error increases. This is illustrated below for a two group problem with 15 subjects per group:

α	β	$1 - \beta$
.10	.37	.63
.05	.52	.48
.01	.78	.22

Notice that as we control on α more severely (from .10 to .01), type II error increases fairly sharply (from .37 to .78). Therefore, the problem for the experimental planner is achieving an appropriate balance between the two types of errors. While we do not intend to minimize the seriousness of making a type I error, we hope to convince the reader throughout the course of this text that much more attention should be paid to type II error. Now, the quantity in the last column of the above table $(1 - \beta)$ is the *power of a statistical test, which is the probability of rejecting the null hypothesis when it is false.* Thus, power is the probability of making a correct decision, or saying the groups differ when in fact they do. Notice from the above table that as the α level decreases, power also decreases. The diagram in Figure 1.1 should help to make clear why this happens.

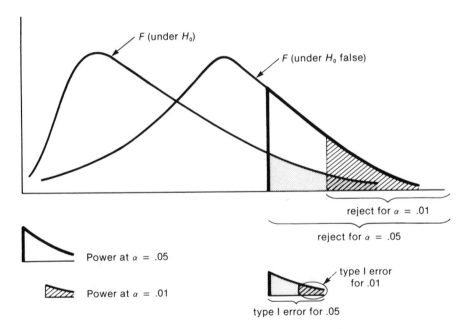

FIG. 1.1. Graph of F Distribution under H_0 and under H_0 False Showing the Direct Relationship Between Type I Error and Power. Since type I error is the probability of rejecting H_0 when true, it is the area underneath the F distribution in critical region for H_0 true. Power is the probability of rejecting H_0 when false; therefore it is the area underneath the F distribution in critical region when H_0 is false.

The power of a statistical test is dependent on three factors:

1. The α level set by the experimenter.

2. Sample size
3. Effect size—How much of a difference the treatments make, or the extent to which the groups differ in the population on the dependent variable(s).

Figure 1.1 has already demonstrated that power is directly dependent on the α level. Power is *heavily* dependent on sample size. Consider a two-tailed test at the .05 level for the t test for independent samples. Estimated effect size for the t test, as defined by Cohen (1977), is simply $\hat{d} = (\bar{x}_1 - \bar{x}_2)/s$, where s is the standard deviation. That is, effect size expresses the difference between the means in standard deviation units. Thus, if $\bar{x}_1 = 6$ and $\bar{x}_2 = 3$ and $s = 6$, then $\hat{d} = (6 - 3)/3 = .5$, or the means differ by ½ standard deviation. Suppose for the above problem we have an effect size of .5 standard deviations. Power changes dramatically as sample size increases (power values from Cohen, 1977):

n (subjects per group)	power
10	.18
20	.33
50	.70
100	.94

As the table suggests, when sample size is large (say 100 or more subjects per group) power is not an issue. It is when one is conducting a study where the group sizes will be small ($n \leq 20$), or when one is evaluating a completed study that had small group size, that it is imperative to be very sensitive to the possibility of poor power (or equivalently, a type II error). Thus, in studies with small group size it can make sense to test at a more liberal level (.10 or .15) to improve power, since (as mentioned earlier) power is directly related to the α level. We explore the power issue in considerably more detail in Chapter 4.

1.3. MULTIPLE STATISTICAL TESTS AND THE PROBABILITY OF SPURIOUS RESULTS

If a researcher sets his $\alpha = .05$ in conducting a single statistical test (say a t test), then the probability of rejecting falsely (a spurious result) is under control. Now consider a five group problem in which the researcher wishes to determine whether the groups differ significantly on some dependent variable. The reader may recall from a previous statistics course that a one way ANOVA is appropriate here. But suppose our researcher is unaware of ANOVA and decides to do 10 tests, each at the .05 level, comparing each pair of groups. His probability of a false rejection is no longer under control for the *set* of 10 t tests. We define the *overall α for a set of tests as the probability of at least one false rejection when* *the null hypothesis is true.* There is an important inequality, called the *Bonferroni Inequality* which gives an upper bound on overall $\overset{.}{\alpha}$:

overall $\alpha \leq .05 + .05 + \ldots + .05 = .50$

Thus, the probability of a few false rejections here could easily be 30 or 35%, i.e., much too high.

In general then, if we are testing k hypotheses at the $\alpha_1, \alpha_2, \ldots, \alpha_k$ levels, the Bonferroni inequality guarantees that

overall $\alpha \leq \alpha_1 + \alpha_2 + \ldots + \alpha_k$

The reader may have been alert to the possibility of spurious results in the above example with multiple t tests, since this problem is pointed out in texts on intermediate statistical methods. Another frequently occurring example of multiple t tests, where overall α gets completely out of control is in comparing two groups on *each* item of a scale (test). For example, comparing males and females on each of 30 items, doing 30 t tests, each at the .05 level.

Multiple statistical tests also arise in various other contexts in which the reader may not readily recognize that the same problem of spurious results exists. And the fact that the researcher may be using a more sophisticated design or more complex statistical tests doesn't mitigate the problem.

As our first illustration, consider a researcher who runs a 4-way ANOVA ($A \times B \times C \times D$). Then 15 statistical tests are being done, one for each effect in the design: A, B, C and D main effects, and AB, AC, AD, BC, BD, CD, ABC, ABD, ACD, BCD, and $ABCD$ interactions. If each of these effects is tested at the .05 level, then all we know from the Bonferroni inequality is that overall $\alpha \leq 15 (.05) = .75$; not very reassuring: Hence, two or three significant results from such a study (if they were *not* predicted ahead of time) could very well be type I errors, i.e., spurious results.

Let us take another common example. Suppose an investigator has a two way ANOVA design ($A \times B$) with 7 dependent variables. Then, there are three effects being tested for significance: A main effect, B main effect and the $A \times B$ interaction. The investigator does separate two-way ANOVAs for each dependent variable. Therefore, the investigator has done a total of 21 statistical tests, and if each of them was conducted at the .05 level, then the overall α has gotten completely out of control. This type of thing is done *very frequently* in the literature, and the reader should be aware of it in interpreting the results of such studies. Little faith should be placed in scattered significant results from such studies.

A third example comes from survey research, where investigators are often interested in relating demographic characteristics of the subjects (sex, age, religion, SES, etc.) to responses to items on a questionnaire. The statistical test for relating each demographic characteristic to response on each item is a two-way

χ^2. Often in such studies 20 or 30 (or many more) two-way χ^2 are run (and it is so easy to get them run on SPSSX). The investigators often seem to be able to explain the frequent small number of significant results perfectly, although seldom have the significant results been predicted a priori.

A fourth fairly common example of multiple statistical tests is in examining the elements of a correlation matrix for significance. Suppose there were 10 variables in one set being related to 15 variables in another set. In this case there are 150 between correlations, and if each of these is tested for significance at the .05 level, then 150 (.05) = 7.5, or about 8 significant results could be expected by chance. Thus, if 10 or 12 of the between correlations are significant, most of them could be chance results, and it is very difficult to separate out the chance effects from the real associations. A way of circumventing this problem is to simply test each correlation for significance at a much more stringent level, say $\alpha = .001$. Then, by the Bonferroni inequality overall $\alpha \leq 150 (.001) = .15$. Naturally, this will cause a power problem (unless n is large), and only those associations that are quite strong will be declared significant. Of course, one could argue that it is only such strong associations that may be of practical significance anyways.

A fifth case of multiple statistical tests occurs when comparing the results of many studies in a given content area. Suppose, for example, that 20 studies have been reviewed in the area of programmed instruction and its effect on math achievement in the elementary grades, and that only 5 studies show significance. Since at least 20 statistical tests were done (there would be more if there was more than a single criterion variable in some of the studies), most of these significant results could be spurious, i.e., type I errors.

Miller (1977) has commented on the tightness of the upper bound for the Bonferroni inequality, "At the time I wrote my book, I knew the Bonferroni inequality was very useful, but over the course of the past 10 years, I have become even more impressed with the tightness of the bound. . . . Although special techniques and distribution theory can improve on it, the improvement is very often only minor" (p. 779). This writer is not aware of any development since Miller made his statement that would change his conclusion.

1.4.   STATISTICAL SIGNIFICANCE VS. PRACTICAL SIGNIFICANCE

The reader may have been exposed to the statistical significance vs. practical significance of results issue in a previous course in statistics, but it is so important we wish to review it here again. Recall from our earlier discussion of power (probability of rejecting H_0 when it is false), that power is heavily dependent on sample size. Thus, given very large sample size (say group sizes > 200), most effects will be declared statistically significant at the .05 level. If significance is found in such a study, then we must decide whether the difference in means is large enough to be of practical significance. One way is to use confidence intervals to determine ranges of values within which the true population mean differences lie. Another way is to use a measure of association or strength of relationship, such as Hayes $\hat{\omega}^2$. Although such measures can be useful, they too have limitations which we discuss in Chapter 4.

Recall also, from our earlier discussion of power, the problem of finding statistical significance with small sample size. Thus, results in the literature that are not statistically significant may be due simply to poor power, while results that are statistically significant, but have been obtained with hugh sample sizes, may not be practically significant.

To focus this, consider a two-group study with 8 subjects per group and an effect size of .8 standard deviations. This is a large effect size (Cohen, 1977), and most researchers would consider this result to be practically significant. However, if testing for significance at the .05 level (two-tailed test), then the chances of finding significance are only about 1 in 3 (.31 from Cohen's [1977] power tables). The danger of not being sensitive to the power problem in such a study is that a researcher may abort a promising line of research, perhaps an effective diet or type of psychotherapy, because significance is not found. And it may also discourage other researchers.

On the other hand, now consider a two-group study with 300 subjects per group and an effect size of .20 standard deviations. In this case, when testing at the .05 level, the researcher is likely to find significance (power = .70 from Cohen's tables). To use a domestic analogy, this is like using a sledgehammer to "pound out" significance. Yet the effect size here would probably not be considered practically significant in most cases. Statistical significance obtained in this type of study can have an equally unsatisfactory effect. Based on such results, for example, a school system may decide to implement an expensive program that may yield only very small gains in achievement.

Also, with various multivariate procedures we consider in this text (such as disciminant analysis and canonical correlation), unless sample size is large relative to the number of variables, the results will not be reliable, i.e., they will not generalize. The main point of the discussion thus far is that *it is critically important to take sample size into account in interpreting results in the literature.*

1.5. OUTLIERS

Outliers are data points that split off or are very different from the rest of the data. Specific examples of outliers would be an I.Q. of 160, or a weight of 350 lbs. in a group for which the median weight is 180 lbs. Outliers can occur because of two fundamental reasons: (1) a data recording or entry error was made, or (2) the subjects are simply different from the rest. The first type of outlier can be identified by always listing the data and checking to make sure the data has been read in accurately.

The importance of listing the data was brought home to me many years ago as a graduate student. A regression problem with 5 predictors, one of which was a set of random scores, was run without checking the data. This was a textbook problem to show the student that the random number predictor would not be related to the dependent variable. However, the random number predictor was significant, and accounted for a fairly large part of the variance on y. This all resulted simply because one of the scores for the random number predictor was mispunched as a 300 rather than as a 3. In this case it was obvious that something was wrong. But, with large data sets the situation will not be so transparent, and the results of an analysis could be completely thrown off by 1 or 2 errant points. The amount of time it takes to list and check the data for accuracy (even if there are 1,000 or 2,000 subjects) is well worth the effort, and the computer cost is minimal.

Statistical procedures in general can be quite sensitive to outliers. This is particularly true for the multivariate procedures that will be considered in this text. *It is very important to be able to identify such outliers and then decide what to do about them.* Why? Because we want the results of our statistical analysis to reflect most of the data, and not to be highly influenced by just 1 or 2 errant data points.

In small data sets with just 1 or 2 variables, such outliers can be relatively easy to spot. We now consider some examples.

Example 1

Consider the following small data set with two variables:

Case Number	x_1	x_2
1	111	68
2	92	46
3	90	50
4	107	59
5	98	50
6	150	66
7	118	54
8	110	51
9	117	59
10	94	97

Cases 6 and 10 are both outliers, but for different reasons. Case 6 is an outlier because the score for Case 6 on x_1 (150) is deviant, while Case 10 is an outlier because the score for that subject on x_2 (97) splits off from the other scores on

x_2. The graphical split off of cases 6 and 10 is quite vivid and is given in Figure 1.2.

FIG. 1.2. Plot of Outliers for Two Variable Example

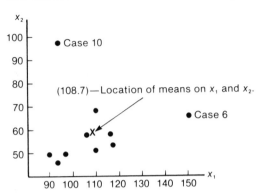

In large data sets involving many variables, however, some outliers are not so easy to spot and could go easily undetected. Now, we give an example of a somewhat more subtle outlier.

Example 2

Consider the following data set on four variables:

Case	x_1	x_2	x_3	x_4
1	111	68	17	81
2	92	46	28	67
3	90	50	19	83
4	107	59	25	71
5	98	50	13	92
6	150	66	20	90
7	118	54	11	101
8	110	51	26	82
9	117	59	18	87
10	94	67	12	69
11	130	57	16	97
12	118	51	19	78
13	155	40	9	58
14	118	61	20	103
15	109	66	13	88

The somewhat subtle outlier here is case 13. Notice that the scores for case 13 on none of the x's really split off dramatically from the other subjects scores. Yet, the scores tend to be low on x_2, x_3, and x_4 and high on x_1, and the cummulative effect of all this is to isolate case 13 from the rest of the cases. We indicate shortly a statistic that is quite useful in detecting multivariate outliers and pursue outliers in more detail in Chapter 3 on multiple regression.

We now give three examples, involving material learned in previous statistics courses, to show the effect outliers can have on some simple statistics.

Example 3

Consider the following small set of data: 2, 3, 5, 6, 44. The last number, 44, is an obvious outlier, i.e., it splits off from the rest of the data. If we were to use the mean (12) as the measure of central tendency for this set of data, it would be quite misleading, as there are no scores around 12. That is why you were told to use the median as the measure of central tendency when there are extreme scores (outliers in our terminology), since the median is unaffected by outliers. That is, it is a "robust" measure of central tendency.

Example 4

In Figure 1.3 we present the scatterplot for 20 subjects measured on variables x and y. The point in the upper right hand corner is an obvious outlier, and it has a dramatic effect on the magnitude of the correlation between x and y. With that point the correlation in .35, while with that point deleted the correlation becomes $-.49$: With the point deleted one can see how the drift of the points is from upper left to lower right, i.e., as the scores on x increase the scores on y decrease, and hence a negative correlation.

Example 5

As a third example, consider the following data from a one-way ANOVA:

Gp 1		Gp 2		Gp 3	
15	21	17	36	6	26
18	27	22	41	9	31
12	32	15	31	12	38
12	29	12	28	11	24
9	18	20	47	11	35
10	34	14	29	8	29
12	18	15	33	13	30
20	36	20	38	30	16
		21	25	7	23

For now, the reader should ignore the second column of numbers. The score of 30 in group 3 is an outlier. With that case in the ANOVA we do not find significance ($F = 2.61, p < .095$) at the .05 level, while with the case deleted we do find significance well beyond the .01 level ($F = 11.18, p < .0004$). Deleting the case has the effect of producing greater separation among the 3 means, since the means with the case included are (13.5, 17.33, and 11.89),

FIG. 1.3 Scatterplot Showing the Effect of an Outlier on the Correlation

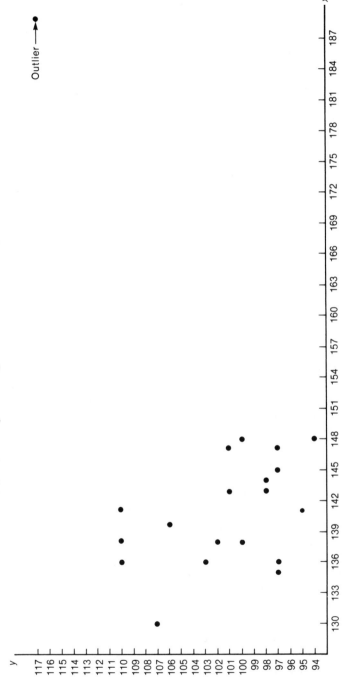

Note: The correlation between x and y is .35 with the outlier included, while with the outlier excluded the correlation changes to $-.49$.

while with the case deleted the means are (13.5, 17.33, and 9.63). It also has the effect of reducing the within variability in group 3 substantially, and hence the pooled within variability (error term for the ANOVA) will be much smaller.

These three examples should convince the reader that outliers can have a profound effect on statistical results, and hence it is crucial to identify them and then decide whether there is a basis for deleting them from the analysis.

Detecting Outliers

We first consider, although briefly, the univariate case. If the variable is approximately normal, then z scores about greater than three in absolute value should be considered as potential outliers. Of course, if n is large (say > 100), then simply by chance we might expect a few subjects to have z scores greater than three and this should be kept in mind. When comparing group differences, as in ANOVA or for a t test, then we want the z scores computed separately for each group. These can be obtained, for example, using the BMDP1D program. Note that the z score for 30 in group three from Example 5, which we indicated was an outlier, has a value around three.

Multivariate outliers can occur in more subtle ways. For instance, as shown in Example 2, a case may be an outlier because the subject is somewhat deviant on several of the variables, although not markedly deviant on any of them. Of course, in some instances, multivariate outliers might be detected by simply examining z scores on each variable. For example, a subject may be a multivariate outlier because he(she) is very deviant on one of the variables, or on a few of the variables. Fortunately, however, there is a statistic (called Mahalanobis Distance) which has an approximate chi-square distribution for large N, which can be used to detect multivariate outliers of any type. It is available in the BMDPAM program.

In Table 1.1 we show the control lines for running the data in Example 2, and the Mahalanobis distances and probabilities associated with each case. For the reader unfamiliar with the BMDP package it will be essential to refer to Table 1.3 where we give some of the basic elements of the BMDP control language, and also Table 1.5 where we provide further discussion. As alluded to earlier, the probability associated with case 13 is quite small ($p = .020$), indicating that it splits of markedly from the vector of means for the 4 variables. Thus, this subject is quite different from what is average for the set of subjects.

The BMDPAM program can also be used to detect multivariate outliers when two or more groups of subjects are being compared. To illustrate this, consider Example 5, which is a three-group multivariate analysis of variance. The control lines and selected output for this run are given in Table 1.2. The output shows that the case in group three with scores of 30 and 16 is an outlier since the probability associated with that case is very small (.0006).

In summary then, always listing the data to check for possible recording errors

TABLE 1.1

BMDPAM Control Lines for Assessing Multivariate Outliers for a
Single Group of Subjects

```
    /PROBLEM TITLE IS ' OBTAINING MAHALANOBIS DISTANCES FOR IDENTIFYING MULTIVARIATE
    OUTLIERS'.
    /INPUT VARIABLES ARE 4. FORMAT IS STREAM.
    /VARIABLE NAMES ARE X1,X2,X3,X4.
①  /ESTIMATE METHOD IS REGR.
②  /PRINT CASE = 15. MATRICES ARE CORR,DIS.
    /END
```

111	68	17	81
92	46	28	67
90	50	19	83
107	59	25	71
98	50	13	92
150	66	20	90
118	54	11	101
110	51	26	82
117	59	18	87
94	67	12	69
130	57	16	97
118	51	19	78
155	40	9	58
118	61	20	103
109	66	13	88

③

OUTPUT

CASE NUMBER	CHI—SQ	CHISQ/DF	D.F.	SIGNIFICANCE	
1	2.428	0.607	4	0.6576	
2	5.619	1.405	4	0.2294	
3	2.497	0.624	4	0.6452	
4	2.820	0.705	4	0.5883	
5	3.825	0.956	4	0.4301	
6	6.264	1.566	4	0.1803	
7	3.772	0.943	4	0.4378	
8	2.561	0.640	4	0.6337	
9	0.178	0.044	4	0.9963	
10	7.146	1.787	4	0.1284	
11	1.805	0.451	4	0.7716	
12	0.515	0.129	4	0.9720	
13	11.630	2.908	4	0.0203	④
14	2.790	0.698	4	0.5935	
15	2.149	0.537	4	0.7084	

①The ESTIMATE paragraph is necessary in order for the Mahalanobis distances to be printed.

②To obtain the correlation matrix for the variables and the distances, we specify MATRICES ARE CORR,DIS. in the PRINT paragraph. The CASE = 15. is necessary to get all the data printed; otherwise the program will just print out the first 5 cases.

③This is Mahalanobis distance.

④Case 13 splits off significantly, at the .05 level, from the measure of central tendency for the 4 variables, i.e., the vector of means. Since statistical distance, as measured by Mahalanobis distance, is different from ordinary (Euclidean) distance, we indicate in the Appendix of this chapter some of the considerations needed in defining a measure of statistical distance.

TABLE 1.2
BMDPAM Control Lines for Assessing Multivariate Outliers in a
Three Group Multivariate Analysis of Variance

```
/PROBLEM TITLE IS ' MULTIVARIATE OUTLIERS
   FOR MULTIVARIATE ANOVA.' .
/INPUT VARIABLES ARE 3. FORMAT IS STREAM.
/VARIABLE NAMES ARE GPID,Y1,Y2. GROUPING IS GPID.
/GROUP CODES(1) ARE 1,2,3. NAMES(1) ARE GP1,GP2,GP3.
/ESTIMATE METHOD IS REGR.
/PRINT CASE = 26. MATRICES ARE CORR,DIS.
/END
```

The control lines here are very similar to those in Table 1.1, except here we must indicate which variable is the grouping variable. This is done in the VARIABLE paragraph by specifying GROUPING IS GPID. Also, there is a GROUP paragraph where a numerical code (1, 2, or 3) and name is given to each group. The 1 in parenthesis refers to the location of the grouping variable in the variable list. Here the grouping variable is the first variable in the list.

OUTPUT

CASE NUMER	GROUP	CHI—SQ	CHISG/DF	D.F.	SIGNIFICANCE
1	GP1	0.794	0.397	2	0.6724
2	GP1	0.757	0.378	2	0.6850
3	GP1	0.623	0.311	2	0.7324
4	GP1	0.174	0.087	2	0.9168
5	GP1	2.466	1.233	2	0.2914
6	GP1	1.483	0.742	2	0.4763
7	GP1	1.754	0.877	2	0.4159
8	GP1	3.410	1.705	2	0.1817
9	GP2	0.069	0.035	2	0.9659
10	GP2	1.823	0.911	2	0.4020
11	GP2	0.432	0.216	2	0.8057
12	GP2	1.923	0.961	2	0.3824
13	GP2	3.738	1.869	2	0.1543
14	GP2	1.012	0.506	2	0.6028
15	GP2	0.239	0.119	2	0.8875
16	GP2	0.580	0.290	2	0.7484
17	GP2	2.233	1.116	2	0.3274
18	GP3	1.395	0.698	2	0.4977
19	GP3	0.487	0.243	2	0.7839
20	GP3	2.098	1.049	2	0.3504
21	GP3	0.370	0.185	2	0.8311
22	GP3	1.047	0.523	2	0.5925
23	GP3	0.579	0.290	2	0.7485
24	GP3	0.133	0.067	2	0.9356
25	GP3	14.929	7.464	2	0.0006*
26	GP3	1.452	0.726	2	0.4837

*There is only one case here which is significantly separated at the .05 level, ie, case 25. The program, however, only specifically flags those observations which have really extreme probabilities ($p < .001$).

and running the data through BMDPAM to check for potential multivariate outliers are both essential parts of the *preliminary data screening* process investigators should routinely do.

1.6. RESEARCH EXAMPLES FOR SOME ANALYSES CONSIDERED IN THIS TEXT

To give the reader somewhat of a feel for several of the statistical analyses considered in succeeding chapters, we present the objectives in doing a multiple regression analysis, a multivariate analysis of variance and covariance, and a canonical correlation analysis, along with illustrative studies from the literature that used each of these analyses.

Multiple Regression

In a previous course simple linear regression was covered, where a dependent variable (say chemistry achievement) is predicted from just one predictor, like I. Q. Now it is certainly reasonable that other factors would also be related to chemistry achievement and that we could obtain better prediction by making use of these other factors, such as previous average grade in science courses, attitude toward education and math ability. Thus, the objective in multiple regression (called multiple since we have multiple predictors) is:

Objective: Predict a dependent variable from a set of independent variables.

Example

Feshbach, Adelman, and Fuller (1977) conducted a longitudinal study on 850 middle class kindergarten children. The children were administered a psychometric battery that included the Wechsler Preschool and Primary Scale of Intelligence, the deHirsch-Jansky Predictive Index (assessing various linguistic and perceptual motor skills) and the Bender Motor Gestalt test. The students were also assessed on a Student Rating Scale (SRS) developed by the authors, which measured various cognitive and affective behaviors and skills. These various predictors were used to predict reading achievement in grades 1, 2, and 3. Reading achievement was measured with the Cooperative Reading Test. The major thrust of the study in the authors words was

> The present investigation evaluates and contrasts one major psychometric predictive index, that developed by deHirsch . . . with an alternative strategy based on a systematic behavioral analysis and ratings made by the kindergarten teacher of academically relevant cognitive and affective behaviors and skills (assessed by the SRS). . . . This approach, in addition to being easier to implement and less costly than psychometric testing, yields assessment data which are more closely linked to intervention and remedial procedures. (p. 300)

The SRS scale proved equal to the deHirsch in predicting reading achievement, and because of the above rationale might well be preferred.

One Way Multivariate Analysis of Variance

In univariate analysis of variance, several groups of subjects were compared to determine whether they differed on the average on a single dependent variable. But, as was mentioned earlier in this chapter, any good treatment(s) generally affects the subjects in several ways. Hence, it makes sense to measure the subjects on those variables and then test whether they differ on the average on the set of variables. This gives a more accurate assessment of the true efficacy of the treatments. Thus, the objective in multivariate analysis of variance is:

Objective: Determine whether several groups differ on the average on a set of dependent variables.

Example

Stevens (1972) conducted a study on National Merit scholars. The classification variable was the educational level of both parents of the scholars. Four groups were formed:

1. Students for whom at least one parent had an eighth grade education or less
2. Students whose both parents were high school graduates
3. Students both of whose parents had gone to college, with at most one graduating
4. Students for whom both parents had at least one college degree

The dependent variables were a subset of the Vocational Personality Inventory: realistic, intellectual, social, conventional, enterprising, artistic, status, and aggression. He found that the parents' educational level was related to their children's personality characteristics, with conventional and enterprising being the key variables. Specifically, scholars whose parents had gone to college tended to be more enterprising and less conventional than scholars whose parents had not gone to college. This example is considered in detail in the chapter on discriminant analysis.

Multivariate Analysis of Covariance

Objective: Determine whether several groups differ on a set of dependent variables after the posttest means have been adjusted for any initial differences on the covariates (which are often pretests).

Example

Friedman, Lehrer, and Stevens (1983) examined the effect of two stress management strategies, directed lecture discussion and self-directed, and the locus of control of teachers on their scores on the State-Trait Anxiety Inventory and on the Subjective Stress Scale. Eighty-five teachers were pretested and posttested on the above measures, with the treatment extending five weeks. Those subjects who received the stress management programs reduced their stress and anxiety more than those in a control group. However, subjects who were in a stress management program compatiable with their locus of control (i.e., externals with lectures and internals with the self-directed) did not reduce stress significantly more than those subjects in the unmatched stress management groups.

Canonical Correlation

With a simple correlation we analyzed the nature of the association between two variables, like anxiety and performance. However, there are many situations where one may want to examine the nature of the association between two *sets* of variables. For example, we may wish to relate a set of interest variables to a set of academic achievement variables, or a set of biological variables to a set of behavioral variables, or a set of stimulus variables to a set of response variables. Canonical correlation is a procedure for breaking down the complex association present in such situations into additive pieces. Thus, the objective in canonical correlation is:

Objective: Determine the number and nature of independent relationships existing between two sets of variables.

Example

Tetenbaum (1975), in a study of the validity of student ratings of teachers, hypothesized that specified student needs would be related to ratings of specific teacher orientations congruent with those needs. Student needs were assessed by the Personality Research Form, and fell into four broad categories: need for control, need for intellectual striving, need for gregariousness, and need for ascendancy. There were a total of 12 need variables. There were also 12 teacher-rating variables. These two sets of variables were analyzed using canonical correlation. The first canonical dimension revealed quite cleanly the intellectual striving—rating correspondence and the ascendancy need—rating correspondence. The second canonical dimenson revealed the control need-rating correspondence, and the third the gregariousness need-rating correspondence. This example is considered in detail in the chapter on canonical correlation.

1.7. THE BMDP AND SPSSX STATISTICAL PACKAGES

The Biomedical (BMDP) and Statistical Package for the Social Sciences (SPSSX) statistical packages were selected for use in this text for several reasons:

1. They are very widely distributed.
2. They are easy to use.
3. They do a very wide range of analyses, from simple descriptive statistics to all types of univariate ANOVA and repeated measures designs (one way, factorial [equal or unequal n], nested designs), to regression and factor analyses, and finally various types of multivariate analyses (multivariate analysis of variance and covariance, multivariate repeated measures). They also do time series analysis and complex analysis of categorical data, i.e., the log linear model.
4. Both packages have been in development for many years, the BMDP since the early 1960's and SPSSX since the mid 1960's.

The control language that is used by both packages is quite natural, and readers will see that with a little practice complex analyses can be run quite easily and with a very small set of control line instructions. Getting output is relatively easy; however, this can be a mixed blessing. Because it is so easy to get output, it is also easy to get "garbage." Hence, although we illustrate the control lines in this text for running various analyses, there are several other facets that are much more important, such as interpretation of printout (in particular, knowing what to focus on in the printout), careful selection of variables, adequate sample size for reliable results, checking for outliers, and knowing what assumptions are important to check for a given analysis.

In Tables 1.3 and 1.4 we present some of the basic rules of the control language for BMDP and SPSSX. Although the points mentioned are basic, they are important. If they are not observed, one will get "booted off" the system. For example, failing to end an instruction in BMDP with a period will cause the specific program to terminate. Or, simply using an invalid name for a variable will cause termination. Similarily, with SPSSX, if a command (like LIST, DATA LIST, or BEGIN DATA) does not begin in column 1, or if a subcommand is not indented at least one column, the program will terminate. Paying careful attention to the information in Tables 1.3 and 1.4 will help considerably in getting programs to run.

Since the use of punched cards is becoming obsolete, we assume in this text that the reader will be using a terminal of some type to access the packages. Thus, instead of referring to control cards or data cards, we talk about control lines or data lines. Also, we only consider examples where the data is part of the control lines. Now, it is true that often in practice data will be accessed from a tape or disk. Hence, the FILE HANDLE command in SPSSX will not be relevant in our use of this package. Accessing data from tape or disk, along with data management (e.g., interleaving or matching files), is a whole other area we do not wish to enter. For those who are interested, however, SPSSX is setup nicely for efficient file manipulation.

In Table 1.5 we have illustrated the control lines for running both a simple

TABLE 1.3
Some Basic Elements of the BMDP Control Language

English based—noncolumn oriented—information can go anywhere in columns 1–80 (if using cards) or columns 1–72 (if using a terminal). The instructions go in as sentences, which *must* end with a period.
Examples: VARIABLES ARE 6. DEPENDENT IS *Y*.
The sentences are grouped into paragraphs, which *must* be separated by a slash, i.e., by /.
Names or values in a list must be separated by commas.
Example: NAMES ARE *X*1, *X*2, *X*3, *X*4.
Each word or value must be separated from the following word or value by one or more blanks or some kind of punctuation.
The words "are" and "=" are interchangeable. That is we could put VARIABLES ARE 6. or VARIABLES = 6.

Names for Variables
They must be eight or less characters.
Names that don't begin with a letter or contain a character that is not a letter or number must be in apostrophes.
Examples: ACHIEV (valid name), INTELLIGENCE (invalid—too long), I. Q. (invalid—the periods are special characters), SOC CLAS (invalid—imbedded blank), *X*1 + *X*2 (invalid—+ is a special character), but ' *X*1 + *X*2 ' is valid.

Different Types of Paragraphs
The PROBLEM, INPUT, VARIABLE, and END paragraphs will be common to all programs. These are the paragraph names.
In the PROBLEM paragraph we are simply giving a title for the analysis.
It can't exceed 160 characters, and *must* be placed in apostrophes if it does not begin with a letter or if it contains a symbol that is neither a letter or number (e.g., a blank or comma). Since a title will virtually always have more than one word with imbedded blanks separating the words, it is best to routinely place the title in apostrophes.
In the INPUT paragraph we indicate the number of variables in the analysis and the format in which the variables appear (e.g., free or fixed).
In the VARIABLE paragraph we give names for the variables, and for the following programs *must* indicate (if comparing groups) which of the variables is the grouping variable: 1D, 3D, 5D, 6D, 7M, AM, 1R, 3S and 1V.
We can also have a GROUP paragraph if we wish to give a label for each group (see BMDP manual, 1983, pp. 43–44).
There will also be program specific paragraphs like REGRESSION and CANONICAL (when doing canonical correlation).

linear regression and a univariate analysis of variance on both packages. This is done for several reasons. First, it shows the structure and flow of control instructions for each package. Secondly, it shows that with a very small set of control instructions one can run complicated analyses. Third, it shows that for each package as we go from one type of analysis (regression) to another type (ANOVA), a good portion of the control lines is very similar. For example, for the BMDP2R and BMDP1V runs, notice the considerable similarity in terms of the PROBLEM, INPUT, and VARIABLE paragraphs. For SPSSX the similarity

TABLE 1.4
Some Basic Elements of the SPSSX Control Language

SPSSX operates on commands and subcommands.

It is column oriented to the extent that each command begins in column 1 and continues for as many lines as needed. All continuation lines are indented at least one column

Examples of commands: TITLE, DATA LIST, MANOVA, REGRESSION

The title is put in apostrophes, and can be up to 60 characters.

All subcommands begin with a keyword followed by an equals sign, then the specifications, and are terminated by a slash.

Each subcommand is indented at least one column.

The subcommands are further specifications for the commands.

For example, if the command is REGRESSION, then DEPENDENT $= Y/$ is a subcommand indicating which of the variables in the analysis is to be predicted. The further subcommand STEPWISE/ indicates that the stepwise selection procedure will be used to select a good set of predictors.

Names for variables must be eight or less characters.

They must begin with a letter, or one of 3 special characters (see SPSSX Users Guide, 1983, p. 33)

The safest course, in terms of having valid names, is to simply use contiguous letters and numbers.

FREE format—the variables must be in the same order for each case but do not have to be in the same location. Also, multiple cases can go on the same line, with the values for the variables separated by blanks or commas.

When the data is part of the command file, then the BEGIN DATA command precedes the first line of data and the END DATA command follows the last line of data.

Can use the keyword TO in specifying a set of consecutive variables, rather than listing all the variables. For example, if we had the six variables $X1,X2,X3,X4,X5,X6$, the following subcommands are equivalent:

VARIABLES $= X1,X2,X3,X4,X5,X6/$ or   VARIABLES $= X1$ to $X6/$

---

of the control lines for TITLE through END DATA is striking. Knowing the details of each analysis is not important in order to appreciate the simplicity, conciseness and similarity of the control lines from analysis to analysis. Fourth, it enables us to introduce three programs (SPSSX MANOVA, BMDP2R and SPSSX REGRESSION) which are used later for more complex analyses. Here they are used in their simplest applications, but to run analyses which the reader was exposed to in previous courses. SPSSX MANOVA is setup to compare groups on several dependent variables simultaneously; in Table 1.5 it is used to compare 4 groups on just 1 dependent variable. BMDP2R and SPSSX REGRESSION are setup to predict a dependent variable from several predictors; in Table 1.5 just 1 predictor is used.

The control lines are complete for running the analyses, except for the systems lines, which can vary from installation to installation. Although we have provided a fair amount of annotation in Table 1.5, it will be helpful to refer to Tables 1.3 and 1.4 in making more sense of the control language. One additional

TABLE 1.5
Comparison of Control Lines for Running One Way ANOVA and
Simple Regression on the BMDP and SPSSX Packages

CONTROL LINES FOR ONE WAY ANOVA

BMDP1V		SPSSX MANOVA	Data Sets			
			1	2	3	4
/PROBLEM TITLE IS ' 4 GROUP ANOVA ' .		TITLE ' 4 GROUP ANOVA '				
/INPUT VARIABLES = 2. FORMAT IS STREAM.	④	DATA LIST FREE/ GP, Y1				
/VARIABLE NAMES ARE GP,Y1.	⑤	LIST	13	9	14	17
GROUPING IS GP.		BEGIN DATA	18	10	21	12
/DESIGN DEPENDENT IS Y1.			23	14	20	11
/END	⑥	DATA LINES	20	8	24	18
1 13 1 18 1 23 1 20 1 19		END DATA	19			19
2 9 2 10 2 14 2 8	⑦	MANOVA Y1 BY GP(1,4)/				
3 14 3 21 3 20 3 24		PRINT = CELLINFO(MEANS)/				
4 17 4 12 4 11 4 18 4 19						

CONTROL LINES FOR REGRESSION

BMDP2R		SPSSX REGRESSION	y	x1
/PROBLEM TITLE IS ' REGRESSION—ONE		TITLE ' REGRESSION—ONE PREDICTOR '	34	8
① PREDICTOR'.		DATA LIST FREE/ Y X1	23	11
/INPUT VARIABLES ARE 2. FORMAT IS STREAM.		LIST	26	12
② /VARIABLE NAMES ARE Y, X1.		BEGIN DATA	31	9
/PRINT DATA.		DATA LINES	27	14
/REGRESSION DEPENDENT IS Y.		END DATA	37	15
③ /END		REGRESSION DESCRIPTIVES =	19	6
34 8 23 11 26 12 31 9		DEFAULT/	29	10
27 14 37 15 19 6 29 10		VARIABLES = Y,X1/		
		DEPENDENT = Y/ STEPWISE/		

①Variables is the total number of variables in the analysis, here it includes Y and X1, whereas in the BMDP1V program it includes the dependent variable and the grouping variable.

①Stream refers to free format, with multiple cases possible on the same line.

②This PRINT paragraph is necessary to obtain a listing of the data.

③This END paragraph simply indicates to the program the end of the control instructions.

④The FREE on this DATA LIST command is a further specification, indicating the data will be in free format.

⑤This LIST command gives a listing of the data.

⑥When the data is part of the command file, it is preceded by BEGIN DATA and terminated by END DATA.

⑦The general form for the MANOVA command is

MANOVA   list of   BY   list of   WITH list of
              dependent vars   factors   covariates

comment concerning the SPSSX programs. The PRINT subcommand is necessary in order to obtain the means and standard deviations for the dependent variable in each of the groups, while the DESCRIPTIVES-DEFAULT serves the same purpose in the REGRESSION program.

To modify any one of the three programs to run more complicated analyses requires only some very modest changes. For example, to modify BMDP2R to run a regression analysis with three predictors ($X1$, $X2$, $X3$) the total number of variables in the INPUT paragraph becomes 4, and in the VARIABLE paragraph we would have

VARIABLE NAMES ARE Y, $X1$, $X2$, $X3./$

It should be understood that although we have given some very important, basic elements of the packages in Tables 1.3 and 1.4, and present complete control lines for running various analyses in this text, our treatment is in no sense a substitute for the BMDP and SPSSX manuals. All the contingencies one might encounter in a practical problem can't be covered in this text; however, a way of dealing with them undoubtedly will be found in the manuals. Also, although certain analyses are done with one package (BMDP) while other analyses are done with SPSSX, this does *not* mean we are advocating that particular package for that analysis. The choice is simply illustrative, unless otherwise indicated.

1.8. MICROCOMPUTERS AND THE STATISTICAL PACKAGES

The BMDP and SPSSX packages were developed in the 1960's, and they were in widespread use during the 1970's on mainframe computers. The emergence of microcomputers in the 1970's had implications for the way in which data would be processed in the future, and some quality software for doing simpler statistics (descriptive, *t* tests, ANOVAS, etc.) was developed in the late 1970's and early 1980's for the Apple.

Vastly increased memory capacity and more sophisticated microprocessors have made it possible for the packages to become available on microcomputers. SPSSX (1983) has a scaled down version of their package for the IBM personal computer. It does descriptive statistics, *t* tests, factorial ANOVAS (equal and unequal *n*), multiple regression, and factor analysis. Also, all the BMDP programs (except BMDP4V) are available on the IBM personal computer, with some modifications. The hardware requirements are 640K, a floating point processor, and a 5 megabyte hard disk. The cost of all of this (with educational discount) is around $4,000; definitely in the personal computer cost range. The days of dependence on the main frame computer, even for the powerful statistical packages, will probably diminish considerably within the next 5 to 10 years. We are truly entering a new era in data processing.

1.9. SOME ISSUES UNIQUE TO MULTIVARIATE ANALYSIS

Many of the techniques discussed in this text are *mathematical maximization procedures*, and hence there is great opportunity for capitalization on chance. Often, as the reader will see as we move along in the text, the results "look great" on a given sample, but do not generalize to other samples. Thus, the results are sample-specific and of limited scientific utility. Reliability of results is a real concern.

The notion of a *linear combination* of variables is fundamental to all of the types of analysis we discuss. A general linear combination for p variables is given by:

$$y = a_1 x_1 + a_2 x_2 + a_3 x_3 + \ldots + a_p x_p,$$

where $a_1, a_2, a_3, \ldots, a_p$ are the coefficients for the variables. The above definition is abstract; however, we give some simple examples of linear combinations that the reader will be familiar with.

Suppose we have a treatment vs. control group design with the subjects pretested and posttested on some variable. Then sometimes analysis is done on the difference scores (gain scores), i.e., posttest-pretest. If we denote the pretest variable by x_1 and the posttest variable by x_2, then the difference variable $y = x_2 - x_1$ is a simple linear combination, where $a_1 = -1$ and $a_2 = 1$.

As another example of a simple linear combination, suppose we wished to sum three subtest scores on a test (x_1, x_2, and x_3). Then the newly created sum variable $y = x_1 + x_2 + x_3$ is a linear combination, where $a_1 = a_2 = a_3 = 1$.

Still another example of linear combinations that the reader has encountered in an intermediate statistics course is that of contrasts among means, as in the Scheffe' post hoc procedure or in planned comparisons. Consider the following 4-group ANOVA, where T_3 is a combination treatment, and T_4 is a control group.

$$\underline{T_1 \ T_2 \ T_3 \ T_4}$$
$$\mu_1 \ \mu_2 \ \mu_3 \ \mu_4$$

Then the following meaningful contrast

$$L_1 = \frac{\mu_1 + \mu_2}{2} - \mu_3$$

is a linear combination, where $a_1 = a_2 = \frac{1}{2}$ and $a_3 = -1$, while the following contrast among means

$$L_2 = \frac{\mu_1 + \mu_2 + \mu_3}{3} - \mu_4$$

is also a linear combination, where $a_1 = a_2 = a_3 = \frac{1}{3}$ and $a_4 = -1$. The notions of mathematical maximization and linear combinations are combined in many of the multivariate procedures. For example, in multiple regression we talk about the linear combination of the predictors that is maximally correlated with the dependent variable, and in principal components analysis the linear combinations of the variables which account for maximum portions of the total variance are considered.

APPENDIX:
DEFINING A MEASURE OF STATISTICAL DISTANCE

Consider two points (x_1, y_1) and (x_2, y_2) in the plane. Then the ordinary (sometimes called Euclidean) distance between them is obtained by use of the Pythagorean theorem, which states that the square of the hypotenuse (side opposite the right angle) is equal to the sum of the squares of the two legs. This is shown below:

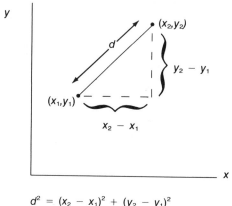

$$d^2 = (x_2 - x_1)^2 + (y_2 - y_1)^2$$
$$d = \sqrt{(x_2 - x_1)^2 + (y_2 - y_1)^2}$$

For example, if the two points were (2,3) and (4,6), then the distance would be $d = \sqrt{(4 - 2)^2 + (6 - 3)^2} = \sqrt{13} = 3.606$.

As Johnson and Wichern (1982) note, "Straight line or Euclidean distance is unsatisfactory for most statistical purposes. This is because each coordinate (variable) contributes equally to the calculation of the Euclidean distance. When the coordinates represent measurements that are subject to random fluctuations of differing magnitudes, it is often desirable to weight coordinates subject to a great deal of variability less heavily than those that are not highly variable (p. 20)." In defining a statistical measure of distance then we must take into account two factors: (1) differing variability for the variables, which can occur simply because the variables have been scaled differently, and (2) the correlation between the variables.

The squared, standardized distance which adjusts for differing variability on the variables is given by:

$$d^{*2} = \frac{(x_{i1} - \bar{x}_1)^2}{s_1^2} + \frac{(x_{i2} - \bar{x}_2)^2}{s_2^2}$$

where x_{i1} and x_{i2} represent the scores for subject i on variables 1 and 2 and $\bar{x}_1$ and $\bar{x}_2$ represent the means on the variables.

To illustrate the above formula, suppose we have two variables x_1 and x_2 with variances of 36 and 100 and that the means are 4 and 6. For the moment, assume that x_1 and x_2 are uncorrelated. We wish to determine the distance of a subject with scores (2,3) from the vector of means, i.e., from (4,6).

$$d^{*2} = \frac{(2 - 4)^2}{36} + \frac{(3 - 6)^2}{100} = .11 + .09 = .20$$

These are the same two points we considered earlier with the unstandardized Euclidean distance formula. It is important to note that using the unstandardized formula it was found that a greater portion of the squared distance (9) was due to x_2 (denoted by y earlier). After appropriate standardization for the different variances, we find that the greater portion of the distance is due to x_1 (.11 of .20).

Now, suppose the variables are moderately correlated, i.e., $r_{x_1 x_2} = .50$. The Mahalanobis distance, which takes correlation into account, is given by

$$D^2 = \frac{1}{1 - r^2} \left[\frac{(x_{i1} - \bar{x}_1)^2}{s_1^2} + \frac{(x_{i2} - \bar{x}_2)^2}{s_2^2} - \frac{2r\,(x_{i1} - \bar{x}_1)(x_{i2} - \bar{x}_2)}{s_1 s_2} \right]$$

Note that if the correlation is positive then the distance is reduced by an amount related to the third term inside the brackets. This is because some of the distance along the second dimension (on the second variable) is predictable from x_2's correlation with x_1.

Now we calculate the distance from (2,3) to (4,6), assuming a correlation of .50:

$$D^2 = \frac{1}{1 - .25} \left[\frac{(2 - 4)^2}{36} + \frac{(3 - 6)^2}{100} - \frac{2(.5)(2 - 4)(3 - 6)}{6(10)} \right]$$

$$D^2 = 1/.75 \,(.11 + .09 - .10) = .133$$

If the correlation is strong (e.g., .71), then the Mahalanobis distance is even smaller:

$$D^2 = \frac{1}{1 - .50} \left[.11 + .09 - \frac{2(.71)(-2)(-3)}{60} \right] = .116$$

On the other hand, if the correlation is negative, then the distance will be *greater* than what it was when the variables were uncorrelated. To illustrate, suppose in the above example that the correlation between x_1 and x_2 was $-.50$. Then the distance is

$$D^2 = \frac{1}{1 - .25} \,(.11 + .09 + .10) = .40$$

After we have covered matrices in Chapter 2, we define the Mahalanobis distance in terms of matrices for the general case of p variables in Chapter 3.

2 Matrix Algebra

2.1. INTRODUCTION

A matrix is simply a rectangular array of elements. The following are examples of matrices:

$$
\begin{bmatrix} 1 & 2 & 3 & 4 \\ 4 & 5 & 6 & 9 \end{bmatrix} \qquad
\begin{bmatrix} 1 & 2 & 1 \\ 2 & 3 & 5 \\ 5 & 6 & 8 \\ 1 & 4 & 10 \end{bmatrix} \qquad
\begin{bmatrix} 1 & 2 \\ 2 & 4 \end{bmatrix}
$$
$$
2 \times 4 \qquad\qquad 4 \times 3 \qquad\qquad 2 \times 2
$$

The numbers underneath each matrix are the dimensions of the matrix, and indicate the size of the matrix. The first number is the number of rows and the second number the number of columns. Thus, the first matrix is a 2×4 since it has 2 rows and 4 columns.

A familiar matrix in educational research is the score matrix. For example, suppose we had measured six subjects on three variables. We could represent all the scores as a matrix:

Variables

		1	2	3
	1	10	4	18
	2	12	6	21
Subjects	3	13	2	20
	4	16	8	16
	5	12	3	14
	6	15	9	13

This is a 6×3 matrix. More generally, we can represent the scores of N subjects on p variables in a $N \times p$ matrix as follows:

Variables

		1	2	3		p
	1	x_{11}	x_{12}	x_{13}	$\cdots$	x_{1p}
	2	x_{21}	x_{22}	x_{23}	$\cdots$	x_{2p}
Subjects		$\vdots$	$\vdots$	$\vdots$		$\vdots$
	N	x_{N1}	x_{N2}	x_{N3}	$\cdots$	x_{Np}

The first subscript indicates the row and the second subscript the column. Thus, x_{12} represents the score of subject 1 on variable 2 and x_{2p} represents the score of subject 2 on variable p.

The *transpose* $\mathbf{A}'$ of a matrix $\mathbf{A}$ is simply the matrix obtained by interchanging rows and columns.

Examples

$$\mathbf{A} = \begin{bmatrix} 2 & 3 & 6 \\ 5 & 4 & 8 \end{bmatrix} \Rightarrow \mathbf{A}' = \begin{bmatrix} 2 & 5 \\ 3 & 4 \\ 6 & 8 \end{bmatrix}$$

The first row of $\mathbf{A}$ has become the first column of $\mathbf{A}'$ and the second row of $\mathbf{A}$ has become the second column of $\mathbf{A}'$.

$$\mathbf{B} = \begin{bmatrix} 3 & 4 & 2 \\ 5 & 6 & 5 \\ 1 & 3 & 8 \end{bmatrix} \rightarrow \mathbf{B}' = \begin{bmatrix} 3 & 5 & 1 \\ 4 & 6 & 3 \\ 2 & 5 & 8 \end{bmatrix}$$

In general, if a matrix **A** has dimensions $r \times s$, then the dimensions of the transpose are $s \times r$.

A matrix with a single row is called a row vector, and a matrix with a single column is called a column vector. Vectors are always indicated by small letters and a row vector by a transpose, i.e., **x'**, **y'** etc. Throughout this text a matrix or vector will be denoted by boldface letters.

Examples

$$\mathbf{x'} = (1, 2, 3)$$
1×3 row vector

$$\mathbf{y} = \begin{bmatrix} 4 \\ 6 \\ 8 \\ 7 \end{bmatrix} \quad 4 \times 1 \text{ column vector}$$

A row vector that is of particular interest to us later is the vector of means for a group of subjects on several variables. For example, suppose we have measured 100 subjects on the California Psychological Inventory and have obtained their average scores on 5 of the subscales. We could represent their 5 means as a column vector, and the transpose of this column vector is a row vector **x'**.

$$\mathbf{x} = \begin{bmatrix} 24 \\ 31 \\ 22 \\ 27 \\ 30 \end{bmatrix} \mapsto \mathbf{x'} = (24, 31, 22, 27, 30)$$

The elements on the diagonal running from upper left to lower right are said to be on the main diagonal of a matrix. A matrix **A** is said to be *symmetric* if the elements below the main diagonal are a mirror reflection of the corresponding elements above the main diagonal. This is saying $a_{12} = a_{21}, a_{13} = a_{31}$ and $a_{23} = a_{32}$ for a 3×3 matrix, since these are the corresponding pairs. This is illustrated below:

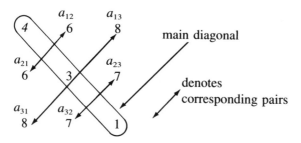

In general, a matrix **A** is symmetric if $a_{ij} = a_{ji}, i \neq j$, i.e., if all corresponding pairs of elements above and below the main diagonal are equal.

An example of a symmetric matrix that is frequently encountered in statistical work is that of a correlation matrix. For example, below is the matrix of inter-correlations for 4 subtests of the Differential Aptitude Test for boys:

	VR	NA	Cler.	Mech.
Verbal Reas.	1.00	.70	.19	.55
Numerical Abil.	.70	1.00	.36	.50
Clerical Speed	.19	.36	1.00	.16
Mechan. Reas.	.55	.50	.16	1.00

This matrix is obviously symmetric since, for example, the correlation between VR and NA is the same as the correlation between NA and VR.

Two matrices **A** and **B** are equal if and only if all corresponding elements are equal. That is to say, 2 matrices are equal only if they are identical.

2.2. ADDITION, SUBTRACTION, AND MULTIPLICATION OF A MATRIX BY A SCALAR

Two matrices **A** and **B** are added by adding corresponding elements

Example

$$\mathbf{A} = \begin{bmatrix} 2 & 3 \\ 3 & 4 \end{bmatrix} \quad \mathbf{B} = \begin{bmatrix} 6 & 2 \\ 2 & 5 \end{bmatrix}$$

$$\mathbf{A} + \mathbf{B} = \begin{bmatrix} 2+6 & 3+2 \\ 3+2 & 4+5 \end{bmatrix} = \begin{bmatrix} 8 & 5 \\ 5 & 9 \end{bmatrix}$$

Notice the elements in the (1, 1) positions, i.e., 2 and 6 have been added, etc.

Only matrices of the same dimensions can be added. Thus addition would not be defined for the matrices below:

$$\begin{bmatrix} 2 & 3 & 1 \\ 1 & 4 & 6 \end{bmatrix} + \begin{bmatrix} 1 & 4 \\ 5 & 6 \end{bmatrix} \quad \text{not defined}$$

Two matrices, of the same dimensions, are subtracted by subtracting corresponding elements.

$$
\overset{\textbf{A}}{\begin{bmatrix} 2 & 1 & 5 \\ 3 & 2 & 6 \end{bmatrix}} - \overset{\textbf{B}}{\begin{bmatrix} 1 & 4 & 2 \\ 1 & 2 & 5 \end{bmatrix}} = \overset{\textbf{A} - \textbf{B}}{\begin{bmatrix} 1 & -3 & 3 \\ 2 & 0 & 1 \end{bmatrix}}
$$

Multiplication of a matrix or a vector by a scalar (number) is accomplished by multiplying each element of the matrix or vector by the scalar.

Examples

$$
2\,(3,\ 1,\ 4) = (6,\ 2,\ 8) \qquad 1/3 \begin{bmatrix} 4 \\ 3 \end{bmatrix} = \begin{bmatrix} 4/3 \\ 1 \end{bmatrix}
$$

$$
4 \begin{bmatrix} 2 & 1 \\ 1 & 5 \end{bmatrix} = \begin{bmatrix} 8 & 4 \\ 4 & 20 \end{bmatrix}
$$

Multiplication of Matrices

In order to multiply two matrices they do not necessarily have to be of the same dimensions, however, there is a restriction as to when two matrices can be multiplied. Consider the product **AB**. Then *the number of columns in* **A** *must equal the number of rows in* **B**. For example, if **A** is 2 × 3, then **B** must have 3 rows, although **B** could have any number of columns. If two matrices can be multiplied they are said to be *conformable*. The dimensions of the product matrix, call it **C**, is simply the number of rows of **A** by number of columns of **B**. In the above example, if **B** were 3 × 4, then **C** would be a 2 × 4 matrix. In general then, if **A** is an $r \times s$ matrix and **B** is an $s \times t$ matrix, then the dimensions of the product **AB** are $r \times t$.

Example

$$
\underset{2 \times 3}{\overset{\textbf{A}}{\begin{bmatrix} 2 & 1 & 3 \\ 4 & 5 & 6 \end{bmatrix}}} \quad \underset{3 \times 2}{\overset{\textbf{B}}{\begin{bmatrix} 1 & 0 \\ 2 & 4 \\ -1 & 5 \end{bmatrix}}} = \underset{2 \times 2}{\overset{\textbf{C}}{\begin{bmatrix} c_{11} & c_{12} \\ c_{21} & c_{22} \end{bmatrix}}}
$$

Notice first that **A** and **B** can be multiplied since the number of columns in **A** is 3 which is equal to the number of rows in **B**. The product matrix **C** is a 2×2, i.e., the outer dimensions of **A** and **B**. To obtain the element c_{11} (in the first row and first column), we multiply corresponding elements of the first row of **A** by the elements of the first column of **B**. Then, we simply add the sum of these products. To obtain c_{12} we take the sum of products of the corresponding elements of the first row of **A** by the second column of **B**. This procedure is presented below for all four elements of **C**:

Element

$$c_{11} \quad (2,\ 1,\ 3) \begin{pmatrix} 1 \\ 2 \\ -1 \end{pmatrix} = 2\,(1) + 1\,(2) + 3\,(-1) = 1$$

$$c_{12} \quad (2,\ 1,\ 3) \begin{pmatrix} 0 \\ 4 \\ 5 \end{pmatrix} = 2\,(0) + 1\,(4) + 3\,(5) = 19$$

$$c_{21} \quad (4,\ 5,\ 6) \begin{pmatrix} 1 \\ 2 \\ -1 \end{pmatrix} = 4\,(1) + 5\,(2) + 6\,(-1) = 8$$

$$c_{22} \quad (4,\ 5,\ 6) \begin{pmatrix} 0 \\ 4 \\ 5 \end{pmatrix} = 4\,(0) + 5\,(4) + 6\,(5) = 50$$

Therefore, the product matrix **C** is: $\mathbf{C} = \begin{bmatrix} 1 & 19 \\ 8 & 50 \end{bmatrix}$

Now we multiply two more matrices to illustrate an important property concerning matrix multiplication

Example

$$\overset{\mathbf{A}}{\begin{bmatrix} 2 & 1 \\ 1 & 4 \end{bmatrix}} \overset{\mathbf{B}}{\begin{bmatrix} 3 & 5 \\ 5 & 6 \end{bmatrix}} = \begin{bmatrix} 2 \cdot 3 + 1 \cdot 5 & 2 \cdot 5 + 1 \cdot 6 \\ 1 \cdot 3 + 4 \cdot 5 & 1 \cdot 5 + 4 \cdot 6 \end{bmatrix} = \overset{\mathbf{AB}}{\begin{bmatrix} 11 & 16 \\ 23 & 29 \end{bmatrix}}$$

$$\overset{\mathbf{B}}{\begin{bmatrix} 3 & 5 \\ 5 & 6 \end{bmatrix}} \overset{\mathbf{A}}{\begin{bmatrix} 2 & 1 \\ 1 & 4 \end{bmatrix}} = \begin{bmatrix} 3 \cdot 2 + 5 \cdot 1 & 3 \cdot 1 + 5 \cdot 4 \\ 5 \cdot 2 + 6 \cdot 1 & 5 \cdot 1 + 6 \cdot 4 \end{bmatrix} = \overset{\mathbf{BA}}{\begin{bmatrix} 11 & 23 \\ 16 & 29 \end{bmatrix}}$$

Notice that $\mathbf{AB} \neq \mathbf{BA}$, i.e., the *order* in which matrices are multiplied makes a difference. The mathematical statement of this is to say that multiplication of matrices is not commutative. Multiplying matrices in two different orders (assuming they are conformable both ways) in general yields different results.

Example

$$
\begin{array}{ccc}
\mathbf{A} & \mathbf{x} & \mathbf{Ax} \\
\begin{bmatrix} 3 & 1 & 2 \\ 1 & 4 & 5 \\ 2 & 5 & 2 \end{bmatrix} & \begin{bmatrix} 2 \\ 6 \\ 3 \end{bmatrix} = & \begin{bmatrix} 18 \\ 41 \\ 40 \end{bmatrix} \\
(3 \times 3) & (3 \times 1) & (3 \times 1)
\end{array}
$$

Notice that multiplying a matrix on the right by a column vector takes the matrix into a column vector.

$$
(2, 5) \begin{bmatrix} 3 & 1 \\ 1 & 4 \end{bmatrix} = (11, 22)
$$

Multiplying a matrix on the left by a row vector results in a row vector. If we are multiplying more than two matrices, then we may *group at will*. The mathematical statement of this is that multiplication of matrices is associative. Thus, if we are considering the matrix product $\mathbf{ABC}$, we get the same result if we multiply $\mathbf{A}$ and $\mathbf{B}$ first (and then the result of that by $\mathbf{C}$) as if we multiply $\mathbf{B}$ and $\mathbf{C}$ first (and then the result of that by $\mathbf{A}$), i.e.,

$$\mathbf{A\ B\ C} = (\mathbf{A\ B})\ \mathbf{C} = \mathbf{A}\ (\mathbf{B\ C})$$

A matrix product that is of particular interest to us in Chapter 4 is of the following form:

$$
\begin{array}{ccc}
\mathbf{x'} & \mathbf{S} & \mathbf{x} \\
1 \times p & p \times p & p \times 1
\end{array}
$$

Note that this product yields a number, i.e., the product matrix is 1×1 or a number. The multivariate test statistic for 2 groups is of this form (except for a scalar constant in front).

Example

$$
(4, 2) \begin{bmatrix} 10 & 3 \\ 3 & 4 \end{bmatrix} \begin{bmatrix} 4 \\ 2 \end{bmatrix} = (46, 20) \begin{bmatrix} 4 \\ 2 \end{bmatrix} = 184 + 40 = 224
$$

2.3. OBTAINING THE MATRIX OF VARIANCES AND COVARIANCES

Now, we show how various matrix operations introduced thus far can be used to obtain a very important quantity in statistical work, i.e., the matrix of variances and covariances for a set of variables. Consider the following set of data

x_1	x_2
1	1
3	4
2	7

$$\bar{x}_1 = 2 \quad \bar{x}_2 = 4$$

First, we form the matrix X_d of deviation scores, i.e., how much each score deviates from the mean on that variable:

$$\mathbf{X}_d = \overset{\mathbf{X}}{\begin{bmatrix} 1 & 1 \\ 3 & 4 \\ 2 & 7 \end{bmatrix}} - \overset{\overline{\mathbf{X}}}{\begin{bmatrix} 2 & 4 \\ 2 & 4 \\ 2 & 4 \end{bmatrix}} = \begin{bmatrix} -1 & -3 \\ 1 & 0 \\ 0 & 3 \end{bmatrix}$$

Next we take the transpose of $\mathbf{X}_d$:

$$\mathbf{X}'_d = \begin{bmatrix} -1 & 1 & 0 \\ -3 & 0 & 3 \end{bmatrix}$$

Now we can obtain the so-called matrix of sums of squares and cross products (SSCP) as the product of $\mathbf{X}'_d$ and $\mathbf{X}_d$:

deviation scores for x_1 $\mathbf{X}'_d$ $\mathbf{X}_d$ deviation scores for x_2

$$\mathbf{SSCP} = \begin{bmatrix} -1 & 1 & 0 \\ -3 & 0 & 3 \end{bmatrix} \begin{bmatrix} -1 & -3 \\ 1 & 0 \\ 0 & 3 \end{bmatrix} = \begin{bmatrix} ss_1 & ss_{12} \\ ss_{21} & ss_2 \end{bmatrix}$$

The diagonal elements are just sums of squares:

$$ss_1 = (-1)^2 + 1^2 + 0^2 = 2$$
$$ss_2 = (-3)^2 + 0^2 + 3^2 = 18$$

Notice that these deviation sums of squares are the numerators of the variances for the variables, since the variance for a variable is

$$s^2 = \sum_i (x_{ii} - \bar{x})^2 / (n - 1).$$

The sum of deviation cross products (ss_{12}) for the two variables is

$$ss_{12} = ss_{21} = (-1)(-3) + 1\,(0) + (0)\,(3) = 3$$

This is just the numerator for the covariance for the two variables, since the definitional formula for covariance is given by:

$$s_{12} = \frac{\sum_{i=1}^{n} (x_{i1} - \bar{x}_1)\,(x_{i2} - \bar{x}_2)}{n - 1},$$

where $(x_{i1} - \bar{x}_1)$ is the deviation score for the ith subject on x_1 and $(x_{i2} - \bar{x}_2)$ is the deviation score for the ith subject on x_2.

Finally, the matrix of variances and covariances **S** is obtained from **SSCP** matrix by multiplying by a constant, namely $1/(n - 1)$:

$$\mathbf{S} = \frac{\mathbf{SSCP}}{n - 1}$$

variance for variable 1

$$\mathbf{S} = \frac{1}{2} \begin{bmatrix} 2 & 3 \\ 3 & 18 \end{bmatrix} = \begin{bmatrix} 1 & 1.5 \\ 1.5 & 9 \end{bmatrix}$$

variance for variable 2

covariance

Thus, in obtaining **S** we have:

1. Represented the scores on several variables as a matrix
2. Illustrated subtraction of matrices—to get $\mathbf{X}_d$
3. Illustrated the transpose of a matrix—to get $\mathbf{X}_d'$
4. Illustrated multiplication of matrices, i.e., $\mathbf{X}_d' \mathbf{X}_d$, to get **SSCP**.
5. Illustrated multiplication of a matrix by a scalar, i.e., by $1/(n - 1)$, to finally obtain **S**.

2.4. DETERMINANT OF A MATRIX

The determinant of a matrix **A** is denoted by $|\mathbf{A}|$ and is a unique number associated with each *square* matrix. There are two interrelated reasons why consideration of determinants is quite important for multivariate statistical analysis. First, the determinant of a covariance matrix represents the *generalized* variance for several variables. That is, it characterizes in a single number how much variability is present on a set of variables. Secondly, because the determinant represents variance for a set of variables, it is intimately involved in several multivariate test statistics. For example, in chapter three on regression analysis we use a test statistic called Wilk's Λ which involves a ratio of two determinants. Also, in k group multivariate analysis of variance the following form of Wilk's Λ ($\Lambda = |\mathbf{W}|/|\mathbf{T}|$) is the most widely used test statistic for determining whether several groups differ on a set of variables. The $\mathbf{W}$ and $\mathbf{T}$ matrices are multivariate generalizations of SS_w (sum of squares within) and SS_t (sum of squares total) from univariate ANOVA, and are defined and described in detail in Chapters 4 and 5.

There is a formal definition for finding the determinant of a matrix, but it is complicated and we do not present it. There are other ways of finding the determinant, and a convenient method for smaller matrices (4×4 or less) is the method of cofactors. For a 2×2 matrix the determinant could be evaluated by the method of cofactors; however, it is evaluated more quickly as simply the difference in the products of the diagonal elements.

Example

$$\mathbf{A} = \begin{bmatrix} 4 & 1 \\ 1 & 2 \end{bmatrix} \Rightarrow |\mathbf{A}| = 4 \cdot (2) - 1 \cdot (1) = 7$$

In general, for a 2×2 matrix $\mathbf{A} = \begin{bmatrix} a & b \\ c & d \end{bmatrix}$ then, $|\mathbf{A}| = ad - bc$.

To evaluate the determinant of a 3×3 matrix we need the method of cofactors and the following definition.

Definition: The *minor* of an element a_{ij} is the determinant of the matrix formed by deleting the ith row and the jth column.

Example

Consider the following matrix

$$\mathbf{A} = \begin{matrix} & a_{12} & a_{13} \\ & \downarrow & \downarrow \\ \begin{bmatrix} 1 & 2 & 3 \\ 2 & 2 & 1 \\ 3 & 1 & 4 \end{bmatrix} \end{matrix}$$

The minor of $a_{12} = 2$ is the determinant of the matrix $\begin{bmatrix} 2 & 1 \\ 3 & 4 \end{bmatrix}$ obtained by

deleting the first row and the second column. Therefore, the minor of 2 is

$$\begin{vmatrix} 2 & 1 \\ 3 & 4 \end{vmatrix} = 8 - 3 = 5.$$

The minor of $a_{13} = 3$ is the determinant of the matrix $\begin{bmatrix} 2 & 2 \\ 3 & 1 \end{bmatrix}$ obtained by

deleting the first row and the third column. Thus, the minor of 3 is $\begin{vmatrix} 2 & 2 \\ 3 & 1 \end{vmatrix} =$

$2 - 6 = -4.$

Definition: The cofactor of $a_{ij} = (-1)^{i+j} \times$ minor

Thus, the cofactor of an element will differ at most from its minor by sign. We now evaluate $(-1)^{i+j}$ for the first 3 elements of the above **A** matrix:

$$a_{11} : (-1)^{1+1} = 1$$
$$a_{12} : (-1)^{1+2} = -1$$
$$a_{13} : (-1)^{1+3} = 1$$

Notice that the signs for the elements in the first row alternate, and this pattern continues for all the elements in a 3×3 matrix. Thus, when evaluating the determinant for a 3×3 matrix it will be convenient to write down the pattern of signs and use it, rather than figuring out what $(-1)^{i+j}$ is for each element. That pattern of signs is:

$$\begin{bmatrix} + & - & + \\ - & + & - \\ + & - & + \end{bmatrix}$$

We denote the matrix of cofactors **C** as follows:

$$\mathbf{C} = \begin{bmatrix} c_{11} & c_{12} & c_{13} \\ c_{21} & c_{22} & c_{23} \\ c_{31} & c_{32} & c_{33} \end{bmatrix}$$

Now, *the determinant is obtained by expanding along any row or column of the matrix of cofactors.* Thus, for example, the determinant of **A** would be given by

$$|\mathbf{A}| = a_{11} c_{11} + a_{12} c_{12} + a_{13} c_{13}$$

(expanding along the first row)

or by

$$|\mathbf{A}| = a_{12} c_{12} + a_{22} c_{22} + a_{32} c_{32}$$

(expanding along the second column)

We now find the determinant of **A** by expanding along the first row:

Element	Minor	Cofactor	Element × Cofactor
$a_{11} = 1$	$\begin{vmatrix} 2 & 1 \\ 1 & 4 \end{vmatrix} = 7$	7	7
$a_{12} = 2$	$\begin{vmatrix} 2 & 1 \\ 3 & 4 \end{vmatrix} = 5$	-5	-10
$a_{13} = 3$	$\begin{vmatrix} 2 & 2 \\ 3 & 1 \end{vmatrix} = -4$	-4	-12

Therefore, $|\mathbf{A}| = 7 + (-10) + (-12) = -15$.

For a 4×4 matrix the pattern of signs is given by:

$$\begin{matrix} + & - & + & - \\ - & + & - & + \\ + & - & + & - \\ - & + & - & + \end{matrix}$$

and the determinant is again evaluated by expanding along any row or column. However, in this case the minors are determinants of 3×3 matrices, and the procedure becomes quite tedious. Thus, we do not pursue it any further here.

In the example in 2.3 we obtained the following covariance matrix

$$S = \begin{bmatrix} 1.0 & 1.5 \\ 1.5 & 9.0 \end{bmatrix}$$

We also indicated at the beginning of this section that the determinant of **S** can be interpreted as the generalized variance for a set of variables.

Now, the generalized variance for the above two variable example is just $|S|$ = $1 \cdot (9) - (1.5 \cdot 1.5) = 6.75$. Since for this example there is a covariance, the generalized variance is reduced by this. That is, some of the variance in variable 2 is accounted for by variance in variable 1. On the other hand, if the variables were uncorrelated (covariance = 0), then we would expect the generalized variance to be larger (since none of the variance in variable 2 can be acounted for by variance in variable 1), and this is indeed the case:

$$|S| = \begin{vmatrix} 1 & 0 \\ 0 & 9 \end{vmatrix} = 9$$

Univariate Notion of Variance

In univariate analysis of variance, the variance of a variable x is given by:

$$s_x^2 = \frac{\sum\limits_{i=1}^{n} (x_i - \bar{x})^2}{n - 1}$$

where n is the number of scores. Variance is thus a measure of dispersion or spread of the scores about the mean. How much the points disperse can be depicted graphically by plotting the points on the number line. Consider the following two sets of scores with the same mean of 5:

1. 4.5,4.5, 4.5, 5,5, 5.5, 5.5, 5.5
2. 0, 0, 2, 4, 5, 6, 8, 10, 10

It is clear that the variance is much greater for set 2, and plotting the points on the number line shows this:

```
              X X X
              X X X

        _____
          4   5   6


     X    x  x  x  x    x    X
     X                       X
   _____
     0    2    4    6    8    10
```

Multivariate Notions of Variance

In MANOVA there are several variables, each of which has a variance. In addition, each pair of variables has a covariance. Thus to represent variance in the multivariate case we must take into account all the variances and covariances. This gives rise to a matrix of these quantities. Consider the simplest case of 2 dependent variables. The population covariance matrix $\sum$ looks like this:

$$\sum = \begin{bmatrix} \sigma_1^2 & \sigma_{12} \\ \sigma_{21} & \sigma_2^2 \end{bmatrix}$$

where σ_1^2 is the population variance for variable 1 and σ_{12} is the population covariance for the two variables.

This population matrix is estimated by a sample covariance matrix (S)

$$\hat{\sum} = S = \begin{bmatrix} s_1^2 & s_{12} \\ s_{12} & s_2^2 \end{bmatrix}$$

where s_1^2 is the sample variance for variable 1, and s_{12} is the covariance for the two variables. Recall that the following relationship holds between the correlation and covariance:

$$r_{12} = \frac{s_{12}}{s_1 s_2}$$

Thus, one multivariate generalization of the univariate notion of variance is to replace the variance for a single variable by the *matrix* of variances and covariances for the set of variables. This multivariate generalization of variance is used to measure within-group variability on p dependent variables for the two-group multivariate analysis of variance test statistic (Hotellings T^2).

The other multivariate generalization of variance is to use the *determinant of the sample covariance matrix* S, i.e., $|S|$ as the measure of spread. This generalization *is called the generalized variance*. As we detail shortly, the determinant of the sample covariance matrix for two variables can be interpreted as the squared area of a parallelogram, whose sides are the standard deviations for the variables. For three variables, the determinant of the covariance matrix (generalized variance) can be interpreted as the squared volume of a parallelotype (the 3 dimensional analogue of the parallelogram).

In summarizing then, *for one variable variance can be interpreted as the spread of the points (scores) on a line, for two variables we can think of variance as squared area in the plane, and for 3 variables we can think of variance as squared volume in 3 space.*

In the following we present a concrete illustration of generalized variance with data.

Example

Consider the following scores on 2 dependent variables for 3 subjects.

Subject	x_1	x_2
1	2	3
2	3	7
3	4	5
Means	3	5

The sample variances for x_1 and x_2 are 1 and 4 respectively, and the covariance is 1, as the reader should confirm. Thus, the covariance matrix **S** is:

$$\mathbf{S} = \begin{bmatrix} 1 & 1 \\ 1 & 4 \end{bmatrix} \Rightarrow |\mathbf{S}| = 3 \text{ generalized variance}$$

Also, the correlation between the variables $r_{12} = \dfrac{1}{1 \cdot 2} = .5$.

Now, it can be shown that the cosine of the angle between the sides of the parallelogram is equal to the correlation between the variables (Bock, 1975, p. 28). Thus, here we have $r_{12} = .5 = \cos \theta$ so that from trigonometry $\theta = 60°$. Therefore, the parallelogram is as follows:

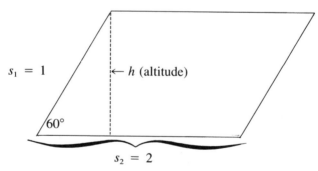

Now,

Area of Parallelogram = base × altitude

Since

$$\sin 60° = \frac{\text{opposite}}{\text{hypothenuse}} = \frac{h}{1} \Rightarrow h = \sin 60° = \frac{\sqrt{3}}{2}$$

$$\text{Area} = 2 \cdot \frac{\sqrt{3}}{2} = \sqrt{3} \Rightarrow \text{Squared area} = 3 = \text{generalized variance}$$

Notice how generalized variance is affected by the correlation between the variables. If, in the above example the angle had been 30° (indicating a higher correlation), then

Area $= b \cdot h = 2 \cdot \frac{1}{2} = 1 \Rightarrow$ generalized variance $= 1^2 = 1$, instead of 3 as above.

In the limiting case (i.e., where the variables were perfectly correlated), we would have $\cos \theta = 1 \Rightarrow \theta = 0°$, or no generalized variance since there would be no area.

2.5. INVERSE OF A MATRIX

The inverse of a square matrix $\mathbf{A}$ is a matrix $\mathbf{A}^{-1}$ which satisfies the following equation:

$$\mathbf{A} \, \mathbf{A}^{-1} = \mathbf{A}^{-1} \, \mathbf{A} = \mathbf{I}_n$$

where $\mathbf{I}_n$ is the identity matrix of order n. The identity matrix is simply a matrix with 1's on the main diagonal and 0's elsewhere.

$$\mathbf{I}_2 = \begin{bmatrix} 1 & 0 \\ 0 & 1 \end{bmatrix} \quad \mathbf{I}_3 = \begin{bmatrix} 1 & 0 & 0 \\ 0 & 1 & 0 \\ 0 & 0 & 1 \end{bmatrix}$$

Why is finding inverses important in statistical work? Because we do not literally have division with matrices, *inversion for matrices is the analogue of division for numbers*. This is why finding inverses is so important. An analogy with univariate ANOVA may be helpful here. In univariate ANOVA recall that the test statistic $F = MS_b/MS_w = MS_b \, (MS_w)^{-1}$, i.e., a ratio of between to within variability. The analogue of this test statistic in multivariate analysis of variance is $\mathbf{BW}^{-1}$, where $\mathbf{B}$ is a matrix which is the multivariate generalization of SS_b (sum of squares between), i.e., it is a measure of how differential the effects of treatments have been on the set of dependent variables. In the multivariate case we also want to "divide" the between-variability by the within-variability, but we don't have division per se. However, multiplying the $\mathbf{B}$ matrix by $\mathbf{W}^{-1}$ accomplishes this for us, since inversion is the analogue of division. Also, as shown in the next chapter, to obtain the regression coefficients for a multiple regression analysis, it is necessary to find the inverse of a matrix product involving the predictors.

Procedure for Finding the Inverse of a Matrix

1. Replace each element of the matrix **A** by it's minor.
2. Form the matrix of cofactors, attaching the appropriate signs from the pattern of signs.
3. Take the transpose of the matrix of cofactors, forming what is called the adjoint.
4. Divide each element of the adjoint by the determinant of **A**.

For symmetric matrices (with which this text deals almost exclusively), taking the transpose is *not* necessary, and hence when finding the inverse of a symmetric matrix step three is omitted.

We apply this procedure first to the simplest case, i.e., finding the inverse of a 2 × 2 matrix.

Example

$$\mathbf{D} = \begin{bmatrix} 4 & 2 \\ 2 & 6 \end{bmatrix}$$

The minor of 4 is the determinant of the matrix obtained by deleting the first row and the first column. What is left is simply the number 6, and the determinant of a number is that number. Thus we obtain the following matrix of minors:

$$\begin{bmatrix} 6 & 2 \\ 2 & 4 \end{bmatrix}$$

Now the pattern of signs for any 2 × 2 matrix is

$$\begin{bmatrix} + & - \\ - & + \end{bmatrix}$$

Therefore, the matrix of cofactors is

$$\begin{bmatrix} 6 & -2 \\ -2 & 4 \end{bmatrix}$$

The determinant of **D** = 6(4) − 2 (2) = 20.

Finally then, the inverse of **D** is obtained by dividing the matrix of cofactors by the determinant, obtaining

$$\mathbf{D}^{-1} = \begin{bmatrix} \dfrac{6}{20} & \dfrac{-2}{20} \\[2ex] \dfrac{-2}{20} & \dfrac{4}{20} \end{bmatrix}$$

To check that $\mathbf{D}^{-1}$ is indeed the inverse of **D**, note that

$$\underset{\mathbf{D}}{\begin{bmatrix} 4 & 2 \\ 2 & 6 \end{bmatrix}} \underset{\mathbf{D}^{-1}}{\begin{bmatrix} \dfrac{6}{20} & \dfrac{-2}{20} \\[2ex] \dfrac{-2}{20} & \dfrac{4}{20} \end{bmatrix}} = \underset{\mathbf{D}^{-1}}{\begin{bmatrix} \dfrac{6}{20} & \dfrac{-2}{20} \\[2ex] \dfrac{-2}{20} & \dfrac{4}{20} \end{bmatrix}} \underset{\mathbf{D}}{\begin{bmatrix} 4 & 2 \\ 2 & 6 \end{bmatrix}} = \underset{\mathbf{I}_2}{\begin{bmatrix} 1 & 0 \\ 0 & 1 \end{bmatrix}}$$

Example

Let us find the inverse for the 3×3 **A** matrix that we found the determinant for in the previous section. Since **A** is a symmetric matrix, it is not necessary to find 9 minors, but only 6, since the inverse of a symmetric matrix is symmetric. Thus we just find the minors for the elements on and above the main diagonal.

$$\mathbf{A} = \begin{bmatrix} 1 & 2 & 3 \\ 2 & 2 & 1 \\ 3 & 1 & 4 \end{bmatrix}$$

Recall again that the minor of an element is the determinant of the matrix obtained by deleting the row and column that the element is in.

Element	Matrix	Minor
$a_{11} = 1$	$\begin{bmatrix} 2 & 1 \\ 1 & 4 \end{bmatrix}$	$2 \cdot 4 - 1 \cdot 1 = 7$
$a_{12} = 2$	$\begin{bmatrix} 2 & 1 \\ 3 & 4 \end{bmatrix}$	$2 \cdot 4 - 1 \cdot 3 = 5$
$a_{13} = 3$	$\begin{bmatrix} 2 & 2 \\ 3 & 1 \end{bmatrix}$	$2 \cdot 1 - 2 \cdot 3 = -4$

$a_{22} = 2$

$$\begin{bmatrix} 1 & 3 \\ 3 & 4 \end{bmatrix}$$

$1 \cdot 4 - 3 \cdot 3 = -5$

$a_{23} = 1$

$$\begin{bmatrix} 1 & 2 \\ 3 & 1 \end{bmatrix}$$

$1 \cdot 1 - 2 \cdot 3 = -5$

$a_{33} = 4$

$$\begin{bmatrix} 1 & 2 \\ 2 & 2 \end{bmatrix}$$

$1 \cdot 2 - 2 \cdot 2 = -2$

Therefore, the matrix of minors for **A** is

$$\begin{bmatrix} 7 & 5 & -4 \\ 5 & -5 & -5 \\ -4 & -5 & -2 \end{bmatrix}$$

Recall that the pattern of signs is

$$\begin{matrix} + & - & + \\ - & + & - \\ + & - & + \end{matrix}$$

Thus, attaching the appropriate sign to each element in the matrix of minors and completing step 2 of finding the inverse we obtain:

$$\begin{bmatrix} 7 & -5 & -4 \\ -5 & -5 & 5 \\ -4 & 5 & -2 \end{bmatrix}$$

Now the determinant of **A** was found to be -15. Therefore, to complete the final step in finding the inverse we simply divide the above matrix by -15, and the inverse of **A** is

$$\mathbf{A}^{-1} = \begin{bmatrix} \dfrac{-7}{15} & \dfrac{1}{3} & \dfrac{4}{15} \\[2ex] \dfrac{1}{3} & \dfrac{1}{3} & \dfrac{-1}{3} \\[2ex] \dfrac{4}{15} & \dfrac{-1}{3} & \dfrac{2}{15} \end{bmatrix}$$

Again we can check that this is indeed the inverse by multiplying it by $\mathbf{A}$ to see if the result is the identity matrix.

Note that for the inverse of a matrix to exist the determinant of the matrix must *not* be equal to 0. This is because in obtaining the inverse each element is divided by the determinant, and division by 0 is not defined. If the determinant of a matrix $\mathbf{B} = 0$, we say $\mathbf{B}$ is *singular*. If $|\mathbf{B}| \neq 0$, we say $\mathbf{B}$ is nonsingular, and its inverse does exist.

2.6.   EIGENVALUES

The eigenvalues (roots) of a $p \times p$ matrix $\mathbf{A}$ are the solutions to the following determinantal equation: $|\mathbf{A} - \lambda\mathbf{I}| = 0$: $\mathbf{A}$ will have p roots, some of which may be 0.

Example

$$\mathbf{A} = \begin{bmatrix} 3 & 1 \\ 1 & 2 \end{bmatrix} \Rightarrow \mathbf{A} - \lambda\mathbf{I} = \begin{bmatrix} 3 & 1 \\ 1 & 2 \end{bmatrix} - \begin{bmatrix} \lambda & 0 \\ 0 & \lambda \end{bmatrix} = \begin{bmatrix} 3 - \lambda & 1 \\ 1 & 2 - \lambda \end{bmatrix}$$

Thus we have to solve the following determinantal equation:

$$\begin{vmatrix} 3 - \lambda & 1 \\ 1 & 2 - \lambda \end{vmatrix} = 0 \Rightarrow \lambda^2 - 5\lambda + 5 = 0,$$

an equation of the second degree which has two roots or solutions

Although we have defined eigenvalues abstractly, they are fundamental to the multivariate analysis of variance problem (MANOVA). In MANOVA we are greatly interested in solving the determinantal equation where $\mathbf{BW}^{-1}$ plays the role of $\mathbf{A}$.

Consider the following between- and within-matrices:

$$\mathbf{B} = \begin{bmatrix} 5 & 3 \\ 3 & 6 \end{bmatrix} \qquad \mathbf{W} = \begin{bmatrix} 2 & 1 \\ 1 & 3 \end{bmatrix}$$

Find the eigenvalues of $\mathbf{BW}^{-1}$.

$$|\mathbf{W}| = 2 \cdot 3 - 1 \cdot 1 = 5$$

$$\text{Pattern of signs} = \begin{bmatrix} + & - \\ - & + \end{bmatrix}$$

$$\text{Matrix of cofactors} = \begin{bmatrix} 3 & -1 \\ -1 & 2 \end{bmatrix}$$

$$\mathbf{W}^{-1} = \frac{1}{5}\begin{bmatrix} 3 & -1 \\ -1 & 2 \end{bmatrix} = \begin{bmatrix} .6 & -.2 \\ -.2 & .4 \end{bmatrix}$$

Thus,

$$\mathbf{BW}^{-1} = \begin{bmatrix} 5 & 3 \\ 3 & 6 \end{bmatrix}\begin{bmatrix} .6 & -.2 \\ -.2 & .4 \end{bmatrix} = \begin{bmatrix} 2.4 & .2 \\ .6 & 1.8 \end{bmatrix}$$

Now, the eigenvalues of $\mathbf{BW}^{-1}$ are solutions to the following determinantal equation:

$$|\mathbf{B}\,\mathbf{W}^{-1} - \lambda\,\mathbf{I}| = 0$$

$$\mathbf{B}\,\mathbf{W}^{-1} - \lambda\mathbf{I} = \begin{bmatrix} 2.4 & .2 \\ .6 & 1.8 \end{bmatrix} - \begin{bmatrix} \lambda & 0 \\ 0 & \lambda \end{bmatrix}$$

$$|\mathbf{BW}^{-1} - \lambda\mathbf{I}| = \begin{vmatrix} 2.4 - \lambda & .2 \\ .6 & 1.8 - \lambda \end{vmatrix} = 0$$

or $(2.4 - \lambda)(1.8 - \lambda) - .2\,(.6) = 0$

$\lambda^2 - 4.2\,\lambda + 4.2 = 0$

This is an equation of the second degree, a so-called quadratic equation. There is a general formula for solving *any* quadratic equation. If the general equation is given by $a\lambda^2 + b\lambda + c = 0$, then the formula for the two roots is:

$$\lambda_i = \frac{-b \pm \sqrt{b^2 - 4\,ac}}{2a}$$

The coefficients for the above equation are: $a = 1, b = -4.2, c = 4.2$. Plugging into the above formula

$$\lambda_i = \frac{-(-4.2) \pm \sqrt{(-4.2)^2 - 4(1)\cdot(4.2)}}{2(1)}$$

$$\lambda_i = (4.2 \pm .92)/2$$

Thus, the roots or eigenvalues are $\lambda_1 = 2.558$, $\lambda_2 = 1.642$.

The sum of the eigenvalues of a matrix is called the *trace*. If the matrix is $\mathbf{BW}^{-1}$, then the trace will have a very important meaning as it will be one of the multivariate test statistics, and will tell us whether the groups differ significantly on the set of dependent variables.

EXERCISES CHAPTER 2

1. Given:

$$\mathbf{A} = \begin{bmatrix} 2 & 4 & 1 \\ 3 & -2 & 5 \end{bmatrix} \quad \mathbf{B} = \begin{bmatrix} 1 & 2 \\ 2 & 1 \\ 3 & 4 \end{bmatrix} \quad \mathbf{C} = \begin{bmatrix} 1 & 3 & 5 \\ 6 & 2 & 1 \end{bmatrix}$$

$$\mathbf{D} = \begin{bmatrix} 4 & 2 \\ 2 & 6 \end{bmatrix} \quad \mathbf{E} = \begin{bmatrix} 1 & -1 & 2 \\ -1 & 3 & 1 \\ 2 & 1 & 10 \end{bmatrix} \quad \mathbf{X} = \begin{bmatrix} 1 & 2 \\ 3 & 1 \\ 4 & 6 \\ 5 & 7 \end{bmatrix}$$

$$\mathbf{u}' = (1, 3), \mathbf{v} = \begin{bmatrix} 2 \\ 7 \end{bmatrix}$$

Find, where meaningful, each of the following:
a) $\mathbf{A} + \mathbf{C}$
b) $\mathbf{A} + \mathbf{B}$
c) $\mathbf{AB}$
d) $\mathbf{AC}$
e) $\mathbf{u}' \mathbf{D} \mathbf{u}$
f) $\mathbf{u}' \mathbf{v}$
g) $(\mathbf{A} + \mathbf{C})'$
h) $3 \mathbf{C}$
i) $|\mathbf{D}|$
j) $\mathbf{D}^{-1}$
k) $|\mathbf{E}|$

l) $\mathbf{E}^{-1}$

m) $\mathbf{u'\, D^{-1} u}$

n) $\mathbf{BA}$ (compare this result with [c])

o) $\mathbf{X'X}$

2. In the next chapter on multiple regression we are interested in predicting each person's score on a dependent variable y from a linear combination of their scores on several predictors (x_i's). If there were 3 predictors, then the prediction equations for N subjects would look like this:

$$y_1 = e_1 + b_0 + b_1 x_{11} + b_2 x_{12} + b_3 x_{13}$$

$$y_2 = e_2 + b_0 + b_1 x_{21} + b_2 x_{22} + b_3 x_{23}$$

$$y_3 = e_3 + b_0 + b_1 x_{31} + b_2 x_{32} + b_3 x_{33}$$

$$\vdots \qquad\qquad \vdots \qquad\qquad \vdots$$

$$y_N = e_N + b_0 + b_1 x_{N1} + b_2 x_{N2} + b_3 x_{N3}$$

Note: The e_i's are the portion of y not predicted by the x's, and the b's are the regression coefficient. Express this set of prediction equations as a single matrix equation. Hint: The right hand portion of the equation will be of the form:

vector + matrix times vector

3. Using the approach detailed in section 2.3, find the matrix of variances and covariances for the following data:

x_1	x_2	x_3
4	3	10
5	2	11
8	6	15
9	6	9
10	8	5

4. Consider the following two situations:

a) $s_1 = 10$, $s_2 = 7$, $r_{12} = .80$

b) $s_1 = 9$, $s_2 = 6$, $r_{12} = .20$

For which situation is the generalized variance larger? Does this surprise you?

5. Calculate the determinant for $\mathbf{A} = \begin{bmatrix} 9 & 2 & 1 \\ 2 & 4 & 5 \\ 1 & 5 & 3 \end{bmatrix}$

Could $\mathbf{A}$ be a covariance matrix for a set of variables? Explain.

3

Multiple Regression

3.1. INTRODUCTION

In multiple regression we are interested in predicting a dependent variable from a set of predictors. In a previous course in statistics the reader probably studied simple regression, predicting a dependent variable from a single predictor. An example would be predicting college GPA from high school GPA. Since human behavior is complex and influenced by many factors, such single predictor studies are necessarily limited in their predictive power. For example, in the above college GPA study, we are able to predict college GPA better by considering other predictors such as scores on a standardized test (verbal, quantitative), and some noncognitive variables, such as study habits, attitude toward education. That is, we look to other predictors (often test scores) which tap other aspects of criterion behavior.

In modeling the relationship between y and the x's, we are assuming a *linear* model is appropriate. Of course, it is possible that a more complex model (curvilinear) may be necessary to predict y accurately. Polynomial regression may be appropriate, or if there is non-linearity in the parameters, then BMDP3R can be used to fit a model.

In this chapter, various ways of selecting a good set of predictors are presented and the importance of cross-validating the regression equation is considered in some detail. Detecting outliers on y and on the set of x's is also detailed. The importance of isolating influential data points, i.e., points which have a profound influence on the regression coefficients, and deciding what to do about them are discussed. Also, the practical implementation of running all the above analyses on BMDP2R and BMDP9R and on SPSSX is illustrated. We first consider, however, simple linear regression, familiar to most readers.

We wish to emphasize that our focus in this chapter is on the use of multiple regression for prediction. Another broad, related area is the use of regression for explanation. Cohen and Cohen (1983) and Pedhazur (1982) have excellent, extended discussions of the use of regression for explanation purposes (e.g., causal modeling).

3.2. SIMPLE REGRESSION

For one predictor the mathematical model is

$$y_i = \beta_0 + \beta_1 x_i + e_i \quad i = 1, 2, \ldots, n$$

where β_0 and β_1 are parameters to be estimated. The e_i's are the errors of prediction, and are assumed to be independent, with constant variance and normally distributed with a mean of 0. If these assumptions are valid for a given set of data, then the estimated errors $(\hat{e}_i)$ should have similar properties. For example, the $\hat{e}_i$ should be normally distributed, or at least approximately normally distributed. This is considered further in section 3.11. The $\hat{e}_i$ are called the residuals. How do we estimate the parameters? The *least squares* criterion is used, i.e., the sum of the squared estimated errors of prediction is minimized:

$$\hat{e}_1^{\,2} + \hat{e}_2^{\,2} + \ldots\ldots + \hat{e}_n^{\,2} = \sum_{i=1}^{n} \hat{e}_i^{\,2} = \min$$

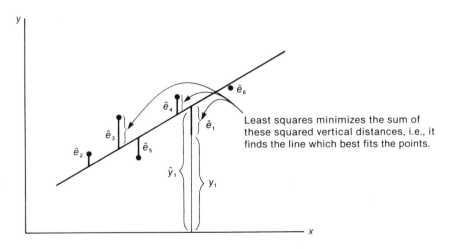

Least squares minimizes the sum of these squared vertical distances, i.e., it finds the line which best fits the points.

FIG. 3.1. Geometrical Representation of Least Squares Criterion.

Now, $\hat{e}_i = y_i - \hat{y}_i$ *where* y_i is the actual score on the dependent variable and $\hat{y}_i$ is the estimated score for the ith subject.

The scores for each subject (x_i, y_i) define a point in the plane. What the least squares criterion does is find the line which best fits the points. Geometrically this corresponds to minimizing the sum of the squared vertical distances $(\hat{e}_i^2)$ of each subject's y score from their estimated y score. This is illustrated in Figure 3.1.

Example

To illustrate simple regression we consider a small part of a "Sesame Street" data base from Glasnapp and Poggio (1985), who present data on many variables, including 12 background variables and 8 achievement variables, for 240 subjects. Sesame Street was developed as a television series aimed mainly at teaching pre-school skills to three to five year old children. Data was collected on many achievement variables both before (pretest) and after (posttest) viewing of the series. We consider here only one of the achievement variables: knowledge of body parts. In particular, we consider pretest and posttest data on body parts for a sample of 80 children.

The control lines for running the simple regression on BMDP9R are given in Table 3.1, along with annotation on how to obtain the scatterplot and plot of residuals in the same run. Figure 3.2 presents the scatterplot for prebody and postbody variables and shows a fair amount of clustering (reflecting the moderate correlation of .5825) about the regression line. The probability value of .000 shows there is a significant correlation at the .05 level, i.e., there is a linear

TABLE 3.1
Control Lines for Simple Regression Example on BMDP9R

```
/PROBLEM TITLE IS 'SIMPLE REGRESSION — DEPENDENT VARIABLE —
POSTTEST ON BODY PARTS, PREDICTOR — PRETEST'.
/INPUT VARIABLES ARE 2. FORMAT IS STREAM.
/VARIABLE NAMES ARE PREBODY,POSTBODY.
①/REGRESS DEPENDENT IS POSTBODY. INDEPENDENT IS PREBODY.
②/PRINT CASE = 80.
③/PLOT HIST. YVAR = POSTBODY. XVAR = PREBODY. STATISTICS.
/END
     DATA (in Appendix at the end of this chapter)
```

---

①In the REGRESSION paragraph we indicate which is the dependent variable and which is the independent (predictor) variable.

②This PRINT paragraph is necessary to obtain a listing of all the data. Without it, only the first 5 cases would be printed.

③With the PLOT paragraph we obtain three important pieces of information. First, HIST yields a histogram of the standardized residuals; recall that an assumption of linear regression is that the raw (and hence standardized) residuals should be normally distributed with a mean of 0. The next part of the paragraph (YVAR = POSTBODY. XVAR = PREBODY.) yields a scatter plot for the data. Finally, STATISTICS yields the correlation and associated significance level, along with the regression line.

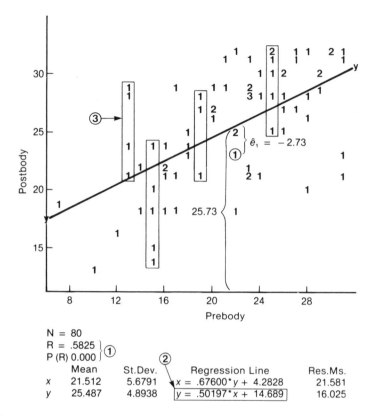

N = 80
R = .5825
P (R) 0.000 } ①

	Mean	St.Dev.	Regression Line	Res.Ms.
x	21.512	5.6791	$x = .67600*y + 4.2828$	21.581
y	25.487	4.8938	$y = .50197*x + 14.689$	16.025

②

①The correlation between postbody and prebody is .5825—a moderate relationship—but significant well beyond the .05 level.

②The prediction equation $\hat{y}_i = .50197\,x_i + 14.689$. Thus, for the point circled on the scatterplot (i.e., (22, 23)) the predicted value for postbody is $\hat{y}_i = .50197\,(22) + 14.689 = 25.73$. For this point the error of estimate is $e_i = 23 - 25.73 = -2.73$.

③The horizontal boxes give a visual representation of variances of postbody scores for different values of prebody—this is related to the homogeneity of residuals assumption for different values of the predictor.

FIG. 3.2. Scatter Plot and Regression Line for Simple Regression Example.

(proportional) relationship between prebody and postbody scores. Incidentally, numbers greater than 1 in the scatterplot mean that number of subjects had the same scores on prebody and postbody. For example, the 3 in the scatterplot occurring at (23, 28) means three subjects have these identical scores, as the reader may verify by checking the data in the Appendix of this chapter.

Table 3.2, which has the histogram of standardized residuals, shows that the

TABLE 3.2
Histogram of Standarized Residuals and Variances of Postbody
Scores for Various Values of the Predictor (Prebody)

HISTOGRAM OF STANDARIZED (STUDENTIZED) RESIDUALS EACH BIN OF THE HISTOGRAM IS LABELED WITH ITS LOWER LIMIT. NOTE THAT IF THE COUNT FOR A BIN EXCEEDS 100, ONLY 100 ASTERISKS WILL BE PRINTED.

−2.4	2	**
−2.2	1	*
−2.0	3	***
−1.8	1	*
−1.6	1	*
−1.4	4	****
−1.2	3	***
−1.0	3	***
−0.8	3	***
−0.6	4	****
−0.4	1	*
−0.2	9	*********
0.0	7	*******
0.2	5	*****
0.4	11	***********
0.6	6	******
0.8	6	******
1.0	4	****
1.2	0	
1.4	3	***
1.6	1	*
1.8	2	**

The distribution of residuals, viewed sideways, is roughly normal, although somewhat negatively skewed.

Prebody Score	Postbody Scores	Variance
13	28, 21, 24, 29	13.67
15	14, 24, 20, 18, 15	16.20
19	28, 27, 21	14.33
25	28, 25, 32, 32, 30, 31	7.47

assumption of normality of residuals is roughly satisfied, although there is certainly some negative skewness.

3.3. MULTIPLE REGRESSION FOR TWO PREDICTORS—MATRIX FORMULATION

The linear model for two predictors is a simple extension of what we had for one predictor:

$$y_i = \beta_0 + \beta_1 x_1 + \beta_2 x_2 + e_i$$

where β_0 (regression constant), β_1 and β_2 are the parameters to be estimated, and e is error of prediction. We consider a small data set to illustrate the estimation process.

y	x_1	x_2
3	2	1
2	3	5
4	5	3
5	7	6
8	8	7

We model each subject's y score as a linear function of the β's:

$$y_1 = 3 = 1 \cdot \beta_0 + 2 \cdot \beta_1 + 1 \cdot \beta_2 + e_1$$

$$y_2 = 2 = 1 \cdot \beta_0 + 3 \cdot \beta_1 + 5 \cdot \beta_2 + e_2$$

$$y_3 = 4 = 1 \cdot \beta_0 + 5 \cdot \beta_1 + 3 \cdot \beta_2 + e_3$$

$$y_4 = 5 = 1 \cdot \beta_0 + 7 \cdot \beta_1 + 6 \cdot \beta_2 + e_4$$

$$y_5 = 8 = 1 \cdot \beta_0 + 8 \cdot \beta_1 + 7 \cdot \beta_2 + e_5$$

This series of equations can be expressed as a single matrix equation:

$$
\mathbf{y} =
\begin{bmatrix} 3 \\ 2 \\ 4 \\ 5 \\ 8 \end{bmatrix}
=
\overset{\mathbf{X}}{
\begin{bmatrix} 1 & 2 & 1 \\ 1 & 3 & 5 \\ 1 & 5 & 3 \\ 1 & 7 & 6 \\ 1 & 8 & 7 \end{bmatrix}}
\overset{\boldsymbol{\beta}}{
\begin{bmatrix} \beta_0 \\ \beta_1 \\ \beta_2 \end{bmatrix}}
+
\overset{\mathbf{e}}{
\begin{bmatrix} e_1 \\ e_2 \\ e_3 \\ e_4 \\ e_5 \end{bmatrix}}
$$

It is pretty clear that the y scores and the e_i define column vectors, while not so clear is how the boxed-in area can be represented as the product of two matrices, i.e., $\mathbf{X} \boldsymbol{\beta}$.

The first column of 1s is used to obtain the regression constant. The remaining two columns contain the scores for the subjects on the two predictors. Thus, the classic matrix equation for multiple regression is:

$$\mathbf{y} = \mathbf{X} \boldsymbol{\beta} + \mathbf{e} \tag{1}$$

Now, it can be shown using the calculus that the least square estimates of the β's are given by:

$$\hat{\boldsymbol{\beta}} = (\mathbf{X'} \mathbf{X})^{-1} \mathbf{X'} \mathbf{y} \tag{2}$$

Thus, for our data the estimated regression coefficients would be:

$$\hat{\beta} = \left\{ \begin{bmatrix} 1 & 1 & 1 & 1 & 1 \\ 2 & 3 & 5 & 7 & 8 \\ 1 & 5 & 3 & 6 & 7 \end{bmatrix} \overset{\mathbf{X}}{\begin{bmatrix} 1 & 2 & 1 \\ 1 & 3 & 5 \\ 1 & 5 & 3 \\ 1 & 7 & 6 \\ 1 & 8 & 7 \end{bmatrix}} \right\}^{-1} \overset{\mathbf{X}'}{\begin{bmatrix} 1 & 1 & 1 & 1 & 1 \\ 2 & 3 & 5 & 7 & 8 \\ 1 & 5 & 3 & 6 & 7 \end{bmatrix}} \overset{\mathbf{y}}{\begin{bmatrix} 3 \\ 2 \\ 4 \\ 5 \\ 8 \end{bmatrix}}$$

Let us do this in pieces. First

$$\mathbf{X'X} = \begin{bmatrix} 5 & 25 & 22 \\ 25 & 151 & 130 \\ 22 & 130 & 120 \end{bmatrix} \text{ and } \mathbf{X'y} = \begin{bmatrix} 22 \\ 131 \\ 111 \end{bmatrix}$$

Furthermore, the reader should show that

$$(\mathbf{X'X})^{-1} = \frac{1}{1016} \begin{bmatrix} 1220 & -140 & -72 \\ -140 & 116 & -100 \\ -72 & -100 & 130 \end{bmatrix}$$

where 1016 is the determinant of $\mathbf{X'X}$. Thus, the estimated regression coefficients are given by

$$\hat{\beta} = \frac{1}{1016} \begin{bmatrix} 1220 & -140 & -72 \\ -140 & 116 & -100 \\ -72 & -100 & 130 \end{bmatrix} \begin{bmatrix} 22 \\ 131 \\ 111 \end{bmatrix} = \begin{bmatrix} .50 \\ 1 \\ -.25 \end{bmatrix}$$

Therefore, the regression (prediction) equation is

$$\hat{y}_i = .50 + x_1 - .25 x_2$$

To illustrate the use of this equation, we find the predicted score for subject 3 and the residual for that subject:

$$\hat{y}_3 = .5 + 5 - .25(3) = 4.75$$
$$\hat{e}_3 = y_3 - \hat{y}_3 = 4 - 4.75 = -.75$$

3.4. MATHEMATICAL MAXIMIZATION NATURE OF LEAST SQUARES REGRESSION

In general then, in multiple regression the *linear combination* of the x's which is maximally correlated with y is sought. Minimizing the sum of squared errors of prediction is equivalent to *maximizing* the correlation between the observed and predicted y scores. This maximized Pearson correlation is called the multiple correlation, i.e., $R = r_{y_i \hat{y}_i}$. Nunnally (1978) characterized the procedure as "wringing out the last ounce of predictive power" (obtained from the linear combination of x's, i.e., from regression equation). Since the correlation is maximum for the sample from which it is derived, when the regression equation is applied to an independent sample from the same population (i.e., cross-validated), the predictive power drops off. If the predictive power drops off sharply, then the equation is of limited utility. That is, it has no generalizability, and hence is of limited scientific value. After all, we derive the prediction equation for the purpose of predicting with it on future (other) samples. If the equation does not predict well on other samples, then it is not fulfilling the purpose for which it was designed.

Sample size (n) and the number of predictors (k) are two crucial factors which determine how well a given equation will cross-validate (i.e., generalize). In particular, the n/k ratio is crucial. For small ratios (5:1 or less) the shrinkage in predictive power can be substantial. A study by Guttman (1941) illustrates this point. He had 136 subjects and 84 predictors, and found the multiple correlation on the original sample to be .73. However, when the prediction equation was applied to an independent sample the new correlation was only .04! In other words, the good predictive power on the original sample was due to capitalization on chance, and the prediction equation had no generalizability.

We return to the cross-validation issue in more detail later in this chapter, where we show that *for social science research, about 15 subjects per predictor are needed for a reliable equation*, i.e., for an equation that will cross-validate with little loss in predictive power.

3.5. BREAKDOWN OF SUM OF SQUARES IN REGRESSION AND F TEST FOR MULTIPLE CORRELATION

In analysis of variance we broke down variability about the grand mean into between- and within-variability. In regression analysis variability about the mean is broken down into variability due to regression and variability about the regression. To get at the breakdown, we start with the following identity:

$$y_i - \hat{y}_i = (y_i - \bar{y}) - (\hat{y}_i - \bar{y})$$

Now we square both sides, obtaining

$$(y_i - \hat{y}_i)^2 = [(y_i - \bar{y}) - (\hat{y}_i - \bar{y})]^2$$

Then we sum over the subjects, from 1 to n:

$$\sum_{i=1}^{n} (y_i - \hat{y}_i)^2 = \sum_{i=1}^{n} [(y_i - \bar{y}) - (\hat{y}_i - \bar{y})]^2$$

By algebraic manipulation (see Draper & Smith, 1981, pp. 17–18), this can be rewritten as:

$$\sum (y_i - \bar{y})^2 \;=\; \sum (y_i - \hat{y}_i)^2 \;+\; \sum (\hat{y}_i - \bar{y})^2 \qquad (3)$$

sum of squares about mean	=	sum of squares about regression (SS_{res})	+	sum of squares due to regression (SS_{reg})
df: $n - 1$	=	$(n - k - 1)$	+	k

This results in the following analysis of variance table and the F test for determining whether the population multiple correlation is different from 0.

Analysis of Variance Table for Regression

Source	SS	df	MS	F
Regression	SS_{reg}	k	S_{reg}/k	
				$\dfrac{MS_{reg}}{MS_{res}}$
Residual (error)	SS_{res}	$n - k - 1$	$SS_{res}/(n - k - 1)$	

Recall that since the residual for each subject is $\hat{e}_i = y_i - \hat{y}_i$, the mean square error term can be written as $MS_{res} = \Sigma \hat{e}_i^2/(n - k - 1)$. Now, R^2 (squared multiple correlation) is given by:

$$R^2 = \frac{\text{sum of squares due to regression}}{\text{sum of squares about the mean}} = \frac{\sum (\hat{y}_i - \bar{y})^2}{\sum (y_i - \bar{y})^2} = \frac{SS_{reg}}{SS_{tot}}$$

Thus, R^2 measures the proportion of total variance on y that is accounted for by the set of predictors. By simple algebra then we can rewrite the F test in terms of R^2 as follows:

$$F = \frac{R^2/k}{(1 - R^2)/(n - k - 1)}, \text{ with } k \text{ and } (n - k - 1) \, df \qquad (4)$$

We feel this test is of limited utility, since it does *not necessarily* imply that the equation will cross-validate well, and this is the crucial issue in regression analysis.

Example 1

An investigator obtains $R^2 = .50$ on a sample of 50 subjects with 10 predictors. Do we reject the null hypothesis that the population multiple correlation $= 0$?

$$F = \frac{.50/10}{(1 - .50)/(50 - 10 - 1)} = 3.9 \text{ with } 10 \text{ and } 39 \, df$$

This is significant at .01 level, since the critical value is 2.8.

However, since the n/k ratio is only 5/1, the prediction equation will probably not predict well on other samples and is therefore of questionable utility.

Example 2

A study by Schutz (1977) on California principals and superintendents illustrates how capitalization on chance in multiple regression (if the researcher is unaware of it) can lead to misleading conclusions. Schutz was interested in validating a "contingency theory of leadership," i.e., that success in administering schools calls for different personality styles depending on the social setting of the school. The theory seems plausible, and in what follows we are not criticizing the theory per se, but the empirical validation of it. Schutz's procedure for validating the theory involved establishing a relationship between various personality attributes (24 predictors) and several measures of administrative success in heterogeneous samples with respect to social setting using multiple regression, that is, find the multiple R for each measure of success on 24 predictors. Then he showed that the magnitude of the relationships was greater for subsamples homogeneous with respect to social setting. The problem was that he had nowhere near adequate sample size for a reliable prediction equation. Below we present the total sample sizes and the subsamples homogeneous with respect to social setting:

	Superintendents	*Principals*
Total	$n = 77$	$n = 147$
Subsample(s)	$n = 29$	$n_1 = 35, n_2 = 61, n_3 = 36$

Indeed, Schutz did find that the R's in the homogeneous subsamples were on the average .34 greater than in the total samples; however, this was an artifact of the multiple regression procedure in this case. As Schutz went from total to his subsamples the number of predictors (k) approached sample size (n). For this situation the multiple correlation increases to 1 *regardless* of whether there is any relationship between y and the set of predictors. And in 3 of 4 of Schutz's subsamples the n/k ratios became dangerously close to 1. In particular it is the case that $E(R^2) = k/(n - 1)$, when the population multiple correlation $= 0$. (Morrison, 1976).

To dramatize this, consider subsample 1 for the principals. Then $E(R^2) = 24/34 = .706$, even when there is *no* relationship between y and set of predictors: The critical value required just for statistical significance of R at .05 is 2.74, which implies $R^2 > .868$, just to be confident that the population multiple correlation is different from 0!

3.6. RELATIONSHIP OF SIMPLE CORRELATIONS TO MULTIPLE CORRELATION

The ideal situation, in terms of obtaining a high R would be to have each of the predictors significantly correlated with the dependent variable and for the predictors to be uncorrelated with each other, so that they measure different constructs and are able to predict different parts of the variance on y. Of course, in practice we will not find this since almost all variables are correlated to some degree. A good situation in practice then would be were most of our predictors correlate significantly with y and the predictors have relatively low correlations among themselves. To illustrate the above points further consider the following three patterns of intercorrelations for 3 predictors.

	X_1	X_2	X_3		X_1	X_2	X_3		X_1	X_2	X_3
(1) Y	.20	.10	.30	(2) Y	.60	.50	.70	(3) Y	.60	.70	.70.
X_1		.50	.40	X_1		.20	.30	X_1		.70	.60
X_2			.60	X_2			.20	X_2			.80

In which of these cases would you expect the multiple correlation to be the largest and the smallest respectively?

Here it is quite clear that R will be the smallest for 1 since the highest correlation of any of the predictors with y is .30, whereas for the other two patterns at least one of the predictors has a correlation of .70 with y. Thus, we know that R will be at least .70 for cases 2 and 3, whereas for case 1 we only know that R will be at least .30. Furthermore, there is no chance that R for case 1 might become larger than that for 2 or 3 because the intercorrelations among the predictors for 1 are approximately as large or larger than those for the other 2 cases.

We would expect R to be largest for case 2 because each of the predictors is moderately to strongly tied to y and there are low intercorrelations (i.e., little redundancy) among the predictors, exactly the kind of situation we would hope to find in practice. We would expect R to be greater in case 2 than in case 3, because in case 3 there is considerable redundancy among the predictors. Although the correlations of the predictors with Y are slightly higher in case 3 (.60, .70, .70) than in case 2 (.60, .50, .70), the much higher intercorrelations among the predictors for case 3 will severely limit the ability of X_2 and X_3 to predict additional variance beyond that of X_1 (and hence significantly increase R), whereas this will not be true for case 2.

When there are high intercorrelations among the predictors, as can be the case when several cognitive measures are used as predictors, the problem is referred to as *multicollinearity*.[1] Multicollinearity poses a real problem for the researcher using multiple regression since (1) it severely limits the size of R and (2) it makes determining the importance of a given predictor difficult because the effects of the predictors are confounded due to the high correlation among them.

A study by Dizney and Gromen (1967) illustrates very nicely how multicollinearity among the predictors limits the size of R. They studied how well reading proficiency (x_1) and writing proficiency (x_2) would predict course grade in college german. The correlation matrix below resulted:

	x_1	x_2	y
x_1	1	.58	.33
x_2		1	.45
y			1

Note the multicollinearity for x_1 and x_2 $(r_{x_1,x_2} = .58)$, and also that x_2 has a simple correlation of .45 with y. The multiple correlation R was only .46. Thus, the relatively high correlation between reading and writing severely limited the ability of reading to add hardly anything (only .01) to the prediction of German grade above and beyond that of writing.

3.7. SEMI-PARTIAL CORRELATIONS—OBTAINING AN ADDITIVE PARTITIONING OF R^2

We now consider a procedure that, for a *given ordering* of the predictors, will enable us to determine the unique contribution each predictor is making in accounting for variance on y. That is, this procedure (the use of semipartial correlations) will disentangle the correlations among the predictors.

The partial correlation between variables 1 and 2 with variable 3 partialled from both 1 and 2 is the correlation with variable 3 held constant, as the reader may recall. The formula for partial correlation is given by

---

[1]There are more subtle types of multicollinearity that can occur. See Belsley, Kuh, and Welsch (1980, chapter 3) for an extensive discussion.

$$r_{12.3} = \frac{r_{12} - r_{13}\, r_{23}}{\sqrt{1 - r_{13}^2}\, \sqrt{1 - r_{23}^2}}$$

We have introduced the partial correlation first for two reasons: (1) the semipartial correlation is a variant of the partial correlation and (2) the partial correlation will be involved in computing more complicated semi-partial correlations.

For breaking down R^2 we will want to work with the semipartial, sometimes called part, correlation. The formula for the semipartial correlation is:

$$r_{12.3(s)} = \frac{r_{12} - r_{13}\, r_{23}}{\sqrt{1 - r_{23}^2}}$$

The only difference between this equation and the previous one is that the denominator here doesn't contain the standard deviation of the partialled scores for variable 1.

In multiple correlation we wish to partial the independent variables (the predictors) from one another, but not from the dependent variable. We wish to leave the dependent variable intact, and not partial any variance attributable to the predictors. Let $R^2_{y.12\ldots k}$ denote the squared multiple correlation for the k predictors, where the predictors appear after the dot. Consider the case of one dependent variable and three predictors. It can be shown that:

$$R^2_{y.123} = r_{y1}{}^2 + r^2_{y2.1(s)} + r^2_{y3.12(s)}$$

where

$$r_{y2.1(s)} = \frac{r_{y2} - r_{y1}\, r_{21}}{\sqrt{1 - r_{21}{}^2}}$$

is the semipartial correlation between y and variable 2, with variable 1 partialled only from variable 2, and $r_{y3.12(s)}$ is the semipartial correlation between y and variable 3 with variables 1 and 2 partialled only from variable 3:

$$r_{y3.12(s)} = \frac{r_{y3.1(s)} - r_{y2.1(s)}\, r_{23.1}}{\sqrt{1 - r_{23.1}{}^2}}$$

Thus, through the use of semipartial correlations we disentangle the correlations among the predictors and determine how much *unique* variance on each predictor is related to variance on y.

We now consider two examples to illustrate the meaning of squared semipartial correlations; the first example being a verbal explanation while the second is a graphical representation.

Example 3—Verbal Explanation of Variance Breakdown

y—freshman college GPA
predictor 1—high school GPA

predictor 2—SAT total score
predictor 3—attitude toward education

$$R^2_{y1.123} = r_{y1}{}^2 + r^2_{y2.1(s)} + r^2_{y3.12(s)}$$

$r_{y1}{}^2$ — gives the variance in college GPA scores that is predictable from variability on high school GPA scores. That is, because of differences in high school GPA the subject will differ (vary) in college GPA.

$r^2_{y2.1(s)}$ — gives the residual variance in SAT scores (i.e., variance *unrelated* to variance on high school GPA) which is related to variance in college GPA.

$r^2_{y3.12(s)}$ — gives the residual variance on attitude (i.e., variance *not* related to its correlations with high school GPA and SAT score) which is related to variance on college GPA.

Example 4—Graphical Representation of Variance Breakdown

This is easiest to see for 2 predictors. Therefore, suppose we have the following: $r_{y1} = .60, r_{y2} = .50$ and $r_{12} = .70$. We will use a Venn diagram, where a circle represents variance for a variable, and overlap between two circles indicates amount of variance the two variables share.

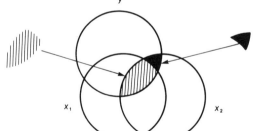

common variance in y that both predictors 1 and 2 account for

variance in y accounted for by predictor 2 after the effect of predictor 1 has been partialled out—this is only 1.2.

Below we present the semipartial correlation, showing how the 1.2% is arrived at:

$$r_{y2.1(s)} = \frac{r_{y2} - r_{y1}\,r_{21}}{\sqrt{1 - r^2_{21}}} = \frac{.50 - .60(.70)}{\sqrt{1 - .49}} = .11 \Rightarrow r^2_{y2.1(s)} = .012$$

3.8. IMPORTANCE OF THE ORDER OF THE PREDICTORS IN REGRESSION ANALYSIS

The order in which the predictors enter a regression equation can make a great deal of difference with respect to how much variance on y they account for, especially for moderate or highly correlated predictors. Only for uncorrelated predictors (which would rarely occur in practice), does the order not make a difference. We give two examples to illustrate.

Example 5

A dissertation by Crowder (1975) attempted to predict ratings of trainably mentally (TMs) retarded individuals using I.Q. (x_2) and scores from a TEST of Social Inference (TSI). He was especially interested in showing that the TSI had incremental predictive validity. The criterion was the average ratings by two individuals in charge of the TMs. The intercorrelations among the variables were:

$$r_{x_1x_2} = .59, \ r_{yx_2} = .54, \ r_{yx_1} = .566$$

Now, consider two orderings for the predictors, one where TSI is entered first, and the other ordering where I.Q. is entered first.

First Ordering % of variance		Second Ordering % of variance	
TSI	32.04	I.Q.	29.16
I.Q.	6.52	TSI	9.40

The first ordering conveys an overly optimistic view of the utility of the TSI scale. Since we know that I.Q. will predict ratings it should be entered first in the equation (as a control variable), and then TSI to see what it's incremental validity is, i.e., how much it *adds* to predicting ratings above and beyond what I.Q. does. Because of the moderate correlation between I.Q. and TSI, the amount of variance accounted for by TSI differs considerably when entered first vs. second (32.04 vs. 9.4).

The 9.4% of variance accounted for by TSI when entered second is obtained through the use of the semipartial correlation previously introduced:

$$r_{y1.2(s)} = \frac{.566 - .54(.59)}{\sqrt{1 - .59^2}} = .306 \Rightarrow r^2_{y1.2(s)} = .094$$

Example 6

Consider the following matrix of correlations for a three predictor problem:

	x_1	x_2	x_3
y	.60	.70	.70
x_1		.70	.60
x_2			.80

Notice that the predictors are strongly intercorrelated.

How much variance in y will x_3 account for if entered first? if entered last?

If x_3 is entered first, then it will account for $(.7)^2 \times 100$ or 49% of variance on y, a sizable amount.

To determine how much variance x_3 will account for if entered last, we need to compute the following second order semipartial correlation:

$$r_{y3.12(s)} = \frac{r_{y3.1(s)} - r_{y2.1(s)} \, r_{23.1}}{\sqrt{1 - r_{23.1}^2}}$$

We show the details below for obtaining $r_{y3.12(s)}$.

$$r_{y2.1(s)} = \frac{r_{y2} - r_{y1} r_{21}}{\sqrt{1 - r_{21}^2}} = \frac{.70 - (.6)(.7)}{\sqrt{1 - .49}}$$

$$r_{y2.1(s)} = \frac{.28}{.714} = .392$$

$$r_{y3.1.(s)} = \frac{r_{y3} - r_{y1} \, r_{31}}{\sqrt{1 - r_{31}^2}} = \frac{.7 - .6(.6)}{\sqrt{1 - .6^2}} = .425$$

$$r_{23.1} = \frac{r_{23} - r_{21} \, r_{31}}{\sqrt{1 - r_{21}^2} \, \sqrt{1 - r_{31}^2}} = \frac{.80 - (.7)(.6)}{\sqrt{1 - .49} \, \sqrt{1 - .36}} = .665$$

$$r_{y3.12(s)} = \frac{.425 - .392(.665)}{\sqrt{1 - .665^2}} = \frac{.164}{.746} = .22$$

$$r_{y3.12(s)}^2 = (.22)^2 = .048$$

Thus, when x_3 enters last it accounts for only 4.8% of the variance on y! This is a tremendous drop from the 49% it accounted for when entered first. Because the 3 predictors are so highly correlated, most of the variance on y that x_3 could have accounted for has already been accounted for by x_1 and x_2.

3.9. SEVERAL REASONS FOR WORKING WITH A SMALL NUMBER OF PREDICTORS

1.   Principle of scientific parsimony
2.   Reducing the number of predictors improves the n/k ratio, and this helps cross validation prospects.
3.   Note the following from Lord and Novick (1968, p. 274). "Experience in psychology and in many other fields of application has shown that it is seldom worthwhile to include very many predictors variables in a regression equation, for the incremental validity of new variables, after a certain point, is usually very low. This is true because tests tend to overlap in content and consequently the addition of a fifth or sixth test may add little that is new to the battery and still relevant to the criterion."

4. If there is initially a large set of predictors, it is often possible to account for most of the variance in this set with a much smaller set of underlying constructs (principal components). These new constructs, the components or rotated factor scores, serve as the predictors. In the chapter on components analysis we illustrate the use of principal components to reduce a set of predictors to a much smaller subset, which are then used as the new predictors in a regression analysis.

Suppressor Variables

Lord and Novick (1968) state the following two rules of thumb for the selection of predictor variables:

1. Choose variables that correlate highly with the criterion but that have low intercorrelations.
2. To these variables add other variables that have low correlations with the criterion but that have high correlations with the other predictors.

At first blush the second rule of thumb may not seem to make sense, but what they are talking about is suppressor variables. To illustrate specifically why a suppressor variable can help in prediction we consider a hypothetical example.

Example 7

Consider a two predictor problem with the following correlations among the variables: $r_{yx_1} = .60$, $r_{yx_2} = 0$, and $r_{x_1x_2} = .50$.

Note that x_1 by itself accounts for $(.6)^2 \times 100$, or 36% of the variance on y. Now consider entering x_2 into the regression equation first. It will of course account for no variance on y, and it may seem like we have gained nothing. But, if we now enter x_1 into the equation (after x_2), it's predictive power is enhanced. This is because there is irrelevant variance on x_1 (i.e., variance that does not relate to y) which is related to x_2. In this case that irrelevant variance is $(.5)^2 \times 100$ or 25%. When this irrelevant variance is partialled out (or suppressed), the remaining variance on x_1 is more strongly tied to y. Calculation of the semipartial correlation shows this:

$$r_{y1.2(s)} = \frac{r_{yx_1} - r_{yx_2} r_{x_1x_2}}{\sqrt{1 - r_{x_1x_2}^2}} = \frac{.60 - 0}{\sqrt{1 - .5^2}} = .693$$

Thus, $r_{y1.2(s)}^2 = .48$, and the predictive power of x_1 has increased from accounting for 36% to accounting for 48% of the variance on y.

3.10. THREE POPULAR PROCEDURES FOR SELECTING A GOOD SET OF PREDICTORS[1]

All three of the prediction selection procedures we discuss, forward, backward, and stepwise, are available on both the BMDP and SPSSX packages.

1. *Forward Selection*—The first predictor to enter the equation is the one which has the largest correlation with y. If this predictor is significant, then the predictor with the largest semipartial correlation with y is considered. If this predictor is also significant, then the predictor with the next largest semipartial correlation with y is considered, etc. At some stage a given predictor will not make a significant contribution to prediction, and the procedure is terminated.

2. *Backward Selection*—The steps are as follows:

a) An equation with all predictors is computed.

b) The partial F is calculated for every predictor, treated as though it were the last predictor to enter the regression equation.

c) The smallest partial F value, say F_1, is compared with a preselected significance value (F_0), or to an F to remove as in the BMDP2R program. If $F_1 < F_0$, remove that predictor and recompute the equation with the remaining variables. Reenter stage B.

If, on the other hand, $F_1 > F_0$, adopt the equation as calculated.

3. *Stepwise Regression*—This is basically a variation on the forward selection procedure. However, at each stage of the procedure, a test is made of the least useful predictor. Thus, a predictor that may have been the best entry candidate earlier may now be superfluous. Most statisticians recommend this procedure. Draper and Smith (1981) offer however the following caveats: "Stepwise regression can easily be abused by the amateur statistician. As with all the procedures discussed, sensible judgment is still required in the initial selection of variables and in the critical examination of the model through examination of residuals" (p. 310).

As shown on the BMDP2R printout (Table 3.1), at each stage of the regression analysis there are "F to Enter" values for each predictor. However, there are no tail probabilities given for these F's to tell us whether a predictor is significant at some alpha level. Why not? The reason is that the ordinary F distribution is *not* appropriate here, because the largest F is being selected out of all F's available. Thus the appropriate critical value will be larger (and can be considerably larger) than would be obtained from the ordinary null F distribution. Draper and Smith (1981, p. 311) note, "Studies have shown, for example, that in some cases where an entry F test was made at the α level, the appropriate

---

[1]A method some statisticians prefer is Mallow's C_k(1973). Good models have $C_k \approx k$ (cf. Weisberg, 1985, pp. 216–17, or Draper and Smith, 1981, pp. 299–301). C_k is available on the BMDP9R program.

probability was $q\alpha$, where there were q entry candidates at that stage." This is saying, for example, that an experimenter may think his probability or erroneously including a predictor is .05, when in fact his *actual* probability of erroneously including the predictor is .50 (if there were 10 entry candidates at that point)!

Thus, *the F tests for all three of the above procedures are positively biased, and the greater the number of predictors the larger the bias. Hence, these F tests should be used only as rough guides as to the usefulness of the predictors chosen.* The acid test is how well the predictors do under cross-validation. It is unwise to use *any* of the above procedures with 20 or 30 predictors and only 100 subjects, since capitalization on chance is great, and the results will not cross-validate well. To find an equation that will cross-validate well, it is best to select a small set of predictors. Then force into the equation first those predictors which have proven themselves from previous literature, and then check the incremental validity of the others. Here, if one has 150 to 200 S's, the equation will validate well.

TABLE 3.3
Control Lines from BMDP2R for Two Predictor Sample Problem

/PROBLEM TITLE IS ' EXAMPLE 1 '.		
①/INPUT VARIABLES ARE 3. FORMAT IS STREAM.		
/VARIABLE NAMES ARE MARK,COMP,CERTIF.		
②/PRINT CORR.DATA.		
③/REGRESSION DEPENDENT IS MARK.		
④/END		
476	111	68
457	92	46
540	90	50
551	107	59
575	98	50
698	150	66
545	118	54
574	110	51
645	117	59
556	94	97
634	130	57
637	118	51
390	91	44
562	118	61
560	109	66

①Variables in this INPUT paragraph refers to the total number variables in the analysis; here it includes the dependent variable and the two predictors.

Recall that STREAM is the name given by the BMDP package to free format, with multiple cases possible on the same line. Thus, if we wished the data for the first 4 subjects could be put on line 1, the data for the next 4 subjects on line 2, etc.

②This PRINT paragraph is necessary in order to obtain the correlation matrix for the variables and to obtain a listing of the data.

③In this REGRESSION paragraph we tell the program which of the variables is to be predicted. Although the dependent variable happens to be first in this example, that is not necessary.

④This END paragraph simply indicates to the program the end of the control instructions.

TABLE 3.4
Selected Printout from BMDP2R for Two Predictor Sample Problem

STEP NO.   1

VARIABLE ENTERED   2 COMP

MULTIPLE R	0.7512
MULTIPLE R-SQUARE	0.5643
ADJUSTED R-SQUARE	0.5308
STD. ERROR OF EST.	53.4933

ANALYSIS OF VARIANCE

	SUM OF SQUARES	DF	MEAN SQUARE	F RATIO
REGRESSION	48186.098	1	48186.10	16.84
RESIDUAL	37199.898 ③	13	2861.531	

①

VARIABLES IN EQUATION FOR MARK   ·   F

VARIABLE	COEFFICIENT	STD. ERROR OF COEFF	STD REG COEFF	TOLERANCE	TO REMOVE	LEVEL
(Y-INTERCEPT	164.25464)					
COMP 2	3.59116	0.8751	0.751	1.00000	16.84	1

VARIABLES NOT IN EQUATION

VARIABLES	PARTIAL CORR.	TOLERANCE	F TO ENTER	LEVEL
CERTIF 3	0.20772	0.98564	0.54	1

CASE NO. LABEL		PREDICTED	RESIDUAL	
1	②	562.9	−86.87	*
2		494.6	−37.64	
3		487.5	52.54	
4		548.5	2.492	
5		516.2	58.81	*
6		702.9	−4.928	
7		588.0	−43.01	
8		559.3	14.72	
9		584.4	60.58	*
10		501.8	54.18	*
11		631.1	2.895	*
12		588.0	48.99	
13		491.0	−101.0	*
14		588.0	−26.01	
15		555.7	4.310	

EACH ASTERISK REPRESENTS ONE STANDARD DEVIATION ④

①Thus, the prediction equation is $\hat{y}_i = 164.255 + 3.591$ COMP

②Applying the above prediction equation for subject 1, we obtain

$$\hat{y}_1 = 164.255 + 3.591(111) = 562.9,$$

and hence the residual for this subject is

$$\hat{e}_1 = y_1 - \hat{y}_1 = 476 - 562.9 = -86.9$$

③$SS_{res} = (-86.87)^2 + (-37.64)^2 + \ldots + (-26.01)^2 + (4.31)^2 = 37189$, which is the value reported within rounding error. It is this sum that is *minimized* in obtaining the regression equation.

④The standard deviation is just square root of mean square residual, i.e., $\sqrt{2861.53} = 53.49$.

Example 8—Stepwise Regression Problem 1

As a simple initial example of the stepwise regression procedure, we consider a two predictor data set from Draper and Smith (1981). The dependent variable (MARK) was scores for students from Great Britain on a General Certificate of Education exam. One predictor was their score on the compulsory papers (COMP) and the other predictor was the score on the School Certificate English Language paper (CERTIF). The control lines for running the analysis on BMDP2R, along with selected printout and annotation is given in Tables 3.3 and 3.4. The data for the problem is in Table 3.3.

The predictor to be considered for entry into the equation first is the one with the highest simple correlation with MARK, which is COMP (correlation = .75). Furthermore, COMP indeed does enter the equation since it's F to enter (16.84) *exceeds* the program default F to enter value of 4. The other predictor does not enter the equation since it's F to enter (.54) is less than 4.

Example 9—Stepwise Regression Problem 2

We illustrate the use of stepwise regression on a data set from Morrison (1983). The dependent variable (y) was instructor course evaluation ($n = 32$) in an MBA course. We focus on the following 5 predictors: clarity, stimulating, knowledge, interest, and course evaluation. The control lines for running the stepwise regression on BMDP2R, along with the correlation matrix for the variables, are given in Table 3.5. The data is given in the appendix of this chapter.

BMDP2R has "F to enter" and "F to remove" values which govern whether

TABLE 3.5
Control Lines for BMDP2R and Correlation Matrix for Stepwise
Regression Problem 2

```
/PROBLEM TITLE IS ' STEPWISE REGRESSION '.
/INPUT VARIABLES = 6. FORMAT IS STREAM.
/VARIABLE NAMES ARE INSTEVAL,CLARITY,STIMUL,KNOWLDGE,INTEREST,COUEVAL.
/PRINT CORR. DATA.
/REGRESSION DEPENDENT IS INSTEVAL. ENTER = 3. REMOVE = 2.   ①
/END
```

DATA LINES

CORRELATION MATRIX

		INSTEVAL	CLARITY	STIMUL	KNOWLDGE	INTEREST	COUEVAL
		1	2	3	4	5	6
INSTEVAL	1	1.0000					
CLARITY	2	0.8618	1.000				
STIMUL	3	0.7394	0.6174	1.0000			
KNOWLDGE	4	0.2818	0.0573	0.0777	1.0000		
INTEREST	5	0.4350	0.2002	0.3169	0.5833	1.0000	
COUEVAL	6	0.7379	0.6510	0.5229	0.0409	0.4477	1.0000

①In our previous example (Table 3.3) we used the default F to ENTER and F to REMOVE values. If we wish to change them, as here, then we do so in the REGRESSION paragraph.

TABLE 3.6   Selected Output from BMDP2R for Stepwise Regression Problem 2

STEP NO. 1 ①

VARIABLE ENTERED	2 CLARITY
MULTIPLE R	0.8618
MULTIPLE R-SQUARE	0.7427
ADJUSTED R-SQUARE	0.7341
STD. ERROR OF EST.	0.4112

ANALYSIS OF VARIANCE

	SUM OF SQUARES	DF	MEAN SQUARE	F RATIO
REGRESSION	14.645519	1	14.64552	86.60
RESIDUAL	5.0733671	30	0.1691122	

VARIABLES IN EQUATION FOR INSTEVAL

VARIABLE	COEFFICIENT	STD. ERROR OF COEFF	STD REG COEFF	TOLERANCE	F TO REMOVE
(Y-INTERCEPT	0.59792)				
CLARITY 2	0.63589	0.0683	0.862	1.00000	86.60

VARIABLES NOT IN EQUATION

VARIABLE	LEVEL*	PARTIAL CORR.	TOLERANCE	F TO ENTER
STIMUL 3	1*	0.51956	0.61883	10.72
KNOWLDGE 4	*	0.45907	0.99672	7.74
INTEREST 5	*	0.52824	0.95993	11.22 ②
COUEVAL 6	*	0.45930	0.57619	7.75

STEP NO. 2

VARIABLE ENTERED	5 INTEREST
MULTIPLE R	0.9025
MULTIPLE R-SQUARE	0.8145
ADJUSTED R-SQUARE	0.8017
STD. ERROR OF EST.	0.3551

ANALYSIS OF VARIANCE

	SUM OF SQUARES	DF	MEAN SQUARE	F RATIO
REGRESSION	16.061157	2	8.030579	63.67
RESIDUAL	3.6577215	29	0.1261283	

VARIABLES IN EQUATION FOR INSTEVAL

VARIABLE	COEFFICIENT	STD. ERROR OF COEFF	STD REG COEFF	TOLERANCE	F TO REMOVE
(Y-INTERCEPT	0.25399)				
CLARITY 2	0.59530	0.0602	0.807	0.95993	97.75
INTEREST 5	0.27701	0.0827	0.273	0.95993	11.22

VARIABLES NOT IN EQUATION

VARIABLE	LEVEL*	PARTIAL CORR.	TOLERANCE	F TO ENTER
STIMUL 3	1*	0.47086	0.57989	7.98 ③
KNOWLDGE 4	1*	0.21810	0.65603	1.40
COUEVAL 6	*	0.30453	0.47122	2.86

①This predictor enters the equation first, since it has the highest simple correlation with the dependent variable INSTEVAL, i.e., .8618.

②INTEREST has the opportunity to enter the equation next since it has the largest partial correlation (.528) with the dependent variable, and does enter since it's F to enter of 11.22 exceeds 3.

③Since STIMUL has the strongest tie to INSTEVAL, after the effects of CLARITY and INTEREST are partialled out, it gets the opportunity to enter the equation next. STIMUL does enter since its $F = 7.98$ exceeds the value of 3 we have set.

TABLE 3.7
Selected Output from BMDP2R for Stepwise Regression Problem 2

STEP NO.   3

VARIABLE ENTERED	3 STIMUL
MULTIPLE R	0.9250
MULTIPLE R-SQUARE	0.8556
ADJUSTED R-SQUARE	0.8402
STD. ERROR OF EST.	0.3189

ANALYSIS OF VARIANCE

	SUM OF SQUARES	DF	MEAN SQUARE	F RATIO
REGRESSION	16.872131	3	5.624043	55.32
RESIDUAL	2.8467541	28	0.1016698	

VARIABLES IN EQUATION FOR INSTEVAL

VARIABLE		COEFFICIENT	STD. ERROR OF COEFF	STD REG COEFF	TOLERANCE	F TO REMOVE	LEVEL*
(Y-INTERCEPT		0.2136)					
CLARITY	2	0.48211	0.0674	0.653	0.61881	51.24	1*
STIMUL	3	0.19474	0.0690	0.266	0.57989	7.98	1*
INTEREST	5	0.22267	0.0767	0.220	0.89951	8.43	1*

* * * * * F LEVELS(3.000, 2.000) OR TOLERANCE INSUFFICIENT FOR FURTHER STEPPING

VARIABLES NO IN EQUATION

VARIABLE		PARTIAL CORR.	TOLERANCE	F TO ENTER	LEVEL
KNOWLDGE	4	0.31248	0.64687	2.92 ①	1*
COUEVAL	6	0.28873	0.46562	2.46	1*

SUMMARY TABLE

STEP NO.	VARIABLE ENTERED	R	RSQ ②	INCREASE IN RSQ	F TO ENTER
1	2 CLARITY	0.8618	0.7427	0.7427	86.6024
2	5 INTEREST	0.9025	0.8145	0.0718	11.2238
3	3 STIMUL	0.9250	0.8556	0.0411	7.9765

SQUARED SEMI PARTIAL CORRELATIONS (→ INCREASE IN RSQ column)

① Since neither of these F to enter values exceeds 3 (the value we have set), the remaining predictors KNOWLDGE and COUEVAL do *not* enter the equation, and the process terminates.

② This column shows how the variance accounted for on dependent variable increases as predictors are added to the equation. With just CLARITY in the equation we account for 74.27%; adding INTEREST increases the variance accounted for to 81.45%; and finally with 3 predictors (STIMUL added) we account for 85.56% of the variance on INSTEVAL.

a predictor will enter the regression equation, and which predictors will be removed (e.g., if using backward selection). The *default* values set by the program are $F = 4$ to enter (i.e., if an F value for a predictor is > 4, then it enters the equation), and $F = 3.9$ to remove (if an F for a predictor is < 3.9, it is removed from the equation. We have set these values somewhat lower in this example ($F = 3$ to enter and $F = 2$ to remove) in order to increase our chances of not leaving out a potentially important predictor.

Examination of the correlation matrix reveals that 3 of the predictors (CLARITY, STIMUL, and COUEVAL) are strongly related to INSTEVAL (simple correlations of .86, .74, and .74 respectively, rounding off to 2 decimal places). Since CLARITY has the highest correlation, it will enter the equation first. Superficially, it might appear that STIMUL or COUEVAL would enter next; however, we must take into account how these predictors are correlated with CLARITY and indeed both have fairly high correlations with CLARITY (.62 and .65 respectively). Thus, they will not account for as much unique variance on INSTEVAL, above and beyond that of CLARITY, as first appeared. On the other hand, INTEREST, which has a considerable lower correlation with INSTEVAL (.44), has a low correlation with CLARITY (.20). Thus, the variance on INSTEVAL it accounts for is relatively independent of the variance CLARITY accounted for. And, as seen in the regression analysis, it is INTEREST that enters the regression equation second.

Examining the selected output for the regression analysis in Tables 3.6 and 3.7, we note that CLARITY enters first, since it has the highest F to enter. The next predictor to enter is the one with the largest F to enter after the effects of CLARITY have been partialled out, and this is the INTEREST variable ($F = 11.22$), just beating out STIMUL ($F = 10.72$). INTEREST enters the equation since it's F value exceeds the "critical value of 3" that we have set. The F test is really a test of significance of the partial correlation, which is .528.

With CLARITY and INTEREST in the equation, the procedure now determines which of the remaining predictors add most, above and beyond these 2, to predicting INSTEVAL. Since the partial correlation for STIMUL is highest (.47) and the associated $F = 7.98$ exceeds the F to enter of 3, STIMUL enters the equation. No other predictors enter the equation since the largest F to enter is 2.92, which is less than the critical value of 3.

Also, note that none of the 3 predictors that entered the equation are later removed, since none of their F to remove values are less than 2.

3.11. CHECKING ASSUMPTIONS
FOR THE REGRESSION MODEL

Recall that in the linear regression model it is assumed that the errors are independent and follow a normal distribution with constant variance. The normality assumption can be checked through use of histogram of the standardized or studentized residuals, as we did in Table 3.2 for the simple regression example. The independence assumption implies that the subjects are responding independently of one another. This is an important assumption. We show in Chapter 6 (in the context of analysis of variance) that if independence is violated only mildly then the probability of a type I error will be *several* times greater than the lvel the experimenter thinks he or she is working at. Thus, instead of rejecting falsely 5% of the time, the experimenter may be rejecting falsely 25 or 30% of the time. We now consider an example were this assumption was violated.

Example 10

Nold and Freedman (1977) had each of 22 college freshmen write four in class essays in two 1 hour sessions separated by a span of several months. In doing a subsequent stepwise regression analysis in predicting quality of essay response (by summing the scores from the four essays), they used an n of 88. However, the responses for each subject on the 4 essays are obviously going to be correlated, so that there are not 88 independent observations, but only 22.

Residual Plots

There are various types of plots that are available for assessing potential problems with the regression model (Draper and Smith, 1981; Weisberg, 1985). One of the most useful plots graphs the studentized residuals (which we denote here by r(i) vs the predicted values ($\hat{y}_i$). If the assumptions of the linear regression model are tenable then the studentized residuals should scatter randomly about a horizontal line defined by $r_{(i)} = 0$,   as shown in Figure 3.3a. *Any systematic pattern or clustering of the residuals suggest a model violation(s).* Three such systematic patterns are indicated in Figures 3.3b to 3.3d. Figure 3.3b shows a systematic quadratic (second degree equation) clustering of the residuals. For Figure 3.3c the variability of the residuals increases systematically as the predicted values increase, suggesting a violation of the constant variance assumption.

In Figure 3.4 we present the residual plots for two real data sets, one of which was discussed earlier (Morrison data, Example 3.9). The first data set in nonlinear, as a simple scatterplot of x vs y would show. The residual plot in Figure 3.4a suggests both nonlinearity and nonconstant variance. The plot is similar to Figure 3.3d, although based on less data. The plot of the Morrison data in Figure 3.4b shows random variation of the residuals about 0, suggesting no violations.

It is important to note that the plots in Figure 3.3 are somewhat idealized, constructed to be clear illustrations of violations. As Weisberg (1985, p. 131) states, "Unfortunately, these idealized plots cover up one very important point; in real data sets, the true state of affairs is rarely this clear."

If nonlinearity or nonconstant variance are found, there are various remedies. For non-linearity perhaps a polynomial model is needed. Or sometimes a transformation of the data will enable a non-linear model to be approximated by a

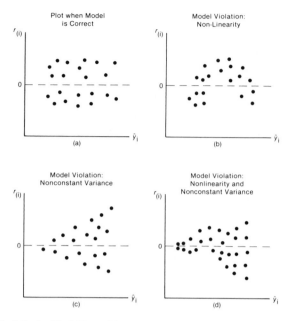

FIG. 3.3. Residual Plots of Studentized Residuals vs Predicted Values.

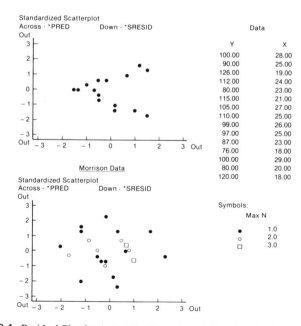

FIG. 3.4. Residual Plot for Actual Nonlinear Data & Plot for Morrison Data.

linear one. For non-constant variance, weighted least squares is one possibility, or more commonly, use of a variance stabilizing transformation (such as square root or log). We refer the reader to Weisberg (1985, Chapter 6) for an excellent discussion of remedies for regression model violations.

3.12. CONTROLLING THE ORDER OF ENTRY OF PREDICTORS IN REGRESSION EQUATION

With the forward and stepwise selection procedures, the order of entry of predictors into the regression equation is determined via a mathematical maximization procedure. That is, the first predictor to enter is the one with the largest (maximized) correlation with y, the second to enter is the predictor with the largest semipartial correlation, etc. However, there are situations where one may not want the mathematics to determine the order of entry of the predictors.

TABLE 3.8
Controlling the Order of Predictors and Forcing Predictors into the
Equation with BMDP2R and SPSSX Regression

BMDP2R

/PROBLEM TITLE IS ' MULT REG- X3 AND X4 ARE PROVEN PREDICTORS'.
/INPUT VARIABLES ARE 6. FORMAT IS STREAM.
/VARIABLE NAMES ARE X1,X2,X3,X4,X5,Y.
/PRINT CORR. DATA.
/REGRESSION DEPENDENT IS Y.
① LEVELS ARE 3,3,1,2,3.
② FORCE = 2.
/END
    DATA

SPSSX REGRESSION

TITLE 'FORCING X3 AND X4 AND USING FORWARD SELECTION FOR OTHERS'
DATA LIST FREE/ Y X1 X2 X3 X4 X5
LIST
BEGIN DATA
  DATA LINES
END DATA
REGRESSION VARIABLES = Y X1 X2 X3 X4 X5/
  DEPENDENT = Y/
③ENTER X3/ ENTER X4/ FORWARD/

---

①Variables with smaller level values are entered before those with larger level values. Therefore, here, proven predictor X3 will enter first, then proven predictor X4 will enter second.

②Variables with LEVEL ≤ FORCE are forced into the equation. This implies here that proven predictors X3 and X4 will be forced into the equation.

③These two ENTER subcommands will force the predictors in the specific order indicated. Then the FORWARD subcommand will determine whether any of the remaining predictors (X1, X2, or X5) have semi-partial correlations large enough to be "significant." If we wished to completely a priori have the predictors enter as in the variable list above, then we would use five ENTER subcommands: ENTER X1/ ENTER X2/ ENTER X3/ ENTER X4/ ENTER X5/

For example, suppose we have a five predictor problem, with two proven predictors from previous research. The other three predictors are included to see if they have any incremental validity. In this case we would want to enter the two proven predictors in the equation first (as control variables), and then let the remaining 3 predictors "fight it out" to determine whether any of them add anything significant to predicting y above and beyond the proven predictors.

With BMDP2R or SPSSX REGRESSION we can, on an a priori basis, totally, partially, or not at all control the order of entry of predictors into the equation. (see BMDP manual, 1983, pp 257–258, and SPSSX User's Guide, 1983, pp 604–605). This gives us complete flexibility to fit any situation, which is very desirable. In Table 3.8 we illustrate the use of BMDP2R and SPSSX REGRESSION for the above 5 predictor problem, where we are partially controlling the order of entry.

3.13   CROSS VALIDATION AND THE SHRINKAGE FORMULAS

We indicated earlier that it was crucial for the researcher to cross-validate the prediction equation to see whether it would predict well on an independent sample. That is, it was important to determine whether the equation had generalizability.

How is the cross-validation done? The sample is randomly split in half. The regression equation is found on the so-called derivation sample (also called the screening sample). This prediction equation is then applied to the other sample (validation or calibration) to see how well it predicts the y scores there. We give a hypothetical example below, randomly splitting 100 subjects.

Derivation Sample	Validation Sample		
$n = 50$	$n = 50$		
Prediction Equation $\hat{y}_i = 4 + .3x_1 + .7x_2$	y	x_1	x_2
	6	1	.5
	4.5	2	.3
	. . . .		
	7	5	.2

Now, using the above prediction equation we predict the y scores in the validation sample:

$$\hat{y}_1 = 4 + .3\,(1) + .7\,(.5) = 4.65$$

$$\hat{y}_2 = 4 + .3\,(2) + .7\,(.3) = 4.81$$

. . . .

$$\hat{y}_{50} = 4 + .3\,(5) + .7(.2) = 5.64$$

The cross-validated R then is the correlation for the following set of scores:

y	$\hat{y}_i$
6	4.65
4.5	4.81
. . . .	
7	5.64

We illustrate the random splitting and cross-validation using the BMDP9R and BMDP6D programs. The 9R program randomly splits the sample (in the TRANSFORM paragraph) and does the regression analysis. The 6D program is used to obtain the cross-validated correlation. In Table 3.9 we present the control lines for randomly splitting and cross validating for a data set having 50 subjects and 5 predictors. The data for this example is given in the appendix of this chapter.

Herzberg (1969) presents a discussion of various formulas that have been used to estimate the amount of shrinkage found in R^2. The one most commonly used (and due to Wherry) is:

$$\hat{\rho}^2 = 1 - (n - 1)/n - k - 1)(1 - R^2) \tag{8}$$

TABLE 3.9
Control Lines for Randomly Splitting the Sample and Cross
Validating the Regression Equation with BMDP9R

```
//   EXEC BIMED, PROG = BMDP9R
//SYSIN DD *
/PROBLEM TITLE IS 'CROSS VALIDATION'.
/INPUT VARIABLES ARE 6. FORMAT IS STREAM.
/VARIABLE ADD IS 1. WEIGHT IS 7.
/REGRESSION DEPENDENT IS 1. INDEPENDENT ARE 2 TO 6. METHOD IS NONE
/PRINT MATRICES = CORR.RESID.
/TRANSFORM TEMP IS RNDU(1232557). X(7) IS TEMP LT. .5.    ①
/SAVE UNIT = 3. NEW.CODE IS RESID.
/END

    DATA

//   EXEC BIMED,PROG = BMDP6D
//SYSIN DD *
/PROBLEM TITLE IS 'PLOT'.
/INPUT UNIT = 3. CODE = RESID.
/VARIABLE GROUPING IS 7.
/GROUP CODES(7) ARE 0,1. NAMES(7) ARE VALID,DERIV.
/PLOT YVAR = 1. XVAR = PREDICTD. GROUP IS VALID. GROUP IS DERIV. STATISTICS.
/END
```

①In the TRANSFORM paragraph we randomly split the sample. A dummy variable taking on the values 0 and 1 is created to label the members of the derivation and validation samples. The fact that we are adding a new variable to the file is indicated by ADD IS 1 in the VARIABLE paragraph. The number in parentheses after the random number routine RNDU is a large positive *odd* integer which is used to start the random number sequence. The random number routine generates numbers on the interval from 0 to 1. Those cases that are associated with random numbers less than .5 are put in the derivation sample, with the remaining cases constituting the validation sample.

where $\hat{\rho}$ is the estimate of ρ, the population multiple correlation coefficient. This is the adjusted R^2 printed out by BMDP2R and by SPSSX REGRESSION. Draper and Smith (1981) comment on Equation 8: "A related statistic . . . is the so-called adjusted R (R_a^2), the idea being that the statistic R_a^2 can be used to compare equations fitted not only to a specific set of data but also to 2 or more entirely different sets of data. The value of this statistic for the latter purpose is, in our opinion, not high" (p. 92).

Herzberg notes that, "In applications, the population regression function can never be known and one is more interested in how effective the *sample* regression function is in *other* samples. A measure of this effectiveness is r_c, the sample cross validity. For any given regression function r_c will vary from validation sample to validation sample. The average value of r_c will be approximately equal to the correlation, in the *population*, of the sample regression function with the criterion. This correlation is the population cross-validity, ρ_c. Wherry's formula estimates ρ rather than ρ_c." (p.4).

There are two possible models for the predictors: (1) regression—the values of the predictors are fixed, i.e., we study y only for certain values of x, and (2) correlation—the predictors are random variables—this is a much more reasonable model for social science research. Herzberg presents the following formula for estimating ρ_c^2 under the correlation model:

$$\hat{\rho}_c^2 = 1 - \left(\frac{n-1}{n-k-1}\right)\left(\frac{n-2}{n-k-2}\right)\left(\frac{n+1}{n}\right)(1 - R^2) \tag{9}$$

where n is sample size and k is the number of predictors. It can be shown that $\rho_c < \rho$.

Herzberg gives the following formula for estimating the amount of shrinkage to be expected under cross-validation for the regression model:

$$\hat{\rho}_c^2 = 1 - \frac{(n-1)}{(n-k-1)}\frac{(n+k+1)}{n}(1 - R^2) \tag{10}$$

We feel Equation 9 is more relevant than the Wherry formula (Equation 8) and should be used by investigators for it yields a more severe and realistic estimate of how much prediction power is lost.

For example, suppose $n = 50$, $k = 10$, and $R^2 = .50$. Then using Equation (8) we obtain

$$\hat{\rho}^2 = 1 - 49/39 \ (.50) = .372,$$

whereas with Equation 9, the Herzberg formula, we obtain

$$\hat{\rho}_c^2 = 1 - (49/39)(48/38)(51/50)(.50) = .191$$

Thus, the Herzberg formula indicates the loss in predictive power will be over *twice* as great (.309) as the other formula suggests (.128)!

TABLE 3.10
Estimated Predictive Power Using the Herzberg Formulas for Small
to Fairly Large Subject/Variable Ratios

Subject/Variable Ratio	Herzberg Estimate	Comment
Small (5:1) $n = 50$, $k = 10$ $R^2 = .50$ ②	$\hat{\rho}_c^2 = 1 - (n-1/n-k-1)(n+k$ $+ 1/n)(1-R^2)$ $= 1 - 49/39 \, (61/50) \, (.50)$ $= .234$① *Correlation Model* $\hat{\rho}_c^2 = 1$ $- \left(\dfrac{n-1}{n-k-1}\right)\left(\dfrac{n-2}{n-k-2}\right)\left(\dfrac{n+1}{n}\right)(1$ $-R^2)$ $= 1 - 49/39 \, (48/38) \, (51/50) \, (.5)$ $= .191$	The estimated amount of shrinkage is great, i.e., on the average we expect the predictive power to be reduced by over 50%.
Moderate (10:1) $n = 100$, $k = 10$ $R^2 = .50$	$\hat{\rho}_c^2 = 1 - 99/89 \, (111/100) \, (.50) = .383$ *Correlation Model* $\hat{\rho}_c^2 = 1 - 99/89 \, (98/88) \, (101/100) \, (.5)$ $= .374$	The shrinkage is still fairly substantial.
Fairly Large (15:1) $n = 150$, $k = 10$ $R^2 = .50$	$\hat{\rho}_c^2 = 1 - 149/139 \, (161/150) \, (.50)$ $= .427$ *Correlation Model* $\hat{\rho}_c^2 = 1$ $- 149/139 \, (148/138) \, (151/150) \, (.5)$ $= .421$	We finally reach a point where the expected amount of shrinkage is fairly small, i.e., about 12%.

①If we were to apply the prediction equation to many other samples from the same population, then on the *average* we would account for 23.4% of the variance on y.

②We have chosen this value to illustrate since the typical R^2 values found in social science are often around .50.

Table 3.10 shows how the estimated predictive power drops off using the Herzberg formula for small to fairly large subject/variable ratios, if $R^2 = 50$.

We indicated earlier that about 15 subjects per predictor are needed for a reliable regression equation, i.e., an equation that will cross validate well. There are three converging lines of evidence that support this conclusion:

1. The Herzberg formula for estimated shrinkage (cf. Table 3.10).
2. Our own experience.
3. A study by Park and Dudycha (1974) which considered from 3 to 25 random variable predictors, and found that with about 15 subjects per

TABLE 3.11

Sample Size such that the Difference Between the Squared Multiple Correlation and Squared Cross Validated Correlation is Arbitrarily Small with Given Probability

Three Predictors

ρ^2	ϵ	γ .99	.95	.90	.80	.60	.40
.05	.01	858	554	421	290	158	81
	.03	269	166	123	79	39	18
.10	.01	825	535	410	285	160	88
	.03	271	174	133	91	50	27
	.05	159	100	75	51	27	14
.25	.01	693	451	347	243	139	79
	.03	232	151	117	81	48	27
	.05	140	91	71	50	29	17
	.10	70	46	36	25	15	7
	.20	34	22	17	12	8	6
.50	.01	464	304	234	165	96	55
	.03	157	104	80	57	34	21
	.05	96	64	50	36	22	14
	.10	50	34	27	20	13	9
	.20	27	19	15	12	9	7
.75	.01	235	155	120	85	50	30
	.03	85	55	43	31	20	13
	.05	51	35	28	21	14	10
	.10	28	20	16	13	9	7
	.20	16	12	10	9	7	6
.98	.01	23	17	14	11	9	7
	.03	11	9	8	7	6	6
	.05	9	7	7	6	6	5
	.10	7	6	6	5	5	5
	.20	6	6	5	5	5	5

Four Predictors

ρ^2	ϵ	γ .99	.95	.90	.80	.60	.40
.05	.01	1041	707	559	406	245	144
	.03	312	201	152	103	54	27
.10	.01	1006	691	550	405	253	155
	.03	326	220	173	125	74	43
	.05	186	123	95	67	38	22
.25	.01	853	587	470	348	221	140
	.03	283	195	156	116	73	46
	.05	168	117	93	69	43	28
	.10	84	58	46	34	20	14
	.20	38	26	20	15	10	7
.50	.01	573	396	317	236	152	97
	.03	193	134	108	81	53	35
	.05	117	82	66	50	33	23
	.10	60	43	35	27	19	13
	.20	32	23	19	15	11	9
.75	.01	290	201	162	121	78	52
	.03	100	70	57	44	30	21
	.05	62	44	37	28	20	15
	.10	34	25	21	17	13	11
	.20	19	15	13	11	9	7
.98	.01	29	22	19	15	12	10
	.03	14	11	10	9	8	7
	.05	10	9	8	8	7	7
	.10	8	8	7	7	7	6
	.20	7	7	7	6	6	6

Eight Predictors

ρ^2	ϵ	γ = .99	.95	.90	.80	.60	.40
.05	.01	1640	1226	1031	821	585	418
	.03	447	313	251	187	116	71
.10	.01	1616	1220	1036	837	611	450
	.03	503	373	311	246	172	121
	.05	281	202	166	128	85	55
.25	.01	1376	1047	893	727	538	404
	.03	453	344	292	237	174	129
	.05	267	202	171	138	101	74
	.10	128	95	80	63	45	33
	.20	52	37	30	24	17	12
.50	.01	927	707	605	494	368	279
	.03	312	238	204	167	125	96
	.05	188	144	124	103	77	59
	.10	96	74	64	53	40	31
	.20	49	38	33	28	22	18
.75	.01	470	360	308	253	190	150
	.03	162	125	108	90	69	54
	.05	100	78	68	57	44	35
	.10	54	43	38	32	26	22
	.20	31	25	23	20	17	15
.98	.01	47	38	34	29	24	21
	.03	22	19	18	16	15	14
	.05	17	16	15	14	13	12
	.10	14	13	12	12	11	11
	.20	12	11	11	11	11	10

Fifteen Predictors

ρ^2	ϵ	γ = .99	.95	.90	.80	.60	.40
.05	.01	2523	2007	1760	1486	1161	918
	.03	640	474	398	316	222	156
.10	.01	2519	2029	1794	1532	1220	987
	.03	762	600	524	438	337	263
	.05	403	309	265	216	159	119
.25	.01	2163	1754	1557	1339	1079	884
	.03	705	569	504	431	345	280
	.05	413	331	292	249	198	159
	.10	191	151	132	111	87	69
	.20	76	58	49	40	30	24
.50	.01	1461	1188	1057	911	738	608
	.03	489	399	355	306	249	205
	.05	295	261	214	185	151	125
	.10	149	122	109	94	77	64
	.20	75	62	55	48	40	34
.75	.01	741	605	539	466	380	315
	.03	255	210	188	164	135	113
	.05	158	131	118	103	86	73
	.10	85	72	65	58	49	43
	.20	49	42	39	35	31	28
.98	.01	75	64	59	53	46	41
	.03	36	33	31	29	27	25
	.05	28	26	25	24	23	22
	.10	23	21	21	20	20	19
	.20	20	19	19	19	18	18

*Entries in the body of the table are the sample size such that $P(\rho^2 - \rho_c^2 < \epsilon) = \gamma$ where ρ is population multiple correlation, ϵ is some tolerance and γ is the probability.

predictor the amount of shrinkage is small ($< .05$) with high probability (.90), if ρ^2 (squared population multiple correlation) is .50.

In Table 3.11 we present selected results from Park and Dudycha, for 3, 4, 8, and 15 predictors.

To use Table 3.11 we need an estimate of ρ^2, i.e., the squared population multiple correlation. Unless an investigator has a good estimate from a previous study which used similar subjects and predictors, we feel taking $\hat{\rho}^2 = .50$ is a reasonable guess for social science research (in the physical sciences estimates $\geq .75$ are quite reasonable). If we set $\hat{\rho}^2 = .50$ and want the loss in prediction to be less than 5% with probability $= .90$, then the sample sizes are displayed below:

$\hat{\rho}^2 = .50 \quad \epsilon = .05$	Number of Predictors			
	3	4	8	15
n	50	66	124	214
n/k ratio	16.7	16.7	15.5	14.3

The n/k ratios in all 4 cases are around 15/1.

Notice also from Table 3.11 that *the magnitude of ρ (population multiple correlation) strongly affects how many S's will be needed for a reliable regression equation.* For example, if $\rho^2 = .75$, then for 3 predictors only 28 subjects are needed whereas 50 subjects were needed for the same case above when $\rho^2 = .50$.

Now, we wish to return to the stepwise regression (example 2) and specifically Table 3.7. The summary table indicates that with 3 predictors in the equation we account for 85.56% of the variance on insteval. The adjusted R^2 (under Step No. 3) is .8402; this is the Wherry estimate (cf. Equation 8). The Herzberg adjusted R^2 in this case is

$$\hat{\rho}_c^{\,2} = 1 - \left(\frac{31}{28}\right)\left(\frac{30}{27}\right)\left(\frac{33}{32}\right)(1 - .856) = .82$$

This is not very different from the BMDP adjusted R^2 of .84 in this particular case, because the association between y and the set of predictors is *very* strong. Recall from an earlier example, however, that the Herzberg estimate can be quite different from the BIMED adjusted R^2 when R^2 is smaller (.5 or less), which is often the case in social science research. Thus, *if one is going to report an adjusted* R^2, *we strongly recommend the Herzberg estimate.*

Finally, for this example the equation will cross validate well. Reference to the Park and Dudycha results (Table 3.11; 3 predictors), indicates that $n = 28$ will guarantee that the shrinkage should be less than .05 with probability .90 for $\hat{\rho}^2 = .75$, and our $\hat{\rho}^2$ is slightly greater. Thus, we would expect to account for about 80% of variance on y if the equation were cross-validated.

3.14. PRESELECTION OF PREDICTORS

An industrial psychologist hears about the predictive power of multiple regression and is excited. He wants to predict success on the job, and gathers data for 20 potential predictors on 70 subjects. He obtains the correlation matrix for the variables, and then picks out 6 predictors which correlate significantly with success on the job and which have low intercorrelations among themselves. The analysis is run, and the R^2 is highly significant. Furthermore, he is able to explain 52% of the variance on y (more than other investigators have been able to do). Are these results generalizable? Probably not, since what he did involves a *double* capitalization on chance:

1. First, in preselecting the predictors from a larger set, he is capitalizing on chance. Some of these variables would have high correlations with y because of sampling error, and consequently their correlations would tend to be lower in another sample.

2. Secondly, the mathematical maximization involved in obtaining the multiple correlation involves capitalizing on chance.

Preselection of predictors is common among many researchers, who are unaware of the fact that this tends to make their results sample specific. Nunnally (1978) has a nice discussion of the preselection problem, and Wilkinson (1979) has shown the considerable positive bias preselection can have on the test of significance of R^2 in forward selection. The following example from his tables illustrates. The critical value for a 4 predictor problem ($n = 35$) at .05 level is .26, while the appropriate critical value for the *same* n and α level, when preselecting 4 predictors from a set of 20 predictors is .51! Unawareness of the positive bias has led to many results in the literature which are not replicable, for as Wilkinson notes, "A computer assisted search for articles in psychology using stepwise regression from 1969 to 1977 located 71 articles. Out of these articles, 66 forward selections analyses reported as significant by the usual F tests were found. Of these 66 analyses, 19 were *not* significant by [his] Table 1."

It is important to note that both the Wherry and Herzberg formulas do *not* take into account preselection. Hence, the following from Cohen and Cohen (1983) should be seriously considered: "A more realistic estimate of the shrinkage is obtained by substituting for k the *total* number of predictors from which the selection was made." (p. 107) In other words, they are saying if 4 predictors were selected out of 15, use $k = 15$ in the Herzberg formula. While this may be conservative, using 4 will certainly lead to a positive bias. Probably a median value between 4 and 15 would be closer to the mark, although this needs further investigation.

3.15. OUTLIERS AND INFLUENTIAL DATA POINTS

Since multiple regression is a mathematical maximization procedure, it can be very sensitive to data points within "split off" or are different from the rest of the points, i.e., to outliers. Just 1 or 2 such points can affect the interpretation of results, and it is certainly moot as to whether 1 or 2 points should be permitted to have such a profound influence. Therefore, it is important to be able to detect outliers and influential points. There is a distinction between the two because a point that is an outlier (either on y or for the predictors) will *not necessarily* be influential in affecting the regression equation.

The fact that a simple examination of summary statistics can result in misleading interpretations was illustrated by Anscombe (1973). He presented three data sets that yielded the same summary statistics (i.e., regression coefficients and same $r^2 = .667$). In one case linear regression was perfectly appropriate. In the second case, however, a scatter plot showed that curvilinear regression was appropriate. In the third case, linear regression was appropriate for 10 of 11 points, but the other point was an outlier and possibly should have been excluded from the analysis.

There are two basic approaches that can be used in dealing with outliers and influential points. We consider the approach of having an arsenal of tools for isolating these important points for further study, with the possibility of deleting some or all of the points from the analysis. The other approach is to develop procedures that are relatively insensitive to wild points (i.e., robust regression techniques). (Some pertinent references for robust regression are Hogg, 1979; Huber, 1977; Mosteller & Tukey, 1977). It is important to note that even robust regression may be ineffective when there are outliers in the space of the predictors (Huber, 1977). Thus, even in robust regression there is a need for case analysis. Also, a modification of robust regression, called bounded-influence regression, has been developed by Krasker and Welsch (1979).

Data Editing

Outliers and influential cases can occur because of recording errors. Consequently, researchers should give more consideration to the data editing phase of the data analysis process (i.e., *always* listing the data and examining the list for possible errors). There are many possible sources of error from the initial data collection to the final keypunching. First, some of the data may have been recorded incorrectly. Second, even if recorded correctly, when all of the data are transferred to a single sheet or a few sheets in preparation for keypunching, errors may be made. Finally, even if no errors are made in these first two steps, an error(s) could be made in putting the data on cards or into the terminal.

Measuring Outliers on y

The raw residuals, $\hat{e}_i = y_i - \hat{y}_i$, in linear regression are assumed to be independent, to have a mean of 0, to have constant variance, and to follow a normal
distribution. However, because the n residuals have only $n-k$ degrees of freedom
(k degrees of freedom were lost in estimating the regression parameters), they
can't be independent. If n is large relative to k, however, then the $\hat{e}_i$ are essentially
independent. Also, the residuals have different variances. It can be shown (cf.
Draper & Smith, 1981, p. 144) that the variance for the ith residual is given by:

$$s_{e_i}^2 = \hat{\sigma}^2 (1 - h_{ii}) \tag{11}$$

where $\hat{\sigma}^2$ is the estimate of variance not predictable from the regression (MS_{res}),
and h_{ii} is the ith diagonal element of the hat matrix $\mathbf{X}(\mathbf{X}'\mathbf{X})^{-1}\mathbf{X}'$. Recall that $\mathbf{X}$
is the score matrix for the predictors. The h_{ii} play a key role in determining the
predicted values for the subjects. Recall that

$$\boldsymbol{\beta} = (\mathbf{X}'\mathbf{X})^{-1}\mathbf{X}'\mathbf{y} \text{ and } \hat{\mathbf{y}} = \mathbf{X}\boldsymbol{\beta}$$

Therefore, $\hat{\mathbf{y}} = \mathbf{X}(\mathbf{X}'\mathbf{X})^{-1}\mathbf{X}'\mathbf{y}$, by simple substitution. Thus, the predicted values
for y are obtained by postmultipling the hat matrix by the column vector of
observed scores on y.

Since the predicted values ($\hat{y}_i$) and the residuals are related by $\hat{e}_i = y_i - \hat{y}_i$,
it should not be surprising in view of the above that the variability of the $\hat{e}_i$
would be affected by the h_{ii}.

Since the residuals have different variances, we need to standardize to meaningfully compare them. This is completely analogous to what is done in comparing raw scores from distributions with different variances and different means.
There, one means of standardizing was to convert to z scores, using $z_i = (x_i - \bar{x})/s$. Here we also subtract off the mean (which is 0 and hence has no
effect) and then divide by the standard deviation. The standard deviation is the
square root of Equation 11. Therefore,

$$r_i = \frac{\hat{e}_i - 0}{\hat{\sigma}\sqrt{1 - h_{ii}}} = \frac{\hat{e}_i}{\hat{\sigma}\sqrt{1 - h_{ii}}} \tag{12}$$

Because the r_i are assumed to have a normal distribution with a mean of 0
(if the model is correct), then about 99% of the r_i should lie within 3 standard
deviations of the mean.

Weisberg (1980) has given the following t statistic for testing an outlier on
y for significance:

$$t_i = r_i \sqrt{\frac{n - p' - 1}{n - p' - r_i^2}} \tag{13}$$

where r_i is the standardized residual, n is sample size, p' is the number of

TABLE 3.12
Critical Values for Weisberg Outlier Test with Overall $\alpha = .05$

$p' = k + 1$

n	1	2	3	4	5	6	7	8	9	10	11	12	13	14	15	20	25	30
6	4.85	6.23	10.89	76.39														
7	4.38	5.07	6.58	11.77	89.12													
8	4.12	4.53	5.26	6.90	12.59	101.9												
9	3.95	4.22	4.66	5.44	7.18	13.36	114.6											
10	3.83	4.03	4.32	4.77	5.60	7.45	14.09	127.3										
11	3.75	3.90	4.10	4.40	4.88	5.75	7.70	14.78	140.1									
12	3.69	3.81	3.96	4.17	4.49	4.98	5.89	7.94	15.44	152.8								
13	3.65	3.74	3.86	4.02	4.24	4.56	5.08	6.02	8.16	16.08	165.5							
14	3.61	3.69	3.79	3.91	4.07	4.30	4.63	5.16	6.14	8.37	16.69	178.2						
15	3.58	3.65	3.73	3.83	3.95	4.12	4.36	4.70	5.25	6.25	8.58	17.28	191.0					
16	3.56	3.62	3.68	3.77	3.87	4.00	4.17	4.41	4.76	5.33	6.36	8.77	17.85	203.7				
17	3.54	3.59	3.65	3.72	3.80	3.90	4.04	4.21	4.46	4.82	5.40	6.47	8.95	18.40	216.4			
18	3.53	3.57	3.62	3.68	3.75	3.83	3.94	4.08	4.26	4.51	4.88	5.47	6.47	9.13	18.93			
19	3.52	3.56	3.60	3.65	3.71	3.78	3.86	3.97	4.11	4.30	4.55	4.93	5.54	6.67	9.30			
20	3.51	3.54	3.58	3.62	3.67	3.73	3.81	3.89	4.00	4.15	4.33	4.59	4.98	5.60	6.76			
21	3.50	3.53	3.57	3.60	3.65	3.70	3.76	3.83	3.92	4.03	4.18	4.37	4.64	5.03	5.67			
22	3.50	3.52	3.55	3.59	3.63	3.67	3.72	3.78	3.86	3.95	4.06	4.21	4.40	4.68	5.08	280.1		
23	3.49	3.52	3.54	3.57	3.61	3.65	3.69	3.75	3.81	3.88	3.98	4.09	4.24	4.44	4.71	21.41		
24	3.49	3.51	3.53	3.56	3.59	3.63	3.67	3.71	3.77	3.83	3.91	4.00	4.12	4.27	4.47	10.07		
25	3.48	3.50	3.53	3.55	3.58	3.61	3.65	3.69	3.73	3.79	3.85	3.93	4.02	4.14	4.30	7.17		
26	3.48	3.50	3.52	3.54	3.57	3.60	3.63	3.66	3.70	3.75	3.81	3.87	3.95	4.05	4.17	5.95		
27	3.48	3.50	3.52	3.54	3.56	3.58	3.61	3.65	3.68	3.72	3.77	3.83	3.89	3.97	4.07	5.29	353.80	
28	3.48	3.50	3.51	3.53	3.55	3.58	3.60	3.63	3.66	3.70	3.74	3.79	3.84	3.91	3.99	4.88	23.63	
29	3.48	3.49	3.51	3.53	3.55	3.57	3.59	3.62	3.64	3.68	3.71	3.76	3.81	3.86	3.93	4.61	10.74	
30	3.48	3.49	3.51	3.52	3.54	3.56	3.58	3.60	3.63	3.66	3.69	3.73	3.77	3.82	3.88	4.42	7.53	
31	3.48	3.49	3.50	3.52	3.54	3.55	3.57	3.59	3.62	3.64	3.67	3.71	3.74	3.79	3.84	4.28	6.18	
32	3.48	3.49	3.50	3.52	3.53	3.55	3.57	3.59	3.61	3.63	3.66	3.69	3.72	3.76	3.80	4.17	5.47	407.4

33	3.48	3.49	3.50	3.52	3.53	3.54	3.56	3.58	3.60	3.62	3.64	3.67	3.70	3.74	3.77	4.08	5.03	25.66
34	3.48	3.49	3.50	3.51	3.53	3.54	3.56	3.57	3.59	3.61	3.63	3.66	3.68	3.71	3.75	4.01	4.74	11.34
35	3.48	3.49	3.50	3.51	3.52	3.54	3.55	3.47	3.58	3.60	3.62	3.64	3.57	3.70	3.73	3.96	4.53	7.84
36	3.48	3.49	3.50	3.51	3.52	3.54	3.55	3.56	3.58	3.60	3.61	3.63	3.66	3.68	3.71	3.91	4.37	6.39
37	3.48	3.49	3.50	3.51	3.52	3.53	3.55	3.56	3.57	3.59	3.61	3.62	3.65	3.67	3.69	3.87	4.26	5.62
38	3.49	3.49	3.50	3.51	3.52	3.53	3.54	3.56	3.58	3.60	3.62	3.60	3.66	3.68	3.84	4.16	5.16	
39	3.49	3.49	3.50	3.51	3.52	3.53	3.54	3.55	3.57	3.58	3.59	3.61	3.63	3.65	3.67	3.81	4.09	4.84
40	3.49	3.49	3.50	3.51	3.52	3.53	3.54	3.55	3.56	3.59	3.60	3.62	3.64	3.66	3.79	4.03	4.62	
50	3.51	3.51	3.51	3.52	3.53	3.55	3.54	3.54	3.55	3.56	3.57	3.57	3.58	3.59	3.60	3.66	3.75	3.88
60	3.53	3.53	3.53	3.54	3.54	3.54	3.55	3.55	3.56	3.56	3.57	3.57	3.58	3.58	3.59	3.62	3.67	3.73
70	3.55	3.55	3.55	3.55	3.56	3.56	3.56	3.56	3.57	3.57	3.57	3.58	3.58	3.59	3.59	3.61	3.64	
80	3.57	3.57	3.57	3.57	3.57	3.58	3.58	3.58	3.58	3.58	3.59	3.59	3.59	3.60	3.60	3.61	3.63	3.66
90	3.58	3.59	3.59	3.59	3.59	3.59	3.59	3.60	3.60	3.60	3.60	3.60	3.60	3.61	3.61	3.62	3.63	3.65
100	3.60	3.60	3.60	3.60	3.61	3.61	3.61	3.61	3.61	3.61	3.61	3.62	3.62	3.62	3.62	3.63	3.64	3.65
200	3.73	3.73	3.73	3.73	3.73	3.73	3.73	3.73	3.73	3.73	3.73	3.73	3.73	3.73	3.74	3.74	3.74	3.74
300	3.81	3.81	3.81	3.81	3.81	3.81	3.81	3.81	3.81	3.81	3.82	3.82	3.82	3.82	3.82	3.82	3.82	3.82
400	3.87	3.87	3.87	3.87	3.87	3.87	3.87	3.88	3.88	3.88	3.88	3.88	3.88	3.88	3.88	3.88	3.88	3.88
500	3.92	3.92	3.92	3.92	3.92	3.92	3.92	3.92	3.92	3.92	3.92	3.92	3.92	3.92	3.92	3.92	3.92	3.92

parameters (including the regression constant), and df $= n - p' - 1$. Although t_i is not given on the printout from BMDP, or SPSSX, r_i is given and therefore t_i is found by plugging into Equation 13.

Assessing the significance of the case with the largest value of t_i is equivalent to performing n significance tests, one for each of the n cases. To control the resulting inflated Type I error rate, the somewhat conservative Bonferroni inequality is used, doing each test at the α/n level of significance. Table 3.12 gives the critical values (Weisberg, 1980) for various n and p', which keeps overall $\alpha = .05$.

Example 10

Consider a regression analysis with 4 predictors on 50 subjects; the largest $r_i = 2.8$. Is this a statistically significant deviation (overall $\alpha = .05$) according to the Weisberg test?

$$t_i = r_i \sqrt{\frac{n - p' - 1}{n - p' - r_i^2}}$$

$$= 2.8 \sqrt{\frac{50 - 5 - 1}{50 - 5 - 7.84}}$$

$$= 2.8(1.088) = 3.047.$$

Because the critical value is 3.53, this is not a significant deviation.

Measuring Outliers on the Predictors

The h_{ii}'s are one measure of the extent to which the ith observation is an outlier for the predictors. The h_{ii}'s are important because they can play a key role in determining the predicted values for the subjects. Recall that

$$\hat{\beta} = (X'X)^{-1}X'y \text{ and } \hat{y} = X\hat{\beta}$$

Therefore, $\hat{y} = X(X'X)^{-1}X'y$ by simple substitution.

Thus, the predicted values for y are obtained by postmultiplying the hat matrix by the column vector of observed scores on y. It can be shown that the h_{ii}'s lie between 0 and 1, and that the average value for $h_{ii} = p/n$. From Equation 11 it may be seen that when h_{ii} is large (i.e., near 1), then the variance for the ith residual is near 0. This means that $y_i \approx \hat{y}_i$. In other words, an observation may fit the linear model well and yet be an influential data point. This second diagnostic, then, is "flagging" observations that need to be examined carefully because they may have an unusually large influence on the regression coefficients.

What is a significant value for the h_{ii}? Hoaglin and Welsch (1978) suggest that $2p/n$ may be considered large. Belsey et al. (1980, pp. 67–68) show that when the set of predictors is multivariate normal, then $(n - p) [h_{ii} - 1/n]/$ $(1 - h_{ii})(p - 1)$ is distributed as F with $(p - 1)$ and $(n - p)$ degrees of freedom. *Rough, quick, approximate critical values* (for $\alpha = .05$) *are available to cover most situations. For $3 \leq p \leq 9$ and $25 < n - p < 50$, 3p/n can be used, whereas for* $p > 10$ *and* $n - p > 50$*, 2p/n is appropriate.*

An important point to remember concerning the hat elements is that the points they identify will not necessarily be influential in affecting the regression coefficients.

Mahalanobis' distance for case i (D_i^2) indicates how far the case is from the centroid of all cases for the predictor variables. A large distance indicates an observation that is an outlier for the predictors. The Mahalanobis distance can be written in terms of the covariance matrix $\mathbf{S}$ as

$$D_i^2 = (\mathbf{x}_i - \bar{\mathbf{x}})'\mathbf{S}^{-1}(\mathbf{x}_i - \bar{\mathbf{x}}), \tag{14}$$

where $\mathbf{X}_i$ is the vector of the data for case i and $\bar{\mathbf{x}}$ is the vector of means (centroid) for the predictors.

For a better understanding of D_i^2, consider two small data sets. The first set has two predictors. In Table 3.13, the data is presented, as well as the D_i^2 and the descriptive statistics (including $\mathbf{S}$). The D_i^2 for Cases 6 and 10 are large because the score for Case 6 on x_i (150) was deviant, whereas for Case 10 the score on x_2 (97) was very deviant. The graphical split-off of Cases 6 and 10 is quite vivid and is displayed in Figure 1.2.

In the previous example, because the numbers of predictors and subjects were few, it would have been fairly easy to spot the outliers even without the Mahalanobis distance. However, in practical problems with 200 or 300 subjects and 10 predictors, outliers are not always easy to spot and can occur in more subtle ways. For example, a case may have a large distance because there are moderate to fairly large differences on many of the predictors. The second small data set with 4 predictors and $N = 15$ in Table 3.13 illustrates this latter point. The D_i^2 for case 13 is quite large (7.97) even though the scores for that subject do not split off in a striking fashion for any of the predictors. Rather, it is a cumulative effect that produces the separation.

How large must D_i^2 be before one can say that case i is significantly separated from the rest of the data at the .05 level of significance? If it is tenable that the predictors came from a multivariate normal population, then the critical values (Barnett & Lewis, 1978) are given in Table 3.14 for 2 through 5 predictors. An easily implemented graphical test for multivariate normality is available (Johnson & Wichern, 1982). The test involves plotting ordered Mahalanobis distances against chi-square percentile points. The D_i^2 can be obtained from the BMDP9R program.

Referring back to the example with 2 predictors and $n = 10$, if we assume multivariate normality, then Case 6 ($D_i^2 = 5.48$) is not significantly separated

TABLE 3.13
Raw Data and Mahalanobis Distances for Two Small Data Sets

Case	Y	X_1	X_2	X_3	X_4		D_i^2
1	476	111	68	17	81		0.30
2	457	92	46	28	67		1.55
3	.540	90	50	19	83		1.47
4	551	107	59	25	71		0.01
5	575	98	50	13	92	①	0.76
6	698	150	66	20	90		5.48
7	545	118	54	11	101		0.47
8	574	110	51	26	82		0.38
9	645	117	59	18	87		0.23
10	556	94	97	12	69		7.24
11	634	130	57	16	97		
12	637	118	51	19	78		
13	390	91	44	14	64		
14	562	118	61	20	103		
15	560	109	66	13	88		
Summary statistics							
M	561.70000	108.70000	60.00000				
SD	70.74846	17.73289	14.84737				

$$S = \begin{bmatrix} 314.455 & 19.483 \\ 19.483 & 220.444 \end{bmatrix}$$

Note: Boxed-in entries are the first data set and corresponding D_i^2. The 10 case numbers having the largest D_i^2 for a four-predictor data set are: 10, 10.859; 13, 7.977; 6, 7.223; 2, 5.048; 14, 4.874; 7, 3.514; 5, 3.177; 3, 2.616; 8, 2.561; 4, 2.404.

① Calculation of D_i^2 for Case 6:

$$D_6^2 = (41.3, 6) \begin{bmatrix} 314.455 & 19.483 \\ 19.483 & 220.440 \end{bmatrix}^{-1} \binom{41.3}{6}$$

$$S^{-1} = \begin{bmatrix} .00320 & -.00029 \\ -.00029 & .00456 \end{bmatrix} \rightarrow D_6^2 = 5.484$$

from the rest of the data at .05 level because the critical value equals 6.32. In contrast, Case 10 is significantly separated.

(Weisberg, 1980, p. 104) has shown that if n is even moderately large (50 or more), then D_i^2 is approximately proportional to h_{ii}:

$$D_i^2 \approx (n - 1)h_{ii} \tag{15}$$

Thus, with large n, either measure may be used. Also, because we have previously indicated what would correspond roughly to a significant h_{ii} value, from Equation 15 we can immediately determine the corresponding significant D_i^2 value. For example, if $p = 7$ and $n = 50$, then a large $h_{ii} = .42$ and the corresponding large $D_i^2 = 20.58$. If $p = 20$ and $n = 200$, then a large $h_{ii} = 2p/n = .20$ and the corresponding large $D_i^2 = 39.90$.

TABLE 3.14
Critical Values for an Outlier on the Predictors as Judged by
Mahalanobis D^2

	Number of Predictors							
	$p = 2$		$p = 3$		$p = 4$		$p = 5$	
n	5%	1%	5%	1%	5%	1%	5%	1%
5	3.17	3.19						
6	4.00	4.11	4.14	4.16				
7	4.71	4.95	5.01	5.10	5.12	5.14		
8	5.32	5.70	5.77	5.97	6.01	6.09	6.11	6.12
9	5.85	6.37	6.43	6.76	6.80	6.97	7.01	7.08
10	6.32	6.97	7.01	7.47	7.50	7.79	7.82	7.98
12	7.10	8.00	7.99	8.70	8.67	9.20	9.19	9.57
14	7.74	8.84	8.78	9.71	9.61	10.37	10.29	10.90
16	8.27	9.54	9.44	10.56	10.39	11.36	11.20	12.02
18	8.73	10.15	10.00	11.28	11.06	12.20	11.96	12.98
20	9.13	10.67	10.49	11.91	11.63	12.93	12.62	13.81
25	9.94	11.73	11.48	13.18	12.78	14.40	13.94	15.47
30	10.58	12.54	12.24	14.14	13.67	15.51	14.95	16.73
35	11.10	13.20	12.85	14.92	14.37	16.40	15.75	17.73
40	11.53	13.74	13.36	15.56	14.96	17.13	16.41	18.55
45	11.90	14.20	13.80	16.10	15.46	17.74	16.97	19.24
50	12.23	14.60	14.18	16.56	15.89	18.27	17.45	19.83
100	14.22	16.95	16.45	19.26	18.43	21.30	20.26	23.17
200	15.99	18.94	18.42	21.47	20.59	23.72	22.59	25.82
500	18.12	21.22	20.75	23.95	23.06	26.37	25.21	28.62

3.16. A MEASURE FOR INFLUENTIAL DATA POINTS

Cook's Distance.

Cook's distance (CD) is a measure of the change in the regression coefficients that would occur if this case was omitted, thus revealing which cases are most influential in affecting the regression equation. It is affected by both the case being an outlier on y and on the set of the predictors. Cook's distance is given by

$$CD_i = (\hat{\boldsymbol{\beta}} - \hat{\boldsymbol{\beta}}_{(-i)})'\mathbf{X}'\mathbf{X}(\hat{\boldsymbol{\beta}} - \hat{\boldsymbol{\beta}}_{(-i)})/(k + 1)\, MS_{\text{res}} \qquad (16)$$

where $\hat{\boldsymbol{\beta}}_{(-i)}$ is the vector of estimated regresson coefficients with the ith data point deleted, k is the number of predictors, and MS_{res} is the residual (error) variance for the full data set.

Removing the ith data point should keep $\hat{\beta}_{(-i)}$ close to $\hat{\beta}$ unless the ith observation is an outlier.

Cook and Weisberg (1982, p. 118) indicate that *a CD_i of about 1 would generally be considered large.*

Cook's distance can be written in an alternative revealing form.

$$CD_i = \frac{1}{(p + 1)} r_i^2 \frac{h_{ii}}{1 - h_{ii}}, \tag{17}$$

where r_i is the standardized residual and h_{ii} is the hat element. Thus, *Cook's distance measures the joint (combined) influence of the case being an outlier on y and on the set of predictors.* A case may be influential because it is a significant outlier only on y, for example,

$$(p = 5, n = 40, r_i = 4, h_{ii} = .3 \Rightarrow CD_i > 1.),$$

or because it is a significant outlier only in the space of the predictors, for example,

$$(p = 5, n = 40, r_i = 2, h_{ii} = .7 \Rightarrow CD_i > 1.).$$

Note, however, that a case may not be a significant outlier on either y or in the space of the predictors, but may still be influential as in the following:

$$(p = 3, n = 20, h_{ii} = 4, r_i = 2.5 \Rightarrow CD_i > 1).$$

Summary

In summarizing then, use of the Weisberg test (with standardized residuals) will detect y outliers, and the hat elements or the Mahalanobis distances will detect outliers on the predictors. Such outliers will not necessarily be influential points. To determine which outliers are influential, find those whose Cook distances are > 1. Those points that are flagged as influential by Cook's distance need to be examined carefully to determine whether they should be deleted from the analysis. If there is a reason to believe that these cases arise from a process different from that for the rest of the data, then the cases should be deleted. For example, the failure of a measuring instrument, a power failure, or the occurrence of an unusual event (perhaps inexplicable) would be instances of a different process.

If a point is a significant outlier on y, *but it's Cook distance is* < 1, *there is no real need to delete the point since it does not have a large effect on the regression analysis. However, one should still be interested in studying such points further to understand why they did not fit the model.* After all, the purpose of any study is to understand the data. In particular, one wants to ascertain if there are any communalities among the S's corresponding to such outliers, suggesting that perhaps these subjects come from a different population. For an excellent, readable, and extended discussion of outliers, influential points, identification of and remedies for, see Weisberg (1980, chapters 5 and 6).

In concluding this summary the following from Belsley, Kuh, and Welsch (1980) is appropriate:

> A word of warning is in order here, for it is obvious that there is room for misuse of the above procedures. High-influence data points could conceivably be removed solely to effect a desired change in a particular estimated coefficient, its t value, or some other regression output. While this danger exists, it is an unavoidable consequence of a procedure that successfully highlights such points . . . the benefits obtained from information on influential points far outweigh any potential danger. (pp. 15–16)

Example 11

We now consider the data in Table 3.13 with 4 predictors ($n = 15$). This data was run on SPSSX REGRESSION; the control lines and summary statistics

TABLE 3.15
SPSSX Control Lines for Sample Problem
on Outliers and Influential Points

```
DATA LIST FREE/ Y X1 X2 X3 X4
LIST
BEGIN DATA

DATA LINES

END DATA
TITLE 'MULT REGRESSION — OUTLIERS AND INFLUENTIAL POINTS '
① REGRESSION DESCRIPTIVES = DEFAULT/
     VARIABLES = Y X1 X2 X3 X4/
     DEPENDENT = Y/
②ENTER/
③ RESIDUALS = OUTLIERS (ZRESID,SRESID,SDRESID,MAHAL,COOK,LEVER)/
```

	MEAN	STD DEV
Y	560.000	78.096
X1	110.200	16.337
X2	58.600	12.922
X3	18.067	5.203
X4	83.533	12.171

CORRELATION:

	Y	X1	X2	X3	X4
Y	1.000	.751	.226	.005	.530
X1	.751	1.000	.120	.019	.591
X2	.226	.120	1.000	−.341	−.037
X3	.005	.019	−.341	1.000	−.300
X4	.530	.591	−.037	−.300	1.000

①Descriptives is necessary in order to obtain the means, standard deviations and the correlation matrix for the variables.

②ENTER is the keyword to force all the predictors into the equation.

③This RESIDUALS subcommand is necessary in order to obtain the outlier statistics. The first three labels within the parentheses are abbreviations for standardized residual, studentized residual and the studentized, deleted residual—all of which are for locating outliers on y. MAHAL is an abbreviation for the Mahalanobis distance, and LEVER is for leverage value (a term sometimes used for the hat elements)–both which are used for locating outliers on the set of predictors. COOK is for Cook's distance, used for locating influential data points.

appearing in Table 3.15. SPSSX has been used here since it compactly and conveniently presents all the outlier information on a single page. The regression with all 4 predictors is significant at .05 level ($F = 3.94$, $p < .0358$) (cf. Table 3.16). However, we wish to focus our attention here on the outlier analysis, a summary of which is given in Table 3.17. Examination of the studentized residuals shows there are no significant outliers on y. To determine whether there are any significant outliers on set of predictors we examine the Mahalanobis distances. Case 10 is an outlier on the x's since the critical value from Table 3.14 is 10, while case 13 is not significant. Cook's distances reveal that both cases 10 and 13 are influential data points, since both are > 1. Note that case 13 is an influential point even though it is *not* a significant outlier on either y or set of x's. We indicated that this is possible, and indeed it has occurred

TABLE 3.16
Selected Output for Sample Problem on Outliers
and Influential Points

BEGINNING BLOCK NUMBER 1. METHOD: ENTER

VARIABLES(S) ENTERED ON STEP NUMBER   1··   X4
                                      2··   X2
                                      3··   X3
                                      4··   X1

MULTIPLE R	.78212	ANALYSIS OF VARIANCE			
R SQUARE	.61171		DF	SUM OF SQUARES	MEAN SQUARE
ADJUSTED R SQUARE	.45639	REGRESSION	4	52231.50225	13057.87556
STANDARD ERROR	57.57994	RESIDUAL	10	33154.49775	3315.44977

F = 3.93849   SIGNIF F = .0358

---------VARIABLES IN THE EQUATION-----------

VARIABLE	B	SE B	BETA	T	SIG T
X4	1.48832	1.78548	.23194	.834	.4240
X2	1.27014	1.34394	.21016	.945	.3669
X3	2.01747	3.55943	.13440	.567	.5833
X1	2.80343	1.26554	.58644	2.215	.0511
(CONSTANT)	15.85866	180.29777		.088	.9316

FOR BLOCK NUMBER 1 ALL REQUESTED VARIABLES ENTERED.

REGRESSION COEFFICIENTS WITH CASE 10 DELETED

VARIABLE	B
X4	2.07788
X2	-1.48076
X3	2.75130
X1	3.52924
(CONSTANT)	23.36214

REGRESSION COEFFICIENTS WITH CASE 13 DELETED

VARIABLE	B
X4	-1.33883
X2	-.70800
X1	3.41539
X3	-3.45596
(CONSTANT)	410.45740

TABLE 3.17
Selected Output for Sample Problem on Outliers
and Influential Points

OUTLIERS—STANDARDIZED RESIDUAL			OUTLIERS—STUDENTIZED RESIDUAL	
CASE #	*ZRESID		CASE #	*SRESID
1	−1.60229		13	−1.73853
12	1.23548		1	−1.69609
9	1.04904		12	1.39104
13	−1.04818		14	−1.26662
5	1.00288		5	1.19324
14	−.96888		10	1.15951
3	.80693		9	1.09324
7	−.74268		3	.93397
2	−.54545		7	−.89911
10	.46043		2	−.72075

OUTLIER—STUDENTIZED DELETED (PRESS) RESIDUAL			OUTLIERS—MAHALANOBIS' DISTANCE	
CASE #	*SDRESID		CASE #	*MAHAL
13	−1.97449		10	10.85912
1	−1.90647		13	7.97770
12	1.46946		6	7.22347
14	−1.31142		2	5.04841
5	1.22237		14	4.87493
10	1.18236		7	3.51446
9	1.10529		5	3.17728
3	.92741		3	2.61511
7	−.88969		8	2.56197
2	−.70224		4	2.40401

OUTLIERS—COOK'S DISTANCE			OUTLIERS—LEVERAGE	
CASE #	*COOK D	SIG F	CASE #	*LEVER
10	1.43639	.2922	10	.77565
13	1.05851	.4370	13	.56984
14	.22751	.9420	6	.51596
5	.11837	.9853	2	.36060
12	.10359	.9891	14	.34821
2	.07751	.9943	7	.25103
7	.07528	.9947	5	.22695
1	.06934	.9956	3	.18686
3	.05925	.9970	8	.18300
9	.02057	.9998	4	.17172

here. This is the more subtle type of influential points which Cook's distance brings to our attention.

In Table 3.16 we have presented the regression coefficients that resulted when cases 10 and 13 were deleted. There is a fairly dramatic shift in the coefficients in each case. For Case 10 the dramatic shift occurs for x_2, where the coefficient changes from 1.27 (for all data points) to −1.48 (with case 10 deleted). This is a shift of just over 2 standard errors (standard error for x_2 on printout is 1.34). For case 13 the coefficients change in sign for 3 of the 4 predictors (x_4, x_2, and x_3).

3.17.   OTHER TYPES OF REGRESSION ANALYSIS

Least squares regression is only one (although the most prevalent) way of conducting a regression analysis. The least squares estimator has two desirable statistical properties, i.e., it is an unbiased, minimum variance estimator. Mathematically, unbiased means that $E(\hat{\beta}) = \beta$, the expected value of the vector of estimated regression coefficients is the vector of population regression coefficients. To elaborate on this a bit, unbiased means that the estimate of the population coefficients will not be consistently high or low, but will "bounce around" the population values. And, if we were to average the estimates from many repeated samplings, the averages would be very close to the population values.

The minimum variance notion can be misleading. It does not mean that the variance of the coefficients for the least squares estimator is small per se, but that *among the class* of unbiased estimators $\hat{\beta}$ has the minimum variance. The fact that the variance of $\hat{\beta}$ can be quite large led Hoerl and Kenard (1970a, 1970b) to consider a biased estimator of β which has considerably less variance, and the development of their ridge regression technique. Ridge regression is available on the BMDP package. Although ridge regression has been strongly endorsed by some, it has also been criticized (Draper & Smith, 1981; Morris, 1982; Smith & Campbell, 1980). Morris, for example, found that ridge regression never cross-validated better than other types of regression (least squares, equal weighting of predictors, reduced rank) for a set of data situations.

Another class of estimators are the James–Stein (1961) estimators. Regarding the utility of these, the following from Weisberg (1980) is relevant, "the improvement over least squares will be very small whenever the parameter β is well estimated, i.e., collinearity is not a problem and β is not too close to $\mathbf{0}$."

Since, as we have indicated earlier, least square regression can be quite sensitive to outliers, some researchers prefer regression techniques that are relatively insensitive to outliers, i.e., robust regression techniques. Since the early 1970s the literature on these techniques has grown considerably (Hogg, 1979; Huber, 1977; Mosteller & Tukey, 1977). Although these techniques have merit, we feel that use of least squares, along with the appropriate identification of outliers and influential points, is a quite adequate procedure.

3.18.   A SUMMARY OF THE MOST SALIENT POINTS REGARDING REGRESSION ANALYSIS

Since there are so many details in this chapter, it may be easy for the reader to get lost in the forest because of the trees. Therefore, here we present in concise form the main things a researcher should be considering in regression analysis.

1. Always list the data to make sure it has been read in correctly. Recall, that just 1 or 2 errant points can substantially affect the regression equation.

2. A particularly good situation for multiple regression is where each of the predictors is correlated with y and the predictors have low intercorrelations, for then each of the predictors is accounting for a relatively distinct piece of the variance on y.

3. Since multiple regression is a mathematical maximization procedure, there is considerably opportunity for capitalization on chance. About 15 subjects per predictor are needed for a reliable regression equation, i.e., one which will cross-validate with little loss in predictive power.

4. Unless one has several hundred subjects, working with 30 or 40 predictors is not likely to produce a reliable equation. Besides, several reasons were given for generally working with a small number of predictors.

5. Preselecting a small set of predictors (by examining a correlation matrix) from a large initial set, or using one of the selection procedures (forward, stepwise) to select a small set, is quite likely to produce an equation which is sample specific. If one is going to insist on doing this, and we don't recommend it, then the onus is on them to demonstrate that the equation cross-validates on an independent sample.

6. Talking about the unique contribution of a given predictor in general is meaningless if the predictors are correlated (virtually always the case in practice), since how much variance a predictor accounts for depends on when it enters the equation. On the other hand, it is meaningful to talk about the unique contribution for a *single* ordering.

7. In evaluating studies in the literature that used multiple regression and didn't cross-validate (which is most studies), use the Herzberg formula to estimate how good the predictive power of the equation will be on the average for other samples. That is, check the generalizability of the equation.

8. Use the Weisberg test (for y) and either Mahalanobis D^2 or the hat elements (for the x's) to check for outliers. Use Cook's distance to check for influential data points; points which have a considerable effect on the regression equation. Outliers on y that are not influential should still be examined closely to explain why those subjects didn't fit the model. Outliers that are influential (i.e., have Cook distances > 1) need to be examined very carefully to determine whether the process involved in generating these points was different than for the rest of the data. If it was, then those points should be deleted from the analysis.

3.19 MULTIVARIATE REGRESSION

In multivariate regression we are interested in predicting several dependent variables from a set of predictors. The dependent variables might be differentiated aspects of some variable. For example, Finn (1974) broke Grade Point Average

(GPA) up into GPA required and GPA elective, and considered predicting these two dependent variables from high school GPA, a general knowledge test score, and attitude toward education. Or, one might measure "success as a professor" by considering various aspects of success such as : rank (assistant, associate, full), rating of institution working at, salary, rating by experts in the field and number of articles published. These would constitute the multiple dependent variables.

Mathematical Model

In multiple regression (one dependent variable), the model was

$$\mathbf{y} = \mathbf{X}\,\boldsymbol{\beta} + \mathbf{e},$$

where $\mathbf{y}$ was the vector of scores for the subjects on the dependent variable, $\mathbf{X}$ was the matrix with the scores for the subjects on the predictors, and $\mathbf{e}$ was the vectors of errors and $\boldsymbol{\beta}$ was vector of regression coefficients.

In multivariate regresson the $\mathbf{y}$, $\boldsymbol{\beta}$, and $\mathbf{e}$ vectors become matrices, which we denote by $\mathbf{Y}$, B, and $\mathbf{E}$:

$$\mathbf{Y} = \mathbf{XB} + \mathbf{E}$$

$$
\underset{\mathbf{Y}}{\begin{bmatrix} y_{11} & y_{12} & \cdots & y_{1p} \\ y_{21} & y_{22} & \cdots & y_{2p} \\ \cdots & \cdots & \cdots & \\ y_{n1} & y_{n2} & & y_{np} \end{bmatrix}}
=
\underset{\mathbf{X}}{\begin{bmatrix} 1 & x_{12} & \cdots & x_{1k} \\ 1 & x_{22} & \cdots & x_{2k} \\ \cdots & \cdots & \cdots & \\ 1 & x_{n2} & & x_{nk} \end{bmatrix}}
\underset{\mathbf{B}}{\begin{bmatrix} b_{01} & b_{02} & \cdots & b_{1p} \\ b_{11} & b_{12} & \cdots & b_{1p} \\ \cdots & \cdots & \cdots & \\ b_{k1} & b_{k2} & \cdots & b_{kp} \end{bmatrix}}
+
\underset{\mathbf{E}}{\begin{bmatrix} e_{11} & e_{12} & \cdots & e_{1p} \\ e_{21} & e_{22} & \cdots & e_{2p} \\ & & & \\ e_{n1} & e_{n2} & \cdots & e_{np} \end{bmatrix}}
$$

The first column of $\mathbf{Y}$ gives the scores for the subjects on the first dependent variable, the second column the scores on the second dependent variable, etc. The first column of $\mathbf{B}$ gives the set of regression coefficients for the first dependent variable, the second column the regression coefficients for the second dependent variable, etc.

Example 12

As an example of multivariate regression, we consider part of a data set from Timm (1975). The dependent variables are Peabody Picture Vocabulary Test score and score on the Ravin Progressive Matrices Test. The predictors were scores from different types of paired associate learning tasks, called "named still (ns)," named action (na)," and "sentence still (ss)." The control lines for running the analysis on SPSSX MANOVA are given in Table 3.18, along with annotation. In understanding the annotation the reader should refer back to Table 1.4, where we indicated some of the basic elements of the SPSSX control language.

TABLE 3.18
Control Lines for Multivariate Regression Analysis of Timm Data—
Two Dependent Variables and Three Predictors

```
TITLE 'MULTIVARIATE REGRESSION — 2 DEP VAR AND 3 PREDS'
DATA LIST FREE/ PEVOCAB RAVIN NS NA SS   ①
LIST   ②
BEGIN DATA   ③
```

48.00	8.00	6.00	12.00	16.00
76.00	13.00	14.00	30.00	27.00
40.00	13.00	21.00	16.00	16.00
52.00	9.00	5.00	17.00	8.00
63.00	15.00	11.00	26.00	17.00
82.00	14.00	21.00	34.00	25.00
71.00	21.00	20.00	23.00	18.00
68.00	8.00	10.00	19.00	14.00
74.00	11.00	7.00	16.00	13.00
70.00	15.00	21.00	26.00	25.00
70.00	15.00	15.00	35.00	24.00
61.00	11.00	7.00	15.00	14.00
54.00	12.00	13.00	27.00	21.00
55.00	13.00	12.00	20.00	17.00
54.00	10.00	20.00	26.00	22.00
40.00	14.00	5.00	14.00	8.00
66.00	13.00	21.00	35.00	27.00
54.00	10.00	6.00	14.00	16.00
64.00	14.00	19.00	27.00	26.00
47.00	16.00	15.00	18.00	10.00
48.00	16.00	9.00	14.00	18.00
52.00	14.00	20.00	26.00	26.00
74.00	19.00	14.00	23.00	23.00
57.00	12.00	4.00	11.00	8.00
57.00	10.00	16.00	15.00	17.00
80.00	11.00	18.00	28.00	21.00
78.00	13.00	19.00	34.00	23.00
70.00	16.00	9.00	23.00	11.00
47.00	14.00	7.00	12.00	8.00
94.00	19.00	28.00	32.00	32.00
63.00	11.00	5.00	25.00	14.00
76.00	16.00	18.00	29.00	21.00
59.00	11.00	10.00	23.00	24.00
55.00	8.00	14.00	19.00	12.00
74.00	14.00	10.00	18.00	18.00
71.00	17.00	23.00	31.00	26.00
54.00	14.00	6.00	15.00	14.00

```
END DATA
MANOVA PEVOCAB RAVIN WITH NS NA SS/   ④
   PRINT = CELLINFO(MEANS,COR)/
```

①The variables are separated by blanks; they could also have been separated by commas.

②This LIST command is to get a listing of the data.

③The data is preceded by the BEGIN DATA command and followed by the END DATA command.

④The predictors follow the keyword WITH in the MANOVA command.

TABLE 3.19

Multivariate and Univariate Tests of Significance and Regression Coefficients for Timm Data

EFFECT .. WITHIN CELLS REGRESSION

MULTIVARIATE TESTS OF SIGNIFICANCE (S = 2, M = 0, N = 15)

TEST NAME	VALUE	APPROX. F	HYPOTH. DF	ERROR DF	SIG. OF F
PILLAIS	.57254	4.41203	6.00	66.00	.001
HOTELLINGS	1.00976	5.21709	6.00	62.00	.000
WILKS	.47428	4.82197	6.00	64.00	.000
ROYS	.47371				

This test indicates there is a significant (at $\alpha = .05$) regression of the set of 2 dependent variables on the three predictors.

UNIVARIATE F-TESTS WITH (3.33) D. F.

VARIABLE	SQ. MUL. R.	MUL. R	ADJ. R-SQ.	F	SIG. OF F
PEVOCAB	.46345	.68077	.41467	① 9.50121	.000
RAVIN	.19429	.44078	.12104	2.65250	.065

These results show there is a significant regression for PEVOCAB, but RAVIN is not significantly related to the three predictors at .05, since .065 > .05.

DEPENDENT VARIABLE .. PEVOCAB

COVARIATE	B	BETA	STD. ERR.	T-VALUE	SIG. OF T.
NS	-.2056372599	-.1043054487	.40797	-.50405	.618
NA	② 1.01272293634	.5856100072	.37685	2.68737	.011
SS	.3977340740	.2022598804	.47010	.84606	.404

DEPENDENT VARIABLE .. RAVIN

COVARIATE	B	BETA	STD. ERR.	T-VALUE	SIG. OF T
NS	.2026184278	.4159658338	.12352	1.64038	.110
NA	.0302663367	.0708355423	.11410	.26527	.792
SS	-.0174928333	-.0360039904	.14233	-.12290	.903

①Using Equation 4, $F = \dfrac{R^2/k}{(1 - R^2)/(n - k - 1)} = \dfrac{.46345/3}{.53655/(37 - 3 - 1)} = 9.501$

②These are the raw regression coefficients for predicting PEVOCAB from the 3 predictors, excluding the regression constant.

Selected output from the multivariate regression analysis run is given in Table 3.19. The multivariate test determines whether there is a significant relationship between the two *sets* of variables, i.e., the two dependent variables and the three predictors. At this point, the reader should focus on Wilk's Λ, the most commonly used multivariate test statistic. We have more to say about the other multivariate tests in Chapter 5. Wilk's Λ here is given by:

$$\Lambda = \frac{|SS_{resid}|}{|SS_{tot}|} = \frac{|SS_{resid}|}{|SS_{reg} + SS_{resid}|}, \ 0 \le \Lambda \le 1$$

Recall from the matrix algebra chapter that the determinant of a matrix served as a multivariate generalization for the variance of a set of variables. Thus, $|SS_{resid}|$ indicates the amount of variability for the set of 2 dependent variables that is not accounted for by regression, and $|SS_{tot}|$ gives the total variability for the 2 dependent variables about their means. The sampling distribution of Wilk's Λ is quite complicated, however, there is an excellent F approximation (due to Rao), which is what appears in Table 3.19. Note that the multivariate $F = 4.82$, $p < .000$, which indicates a significant relationship between the dependent variables and the 3 predictors beyond the .01 level.

The univariate F's are the tests for the significance of the regression of each dependent variable separately. They indicate that PEVOCAB is significantly related to the set of predictors at the .05 level ($F = 9.501$, $p < .000$), while RAVIN is not significantly related at the .05 level ($F = 2.652$, $p < .065$). Thus, the overall multivariate significance is primarily attributable to PEVO-CAB's relationship with the three predictors.

It is important for the reader to realize that although the multivariate tests take into account the correlations among the dependent variables, the regression equations that appear in Table 3.19 are those that would be obtained if each dependent variable were regressed *separately* on the set of predictors. That is, in deriving the prediction equations, the correlations among the dependent variables are ignored, or not taken into account.

We indicated earlier in this chapter that an R^2 value around .50 occurs quite often with educational and psychological data, and this is precisely what has occurred here with the PEVOCAB variable ($R^2 = .463$). Also, we can be fairly confident that the prediction equation for PEVOCAB will cross-validate, since the n/k ratio is $37/3 = 12.33$, which is close to the 15/1 ratio we indicated is necessary.

Appendix
Sesame Street Data for Example 1

Case No. Label	Viewing	Prebody	Postbody
1	1	16	18
2	1	23	21
3	3	23	22
4	3	30	32
5	1	28	20
6	3	25	28
7	3	25	32
8	4	25	32
9	2	15	14
10	4	17	21
11	3	24	21
12	3	23	29
13	3	27	32
14	2	31	21
15	3	23	29
16	4	14	29
17	4	26	24
18	4	25	30
19	2	16	21
20	1	25	25
21	4	20	27
22	2	23	28
23	3	31	31
24	4	27	31
25	4	29	30
26	4	31	23
27	2	31	32
28	3	30	32
29	3	24	28
30	2	23	28
31	2	22	25
32	4	21	29
33	4	22	32
34	1	17	18
35	4	21	31
36	2	26	27
37	4	28	32
38	3	22	25
39	1	19	28
40	3	14	18
41	3	22	23
42	1	7	19
43	2	26	28
44	4	17	29
45	2	12	16
46	2	18	25

Appendix
Sesame Street Data for Example 1

Case No. Label	Viewing	Prebody	Postbody
47	3	29 .	29
48	3	13	28
49	4	19	27
50	4	28	28
51	4	18	23
52	2	20	26
53	4	23	31
54	4	26	30
55	3	15	24
56	3	10	13
57	4	23	21
58	2	16	22
59	1	15	20
60	1	13	21
61	1	13	24
62	3	25	31
63	2	24	30
64	1	28	26
65	1	19	21
66	1	22	18
67	3	29	30
68	4	23	28
69	2	20	27
70	1	14	22
71	4	27	27
72	3	18	24
73	1	26	25
74	2	16	24
75	1	15	18
76	1	15	15
77	2	20	29
78	4	26	30
79	2	16	22
80	1	13	29

This is a subset of data from the first year evaluation of "Sesame Street." It is used with the permission of the Children's Television Workshop. This subset may not represent the full data set, and therefore, generalizations should not be drawn.

Data for Example 9

Student	Y	Predictors				
		1	2	3	4	5
1	1	1	2	1	1	2
2	1	2	2	1	1	1
3	1	1	1	1	1	2
4	1	1	2	1	1	2
5	2	1	3	2	2	2
6	2	2	4	1	1	2
7	2	3	3	1	1	2
8	2	3	4	1	2	3
9	2	2	3	1	3	3
10	2	2	2	2	2	2
11	2	2	3	2	1	2
12	2	2	2	3	3	2
13	2	2	2	1	1	2
14	2	2	4	2	2	2
15	2	3	3	1	1	3
16	2	3	4	1	1	2
17	2	3	2	1	1	2
18	3	4	4	3	2	2
19	3	4	3	1	1	4
20	3	4	3	1	2	3
21	3	4	3	2	2	3
22	3	3	4	2	3	3
23	3	3	4	2	3	3
24	3	4	3	1	1	2
25	3	4	5	1	1	3
26	3	3	5	1	2	3
27	3	4	4	1	2	3
28	3	4	4	1	1	3
29	3	3	3	2	1	3
30	3	3	5	1	1	2
31	4	5	5	2	3	4
32	4	4	5	2	3	4

*Key:
Y—instructor evaluation
1—clarity
2—stimulating
3—knowledge
4—interesting
5—course evaluation

Data for Cross Validation—Table 3.9

Case No. Label	Y	x_2	x_3	x_4	x_5	x_6
1	4	87	39	9	12	9
2	5	76	15	7	10	10
3	5	90	28	8	12	9
4	3	82	47	13	14	12
5	1	76	33	9	12	9
6	2	99	46	18	20	15
7	4	93	42	10	17	13
8	2	79	38	14	18	11
9	2	82	32	10	18	8
10	5	76	34	7	9	5
11	4	91	41	11	12	11
12	1	86	43	5	11	11
13	1	92	43	12	15	12
14	1	92	43	16	19	12
15	4	83	36	14	16	12
16	1	97	45	10	16	11
17	1	99	39	9	17	11
18	2	96	44	18	15	10
19	3	83	33	7	15	11
20	1	89	43	18	17	10
21	1	104	47	8	13	14
22	4	88	42	13	12	14
23	1	85	41	15	19	12
24	3	82	36	12	16	11
25	1	94	40	13	15	6
26	4	92	37	14	18	11
27	1	108	46	10	11	14
28	5	79	15	13	5	5
29	5	80	21	4	11	7
30	5	86	23	4	4	8
31	1	95	40	10	9	11
32	5	87	28	6	6	6
33	5	78	23	9	10	12
34	3	98	45	8	9	9
35	2	96	42	13	13	13
36	1	84	24	11	7	9
37	1	102	45	13	11	11
38	4	84	25	12	10	7
39	1	91	39	11	9	7
40	5	83	32	3	4	3
41	1	104	43	13	17	14
42	5	98	43	15	18	13
43	1	91	43	12	8	9
44	5	107	42	17	13	12
45	2	103	45	15	14	11
46	5	104	42	11	13	9
47	5	79	28	8	10	12
48	4	72	14	12	4	9
49	1	94	32	11	11	8
50	4	96	44	13	14	12

REGRESSION EXERCISES—CHAPTER 3

1. Recall from the text that $E(R^2) = k/(n - 1)$ when the population $R^2 = 0$, where k is the number of predictors and n is sample size. Explain what this means geometrically for the following cases: (a) $k = 1$, $n = 2$ and (b) $k = 2$, $n = 3$.

2. Consider the following correlation matrix:

	y	x_1	x_2
y	1.0	.60	.50
x_1	.60	1.0	.80
x_2	.50	.80	1.0

a) How much variance on y will x_1 account for if entered first?
b) How much variance on y will x_1 account for if entered second?
c) What, if anything, do the above results have to do with the multicollinearity problem?

3. The data is as follows schematically for a 7 predictor regression:

y	x_1	x_2	x_3	x_4	x_5	x_6	x_7
21	6	106	38	2.1	1.89	17	.16
17	8	104	41	3.7	2.16	18	.24
28	5	97	33	4.6	3.52	14	.89

Suppose there is solid evidence from previous literature that x_2, x_3 and x_5 are good predictors of y. There is some evidence that x_1 and x_4 will predict y, and we wish to determine whether x_6 and x_7 have any incremental validity.

Show the set up of the control lines for running this problem on BMDP2R, where x_2, x_3, and x_5 are forced into the equation, x_1 and x_4 are entered next (but *not* forced in), and finally, x_6 and x_7 are entered.

4. Consider the 5 predictor data set in the Appendix for this chapter. Obtain three random splits (use three different odd 7 digit numbers) and the resulting regression analysis with the BMDP9R program and the cross validated correlations from the BMDP6D program. Compare the average of the three cross validated correlations against the average of the three maximized R's. Did you expect considerable shrinkage in this case?

5. Consider again the Sesame Street data set analyzed in 3.2 where we predicted knowledge of body parts (postbody) after viewing the series from previous knowledge of body parts (prebody). Now we add another predictor, amount of time the children viewed the Sesame Street series (scaled from 1 to 4, with 4 meaning more viewing time), to see if postbody can be predicted better from prebody and viewing.

a) Run the multiple regression on SPSSX REGRESSION, using the stepwise procedure. Are both predictors "significant"?

b) How much variance on postbody is accounted for by the significant predictor(s)?

c) Write out the prediction equation.

d) Would you be confident of the generalizability of the equation? Explain.

e) Are there any standardized or studentized residuals > 2?

f) Are there any standardized residuals that would be significant at overall $\alpha = .05$, i.e., using the Bonferroni inequality?

g) Are there any significant ($\alpha = .05$) outliers for the predictors according to Mahalanobis distance?

h) Using Cook's distance, are there any influential data points?

6. Consider the following RESULTS section from a study by Sharp (1981):

The regression was performed to determine the extent to which a linear combination of two or more of the five predictor variables could account for the variance in the dependent variable (posttest). Three steps in the multiple regression were completed before the contributions of additional predictor variables were deemed insignificant ($p < .05$). In Step #1, the pretest variable was selected as the predictor variable that explained the greatest amount of variance in posttest scores. The R^2 value using this single variable was .25. The next predictor variable chosen (Step #2) in conjunction with pretest, was interest in participating in the CTP. The R^2 value using these two variables was .36. The final variable (Step #3), which significantly improved the prediction of posttest scores, was the treatment—viewing the model videotape (Tape). The multiple regression equation, with all three significant predictor variables entered, yielded an R^2 of .44. The other two predictor variables, interest and relevance, were not entered into the regression equation as both failed to meet the statistical significance criterion.

Correlations Among Criterion and Predictor Variables

	Posttest	Pretest	Tape	Campus Teaching Program	Interest	Relevancy
Posttest	1.0					
Pretest	.50*	1.0				
Tape	.27	− .02	1.0			
Campus Teaching Program	.35*	.06	− .07	1.0		
Interest	− .02	.14	.07	− .06	1.0	
Relevance	− .06	− .02	.07	.05	.31	1.0

Note. N = 37.
*$p < .05$.

a) Which specific predictor selection procedure were the authors using?

b) They give the R^2 for the first predictor as .25. How did they arrive at this figure?

c) The R^2 for the first two predictors was .36, an increase of .11 over the R^2 for just the first predicter. Using the appropriate correlations in the Table show how the value of .11 is obtained.

d) Is there evidence of multicollinearity among the predictors? Explain.

e) Do you think the author's regression equation would cross-validate well? Explain.

7.   Plante and Goldfarb (1984) predicted social adjustment from Cattell's 16 personality factors. There were 114 subjects, consisting of students and employees from two large manufacturing companies. They state in their RESULTS section:

> Stepwise multiple regression was performed. . . . The index of social adjustment significantly correlated with 6 of the primary factors of the 16 PF. . . . Multiple regression analysis resulted in a multiple correlation of $R = .41$ accounting for 17% of the variance with these 6 factors. The multiple R obtained while utilizing all 16 factors was $R = .57$, thus accounting for 32% of the variance.

a) Would you have much faith in the reliability of either of the above regression equations?

b) Apply the Herzberg formula for random predictors (Equation 9) to the 16 variable equation to estimate how much variance on the average we could expect to account for if the equation were cross validated on many other random samples.

8.   A medical school admissions official has two proven predictors (x_1 and x_2) of success in medical school. He has two other predictors under consideration (x_3 and x_4), of which he wishes to choose just one which will add the most (beyond what x_1 and x_2 already predict) to predicting success. Below is the matrix of intercorrelations he has gathered on a sample of 100 medical students:

	x_1	x_2	x_3	x_4
y	.60	.55	.60	.46
x_1		.70	.60	.20
x_2			.80	.30
x_3				.60

a) What procedure would he use to determine which predictor has the greater incremental validity? Do *not* go into any numerical details, just indicate the general procedure. Also, what is your educated guess as to which predictor (x_3 or x_4) will probably have the greater incremental validity.

b) Suppose the investigator has found his third predictor, runs the regression and finds $R = .76$. Apply the Herzberg formula (use $k = 3$), and tell exactly what the resulting number represents.

9. In a study from a major journal (Bradley, Caldwell, and Elardo, 1977) the investigators were interested in predicting I.Q. of 3-year-old children from four measures of socioeconomic status and six environmental process variables (as assessed by a HOME inventory instrument). Their total sample size was 105. They were also interested in determining whether the prediction varied depending on sex and on race. The following is from their PROCEDURE section:

> To examine the relations among SES, environmental process, and IQ data, three multiple correlation analyses were performed on each of five samples: total group, males, females, whites, and blacks. First, four SES variables (maternal education, paternal education, occupation of head of household, and father absence) plus six environmental process variables (the six HOME inventory subscales) were used as a set of predictor variables with IQ as the criterion variable. Third, the six environmental process variables were used as the predictor set with IQ as the criterion variable.

Below is the table they present with the 15 multiple correlations:

Multiple Correlations Between Measures
of Environmental Quality and IQ

Measure	Males (n = 57)	Females (n = 48)	Whites (n = 37)	Black (n = 68)	Total (N = 105)
Status variables (A)	.555	.636	.582	.346	.556
HOME inventory (B)	.647	.790	.622	.576	.742
A and B	.682	.825	.683	.614	.765

a) The authors state that all of the above multiple correlations are statistically significant (.05 level) except for .346 obtained for Blacks with Status variables. Show that .346 is not significant at .05 level.

b) For Males, does the addition of the Home inventory variables to the prediction equation significantly increase (use .05 level) predictive power beyond that of the Status variables?

The following F statistic is appropriate for determining whether a set B significantly adds to the prediction beyond what set A contributes:

$$F = \frac{(R^2_{y \cdot AB} - R^2_{y \cdot A})/k_b}{(1 - R^2_{y \cdot AB})/(n - k_A - k_B - 1)}$$

Where k_A and k_B represent the number of predictors in sets A and B respectively.

d) For Females the multiple correlation for all predictors is quite high, i.e., .825. How much *variance* would you expect to account for in I.Q. from all 10 predictors if the prediction equation were cross validated?

e) The authors make the statement that, "environmental quality (as assessed by the HOME inventory) is more strongly associated with I.Q. among whites than blacks and among females than males." After correcting each of the multiple correlations for predictive power expected on the average in population, then apply (as a rough test) the test for a difference in correlations from independent samples to see if either part of the authors assertion is tenable. The appropriate statistic is $z = \dfrac{Z_1 - Z_2}{\sqrt{1/(n_1 - 3) + 1/(n_2 - 3)}}$, where Z_i are Fisher transformed values of correlations.

10. A regression analysis for 52 subjects with 3 predictors yielded the following summary statistics:

Correlation Matrix				Means	Variances
	x_1	x_2	x_3		
x_1	1	.67	.53	x_1 2.78	1.2
x_2		1	.15	x_2 14.12	3.5
x_3			1	x_3 38.54	16.8

J. R. obtained the following scores on the 3 predictors 1.6, 11.4 and 41.7. Calculate Mahalanobis D^2 for J. R. and determine whether he is an outlier on the set of predictors at the .05 level.

4 Two Group Multivariate Analysis of Variance

4.1. INTRODUCTION

In this chapter we consider the statistical analysis of two groups of subjects on several dependent variables simultaneously, focusing on cases where the variables are correlated and share a common conceptual meaning. That is, the dependent variables considered together make sense as a group. For example, they may be different dimensions of self concept (physical, social, emotional, academic), teacher effectiveness, speaker credibility, or reading (blending, syllabication, comprehension, etc.). We consider the multivariate tests along with their univariate counterparts and show that the multivariate two-group test (Hotelling's T^2) is a natural generalization of the univariate t test. We initially present the traditional analysis of variance approach for the two-group multivariate problem, and then later present and compare a regression analysis of the same data. In the next chapter studies with more than two groups are considered, where multivariate tests are employed that are generalizations of Fisher's F found in a univariate one way ANOVA.

There are two reasons one should be interested in using more than one dependent variable when comparing two treatments:

1. Any treatment "worth it's salt" will affect the subjects in more than one way; hence the need for several criterion measures.
2. Through the use of several criterion measures we can obtain a more complete and detailed description of the phenomenon under investigation, whether it is reading achievement, math achievement, self concept, physiological stress, or teacher effectiveness or counselor effectiveness.

If we were comparing two methods of teaching second-grade reading, we would obtain a more detailed and informative breakdown of the differential effects of the methods if reading achievement were split into its subcomponents: syllabication, blending, sound discrimination, vocabulary, comprehension, and reading rate. Comparing the two methods only on total reading achievement might yield no significant difference; however, the methods may be making a difference. The differences may be confined to only the more basic elements of blending and syllabication. Similarly, if two methods of teaching sixth-grade mathematics were being compared, it would be more informative to compare them on various levels of mathematics achievement (computations, concepts, and applications).

4.2.   FOUR STATISTICAL REASONS FOR PREFERRING A MULTIVARIATE ANALYSIS

1.   The use of fragmented univariate tests leads to a greatly inflated overall type I error rate, i.e., the probability of at least one false rejection. Consider a two-group problem with 10 dependent variables. What is the probability of one or more spurious results, if we do 10 t tests, each at the .05 level of significance? If we assume the tests are independent as an approximation (since the tests are not independent), then the probability of *no* type I errors is:

$$\underbrace{(.95)(.95) \ldots \ldots (.95)}_{10 \text{ times}} \approx .60$$

since the probability of not making a type I error for each test is .95, and with the independence assumption we can multiply probabilities. Therefore, the probability of at least one false rejection is $1 - .60 = .40$, which is unacceptably high. Thus, with the univariate approach not only does overall α become too high, but we can't even accurately estimate it!

2.   The univariate tests ignore important information, i.e., the correlations among the variables. The multivariate test incorporates the correlations (via the covariance matrix) right into the test statistic, as is shown in the next section.

3.   Although the groups may not be significantly different on any of the variables individually, *jointly* the set of variables may reliably differentiate the groups. That is, small differences on several of the variables may combine to produce a reliable overall difference. Thus, the multivariate test will be more powerful in this case.

4.   It is sometimes argued that the groups should be compared on total test score first to see if there is a difference. If so, then compare the groups further on subtest scores to locate the sources responsible for the global difference. On the other hand, if there is no total test score difference, then stop. This procedure

could definitely be misleading. Suppose, for example, that the total test scores were not significantly different, but that on subtest 1 group 1 was quite superior, on subtest 2 group 1 was somewhat superior, on subtest 3 there was no difference, and on subtest 4 group 2 was quite superior. Then it would be clear why the univariate analysis of total test score found nothing; because of a cancelling out effect. But the two groups do differ substantially on 2 of the 4 subtests, and to some extent on a third. A multivariate analysis of the subtests would reflect these differences and would show a significant difference.

Many investigators, especially when they first hear about multivariate analysis of variance (MANOVA), will lump all the dependent variables in a single analysis. This is not necessarily a good idea. If several of the variables have been included without any strong rationale (empirical and/or theoretical), then small or negligible differences on these variables may obscure a real difference(s) on some of the other variables. That is, the multivariate test statistic detects mainly error in the system (i.e., in the set of variables), and therefore declares no reliable overall difference. In a situation such as this what is called for are two separate multivariate analyses, one multivariate analysis for the variables for which there is solid support and a separate multivariate analysis for the variables which are being tested on a heuristic basis.

4.3.   THE MULTIVARIATE TEST STATISTIC AS A GENERALIZATION OF UNIVARIATE t

For the univariate t test the null hypothesis is:

$H_0 : \mu_1 = \mu_2$ (population means are equal)

In the multivariate case the null hypothesis is:

$$H_0 : \begin{pmatrix} \mu_{11} \\ \mu_{21} \\ \vdots \\ \mu_{p1} \end{pmatrix} = \begin{pmatrix} \mu_{12} \\ \mu_{22} \\ \vdots \\ \mu_{p2} \end{pmatrix} \quad \text{(population mean vectors are equal)}$$

Saying that the vectors are equal implies that the groups are equal on all p dependent variables. The first part of the subscript refers to the variable and the second part to the group. Thus, μ_{21} refers to the population mean for variable 2 in group 1.

Now, for the univariate t test the reader should recall that there are 3 assumptions involved: (1) independence of the observations, (2) normality, and (3) equality of the population variances (homogeneity of variance). In testing the multivariate null hypothesis the corresponding assumptions are: (1) independence of the observations, (2) multivariate normality on the dependent variables in each population, and (3) equality of the covariance matrices.

The latter two multivariate assumptions are much more stringent than the corresponding univariate assumptions. For example, saying that two covariance matrices are equal for 4 variables implies that the variances are equal for each of the variables *and* that the 6 covariances for each of the groups are equal. Consequences of violating the multivariate assumptions are discussed in detail in Chapter 6.

We now show how the multivariate test statistic arises naturally from the univariate t by replacing scalars (numbers) by vectors and matrices. The univariate t is given by:

$$t = \frac{\bar{y}_1 - \bar{y}_2}{\sqrt{\frac{(n_1 - 1) s_1^2 + (n_2 - 1) s_2^2}{n_1 + n_2 - 2} \left(\frac{1}{n_1} + \frac{1}{n_2}\right)}} \tag{1}$$

where s_1^2 and s_2^2 are the sample variances for groups 1 and 2 respectively. The quantity under the radical, excluding the sum of the reciprocals, is the pooled estimate of the assumed common within population variance, call it s^2. Now, replacing that quantity by s^2 and squaring both sides, we obtain:

$$t^2 = \frac{(\bar{y}_1 - \bar{y}_2)^2}{s^2 \left(\frac{1}{n_1} + \frac{1}{n_2}\right)}$$

$$= (\bar{y}_1 - \bar{y}_2) \left[s^2 \left(\frac{1}{n_1} + \frac{1}{n_2}\right) \right]^{-1} (\bar{y}_1 - \bar{y}_2)$$

$$= (\bar{y}_1 - \bar{y}_2) \left[s^2 \left(\frac{n_1 + n_2}{n_1 n_2}\right) \right]^{-1} (\bar{y}_1 - \bar{y}_2)$$

$$t^2 = \frac{n_1 n_2}{n_1 + n_2} (\bar{y}_1 - \bar{y}_2) (s^2)^{-1} (\bar{y}_1 - \bar{y}_2)$$

Hotelling's T^2 is obtained by replacing the means on each variable by the vectors of means in each group, and by replacing the univariate measure of within variability s^2 by it's multivariate generalization **S** (the estimate of the assumed common population covariance matrix). Thus we obtain:

$$T^2 = \frac{n_1 n_2}{n_1 + n_2} (\bar{\mathbf{y}}_1 - \bar{\mathbf{y}}_2)' \mathbf{S}^{-1} (\bar{\mathbf{y}}_1 - \bar{\mathbf{y}}_2) \tag{2}$$

Recall that the matrix analogue of division is inversion; thus $(s^2)^{-1}$ is replaced by the inverse of **S**.

Hotelling (1931) showed that the following transformation of T^2 yields an exact F distribution:

$$F = \frac{n_1 + n_2 - p - 1}{(n_1 + n_2 - 2)\,p}\,T^2 \qquad (3)$$

with p and $(N - p - 1)$ degrees of freedom, where p is the number of dependent variables and $N = n_1 + n_2$, i.e., total number of subjects.

We can rewrite T^2 as:

$$T^2 = k\,\mathbf{d}'\mathbf{S}^{-1}\,\mathbf{d}$$

where k is a constant involving the group sizes, $\mathbf{d}$ is the vector of mean differences and $\mathbf{S}$ is the covariance matrix. Thus, what we have reflected in T^2 is a comparison of between-variability (given by the $\mathbf{d}$ vectors) to within-variability (given by $\mathbf{S}$). This is perhaps not obvious, since we are not literally dividing between by within as in the univariate case (i.e., $F = MS_b/MS_w$). However, recall again that inversion is the matrix analogue of division, so that multiplying by $\mathbf{S}^{-1}$ is in effect "dividing" by the multivariate measure of within variability.

4.4. NUMERICAL CALCULATIONS FOR A TWO-GROUP PROBLEM

We now consider a small example to illustrate the calculations associated with Hotelling's T^2. The ficticious data shown below represent scores on two measures of counselor effectiveness, client satisfaction (SA) and client self acceptance (CSA). Six subjects were originally randomly assigned to counselors who used either Rogerian or Adlerian methods, however, three in the Rogerian group were unable to continue for reasons unrelated to the treatment.

Rogerian		Adlerian	
SA	CSA	SA	CSA
1	3	4	6
3	7	6	8
2	2	6	8
$\bar{y}_{11} = 2$	$\bar{y}_{21} = 4$	5	10
		5	10
		4	6
		$\bar{y}_{12} = 5$	$\bar{y}_{22} = 8$

Recall again that the first part of the subscript denotes the variable and the second part the group, i.e., $\bar{y}_{12}$ is the mean for variable 1 in group 2.

In words, our multivariate null hypothesis is "There is no difference between the Rogerian and Adlerian groups when they are compared simultaneously on client satisfaction and client self acceptance." Let client satisfaction be variable 1 and client self acceptance be variable 2. Then the multivariate null hypothesis in symbols is:

$$H_0 : \begin{pmatrix} \mu_{11} \\ \mu_{21} \end{pmatrix} = \begin{pmatrix} \mu_{12} \\ \mu_{22} \end{pmatrix}$$

That is, we wish to determine whether it is tenable that the population means are equal for variable 1 ($\mu_{11} = \mu_{12}$) and that the population means for variable 2 are equal ($\mu_{21} = \mu_{22}$). To test the multivariate null hypothesis we need to calculate F in Equation 3. But to obtain this we first need T^2, and the tedious part of calculating T^2 is in obtaining $\mathbf{S}$, which is our pooled estimate of within-group variability on the set of two variables, i.e., our estimate of error. Before we begin calculating $\mathbf{S}$ it will be helpful to go back to the univariate t test (Equation 1) and recall how the estimate of error variance was obtained there. The estimate of the assumed common within population variance (σ^2) (i.e., error variance) is given by

$$s^2 = \frac{(n_1 - 1) s_1^2 + (n_2 - 1) s_2^2}{n_1 + n_2 - 2} = \frac{ss_{g_1} + ss_{g_2}}{n_1 + n_2 - 2} \qquad (4)$$

(cf. Equation 1)   (from the definition of variance)

where ss_{g_1} and ss_{g_2} are the within sums of squares for groups 1 and 2. In the multivariate case (i.e., in obtaining $\mathbf{S}$) we replace the univariate measures of

TABLE 4.1
Estimation of Error Term for t Test and Hotelling's T^2

	t test (univariate)	T^2 (multivariate)
Assumption	Within group population variances are equal, i.e., $\sigma_1^2 = \sigma_2^2$ Call the common value σ^2	Within group population covariance matrices are equal $\Sigma_1 = \Sigma_2$ Call the common value Σ
	To estimate these assumed common population values we employ the three steps indicated below:	
Calculate the within group measures of variability.	ss_{g_1} and ss_{g_2}	$\mathbf{W}_1$ and $\mathbf{W}_2$
Pool the above estimates	$ss_{g_1} + ss_{g_2}$	$\mathbf{W}_1 + \mathbf{W}_2$
Divide by the degrees of freedom	$\dfrac{ss_{g_1} + ss_{g_2}}{n_1 + n_2 - 2} = \hat{\sigma}^2$	$\dfrac{\mathbf{W}_1 + \mathbf{W}_2}{n_1 + n_2 - 2} = \Sigma = \mathbf{S}$

The rationale for pooling is that if we are measuring the same variability in each group (which is the assumption), then we obtain a better estimate of this variability by combining our estimates.

within-group variability (ss_{g_1} and ss_{g_2}) by their matrix multivariate generalizations, which we call $\mathbf{W}_1$ and $\mathbf{W}_2$.

$\mathbf{W}_1$ will be our estimate of within variability on the two dependent variables in group 1. Since we have two variables, there is variability on each, which we denote by ss_1 and ss_2, and covariability, which we denote by ss_{12}. Thus, the matrix $\mathbf{W}_1$ will look as follows:

$$\mathbf{W}_1 = \begin{bmatrix} ss_1 & ss_{12} \\ ss_{21} & ss_2 \end{bmatrix}$$

Similarly, $\mathbf{W}_2$ will be our estimate of within variability (error) on variables in group 2. After $\mathbf{W}_1$ and $\mathbf{W}_2$ have been calculated, we will pool them (i.e., add them) and divide by the degrees of freedom, as was done in the univariate case (cf. Equation 4), to obtain our multivariate error term, the covariance matrix $\mathbf{S}$. Table 4.1 shows schematically the procedure for obtaining the pooled error terms for both the univariate t test and for Hotelling's T^2.

Calculation of the Multivariate Error Term $\mathbf{S}$

First we calculate $\mathbf{W}_1$, the estimate of within variability for group 1.

Now, ss_1 and ss_2 are just the sum of the squared deviations about the means for variables 1 and 2 respectively. Thus,

$$ss_1 = \sum_{i=1}^{3} (y_{1(i)} - \bar{y}_{11})^2 = (1 - 2)^2 + (3 - 2)^2 + (2 - 2)^2 = 2$$

($y_{1(i)}$ denotes the score for the ith subject on variable 1)

and

$$ss_2 = \sum_{i=1}^{3} (y_{2(i)} - \bar{y}_{21})^2 = (3 - 4)^2 + (7 - 4)^2 + (2 - 4)^2 = 14$$

Finally, ss_{12} is just the sum of deviation cross products:

$$ss_{12} = \sum_{i=1}^{3} (y_{1(i)} - 2)(y_{2(i)} - 4)$$

$$= (1 - 2)(3 - 4) + (3 - 2)(7 - 4) + (2 - 2)(2 - 4) = 4$$

Therefore, the within SSCP matrix for group 1 is

$$\mathbf{W}_1 = \begin{bmatrix} 2 & 4 \\ 4 & 14 \end{bmatrix}$$

Similarly, as we leave for the reader to show, the within matrix for group 2 is

$$\mathbf{W}_2 = \begin{bmatrix} 4 & 4 \\ 4 & 16 \end{bmatrix}$$

Thus, the multivariate error term (i.e., the pooled within covariance matrix) is calculated as:

$$\mathbf{S} = \frac{\mathbf{W}_1 + \mathbf{W}_2}{n_1 + n_2 - 2} = \frac{\begin{bmatrix} 2 & 4 \\ 4 & 14 \end{bmatrix} + \begin{bmatrix} 4 & 4 \\ 4 & 16 \end{bmatrix}}{7} = \begin{bmatrix} 6/7 & 8/7 \\ 8/7 & 30/7 \end{bmatrix}$$

Note that 6/7 is just the sample variance for variable 1, 30/7 is the sample variance for variable 2, and 8/7 is the sample covariance.

Calculation of the Multivariate Test Statistic

To obtain Hotelling's T^2 we need the inverse of $\mathbf{S}$ as follows:

$$\mathbf{S}^{-1} = \begin{bmatrix} 1.811 & -.483 \\ -.483 & .362 \end{bmatrix}$$

From Equation 2 then, Hotelling's T^2 is

$$T^2 = \frac{n_1 n_2}{n_1 + n_2} (\bar{\mathbf{y}}_1 - \bar{\mathbf{y}}_2)' \, \mathbf{S}^{-1} \, (\bar{\mathbf{y}}_1 - \bar{\mathbf{y}}_2)$$

$$T^2 = \frac{3(6)}{3 + 6} (2 - 5, 4 - 8) \begin{bmatrix} 1.811 & -.483 \\ -.483 & .362 \end{bmatrix} \begin{pmatrix} 2 - 5 \\ 4 - 8 \end{pmatrix}$$

$$T^2 = (-6, -8) \begin{pmatrix} -3.501 \\ .001 \end{pmatrix} = 21$$

The exact F transformation of T^2 is then

$$F = \frac{n_1 + n_2 - p - 1}{(n_1 + n_2 - 2) p} T^2 = \frac{9 - 2 - 1}{7 \, (2)} (21) = 9,$$

where F has 2 and 6 degrees of freedom (cf. Equation 3).

If we were testing the multivariate null hypothesis at the .05 level, then we would reject (since the critical value $= 5.14$) and conclude that the two groups differ on the set of two variables.

After finding that the groups differ, we would now like to determine which of the variables are contributing to the overall difference, i.e., a post hoc procedure is needed. This is similar to the procedure followed in a one way ANOVA, where first an overall F test is done. If F is significant, then a post hoc technique (such as Scheffe's or Tukey's) is used to determine which specific groups differed, and thus contributed to the overall difference. Here, instead of groups, we wish to know which variables contributed to the overall multivariate significance.

Now, multivariate significance implies there is a linear combination of the dependent variables (the discriminant function) that is significantly separating the groups. We defer extensive discussion of discriminant analysis to chapter 7. Harris (1985, p. 9) argues vigorously for focusing on such linear combinations," Multivariate statistics can be of considerable value in suggesting new, emergent variables of this sort that may not have been anticipated-but the researcher must be prepared to think in terms of such combinations. . ." While we agree that discriminant analysis can be of value, there are at least 3 factors that can mitigate it's usefulness in many instances:

1) There is no guarantee that the linear combination (the discriminant function) will be a meaningful variate, i.e., that it will make substantive or conceptual sense.

2) Sample size must be considerably larger than many investigators realize in order for the results of a discriminant analysis to be reliable. More details on this later.

3) The investigator may be more interested in what specific variables contributed to treatment differences, rather than on some combination of them.

4.5.   THREE POST HOC PROCEDURES

We now consider three possible post hoc approaches. One approach is to use the Roy-Bose simultaneous confidence intervals. These are a generalization of the Scheffe' intervals, and are illustrated in Morrison (1976) and in Johnson and Wichern (1982). The intervals are nice in that we can not only determine whether a pair of means is different, but in addition can obtain a range of values within which the population mean differences probably lie. Unfortunately, however, the procedure is extremely conservative (Hummel & Sligo, 1971), and this will hurt power (sensitivity for detecting differences).

As Bock (1975, p. 422) has noted, "Their [Roy-Bose intervals] use at the conventional 90% confidence level will lead the investigator to overlook many differences that should be interpreted and defeat the purposes of an exploratory comparative study." What Bock says applies with particularly great force to a very large number of studies in social science research where the group and/or effect sizes are small or moderate. In these studies power will be poor or not adequate to begin with. To be more specific, consider the power table from Cohen (1977, p. 36) for a two-tailed t test at the .05 level of significance. For group sizes $\leq$ 20 and small or medium effect sizes through .60 standard deviations, which is a quite common class of situations, the *largest* power is .45! The use of the Roy-Bose intervals will dilute the power even further to extremely low levels.

A second, less conservative post hoc procedure is to follow a significant multivariate result by univariate t's, but to do each t test at the α/p level of significance. Then we are assured by the Bonferroni inequality that the overall type I error rate for the set of t tests will be less than α. This is a good procedure, if the number of dependent variables is small (say $\leq$ 7). Thus, if there were 4 variables and we wished to take at most a 10% chance of one or more false rejections, this can be assured by setting α = .10/4 = .025 for each t test. Recall that the Bonferroni inequality simply says that the overall α level for a set of tests is less than or equal to the sum of the α levels for each test.

The third post hoc procedure we consider is following a significant multivariate test at the .05 level by univariate tests, each at the .05 level. The results of a Monte Carlo study by Hummel and Sligo (1971) indicate that, if the multivariate null hypothesis is true, then this procedure keeps the overall α level under control for the set of t tests. This procedure has greater power for detecting differences than the two previous approaches, and this is an important consideration when small or moderate sample sizes are involved. Timm (1975) has noted that if the multivariate null hypothesis is only partially true (e.g., for only 3 of 5 variables there are no differences in the population means), and the multivariate null hypothesis is likely to be rejected, then the Hummel and Sligo results are not directly applicable. He suggested use of the second approach we mentioned. While this approach will guard against spurious results, power will be severely attenuated if the number of dependent variables is even moderately large. For example, if p = 15 and we wish to set overall α = .05, then each univariate test must be done at the .05/15 = .0033 level of significance! There are two things that can be done to improve power and yet provide reasonably good protection against type I errors. First, there are several reasons (which we detail in Chapter 5) for *generally* preferring to work with a relatively small number of dependent variables (say $\leq$10). Secondly, in many cases it may be possible to divide the dependent variables up into 2 or 3 of the following categories: (1) those variables likely to show a difference, (2) those variables (based on past research) that may show a difference, and (3) those variables that are being tested on a heuristic basis.

As an example, suppose we conduct a study, limiting the number of variables to 8. There is solid or fairly solid evidence from the literature that 3 of the variables will be significant, and the other 5 are being tested on a heuristic basis. In this situation, as indicated in 4.2, two multivariate tests should be done. If the multivariate test for the 3 solid variables is significant at the .05 level, then we would test each of the individual variables at the .05 level. Here we are not as worried about type I errors in the followup phase, since there is prior reason to believe that the variables will be significant. A separate multivariate test is done for the 5 heuristic variables. If this is significant, then we would employ the Timm approach, but set overall α somewhat higher for better power (especially if sample size is small or moderate). For example, set overall $\alpha = .15$, and thus test each variable for significance at the $.15/5 = .03$ level of significance.

4.6.   HUMMEL AND SLIGO STUDY

Hummel and Sligo considered the two-group MANOVA case for equal group sizes of 10, 30, and 50, and for 3, 6, and 9 variables. Various correlational structures among the variables were considered, from weak to very strong. A weak structure had proportion of variance in common for each pair of variables equal to .10 (i.e., the correlation in each case was .315), while a very strong structure had proportion of variance in common of .70 (i.e., the correlation in each case was .84). Their study was designed to examine the effect (if any) of group size, number of variables, and correlational structure on experimentwise error rate (probability of at least one false rejection when the null hypothesis is true—this is what we have called overall α). Part of the main results of Hummel and Sligo are presented in Table 4.2.

Table 4.2 shows why analyzing multivariate data with only univariate tests can lead to seriously inflated error rates. Note, in particular, that for 6 and 9 variables (with proportion of variance in common through .50), in all but three cases the error rates are $\geq .19$. That is, the error rate is about four times greater than the nominal value of .05; the value the experimenter thinks he or she is working at!

The other part of Table 4.2 shows why Hummel and Sligo recommended the combination (a significant multivariate test, followed by univariate tests) approach for analyzing multivariate data. The error rates are quite homogeneous, and most importantly close to the nominal value of .05, although there is a trend toward

TABLE 4.2

Experimentwise Error Rates for Analyzing Multivariate Data with
only Univariate Tests and with a Multivariate Test followed by
Univariate Tests*

Sample Size	Number of Variables	Univariate Tests Only Proportion of variance in common			
		.10	.30	.50	.70
10	3	.145	.112	.114	.077
10	6	.267	.190	.178	.111
10	9	.348	.247	.209	.129
30	3	.115	.119	.117	.085
30	6	.225	.200	.176	.115
30	9	.296	.263	.223	.140
50	3	.138	.124	.102	.083
50	6	.230	.190	.160	.115
50	9	.324	.258	.208	.146
Multivariate Test Followed by Univariate Tests					
10	3	.044	.029	.035	.022
10	6	.046	.029	.030	.017
10	9	.050	.026	.025	.018
30	3	.037	.044	.029	.025
30	6	.037	.037	.032	.021
30	9	.042	.042	.030	.021
50	3	.038	.041	.033	.028
50	6	.037	.039	.028	.027
50	9	.036	.038	.026	.020

*Nominal $\alpha = .05$.

conservativeness (i.e., the actual type I error rate is less than the nominal value).

Recall for our sample problem that the multivariate test was significant at the .05 level. If we perform the univariate t test on each variable we find for client satisfaction ($t = -4.58$) and for client self acceptance ($t = -2.73$), both of which are significant at the .05 level. Furthermore, given the Hummel and Sligo results we can also be confident that the probability of at least one false rejection for these two tests is close to the .05 level we think we are working at.

An illustration of the importance of recognizing that the multivariate F must be significant before interpreting univariate F's (or t's) is brought out by a study by Griesinger (1977). He had a 2×2 design (treatments by sex) with four criterion measures. All three multivariate F's were not significant ($F = 1.09$, $p < .44$ for treatments; $F = 1.47$, $p < .32$ for sex; and $F = .216$, $p < .92$ for interaction). Thus, the univariate F's were not interpreted. Now, it turned out that one of the univariate F's was 3.95, $p < .078$ for treatment, and a different variable had a univariate $F = 5.65$, $p < .04$ for sex. It is very tempting for a researcher to interpret these as real effects. However, 12 univariate tests were done, and the probability of two significant results by chance is fairly high. *The importance of requiring multivariate significance before interpreting univariate F's is that it provides an extra measure of protection against researchers interpreting effects which are probably spurious.*

4.7. OUTPUT FOR SAMPLE PROBLEM FROM BMDP3D

Table 4.3 presents the control lines for running the sample problem on both BMDP3D and on SPSSX MANOVA, and Table 4.4 presents the BMDP3D output for our sample problem. The first test given is the multivariate test ($F = 9$, $p < .0156$), which shows that the groups differ on the set of two variables at the .05 level. The p value on the printout is an exact probability of a type I error. Therefore, if this value is less than the α level we have set a priori (nominal value), we can reject H_0. The exact probability (sometimes called a tail probability) being less than the α level set by the experimenter means that the value of the test statistic is in the critical region. These exact probabilities obviate the

TABLE 4.3
BMDP3D and SPSSX MANOVA Control Lines for Two-Group
MANOVA Sample Problem

BMDP3D ①		SPSSX MANOVA
	/PROBLEM TITLE IS 'TWO GROUP MANOVA'.	TITLE 'TWO GROUP MANOVA'
	/INPUT VARIABLES = 3. FORMAT IS STREAM.	DATA LIST FREE/GP,Y1,Y2
	/VARIABLE NAMES ARE GP,Y1,Y2.	LIST
	GROUPING IS GP.	BEGIN DATA
②	/TEST VARIABLES ARE Y1,Y2, HOTELLING.	1 1 3 1 3 7 1 2 2
	/END	2 4 6 2 6 8 2 6 8
	1 1 3 1 3 7 1 2 2	2 5 10 2 5 10 2 4 6
	2 4 6 2 6 8 2 6 8	END DATA
	2 5 10 2 5 10 2 4 6	③ MANOVA Y1 Y2 BY GP(1,2)/
		④ PRINT = CELLINFO(MEANS)/

①The reader may find it very helpful to refer back to Tables 1.3 and 1.4 (where we present some of the basic elements of the control language for BMDP and SPSSX), and Table 1.5, where we present an example of the control lines for running SPSSX MANOVA for a single dependent variable. Also, in Table 1.5 we discuss the INPUT paragraph.

②This TEST paragraph is necessary to obtain the multivariate test, with HOTELLING being the keyword that is used to request the multivariate test.

③The general form for the MANOVA command is

MANOVA	list of dependent	BY list of	WITH list of
	variables	factors	covariates

④This PRINT subcommand is to obtain the means and standard deviations for the variables.

TABLE 4.4
Selected Output from BMDP3D for Sample Two-Group MANOVA Problem

BMDP3D TWO GP MANOVA-FROM CHAP 4

DIFFERENCES AMONG GROUPS MEANS USING ALL VARIABLES
FOR THE FOLLOWING GROUPS

* *1.00000 *
* *2.00000 *
••••••••

This is the multivariate test, indicating the groups differ on the set of two variables at the .05 level.

MAHALANOBIS D SQUARE	10.5000	
HOTELLING T SQUARE	21.0000	
F VALUE	9.0000	
DEGREES OF FREEDOM 2.	6.0	P-VALUE 0.0156 6.0

① DIFFERENCES ON SINGLE VARIABLES

••••••••	VARIABLE NUMBER		2			1	*1.00000	2	*2.00000
* SA *					GROUP		2.0000		5.0000
••••••••					MEAN				

STATISTICS		P-VALUE	DF		STD DEV	1.000	0.8944
					S.E.M.	0.5774	0.3651
T (SEPARATE)	-4.39	0.0141	3.7		SAMPLE SIZE	3	6
T (PCOLED)	-4.58	0.0025	7		MAXIMUM	3.0000	6.0000
					MINIMUM	1.0000	4.0000

F(FOR ②
VARIANCES)
LEVENE   0.00   1.0000   1. 7

••••••••	VARIABLE NUMBER		3			1	*1.00000	2	*2.00000
* CSA *					GROUP		4.0000		8.0000
••••••••					MEAN				

STATISTICS		P-VALUE	DF		STD DEV	2.6458	1.7889
					S.E.M.	1.5275	0.7303
T (SEPARATE)	-2.36	0.1004	3.0		SAMPLE SIZE	3	6
T (POOLED)	-2.73	0.0292	7		MAXIMUM	7.0000	10.0000
					MINIMUM	2.0000	6.0000

F(FOR
VARIANCES)
LEVENE   0.85   0.3876   1. 7

①The *T* (SEPARATE) and *T* (POOLED) that follow are the univariate *t* tests for the variables.

②Since this test is not significant at .05 level, the *T* (POOLED) is appropriate in each case. (See the discussion in the body of the text). The *T* (POOLED) values indicate that both variables are significant at the .05 level, since the exact probabilities (*P*-VALUE) are less than .05.

need of looking up critical values. They are printed out on all three major statistical packages (BMDP, SPSSX, and SAS).

Two different univariate t's are printed for each variable below the multivariate test. One should use the separate t value only if the F test for variances is significant *and* the group sizes are sharply unequal (larger group size/smaller group size >1.5). For this case various studies have shown that the separate t will keep the actual type I error rate close to the nominal value, whereas the type I error rate for the pooled t will differ somewhat from the nominal value. For the present example, neither F test for variances is significant (at .05), so it is appropriate to use the pooled t values. These indicate that both variables are contributing to the overall multivariate significance ($t_{SA} = -4.58, p < .0025$ and $t_{CSA} = -2.73, p < .029$).

It is important to note here that some frequently used tests for homogeneity of variance, such as Bartlett's Cochran's, and Hartley's F_{max}, are quite sensitive to non-normality. That is, with these tests one may reject and erroneously conclude that the population variances are different when in fact the rejection was due to non-normality in the underlying populations. The Levene test on the BMDP3D printout was designed to be robust against non-normality. The test statistic is formed by deviating the scores for the subjects in each group from the group mean, and then taking the absolute values. Thus, $z_{ij} = |y_{ij} - \bar{y}_j|$, where $\bar{y}_j$ represents the mean for the jth group, and then an ANOVA is done on the z_{ij}'s. Although the Levene test is somewhat more robust, an extensive Monte Carlo study by Conover, Johnson, and Johnson (1981) showed that if considerable skewness is present, a modification of the Levene test is necessary for it to remain robust. The mean for each group is replaced by the *median* ($y_{j(med)}$) and the ANOVA is done on $z_{ij}^* = |y_{ij} - y_{j(med)}|$. This modification produces a robust test with good power.

We have indicated that both variables are contributing to the overall multivariate significance. It needs to be emphasized, however, that *since the univariate t's ignore how a given variable is correlated with the others in the set, they do not give an indication of the relative importance of that variable to group differentiation.* A technique for determining the relative importance of each variable to group separation is discriminant analysis, discussed in Chapter 7. To obtain reliable results with discriminant analysis, however, a large subject to variable ratio is needed, i.e., about 20 subjects per variable are required.

4.8. TWO-GROUP MATCHED PAIRS

In many studies comparing a treatment group vs. a control group or in comparing treatments, it is not possible to randomly assign subjects to the groups. Hence, a nice, clean cause-effect interpretation is not possible. However, by matching (pairing) subjects on certain key variables, known or suspected, to be related to performance on the dependent variable(s), an investigator makes it more plausible that if a significant difference is found, it was the treatment that made the difference.

Now, when the subjects are matched on variables their scores on the dependent variable(s) within each pair become correlated, and hence the analysis considered earlier is not applicable (since it assumes independence). To illustrate, consider a study investigating the effect of kindergarten on first grade readiness. Sixteen girl beginners, some of which had attended kindergarten and others who had not, are matched on I. Q., socioeconomic status, and number of children in the family, and then compared on their first grade readiness scores. Schematically then, we have:

Pairs	Kind	No. Kind.	I. Q.	SES	No. of Children
1	Jane	Joan	103, 105	M, M	3, 3
2	Sue	Ellen	115, 112	L, L	2, 2
		....			
8	Marg	Kathy	121,124	U,U	1, 1

Since within each pair the subjects are similar on variables related to first grade readiness, we would expect their scores to be somewhat similar or correlated. The reader should recall that the t test for correlated or dependent samples is appropriate here. For the case of several dependent variables, a multivariate generalization of the t test for correlated samples is used. We defer discussion of this to Chapter 13, where we treat correlated observations.

4.9. MULTIVARIATE SIGNIFICANCE BUT NO UNIVARIATE SIGNIFICANCE

If the multivariate null hypothesis is rejected, then *generally* at least one of the univariate t's will be significant, as in our previous example. This will not always be the case. It is possible to reject the multivariate null hypothesis and yet for none of the univariate t's to be significant. As Timm (1975, p. 166) has pointed out, "Furthermore, rejection of the multivariate test does not guarantee that there exists at least one significant univariate F ratio. For a given set of data, the significant comparison may involve some linear combination of the variables." This is analogous to what happens occasionally in univariate analysis of variance. The overall F is significant, but when say the Tukey procedure is used to determine which pairs of groups are significantly different none are found. Again, all the significant F guarantees is that there is at least one comparison among the group means that is significant at or beyond the same α level: The particular comparison may be a complex one, and may or may not be a meaningful one.

One way of seeing that there will be no necessary relationship between multivariate significance and univariate significance is to observe that the tests make use of different information. For example, the multivariate test takes into account the correlations among the variables whereas the univariate don't. Also, the multivariate test considers the differences on all variables jointly, while the univariate tests consider the difference on each variable separately.

We now consider a specific example, explaining in a couple of ways why multivariate significance was obtained but univariate significance was not.

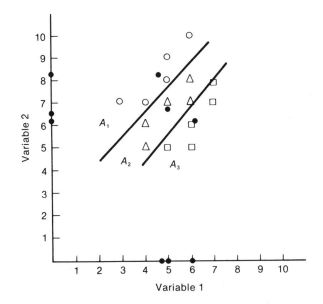

Data for Above Plot

A_1		A_2		A_3	
1	2	1	2	1	2
3	7	4	5	5	5
4	7	4	6	6	5
5	8	5	7	6	6
5	9	6	7	7	7
6	10	6	8	7	8

FIG. 4.1. Graphical Plot of Scores for Three-Group Case with Multivariate Significance but no Univariate Significance.

Example

Kerlinger and Pedhazur (1973) present a three-group, two dependent variable example where the MANOVA test is significant at the .001 level, yet neither univariate test is significant, even at the .05 level. To explain this geometrically they plot the scores for the variables in the plane (cf. Figure 4.1), along with the means for the groups in the plane (the problem considered as two-dimensional, i.e., multivariate). The separation of the means for the groups along each axis (i.e., when the problem is considered as two unidimensional or univariate analyses) is also given in Figure 4.1. Note that the separation of the groups in the plane is clearly greater than the separation along either axis, and in fact yielded multivariate significance. Thus, the smaller unreliable differences on each of the variables combined to produce a cumulative reliable overall difference when the variables are considered jointly.

We wish to dig a bit more deeply into this example, for there are two factors present which make it a near optimal situation for the multivariate test. First, treatments affected the dependent variables in different ways, i.e., the across-groups association between the variables was weak, so each variable was adding something relatively unique to group differentiation. This is analogous to having low intercorrelations among the predictors in a multiple regression situation. Each predictor is then adding something relatively unique to prediction of y. The pattern of means for the problem is presented below:

	Gp 1	Gp 2	Gp 3
Dep. 1	4.6	5.0	6.2
Dep. 2	8.2	6.6	6.2

The second factor that contributed to a particularly sensitive multivariate test is that the variables had a very strong *within* group correlation (.88). This is important, because it produced a smaller generalized error term against which multivariate significance was judged. The error term in MANOVA which corresponds to MS_w in ANOVA is $|\mathbf{W}|$. That is, $|\mathbf{W}|$ is a measure of how much the subjects scores vary within groups on the set of variables.

Consider the following two $\mathbf{W}$ matrices (the first matrix is from the above example) whose off diagonal elements differ because the correlation between the variables in the first case is .88 while in the other case it is .33.

$$\mathbf{W}_1 = \begin{bmatrix} 12.0 & 13.2 \\ 13.2 & 18.8 \end{bmatrix} \quad \mathbf{W}_2 = \begin{bmatrix} 12.0 & 5.0 \\ 5.0 & 18.8 \end{bmatrix}$$

The multivariate error term in the first situation is $|\mathbf{W}_1| = 12 (18.8) - 13.2^2 = 51.36$, while for $\mathbf{W}_2$ the error term is 200.6, i.e., almost four times greater! Thus, the size of the correlation can make a considerable difference in the magnitude of the multivariate error term. If the correlation is weak, then most of the error on the second variable cannot be accounted for by error on the first, and all that additional error becomes part of the multivariate error. On the other hand, when the correlation is strong the second variable adds little additional error, and therefore the multivariate error term is much smaller.

Summarizing then, in the Kerlinger and Pedhazur example it was the *combination* of weak across group association (meaning each variable was making a relatively unique contribution to group differentiation) coupled with a strong within group correlation (producing a small multivariate error term) that yielded an excellent situation for the multivariate test.

4.10. MULTIVARIATE REGRESSION ANALYSIS FOR THE SAMPLE PROBLEM

This section is presented to show that ANOVA and MANOVA are special cases of regression analysis, i.e., of the so-called general linear model. Cohen's (1968) seminal article was primarily responsible for bringing the general linear model to the attention of social science researchers. The regression approach to MANOVA is accomplished by dummy coding group membership. This amounts, for the two-group problem, to coding the subjects in group 1 by some numerical value, say 1, and the subjects in group 2 by another numerical value, say 0. Thus, the data for our sample problem would look like this:

y_1	y_2	x	
1	3	1	Group 1
3	7	1	
2	2	1	
4	6	0	Group 2
4	6	0	
5	10	0	
5	10	0	
6	8	0	
6	8	0	

In a typical regression problem, as considered in the previous chapters, the predictor(s) have been continuous variables. Here, for MANOVA the predictor is a categorical or nominal variable, and is used to determine how much of the variance in the dependent variables is accounted for by group membership. It should be noted that values other than 1 and 0 could have been used as the dummy codes without affecting the results. For example, the subjects in group 1 could have been coded as 1's and the subjects in group 2 as 2's. All that is necessary is to distinguish between the subjects in the two groups by two different values.

The setup of the two-group MANOVA as a multivariate regression may seem somewhat strange since there are two dependent variables and only one predictor. In the previous chapters there has been either one dependent variable and several predictors, or several dependent variables and several predictors. However, the examination of the association is done in the same way. Recall, that Wilk's Λ was the statistic for determining whether there is a significant association between the dependent variables and the predictor(s):

$$\Lambda = \frac{|\mathbf{S}_e|}{|\mathbf{S}_e + \mathbf{S}_r|}$$

where $\mathbf{S}_e$ is the error SSCP matrix, i.e., the sum of square and cross-products not due to regression (or the residual), and $\mathbf{S}_r$ is the regression SSCP matrix, i.e., an index of how much variability in the dependent variables is due to regression. In this case variability due to regression is variability in the dependent variables due to group membership, since the predictor is group membership.

Part of the output from SPSSX for the two-group MANOVA, set up and ran as a regression, is presented in Table 4.5. The error matrix $\mathbf{S}_e$ is called adjusted within cells sum of squares and cross products, and the regression SSCP matrix is called adjusted hypothesis sum of squares and cross products. Using these matrices, we can form Wilk's Λ (and see how the value of .25 is obtained):

$$\Lambda = \frac{|\mathbf{S}_e|}{|\mathbf{S}_e + \mathbf{S}_r|} = \frac{\begin{vmatrix} 6 & 8 \\ 8 & 30 \end{vmatrix}}{\left| \begin{bmatrix} 6 & 8 \\ 8 & 30 \end{bmatrix} + \begin{bmatrix} 18 & 24 \\ 24 & 32 \end{bmatrix} \right|}$$

$$\Lambda = \frac{\begin{vmatrix} 6 & 8 \\ 8 & 30 \end{vmatrix}}{\begin{vmatrix} 24 & 32 \\ 32 & 62 \end{vmatrix}} = \frac{116}{464} = .25$$

Note first that the multivariate F's are *identical* on BMDP3D (Table 4.4) and on SPSSX (Table 4.5); thus, significant separation of the group mean vectors is equivalent to significant association between group membership (dummy coded) and the set of dependent variables. SPSSX gives four multivariate test statistics (Pillais, Hotellings, Wilks, and Roys). All the reader need know at this point is that for two groups they are equivalent (cf. Table 4.5). For k groups they can yield different results, and this is discussed in the k group chapter.

TABLE 4.5

Selected Output from SPSSX for Regression Analysis on Two-Group MANOVA with Group Membership as Predictor

EFFECT .. WITHIN CELL REGRESSION

ADJUSTED WITHIN CELLS SUM-OF-SQUARES AND CROSS-PRODUCTS

	Y1	Y2
Y1	6.0000	
Y2	8.0000	30.00000

ADJUSTED HYPOTHESIS SUM-OF-SQUARES AND CROSS-PRODUCTS

	Y1	Y2
Y1	18.00000	
Y2	24.00000	32.00000

MULTIVARIATE TESTS OF SIGNIFICANCE (S = 1, M = 0, N = 2)

TEST NAME	VALUE	APPROX. F.	HYPOTH. DF	ERROR DF	SIG. OF F
PILLAIS	.75000	9.00000	2.00	6.00	.016
HOTELLINGS	3.00000	9.00000	2.00	6.00	.016
WILKS	.25000	9.00000	2.00	6.00	.016
ROYS	.75000				

UNIVARIATE F-TESTS WITH (1,7) D.F.

VARIABLE	SQ. MUL. R	MUL. R	ADJ. R-SQ.	HYPOTH. MS	ERROR MS	F	SIG. OF F
Y1	.75000	.86603	.71429	18.00000	.85714	21.00000	.003
Y2	.51613	.71842	.44700	32.00000	4.28571	7.46667	.029

The univariate results from BMDP3D and SPSSX are also identical, although this is not obvious. That is, the F values from SPSSX are simply the squares of the pooled t values from BMDP3D (recall that $F = t^2$, i.e., analysis of variance on two groups is equivalent to a two-tailed t test). Thus, $t_{SA} = -4.58 \Rightarrow t^2 = F = 21$, while $t_{CSA} = -2.73 \Rightarrow t^2 = 7.45 = F$ (within rounding error).

In traditional ANOVA, the total sum of squares (ss_t) is partitioned as:

$$ss_t = ss_b + ss_w$$

while in regression analysis the total sum of squares is partitioned as follows:

$$ss_t = ss_{reg} + ss_{resid}$$

The corresponding F ratios, for determining whether there is significant group separation and for determining whether there is a significant regression are:

$$F = \frac{ss_b/df_b}{ss_w/df_w} \text{ and } F = \frac{ss_{reg}/df_{reg}}{ss_{resid}/df_{resid}}$$

To see that these F ratios are equivalent, note that since the predictor variable is group membership, ss_{reg} is just the amount of variability between groups or ss_b, while ss_{resid} is just the amount of variability not accounted for by group membership, or the variability of the scores within each group (i.e., ss_w).

The regression output from SPSSX also gives some information *not* on the traditional MANOVA output, ie., the squared multiple R's for each dependent variable. Since in this case there is just one predictor, these multiple R's are just squared Pearson correlations. In particular, they are squared pt-biserial correlations since one of the variables is dichotomous (dummy coded group membership). The relationship between the pt biserial correlation and the F statistic is given by:

$$r_{pb} = \sqrt{\frac{F}{F + df_w}} \quad \text{(Welkowitz, Ewen, \& Cohen, 1982)}$$

$$r_{pb}^2 = \frac{F}{F + df_w}$$

Thus, for dependent variable 1, we have

$$r_{pb}^2 = \frac{21}{21 + 7} = .75$$

This squared correlation has a very meaningful and important interpretation. It tells us that 75% of the variance in the dependent variable is accounted for by group membership. Thus, we not only have a statistically significant relationship, as indicated by the F ratio, but in addition the relationship is very strong. It should be recalled that it is important to have a measure of strength of relationship *along* with a test of significance, as significance resulting from large sample size might indicate a very weak relationship, and therefore one that may be of little practical significance.

Various textbook authors have recommended measures of association or strength of relationship measures (Cohen & Cohen, 1975; Hays, 1981; Kerlinger & Pedhazur, 1973; Kirk, 1982). We also feel that they can be useful, but they also have limitations.

For example, simply because a strength of relationship indicates that say only 10% of variance is accounted for does not *necessarily* imply that the result has no practical significance, as O'Grady(1982) has indicated in an excellent review on measures of association. There are several factors that affect such measures. One very important factor is context, i.e., 10% of variance accounted for in certain research areas may indeed be practically significant.

A good example illustrating this point is provided by Rosenthal and Rosnow (1984). They consider the comparison of a treatment and control group where the dependent variable is dichotomous, whether the subjects survive or die. The following table is presented:

	Treatment Outcome		
	Alive	Dead	
Treatment	66	34	100
Control	34	66	100
	100	100	

Since both variables are dichotomous, the phi coefficient (a special case of the Pearson correlation for two dichotomous variables, Glass and Hopkins, 1984) measures the relationship between them

$$\phi = \frac{34^2 - 66^2}{\sqrt{100\ (100)(100)(100)}} = -.32 \Rightarrow \phi^2 = .10$$

Thus, even though the treatment-control distinction accounts for "only" 10% of the variance in the outcome, it increases the survival rate from 34% to 66%, far from trivial! The same type of interpretation would hold if we considered some less dramatic type of outcome like improvement vs. no improvement, where treatment was a type of psychotherapy. Also, the interpretation is *not* confined to a dichotomous outcome measure. Another factor to consider is the design of the study. As O'Grady (1982) notes, "Thus, true experiments will frequently produce smaller measures of explained variance than will correlational studies. At the least this implies that consideration should be given to whether an investigation involves a true experiment or a correlational approach in deciding whether an effect is weak or strong." Another point to keep in mind is that since most behaviors have multiple causes, it will be difficult in these cases to account for a large percent of variance with just a single cause (say treatments). Still another factor is the homogeneity of the population sampled. Since measures of association are correlational type measures, the more homogeneous the population the smaller the correlation will tend to be, and therefore the smaller the percent of variance accounted for can potentially be (this is the restriction of range phenomenon).

Finally, we focus on a topic that is generally neglected in texts on MANOVA, i.e., estimation of power. We start at a basic level, reviewing what power is, factors affecting power, and reasons why estimation of power is important. Then the notion of effect size for the univariate t test is given, followed by the multivariate effect size concept for Hotelling's T^2.

4.11. POWER ANALYSIS[1]

Type I error, or the level of significance (α), is familiar to all readers. This is the probability of rejecting the null hypothesis when it is true, i.e., saying the groups differ when in fact they don't. The α level set by the experimenter is a subjective decision, but is usually set at .05 or .01 by most researchers to minimize the probability of making this kind of error. There is however another type of error that one can make in conducting a statistical test, and this is called a type II error. Type II error, denoted by β, is the probability of accepting H_0 when it is false, i.e., saying the groups don't differ when they do. Now, not only can either of these errors occur, but in addition they are inversely related. Thus, as we control on type I error, type II error increases. This is illustrated below for a two-group problem with 15 subjects per group:

α	β	$1 - \beta$
.10	.37	.63
.05	.52	.48
.01	.78	.22

Notice that as we control on α more severely (from .10 to .01), type II error increases fairly sharply (from .37 to .78). Therefore, the problem for the experimental planner is achieving an appropriate balance between the two types of errors. While we do not intend to minimize the seriousness of making a type I error, we hope to convince the reader that much more attention should be paid to type II error. Now, the quantity in the last column is the *power* of a statistical test, and is the probability of rejecting the null hypothesis when it is false. Thus, power is the probability of making a correct decision. In the above example if

---

[1]Much of the material in this section is identical to that presented in 1.2; however, it was felt worth repeating in this more extensive discussion of power.

we are willing to take a 10% chance of rejecting H_0 falsely, then we have a 63% chance of finding a difference of a specified magnitude in the population (more specifics on this shortly). On the other hand, if we insist on only a 1% chance of rejecting H_0 falsely, then we have only about 2 chances out of 10 of finding the difference. This example with small sample size suggests that in this case it might be prudent to abandon the traditional α levels of .01 or .05 to a more liberal α level to improve power sharply. Of course, one does not get something for nothing. We are taking a greater risk of rejecting falsely, but that increased risk is *more than balanced* by the increase in power.

There are two types of power estimation, a priori and post hoc, and very good reasons why each of them should be considered seriously. If a researcher is going to invest a great amount of time and money in carrying out a study, then he or she would certainly want to have a 70% or 80% chance (i.e., power of .70 or .80) of finding a difference if one is there. Thus, the a priori estimation of power will alert the researcher to how many subjects per group will be needed for adequate power. Later on we consider an example of how this is done in the multivariate case.

The post hoc estimation of power is important in terms of how one interprets the results of completed studies. Researchers not sufficiently sensitive to power may interpret nonsignificant results from studies as demonstrating that treatments made no difference. In fact, it may be that treatments did make a difference but that the researchers had poor power for detecting the difference. The poor power may result from small sample size and/or effect size. The following example shows how important an awareness of power can be. Cronbach and Snow had written a report on aptitude-treatment interaction research, not being fully cognizant of power. By the publication of their text, *Aptitudes and Instructional Methods* (1977) on the same topic, they acknowledged the importance of power, stating in the preface, "[We] . . . became aware of the critical relevance of statistical power, and consequently changed our interpretations of individual studies and sometimes of whole bodies of literature." Why would they change their interpretation of a whole body of literature? Because, prior to being sensitive to power when they found most studies in a given body of literature had nonsignificant results, they concluded no effect existed. However, after being sensitized to power they took into account the sample sizes in the studies, and also the magnitude of the effects. If the sample sizes were small in most of the studies with nonsignificant results, then lack of significance is due to poor power. Or, in other words, several low power studies that report nonsignificant results of the same character *are* evidence for an effect.

The power of a statistical test is dependent on three factors:

1. The α level set by the experienter
2. Sample size
3. Effect size—How much of a difference the treatments make, or the extent

to which the groups differ in the population on the dependent variable(s).

For the univariate independent samples t test, Cohen (1977) has defined the population effect size as $d = (\mu_1 - \mu_2)/\sigma$, where σ is the assumed common population standard deviation. Thus, effect size simply indicates how many standard deviation units the group means are separated by.

Power is *heavily* dependent on sample size. Consider a two-tailed test at the .05 level for the t test for independent samples. Suppose we have an effect size of .5 standard deviations. The table below shows how power changes dramatically as sample size increases.

n (subjects per group)	power
10	.18
20	.33
50	.70
100	.94

As the above example suggests, when sample size is large (say 100 or more subjects per group) power is not an issue. It is when one is conducting a study where the group sizes are small (n ≤ 20), or when one is evaluating a completed study that had small group size, that it is imperative to be very sensitive to the possibility of poor power (or equivalently, a type II error).

We have indicated that power is also influenced by effect size. For the t test, Cohen (1977) has suggested as a rough rule of thumb that an effect size around .20 is small, an effect size around .50 is medium, and an effect size > .80 is large. The difference in the mean I.Q.'s between Ph.D's and the typical college freshmen is an example of a large effect size (about .8 of a standard deviation). *It is quite important to realize that small or moderate effect sizes are very common in social science research.* A direct implication is that in these studies large group size or very sensitive designs will be required to detect these effects (i.e., to have adequate power).

4.12. WAYS OF IMPROVING POWER

Given how poor power generally is with less than 20 subjects per group, the following 4 methods of improving power should be seriously considered:

1. Adopt a more lenient α level, perhaps $\alpha = .10$ or $\alpha = .15$.
2. Use one-tailed tests where the literature supports a directional hypothesis. This option is not available for the multivariate tests since they are inherently two-tailed.
3. Consider ways of reducing within-group variability, so that one has a

more sensitive design. One way is through sample selection; more homogeneous subjects tend to vary less on the dependent variable(s). For example, use just males, rather than males and females, or use only 6 and 7 year old children rather than 6 through 9 year old children. A second way is through the use of factorial designs, which we consider in Chapter 8. A third way of reducing within-group variability is through the use of analysis of covariance, which we consider in Chapter 9. Covariates which have low correlations with each other are particularly helpful since then each is removing a somewhat different part of the within-group (error) variance. A fourth means is through the use of repeated measures designs. These designs are particularily helpful since all individual differences due to the average response of subjects is removed from the error term, and individual differences are the main reason for within group variability.

4. Make sure there is a strong linkage between the treatments and the dependent variable(s), and that the treatments extend over a long enough period of time to produce a large or at least fairly large effect size.

Using these methods *in combination* can make a considerable difference in effective power. To illustrate we consider a two-group situation with 18 subjects per group and one dependent variable. Suppose a two tailed test was done at the .05 level, and that the effect size was

$$\hat{d} = (\bar{x}_1 - \bar{x}_2)/s = (8 - 4)/10 = .40,$$

where s is pooled within standard deviation. Then, from Cohen (1977, p. 36), power $= .21$, which is very poor.

Now, suppose that through the use of two good covariates we are able to reduce pooled within variability (s^2) by 60%, from 100 (as above) to 40. This is a definite realistic possibility in practice. Then our new estimated effect size would be $\hat{d} \approx 4/\sqrt{40} = .61$.[1] Suppose in addition that a one tail test was really appropriate, and that we also take a somewhat greater risk of a type I error, i.e., $\alpha = .10$. Then, our new estimated power changes dramatically to .69 (Cohen, 1977, p. 32)!

4.13. MULTIVARIATE ESTIMATION OF POWER

Stevens (1980) has discussed estimation of power in MANOVA at some length, and in what follows we borrow heavily from his work. Below we present the univariate and multivariate measures of effect size for the two-group problem. Recall, that the univariate measure was presented earlier.

---

[1]In covariance the means are replaced by adjusted means (Chapter 9), but assuming a randomized study here the expected difference between the adjusted means should be 4.

Measures of Effect Size

| *Univariate* | *Multivariate* |

$$d = \frac{\mu_1 - \mu_2}{\sigma} \qquad D^2 = (\mu_1 - \mu_2)'\Sigma^{-1}(\mu_1 - \mu_2)$$

$$\hat{d} = \frac{\bar{y}_1 - \bar{y}_2}{s} \qquad \hat{D}^2 = (\bar{y}_1 - \bar{y}_2)'\, S^{-1}\, (\bar{y}_1 - \bar{y}_2)$$

The first row gives the population values, and the second row the estimated effect sizes. Notice that the multivariate measure $\hat{D}^2$ is Hotelling's T^2 without the sample sizes (cf. Equation 2), i.e., it is a measure of separation of the groups that is *independent* of sample size. D^2 is called in the literature Mahalanobis distance. Note also that the multivariate measure $\hat{D}^2$ *is a natural squared generalization of the univariate measure* d, *where the means have been replaced by mean vectors and* s *(standard deviation) has been replaced by its squared multivariate generalization of within variability, the sample covariance matrix* **S**.

Table 4.6 from Stevens (1980) provides power values for two-group MANOVA for 2 through 7 variables, with group size varying from small (15) to large (100), and with effect size varying from small ($D^2 = .25$) to very large ($D^2 = 2.25$). Earlier, we had indicated that small and/or moderate group and effect sizes produce inadequate power for the univariate t test. Inspection of Table 4.6 shows that a similar situation exists for MANOVA. The following from Stevens (1980, p. 731) provides a summary of the results in Table 4.6:

> For values of $D^2 \leq .64$ and $n \leq 25$, . . . power is generally poor ($< .45$) and never really adequate (i.e., $> .70$) for $\alpha = .05$. Adequate power (at $\alpha = .10$) for two through seven variables at a moderate overall effect size of .64 would require about 30 subjects per group. When the overall effect size is large ($D \geq 1$), then 15 or more subjects per group is sufficient to yield power values $\geq .60$ for two through seven variables at $\alpha = .10$ (p. 731)

Post Hoc Estimation of Power

We consider two examples to illustrate how to use Table 4.6 when (a) the number of dependent variables is not explicitly given in Table 4.6 and (b) the type of adjustment to make when the group sizes are not equal.

Example 1

Consider a two-group study with 25 subjects per group and having 4 dependent variables. First, notice that BMDP3D yields Mahalanobis D^2 as part of the standard output (cf. Table 4.4). Suppose the printout from this study shows

TABLE 4.6

Power of Hotelling's T^2 at $\alpha = .05$ and $.10$ for Small Through Large
Overall Effect and Group Sizes

No. of Variables	n^*	D^2** .25	.64	1	2.25
2	15	26 (32)	44 (60)	65 (77)	95***
2	25	33 (47)	66 (80)	86	97
2	50	60 (77)	95	1	1
2	100	90	1	1	1
3	15	23 (29)	37 (55)	58 (72)	91
3	25	28 (41)	58 (74)	80	95
3	50	54 (65)	93 (98)	1	1
3	100	86	1	1	1
5	15	21 (25)	32 (47)	42 (66)	83
5	25	26 (35)	42 (68)	72	96
5	50	44 (59)	88	1	1
5	100	78	1	1	1
7	15	18 (22)	27 (42)	37 (59)	77
7	25	22 (31)	38 (62)	64 (81)	94
7	50	40 (52)	82	97	1
7	100	72	1	1	1

Note—Power values at $\alpha = .10$ are in parentheses.
*Equal group sizes are assumed.
**$D^2 = (\mu_1 - \mu_2)'\Sigma^{-1}(\mu_1 - \mu_2)$
***Decimal points have been omitted. Thus, 95 means a power of .95. Also, a value of 1 means the power is approximately equal to 1.

$\hat{D}^2 = .98$, a large multivariate effect size. Table 4.6 does not have the power values for 4 variables, but interpolating between the values for 3 and 5 variables gives a good approximation. Using $D^2 = 1$ in Table 4.6 we find:

No. of Variables	n	$D^2 = 1$
3	25	.80
5	25	.72

Thus, a good approximation to the power is .76, which is adequate power. Here, as in univariate analysis, with a large effect size not many subjects are needed per group to have adequate power.

Example 2

For our second example we consider a researcher who had run a two-group MANOVA on BMDP3D having seven dependent variables and 18 subjects in one group and 30 in the other group. Since Table 4.6 assumes equal group sizes, we must make an adjustment for the unequal group sizes here. Following Cohen (1977), we use the harmonic mean as the n with which to enter the table. The harmonic mean for two groups is given by $\tilde{n} = 2 n_1 n_2/(n_1 + n_2)$. Thus, for this case $\tilde{n} = 2 (18)(30)/(18 + 30) = 22.5$. Suppose that $D^2 = .51$ on the printout. Then, by using $n = 25$ (as a fairly rough approximation) to enter Table 4.6, and interpolating between $D^2 = .25$ and $D^2 = .64$, we obtain power $\approx .30$ at $\alpha = .05$. The conclusion is that the researcher had a very poor chance of finding a significant difference in this case.

A Priori Estimation of Sample Size

Suppose that from a pilot study or from a previous study that used the same kind of subjects, an investigator had obtained the following pooled within-group covariance matrix for three variables:

$$S = \begin{bmatrix} 16 & 6 & 1.6 \\ 6 & 9 & .9 \\ 1.6 & .9 & 1 \end{bmatrix}$$

Recall that the elements on the main diagonal of S are the variances for the variables, i.e., 16 is the variance for variable 1, etc.

To complete the estimate of D^2 the difference in the mean vectors must be estimated. This amounts to estimating the mean difference expected for each variable. Suppose that on the basis of previous literature, the investigator hypothesizes that the mean differences on variables 1 and 2 will be 2 and 1.5. Thus, they will correspond to moderate effect sizes of .5 standard derivations. Why? The investigator further expects the mean difference on variable 3 will be .2, i.e., .2 of a standard deviation, or a small effect size. How many subjects per group are required, at $\alpha = .10$, for detecting this set of differences if power = .70 is desired?

To answer this question we first need to estimate D^2:

$$\hat{D}^2 = (2, 1.5, .2) \begin{bmatrix} .0917 & -.0511 & -.1008 \\ -.0511 & .1505 & -.0538 \\ -.1008 & -.0538 & 1.2100 \end{bmatrix} \begin{pmatrix} 2.0 \\ 1.5 \\ .2 \end{pmatrix} = .3347$$

The middle matrix is the inverse of S. Since moderate and small univariate effect sizes produced this $\hat{D}^2$ value of .3347, such a numerical value for D^2 would probably occur fairly frequently in social science research. Recall that small and moderate univariate effect sizes are very common.

Now, to determine the n required for power = .70, we enter Table 4.6 for 3 variables and use the values in parentheses. For $n = 50$ and 3 variables, note that power = .65 for $D^2 = .25$ and power = .98 for $D^2 = .64$. That an $n = 50$

per group yields power $\approx .70$ in the present situation can be seen by interpolating:

$$\text{Power } (D^2 = .33) = \text{Power } (D^2 = .25) + \frac{.08}{.39} \, (.33)$$

$$\text{Power} = .65 + .07 = .72$$

4.14. SUMMARY

In this chapter we have considered the statistical analysis of two groups on several dependent variables simultaneously. Among the reasons for preferring a MANOVA over separate univariate analyses were (a) MANOVA takes into account important information, i.e., the intercorrelations among the variables, (b) MANOVA keeps the overall α level under control, and (c) MANOVA has greater sensitivity for detecting differences in certain situations. It was shown how the multivariate test (Hotelling's T^2) arises naturally from the univariate t by replacing the means with mean vectors and by replacing the pooled within-variance by the covariance matrix. An example indicated the numerical details associated with calculating T^2.

Three post hoc procedures, for determining which of the variables contributed to the overall multivariate significance, were considered. The Roy-Bose simultaneous confidence interval approach was rejected because it is extremely conservative, and hence has poor power for detecting differences. The approach of testing each variable at the α/p level of significance was considered a good procedure if the number of variables is small. In an exploratory study, testing each variable for significance at the .05 level, after a significant multivariate result, is a reasonable procedure. Based on the multivariate significance and the Hummel and Sligo results, we have a fair amount of protection against type I errors, and better power than for the other 2 procedures.

An example where multivariate significance was obtained but not univariate significance was considered in detail. Examination showed that the example was a near optimal situation for the multivariate test since the treatments affected the dependent variables in different ways (thus each variable was making a relatively unique contribution to group differentiation), while the dependent variables were strongly correlated within groups (providing a small multivariate error term).

Group membership for the sample problem was dummy coded, and it was run as a regression analysis. This yielded the same multivariate and univariate results as when the problem was run as a traditional MANOVA. This was done to show that MANOVA is a special case of regression analysis, i.e., of the general linear model. It was noted that the regression output also provided useful strength of relationship measures for each variable (R^2's). However, the reader was warned against concluding that a result is of little practical significance simply because the R^2 value is small (say .10). Several reasons were given for this; one of the most important being context. Thus, 10% variance accounted for in some research areas may indeed be practically significant.

Finally, both post hoc estimation of power and a priori estimation of sample size required for a given power in MANOVA were considered. A table covering a wide range of situations (2 to 7 variables, and small to large group and effect sizes) was provided to facilitate power calculations. It was noted that the power of T^2 with small to moderate group and effect sizes is generally inadequate, as is true for the univariate t test.

EXERCISES—CHAPTER 4

1.   Which of the following are multivariate studies, i.e., involve several correlated dependent variables?

a) An investigator classifies high school freshmen by sex, socioeconomic status, and teaching method, and then compares them on total test score on the Lankton algebra test.

b) A treatment and control group are compared on measures of reading speed and reading comprehension.

c) An investigator is predicting success on the job from high school gpa and a battery of personality variables.

d) An investigator has administered a 50-item scale to 200 college freshmen and he wished to determine whether a smaller number of underlying constructs account for most of the variance in the subjects responses to the items.

e) The same middle and upper class children have been measured in grades 6, 7, and 8 on reading comprehension, math ability, and science ability. The researcher wishes to determine whether there are social class differences on these variables and if the differences change over time.

2.   In Table 4.2 (results from the Hummel and Sligo study) the experimentwise error rates for analyzing multivariate data with univariate tests only show a definite decrease as the proportion of variance the variables have in common increases. Can you explain why this happened?

3.   An investigator has a 50-item scale. He wishes to compare two groups of subjects on the scale. He has heard about MANOVA, and realizes that the items will be correlated. Therefore, he decided to do such an analysis. The scale is administered to 45 subjects, and the analysis is run on SPSSX. However, he finds that the analysis is aborted. Why? What might the investigator consider doing before running the analysis?

4.   Suppose you come across a journal article where the investigators have a

three-way design and five correlated dependent variables. They report the results in five tables, having done a univariate analysis on each of the five variables. They find four significant results at the .05 level. Would you be impressed with these results? Why, or why not? Would you have more confidence if the significant results had been hypothesized a priori? What else could they have done that would have given you more confidence in their significant results?

5.   An investigator compared two groups of subjects (30 per group) on six dependent variables using six univariate analyses, and found two of them significant at $\alpha = .05$. Suppose that the pooled within-correlation matrix for the variables is as follows:

	1	2	3	4	5	6
1	1	.45	.50	.60	.40	.55
2		1	.47	.60	.53	.45
3			1	.58	.61	.50
4				1	.50	.43
5					1	.70
6						1

a) What is a good estimate of the experimentwise error rate the investigator is operating at?
b) What would the experimentwise error rate have been had he first found a significant multivariate difference, and then found two significant univariate results?

6.   Consider the following data for a two-group two-dependent variable problem:

	T_1		T_2	
	y_1	y_2	y_1	y_2
	1	9	4	8
	2	3	5	6
	3	4	6	7
	5	4		
	2	5		

a) Compute **W**, i.e., the pooled within-SSCP matrix
b) Find the pooled within covariance matrix, and indicate what each of the elements in the matrix represents.
c) Find Hotelling's T^2.
d) What is the multivariate null hypothesis in symbolic form?
e) Test the null hypothesis at the .05 level. What is your decision?

7.   The following are the means, standard deviations, and pooled within-group correlation matrix from a study by Crocker and Benson (1976).

Group		Achievement without penalty	Achievement with penalty	Guess	Risk
Norm Referenced	$\bar{x}=$	6.375	6.821	5.526	2.885
Instructions	$sd=$	2.496	1.774	3.242	2.528
(n = 78)					
Criterion Referenced	$\bar{x}=$	5.821	5.670	5.525	2.756
Instructions	$sd=$	2.577	2.519	3.500	2.801
(n = 78)					

Correlation Matrix

	Achievement without penalty	Achievement with penalty	Guess	Risk
Achievement without penalty	1	.45	.20	.015
Achievement with penalty		1	.16	.20
Guess			1	.51
Risk				1

Run the two-group MANOVA on SPSSX. If the multivariate F is significant, then which of the variables are contributing to this overall difference?

8.   Suppose we have two groups, with 30 subjects in each group. The means for the two criterion measures in group 1 are 10 and 9, while the means in group 2 are 9 and 9.5. The pooled within sample variances are 9 and 4 for variables 1 and 2, while the pooled within correlation is .70.

a) Show that each of the univariate t's is not significant at .05 (2-tailed test), but that the multivariate test is significant at .05.

b) Now change the pooled within correlation to .20 and determine whether the multivariate test is still significant at .05. Explain.

9.   Consider the following set of data for two groups of subjects on two dependent variables:

Group 1		Group 2	
y_1	y_2	y_1	y_2
3	9	8	13
5	15	4	9
5	15	4	7
4	13	2	7
1	8	9	15

a) Analyze this data using the traditional MANOVA approach. Does anything interesting happen?

b) Use the regression approach (i.e., dummy coding of group membership) to analyze the data and compare the results.

10.   An investigator ran a two-group MANOVA with 3 dependent variables on SPSSX. There were 12 subjects in group 1 and 26 subjects in group 2. The following selected output gives the results for the multivariate tests (remember that for 2 groups they are equivalent). Note that the multivariate F is significant at the .05 level. Estimate what power the investigator had at the .05 level for finding a significant difference.

EFFECT . . TREATS
MULTIVARIATE TESTS OF SIGNIFICANCE (S = 1, M = 1/2, N = 16)

TEST NAME	VALUE	APPROX. F	HYPOTH. DF	ERROR DF	SIG. DF
PILLAIS	.33083	5.60300	3.00	34.00	.000
HOTELLINGS	.49438	5.60300	3.00	34.00	.000
WILKS	.66917	5.60300	3.00	34.00	.000
ROYS	.33083				

Hint: One would think that the value for "Hotellings" could be used directly in conjunction with Equation 2. However, the value for Hotellings must first be multiplied by $(N - k)$, where N is total number of subjects and k is the number of groups.

11.   An investigator has an estimate of $D^2 = .61$ from a previous study that used the same 4 dependent variables on a similar group of subjects. How many subjects per group are needed to have power = .70 at $\alpha = .10$?

12.   A two-group MANOVA having 5 dependent variables is run on BMDP3D. There are 30 subjects per group, Mahalanobis $D^2 = .48$ on the printout, and multivariate significance is not found at the .05 level. What power did the investigator have?

13.   From a pilot study, a researcher has the following pooled within covariance matrix for two variables

$$S = \begin{bmatrix} 8.6 & 10.4 \\ 10.4 & 21.3 \end{bmatrix}$$

From previous research a moderate effect size of .5 standard deviations on variable 1 and a small effect size of $\frac{1}{3}$ standard deviations on variable 2 are anticipated. For the researcher's main study, how many subjects per group are needed for power = .70 at the .05 level? At the .10 level?

14.   Ambrose (1985) compared elementary school children who received instruction on the clarinet via programmed instruction (experimental group) vs those who received instruction via traditional classroom instruction on the following six performance aspects: interpretation (interp), tone, rhythm, intonation (inton), tempo, and articulation (artic). The data, representing the average of two judges ratings, is listed below, with GPID = 1 referring to the experimental group and GPID = 2 referring to the control group:

GPID	INTERP	TONE	RHYTHM	INTON	TEMPO	ARTIC
1.00	4.20	4.10	3.20	4.20	2.80	3.50
1.00	4.10	4.10	3.70	3.90	3.10	3.20
1.00	4.90	4.70	4.70	5.00	2.90	4.50
1.00	4.40	4.10	4.10	3.50	2.80	4.00
1.00	3.70	2.00	2.40	3.40	2.80	2.30
1.00	3.90	3.20	2.70	3.10	2.70	3.60
1.00	3.80	3.50	3.40	4.00	2.70	3.20
1.00	4.20	4.10	4.10	4.20	3.70	2.80
1.00	3.60	3.80	4.20	3.40	4.20	3.00
1.00	2.60	3.20	1.90	3.50	3.70	3.10
1.00	3.00	2.50	2.90	3.20	3.30	3.10
1.00	2.90	3.30	3.50	3.10	3.60	3.40
2.00	2.10	1.80	1.70	1.70	2.80	1.50
2.00	4.80	4.00	3.50	1.80	3.10	2.20
2.00	4.20	2.90	4.00	1.80	3.10	2.20
2.00	3.70	1.90	1.70	1.60	3.10	1.60
2.00	3.70	2.10	2.20	3.10	2.80	1.70
2.00	3.80	2.10	3.00	3.30	3.00	1.70
2.00	2.10	2.00	2.20	1.80	2.60	1.50
2.00	2.20	1.90	2.20	3.40	4.20	2.70
2.00	3.30	3.60	2.30	4.30	4.00	3.80
2.00	2.60	1.50	1.30	2.50	3.50	1.90
2.00	2.50	1.70	1.70	2.80	3.30	3.10

a) Run the two-group MANOVA on these data using BMDP3D. Is the multivariate null hypothesis rejected at the .05 level?

b) What is the value of Mahalanobis D^2? How would you characterize the magnitude of this effect size? Given this, is it surprising that the null hypothesis was rejected?

c) Setting overall $\alpha = .05$ and using the Bonferroni inequality approach, which of the individual variables are significant, and hence contributing to the overall multivariate significance.

5

K Group MANOVA:
A Priori and Post Hoc
Procedures

5.1. INTRODUCTION

In this chapter we consider the case where more than two groups of subjects are
being compared on several dependent variables simultaneously. We first show
how the MANOVA can be done within the regression model by dummy coding
group membership for a small sample problem and using it as a nominal predictor.
In doing this we build upon the multivariate regression analysis of two-group
MANOVA which was presented in the last chapter. Then we consider the traditional analysis of variance for MANOVA, introducing the most familiar multivariate test statistic Wilk's Λ. Three post hoc procedures, for determining which
groups and which variables are contributing to overall multivariate significance,
are discussed. The first two employ Hotelling T^2's, to locate which pairs of
groups differ significantly on the set of variables. The first post hoc procedure
then uses univariate t's to determine which of the variables are contributing to
the significant pairwise differences that are found, while the second procedure
uses the Tukey simultaneous confidence interval approach to identify the variables. As a third procedure, we consider the Roy-Bose multivariate simultaneous
confidence intervals.

Next we consider a different approach to the k group problem, that of using
planned comparisons rather than an omnibus F test. Hays (1981) has an excellent
discussion of this approach for univariate ANOVA. Our discussion of multivariate planned comparisons is extensive and is made quite concrete through the
use of several examples, including two studies from the literature. The setup of
multivariate contrasts on SPSSX MANOVA is illustrated and some printout is
discussed.

149

We then consider the important problem of a priori determination of sample size for 3, 4, 5, and 6 group MANOVA for the number of dependent variables ranging from 2 to 15, using extensive tables developed by Lauter (1978). Finally, the chapter concludes with a discussion of some considerations which mitigate generally against the use of a large number of criterion variables in MANOVA.

5.2.   MULTIVARIATE REGRESSION ANALYSIS FOR A SAMPLE PROBLEM

In the previous chapter we indicated how analysis of variance can be incorporated within the regression model by dummy coding group membership and using it as a nominal predictor. For the two group case just one dummy variable (predictor) was needed, which took on the value 1 for subjects in group 1 and was 0 for the subjects in the other group. For our three group example we need two dummy variables (predictors) to identify group membership. The first dummy variable (x_1) is 1 for all subjects in group 1 and 0 for all other subjects. The other dummy variable (x_2) is one for all subjects in group 2 and 0 for all other subjects. A third dummy variable is *not* needed since the subjects in group 3 are identified by 0's on x_1 and x_2, i.e., not in group 1 or group 2. Therefore, by default, those subjects must be in group 3. In general, for k groups, the number of dummy variables needed is $(k - 1)$, corresponding to the between degrees of freedom.

The data for our two-dependent variable, three-group problem is presented below:

Dep. 1	Dep. 2	x_1	x_2	
2	3	1	0	Group 1
3	4	1	0	
5	4	1	0	
2	5	1	0	
4	8	0	1	Group 2
5	6	0	1	
6	7	0	1	
7	6	0	0	Group 3
8	7	0	0	
10	8	0	0	
9	5	0	0	
7	6	0	0	

Thus, cast in a regression mold, we are relating two sets of variables, the two dependent variables and the two predictors (dummy variables). The regression analysis will then determine how much of the variance on the dependent variables is accounted for by the predictors, i.e., by group membership.

In Table 5.1 we present the control lines for running the sample problem as a multivariate regression on SPSSX MANOVA, and the lines for running the

TABLE 5.1

SPSSX MANOVA Control Lines for Running Sample Problem as
Multivariate Regression and as MANOVA

```
     TITLE' THREE GROUP MANOVA RUN AS MULTIVARIATE REGRESSION '
     DATA LIST FREE/ DEP1 DEP2 X1 X2
     LIST
     BEGIN DATA
①   2 3 1 0
     3 4 1 0
     5 4 1 0
     2 5 1 0
     4 8 0 1
     5 6 0 1
     6 7 0 1
     7 6 0 0
     8 7 0 0
     10 8 0 0
     9 5 0 0
     7 6 0 0
     END DATA
     MANOVA DEP1 DEP2 WITH X1 X2/


     TITLE ' MANOVA RUN ON SAMPLE PROBLEM '
     DATA LIST FREE/ DEP1 DEP2 GPS
     LIST
     BEGIN DATA
②   2 3 1
     3 4 1
     5 4 1
     2 5 1
     4 8 2
     5 6 2
     6 7 2
     7 6 3
     8 7 3
     10 8 3
     9 5 3
     7 6 3
     END DATA
     MANOVA DEP1 DEP2 BY GPS(1,3)/
        PRINT = CELLINFO (MEANS,COV,COR) HOMOGENEITY (COCHRAN,BOXM)/
```

①The last two columns of data are for the dummy variables $X1$ and $X2$, which identify group membership (cf the data display in Section 5.2).

②The last column of data identifies group membership—again compare the data display in 5.2.

problem as a traditional MANOVA. The reader may verify by running both analyses that the multivariate F's for the regression analysis are identical to those obtained from the MANOVA run.

5.3.   TRADITIONAL MULTIVARIATE ANALYSIS OF VARIANCE

In the k group MANOVA case we are comparing the groups on p dependent variables simultaneously. For the univariate case, the null hypothesis is:

H_0: $\mu_1 = \mu_2 = \ldots = \mu_k$ (population means are equal)

while for MANOVA the null hypothesis is

H_0: $\mu_1 = \mu_2 = \ldots = \mu_k$ (population mean vectors are equal)

For univariate analysis of variance the F statistic ($F = MS_b/MS_w$) is used for testing the tenability of H_0. What statistic do we use for testing the multivariate null hypothesis? There is no single answer, as several test statistics are available (Olson, 1974). The one which is most widely known is Wilk's Λ, where Λ is given by:

$$\Lambda = \frac{|\mathbf{W}|}{|\mathbf{T}|} = \frac{|\mathbf{W}|}{|\mathbf{B} + \mathbf{W}|}, \quad 0 \leq \Lambda \leq 1$$

$|\mathbf{W}|$ and $|\mathbf{T}|$ are the determinants of the within and total sum of squares and cross-products matrices. $\mathbf{W}$ has already been defined for the two-group case, where the observations in each group are deviated about the individual group means. Thus $\mathbf{W}$ is a measure of within-group variability and is a multivariate generalization of the univariate sum of squares within (SS_w). In $\mathbf{T}$ the observations in each group are deviated about the *grand* mean for each variable. $\mathbf{B}$ is the between sum of squares and cross-products matrix, and is the multivariate generalization of the univariate sum of squares between (SS_b). Thus, $\mathbf{B}$ is a measure of how differential the effect of treatments has been on a set of dependent variables. We define the elements of $\mathbf{B}$ shortly. We need matrices to define within, between, and total variability in the multivariate case since there is variability on each variable (these variabilities will appear on the main diagonals of the $\mathbf{W}$, $\mathbf{B}$, and $\mathbf{T}$ matrices) as well as covariability for each pair of variables (these will be the off diagonal elements of the matrices).

Since Wilk's Λ is defined in terms of the determinants of $\mathbf{W}$ and $\mathbf{T}$, it is important to recall from the matrix algebra chapter (Chapter 2) that the determinant of a covariance matrix is called the *generalized variance* for a set of variables. Now, since $\mathbf{W}$ and $\mathbf{T}$ only differ from their corresponding covariance matrices by a scalar we can think of $|\mathbf{W}|$ and $|\mathbf{T}|$ in the same basic way. Thus, the determinant neatly characterizes within and total variability in terms of *single* numbers. It may also be helpful for the reader to recall that geometrically the generalized variance for two variables is the square of the area of a parallelogram whose sides are the standard deviations for the variables, and that for three variables the generalized variance is the square of the volume of a three dimensional parallelogram whose sides are the standard deviations for the variables. Although it is not clear why the generalized variance is square of the area of a parallelogram, the important fact here is the area interpretation of variance for two variables.

For one variable variance indicates how much scatter there is about the mean on a line, i.e., in one dimension. For two variables the scores for each subject on the variables defines a point in the plane, and thus generalized variance indicates how much the points (subjects) scatter in the plane, i.e., in two dimensions. For three variables the scores for the subjects define points in three space, hence generalized variance shows how much the subjects scatter (vary) in three dimensions. An excellent, extended discussion of generalized variance for the more mathematically inclined is provided in Johnson and Wichern (1982, pp. 103–112).

For univariate ANOVA the reader may recall that

$$SS_t = SS_b + SS_w,$$

where SS_t is the total sum of squares.

For MANOVA the corresponding matrix analogue holds

$$T = B + W$$

Total SSCP = Between SSCP + Within SSCP

Matrix   Matrix   Matrix

Notice that Wilk's Λ is an inverse criterion, i.e., the smaller the value of Λ the more evidence for treatment effects (between group association). If there were no treatment effect, then $B = 0$ and $\Lambda = \dfrac{|W|}{|0 + W|} = 1$, whereas if B were very large relative to W then Λ would approach 0.

The sampling distribution of Λ is very complicated, and generally an approximation is necessary. Two approximations are available: (1) Bartlett's χ^2 and (2) Rao's F. Bartlett's χ^2 is given by:

$$\chi^2 = -[(N - 1) - .5(p + k)] \ln \Lambda, \qquad p(k - 1) \, df$$

where N is total sample size, p is the number of dependent variables, and k is the number of groups. Barlett's χ^2 is a good approximation for moderate to large sample sizes. For smaller sample size, Rao's F is a better approximation (Lohnes, 1961), although generally the two statistics will lead to the same decision on H_0. The multivariate F given on SPSSX and on BMDP is the Rao F. The formula for Rao's F is complicated and is presented later. We point out, now, however, that the degrees of freedom for error with Rao's F can be *non-integer*, so that the reader should not be alarmed if this happens on the computer printout.

As alluded to above, there are certain values of p and k for which a function of Λ is exactly distributed as an F ratio (for example, $k = 2$ or 3 and any p; see Tatsuoka, 1971, p. 89).

5.4.   MULTIVARIATE ANALYSIS OF VARIANCE FOR SAMPLE DATA

We now consider the MANOVA of the data given earlier. For convenience, we present the data again below, with the means for the subjects on the two dependent variables in each group:

T_1		T_2		T_3	
y_1	y_2	y_1	y_2	y_1	y_2
2	3	4	8	7	6
3	4	5	6	8	7
5	4	6	7	10	8
2	5	$\bar{y}_{12} = 5$	$\bar{y}_{22} = 7$	9	5
$\bar{y}_{11} = 3$	$\bar{y}_{21} = 4$			7	6
				$\bar{y}_{13} = 8.2$	$\bar{y}_{23} = 6.4$

We wish to test the multivariate null hypothesis with the χ^2 approximation for Wilk's Λ. Recall that $\Lambda = |\mathbf{W}|/|\mathbf{T}|$, so that $\mathbf{W}$ and $\mathbf{T}$ are needed. $\mathbf{W}$ is the pooled estimate of within variability on the set of variables, i.e., our multivariate error term.

Calculation of W

Calculation of $\mathbf{W}$ proceeds in exactly the same way as we obtained $\mathbf{W}$ for Hotelling's T^2 in the two-group MANOVA case in Chapter 4. That is, we determine how much the subjects scores vary on the dependent variables within *each* group, and then pool (add) these together. Symbolically, then

$$\mathbf{W} = \mathbf{W}_1 + \mathbf{W}_2 + \mathbf{W}_3$$

where $\mathbf{W}_1$, $\mathbf{W}_2$, and $\mathbf{W}_3$ are the within sums of squares and cross-products matrices for groups 1, 2, and 3. As in the two-group chapter, we denote the elements of $\mathbf{W}_1$ by ss_1 and ss_2 (measuring the variability on the variables within group 1) and ss_{12} (measuring the covariability of the variables in group 1).

$$\mathbf{W}_1 = \begin{bmatrix} ss_1 & ss_{12} \\ ss_{21} & ss_2 \end{bmatrix}$$

Then, we have

$$ss_1 = \sum_{j=1}^{4} (y_{1(j)} - \bar{y}_{11})^2$$

$$= (2 - 3)^2 + (3 - 3)^2 + (5 - 3)^2 + (2 - 3)^2 = 6$$

$$SS_2 = \sum_{j=1}^{4} (y_{2(j)} - \bar{y}_{21})^2$$

$$= (3 - 4)^2 + (4 - 4)^2 + (4 - 4)^2 + (5 - 4)^2 = 2$$

$$SS_{12} = SS_{21} = \sum_{j=1}^{4} (y_{1(j)} - \bar{y}_{11})(y_{2(j)} - \bar{y}_{21})$$

$$= (2 - 3)(3 - 4) + (3 - 3)(4 - 4) + (5 - 3)(4 - 4)$$
$$+ (2 - 3)(5 - 4) = 0$$

Thus, the matrix which measures within variability on the two variables in group 1 is given by:

$$\mathbf{W}_1 = \begin{bmatrix} 6 & 0 \\ 0 & 2 \end{bmatrix}$$

In exactly the same way the within SCCP matrices for groups 2 and 3 can be shown to be:

$$\mathbf{W}_2 = \begin{bmatrix} 2 & -1 \\ -1 & 2 \end{bmatrix} \qquad \mathbf{W}_3 = \begin{bmatrix} 6.8 & 2.6 \\ 2.6 & 5.2 \end{bmatrix}$$

Therefore, the pooled estimate of within variability on the set of variables is given by

$$\mathbf{W} = \mathbf{W}_1 + \mathbf{W}_2 + \mathbf{W}_3 = \begin{bmatrix} 14.8 & 1.6 \\ 1.6 & 9.2 \end{bmatrix}$$

Calculation of T

Recall, from earlier in this chapter, that $\mathbf{T} = \mathbf{B} + \mathbf{W}$. We will find the $\mathbf{B}$ (between) matrix, and then obtain the elements of $\mathbf{T}$ by adding the elements of $\mathbf{B}$ to the elements of $\mathbf{W}$.

The diagonal elements of $\mathbf{B}$ are defined as follows:

$$b_{ii} = \sum_{j=1}^{k} n_j (\bar{y}_{ij} - \bar{\bar{y}}_i)^2,$$

where n_j is the number of subjects in group j, $\bar{y}_{ij}$ is the mean for variable i in group j, and $\bar{\bar{y}}_i$ is the grand mean for variable i. Notice that for any particular variable, say variable 1, b_{11} is simply the sum of squares between for a univariate analysis of variance on that variable.

The off diagonal elements of **B** are defined as follows:

$$b_{mi} = b_{im} = \sum_{j=1}^{k} n_j \, (\bar{y}_{ij} - \bar{\bar{y}}_i)(\bar{y}_{mj} - \bar{\bar{y}}_m)$$

To find the elements of **B** we need the grand means on the two variables. These are obtained by simply adding up all the scores on each variable and then dividing by the total number of scores. Thus, $\bar{\bar{y}}_1 = 68/12 = 5.67$, and $\bar{\bar{y}}_2 = 69/12 = 5.75$

Now we find the elements of the **B** (between) matrix:

$$b_{11} = \sum_{j=1}^{3} n_j \, (\bar{y}_{1j} - \bar{\bar{y}}_1)^2, \text{ where } \bar{y}_{1j} \text{ is the mean of variable 1 in group } j.$$

$$= 4(3 - 5.67)^2 + 3(5 - 5.67)^2 + 5(8.2 - 5.67)^2 = 61.87$$

$$b_{22} = \sum_{j=1}^{3} n_j \, (\bar{y}_{2j} - \bar{\bar{y}}_2)^2$$

$$= 4(4 - 5.75)^2 + 3(7 - 5.75)^2 + 5(6.4 - 5.75)^2 = 19.05$$

$$b_{12} = b_{21} = \sum_{j=1}^{3} n_j \, (\bar{y}_{1j} - \bar{\bar{y}}_1)(\bar{y}_{2j} - \bar{\bar{y}}_2)$$

$$= 4(3 - 5.67)(4 - 5.75) + 3(5 - 5.67)(7 - 5.75) +$$
$$5(8.2 - 5.67)(6.4 - 5.75) = 24.4$$

Therefore, the **B** matrix is

$$\mathbf{B} = \begin{bmatrix} 61.87 & 24.40 \\ 24.40 & 19.05 \end{bmatrix}$$

and the diagonal elements 61.87 and 19.05 represent the between sum of squares that would be obtained if separate univariate analyses had been done on variables 1 and 2.

Since $\mathbf{T} = \mathbf{B} + \mathbf{W}$, we have

$$\mathbf{T} = \begin{bmatrix} 61.87 & 24.40 \\ 24.40 & 19.05 \end{bmatrix} + \begin{bmatrix} 14.80 & 1.6 \\ 1.6 & 9.2 \end{bmatrix} = \begin{bmatrix} 76.72 & 26.00 \\ 26.00 & 28.25 \end{bmatrix}$$

Calculation of Wilks Λ and the Chi-Square Approximation

Now we can obtain Wilk's Λ:

$$\Lambda = \frac{|\mathbf{W}|}{|\mathbf{T}|} = \frac{\begin{vmatrix} 14.8 & 1.6 \\ 1.6 & 9.2 \end{vmatrix}}{\begin{vmatrix} 76.72 & 26 \\ 26 & 28.25 \end{vmatrix}} = \frac{14.8(9.2) - 1.6^2}{76.72(28.25) - 26^2} = .0897$$

Finally, we can compute the chi-square test statistic:

$$\chi^2 = -[(N - 1) - .5(p + k)] \ln \Lambda, \text{ with } p(k - 1) \, df$$

$$\chi^2 = -[(12 - 1) - .5(2 + 3)] \ln (.0897)$$

$$\chi^2 = -8.5 \, (-2.4116) = 20.4987, \text{ with } 2(3 - 1) = 4 \, df$$

The multivariate null hypothesis here is:

$$\begin{pmatrix} \mu_{11} \\ \mu_{21} \end{pmatrix} = \begin{pmatrix} \mu_{12} \\ \mu_{22} \end{pmatrix} = \begin{pmatrix} \mu_{13} \\ \mu_{23} \end{pmatrix}$$

i.e., that the population means in the three groups on variable 1 are equal, and similarily that the population means on variable 2 are equal. Since the critical value at .05 is 9.49, we reject the multivariate null hypothesis and conclude that the three groups differ overall on the set of two variables. Table 5.2 gives the multivariate F's and the univariate F's from the SPSSX MANOVA run on the sample problem and presents the formula for Rao's F approximation and also relates some of the output from the univariate F's to the $\mathbf{B}$ and $\mathbf{W}$ matrices that we computed. After overall multivariate significance one would like to know which groups and which variables were responsible for the overall association, i.e., a more detailed breakdown. This is considered next.

5.5. POST HOC PROCEDURES

Since pairwise differences are easy to interpret and often the most meaningful, we concentrate on procedures for locating significant pairwise differences, both multivariate and univariate. We consider three procedures, from least to most conservative, in terms of protecting against type I error.

Procedure 1—Hotelling T^2's and Univariate t Tests

Follow a significant overall multivariate result by all pairwise multivariate tests (T^2's) to determine which pairs of groups differ significantly on the set of variables. Then use univariate t tests, each at the .05 level, to determine which of

TABLE 5.2
Multivariate F's and Univariate F's for Sample Problem from SPSSX
MANOVA

EFFECT .. GPID

MULTIVARIATE TESTS OF SIGNIFICANCE (S = 2, M = $-\frac{1}{2}$, N = 3)

TEST NAME	VALUE	APPROX. F	HYPOTH. DF	ERROR DF	SIG. OF F
PILLAIS	1.30178	8.38990	4.00	18.00	.001
HOTELLINGS	5.78518	10.12581	4.00	14.00	.000
WILKS	.08967	9.35751	4.00	16.00	.000
ROYS	.83034				

$$\frac{1 - \Lambda^{1/s}}{\Lambda^{1/s}} \frac{ms - p(k-1)/2 + 1}{p(k-1)}, \text{ where } m = N - 1 - (p+k)/2 \text{ and}$$

$$s = \sqrt{\frac{p^2(k-1)^2 - 4}{p^2 + (k-1)^2 - 5}},$$

is approximately distributed as F with $p(k-1)$ and $ms - p(k-1)/2 + 1$ degrees of freedom. Here Wilk's $\Lambda = .08967$, $p = 2$, $k = 3$ and $N = 12$. Thus, we have $m = 12 - 1 - (2 + 3)/2 = 8.5$ and

$$s = \sqrt{\{4(3 - 1)^2 - 4\}/\{4 + (2)^2 - 5\}} = \sqrt{12/3} = 2,$$

and

$$F = \frac{1 - \sqrt{.08967}}{\sqrt{.08967}} \frac{8.5(2) - 2(2)/2 + 1}{2(3 - 1)} = \frac{1 - .29945}{.29945} \cdot \frac{16}{4} = 9.357,$$

as given on printout above. The pair of degrees of freedom is $p(k-1) = 2(3-1) = 4$ and $ms - p(k-1)/2 + 1 = 8.5(2) - 2(3-1)/2 + 1 = 16$.

UNIVARIATE F-TESTS WITH (2,9) D. F.

VARIABLE	HYPOTH. SS	ERROR SS	HYPOTH. MS	ERROR MS	F	SIG. OF F.
Y1	① 61.86667	② 14.80000	30.93333	1.64444	18.81081	.001
Y2	19.05000	9.20000	9.52500	1.02222	9.31793	.006

①These are the diagonal elements of the **B** (between) matrix we computed in the example:

$$\mathbf{B} = \begin{bmatrix} 61.87 & 24.40 \\ 24.40 & 19.05 \end{bmatrix}$$

②Recall that the pooled within matrix computed in the example was

$$\mathbf{W} = \begin{bmatrix} 14.8 & 1.6 \\ 1.6 & 9.2 \end{bmatrix}$$

and these are the diagonal elements of **W**. The univariate F ratios are formed from the elements on the main diagonals of **B** and **W**. Dividing the elements of **B** by hypothesis degrees of freedom gives the hypothesis mean squares, while dividing the elements of **W** by error degrees of freedom gives the error mean squares. Then, dividing hypothesis mean squares by error mean squares yields the F ratios. Thus, for Y1 we have

$$F = \frac{30.933}{1.644} = 18.81$$

the individual variables are contributing to the significant multivariate pairwise differences. To keep the overall α for the set of pairwise multivariate tests under some control (and still maintain reasonable power) we may want to set overall $\alpha = .15$. Thus, for 4 groups there will be 6 Hotelling T^2's, and we would do each T^2 at the $.15/6 = .025$ level of significance. This procedure has fairly good control on type I error for the first two parts, and not as good control for the last part (i.e., identifying the significant individual variables). It has the best power of the three procedures we discuss, and as long as we recognize that the individual variables identified must be treated somewhat tenuously, it has merit.

Procedure 2—Hotelling T^2's and Tukey Confidence Intervals

Once again we follow a significant overall multivariate result by all pairwise multivariate tests, but then we apply the Tukey simultaneous confidence interval technique to determine which of the individual variables are contributing to each pairwise significant multivariate result. This procedure affords us better protection against type I errors, especially if we set the experimentwise error rate (EER) for each variable that we are applying the Tukey to such that the overall α is *at maximum* .15. Thus, depending on how large a risk of spurious results (within the .15) we can tolerate, we may set EER at .05 for each variable in a 3 variable problem, at .025 for each variable in a 6 variable problem, variable, or at .01 for each variable in an 8 variable study. As we shall see in an example shortly, the 90%, 95%, and 99% confidence intervals, corresponding to EER's of .10, .05, and .01, are easily obtained from the BMDP7D program.

Procedure 3—Roy-Bose Simultaneous Confidence Intervals

In exploratory research in univariate ANOVA after the null hypothesis has been rejected, one wishes to determine where the differences lie with some post hoc procedure. One of the more popular post hoc procedures is the Scheffe', with which a wide variety of comparisons can be made. For example, all pairwise comparisons as well as complex comparisons such as $\mu_1 - (\mu_2 + \mu_3)/2$ or $(\mu_1 + \mu_2) - (\mu_3 + \mu_4)$ can be tested. The Scheffe' allows one to examine *any* complex comparison, as long as the sum of the coefficients for the means is 0. All these comparisons can be made with the assurance that overall type I error is controlled (i.e., the probability of one or more type I errors) at a level set by the experimenter. Importantly, however, the price one pays for being allowed to do all this data snooping is loss of power for detecting differences. This is due to the basic principle that as one type of error (in this case Type I) is controlled, the other type (type II here) increases and therefore power decreases, since power $= 1 -$ type II error. Glass and Hopkins (1984, p. 382) note, "The

Scheffe' method is the most widely presented MC (multiple comparison) method in textbooks of statistical methods; ironically it is rarely the MC method of choice for the questions of interest in terms of power efficiency."

The Roy-Bose intervals are the multivariate generalization of the Scheffe' univariate intervals. After the multivariate null hypothesis has been rejected, the Roy-Bose intervals can be used to examine all pairwise group comparisons as well as all complex comparisons for *each* dependent variable. In addition to all these comparisons, one can examine pairwise and complex comparisons on various linear combinations of the variables (such as the difference of two variables). Thus, *the Roy-Bose approach controls on overall α for an enormous number of comparisons. To do so power has to suffer, and it suffers considerably, especially for small or moderate sized samples.* Hummel and Sligo (1971) found the Roy-Bose procedure to be extremely conservative, and recommended generally against it's use. We agree. In many studies the sample sizes are small or relatively small *and* the effect sizes are small. In these circumstances power will be far from adequate to begin with, and the use of Roy-Bose intervals will further sharply diminish the researchers chances of finding any differences. In addition, there is the question of why one would want to examine all or most of the comparisons allowed by the Roy-Bose procedure. As Bird commented (1975, p. 344), "a completely unrestricted analysis of multivariate data, however, would be extremely unusual."

Example—Illustrating Post Hoc Procedures 1 and 2

We illustrate first the use of post hoc procedure 1 on social psychological data collected by Novince (1977). She was interested in improving the social skills of college females and reducing their anxiety in heterosexual encounters. There were three groups in her study: control group, behavioral reheral, and a behavioral rehearsal + cognitive restructuring group. We consider the analysis on the following set of dependent variables: (1) anxiety—physiological anxiety in a series of heterosexual encounters, (2) measure of social skills in social interactions, (3) appropriateness, and (4) assertiveness. The raw data for this problem is given in the Appendix of this chapter.

The control lines for running the overall multivariate test on SPSSX MANOVA, along with the MANOVA test statistics and the univariate results are given in Table 5.3. Wilk's Λ is significant at .05 ($F = 4.361$, p $< .000$), indicating that the three groups differ on the set of 4 variables. The univariate F's are all significant at the .05 level, showing that all of the variables contributed to the multivariate significance. To isolate more specifically where the differences lie the two parts of our post hoc procedure were applied, i.e., all pairwise multivariate T^2's and the univariate t's were obtained using the BMDP3D program. The control lines for accomplishing this, along with the significant T^2's and univariate t's are presented in Table 5.4. The results show (since group 2 was the control) that each treatment group differed from the control, and that

TABLE 5.3
SPSSX MANOVA Control Lines and Selected Printout for Novince Study*

```
TITLE ' THREE GROUP MANOVA-NOVINCE DATA '
DATA LIST FREE/ GPID,ANX,SOCSKLS,APPROP,ASSERT
LIST
BEGIN DATA

  DATA

END DATA
MANOVA ANX,SOCSKLS,APPROP,ASSERT BY GPID(1,3)/
  PRINT = CELLINFO(MEANS,COV,COR) HOMOGENEITY(COCHRAN,BOXM)/
```

EFFECT .. GPID

MULTIVARIATE TESTS OF SIGNIFICANCE (S = 2, M = 1/2, N = 12 1/2)

TEST NAME	VALUE	APPROX. F	HYPOTH. DF	ERROR DF	SIG. OF F
PILLAIS	.67980	3.60443	8.00	56.00	.002
HOTELLINGS	1.57723	5.12600	8.00	52.00	.000
WILKS	.36906	① 4.36109	8.00	54.00	.000
ROYS	.59812				

UNIVARIATE F-TESTS WITH (2.30) D.F.

VARIABLE	HYPOTH. SS	ERROR SS	HYPOTH. MS	ERROR MS	F	SIG. OF F
ANX	12.06061	11.81818	6.03030	.39394	15.30769	.000
SOCSKLS	23.09091	23.45455	11.54545	.78182	14.76744	.000
APPROP	20.78788	18.54545	10.39394	.61818	16.81373	.000
ASSERT	14.96970	19.27273	7.48485	.64242	11.65094	.000

*The reader should compare the control lines for this example with the control lines for the two-group MANOVA (with two dependent variables) that we ran in Table 4.3, along with the annotation there. The similarity is striking, although here we have requested the univariate (COCHRAN) and multivariate (BOXM) tests for homogeneity of variance and covariance matrices. These we discuss in detail in the next chapter.

all 4 variables in each case were contributing to the multivariate significance.

A few comments on the BMDP3D control lines. The TEST paragraph is used to indicate which of the dependent variables are to be in the analysis. In this case we wished to use all of them. HOTELLING is the keyword to obtain all pairwise multivariate tests.

5.6.   THE TUKEY PROCEDURE

The Tukey procedure (Glass & Hopkins, 1984, p. 370) enables us to examine *all* pairwise group differences on a variable with experimentwise error rate held in check. The studentized range statistic (which we denote by q) is used in the procedure, and the critical values for it are in Table D of the statistical tables

TABLE 5.4
BMDP3D Control Lines for Obtaining all Pairwise Multivariate T^2's and Multivariate and Univariate Results for Significant Pairwise Comparisons

```
/PROBLEM TITLE IS ' NOVINCE-AUDIO JUDGE VARS-ALL PAIR MULT '.
/INPUT VARIABLES ARE 5. FORMAT IS STREAM.
/VARIABLE NAMES ARE GP,ANX,SOCIAL,APPROP,ASSERT. GROUPING IS GP.
/TEST VARIABLES ARE ANX TO ASSERT. HOTELLING.
/END
```

DATA

```
************              ************
* *1.00000 *              * *2.00000 *
* *2.00000 *              * *3.00000 *
************              ************
```

MAHALANOBIS D SQUARE		7.6262	MAHALANOBIS D SQUARE			6.5494
HOTELLING T SQUARE		41.9442	HOTELING T SQUARE			36.0219
F VALUE		8.9131	F VALUE			7.6547
DEGREES OF FREEDOM	4,	17.00	DEGREES OF FREEDOM		4,	17.00
P-VALUE	0.0005		P-VALUE	0.0010		

DIFFERENCES ON SINGLE VARIABLES   DIFFERENCES ON SINGLE VARIABLES

```
*********                               *********
* ANX   * VARIABLE    NUMBER   2        * ANX   * VARIABLE    NUMBER   2
*********                               *********
```

	STATISTICS	P-VALUE	DF		STATISTICS	P-VALUE	DF
T (SEPARATE)	−4.24	0.0005	18.9	T (SEPARATE)	4.62	0.0002	17.7
T (POOLED)	−4.24	0.0004	20	T (POOLED)	4.62	0.0002	20
F(FOR VARIANCES)				F(FOR VARIANCES)			
LEVENE	0.01	0.9201	1, 20	LEVENE	0.95	0.3422	1, 20

```
************                            ************
* SOCIAL * VARIABLE    NUMBER   3       * SOCIAL * VARIABLE    NUMBER   3
************                            ************
```

	STATISTICS	P-VALUE	DF		STATISTICS	P-VALUE	DF
T(SEPARATE)	5.56	0.0000	17.6	T(SEPARATE)	−5.14	0.0001	20.0
T(POOLED)	5.56	0.0000	20	T(POOLED)	−5.14	0.0001	20
F(FOR VARIANCES)				F(FOR VARIANCES)			
LEVENE	0.88	0.3599	1, 20	LEVENE	0.10	0.7535	1, 20

```
************                            ************
* Ar ROP * VARIABLE    NUMBER   4       * APPROP * VARIABLE    NUMBER   4
************                            ************
```

	STATISTICS	P-VALUE	DF		STATISTICS	P-VALUE	DF
T (SEPARATE)	5.15	0.0001	18.2	T (SEPARATE)	−5.65	0.0000	19.6
T(POOLED)	5.15	0.0000	20	T(POOLED)	−5.65	0.0000	20
F(FOR VARIANCES)				F(FOR VARIANCES)			
LEVENE	0.76	0.3924	1, 20	LEVENE	0.36	0.5531	1, 20

```
************                            ************
* ASSERT * VARIABLE    NUMBER   5       * ASSERT * VARIABLE    NUMBER   5
************                            ************
```

	STATISTICS	P-VALUE	DF		STATISTICS	P-VALUE	DF
T (SEPARATE)	4.24	0.0004	19.6	T (SEPARATE)	−4.67	0.0001	20.0
T (POOLED)	4.24	0.0004	20	T (POOLED)	−4.67	0.0001	20
F(FOR VARIANCES				F(FOR VARIANCES)			
LEVENE	0.04	0.8363	1, 20	LEVENE	0.00	0.9928	1, 20

in the Appendix of this volume. If there are k groups and the total sample size is N, then any two means are declared significantly different at the .05 level if the following inequality holds:

$$|\bar{y}_i - \bar{y}_j| > q_{.05;k,N-k} \sqrt{\frac{MS_w}{n}}$$

where MS_w is the error term for a one-way ANOVA, and n is the common group size.

Equivalently, and somewhat more informative, we can determine whether the population means for groups i and j (μ_i and μ_j) differ if the following confidence interval does *not* include 0:

$$\bar{y}_i - \bar{y}_j \mp q_{.05;k,N-k} \sqrt{\frac{MS_w}{n}}$$

i.e.,

$$\bar{y}_i - \bar{y}_j - q_{.05;k,N-k} \sqrt{\frac{MS_w}{n}} < \mu_i - \mu_j < \bar{y}_i - \bar{y}_j + q_{.05;k,N-k} \sqrt{\frac{MS_w}{n}}$$

If the confidence interval includes 0, we conclude the population means are not significantly different. Why? Because if the interval includes 0 that means 0 is a likely value for $\mu_i - \mu_j$, which is to say it is likely that $\mu_i = \mu_j$.

Example

To illustrate numerically the Tukey procedure we consider obtaining the confidence interval for the anxiety (ANX) variable from the Novince study in Table 5.3. In particular we obtain the 95% confidence interval for groups 1 and 2. The mean difference, not given in Table 5.3, is -1.18. Recall that the common group size in this study is $n = 11$. MS_w, denoted by ERROR MS in Table 5.3, is .39394 for ANX. Finally, from Table D the critical value for the studentized range statistic is $q_{.05;3,30} = 3.49$. Thus, the confidence interval is given by

$$-1.18 - 3.49 \sqrt{\frac{.39394}{11}} < \mu_1 - \mu_2 < -1.18 + 3.49 \sqrt{\frac{.39394}{11}}$$

$$-1.84 < \mu_1 - \mu_2 < -.52$$

Since this interval does not cover 0, we conclude that the population means for the anxiety variable in groups 1 and 2 are significantly different. Why is the confidence interval approach more informative, as indicated earlier, then simply testing whether the means are different? Because the confidence interval not only tells us whether the means differ, but it also gives us a range of values within which the mean difference probably lies. This tells us the precision with which we have captured the mean difference, and can be used in judging the practical significance of a result. In the above example the mean difference could be anywhere in the range from -1.84 to $-.52$. If the investigator had decided on some grounds that a difference of at least 1 had to be established for practical significance, then the statistical significance found would not be sufficient.

The Tukey procedure assumes that the variances are homogeneous and it also assumes equal group sizes. If the group sizes are unequal, even very sharply unequal, then various studies (e.g., Dunnett, 1980; Kesselman, Murray, & Rogan, 1976) indicate that the procedure is still appropriate provided that n is replaced by the harmonic mean for each pair of groups *and* provided that the variances are homogeneous. Thus, for groups i and j with sample sizes n_i and n_j, we replace n by $\dfrac{2}{\dfrac{1}{n_i} + \dfrac{1}{n_j}}$. The studies cited above showed that under the conditions given the type I error rate for the Tukey procedure is kept very close to the nominal α, and always less than nominal α (within .01 for $\alpha = .05$ from the Dunnett study).

When both the group sizes and the variances are unequal, then some appropriate procedures have been developed (see Kirk, 1982, pp. 120–21).

We indicated earlier that the Tukey intervals can be easily obtained using the BMDP7D program. Below are the control lines for obtaining the 95% confidence intervals for the Novince data:

```
/PROBLEM TITLE IS ' TUKEY INTERVALS AT .05 LEVEL FOR NOVINCE DATA'.
/INPUT VARIABLES ARE 5. FORMAT IS STREAM.
/VARIABLE NAMES ARE GP,ANX,SOCIAL,APPROP,ASSERT.
/HISTOGRAM GROUPING = GP.
/COMPARISON TUKEY. CONFIDENCE.
/END
```

In the HISTOGRAM paragraph we indicate the grouping variable. It is in the COMPARISON paragraph that we choose which multiple comparison procedure we wish (the Bonferroni, Scheffe', and Dunnett are also available). The .01, .05 and .10 levels of significance are available, with .05 being the default option, if a level of significance is not specified. If confidence intervals are desired, then we must specify CONFIDENCE in the COMPARISON paragraph.

The 95% confidence intervals for each of the 4 variables in the Novince study are given in Tables 5.5 and 5.6. The BMDP7D program uses the Tukey-Cramer procedure for unequal group sizes, i.e., use of harmonic mean.

Tukey 95% Confidence Intervals from BMDP7D for Novince Data

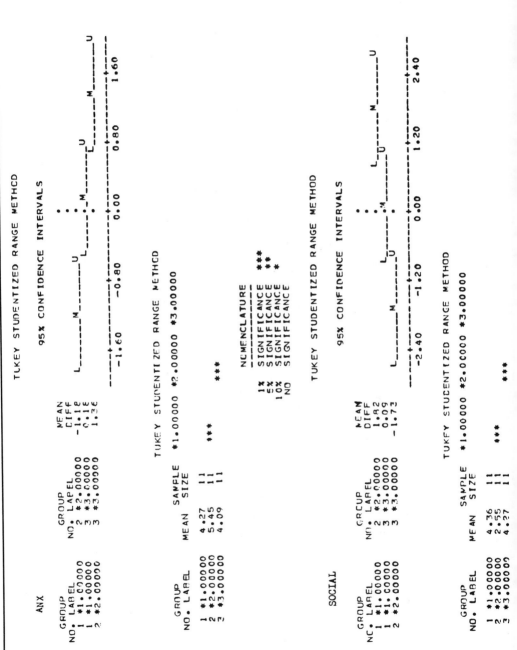

TABLE 5.6
Tukey 95% Confidence Intervals from BMDP7D for Novince Data (cont.)

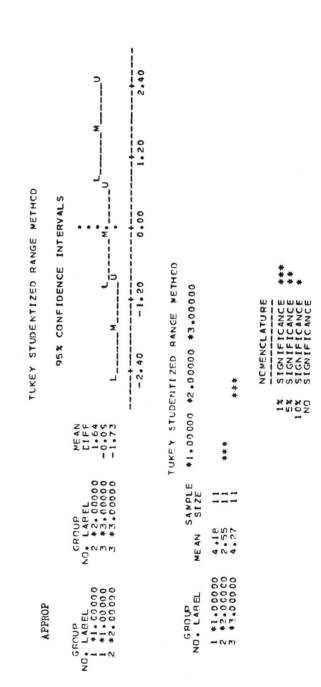

APPROP

TUKEY STUDENTIZED RANGE METHOD

95% CONFIDENCE INTERVALS

GROUP		MEAN
NO. LABEL	GROUP NO. LABEL	DIFF
1 *1.00000	2 *2.00000	1.64
1 *1.00000	3 *3.00000	-0.05
2 *2.00000	3 *3.00000	-1.73

TUKEY STUDENTIZED RANGE METHOD

*1.00000 *2.00000 *3.00000

GROUP	MEAN	SAMPLE SIZE		
NO. LABEL				
1 *1.00000	4.18	11		
2 *2.00000	2.55	11	***	
3 *3.00000	4.27	11		***

NOMENCLATURE
1% SIGNIFICANCE	***
5% SIGNIFICANCE	**
10% SIGNIFICANCE	*
NO SIGNIFICANCE	

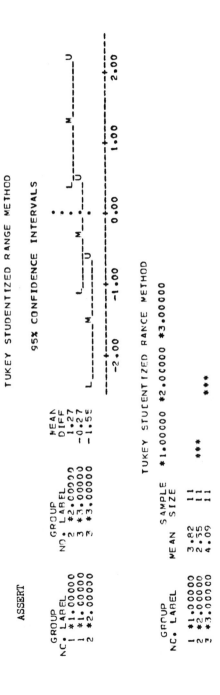

TUKEY STUDENTIZED RANGE METHOD

95% CONFIDENCE INTERVALS

ASSERT

GROUP
NO. LABEL
1 *1.00000
1 *1.00000
2 *2.00000

GROUP
NO. LABEL
2 *2.00000
3 *3.00000
3 *3.00000

MEAN
DIFF
1.27
-0.27
-1.55

TUKEY STUDENTIZED RANGE METHOD

TUKEY STUDENTIZED RANGE METHOD *1.00000 *2.00000 *3.00000

GROUP
NO. LABEL
1 *1.00000
2 *2.00000
3 *3.00000

MEAN
3.82
2.55
4.09

SAMPLE
SIZE
11
11
11

***

***

***

5.7. PLANNED COMPARISONS

One approach to the analysis of data is to first demonstrate overall significance, and then follow this up to assess the subsources of variation (i.e., which particular groups and/or variables) were primarily responsible for the overall significance. One such procedure using pairwise T^2's has been presented. This approach is appropriate in exploratory studies where the investigator first has to establish that an effect exists. However, in many instances there is more of an empirical and/or theoretical base and the investigator is conducting a confirmatory study. Here the existence of an effect may be taken for granted, and the investigator has specific questions he wishes to ask of the data. Thus, rather than examining all 10 pairwise comparisons for a five-group problem, there may be only 3 or 4 comparisons (which may or may not be paired comparisons) of interest. It is important to use planned comparisons when the situation justifies them, since performing a small number of statistical tests cuts down on the probability of spurious results (type I errors), which can result much more readily when a large number of tests are done.

Hays (1981) has shown in univariate ANOVA that the test is more powerful when the comparison is planned. This would carry over to MANOVA. This is a very important factor weighing in favor of planned comparisons. Many studies in educational research have only 10 to 20 subjects per group. With these sample sizes, power is generally going to be poor unless the treatment effect is large (Cohen, 1977). *If we plan a small or moderate number of contrasts that we wish to test, then power can be improved considerably, while control on overall α can be maintained through the use of the Bonferroni Inequality.* Recall this inequality states that if k hypotheses, k planned comparisons here, are tested separately with type I error rates of $\alpha_1, \alpha_2, \ldots, \alpha_k$, then

$$\text{Overall } \alpha \le \alpha_1 + \alpha_2 + \ldots + \alpha_k,$$

where overall α is the probability of one or more type I errors when all the hypotheses are true. Therefore, if 3 planned comparisons were tested each at $\alpha = .01$, then the probability of one or more spurious results can be no greater than .03 for the *set* of 3 tests.

Let us now consider two situations where planned comparisons would be appropriate:

1. Suppose an investigator wishes to determine whether each of two drugs produces a differential effect on three measures of task performance over a placebo. Then if we denote the placebo as group 2, the following set of planned comparisons would answer the investigator's questions:

$$\psi_1 = \mu_1 - \mu_2 \text{ and } \psi_2 = \mu_2 - \mu_3$$

2.   Secondly, consider the following four-group schematic design:

	Groups			
control	T_1 & T_2 combined	T_1	T_2	(T_1 and T_2 represent two treatments)
μ_1	μ_2	μ_3	μ_4	

As outlined this could represent the format for a variety of studies (e.g., if T_1 and T_2 were two methods of teaching reading, or if T_1 and T_2 were two counseling approaches). Then the three most relevant questions the investigator wishes to answer are given by the following planned and so called Helmert contrasts:

1.   Do the treatments as a set make a difference?

$$\psi_1 = \mu_1 - \frac{\mu_2 + \mu_3 + \mu_4}{3}$$

2.   Is the combination of treatments more effective than either treatment alone?

$$\psi_2 = \mu_2 - \frac{\mu_3 + \mu_4}{2}$$

3.   Is one treatment more effective than the other treatment?

$$\psi_3 = \mu_3 - \mu_4$$

Assuming equal n per group, the above two situations represent dependent vs. independent planned comparisons. Two comparisons among means are *independent* if the sum of the products of the coefficients is 0. We represent the contrasts for situation 1 as follows:

	Groups		
	1	2	3
ψ_1	1	-1	0
ψ_2	0	1	-1

These contrasts are dependent since the sum of products of the coefficients $\neq 0$ as shown below:

sum of products $= 1\,(0) + (-1)(1) + 0\,(-1) = -1$

Now consider the contrasts from situation 2:

| | \multicolumn{4}{c}{Groups} |
	1	2	3	4
ψ_1	1	$-\frac{1}{3}$	$-\frac{1}{3}$	$-\frac{1}{3}$
ψ_2	0	1	$-\frac{1}{2}$	$-\frac{1}{2}$
ψ_3	0	0	1	-1

Below we show that these contrasts are pairwise independent by demonstrating that the sum of the products of the coefficients in each case = 0:

ψ_1 and ψ_2 : $1(0) + (-\frac{1}{3})(1) + (-\frac{1}{3})(-\frac{1}{2}) + (-\frac{1}{3})(-\frac{1}{2}) = 0$

ψ_1 and ψ_3 : $1(0) + (-\frac{1}{3})(0) + (-\frac{1}{3})(1) + (-\frac{1}{3})(-1) = 0$

ψ_2 and ψ_3 : $0(0) + 1(0) + (-\frac{1}{2})(1) + (-\frac{1}{2})(-1) = 0$

Now consider two general contrasts for k groups:

$$\psi_1 = c_{11}\mu_1 + c_{12}\mu_2 + \ldots\ldots + c_{1k}\mu_k$$

$$\psi_2 = c_{21}\mu_1 + c_{22}\mu_2 + \ldots\ldots + c_{2k}\mu_k$$

The first part of the c subscript refers to the contrast number and the second part to the group. The condition for independence in symbols then is:

$$c_{11}c_{21} + c_{12}c_{22} + \ldots\ldots + c_{1k}c_{2k} = \sum_{j=1}^{k} c_{1j}c_{2j} = 0$$

If the sample sizes are not equal, then the condition for independence is more complicated and becomes:

$$\frac{c_{11}c_{21}}{n_1} + \frac{c_{12}c_{22}}{n_2} + \ldots\ldots + \frac{c_{1k}c_{2k}}{n_k} = 0$$

It is very desirable, both statistically and substantively, to have orthogonal multivariate planned comparisons. Since the comparisons are uncorrelated, we obtain a nice additive partitioning of the total between group association (Stevens, 1972). The reader may recall that in univariate ANOVA the between sum of squares is split into additive portions by a set of orthogonal planned comparisons (see Hays, 1981, chapter 14). Exactly the same type of thing is accomplished in the multivariate case, however, now the between matrix is split into additive portions, which yield nonoverlapping pieces of information. Since the orthogonal comparisons are uncorrelated, the interpretation is clear and straightforward.

Although it is desirable to have orthogonal comparisons, the set to impose depends on the questions which are of primary interest to the investigator. The first example we gave of planned comparisons was not orthogonal, but corresponded to the important questions the investigator wanted answered. The interpretation of correlated contrasts requires some care, however, and we consider these in more detail later on in this chapter.

5.8.   TEST STATISTICS FOR PLANNED COMPARISONS

Univariate Case

The reader may have been exposed to planned comparisons for a single dependent variable, i.e., the univariate case. For k groups, with population means μ_1, μ_2, . . . , μ_k, a constrast among the population means is given by

$$\psi = c_1\mu_1 + c_2\mu_2 + \ldots + c_k\mu_k$$

where the sum of the coefficients (c_i) must equal 0.

This contrast is estimated by replacing the population means by the sample means, yielding

$$\hat{\psi} = c_1\bar{x}_1 + c_2\bar{x}_2 + \ldots + c_k\bar{x}_k$$

To test whether a given contrast is significantly different from 0, i.e., to test

$$H_0 : \psi = 0 \qquad \text{vs. } H_1 : \psi \neq 0$$

we need an expression for the standard error of a constrast. It can be shown that the variance for a contrast is given by

$$\hat{\sigma}_{\hat{\psi}}^2 = MS_w \cdot \sum_{i=1}^{k} \frac{c_i^2}{n_i} \tag{1}$$

where MS_w is the error term from all the groups (the denominator of the F test) and n_i are the group sizes. Thus, the standard error of a contrast is simply the square root of (1) and the following t statistic can be used to determine whether a contrast is significantly different from 0:

$$t = \frac{\hat{\psi}}{\sqrt{MS_w \cdot \sum_{i=1}^{k} \frac{c_i^2}{n_i}}}$$

SPSSX MANOVA reports the univariate results for contrasts as F values. Recall, that since $F = t^2$, the following F test with 1 and $N - k$ degrees of freedom is equivalent to a two-tailed t test at the same level of significance:

$$F = \frac{\hat{\psi}^2}{MS_w \cdot \sum_{i=1}^{k} \frac{c_i^2}{n_i}}$$

If we rewrite the above as

$$F = \frac{\hat{\psi}^2 \Big/ \sum_{i=1}^{k} \frac{c_i^2}{n_i}}{MS_w} \tag{2}$$

we can think of the numerator of (2) as the sum of squares for a contrast, and this will appear as hypothesis sum of squares (HYPOTH. SS specifically) on the SPSSX printout. MS_w will appear under the heading ERROR MS.

Let us consider a special case of Equation 2. Suppose the group sizes are equal and we are making a simple paired comparison. Then the coefficient for one mean will be 1 and the coefficient for the other mean will be -1, and $\Sigma c_i^2 = 2$. Then the above F statistic can be written as

$$F = \frac{n\hat{\psi}^2/2}{MS_w} = \frac{n}{2} \hat{\psi} (MS_w)^{-1} \hat{\psi} \tag{3}$$

We have rewritten the test statistic in the form on the extreme right because we will be able to relate it more easily to the multivariate test statistic for a two-group planned comparison.

Multivariate Case

All contrasts, whether univariate or multivariate, can be thought of as fundamentally "two-group" comparisons. We are literally comparing two groups, or we are comparing one set of means vs another set of means. In the multivariate case this means that Hotelling's T^2 will be appropriate for testing the multivariate contrasts for significance.

We now have a contrast among the population mean vectors $\boldsymbol{\mu}_1$, $\boldsymbol{\mu}_2$, ... , $\boldsymbol{\mu}_k$, given by

$$\boldsymbol{\psi} = c_1\boldsymbol{\mu}_1 + c_2\boldsymbol{\mu}_2 + \ldots + c_k\boldsymbol{\mu}_k$$

This contrast is estimated by replacing the population mean vectors by the sample mean vectors:

$$\hat{\boldsymbol{\psi}} = c_1\bar{\mathbf{x}}_1 + c_2\bar{\mathbf{x}}_2 + \ldots . + c_k\bar{\mathbf{x}}_k$$

We wish to test that the contrast among the population mean vectors is the null vector:

$$H_0 : \boldsymbol{\psi} = \mathbf{0}$$

Our estimate of error is $\mathbf{S}$, the estimate of the assumed common within group population covariance matrix $\boldsymbol{\Sigma}$, and the general test statistic is

$$T^2 = \left(\sum_{i=1}^{k} \frac{c_i^2}{n_i} \right)^{-1} \hat{\boldsymbol{\psi}}' \mathbf{S}^{-1} \hat{\boldsymbol{\psi}} \tag{4}$$

where, as in the univariate case, the n_i refer to the group sizes. Suppose we wish to contrast group 1 against the average of groups 2 and 3. If the group sizes are 20, 15, and 12, then the term in parenthesis would be evaluated as $[1^2/20 + (-.5)^2/15 + (-.5)^2/12]$. Complete evaluation of a multivarate contrast is given in Table 5.10. Note that the first part of Equation 4, involving the summation, is exactly the same as in the univariate case (cf. Equation 2). Now, however, there are matrices instead of scalars. For example, the univariate error term MS_w has been replaced by the matrix **S**.

Again, as in the two-group MANOVA chapter, we have an exact F transformation of T^2, which is given by

$$F = \frac{(n_e - p + 1)}{n_e \ p} \ T^2, \text{ with } p \text{ and } (n_e - p + 1) \text{ degrees of freedom} \quad (5)$$

In Equation 5, $n_e = N - k$, i.e., the degrees of freedom for estimating the pooled within covariance matrix. Note that for $k = 2$, (5) reduces to Equation 3 in Chapter 4.

For equal n per group and a simple paired comparison, observe that (4) can be written as

$$T^2 = \frac{n}{2} \ \hat{\psi}' \mathbf{S}^{-1} \hat{\psi} \quad (6)$$

Note the analogy with the univariate case in Equation 3, except that now we have matrices instead of scalars. The estimated contrast has been replaced by the estimated mean vector contrast ($\hat{\psi}$) and the univariate error term (MS_w) has been replaced by the corresponding multivariate error term **S**.

5.9. MULTIVARIATE PLANNED COMPARISONS ON SPSSX MANOVA

SPSSX MANOVA is set up very nicely for running multivariate planned comparisons. The following type of contrasts are automatically generated by the program: Helmert (which we have discussed), Simple, Repeated (comparing adjacent levels of a factor), Deviation, and Polynomial. Thus, if we wish Helmert contrasts, it is not necessary to set up the coefficients, the program does this automatically. All we need do is give the following CONTRAST SUBCOMMAND:

CONTRAST(FACTORNAME) = HELMERT/

We remind the reader that all subcommands are indented at least one column and begin with a keyword (in this case CONTRAST) followed by an equals sign, then the specifications, and are terminated by a slash.

An example of where Helmert contrasts are very meaningful has already been given. Simple contrasts involve comparing each group against the last group. A situation where this set of contrasts would make sense is if we were mainly interested in comparing each of several treatment groups against a control group (labeled as the last group). Repeated contrasts might be of considerable interest in a repeated measures design where a single group of subjects is measured at say 5 points in time (a longitudinal study). We might be particularily interested in differences at adjacent points in time. For example, a group of elementary school children is measured on a standardized achievement test in grades 1, 3, 5, 7, and 8. We wish to know the extent of change from grade 1 to 3, from grade 3 to 5, from grade 5 to 7, and from grade 7 to 8. The coefficients for the contrasts would be as follows:

	Grade			
1	3	5	7	8
1	-1	0	0	0
0	1	-1	0	0
0	0	1	-1	0
0	0	0	1	-1

Polynomial contrasts are useful in trend analysis, i.e., where we wish to determine whether there is a linear, quadratic, cubic, etc. trend in the data. Again, these contrasts can be of great interest in repeated measures designs in growth curve analysis, where we wish to model the mathematical form of the growth. To reconsider the previous example, some investigators may be more interested in whether the growth in some basic skills areas like reading and mathematics is linear (proportional) during the elementary years, or perhaps curvilinear. For example, maybe growth is linear for a while and then somewhat levels off, suggesting an overall curvilinear trend.

If none of the above automatically generated contrasts answer the research questions, then one can set up their own contrasts using SPECIAL as the code name. Special contrasts are "tailor made" comparisons for the group comparisons suggested by your hypotheses. In setting these up, however, remember that for k groups there are only $(k - 1)$ between degrees of freedom, so that only $(k - 1)$ non-redundant contrasts can be run. The coefficients for the contrasts are enclosed in parentheses after special:

CONTRAST(FACTORNAME) = SPECIAL(1, 1, . . . , 1 coefficients for contrasts)/

There *must* first be as many 1's as there are groups (see SPSSX User's Guide, 1983, p. 485). We give an example illustrating special contrasts shortly.

Example 1—Helmert contrasts

An investigator has a three-group, two-dependent variable problem with 5 subjects per group. The first is a control group, and the remaining two groups are treatment groups. The Helmert contrasts test each level (group) against the average of the remaining levels. In this case the two single degree of freedom Helmert contrasts, corresponding to the two between degrees of freedom, are very meaningful. The first tests whether the control group differs from the average of the treatment groups on the set of variables. The second Helmert contrast tests whether the treatments are differentially effective. In Table 5.7 we present the control lines, along with the data as part of the command file, for running

TABLE 5.7

SPSSX MANOVA Control Lines for Multivariate Helmert
Contrasts

```
          TITLE ' MULTIVARIATE HELMERT CONTRASTS FOR THREE GROUPS'
          DATA LIST FREE/ Y1 Y2 GPS
          LIST
          BEGIN DATA
          5  6  1
          6  7  1
          6  7  1
          4  5  1
          5  4  1
          2  2  2
          3  3  2
          4  4  2
          3  2  2
          2  1  2
          4  3  3
          6  7  3
          3  3  3
          5  5  3
          5  5  3

          END DATA
          MANOVA Y1 Y2 BY GPS(1,3)/
             CONTRAST(GPS) = HELMERT/
   ①       PARTITION(GPS)/
   ②       DESIGN = GPS(1),GPS(2)/
             PRINT = CELLINFO(MEANS,COV,COR)/
```

①In general, for k groups, the between degrees of freedom could be partitioned in various ways. If we wish all single degree of freedom contrasts, as here, then we could put PARTITION(GPS) = (1,1)/. Or, this can be abbreviated to PARTITION(GPS)/.

②This DESIGN subcommand specifies the effects we are testing for significance, in this case the two single degree of freedom multivariate contrasts. The numbers in parentheses refer to the part of the partition. Thus, GPS(1) refers to the first part of the partition (the first Helmert contrast) and GPS(2) refers to the second part of the partition, i.e., the second Helmert contrast.

the contrasts. Recall that when the data is part of the command file it is preceded by the BEGIN DATA command and the data is followed by the END DATA command.

The means, standard deviations and pooled within covariance matrix **S** are presented in Table 5.8. In Table 5.8 we also calculate $\mathbf{S}^{-1}$ which will serve as the error term for the multivariate contrasts (cf. Equation 4). Table 5.9 presents the output for the multivariate and univariate Helmert contrasts comparing the treatment groups against the control group. The multivariate contrast is significant at the .05 level ($F = 4.303$, $p < .042$), indicating that something is better than

TABLE 5.8
Means, Standard Deviations and Pooled Within Covariance Matrix
for Helmert Contrast Example

CELL MEANS AND STANDARD DEVIATIONS

VARIABLE ... Y1

FACTOR	CODE	MEAN	STD. DEV.
GPS	1	5.20000	.83666
GPS	2	2.80000	.83666
GPS	3	4.60000	1.14018
FOR ENTIRE SAMPLE		4.20000	1.37321

VARIABLE .. Y2

FACTOR	CODE	MEAN	STD. DEV.
GPS	1	5.80000	1.30384
GPS	2	2.40000	1.14018
GPS	3	4.60000	1.67332
FOR ENTIRE SAMPLE		4.26667	1.94447

POOLED WITHIN-CELLS VARIANCE-COVARIANCE MATRIX

	Y1	Y2
Y1	.90000	
Y2	1.15000	1.93333

DETERMINANT OF POOLED VARIANCE-COVARIANCE MATRIX   .41750

To compute the multivariate test statistic for the contrasts we need the inverse of this covariance matrix **S**; compare Equation 4.

The procedure for finding the inverse of a matrix was given in section 2.5. We obtain the matrix of cofactors and then divide by the determinant. Thus, here we have

$$\mathbf{S}^{-1} = \frac{1}{.4175}\begin{bmatrix} 1.933 & -1.15 \\ -1.15 & 9 \end{bmatrix} = \begin{bmatrix} 4.631 & -2.755 \\ -2.755 & 2.156 \end{bmatrix}$$

TABLE 5.9

Multivariate and Univariate Tests for Helmert Contrast Comparing the Control Group Against the Two Treatment Groups

EFFECT .. GPID(1)

MULTIVARIATE TESTS OF SIGNIFICANCE (S = 1, M = 0, N = 4 1/2)

TEST NAME	VALUE	APPROX. F	HYPOTH. DF	ERROR DF	SIG. OF F
PILLAIS	.43897	4.30339	2.00	11.00	.042
HOTELLINGS	.78244	4.30339	2.00	11.00	.042 ①
WILKS	.56103	4.30339	2.00	11.00	.042
ROYS	.43897				

UNIVARIATE F-TESTS WITH (1,12) D. F.

VARIABLE	HYPOTH. SS	ERROR SS	HYPOTH. MS	ERROR MS	F	SIG. OF F
Y1	7.50000	10.80000	7.50000	.90000	8.33333	.014
Y2	17.63333	23.20000	17.63333	1.93333	9.12069	.011

The univariate contrast for $Y1$ is given by $\Psi_1 = \mu_1 - (\mu_2 + \mu_3)/2$

Using the boxed in means of Table 5.8, we obtain the following estimate for the contrast: $\hat{\Psi}_1 = 5.2 - (2.8 + 4.6)/2 = 1.5$.

Recall from Equation 2 that the hypothesis sum of squares is given by $\Psi^2 / \sum_{i=1}^{k} \dfrac{c_i^2}{n_i}$. For equal group sizes, as here, this becomes $n\Psi^2 / \sum_{i=1}^{k} c_i^2$. Thus,

$$\text{HYPOTH } SS = \frac{5(1.5)^2}{1^2 + (-.5)^2 + (-.5)^2} = 7.5.$$

The error term for the contrast is MS_w appears under ERROR MS and is .900. Thus, the F ratio for $Y1$ is $7.5/.90 = 8.333$. Notice that both variables are significant at the .05 level.

① This indicates that the multivariate contrast $\Psi_1 = \mu_1 - (\mu_2 + \mu_3)/2$ is significant at the .05 level (since .042 < .05). That is, the control group differs significantly from the average of the two treatment groups on the set of two variables.

TABLE 5.10
Multivariate and Univariate Tests for Helmert Contrast Comparing the Two Treatment Groups

EFFECT .. GPID(2)

MULTIVARIATE TESTS OF SIGNIFICANCE (S = 1, M = 0, N = 4 1/2)

TEST NAME	VALUE	APPROX. F	HYPOTH. DF	ERROR DF	SIG. OF F
PILLAIS	.43003	4.14970	2.00	11.00	.045
HOTELLINGS	.75449	4.14970	2.00	11.00	① .045
WILKS	.56997	4.14970	2.00	11.00	.045
ROYS	.43003				

Recall from Table 5.8 that the inverse of pooled within covariance matrix is

$$\mathbf{S}^{-1} = \begin{bmatrix} 4.631 & -2.755 \\ -2.755 & 2.156 \end{bmatrix}$$

Since this is a simple contrast with equal n, we can use Equation 6:

$$T^2 = \frac{n}{2}\hat{\Psi}'\mathbf{S}^{-1}\hat{\Psi} = \frac{n}{2}(\bar{\mathbf{x}}_2 - \bar{\mathbf{x}}_3)'\mathbf{S}^{-1}(\bar{\mathbf{x}}_2 - \bar{\mathbf{x}}_3) = \frac{5}{2}\left[\begin{pmatrix} 2.8 \\ 2.4 \end{pmatrix} - \begin{pmatrix} 4.6 \\ 4.6 \end{pmatrix}\right]'\begin{bmatrix} 4.631 & -2.755 \\ -2.755 & 2.156 \end{bmatrix}\begin{pmatrix} -1.8 \\ -2.2 \end{pmatrix} = 9.0535$$

To obtain the value of HOTELLING given on printout above we simply divide by error df, i.e., 9.0535/12 = .75446. To obtain the F we use Equation 5:

$$F = \frac{(n_e - p + 1)}{n_e p}T^2 = \frac{(12 - 2 + 1)}{12(2)}(9.0535) = 4.1495,$$

with degrees of freedom $p = 2$ and $(n_e - p + 1) = 11$ as given above.

UNIVARIATE F-TESTS WITH (1,12) D. F.

VARIABLE	HYPOTH. SS	ERROR SS	HYPOTH. MS	ERROR MS	F	SIG. OF F
Y1	8.10000	10.80000	8.10000	.90000	9.00000	② .011
Y2	12.10000	23.20000	12.10000	1.93333	6.25862	.028

①This multivariate test indicates that treatment groups do differ significantly at the .05 level (since .045 < .05) on the *set* of two variables.
②These results indicate that both univariate contrasts are significant at .05 level, i.e., both variables are contributing to overall multivariate significance.

nothing. Note also that the F's for all the multivariate tests are the *same*, since this is a single degree of freedom comparison and thus effectively a two-group comparison. The univariate results show that each of the two variables is significant at .05, and are thus contributing to overall multivariate significance. We also show in Table 5.9 how the hypothesis sum of squares is obtained for the first univariate Helmert contrast (i.e., for $Y1$).

In Table 5.10 we present the multivariate and univariate Helmert contrasts comparing the two treatment groups. As the annotation indicates, both the multivariate and univariate contrasts are significant at the .05 level. Thus, the treatment groups differ on the set of variables and both variables are contributing to multivariate significance. In Table 5.10 we also show in detail how the F value for the multivariate Helmert contrast is arrived at.

Example 2—Special Contrasts

We indicated earlier that researchers can set up their own contrasts on MANOVA. We now illustrate this for a four-group, five-dependent variable example. There are two control groups, one of which is a Hawthorne control, and two treatment groups. Three very meaningful contrasts are indicated schematically below:

	T_1 (control)	T_2 (Hawthorne)	T_3	T_4
ψ_1	−.5	−.5	.5	.5
ψ_2	0	1	−.5	−.5
ψ_3	0	0	1	−1

TABLE 5.11
SPSSX MANOVA Control Lines for Special Multivariate Contrasts

```
    TITLE 'SPECIAL MULTIVARITE CONTRASTS. '
①   DATA LIST/ GPS 1 Y1 3–4 Y2 6–7(1) Y3 9–11(2) Y4 13–15 Y5 17–18
    LIST
    BEGIN DATA
    1 28 13 476 215 74
    1 33 26 513 398 65
        .    .    .
        .    .    .
    4 42 19 246 417 83
        .    .    .
        .    .    .
    4 24 31 668 355 56
    END DATA
    MANOVA Y1 TO Y5 BY GPS(1,4)/
        CONTRASTS(GPS) = SPECIAL(1 1 1 1 − .5 − .5 .5 .5 0 1 − .5 − .5 0 0 1 − 1)/
        PARTITION(GPS)/
        DESIGN = GPS(1),GPS(2),GPS(3)/
        PRINT = CELLINFO(MEANS,COV,COR)/
```

①Here we have used column input. This first number(s) gives the column(s) in which the scores for the variable appears, and the number in parentheses gives the number of implied decimal places. Thus, $Y1$ is in columns three and four, with no decimal places, while $Y2$ is in columns 6 and 7, with 1 implied decimal place. Therefore, the actual data for subject 1 is 28 1.3 4.76 215 74.

The control lines for running these contrasts on SPSSX MANOVA are presented in Table 5.11. (In this case I have just put in some data schematically and have used column input, simply to illustrate it). As indicated earlier, note that the first 4 numbers in the CONTRAST subcommand are 1's, corresponding to the number of groups. The next 4 numbers define the first contrast, where we are comparing the control groups against the treatment groups. The following 4 numbers define the second contrast, and the last 4 numbers define the third contrast.

5.10. CORRELATED CONTRASTS

The Helmert contrasts we considered in Example 1 are, for equal n, uncorrelated. This is important in terms of clarity of interpretation since significance on one Helmert contrast implies nothing about significance on a different Helmert contrast. For correlated contrasts this is not true. To determine the unique contribution a given contrast is making we need to partial out its correlations with the other contrasts. We will illustrate how this is done on MANOVA.

Correlated contrasts can arise in two ways: (1) the sum of products of the coefficients $\neq 0$ for the contrasts, and (2) the sum of products of coefficients $= 0$, but the group sizes are not equal.

Example 3—Correlated Contrasts

We consider an example with 4 groups and 2 dependent variables. The contrasts are indicated schematically below, with the group sizes in parentheses:

	T_1 & T_2 (12) combined	Hawthorne (14) control	T_1 (11)	T_2 (8)
ψ_1	0	1	-1	0
ψ_2	0	1	$-.5$	$-.5$
ψ_3	1	0	0	1

Notice that ψ_1 and ψ_2 as well as ψ_2 and ψ_3 are correlated since the sum of products of coefficients in each case $\neq 0$. However, ψ_1 and ψ_3 are also correlated since group sizes are unequal. The data for this problem are given in the Appendix of this chapter. The set up of the control lines for this problem would be similar to that for Example 2, except that we would insert METHOD = SSTYPE(UNIQUE)/ before the DESIGN subcommand to obtain the unique contribution of each contrast to between variation.

For illustrative purposes, and to show how default options on the packages may give misleading results, we tested these contrasts for significance in two ways:

1.   We used the SSTYPE(UNIQUE) method mentioned above. This gives

TABLE 5.12

Multivariate Tests for Unique Contribution of Each Correlated Contrast to Between Variation*

EFFECT .. GPS(3)

MULTIVARIATE TESTS OF SIGNIFICANCE (S = 1, M = 0, N = 19)

TEST NAME	VALUE	APPROX. F	HYPOTH. DF	ERROR DF	SIG. OF F
PILLAIS	.14891	3.49930	2.00	40.00	.040
HOTELLINGS	.17496	3.49930	2.00	40.00	.040
WILKS	.85109	3.49930	2.00	40.00	.040
ROYS	.14891				

EFFECT .. GPS(2)

MULTIVARIATE TESTS OF SIGNIFICANCE (S = 1, M = 0, N = 19)

TEST NAME	VALUE	APPROX. F	HYPOTH. DF	ERROR DF	SIG. OF F
PILLAIS	.18228	4.45832	2.00	40.00	.018
HOTELLINGS	.22292	4.45832	2.00	40.00	.018
WILKS	.81772	4.45832	2.00	40.00	.018
ROYS	.18228				

EFFECT .. GPS(1)

MULTIVARIATE TESTS OF SIGNIFICANCE (S = 1, M = 0, N = 19)

TEST NAME	VALUE	APPROX. F	HYPOTH. DF	ERROR DF	SIG. OF F
PILLAIS	.03233	.66813	2.00	40.00	.518
HOTELLINGS	.03341	.66813	2.00	40.00	.518
WILKS	.96767	.66813	2.00	40.00	.518
ROYS	.03233				

*Each contrast is adjusted for it's correlations with the other contrasts.

TABLE 5.13

Multivariate Tests of Correlated Contrasts for Hierarchical Default Option of SPSSX MANOVA*

EFFECT .. GPS(3)

MULTIVARIATE TESTS OF SIGNIFICANCE (S = 1, M = 0, N = 19)

TEST NAME	VALUE	APPROX. F	HYPOTH. DF	ERROR DF	SIG. OF F
PILLAIS	.14891	3.49930	2.00	40.00	.040
HOTELLINGS	.17496	3.49930	2.00	40.00	.040
WILKS	.85109	3.49930	2.00	40.00	.040
ROYS	.14891				

EFFECT .. GPS(2)

MULTIVARIATE TESTS OF SIGNIFICANCE (S = 1, M = 0, N = 19)

TEST NAME	VALUE	APPROX. F	HYPOTH. DF	ERROR DF	SIG. OF F
PILLAIS	.10542	2.35677	2.00	40.00	.108
HOTELLINGS	.11784	2.35677	2.00	40.00	.108
WILKS	.89458	2.35677	2.00	40.00	.108
ROYS	.10542				

EFFECT .. GPS(1)

MULTIVARIATE TESTS OF SIGNIFICANTS (S = 1, M = 0, N = 19)

TEST NAME	VALUE	APPROX. F	HYPOTH. DF	ERROR DF	SIG. OF F
PILLAIS	.13641	3.15905	2.00	40.00	.053
HOTELLINGS	.15795	3.15905	2.00	40.00	.053
WILKS	.86359	3.15905	2.00	40.00	.053
ROYS	.13641				

*Each contrast is adjusted *only* for all contrasts to left of it in the DESIGN subcommand.
It is important to note that starting with Release 2.1 of SPSSX the unique sum of squares is the default option.

the unique contribution of the contrast to between variation, i.e., each contrast is adjusted for it's correlations with the other contrasts.

2. We used the hierarchical default option with DESIGN subcommand as follows:

DESIGN = GPS(1),GPS(2),GPS(3)/

With this option each contrast is adjusted only for all contrasts to the *left* of it in the DESIGN subcommand. Since GPS(3) is the last effect, it will be adjusted for all other contrasts and the value of the multivariate test statistics for GPS(3) will be the *same* as we will obtain using SSTYPE(UNIQUE). However, the value of the test statistics for GPS(2) and GPS(1) will differ from those obtained using SSTYPE(UNIQUE), since GPS(2) is only adjusted for GPS(1) and GPS(1) is not adjusted for either of the other two constants.

The multivariate test statistics for the contrasts using the unique decomposition are presented in Table 5.12, while the statistics for the hierarchical decomposition are given in Table 5.13. As explained earlier, the results for ψ_3 are identical for both approaches, and indicate significance at the .05 level ($F = 3.499, p < .04$). That is, the combination of treatments differs from T_2 alone. The results for the other two contrasts, however, are quite different for the two approaches. The unique breakdown indicates that ψ_2 is significant at .05 (treatments differ from Hawthorne control) and ψ_1 is not significant (T_1 is not different from Hawthorne control). The results in Table 5.12 for the hierarchical approach yield exactly the opposite conclusion! Obviously the conclusions one draws in this study would depend on which approach was used to test the contrasts for significance. We would express a preference in general for the unique approach.

It should be noted that the unique contribution of each contrast can be obtained using the heirarchical approach; however, in this case three DESIGN subcommands would be required, with each of the contrasts ordered last in one of the subcommands:

DESIGN = GPS(1),GPS(2),GPS(3)/

DESIGN = GPS(2),GPS(3),GPS(1)/

DESIGN = GPS(3),GPS(1),GPS(2)/

All three orderings can be done in a single run.

5.11. STUDIES USING MULTIVARIATE PLANNED COMPARISONS

Clifford (1972) was interested in the effect of competition as a motivational technique in the classroom. The subjects were primarily white, average I.Q., fifth graders, with about half of each sex. A two week vocabulary learning task was given under three conditions:

1. Control—a noncompetitive atmosphere in which no score comparisons among classmates were made.
2. Reward Treatment—comparisons among relatively homogeneous subjects were made and accentuated by the rewarding of candy to high scoring subjects.
3. Game Treatment—again comparisons were made among relatively homogeneous subjects and accentuated in a followup game activity. Here high scoring subjects received an advantage in a game which was played immediately after the vocabulary task was scored.

The three dependent variables were performance, interest, and retention. The retention measure was given two weeks after the completion of treatments. Clifford had the following two planned comparisons:

1. Competition is more effective than noncompetition. Thus, she was testing the following contrast for significance:

$$\psi_1 = \frac{\mu_2 + \mu_3}{2} - \mu_1$$

2. Game competition is as effective as reward with respect to performance on the dependent variables. Thus, she was predicting the following contrast would *not* be significant:

$$\psi_2 = \mu_2 - \mu_3$$

Clifford's results are presented in Table 5.14.

As predicted, competition was more effective than noncompetition for the set of three dependent variables. Estimation of the univariate results in Table 5.14 shows that the multivariate significance is primarily due to a significant difference on the interest variable. Clifford's second prediction was also confirmed, i.e., there was no difference in the relative effectiveness of reward vs. game treatments ($F = .84$, $p < .47$).

A second study involving multivariate planned comparisons was conducted by Stevens (1972). He was interested in studying the relationship between parent's educational level and eight personality characteristics of their National Merit scholar children. Part of the analysis involved the following set of orthogonal comparisons (75 subjects per group):

1. Group 1 (parents' education eight grade or less) vs. group 2 (parents' both high school graduates).
2. Groups 1 and 2 (no college) vs. groups 3 and 4 (college for both parents).
3. Group 3 (both parents attended college) vs. group 4 (both parents at least one college degree).

TABLE 5.14
Means and Multivariate and Univariate Results for Two Planned
Comparisons in Clifford Study

	df	MS	F	p
1st Planned Comparison (Control vs. Reward and Game.)				
Multivariate Test	3/61		10.04	.0001
Univariate Tests				
Performance	1/63	.54	.64	.43
Interest	1/63	4.70	29.24	.0001
Retention	1/63	4.01	.18	.67
2nd Planned Comparison (Reward vs. Game)				
Multivariate Test	3/61		.84	.47
Univariate Tests				
Performance	1/63	.002	.003	.96
Interest	1/63	.37	2.32	.13
Retention	1/63	1.47	.07	.80

	Means for the Groups		
	Control	Reward	Games
Variable			
Performance	5.72	5.92	5.90
Interest	2.41	2.63	2.57
Retention	30.85	31.55	31.19

This set of comparisons corresponds to a very meaningful set of questions: Which differences in degree of education produce differential effects on the children's personality characteristics?

Another set of orthogonal contrasts that could have been of interest in this study looks like this schematically:

	Groups			
	1	2	3	4
ψ_1	1	−.33	−.33	−.33
ψ_2	0	0	1	−1
ψ_3	0	1	−.50	−.50

This would have resulted in a different meaningful, additive breakdown of the between association. However, one set of orthogonal contrasts does not have an empirical superiority over another (after all, they both additively partition the between association). In terms of choosing one set over the other, it is a matter of which set best answers the experimenter's research hypotheses.

5.12. STEPDOWN ANALYSIS

We have just finished discussing one type of focused inquiry, planned comparisons, in which specific questions were asked of the data. Another type of directed inquiry in the MANOVA context, but which focuses on the dependent variables rather than the groups, is stepdown analysis. Here, based on previous research and/or theory, we are able to a priori order the dependent variables, and test in that specific order for group discrimination. As an example, let the independent variable be three teaching methods and the dependent variables be the three subtest scores on a common achievement test covering the three lowest levels in Bloom's taxonomy: knowledge, comprehension, and application. An assumption of the taxonomy is that learning at a lower level is a necessary but not sufficient condition for learning at a higher level. Because of this, there is a theoretical rationale for ordering the dependent variables in the above specified way and to test first whether the methods have had a differential effect on knowledge: Then, if so, whether the methods differentially affect comprehension, with knowledge held constant (used as a covariate) etc. Since stepdown analysis is just a series of analyses of covariance, we defer a complete discussion of it to Chapter 10, i.e., until we have covered analysis of covariance in Chapter 9.

5.13. OTHER MULTIVARIATE TEST STATISTICS

In addition to Wilk's Λ, there are three other multivariate test statistics that are in use and are printed out on the packages:

1. Roy's largest root (eigenvalue) of $\mathbf{BW}^{-1}$
2. The Hotelling-Lawley trace, i.e., the sum of the eigenvalues of $\mathbf{BW}^{-1}$.
3. The Pillai-Bartlett trace, i.e., the sum of the eigenvalues of $\mathbf{B}\,\mathbf{T}^{-1}$.

Notice that the Roy and Hotelling-Lawley multivariate statistics are natural generalizations of the univariate F statistic. In univariate ANOVA the test statistic is $F = MS_b/MS_w$, i.e., a measure of between- to within-association. The multivariate analogue of this is $\mathbf{BW}^{-1}$, which is a "ratio" of between- to within-association. With matrices there is no division, so we don't literally divide the between by the within as in the univariate case, however, the matrix analogue of division is inversion.

Since Wilk's Λ can be expressed as a product of eigenvalues of $\mathbf{WT}^{-1}$, *we see that all four of the multivariate test statistics are some function of an eigenvalue(s) (sum, product). Thus, eigenvalues are fundamental to the multivariate problem.* We show in Chapter 7 on discriminant analysis that there are quantities corresponding to the eigenvalues (the discriminant functions) which are linear combinations of the dependent variables and which characterize major differences among the groups.

The reader might well ask at this point, "Which of these four multivariate test statistics should be used in practice?" This is a somewhat complicated question which for full understanding requires a knowledge of discriminant analysis and of the robustness of the four statistics to the assumptions in MANOVA. Nevertheless, the following will provide guidelines for the researcher. In terms of robustness with respect to type I error for the homogeneity of covariance matrices assumption, Stevens (1979) found that *any* of the following three can be used: Pillai-Bartlett trace, Hotelling-Lawley trace, or Wilk's Λ. For subgroup variance differences likely to be encountered in social science research, these three are equally quite robust, provided the group sizes are equal or approximately equal ($\frac{\text{largest}}{\text{smallest}} < 1.5$). In terms of power, no one of the four statistics is always most powerful; which depends on how the null hypothesis is false. Importantly, however, Olson (1973) found that *power differences among the four multivariate test statistics are generally quite small* ($< .06$). So as a general rule, it won't make that much of a difference which of the statistics is used. But, if the differences among the groups are concentrated on the first discriminant function, which does occur quite often in practice (Bock, 1975, p. 154), then Roy's statistic technically would be preferred since it is most powerful. However, Roy's statistic should only be used in this case if there is evidence to suggest that the homogeneity of covariance matrices assumption is tenable. Finally, when the differences among the groups involves two or more discriminant functions, the Pillai-Bartlett trace is most powerful, although it's power advantage tends to be slight.

5.14. HOW MANY DEPENDENT VARIABLES FOR A MANOVA?

Of course, there is no simple answer to this question. However, the following considerations mitigate *generally* against the use of a large number of criterion variables:

1. If a large number of dependent variables are included without any strong rationale (empirical and/or theoretical), then small or negligible differences on

most of them may obscure a real difference(s) on a few of them. That is, the multivariate test detects mainly error in the system, i.e., in the set of variables, and therefore declares no reliable overall difference.

2. The power of the multivariate tests generally declines as the number of dependent variables is increased (DasGupta & Perlman, 1973).

3. The reliability of variables can be a problem in behavioral science work. Thus, given a large number of criterion variables, it probably will be wise to combine (usually add) highly similar response measures, particularly when the basic measurements tend individually to be quite unreliable (Pruzek, 1971). As Pruzek states,

> . . . one should always consider the possibility that his variables include errors of measurement which may attenuate F ratios and generally confound interpretations of experimental effects. Especially when there are several dependent variables whose reliabilities and mutual intercorrelations vary widely, inferences based on fallible data may be quite misleading. (p. 187)

4. Based on his Monte Carlo results, Olson had some comments on the design of multivariate experiments which are worth remembering: For example, one generally will not do worse by making the dimensionality p smaller, insofar as it is under experimenter control. Variates should not be thoughtlessly included in an analysis just because the data are available. Besides aiding robustness, a small value of p is apt to facilitate interpretation. (p. 906)

5. Given a large number of variables, one should always consider the possibility that there are a much smaller number of underlying constructs which will account for most of the variance on the original set of variables. Thus, the use of principal components analysis as a preliminary data reduction scheme before the use of MANOVA should be contemplated.

5.15. POWER ANALYSIS—A PRIORI DETERMINATION OF SAMPLE SIZE

There have been several studies that have dealt with power in MANOVA (e.g., Ito, 1962; Pillai & Jayachandian, 1967; Olson, 1974; Laüter, 1978). Olson examined power for small and moderate sample size, but expressed the non-centrality parameter (which measures the extent of deviation from the null hypothesis) in terms of eigenvalues. Also, there were many gaps in his tables; no power values for 4, 5, 7, 8, and 9 variables or for 4 or 5 groups. The Laüter study is much more comprehensive, giving sample size tables for a very wide range of situations:

1. for $\alpha = .05$ or .01
2. for 2, 3, 4, 5, 6, 8, 10, 15, 20, 30, 50 and 100 variables

3. for 2, 3, 4, 5, 6, 8 and 10 groups
4. for power = 70, .80, .90 and .95

His tables are specifically for the Hotelling-Lawley trace criterion, and this might seem to limit their utility. However, as Morrison (1967) has noted for large sample size, and as Olson (1974) showed for small and moderate sample size, the power differences among the four main multivariate test statistics are generally quite small. Thus, the sample size requirements for Wilk's Λ, the Pillaz-Bartlett trace and Roy's largest root will be very similar to those for the Hotelling-Lawley trace for the vast majority of situations.

Laüter's tables are set up in terms of a certain *minimum* deviation from the multivariate null hypothesis, which can be expressed in the following three forms:

There exists a variable i such that $\dfrac{1}{\sigma^2} \sum\limits_{j=1}^{J} (\mu_{ij} - \mu_{i.}) \geq q^2$, where $\mu_{i.}$ is the total mean and σ^2 is variance.

There exists a variate i such that $1/\sigma_i |\mu_{ij_1} - \mu_{ij_2}| \geq d$, for two groups j_1 and j_2.

There exists a variate i such that for *all* pairs of groups 1 and m we have $1/\sigma_i |\mu_{il} - \mu_{im}| \geq c$.

In Table E at the end of this volume we present selected situations and power values which it is felt would be of most value to social science researchers: for 2, 3, 4, 5, 6, 8, 10, and 15 variables, with 3, 4, 5, and 6 groups, and for power = .70, .80 and .90. We have also characterized the four different minimum deviation patterns as very large, large, moderate, and small effect sizes. Although the characterizations may be somewhat rough, they are reasonable in the following senses. They agree with Cohen's definitions of large, medium and small effect sizes for one variable (Laüter included the univariate case in his tables), and with Stevens (1980) definitions of large, medium and small effect sizes for the two group MANOVA case.

It is important to note that there could be several ways, other than that specified by Laüter, in which a large, moderate, or small multivariate effect size could occur. But the essential point is how many subjects will be needed for a given effect size, regardless of the combination of differences on the variables that produced the specific effect size. Thus, the tables do have broad applicability. We will consider shortly a few specific examples of the use of the tables, but first we present a compact table which should be of great interest to applied researchers:

		Groups			
		3	4	5	6
	very large	12–16	14–18	15–19	16–21
EFFECT	large	25–32	28–36	31–40	33–44
SIZE	medium	42–54	48–62	54–70	58–76
	small	92–120	105–140	120–155	130–170

This table gives the range of sample sizes needed per group for adequate power (.70) at $\alpha = .05$ when there are three to six variables.

Thus, if we expect a large effect size and have 4 groups, 28 subjects per group are needed for power $= .70$ with three variables, while 36 subjects per group are required if there were 6 dependent variables.

Now we consider two examples to illustrate the use of the Lauter sample size tables in the appendix.

Example 1

An investigator has a 4-group MANOVA with 5 dependent variables. He wishes power $= .80$ at $\alpha = .05$. From previous research and his knowledge of the nature of the treatments, he anticipates a moderate effect size. How many subjects per group will he need? Reference to Table E (for 4 groups) indicates that 70 subjects per group are required.

Example 2

A team of researchers has a 5 group, 7 dependent variable MANOVA. They wish power $= .70$ at $\alpha = .05$. From previous research they anticipate a large effect size. How many subjects per group are needed? Interpolating in Table E (for 5 groups) between 6 and 8 variables, we see that 43 subjects per group are needed, or a total of 215 subjects.

5.16. SUMMARY

Cohen's (1968) seminal article showed social science researchers that univariate ANOVA could be considered as a special case of regression, by dummy coding group membership. In this chapter we have pointed out that MANOVA can also be considered as a special case of regression analysis, except that for MANOVA it is multivariate regression since there are several dependent variables being predicted from the dummy variables. That is, separation of the mean vectors is equivalent to demonstrating that the dummy variables (predictors) significantly predict the scores on the dependent variables.

For exploratory research, three post hoc procedures were given for determining which of the groups and/or variables are responsible for an overall difference. One procedure used Hotelling T^2's to determine the significant pairwise multivariate differences, and then univariate t's to determine which of the variables are contributing to the significant pairwise multivariate differences. The second procedure also used Hotelling T^2's, but then used the Tukey intervals to determine which variables were contributing to the significant pairwise multivariate differences. The third post hoc procedure, the Roy-Bose multivariate confidence interval approach (the generalization of the univariate Scheffe' intervals) was discussed and rejected. It was rejected because the power for detecting differences with this approach is quite poor, especially for small or moderate sample size.

For confirmatory research, planned comparisons were discussed. The setup of multivariate contrasts on SPSSX MANOVA was illustrated. Although uncorrelated contrasts are very desirable because of ease of interpretation and the nice additive partitioning they yield, it was noted that often the important questions an investigator has will yield correlated contrasts. The use of SPSSX MANOVA to obtain the unique contribution of each correlated contrast was illustrated.

It was noted that the Roy and Hotelling-Lawley statistics are natural generalizations of the univariate F ratio. In terms of which of the four multivariate test statistics to use in practice, two criteria can be used: robustness and power. Wilk's Λ, the Pillai-Bartlett trace, and Hotelling-Lawley statistics are equally robust (for equal or approximately equal group sizes) with respect to the homogeneity of covariance matrices assumption, and therefore anyone of them can be used. The power differences among the four statistics are in general quite small ($< .06$), so that there is no strong basis for preferring anyone of them over the others on power considerations.

The important problem, in terms of experimental planning, of a priori determination of sample size was considered for 3-, 4-, 5- and 6-group MANOVA for the number of dependent variables ranging from 2 to 15.

APPENDIX

NOVINCE (1977) DATA FOR MULTIVARIATE ANALYSIS OF VARIANCE PRESENTED IN TABLES 5.3 & 5.4

DATA

	Behavioral Rehearsal		
ANX	SOCSKLS	APPROP	ASSERT
5.	3.	3.	3.
5.	4.	4.	3.
4.	5.	4.	4.
4.	5.	5.	4.
3.	5.	5.	5.
4.	5.	4.	4.
4.	4.	5.	5.
4.	4.	4.	4.
5.	4.	4.	3.
5.	4.	4.	3.
4.	4.	4.	4.

		Control Group		
ANX	SOCSKLS	APPROP	ASSERT
6.	2.	1.	1.
6.	2.	2.	2.
5.	2.	3.	3.
6.	2.	2.	2.
4.	4.	4.	4.
7.	1.	1.	1.
5.	4.	3.	3.
5.	2.	3.	3.
5.	3.	3.	3.
5.	4.	3.	3.
6.	2.	3.	3.

		Behavioral Rehearsal + Cognitive Restructuring		
ANX	SOCSKLS	APPROP	ASSERT
4.	4.	4.	4.
4.	3.	4.	3.
4.	4.	4.	4.
4.	5.	5.	5.
4.	5.	5.	5.
4.	4.	4.	4.
4.	5.	4.	4.
4.	6.	6.	5.
4.	4.	4.	4.
5.	3.	3.	3.
4.	4.	4.	4.

DATA FOR MULTIVARIATE CORRELATED CONTRASTS

GPS	V1	V2
1.	18.	5.
1.	13.	6.
1.	20.	4.
1.	22.	8.
1.	21.	9.
1.	19.	0.
1.	12.	6.
1.	12.	6.
1.	10.	5.
1.	15.	4.
1.	15.	5.
1.	14.	0.
2.	18.	9.
2.	20.	5.
2.	17.	10.
2.	24.	4.
2.	19.	4.
2.	18.	4.
2.	15.	7.
2.	16.	7.
2.	16.	5.
2.	14.	3.
2.	18.	2.
2.	14.	4.
2.	19.	6.

2.	23.	2.
3.	17.	5.
3.	13.	3.
3.	22.	7.
3.	22.	5.
3.	13.	9.
3.	13.	5.
3.	11.	5.
3.	12.	6.
3.	23.	3.
3.	17.	7.
3.	18.	7.
4.	13.	3.
4.	9.	3.
4.	9.	3.
4.	15.	5.
4.	13.	4.
4.	12.	4.
4.	13.	5.
4.	12.	3.

EXERCISES—CHAPTER 5

1. Consider the following data for a three group, three dependent variable problem:

	Gp 1			Gp 2			Gp 3	
y_1	y_2	y_3	y_1	y_2	y_3	y_1	y_2	y_3
2.0	2.5	2.5	1.5	3.5	2.5	1.0	2.0	1.0
1.5	2.0	1.5	1.0	4.5	2.5	1.0	2.0	1.5
2.0	3.0	2.5	3.0	3.0	3.0	1.5	1.0	1.0
2.5	4.0	3.0	4.5	4.5	4.5	2.0	2.5	2.0
1.0	2.0	1.0	1.5	4.5	3.5	2.0	3.0	2.5
1.5	3.5	2.5	2.5	4.0	3.0	2.5	3.0	2.5
4.0	3.0	3.0	3.0	4.0	3.5	2.0	2.5	2.5
3.0	4.0	3.5	4.0	5.0	5.0	1.0	1.0	1.0
3.5	3.5	3.5				1.0	1.5	1.5
1.0	1.0	1.0				2.0	3.5	2.5
1.0	2.5	2.0						

Run the one-way MANOVA on SPSSX.

a) What is the multivariate null hypothesis? Do you reject it at $\alpha = .05$?

b) If you reject in part (a), then obtain the pairwise multivariate tests using BMDP3D. Which pairs of groups are significantly different at the .05 level?

c) For the pairs of groups which are significantly different, which of the dependent variables are contributing (at the .05 level) to the overall multivariate significance?

2. Consider the following data from Wilkinson (1975):

Group A			Group B			Group C		
5	6	4	2	2	7	4	3	4
6	7	5	3	3	5	6	7	5
6	7	3	4	4	6	3	3	5
4	5	5	3	2	4	5	5	5
5	4	2	2	1	4	5	5	4

a) Run a one-way MANOVA on SPSSX. Do the various multivariate test statistics agree in a decision on H_0?

b) Below are the multivariate (Roy-Bose) and univariate (Scheffe') 95% simultaneous confidence intervals for the 3 variables for the 3 paired comparisons.

Contrast	Variable	Multivariate Intervals	Univariate Intervals
A–B	1	$-.1 \leq 2.4 \leq 4.9$	$.7 \leq 2.4 \leq 4.1$
	2	$-.3 \leq 3.4 \leq 7.1$	$.9 \leq 3.4 \leq 5.6$
	3	$-4.4 \leq -1.4 \leq 1.6$	$-3.4 \leq -1.4 \leq .6$
A–C	1	$-1.9 \leq .6 \leq 3.1$	$-1.1 \leq .6 \leq 2.3$
	2	$-2.5 \leq 1.2 \leq 4.9$	$-1.3 \leq 1.2 \leq 3.7$
	3	$-3.8 \leq -.8 \leq 2.2$	$-2.8 \leq -.8 \leq 1.2$
B–C	1	$-4.3 \leq -1.8 \leq .7$	$-3.5 \leq -1.8 \leq -.1$
	2	$-5.9 \leq -2.2 \leq 1.5$	$-4.7 \leq -2.2 \leq .3$
	3	$-2.4 \leq .6 \leq 3.6$	$-1.4 \leq .6 \leq 2.6$

Note: Estimates of the contrasts are given at the center of the
inequalities.

Comment on the multivariate intervals relative to the decision reached by the test statistics on H_0. Why is the situation different for the univariate intervals?

3. Skilbeck et al. (1984) examined differences among black, Hispanic and white applicants for outpatient therapy, using symptoms reported on the Symptom Checklist 90-revised. They report the following results, having done 12 univariate ANOVAS.

SCL 90-R Ethnicity Main Effects

	Group					
	Black $N = 48$	Hispanic $N = 60$	White $N = 57$			
Dimension	$\bar{x}$	$\bar{x}$	$\bar{x}$	F	df	Significance
Somatization	53.7	53.2	53.7	.03	2,141	ns
Obsessive-Compulsive	48.7	53.9	52.2	2.75	2,141	ns
Interpersonal Sensitivity	47.3	51.3	52.9	4.84	2,141	$p < .01$

Depression	47.5	53.5	53.9	5.44	2,141	$p < .01$
Anxiety	48.5	52.9	52.2	1.86	2,141	ns
Hostility	48.1	54.6	52.4	3.82	2,141	$p < .03$
Phobic Anxiety	49.8	54.2	51.8	2.08	2,141	ns
Paranoid Ideation	51.4	54.7	54.0	1.38	2,141	ns
Psychoticism	52.4	54.6	54.2	.37	2,141	ns
Global Severity Index	49.7	54.4	54.0	2.55	2,141	ns
Positive Symptom						
Distress Index	49.3	55.8	53.2	3.39	2,141	$p < .04$
Positive Symptom Total	50.2	52.9	54.4	1.96	2,141	ns

a) Could we be confident that these results would replicate? Explain.

b) Check the article to see if the authors a priori hypothesized differences on the specific variables for which significance was found.

c) What would have been a better method of analysis?

4.   A researcher is testing the efficacy of 4 drugs in inhibiting undesirable responses in mental patients. Drugs A and B are similar in composition, whereas drugs C and D are distinctly different in composition than A and B, although similar in their basic ingredients. He takes 100 patients and randomly assigns them to 5 gps: gp 1—control, gp 2—drug A, gp 3—drug B, gp 4—drug C, and gp 5—drug D. The following would be 4 very relevant planned comparisons to test:

		Control	Drug A	Drug B	Drug C	Drug D
	1	1	$-.25$	$-.25$	$-.25$	$-.25$
Contrasts	2	0	1	1	-1	-1
	3	0	1	-1	0	0
	4	0	0	0	1	-1

a) Show that these contrasts are orthogonal.

Now, consider the following set of contrasts, which might also be of interest in the above study:

		Control	Drug A	Drug B	Drug C	Drug D
	1	1	$-.25$	$-.25$	$-.25$	$-.25$
Contrasts	2	1	$-.50$	$-.50$	0	0
	3	1	0	0	$-.5$	$-.5$
	4	0	1	1	-1	-1

b) Show that these contrasts are not orthogonal.

c) Since neither of the above 2 sets of contrasts are one of the standard sets that come out of SPSSX MANOVA, it would be necessary to use the special contrast feature to test each set. Show the control lines for doing this for each set. Assume 4 criterion measures.

5. Consider the following three-group MANOVA with two dependent varia-bles. Run the MANOVA on SPSSX. Is it significant at the .05 level? Examine the univariate F's at the .05 level. Are any of them significant? How would you explain this situation?

Gp 1		Gp 2		Gp 3	
y_1	y_2	y_1	y_2	y_1	y_2
3	7	4	5	5	5
4	7	4	6	6	5
5	8	5	7	6	6
5	9	6	7	7	7
6	10	6	8	7	8

6. Consider the following data from a two-group MANOVA with five depend-ent variables. Run the MANOVA. Is it significant at the .05 level? Examine the univariate F's at the .01 level? Are any of them significant? How would you explain this situation?

Variables

	1.0000	7.0000	10.0000	10.0000	17.0000
	1.0000	6.0000	7.0000	6.0000	14.0000
Gp 1	5.0000	3.0000	13.0000	12.0000	20.0000
	7.0000	3.0000	5.0000	6.0000	18.0000
	1.0000	1.0000	7.0000	6.0000	18.0006
	10.0000	13.0000	15.0000	17.0000	10.0000
	12.0000	13.0000	18.0000	12.0000	13.0000
Gp 2	9.0000	13.0000	18.0000	14.0000	10.0000
	10.0000	10.0000	18.0000	13.0000	8.0000
	6.0000	6.0000	11.0000	13.0000	16.0000

7. Show that the within sums of squares and cross products matrices (SSCP) for the sample problem at the beginning of the chapter are

$$W_2 = \begin{bmatrix} 2 & -1 \\ -1 & 2 \end{bmatrix} \text{ and } W_3 = \begin{bmatrix} 6.8 & 2.6 \\ 2.6 & 5.2 \end{bmatrix}$$

8. We have a five-group MANOVA and wish to show through dummy coding of group membership that a multivariate regression analysis will yield the same multivariate F's. Fill in the table below schematically to indicate what the coding would be

	x_1	x_2	x_3	x_4
Group 1 s_1				
s_{n_1}				
Group 2 s_1				
s_{n_2}				
Group 3 $\mathbf{s}_1$				
$\mathbf{s}_{n_3}$				
Group 4 s_1				
s_{n_4}				
Group 5 s_1				
s_{n_5}				

6 Assumptions in MANOVA

6.1. INTRODUCTION

The reader may recall that one of the assumptions in analysis of variance is normality, i.e., the scores for the subjects in each group are normally distributed. Why should we be interested in studying assumptions in ANOVA and MANOVA? Because in ANOVA and MANOVA we set up a mathematical model, based on these assumptions, and all mathematical models are approximations to reality. Therefore, violations of the assumptions are inevitable. The salient question becomes, "How radically must a given assumption be violated before it has a serious effect on type I and type II error rates?" "Thus, we may set our $\alpha = .05$ and think we are rejecting falsely 5% of the time, but if a given assumption is violated, may be rejecting falsely 10%, or if another assumption is violated, may be rejecting falsely 40% of the time. For these kind of situations we would certainly want to be able to detect such violations and take some corrective action. But all violations of assumptions are not serious, and hence it is crucial to know *which* assumptions to be particularly concerned about, and under what conditions.

In this chapter we consider in detail what effect violating the assumptions has on type I error rate and on power. There has been a fairly substantial amount of research on violations of assumptions in MANOVA on which to base conclusions. First, however, we review the assumptions in univariate anova and the consequences of violating them. As we will see, what happens in the univariate case is a pretty good clue as to what happens in the multivariate case. In reviewing the univariate case we cover some basic terminology that is needed to discuss the results of simulation (i.e., Monte Carlo) studies, whether univariate or multivariate.

6.2. REVIEW OF ASSUMPTIONS IN UNIVARIATE ANALYSIS OF VARIANCE

Univariate analysis of variance is based on the following three assumptions:

1. The observations are normally distributed on the dependent variable in each group.
2. The population variances for the groups are equal (homogeneity of variance).
3. The observations are independent.

What has been found regarding violations of assumptions in ANOVA? Glass, Peckham, and Sanders (1972) conducted an excellent review of the literature, and a summary of their conclusions are given in Table 6.1. We remind the reader of what some of the terminology in Table 6.1 means. The nominal α (level of significance) is the level set by the experimenter, and is the percent of time one is rejecting falsely when *all* assumptions are met. The actual α is the percent of time one is rejecting falsely if one or more of the assumptions is violated. Table 6.1 indicates that type I error rate is essentially unaffected by non-normality. We say the F statistic is *robust* with respect to the normality assumption. Robust means that the actual α is very close to the nominal α. For example, the actual α's for some quite non-normal populations were only .055 or .06, very minor deviations from the nominal level of .05.

The reader may be puzzled as to how this can be. The basic reason is the *Central Limit Theorem*, which states that the sum of independent observations having any distribution whatsoever approaches a normal distribution as the number of observations increases. To be somewhat more specific, Bock (1975) notes, "even for distributions which depart markedly from normality, sums of 50 or more observations approximate to normality. For moderately non-normal distributions the approximation is good with as few as 10 to 20 observations" (p. 111). Now, since the sums of independent observations approach normality rapidly, so do the means, and the sampling distribution of F is based on means. Thus, the sampling distribution of F is only slightly affected, and therefore the critical values when sampling from normal and non-normal distributions will not differ by much.

Table 6.1 also indicates that when group sizes are equal, the F statistic is robust against heterogenous variances. We would extend this a bit further. As long as the group sizes are approximately equal (largest/smallest < 1.5), F is robust. On the other hand, when the group sizes are sharply unequal *and* the

TABLE 6.1
Consequences of Violating the Assumptions for Univariate ANOVA

Type of Violation	Equal n's		Unequal n's	
	Effect on α	*Effect on Power*	*Effect on α*	*Effect on Power*
Nonindependence of errors	Nonindependence of errors seriously affects both the level of significance and power of the F-test whether or not n's are equal			
Nonnormality: Skewness	Skewed populations have very little effect on either the level of significance or the power of the fixed-effects model F-test; distortions of nominal significance levels of power values are rarely greater than a few hundredths. (However, skewed populations can seriously affect the level of significance and power of *directional* or "one-tailed" tests.)			
Kurtosis	① Actual α is less than nominal α when populations are leptokurtic (i.e., $\gamma_2 > 0$). Actual α exceeds nominal α for platykurtic populations. (Effects are slight.) ②	Actual power is less than nominal power when populations are platykurtic. Actual power exceeds nominal power when populations are leptokurtic. Effects can be substantial for small n.	Actual α is less than nominal α when populations are leptokurtic (i.e., $\gamma_2 > 0$). Actual α exceeds nominal α for platykurtic populations. (Effects are slight.)	Actual power is less than nominal power when populations are platykurtic. Actual power exceeds nominal power when populations are leptokurtic. Effects can be substantial for small n's.

TABLE 6.1 (*Continued*)
Consequences of Violating the Assumptions for Univariate ANOVA

Type of Violation	Equal n's		Unequal n's	
	Effect on α	*Effect on Power*	*Effect on α*	*Effect on Power*
Heterogeneous	Very slight effect on α, which is seldom distorted by more than a few hundredths. Actual α seems always to be slightly increased over the nominal α.	(No theoretical power value exists when variances are heterogeneous.)	α may be seriously affected. Actual α exceeds nominal α when smaller samples are drawn from more variable populations; actual α is less than nominal α when smaller samples are drawn from less variable populations.	(No theoretical power value exists when variances are heterogeneous.)
Combined nonnormality and heterogeneous variances	Nonnormality and heterogenous variances appear to combine additively ("noninteractively") to affect either level of significance or power. (For example, the depressing effect on α of leptokurtosis could be expected to be counteracted by the elevating effect or α of having drawn smaller samples from the more variable, leptokurtic populations.)			

① Peaked distribution relative to the normal distribution
② Flattened distribution relative to the normal distribution

population variances are different, then if the large sample variances are associated with the small group sizes, the F statistic is liberal. A statistic being liberal means we are rejecting falsely too often, i.e., the actual α > nominal α. Thus, the experimenter may think he is rejecting falsely 5% of time (nominal α), but in fact his true rejection rate may be 11% (actual α). When the large variances are associated with the large group sizes, then the F statistic is conservative. This means the actual α < nominal α. Many researchers would not consider this serious, however, note that the smaller α will cause a decrease in power. And in many studies we can ill afford to have the power further attentuated.

The Independence Assumption

Although we have listed *the independence assumption* last, it *is by far the most important assumption, for even a small violation of it produces a substantial effect on both the level of significance and the power of the* F *statistic.* Just a small amount of dependence among the observations causes the actual α to be several times greater than the nominal α. Dependence among the observations is measured by the intraclass correlation R, where:

$$R = \frac{MS_b - MS_w}{MS_b + (n - 1) MS_w}$$

and MS_b and MS_w are the numerator and denominator from the F statistic and n is the number of subjects per group. Table 6.2 (Barcikowski, 1981) shows precisely how dramatic of an effect dependence has on type I error. For example,

TABLE 6.2
Actual Type I Error Rates for Dependent Observations with Two
Groups and Nominal $\alpha = .05$.*

	\ *Intraclass Correlation*									
	.00	.01	.05	.10	.20	.30	.40	.50	.60	.70
n per group										
10	.05	.06	.11	.17	.28	.37	.46	.53	.61	.68
20	.05	.07	.17	.27	.41	.52	.60	.66	.72	.77
25	.05	.08	.19	.31	.46	.56	.63	.70	.75	.80
30	.05	.08	.22	.34	.50	.59	.66	.72	.77	.81
35	.05	.09	.24	.37	.52	.62	.69	.74	.79	.83
40	.05	.10	.26	.40	.55	.64	.71	.76	.80	.84
50	.05	.11	.30	.44	.59	.68	.74	.78	.82	.86
100	.05	.17	.43	.57	.70	.77	.81	.84	.87	.90

*Dependence among the observations is measured by the intraclass correlation.

for moderate dependence ($n = 30$, intraclass correlation $= .30 \Rightarrow$ actual $\alpha = .59$), while for small dependence ($n = 30$, intraclass correlation $= .10 \Rightarrow$ actual $\alpha = .34$), for nominal $\alpha = .05$: Thus, for very small dependence the actual probability of rejecting falsely is essentially 7 times greater than the experimenter thinks.

Teaching methods studies constitute a broad class of situations where dependence among the observations is undoubtedly present. For example, a few troublemakers in a classroom would have a detrimental effect on the achievement of many children in the classroom. Thus, their posttest achievement would be at least partially dependent on the disruptive classroom atmosphere. On the other hand, even in a good classroom atmosphere, dependence is introduced, for the achievement of many of the children will be enhanced by the positive learning situation. Therefore, in either case (positive or negative classroom atmosphere), the achievement of the children is not independent of the other children in the classroom.

Another situation I came across recently in which dependence among the observations was present was a study comparing the achievement of the students working in pairs at microcomputers vs. students working in groups of three at the micros. Here, if Bill and John are working at the same microcomputer, then obviously Bill's achievement is partially influenced by John. The proper unit of analysis in this study is the *mean* achievement for each pair and triplet of students, as it is plausible to assume that the achievement of students on one micro is independent of the students working at the other micros.

Glass and Hopkins (1984) make the following statement concerning situations where independence may or may not be tenable, "Whenever the treatment is individually administered, observations are independent. But where treatments involve interaction among persons, such as "discussion" method or group counseling, the observations may influence each other" (p. 353).

As a final example of dependence, we consider an industrial example. Suppose we were interested in comparing how far a part being produced by two machines is from an ideal diameter. If one (or both) machines started "drifting" systematically high (missing tolerance), then the observations will be serially correlated. Thus, a t test comparing the two machines would be inappropriate as the dependence would very seriously inflate the type I error rate.

We are emphasizing the independence assumption here because of the serious effect it has on error rates, and because a violation of it is equally serious in MANOVA, although we do not discuss it again. It is important for the reader to distinguish the dependence that is naturally present in MANOVA from the independence we are focusing on here. The dependence refers to the correlations among the subjects scores on the dependent variables, i.e., within each subject we expect their scores to be related on the dependent variables. The independence assumption says there is no dependence *across* subjects. Thus, although we expect Bill's scores on three measures of achievement to be related, we do not want Bill's achievement scores to be influenced by John who is in the same treatment group.

In summary, then, univariate ANOVA is robust against non-normality for type I error, and for power with skewed distributions. It is also robust against heterogeneous variances if the group sizes are equal or approximately equal. In contrast, both type I error and power are seriously affected if the independence assumption is violated.

Group Mean as the Unit of Analysis

Using the group mean as the unit of analysis, rather than the individual subject scores, does not cause as drastic a loss in power as some have feared. The reason is that the means are much more stable than individual observations and hence the within variability will be far less, even though the effective n will be much smaller. Table 6.3 from Barcikowski (1981) shows if effect size is medium or large that the number of groups needed per treatment for power $\geq$ .80 doesn't

TABLE 6.3
Number of Groups per Treatment Necessary for Power $\geq$ .80 in a
Two Treatment Level Design

				Intraclass Correlation			
			.10			.20	
Effect Size		.20	.50	.80	.20	.50	.80*
α level	Number per group						
	10	73	13	6	107	18	8
	15	62	11	5	97	17	8
	20	56	10	5	92	16	7
.05	25	53	10	5	89	16	7
	30	51	9	5	87	15	7
	35	49	9	5	86	15	7
	40	48	9	5	85	15	7
	10	57	10	5	83	14	7
	15	48	9	4	76	13	6
	20	44	8	4	72	13	6
.10	25	41	8	4	69	12	6
	30	39	7	4	68	12	6
	35	38	7	4	67	12	5
	40	37	7	4	66	12	5

*.20—small effect size
.50—medium effect size
.80—large effect size.

have to be that large. For example, at $\alpha = .10$, intraclass correlation $= .10$ and medium effect size, only 8 groups (of 20 entities each) are needed per treatment. Or, at $\alpha = .05$, intraclass correlation $= .20$ and large effect size, only 7 groups (of 20 entities each) are needed per treatment.

Barcikowski (1981) indicates that a value for the intraclass correlation around .20 is reasonable in the case where students are assigned to groups based on no strong criterion. His tables cover a wide range of intraclass correlation values (from .01 to .80), small, medium, and large effect sizes, and significance levels of .01, .05, and .10.

6.3.   MULTIVARIATE ANALYSIS OF VARIANCE ASSUMPTIONS

The assumptions in MANOVA are:

1. The observations on the p dependent variables follow a multivariate normal distribution in each group.
2. The population covariance matrices for the p dependent variables in each group are equal.
3. The observations are independent.

Since we have already emphasized how important the independence assumption is, we focus our attention on the first two assumptions. The multivariate normality assumption is a much more stringent assumption than the corresponding assumption of normality on a single variable in univariate ANOVA. Although it is difficult to completely characterize multivariate normality, *normality on each of the variables separately is a necessary but not sufficient condition for multivariate normality to hold.* That is, each of the individual variables must be normally distributed, plus more, for the variables to follow a multivariate normal distribution. A couple of other properties of a multivariate normal distribution are: (1) any linear combination of the variables will be normally distributed, and (2) all subsets of the set of variables will have a multivariate normal distribution. This latter property implies, among other things, that all pairs of variables must be bivariate normal. Bivariate normality, for correlated variables, implies that the scatterplots for each pair of variables will be elliptical; the higher the correlation the thinner the ellipse. Thus, as a partial check on multivariate normality, one could obtain the scatterplots for pairs of variables from SPSSX or BMDP and see if they are approximately elliptical. For two variables, a graph of the bivariate normal distribution somewhat resembles a "Texan Hat." Two bivariate normal distributions (from Johnson & Wichern, 1982) are given in Figure 6.1. We give procedures for assessing multivariate and univariate normality, but first

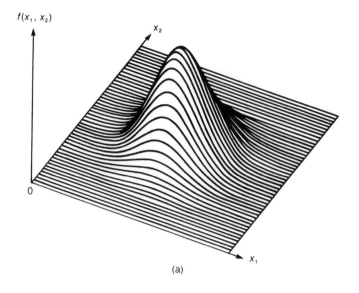

(a)

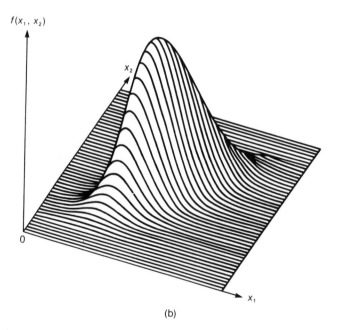

(b)

FIG. 6.1. Two Bivariate Normal Distributions. (a) Equal variances on uncorrelated variables x_1 and x_2. (b) Equal variances with a correlation of .75 between x_1 and x_2.

we briefly review what effect lack of multivariate normality has on type I error and power.

6.4. EFFECT OF NON-MULTIVARIATE NORMALITY ON TYPE I ERROR AND POWER

Results from various studies that considered up to 10 variables and small or moderate sample sizes (Everitt, 1979; Hopkins & Clay, 1963; Mardia, 1971; Olson, 1973) indicate that *deviation from multivariate normality has only a small effect on type I error*. In almost all cases in these studies the actual α was within .02 of the nominal α (the value the experimenter thinks he is working at) for nominal α's of .05 and .10.

Olson found, however, that platykurtosis does have an effect on power, and the severity of the effect increases as platykurtosis spreads from one to all groups. For example, in one specific instance power was close to 1 under no violation. With kurtosis present in just one group the power dropped to about .90. When kurtosis was present in all 3 groups, the power dropped substantially to .55.

The reader should note that what has been found in MANOVA is consistent with what had been found in univariate ANOVA, in which the F statistic was robust with respect to type I error against non-normality, making it plausible that this robustness might extend to the multivariate case, and this indeed is what has been found. Incidentally, there is a multivariate extension of the Central Limit Theorem which also makes the multivariate results not entirely surprising. Secondly, the Olson result of platykurtosis having a substantial effect on power should not be surprising, given that platykurtosis had been shown in univariate ANOVA to have a substantial effect on power for small n (cf. Table 6.1).

With respect to skewness, Table 6.1 indicates that distortions of power values are rarely greater than a few hundreths for univariate ANOVA, even with considerably skewed distributions. Thus, it could well be the case that multivariate skewness also has a negligible effect on power, although this writer has not located any studies bearing on this issue.

6.5. A GRAPHICAL TEST FOR MULTIVARIATE NORMALITY

There are several empirical and graphical techniques available for checking multivariate normality (Gnanedesikan, 1977, pp. 168–175), however, they tend to be difficult to implement unless a special purpose program is written. And, unfortunately, none of the major statistical packages (SPSSX, BMDP or SAS) have a test of multivariate normality. Mardia (1974) has developed multivariate measures of skewness and kurtosis, however, critical values are not available for more than two variables, which severely limits their utility.

The graphical test we propose is based on the Mahalanobis distances for the subjects in each group, and involves plotting these distances against chi-square percentiles. The reason the test is fairly easily implemented is that the distances can be readily obtained from the BMDP7M (Stepwise Discriminant Analysis) program. We now examine the details for the test. First, the Mahalanobis distance for each subject j is given by:

$$D_j^2 = (\mathbf{x}_j - \bar{\mathbf{x}})' \mathbf{S}^{-1} (\mathbf{x}_j - \bar{\mathbf{x}}),$$

where $\mathbf{x}_j$ is the vector of scores for the jth subject, $\bar{\mathbf{x}}$ is the vector of means for the variables, and $\mathbf{S}$ is the covariance matrix. When the population is multivariate normal and both N and $N - p$ are greater than about 25, each of the Mahalanobis distances should behave like a chisquare variable (Johnson & Wichern, 1982). Therefore, we construct for each group a chi-square plot as follows:

1. The distances are ordered from smallest to largest as

$$D_{(1)}{}^2, D_{(2)}{}^2, \ldots, D_{(N)}{}^2$$

2. Then we graph the pairs $(D)_{(j)}{}^2$, $\chi_p^2 ((j - .5)/N)$, where the χ^2 is the $100(j - .5)/n$ percentile of the chi-square distribution with p degrees of freedom.

The plot for each group should resemble a straight line if the population is multivariate normal.

General use of this test requires extensive chi-square percentile points, essentially for each percentile from 1 to 99. The chi-square percentiles found in textbooks and journals fall far short of what is needed. For the reader's convenience, we have computed the appropriate χ^2 values in Table 6 at the end of this book for 3 through 8 variables and for group sizes ranging from 20 to 30. These tables cover a fair range of situations encountered in practice. For $n >$ 30, the appropriate χ^2 values can be obtained by interpolating between the χ^2 percentile points given in Table 6, or by obtaining the values from the SAS package. To illustrate the use of our tables, suppose an investigator had a 4 variable problem with 28 cases in a given group, and wished to determine whether multivariate normality was tenable for that group. Referring to Table 6 at the end of this volume we move across to the column headed $n = 28$ and the subcolumn headed $p = 4$. The appropriate χ^2 values are then read off as: .43, .71, .99, 1.24, etc.

Example 1

To illustrate the use of the graphical test, we consider a sample of data from a study by Pope, Lehrer, & Stevens (1980). Children in kindergarten were measured with various instruments to determine whether they could be classified as low risk or high risk with respect to having reading problems five years later. The children were measured in the fifth grade on the word identification, word comprehension, and passage comprehension subtests of the Woodcock reading test. Thus, there were two groups and three dependent variables, with 26 cases in the low risk group and 12 cases in the high risk group. The raw data, along with the Mahalanobis distances (from BMDP7M) for the low and high risk groups, are presented in Table 6.4.

We have done the plot only for the low risk group, since only there is the

TABLE 6.4
Data and Mahalanobis Distances for Low and High Risk Groups*

Low Risk			High Risk			Unordered Distances	
WI	WC	PC	WI	WC	PC	Low Risk	High Risk
5.8	9.7	8.9	2.4	2.1	2.4	6.8	2.0
10.6	10.9	11.0	3.5	1.8	3.9	6.5	.6
8.6	7.2	8.7	6.7	3.6	5.9	2.8	3.1
4.8	4.6	6.2	5.3	3.3	6.1	1.7	1.8
8.3	10.6	7.8	5.2	4.1	6.4	3.2	1.6
4.6	3.3	4.7	3.2	2.7	4.0	2.4	.2
4.8	3.7	6.4	4.5	4.9	5.7	3.5	.7
6.7	6.0	7.2	3.9	4.7	4.7	.8	.7
7.1	8.4	8.4	4.0	3.6	2.9	1.4	3.0
6.2	3.0	4.3	5.7	5.5	6.2	6.3	.9
4.2	5.3	4.2	2.4	2.9	3.2	2.5	1.3
6.9	9.7	7.2	2.7	2.6	4.1	2.3	.7
5.6	4.1	4.3				3.4	
4.8	3.8	5.3				1.7	
2.9	3.7	4.2				3.3	
6.1	7.1	8.1				2.4	
12.5	11.2	8.9				13.5	
5.2	9.3	6.2				4.6	
5.7	10.3	5.5				8.8	
6.0	5.7	5.4				1.0	
5.2	7.7	6.9				1.8	
7.2	5.8	6.7				1.2	
8.1	7.1	8.1				1.5	
3.3	3.0	4.9				3.6	
7.6	7.7	6.2				2.1	
7.7	9.7	8.9				2.2	

*The control lines for obtaining the Mahalanobis distances are given in Table 7.5 on p. 252.

Ordered Distances	Chi-Square Value
.8	.19
1.0	.40
1.2	.58
1.4	.75
1.5	.87
1.7	1.04
1.7	1.21
1.8	1.38
2.1	1.56
2.2	1.69
2.3	1.87
2.4	2.07
2.4	2.27
2.5	2.49
2.8	2.72
3.2	2.95
3.3	3.17
3.4	3.45
3.5	3.77
3.6	4.16
4.6	4.54
6.3	5.13
6.5	5.60
6.8	6.25
8.8	7.50
13.5	9.84

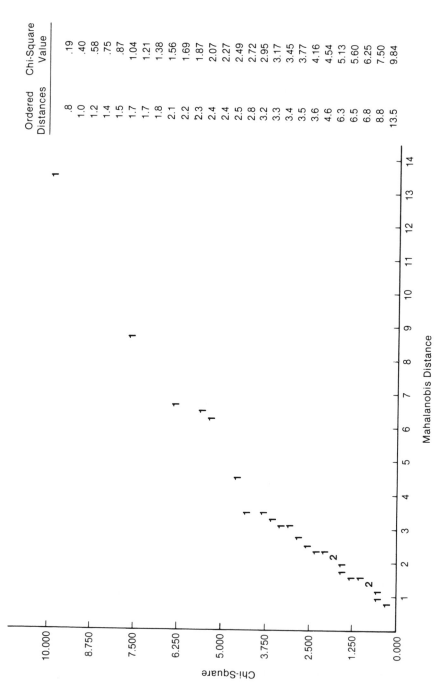

FIG. 6.2. Plot Check for Multivariate Normality

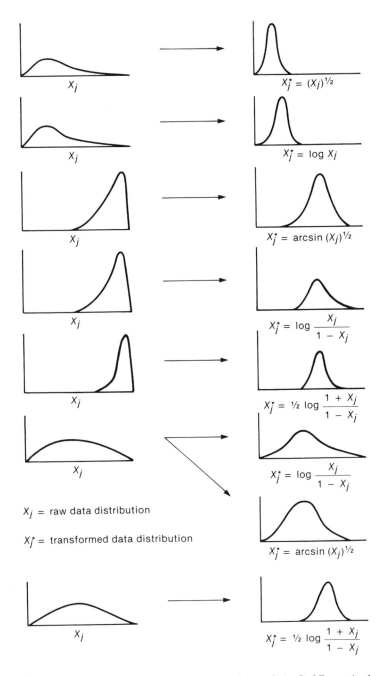

FIG. 6.3. Distributional Transformations. (From Rummel, *Applied Factor Analysis*, 1970).

group size adequate. In Figure 6.2 we present the ordered distances along with the corresponding chi-square percentiles (from Table G) and the plot. The plot resembles a straight line quite well, so that the assumption of multivariate normality for the low risk group is tenable.

If the multivariate graphical plots show systematic curvature, and subjective judgement is required here, then some corrective action is needed. Daniel and Wood (1971) present many "training" probability plots for the univariate normal case. Examination of these will give the reader a lower bound as to how much random variation might be expected even when normality is present.

When systematic curvature is found, then one might examine the shewness and kurtosis coefficients of the individual variables to detect specific types of departure from normality. We show the reader how this is done in the next section. Then distributional transformations can be employed where needed (cf. Figure 6.3). After transformations are completed, the multivariate graphical test can be reapplied to determine whether multivariate normality is then tenable.

Finally since N (group size) and $N - p$ should be greater than about 25 for the distances to behave like a chi-square variable, the reader should treat a multivariate graphical test on an N of 20 with 3 or 4 variables as somewhat rough.

6.6.   ASSESSING UNIVARIATE NORMALITY

There are three reasons why assessing univariate normality is of interest:

1.   We may not have a large enough n to feel comfortable doing the graphical test for multivariate normality.
2.   As Gnanadesikan (1977) stated, "In practice, except for rare or pathological examples, the presence of joint (multivariate) normality is likely to be detected quite often by methods directed at studying the marginal (univariate) normality of the observations on each variable (p. 168).
3.   Since the Box test for the homogeneity of covariance matrices is quite sensitive to non-normality, we wish to detect non-normality on the individual variables and transform to normality to bring the joint distribution much closer to multivariate normality so that the Box test is not unduely affected.

Now, there are many tests, graphical and non-graphical, for assessing univariate normality. One of the most popular graphical tests is the normal probability plot, where the observations are arranged in increasing order of magnitude and then plotted against expected normal distribution values. The plot should resemble a straight line if normality is tenable. These normal probability plots are available in BMDP5D, and are illustrated in Bock (1975) and in Johnson and Wichern (1982). Another graphical procedure is to simply examine the histogram for each dependent variable in each group, which can be obtained with BMDP7D. This does give some indication whether normality might be violated. However, with small or moderate sample size, it is difficult to tell whether the nonnormality is real or apparent, because of considerable sampling error. Although the normal probability plot has value, we prefer a non-graphical test.

Among the non-graphical tests are the chi-square goodness of fit, Kolmogorov-Smirnov, the Shapiro-Wilk test, and the use of the skewness and kurtosis coefficients. The chi-square test suffers from the defect of depending on the number of intervals used for the grouping, whereas the Kolmogorov-Smirnov test was shown not to be as powerful as the Shapiro-Wilk test or the combination of using the skewness and kurtosis coefficients in an extensive Monte Carlo study by Wilk, Shapiro, and Chen (1968). These investigators studied 44 different distributions, with sample sizes ranging from 10 to 50, and found that the combination of using skewness and kurtosis coefficients and the Shapiro-Wilk test were the most powerful in detecting departures from normality. They also found that extreme non-normality can be detected, with sensitive procedures (like the two just mentioned), with sample sizes of less than 20. This is important, since in many practical problems the group sizes are quite small.

On power considerations then, one could defend using either the Shapiro-Wilk statistic or the combination of skewness and kurtosis coefficients. We prefer using the skewness and kurtosis coefficients because we wish to separate out these two types of non-normality, whereas the Shapiro-Wilk statistic combines them. The reason we wish to separate them out is because kurtosis has been shown in both the univariate and multivariate cases to have an effect on power, whereas skewness has been shown not to effect power (at least in the univariate case). Thus, we would be more worried about violations due to kurtosis, especially platykurtosis. For those, however, who may still wish to use the Shapiro-Wilk statistic, it is available on the SAS statistical package in their UNIVARIATE procedure.

We now give an example to illustrate how to obtain the skewness and kurtosis coefficients for each group, and how to test them for significance.

Example 2

Consider a three-group problem having 3 dependent variables, with 15 subjects in each of the first two groups and 30 subjects in the third group. The skewness and kurtosis values for the variables in each group were obtained using the BMDPAM program: (with following control lines)

BMDPAM Control Lines

```
/PROBLEM TITLE IS 'OBTAINING SKEWNESS AND KURTOSIS FOR 3 VARS '.
/INPUT VARIABLES ARE 4. FORMAT IS STREAM.
/VARIABLE NAMES ARE GPID, VAR1,VAR2,VAR3. GROUPING IS GPID.
/GROUP CODES(1) ARE 1,2,3. NAMES(1) ARE GP1,GP2,GP3.
/END
```

The critical values needed for testing the skewness and kurtosis values (given below) for significance are presented in Table 6.5. Also, it is necessary to add 3 to each kurtosis value from the BMDPAM program *before* using Table 6.5, because of the formula used by the program. These values are in parenthesis:

Variable	Group 1 (15)		Group 2 (15)		Group 3 (30)	
	Skewness	Kurtosis	Skewness	Kurtosis	Skewness	Kurtosis
1	.68	1.4 (4.4)	1.14	1.1 (4.1)	.56	.70(3.7)
2	.20	−1.2(1.8)	.11	−.83(2.17)	.43	−1.80(1.2)
3	1.61	.42(3.42)	1.87	.85(3.85)	1.31	.31(3.31)

Now, in performing two tests for each variable in each group, even for a small number of variables (3 here) and small number of groups (3 here), the total number of tests is 18. Thus, it is advisable to do each test at a more stringent alpha level (.01) to keep the overall type I error rate (i.e., the probability of at least one false rejection) somewhat under control. For example, overall $\alpha <$ .18, which is still somewhat high. Therefore, a few rejections should not be of concern unless a priori non-normality had been strongly suspected on those variables.

We now proceed to the testing. The critical value for skewness at $\alpha = .01$ and $n = 15$ is 1.462 (cf. Table 6.5). Thus, only variable 3 is positively skewed in groups 1 and 2. Now, turning to group 3, the critical value for $n = 30$ is 1.114, and therefore variable 3 is also positively skewed in group 3. Referring to Figure 6.3, we find that either the square root or log transformations will normalize variable 3.

For kurtosis in groups 1 and 2, we need to distinguish between platykurtosis and leptokurtosis. The critical value for platykurtosis is 1.55; thus if the value of kurtosis is *less than* 1.55 we conclude platykurtosis exists. This is not the case for any of the variables in groups 1 or 2. The critical value for leptokurtosis in groups 1 and 2 is 5.3; thus if the value of kurtosis is greater than 5.3 we conclude the variable is leptokurtic. Once again, this is not the case for any of the variables. For group 3 ($n = 30$) the critical value for platykurtosis is 1.79, so that variable 2 is platykurtotic (since $1.2 < 1.79$). None of the variables in group 3 are leptokurtotic since the kurtosis values don't exceed the critical value of 5.21. We are not concerned about the platykurtosis here for two reasons. First, it only occurs on one variable in one group and hence wouldn't have much of an effect on power. Secondly, it could be a spurious result, since overall α is fairly high. On the other hand, if we had found platykurtosis on two variables in 2 or more groups, then we would have been concerned and would have applied the last transformation in Figure 6.3, i. e., $\frac{1}{2} \log \frac{1 + x}{1 - x}$.

TABLE 6.5
Critical Values for Skewness and Kurtosis for Small Sample Sizes
(From D'Agostino & Tietjen, 1971, 1973)

Sample Size	SKEWNESS (s_k) Two tailed test					
	0.20	0.10	0.05	0.02	0.01	0.002
5	0.819	1.058	1.212	1.342	1.396	1.466
6	0.805	1.034	1.238	1.415	1.498	1.642
7	0.787	1.008	1.215	1.432	1.576	1.800
8	0.760	0.991	1.202	1.455	1.601	1.873
9	0.752	0.977	1.189	1.408	1.577	1.866
10	0.722	0.950	1.157	1.397	1.505	1.887
11	0.715	0.929	1.129	1.376	1.540	1.924
13	0.688	0.902	1.099	1.312	1.441	1.783
15	0.648	0.862	1.048	1.275	1.462	1.778
17	0.629	0.820	1.009	1.188	1.358	1.705
20	0.593	0.777	0.951	1.152	1.303	1.614
23	0.562	0.743	0.900	1.119	1.276	1.555
25	0.543	0.714	0.876	1.073	1.218	1.468
30	0.510	0.664	0.804	0.985	1.114	1.410
35	0.474	0.624	0.762	0.932	1.043	1.332

For larger sample size (N), significance is determined by using the following as a unit normal deviate:
$z_1 = s_k\sqrt{(N + 1)(N + 3)/6(N - 2)}$

Sample Size	KURTOSIS (k_r) Percentiles											
	1	2	2–5	5	10	20	80	90	95	97–5	98	99
7	1.25	1.30	1.34	1.41	1.53	1.70	2.78	3.20	3.55	3.85	3.93	4.23
8	1.31	1.37	1.40	1.46	1.58	1.75	2.84	3.31	3.70	4.09	4.20	4.53
9	1.35	1.42	1.45	1.53	1.63	1.80	2.98	3.43	3.86	4.28	4.41	4.82
10	1.39	1.45	1.49	1.56	1.68	1.85	3.01	3.53	3.95	4.40	4.55	5.00
12	1.46	1.52	1.56	1.64	1.76	1.93	3.06	3.55	4.05	4.56	4.73	5.20
15	1.55	1.61	1.64	1.72	1.84	2.01	3.13	3.62	4.13	4.66	4.85	5.30
20	1.65	1.71	1.74	1.82	1.95	2.13	3.21	3.68	4.17	4.68	4.87	5.36
25	1.72	1.79	1.83	1.91	2.03	2.20	3.23	3.68	4.16	4.65	4.82	5.30
30	1.79	1.86	1.90	1.98	2.10	2.26	3.25	3.68	4.11	4.59	4.75	5.21
35	1.84	1.91	1.95	2.03	2.14	2.31	3.27	3.68	4.10	4.53	4.68	5.13
40	1.89	1.96	1.98	2.07	2.19	2.34	3.28	3.67	4.06	4.46	4.61	5.04
45	1.93	2.00	2.03	2.11	2.22	2.37	3.28	3.65	4.00	4.39	4.52	4.94
50	1.95	2.03	2.06	2.15	2.25	2.41	3.28	3.62	3.99	4.33	4.45	4.96

NOTE: Recall that Kurtosis = 3 for a normal distribution. Values > 3 indicate Leptokurtosis (peaked distribution), whereas value < 3 indicate Platykurtosis (flattened distribution). In larger sample size, significance is determined by using as unit normal deviate:

$$z_2 = \{k_r - 3 + 6/(N + 1)\}\sqrt{(N + 1)^2 (N + 3)(N + 5)/24N(N - 2)(N - 3)}$$

6.7. THE HOMOGENEITY OF COVARIANCE MATRICES ASSUMPTION

The assumption of equal (homogeneous) covariance matrices is a very restrictive one. Recall from the matrix algebra chapter that two matrices are equal only if all corresponding elements are equal. Let us consider a two-group problem with 5 dependent variables.

All corresponding elements in the two matrices being equal implies first that the corresponding diagonal elements (which represent the variances for the variables) are equal, i.e., $\sigma_{1(1)}^2 = \sigma_{1(2)}^2$, $\sigma_{2(1)}^2 = \sigma_{2(2)}^2$, . . . , $\sigma_{5(1)}^2 = \sigma_{5(2)}^2$. The number in parentheses refers to the group. Thus, $\sigma_{1(1)}^2$ is the population variance for variable 1 in group 1. Since there are 10 covariances for 5 variables, the equal covariance matrices assumption also implies that the 10 covariances in group 1 are equal to the corresponding 10 covariances in group 2. Thus, for only 5 variables the equal covariance matrices assumption requires that 15 elements of group 1 are equal to their counterparts in group 2. For 8 variables the assumptions would imply that the 8 population variances in group 1 are equal to their counterparts in group 2 *and* that the 28 corresponding covariances in the two matrices are also equal. The restrictiveness of the assumption becomes more strikingly apparent when we realize that the corresponding assumption for the univariate *t* test is that the variances on only a single variable are equal.

Hence, it is very unlikely that the equal covariance matrices assumption would ever literally be satisfied in practice. The relevant question is, "Will the very plausible violations of this assumption that occur in practice have much of an effect on error rates?"

6.8. EFFECT OF HETEROGENEOUS COVARIANCE MATRICES ON TYPE I ERROR AND POWER

There have been three major Monte Carlo studies that have examined the effect of unequal covariance matrices on error rates: Holloway and Dunn (1967) and Hakstian, Roed, and Linn (1979) for the two-group case, and Olson (1974) for the k group case. Holloway and Dunn considered both equal and unequal group size, and modeled moderate to extreme heterogeneity. A representative sampling of their results, presented in Table 6.6, shows that *equal n keeps the actual* α *very close to the nominal (within a few percentage points) for all but the extreme cases.* Sharply unequal group size, for moderate inequality, with the larger variability in the small group size produces a liberal test. As a matter of fact, the test can become very liberal (cf. 3 variables, $N_1 = 35$, $N_2 = 15$, actual $\alpha = .175$). Larger variability in the group with the large group size produces a conservative test.

TABLE 6.6
Effect of Heterogeneous Covariance Matrices on Type I Error for
Hotelling's T^2 (Data from Holloway & Dunn, 1967)   ①

Number of Variables	Number of Observations per Group			Degree of Heterogeneity	
	N_1	N_2 ②	③	$D = 3$ (Moderate)	$D = 10$ (Very Large)
3	15	35		.015	0
3	20	30		.03	.02
3	25	25		.055	.07
3	30	20		.09	.15
3	35	15		.175	.28
7	15	35		.01	0
7	20	30		.03	.02
7	25	25		.06	.08
7	30	20		.13	.27
7	35	15		.24	.40
10	15	35		.01	0
10	20	30		.03	.03
10	25	25		.08	.12
10	30	20		.17	.33
10	35	15		.31	.40

①Nominal α = .05.
②Group 2 is more variable.
③D = 3 means that the population variances for all variables in Group 2 are 3 times as large as the population variances for those variables in Group 1.

Hakstian et al. modeled heterogeneity that was milder (and we believe somewhat more realistic of what is encountered in practice) than that considered in the Holloway and Dunn study. They also considered more disparate group sizes (up to a ratio of 5 to 1) for the 2, 6 and 10 variable cases. The following three heterogeneity conditions were examined:

1. The population variances for the variables in population 2 are only 1.44 times as great as those for the variables in population 1.
2. The population 2 variances and covariances are 2.25 times as great as those for all variables in population 1.
3. The population 2 variances and covariances are 2.25 times as great as those for population 1 for only *half* the variables.

The results in Table 6.7 for the six variable case are representative of what Hakstian et al found. Their results are consistent with the Holloway and Dunn

TABLE 6.7
Effect of Heterogeneous Covariance Matrices with Six Variables on
Type I Error for Hotelling's T^2
(Data from Hakstian, Roed, and Lind, 1979)

$N_1 : N_2$①	Nominal α	Heterog. 1		Heterog. 2		Heterog. 3	
		②POS.	NEG.	POS.	NEG.	POS.	NEG.③
18 : 18	.01	.006		.011		.012	
	.05	.048		.057		.064	
	.10	.099		.109		.114	
24 : 12	.01	.007	.020	.005	.043	.006	.018
	.05	.035	.088	.021	.127	.028	.076
	.10	.068	.155	.051	.214	.072	.158
30 : 6	.01	.004	.036	.000	.103	.003	.046
	.05	.018	.117	.004	.249	.022	.145
	.10	.045	.202	.012	.358	.046	.231

①Ratio of the group sizes.
②Condition in which group with larger generalized variance has larger group size.
③Condition in which group with larger generalized variance has smaller group size.

findings, but extend them in two ways. First, even for milder heterogeneity, sharply unequal group sizes can produce sizable distortions in type I error rate (cf. 24:12, Heterogeneity 2 (negative): actual α = .127 vs. nominal α = .05). Secondly, *severely unequal group sizes can produce sizable distortions in type I error rates even for very mild heterogeneity* (cf. 30:6, Heterogeneity 1 (negative): actual α = .117 vs. nominal α = .05).

The Olson study considered only equal *n*, warning on the basis of the Holloway and Dunn results and some preliminary findings of his own that researchers would be well advised to strain to attain equal group size in the *k* group case. The results of Olson's study should be interpreted with care, since he modeled primarily extreme heterogeneity, i.e., cases where the population variances of all variables in one group are 36 times as great as the variances of those variables in all other groups.

Table 6.8, from Holloway and Dunn (1967), shows that small heterogeneity does have an effect on power, even for *equal* group sizes. For example, for 2 variables, 25 subjects per group and $v^* = 1$, the power was .86 under no heterogeneity. Under small heterogeneity in the above situation the power dropped to .77. While this is not a drastic drop in power, it is large enough to be of some concern, especially since larger heterogeneity will produce a more substantial drop in power. To illustrate, we use the power value for the extreme case (.26) and interpolate for $D = 3$ (a case which could reasonably occur in practice). This yields a further power loss of about .09. Thus, the estimated

TABLE 6.8
Power of Hotelling's T^2 at $\alpha = .05$ Under Covariance Inequality

Number of Variables	Group Sizes	Small Heterogeneity (D = 1.5)				Very Large Heterogeneity (D = 10)			
		①$v = .5$	1	1.5	2.0	.5	1	1.5	2.0
2	$n_1 = 30, n_2 = 20$	.27	.79	.94	.99	.20	.34	.60	.79
2	$n_1 = n_2 = 25$	.23	.77	.94	.99	.15	.26	.52	.74
2	$n_1 = n_2 = 25$	(3.7)	(.86)	(.97)	(≈1)②				
2	$n_1 = 20, n_2 = 30$	.18	.74	.92	.98	.07	.15	.40	.66
3	$n_1 = 30, n_2 = 20$	.28	.73	.92	1	.20	.28	.59	.77
3	$n_1 = n_2 = 25$	.28	.71	.90	1	.12	.23	.46	.68
3	$n_1 = n_2 = 25$	(.33)	(.80)	(.95)	(≈1)				
3	$n_1 = 20, n_2 = 30$	.24	.68	.88	1	.05	.12	.32	.56
7	$n_1 = 30, n_2 = 20$	.17	.59	.94	1	.30	.36	.58	.73
7	$n_1 = n_2 = 25$	.15	.53	.92	1	.12	.18	.40	.57
7	$n_1 = n_2 = 25$	(.22)	(.64)	(.96)	(≈1)				
7	$n_1 = 20, n_2 = 30$	.12	.46	.88	1	.03	.07	.18	.30

①$v^2 = (\mu_1 - \mu_2)' \Sigma^{-1}(\mu_1 - \mu_2)$ – Mahalanobis distance.
②Values in parentheses are power under no heterogeneity, i.e., $D = 1$.

power for $D = 3$, $v* = 1$ is .68, a drop of almost .20 from the power (.86) under no heterogeneity.

6.9. TESTING THE HOMOGENEITY OF COVARIANCE MATRICES ASSUMPTION—THE BOX TEST

Box (1950) has developed a test, which is a generalization of the Bartlett univariate homogeneity of variance test, for determining whether the covariance matrices are equal. The test uses the generalized variances, i.e., the determinants of the within covariance matrices. It is very sensitive to non-normality; thus one may reject with Box test because of a lack of multivariate normality, not because covariance matrices are different. Therefore, *before* employing the Box test, it is important to check the tenability of the multivariate normality assumption using the graphical test we mentioned earlier, if the group size is at least 20. If the group size is smaller than 20, then use the skewness and kurtosis coefficients to determine of which (if any) of the individual variables there is departure from normality. Where there is departure find transformations (using Figure 6.3) to normality.

Box has given a χ^2 approximation and an F approximation for his test statistic, both of which appear on the SPSSX MANOVA output, as an example in the next section shows. The details for calculating both approximations are considerable, and so are given in Appendix A of this chapter. However, many readers will not be interested in all the numerical details, but will want to know when they should pay more attention to the χ^2 approximation, and when the F approximation will be more accurate. When all group sizes are greater than 20 *and* the number of dependent variables < 6 *and* the number of groups is < 6, then the χ^2 approximation is fine. Otherwise, the F approximation is more accurate and should be used.

Example 3

We consider again the Pope data used earlier in this chapter. Recall that there were two groups and three dependent variables, with 26 subjects in the high risk group and 12 subjects in the low risk group. Since the group sizes are sharply unequal ($26/12 > 1.5$), a violation of the homogeneity of covariance matrices assumption will throw the type I error rate off substantially. The control lines for running the analysis are given in Table 6.9. It is in the PRINT subcommand that we obtain the multivariate (Box test) and the univariate tests of homogeneity of variance. The F statistic for Box's test is given in Table 6.10 ($F = 2.11$, $p < .049$). This indicates at $\alpha = .05$ that the homogeneity of covariance matrices assumption is not tenable. Now, we wish to determine whether the multivariate test statistics will be liberal or conservative. To determine this we examine the determinants of the covariance matrices (they are called variance-covariance matrices on the printout). Recall that the determinant of the covariance matrix

TABLE 6.9
SPSSX Control Lines for Sample MANOVA Problem

```
TITLE ' TWO GP MANOVA—CHECKING FOR EQUAL COVARIANCE MATRICES'
DATA LIST FREE/ WI,WC,PC,TREATS
LIST
BEGIN DATA

DATA LINES

END DATA
MANOVA WI,WC,PC BY TREATS(1,2)/
   PRINT = CELLINFO(MEANS,COV,COR) HOMOGENEITY(COCHRAN,BOXM)/
```

Note: By inserting PLOT = CELLPLOT, after the PRINT command, we could obtain a plot of the cell means vs. cell standard deviations. However, it is better to use BMDP7D (1981, version), since it gives not only a plot of the cell means vs. cell standard deviations but also the log of standard deviations vs. log of cell means, along with the regression equation for this plot. The slope (B) of this regression, which is given on the printout, is then used to transform the data. The transformation is simply to raise the dependent variable to the power $(1 - B)$. This transformation will produce approximately equal variances (1981 BMDP Manual, pp. 111–112).

is the generalized variance, i.e., it is the multivariate measure of within-group variability for a set of variables. We note that the generalized variances for the two groups are quite different ($|S_1| = 19.11$ and $|S_2| = .799$), and that the large variability is associated with the large group size. Therefore, the multivariate statistics will be conservative. Since significance was found for treatments ($F = 5.603, p < .003$), the violation here is not of concern, for we would have found signficance at an even more stringent level had the assumption been satisfied.

We now consider two variations on the above results where a violation would have been of concern. If the large generalized variance had been with the small group size, then since the multivariate statistics will be liberal, it wouldn't be clear whether the significance was due to treatments or to the test statistics being liberal. In this case three courses of action are possible. The simplest is merely to test at a more conservative α level, say .01, realizing that the effective α level will be around .05. Another course of action is to isolate which specific variable(s) (using the Cochran tests on the printout) were involved in partially causing the different generalized variances, and attempt to find variance stabilizing transformations for those variables. A third possibility involves a multivariate generalization of Welch's approximate univariate t solution, due to Yao (1965). It is described in Timm (1975, pp. 262–263).

The second variation on the example results that would have been of concern is if the large generalized variance was with the large group size and treatments was *not* significant. Then it wouldn't be clear whether the reason we did not find significance was because of the conservativeness of the test statistic. In this case we could simply test at a more liberal α level, once again realizing that the effective α level will probably be around .05. Or, we could again seek variance-stabilizing transformations.

TABLE 6.10
Selected Output from SPSSX MANOVA for Sample Problem

UNIVARIATE HOMOGENEITY OF VARIANCE TESTS

VARIABLE .. WI
   COCHRANS C(18.2) =   .70236, P = .038 (APPROX.)
   BARTLETT—BOX F(1,2539) =   2.39138, P = .122

VARIABLE .. WC
   COCHRANS C(18.2) =   .84923, P = .000 (APPROX.)
   BARTLETT—BOX F(1,2539) =   8.33321, P = .004

VARIABLE .. PC
   COCHRANS C(18.2) =   .62612, P = .142 (APPROX.)
   BARTLETT—BOX F(1,2539) =   .91148, P = .340

CELL NUMBER .. 1

DETERMINANT OF VARIANCE-COVARIANCE MATRIX =   19.11042
LOG(DETERMINANT) = →   2.95023

MULTIVARIATE GENERALIZATION
OF WITHIN CELL VARIABILITY

TABLE 6.10 (Continued)
Selected Output from SPSSX MANOVA for Sample Problem

CELL NUMBER .. 2

DETERMINANT OF VARIANCE-COVARIANCE MATRIX = .79995
LOG(DETERMINANT) = -.22317

DETERMINANT OF POOLED VARIANCE-COVARIANCE MATRIX 10.77800
LOG(DETERMINANT) = -2.33751

MULTIVARIATE TEST FOR HOMOGENEITY OF DISPERSION MATRICES

BOXS M = 14.28933
F WITH (6.2993) DF = 2.11070, P = .049 (APPROX.)
CHI-SQUARE WITH 6 DF = 12.69285, P = .048 (APPROX.)

EFFECT .. TREATS

MULTIVARIATE TESTS OF SIGNIFICANCE (S = 1, M = 1/2, N = 16)

TEST NAME	VALUE	APPROX. F	HYPOTH. DF	ERROR DF	SIG. OF F
PILLAIS	.33083	5.60300	3.00	34.00	.003
HOTELLINGS	.49438	5.60300	3.00	34.00	.003
WILKS	.66017	5.60300	3.00	34.00	.003

With respect to transformations, there are two possible approaches. If there is a known relationship between the means and the variances, then the following two transformations are helpful. The square root transformation, where the original scores are replaced by $\sqrt{y_{ij}}$, will stabilize the variances if the means and variances are proportional for each group. This can happen when the data is in the form of frequency counts. If the scores are proportions, then the means and variances are related as follows: $\sigma_i^2 = \mu_i (1 - \mu_i)$. This is true because with proportions we have a binomial variable, and for a binomial variable the variance is the above function of it's mean (Meyer, 1965). The arc sine transformation, where the original scores are replaced by arc sin $\sqrt{y_{ij}}$, will stabilize the variances in this case.

If the relationship between the means and variances is not known, then one can let the data decide on an appropriate transformation. In this regard, the note in Table 6.9 is very helpful.

Example 4

Consider the following three-group, two-dependent variable data set:

	Gp 1		Gp 2		Gp 3	
	y_1	y_2	y_1	y_2	y_1	y_2
	.30	5.00	5.00	4.00	14.00	5.00
	3.50	4.00	9.00	5.00	18.00	8.00
	1.10	4.00	5.00	3.00	9.00	10.00
	4.30	7.00	11.00	6.00	21.00	2.00
	5.10	8.00	12.00	6.00	20.00	2.00
	1.90	7.00	5.00	3.00	12.00	2.00
	1.90	6.00	8.00	3.00	16.00	6.00
	2.70	4.00	10.00	4.00	15.00	4.00
	4.30	4.00	13.00	4.00	23.00	9.00
	5.90	7.00	7.00	2.00	12.00	5.00
$\bar{y}$'s	3.1	5.6	8.5	4.0	16	5.3
s^2	3.31	2.49	8.94	1.78	20	8.68

Note that for y_1 as the means increase (from group 1 to group 3) the variances also increase. Also, the ratio of variance to mean is approximately the same for the three groups: $3.31/3.1 = 1.068$, $8.94/8.5 = 1.052$, and $20/16 = 1.25$. Also, the variances for y_2 differ by a fair amount. Thus, it is likely here that the homogeneity of covariance matrices assumption is not tenable. Indeed, when the MANOVA was run on SPSSX the Box test was significant at .05 level ($F = 2.947$, $p < .007$), and the Cochran univariate tests for both variables were also significant at the .05 level (y_1: Cochran $= .62$; y_2: Cochran $= .67$).

Since the means and variances for y_1 were approximately proportional, as mentioned earlier, a square root transformation will stabilize the variances. The control lines for running MANOVA on SPSSX, with the square root transformation on y_1, is given in Table 6.11, along with selected output. A few comments on the control lines. It is in the COMPUTE command that we do the transformation, calling the transformed variable RTY1. We then use the transformed

TABLE 6.11
SPSSX Control Lines for Three Group MANOVA with Unequal
Variances
(Illustrating Square Root Transformation)

```
TITLE 'THREE GROUP MANOVA—TRANSFORMATION ON Y1'.
DATA LIST FREE/ GPID, Y1,Y2
BEGIN DATA

    DATA

END DATA
COMPUTE RTY1 = SQRT(Y1)
LIST
MANOVA RTY1 Y2 BY GPID(1,3)/
   PRINT = CELLINFO(MEANS,COV,COR) HOMOGENEITY(COCHRAN,BOXM)/
```

CELL MEANS AND STANDARD DEVIATIONS

VARIABLE ... RTY 1

FACTOR	CODE	MEAN	STD. DEV.
GPID	1	1.67019	.58732
GPID	2	2.87309	.52210
GPID	3	3.96360	.56750
FOR ENTIRE SAMPLE		2.83563	1.09507

VARIABLE .. Y2

FACTOR	CODE	MEAN	STD. DEV.
GPID	1	5.60000	1.57762
GPID	2	4.00000	1.33333
GPID	3	5.30000	2.94581
FOR ENTIRE SAMPLE		4.96667	2.12511

UNIVARIATE HOMOGENEITY OF VARIANCE TESTS

VARIABLE .. RTY1

COCHRANS C(9.3) =   .36712,

BARTLETT—BOX F(2.1640) =   .06176   p = .940

VARIABLE .. Y2

COCHRANS C(9.3.) =   .67039

BARTLETT—BOX F(2,1640) =   3.17413,   P = .042

BOXS M =   12.47224
F WITH (6.18158) DF =   1.85561,   P = .084 (APPROX.)

CHI SQUARE WITH 6 DF =   11.13777,   P = .084 (APPROX.)

variable RTY1, along with Y2, in the MANOVA command for the analysis. Note the stabilizing effect of the square root transformation on y_1; the standard deviations are now approximately equal (.587, .522, and .567). Also, Box's test is no longer significant ($F = 1.86, p < .084$).

Many other standard transformations such as log, arc sine, can be done as well as complicated transformations, like

$$\frac{1}{2} \log \frac{1 + x}{1 - x}$$

(see SPSSX User's Guide, 1983, pp. 87–93). To run the above analysis on BMDP4V, we would simply insert the TRANSFORM paragraph:

TRANSFORM Y1 = SQRT(Y1)./

See the BMDP manual (1983, pp. 50–55) for information on use of transformations with this package.

6.10.   GENERAL PROCEDURE FOR ASSESSING VIOLATIONS IN MANOVA

We have considered each of the assumptions in MANOVA in some detail individually. Now, we wish to tie together the pieces of information gathered into an overall strategy for assessing assumptions in a practical problem. The flow chart in Figure 6.4 gives an overview of the sequence of decisions to be made and the order in which they should be carried out. In the following, we present verbally much of what is embodied in Figure 6.4, and add some detail.

1. Check to determine whether it is reasonable to assume the subjects are responding independently, as a violation of this assumption is most serious. Logically, from the context in which subjects are receiving treatments, one should be able to make a judgment. Empirically, the intraclass correlation can be used (for a single variable) to assess whether this assumption is tenable. If there is evidence of dependence, then consider using the group mean as the unit of analysis. For example, the classroom means in a teaching methods study, or the small group means in a social psychological study which is investigating different modes of group interaction.

2. Check for multivariate normality using the graphical test described in this chapter, if the group size is adequate (i.e., at least 20). If sample size is not adequate, then check the individual variables for normality using either the normal probability plots, the Shapiro-Wilk statistic, or the combination of skewness and kurtosis coefficients. Transform to normalize where significant deviations from normality are found. Figure 6.3 is helpful here.

3. Apply Box's test to check the assumption of homogeneity of the covariance

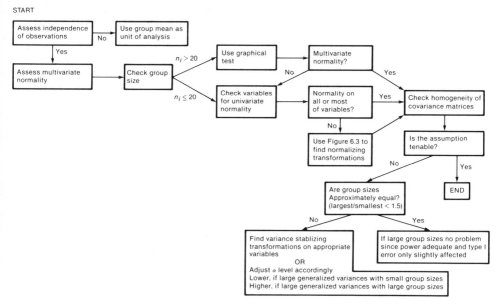

FIG. 6.4. Flow Chart for Assessing Assumptions in MANOVA.

matrices. If in step 2 normality has been achieved on all or most of the variables, then Box's test should be a "clean" test of variance differences. If the Box test is not significant, then all is fine.

4. If the Box test is significant with equal n, then although the type I error rate will be only slightly affected, power will be attenuated to some extent. Hence, look for transformations on the variables that are causing the covariance matrices to differ.

5. If the Box test is significant with sharply unequal n for two groups, then compare the determinants of $\mathbf{S}_1$ and $\mathbf{S}_2$ (the generalized variances for the two groups). If the larger generalized variance is with the smaller group size, then T^2 will be liberal. If the larger generalized variance is with the larger group size, then T^2 will be conservative.

For the k group case, if the Box test is significant, examine the $|\mathbf{S}_i|$ for the groups. If the generalized variances are largest for the groups with the smaller sample sizes, then the multivariate test statistics will be liberal. If the generalized variances are largest for the groups with the larger group sizes, then the statistics will be conservative. It is possible for the k group case that neither of the above two conditions hold. For example, for 3 groups it could happen that the groups with both the smallest and the largest sample sizes both have large generalized variances, with the remaining group variance somewhat smaller. In this case, however, the effect of heterogeneity should not be serious, since the liberal and conservative tendencies co-existing should have somewhat of a cancelling out effect.

Finally, since there are several test statistics in the k group MANOVA case, the relative robustness of them to violations of assumptions could be a criterion for preferring one over the others. In this regard, Olson (1976) argued in favor of the Pillai-Bartlett trace because of it's presumed greater robustness against heterogeneous covariance matrices. For variance differences *likely to occur in practice*, however, Stevens (1979) found that the Pillai-Bartlett trace, Wilk's Λ, and the Hotelling-Lawley trace are essentially equally robust.

APPENDIX
BOX TEST FOR POPE DATA (EXAMPLE 3)

We define the general Box test (for k groups) in parts, and show how the printout in Table 6.10 can be used to obtain each part, and finally both the χ^2 and F approximations.

Let N be total sample size, k be the number of groups, and $v_i = n_i - 1$, i.e., the degrees of freedom for each group. We denote the ith covariance matrix by S_i and the pooled within group estimate of the covariance matrix by S. Then Box's M, which appears on the SPSSX printout in Table 6.10, is defined as:

$$M = (N - k) \, 1n|S| - \sum_{i=1}^{k} v_i \, 1n|S_i|$$

Now, $1n|S_1|$ (log of the determinant of the covariance matrix for group 1), $1n|S_2|$, and $1n|S|$ are given on the printout in Table 6.10. Using these we can easily evaluate M as:

$$M = (38 - 2)(2.3775) - [25(2.9502) + 11(-.22317)] = 14.289$$

Now we define C as follows:

$$C = \frac{2p^2 + 3p - 1}{6(p + 1)(k - 1)} \left(\sum_{i=1}^{k} 1/v_i - 1/(N - k) \right)$$

For the Pope data this is:

$$C = \frac{2(9) + 3(3) - 1}{6(4)(1)} \left[\frac{1}{25} + \frac{1}{11} - \frac{1}{36} \right] = .1117$$

Then Box showed that for sufficiently large $n_i(n_i \geq 20)$ that $M(1 - C)$ is approximately distributed as χ^2 with $v = \dfrac{p(p + 1)(k - 1)}{2}$ d.f. From the above calculations then, $M(1 - C) = 14.289 (1 - .1117) = 12.6929$, which is the value given in Table 6.10, with 6 df. The df is obtained by plugging into $v = \dfrac{p\,(p + 1)(k - 1)}{2} = \dfrac{3(4)(1)}{2} = 6$.

F Approximation

To obtain the F approximation still further calculations are necessary. We define C_0 as

$$C_0 = \frac{(p - 1)(p + 2)}{6(k - 1)}\left[\sum_{i=1}^{k} \frac{1}{v_i^2} - \frac{1}{(N - k)^2}\right]$$

and $v_0 = \dfrac{v + 2}{C_0 - C^2}$.

Then $F = (1 - C - v/v_0)/v$, with v and v_0 df.

Now, $C_0 = \dfrac{2(5)}{6(1)}\left[\dfrac{1}{25^2} + \dfrac{1}{11^2} - \dfrac{1}{36^2}\right] = .0152$

and $v_0 = \dfrac{6 + 2}{.0152 - .1117^2} = 2963$

$$F = \frac{1 - .1117 - 6/2963}{6} = 2.115$$

This F value agrees with that on printout on Table 6.10 within rounding error.

EXERCISES—CHAPTER 6

1. Describe a situation or class of situations where dependence of the observations would be present.

2. An investigator has a treatment vs. control group design with 30 subjects per group. The intraclass correlation is calculated and found to be .15. If testing for significance at .05, estimate what the actual type I error rate is.

3. Consider a 4-group, three dependent variable study. What does the homogeneity of covariance matrices assumption imply in this case?

4. The following covariance matrices are obtained from a two-group study with two dependent variables:

$$\frac{\text{Gp 1 } (n_1 = 41)}{S_1 = \begin{bmatrix} 10 & 3 \\ 3 & 4 \end{bmatrix}} \quad \frac{\text{Gp 2 } (n_2 = 21)}{S_2 = \begin{bmatrix} 2 & 1 \\ 1 & 16 \end{bmatrix}}$$

It might appear that we have a problem here, since the covariance matrices are not equal and the groups sizes are sharply unequal.

a) Compute the determinants of S_1 and S_2, which represent the generalized within group variances for the two groups. Given these results do you think we still have a problem?

5. Consider the following three MANOVA situations. Indicate whether you would be concerned in each case.

a)

Gp 1	Gp 2	Gp 3
$n_1 = 15$	$n_2 = 15$	$n_3 = 15$
$|S_1| = 1.4$	$|S_2| = 18.6$	$|S_3| = 5.9$

Multivariate test for homogeneity of dispersion matrices

$$F = 2.98, p = .027$$

b)

Gp 1	Gp 2
$n_1 = 21$	$n_2 = 57$
$|S_1| = 14.6$	$|S_2| = 2.4$

Multivariate test for homogeneity of dispersion matrices

$$F = 4.82, p = .008$$

c)

Gp 1	Gp 2	Gp 3	Gp 4
$n_1 = 20$	$n_2 = 15$	$n = 40$	$n_4 = 29$
$|S_1| = 42.8$	$|S_2| = 20.1$	$|S_3| = 50.2$	$|S_4| = 15.6$

Multivariate test for homogeneity of dispersion matrices

$$F = 3.79, p = .014$$

6. Consider the data from exercise 4 in Chapter 7, excluding the coast variable.

a) Use the graphical test for multivariate normality to see whether it is tenable for either of the two groups of states.

b) If multivariate normality is not tenable, then which of the transformations in Figure 6.3 might be used to achieve multivariate normality?

7. a) Test the univariate normality of each of the variables in Exercise 1 from

Chapter 5 using the skewness and kurtosis coefficients obtained from running the data on BMDPAM. Use $\alpha = .01$ for each test. Are there any significant departures from normality? If so, make appropriate transformations.

b) Test the homogeneity of covariance matrices assumption. Are you concerned about testing this assumption here because of type I or type II error? Is the Box test significant at the .05 level?

8. Zwick (1984) collected data on incoming clients at a mental health center who were randomly assigned to either an oriented group, which saw a videotape describing the goals and processes of psychotherapy, or a control group. She presents the following data on measures of anxiety, depression, and anger that were collected in a one month follow-up:

Scores			Scores		
Anxiety	Depression	Anger	Anxiety	Depression	Anger
Oriented group ($n_1 = 20$)			Control group ($n_2 = 26$)		
285	325	165	168	190	160
23	45	15	277	230	63
40	85	18	153	80	29
215	307	60	306	440	105
110	110	50	252	350	175
65	105	24	143	205	42
43	160	44	69	55	10
120	180	80	177	195	75
250	335	185	73	57	32
14	20	3	81	120	7
0	15	5	63	63	0
5	23	12	64	53	35
75	303	95	88	125	21
27	113	40	132	225	9
30	25	28	122	60	38
183	175	100	309	355	135
47	117	46	147	135	83
385	520	23	223	300	30
83	95	26	217	235	130
87	27	2	74	67	20
			258	185	115
			239	445	145
			78	40	48
			70	50	55
			188	165	87
			157	330	67

a) Apply the multivariate graphical test to each group to determine whether multivariate normality is tenable in each group.

b) If multivariate normality is not tenable, then what transformations are suggested?

7 Discriminant Analysis

7.1. INTRODUCTION

Discriminant analysis is used for two purposes: (1) describing major differences among the groups in MANOVA, and (2) classifying subjects into groups on the basis of a battery of measurements. Since this text is heavily focused on multivariate tests of group differences, more space is devoted in this chapter to what is called by some descriptive discriminant analysis. We also discuss the use of discriminant analysis for classifying subjects, limiting our attention to the two-group case. The SPSSX package is used for the descriptive discriminant example, and BMDP7M (stepwise discriminant analysis) is used for the classification problem. We also illustrate how to use BMDP7M for randomly splitting the sample and cross-validating the classification function.

7.2. DESCRIPTIVE DISCRIMINANT ANALYSIS

Discriminant analysis is used here to break down the total between association in MANOVA into *additive* pieces, through the use of uncorrelated linear combinations of the original variables (these are the discriminant functions). An additive breakdown is obtained because the discriminant functions are derived to be uncorrelated.

Discriminant analysis has two very nice features: (1) parsimony of description, and (2) clarity of interpretation. It can be quite parsimonious in that in comparing 5 groups on say 10 variables, we may find that the groups differ mainly on only two major dimensions, i.e., the discriminant functions. It has a clarity of interpretation in the sense that separation of the groups along one function is unrelated to separation along a different function. This is all fine, *provided* we can meaningfully name the discriminant functions and that there is adequate sample size so that the results are generalizable.

Recall that in multiple regression we found the linear combination of the predictors that was maximally correlated with the dependent variable. Here in discriminant analysis linear combinations are again used to distinguish the groups. Continuing through the text, it becomes clear that linear combinations are central to many forms of multivariate analysis.

An example of the use of discriminant analysis, which is discussed in complete detail later in this chapter, involved National Merit scholars who were classified in terms of their parents education, from eighth grade or less up to one or more college degrees, yielding four groups. The dependent variables were eight Vocational Personality variables (realistic, conventional, enterprising, sociability, etc.). The major personality differences among the scholars were revealed in one linear combination of variables (the first discriminant function), and showed that the two groups of scholars whose parents had more education were less conventional and more enterprising than the scholars whose parents had less education.

Before we begin a detailed discussion of discriminant analysis, it is important to note that discriminant analysis is a *mathematical maximization* procedure. What is being maximized is made clear shortly. The important thing to keep in mind is that anytime this type of procedure is employed there is a tremendous opportunity for capitalization on chance, especially if the number of subjects is *not large* relative to the number of variables. That is, the results found on one sample may well not replicate on another independent sample. Multiple regression, it will be recalled, was another example of a mathematical maximization procedure. Since discriminant analysis is formally equivalent to multiple regression for two groups (Stevens, 1972), we might expect a similar problem with replicability of results. And indeed, as we see later, this is the case.

If the dependent variables are denoted by $y_1, y_2, \ldots, y_p$, then in discriminant analysis the row vector of coefficients $\mathbf{a}_1'$ is sought which maximizes $\mathbf{a}_1'\mathbf{B}\,\mathbf{a}_1/\mathbf{a}_1'\mathbf{W}\,\mathbf{a}_1$, where $\mathbf{B}$ and $\mathbf{W}$ are the between and the within sum of squares and cross-products matrices. The linear combination of the dependent variables involving the elements of $\mathbf{a}_1'$ as coefficients is the best discriminant function, in that it provides for maximum separation on the groups. Note that both the numerator and denominator in the above quotient are both scalars (numbers). Thus, the procedure finds the linear combination of the dependent variables which maximizes between to within association. The above quotient corresponds to the largest eigenvalue (ϕ_1) of the $\mathbf{BW}^{-1}$ matrix. The next best discriminant, corresponding to the second largest eigenvalue of $\mathbf{BW}^{-1}$, call it ϕ_2, involves the elements of $\mathbf{a}_2'$ in the following ratio: $\mathbf{a}_2'\mathbf{Ba}_2/\mathbf{a}_2'\mathbf{Wa}_2$, as coefficients. This function is derived to be *uncorrelated* with the first discriminant function. It is the next best discriminator among the groups, in terms of separating on them. The third discriminant function would be a linear combination of the dependent variables, derived to be uncorrelated from both the first and second functions, which provides the next maximum amount of separation, etc. The ith discriminant function (z_i) then is given by $z_i = \mathbf{a}_i'\mathbf{y}$, where $\mathbf{y}$ is the column vector of dependent variables.

If k is the number of groups and p is the number of dependent variables, then the number of possible discriminant functions is the minimum of p and $(k - 1)$. Thus, if there were 4 groups and 10 dependent variables, there would be 3 discriminant functions. For 2 groups, no matter how many dependent variables, there will only be one discriminant function. Finally, in obtaining the discriminant functions the coefficients (the a_i) are scaled so that $\mathbf{a}_i'\,\mathbf{a}_i = 1$ for each discriminant function (the so called unit norm condition). This is done so that there is a unique solution for each discriminant function.

7.3. SIGNIFICANCE TESTS

First, it can be shown that Wilk's Λ may be expressed as the following function of eigenvalues (ϕ_i) of $\mathbf{BW}^{-1}$ (Tatsuoka, 1971, p. 164):

$$\Lambda = \frac{1}{1 + \phi_1} \frac{1}{1 + \phi_2} \cdots \frac{1}{1 + \phi_r},$$

where r is the number of possible discriminant functions.

Now, Bartlett showed that the following V statistic can be used for testing the significance of Λ:

$$V = [N - 1 - (p + k)/2] \cdot \sum_{i=1}^{r} \ln (1 + \phi_i),$$

where V is approximately distributed as a χ^2 with $p(k - 1)$ degrees of freedom.

The test procedure for determining how many of the discriminant functions are significant is a residual procedure. First, all of the eigenvalues (roots) are tested together, using the above V statistic. If this is significant, then the largest root (corresponding to the first discriminant function) is removed and a test made of the remaining roots (the first residual) to determine if this is significant. If the first residual (V_1) is not significant, then we conclude that only the first discriminant function is significant. If the first residual is significant, then we examine the second residual, i.e., the V statistic with the largest two roots removed. If the second residual is not significant, then we conclude that only the first two discriminant functions are significant, etc. In general then, when the residual after removing the first s roots is not significant, we conclude that only the first s discriminant functions are significant.

We illustrate this residual test procedure below, also giving the degrees of freedom for each test, for the case of four possible discriminant functions. The constant term, i.e., the term in brackets, is denoted by C for the sake of conciseness.

Residual Test Procedure For Four Possible Discriminant Functions

Name	Test Statistic	df
V	$C \sum_{i=1}^{4} \ln (1 + \phi_i)$	$p(k - 1)$
V_1	$C[\ln (1 + \phi_2) + \ln (1 + \phi_3) + \ln (1 + \phi_4)]$	$(p - 1)(k - 2)$
V_2	$C[\ln (1 + \phi_3) + \ln (1 + \phi_4)]$	$(p - 2)(k - 3)$
V_3	$C[\ln (1 + \phi_4)]$	$(p - 3)(k - 4)$

The general formula for the degrees of freedom for the rth residual is $(p - r)(k - (r + 1))$.

7.4.   INTERPRETING THE DISCRIMINANT FUNCTIONS

There are two methods that are in use for interpreting the discriminant functions:

1.   Examine the standardized coefficients—these are obtained by multiplying the raw coefficient for each variable by the standard deviation for that variable.
2.   Examine the discriminant function—variable correlations, i.e., the correlations between each discriminant function and each of the original variables.

For both of these methods it is the largest (in absolute value) coefficients or correlations that are used for interpretation. It should be noted that the above two methods can give different results, i.e., some variables may have low coefficients and high correlations while other variables may have high coefficients and low correlations. This raises the question of which to use.

Meredith (1964), Porebski (1966) and Darlington, Weinberg, and Walberg (1973) have argued in favor of using the discriminant function—variable correlations for two reasons: (1) the assumed greater stability of the correlations in small- or medium-sized samples, especially when there are high or fairly high intercorrelations among the variables, and (2) the correlations give a direct indication of which variables are most closely aligned with the unobserved trait which the canonical variate (discriminant function) represents. On the other hand, the coefficients are partial coefficients, with the effects of the other variables removed.

Incidentally, the use of discriminant function–variable correlations for interpretation is parallel to what is done in factor analysis, where factor–variable correlations (the so called factor loadings) are used to interpret the factors.

Two Monte Carlo studies (Barcikowski & Stevens, 1975; Huberty, 1975) indicate that unless sample size is large, relative to the number of variables, both the standardized coefficients and the correlations are very unstable. That is, the results obtained in one sample (e.g., interpreting the first discriminant function using variables 3 and 5) will very likely not hold up in another sample from the same population. *The clear implication of both studies is that unless the N (total sample size)/ p (number of variables) ratio is quite large, say 20 to 1, one should be very cautious in interpreting the results.* This is saying, for example, that if there are 10 variables in a discriminant analysis, at least 200 subjects are needed for the investigator to have confidence that the variables he selects as most important in interpreting the discriminant function would again show up as most important in another sample.

Now, given that one has enough subjects to have confidence in the reliability of the index he chooses to use, which should be used? It seems that the following suggestion of Tatsuoka (1973), is very reasonable, "Both approaches are useful, provided we keep their different objectives in mind" (p. 280). That is, use the correlations for substantive interpretation of the discriminant functions, but use the coefficients to determine which of the variables are redundant given that others are in the set. This approach is illustrated in an example later in the chapter.

7.5.   GRAPHING THE GROUPS IN THE DISCRIMINANT PLANE

If there are 2 or more significant discriminant functions, then a useful device for determining directional differences among the groups is to graph them in the discriminant plane. The horizontal direction corresponds to the first discriminant function and thus lateral separation among the groups indicates how much they have been distinguished on this function. The vertical dimension corresponds to the second discriminant function and thus vertical separation tells us which groups are being distinguished in a way unrelated to the way they were separated on the first discriminant function (since the discriminant functions are uncorrelated). Since the functions are uncorrelated, it is quite possible for two groups to differ very little on the first discriminant function and yet show a large separation on the second function.

Since each of the discriminant functions is a linear combination of the original variables, the question arises as to how we determine the mean coordinates of the groups on these linear combinations. Fortunately the answer is quite simple since it can be shown that the mean for a linear combination is equal to the linear combination of the means on the original variables. That is,

$$\bar{z}_1 = a_{11}\bar{x}_1 + a_{12}\bar{x}_2 + \cdots + a_{1p}\bar{x}_p,$$

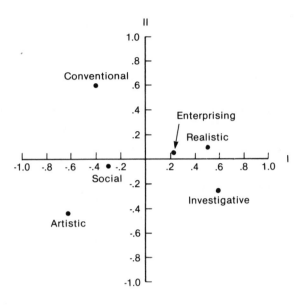

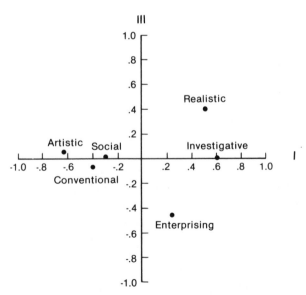

FIG. 7.1. Position of Groups for Holland's Model in Discriminant Planes Defined by Functions 1 & 2 and by Functions 1 & 3

where z_1 is the discriminant function and the x_i are the original variables.

The matrix equation for obtaining the coordinates of the groups on the discriminant functions is given by:

$$\mathbf{Z} = \overline{\mathbf{X}} \, V,$$

where $\overline{\mathbf{X}}$ is the matrix of means for the original variables in the various groups and V is a matrix whose *columns* are the raw coefficients for the discriminant functions (the first column for the first function, etc.). To make this more concrete we consider the case of three groups and four variables. Then the matrix equation becomes:

$$_3\mathbf{Z}_2 = \,_3\overline{\mathbf{X}}_4 \,_4\mathbf{V}_2$$

The specific elements of the matrices would be as follows:

$$\begin{bmatrix} z_{11} & z_{12} \\ z_{21} & z_{22} \\ z_{31} & z_{32} \end{bmatrix} = \begin{bmatrix} \overline{x}_{11} & \overline{x}_{12} & \overline{x}_{13} & \overline{x}_{14} \\ \overline{x}_{21} & \overline{x}_{22} & \overline{x}_{23} & \overline{x}_{24} \\ \overline{x}_{31} & \overline{x}_{32} & \overline{x}_{33} & \overline{x}_{34} \end{bmatrix} \begin{bmatrix} a_{11} & a_{12} \\ a_{21} & a_{22} \\ a_{31} & a_{32} \\ a_{41} & a_{42} \end{bmatrix}$$

In the above equation $\overline{x}_{11}$ gives the mean for variable 1 in group 1, $\overline{x}_{12}$ the mean for variable 2 in group 1, etc. The first row of Z gives the "x" and "y" coordinates of group 1 on the two discriminant functions, the second row gives the location of group 2 in the discriminant plane, etc.

The location of the groups on the discriminant functions appears in all 3 examples from the literature that we present in this chapter. For plots of the groups in the plane, see the Smart study later in this chapter, and specifically Figure 7.1.

Example 1

The data for the example was extracted from the National Merit file (Stevens, 1972). The classification variable was the educational level of both parents of the National Merit scholars. Four groups were formed: (1) those students for whom at least one of their parents had an eighth grade education or less ($n = 90$), (2) those students both of whose parents were high school graduates ($n = 104$), (3) those students both of whose parents had gone to college, with at most one graduating ($n = 115$), and (4) those students both of whose parents had at least one college degree ($n = 75$). The dependent variables, or those we are attempting to predict from the above grouping, were a subset of the Vocational Personality Inventory (VPI): realistic, intellectual, social, conventional, enterprising, artistic, status and aggression.

In Table 7.1 we present the SPSSX control lines necessary to run the DISCRIMINANT program, along with some descriptive statistics, i.e., the means and the correlation matrix for the VPI variables. Many of the correlations are

TABLE 7.1
Control Lines and Selected Output from SPSSX for Discriminant Analysis

```
TITLE 'DISCRIMINANT ANALYSIS ON NATIONAL MERIT DATA— 4 GPS— N=384 '.
DATA LIST FREE/ EDUC REAL INTELL SOCIAL CONVEN ENTERP ARTIS STATUS AGGRESS
LIST
BEGIN DATA

   DATA

END DATA
DISCRIMINANT GROUPS = EDUC(1,4)/         ①
   VARIABLES = REAL TO AGGRESS/

OUTPUT
```

POOLED WITHIN-GROUPS CORRELATION MATRIX

	REAL	INTELL	SOCIAL	CONVEN	ENTERP	ARTIS	STATUS	AGGRESS
REAL	1.00000							
INTELL	0.44541	1.00000						
SOCIAL	0.04860	0.24193	1.00000					
CONVEN	0.32733	0.06629	0.23716	1.00000				
ENTERP	0.35377	0.10396	0.35573	0.54567	1.00000			
ARTIS	.04639	0.23030	0.48143	0.13472	0.37977	1.00000		
STATUS	−0.32954	0.06541	0.38498	0.14731	0.28262	0.40873	1.00000	
AGGRESS	0.32066	0.31931	0.49830	0.32698	0.58887	0.50353	0.43702	1.00000

GROUP MEANS

EDUC	REAL	INTELL	SOCIAL	CONVEN	ENTERP	ARTIS	STATUS	AGGRESS
1	2.35556	4.88889	5.73333	2.64444	2.63333	4.45556	8.67778	5.20000
2	2.01923	4.78846	5.42308	2.32692	2.89423	4.06731	8.41346	5.06731
3	1.96522	5.12174	5.25217	1.91304	3.63478	5.20000	8.92174	5.19130
4	1.44000	4.53333	5.10667	1.29333	2.84000	5.08000	9.08000	4.61333
TOTAL	1.96875	4.86198	5.38261	2.07552	3.04427	4.69531	8.80469	5.04688

①The GROUPS and VARIABLES subcommands are the only subcommands required for running a standard discriminant analysis. There are various other options available, such as a varimax rotation to increase interpretability, and several different types of stepwise discriminant analysis.

TABLE 7.2

Tests of Significance for Discriminant Functions, Discriminant Function—Variable Correlations and Standardized Coefficients

$$73.64\% = \frac{\text{EIGENVALUE}}{\text{SUM OF EIGENVALUES}} \times 100 = \frac{.1097}{.1489} \times 100$$

CANONICAL DISCRIMINANT FUNCTIONS

FUNCTION	EIGENVALUE OF BW^{-1}	PERCENT OF VARIANCE	CUMULATIVE PERCENT	CANONICAL CORRELATION	:	AFTER FUNCTION	WILKS' LAMBDA	CHI-SQUARED	D.F.	SIGNIFICANCE
1*	0.10970	73.64	73.64	0.3144148	:	0	0.8666342	53.876	24	0.0004
2*	0.02871	19.27	92.91	0.1670684	:	1	0.9619271	14.634	14	0.4036
3*	0.01056	7.09	100.00	0.1022387	:	2	0.9895472	3.9614	6	0.4819

*MARKS THE 3 CANONICAL DISCRIMINANT FUNCTION(S) TO BE USED IN THE REMAINING ANALYSIS

STANDARDIZED CANONICAL DISCRIMINANT FUNCTION COEFFICIENTS

	FUNC 1	FUNC 2	FUNC 3
REAL	0.33567	0.92803	0.55970
INTELL	-0.24881	-0.42593	0.18729
SOCIAL	0.36854	0.01669	-0.21222
CONVEN	0.79971	-0.19960	0.33530
ENTERP	-1.07691	-0.66618	0.39790
ARTIS	-0.32335	0.41416	0.20551
STATUS	-0.05005	1.13509	0.38153
AGGRESS	0.41918	-0.55000	-0.27073

RESIDUAL TEST PROCEDURE

Let ϕ_1, ϕ_2, etc denote the eigenvalues of BW^{-1}.

$$\chi^2 = [(N - 1) - (p + k)/2]\sum ln(1 + \phi_i)$$

$$\chi^2 = [(384 - 1) - (8 + 4)/2][ln(1 + .11) + ln(1 + .029) + ln(1 + .0106)];$$

$$\chi^2 = 377(.1429) = 53.88, df = p(k - 1) = 8(3) = 24$$

FIRST RESIDUAL: $\chi_1^2 = 377 [ln(1.029) + ln(1.0106)] = 14.64, df = (p - 1)(k - 2) = 14$

SECOND RESIDUAL: $\chi_2^2 = 377 \, ln(1.0106) = 3.97, df = (p - 2)(k - 3) = 6$

POOLED WITHIN-GROUPS CORRELATION BETWEEN CANONICAL DISCRIMINANT FUNCTIONS AND DISCRIMINATING VARIABLES
VARIABLES ARE ORDERED BY THE FUNCTION WITH LARGEST CORRELATION AND THE MAGNITUDE OF THAT CORRELATION.

	FUNC 1	FUNC 2	FUNC 3
STATUS	-0.17058	0.519084*	0.25516
ENTERP	-0.30649	-0.33095	0.74936
CONVEN	0.47878	-0.24059	0.69316
REAL	0.25946	-0.09310	0.68032
AGGRESS	0.07366	-0.13305	0.47697
INTELL	-0.01297	-0.09701	0.43467
ARTIS	-0.29829	0.27428	0.38834
SOCIAL	0.16516	0.03674	0.19227

CANONICAL DISCRIMINANT FUNCTIONS EVALUATED AT GROUP MEANS (GROUP CENTROIDS)

GROUP	FUNC 1	FUNC 2	FUNC 3
1	0.39158	-0.27492	0.00687
2	0.09873	-0.04190	-0.29200
3	-0.18324	0.27619	0.11148
4	-0.32583	-0.03558	0.22572

in the moderate range (.30 to .58) and clearly significant, indicating that a multivariate analysis is dictated.

At the top of Table 7.2 is the residual test procedure involving Bartlett's Chi-Square tests, to determine the number of significant discriminant functions. Note that there are min $(k - 1, p)$ = min $(3,8)$ = 3 possible discriminant functions. The first line has all 3 eigenvalues (corresponding to the 3 discriminant functions) lumped together, yielding a significant χ^2 at the .0004 level. This tells us there is significant overall association. Now, the largest eigenvalue of $\mathbf{BW}^{-1}$ (i.e., the first discriminant function) is removed, and we test whether the residual, the last two discriminant functions, constitute significant association. The χ^2 for this first residual is not significant ($\chi^2 = 14.63, p < .40$) at the .05 level. The "After Function" column simply means after the first discriminant function has been removed. The third line, testing whether the third discriminant function is significant by itself has a 2 in the "After Function" column. This means, "Is the χ^2 significant after the first *two* discriminant functions have been removed?" To summarize then, only the first discriminant function is significant. The details of obtaining the χ^2, using the eigenvalues of $\mathbf{BW}^{-1}$, which appear in the upper left hand corner of the printout, are given in Table 7.2.

The eigenvalues of $\mathbf{BW}^{-1}$ are .1097, .0287, and .0106. Because the eigenvalues additively partition the total association, since the discriminant functions are uncorrelated, the "Percent of Variance" is simply the given eigenvalue divided by the sum of the eigenvalues. Thus, for the first discriminant function we have:

$$\text{Percent of Variance} = \frac{.1097}{.1097 + .0287 + .0106} \times 100 = 73.64\%$$

The reader should recall from Chapter 5, when we discussed "Other Multivariate Test Statistics," that the sum of the eigenvalues of $\mathbf{BW}^{-1}$ is one of the global multivariate test statistics, i.e., the Hotelling-Lawley trace. Therefore, the sum of the eigenvalues of $\mathbf{BW}^{-1}$ *is* a measure of the total association.

Since the group sizes are sharply unequal (115/75 > 1.5), it is important to check the homogeneity of covariance matrices assumption. The Box test for doing so is part of the printout, although we have not presented it. Fortunately, the Box test is not significant ($F = 1.18, p < .09$) at the .05 level.

The means of the groups on the first discriminant function (Table 7.2) show that it separates those children whose parents have had exposure to college (groups 3 and 4) from children whose parents have not gone to college (groups 1 and 2).

For interpreting the first discriminant function, as mentioned earlier, we use both the standardized coefficients and the discriminant function–variable correlations. We use the correlations for substantive interpretation, i.e., to name the underlying construct which the discriminant function represents. The procedure has empirically clustered the variables. Our task is to determine what the variables that correlate highly with the discriminant function have in common, and thus name the function.

The discriminant function–varible correlations are given in Table 7.2. Examining these for the first discriminant function, we see that it is primarily the conventional variable (correlation = .479) that defines the function, with the enterprising and artistic variables secondarily involved (correlations of − .306 and − .298 respectively). Since the correlations are negative for these variables, this means that the groups that scored higher on the enterprising and artistic variables scored lower on the first discriminant function, i.e., those merit scholars whose parents had a college education.

Now, examining the standardized coefficients to determine which of the variables are redundant given others in the set, we see that the conventional and enterprising variables are *not* redundant (coefficients of .80 and − 1.08 respectively), but that the artistic variable is redundant since it's coefficient is only − .32. Thus, combining the information from the coefficients and the discriminant function–variable correlations, we can say that the first discriminant function is characterizable as a conventional–enterprising continuum. Note, from the group centroid means, that it is the merit scholars whose parents have a college education that tend to be less conventional and more enterprising.

Finally, we can have confidence in the reliability of the results from this study since the subject/variable ratio is very large, i.e., about 50 to 1.

7.6. ROTATION OF THE DISCRIMINANT FUNCTIONS

In factor analysis rotation of the factors often facilitates interpretation. The discriminant functions can also be rotated (varimax) to help interpret them. This is easily accomplished with the SPSSX Discrim program by requesting 13 for "Options." Of course, one should only rotate statistically significant discriminant functions to ensure that the rotated functions are still significant. Also, in rotating, the maximizing property is lost, i.e., the first rotated function will no longer *necessarily* account for the maximum amount of between association. The amount of between association that the rotated functions account for tends to be more evenly distributed. The SPSSX package does print out how much of the canonical variance each rotated factor accounts for.

Up to this point, we have used all the variables in forming the discriminant functions. There is a procedure, called stepwise discriminant analysis, for selecting the best set of discriminators, just as one would select the "best" set of predictors in a regression analysis. It is to this procedure that we turn next.

7.7. STEPWISE DISCRIMINANT ANALYSIS

A popular procedure with both the SPSSX and BMDP packages is stepwise discriminant analysis. In this procedure the first variable to enter is the one which maximizes separation among the groups. The next variable to enter is the one which adds the most to further separating the groups, etc. It should be obvious that this procedure capitalizes on chance in the same way stepwise regression analysis does, where the first predictor to enter is the one which has the maximum correlation with the dependent variable, the second predictor to enter the one which adds the next largest amount to prediction, etc.

The F's to enter and the corresponding significance tests in stepwise discriminant analysis must be interpreted with caution, especially if the subject/variable ratio is small (say ≤ 5). The Wilk's Λ for the "best" set of discriminators is positively biased, and this bias can lead to the following problem (Rencher & Larson, 1980):

> Inclusion of too many variables in the subset. If the significance level shown on a computer output is used as an informal stopping rule, some variables will likely be included which do not contribute to the separation of the groups. A subset chosen with significance levels as guidelines will not likely be stable, i.e., a different subset would emerge from a repetition of the study. (p. 350)

The BMDP manual (1979) warns of the positive bias of the F tests in stepwise regression (p. 403), but does not repeat the warning for stepwise discriminant analysis.

Hawkins (1976) has suggested that a variable be entered only if it is significant at the $\alpha/(k - p)$ level, where α is the desired level of significance, p is the number of variables already included and $(k - p)$ is the number of variables available for inclusion. Although this probably is a good idea if N/p ratio is small, it probably is conservative if $N/p > 10$.

7.8. TWO OTHER STUDIES THAT USED DISCRIMINANT ANALYSIS

McNeil & Karr Study

The first study (McNeil & Karr, 1972) involves four cultural systems of varying degrees of modernization in Sierra Leone. From least to most modernized, these systems were (1) village, (2) modernized village, (3) tribal urban, and (4) Creole urban. There were 20 subjects in each group (10 boys and 10 girls in each case). These groups were compared on the nine subtests of the Illinois Test of Psycholinguistic Abilities (ITPA).

The results of the discriminant analysis, along with the group centroids (the means of the groups on the discriminant functions) are presented in Table 7.3. McNeil and Karr tested each eigenvalue *separately* and found the first two discriminant functions significant at the .01 level. This procedure, at the present state of knowledge, is a questionable practice. Employing the residual test procedure, we still find the first discriminant function significant at the .01 level, but the second function ($\chi^2 = 25$, with 16 df) is only significant at the .10 level. Thus, the evidence for the second discriminant function is weaker, and it would be wise to have this result replicated in another sample before placing a great amount of confidence in it. A second reason for treating this result somewhat skeptically is that the order of the groups on the second discriminant function was *not* as hypothesized.

The correlations between the discriminant functions and the original variables are also given in Table 7.3. These correlations show that the first discriminant function is interpretable as an auditory-vocal construct (since those variables dominate the function). The groups were ordered along this dimension as hypothesized, with the least modernized having the lowest score and the most modernized the highest score. The second discriminant function seems to be interpretable as primarily a motor encoding variable since the correlation of that variable with the discriminant function is quite strong. Furthermore the correlations of the function with the other variables are considerably lower (the next largest being $-.41$).

TABLE 7.3
Discriminant Function–Variable Correlations and Group Centroids for
McNeil-Karr Study

	Functions		
Variables	*1*	*2*	*3*
Auditory-vocal automatic	.94	$-.08$	.12
Visual decoding	.25	.20	$-.21$
Motor encoding	.37	.77	$-.19$
Auditory-vocal association	.87	.06	$-.00$
Visual motor sequencing	.07	$-.01$	.51
Vocal encoding	.57	.37	.34
Auditory vocal sequencing	.33	$-.41$	$-.35$
Visual-motor association	.30	.35	.32
Auditory decoding	.27	.09	$-.08$

	Group Centroids		
	Discriminant Functions		
Groups	*1*	*2*	*3*
Village	8.92	1.71	-3.02
Modernized village	10.81	5.98	-3.46
Tribal urban	12.27	5.47	-2.44
Creole urban	20.21	3.46	-3.09

The one reservation we have about interpreting the discriminant functions as indicated is that the subject/variable ratio is not large, i.e., it is 80/9 or about 9 to 1. We had indicated earlier that unless the ratio was at least 20 to 1 the stability of the results was questionable. Therefore, either replication of these results on another sample or on a combined sample of about 200 or more subjects is essential.

Smart Study

A study by Smart (1976) provides a nice illustration of the use of discriminant analysis to help validate Holland's (1966) theory of vocational choice/personality. Holland's theory assumes that (a) vocational choice is an expression of personality and (b) most people can be classified as one of six primary personality types: realistic, investigative, artistic, social, enterprising, and conventional. Realistic types, for example, tend to be pragmatic, asocial, and possess strong mechanical and technical competencies, while social types tend to be idealistic, sociable, and possess strong interpersonal skills.

Holland's theory further states that there are six related model environments. That is, for each personality type, there is a logically related environment that is characterized in terms of the atmosphere created by the people who dominate it. For example, realistic environments are dominated by realistic personality types and are characterized primarily by the tendencies and competencies these people possess.

Now, Holland and his associates have developed a hexagonal model that defines the psychological resemblances among the six personality types and the environments. The types and environments are arranged in the following clockwise order: realistic, investigative, artistic, social, enterprising, and conventional. The closer any two environments are on the hexagonal arrangement, the stronger they are related. This means, for example, that since realistic and conventional are next to each other they should be much more similar than realistic and social which are the furthest possible distance apart on an hexagonal arrangement.

In validating Holland's theory, Smart nationally sampled 939 academic department chairmen from 32 public universities. The departments could be classified in one of the six Holland environments. We give a sampling here: realistic—civil and mechanical engineering, industrial arts, and vocational education; investigative—biology, chemistry, psychology, mathematics; artistic—classics, music, english; social—counseling, history, sociology, and elementary education; enterprising—government, marketing, and prelaw; conventional—accounting, business education, and finance.

A questionnaire containing 27 duties typically performed by department chairmen was given to all chairmen, and the responses were factor analyzed (principal components with varimax rotation). The six factors that emerged were the dependent variables for the study, and were named: (1) faculty development, (2) external coordination, (3) graduate program, (4) internal administration, (5) instructional, and (6) program management. The independent variable was environments. The overall multivariate $F = 9.65$ was significant at the .001 level. Thus, the department chairmen did devote significantly different amounts of time to the above six categories of their professional duties. A discriminant analysis breakdown of the overall association showed that there were three significant discriminant functions ($p < .001$, $p < .001$ and $p < .02$ respectively). The standardized coefficients, discussed earlier as one of the devices for interpreting such functions, are given in Table 7.4.

Using the italicized weights, Smart gave the following names to the functions: discriminant function 1—curriculum management, discriminant function 2—internal orientation, and discriminant function 3—faculty orientation. The positions of the groups on the discriminant planes defined by functions 1 and 2, and by functions 1 and 3 are given in Figure 7.1. The clustering of the groups in Figure 7.1 is reasonably consistent with Holland's hexagonal model.

In Figure 7.2 we present the hexagonal model, showing how all three discriminant functions empirically confirm different similarities and disparities which should exist, according to the theory. For example, the realistic and investigative groups should be very similar, and the closeness of these groups appears on discriminant function 1. On the other hand, the conventional and artistic groups should be very dissimilar and this is revealed by their vertical separation on discriminant function 2. Also, the realistic and enterprising groups should be somewhat dissimilar and this appears as a fairly sizable separation (vertical) on discriminant function 3 in Figure 7.2.

In concluding our discussion of Smart's study, there are two important points to be made:

1. The issue raised earlier about the lack of stability of the coefficients is *not* a problem in this study. Smart had 932 subjects and only six dependent variables, so that his subject/variable ratio was very large.

TABLE 7.4
Standardized Coefficients for Smart Study

Variables	Function 1	Function 2	Function 3
Faculty development	.22	− .20	− .62
External coordination	− .14	.56	.34
Graduate program	.36	.45	.17
Internal administration	.17	− .58	.69
Instructional	− .82	.15	.06
Program management	− .46	− .35	− .09

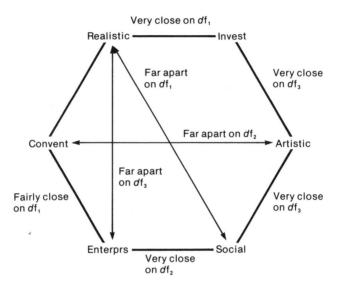

df_1, df_2 and df_3 refer to the first, second and third discriminant functions respectively

FIG. 7.2. Empirical Fit of the Groups as Determined by the Three Discriminant Functions to Holland's Hexagonal Model.

2.   Smart did not use the discriminant function-variable correlations in combination with the coefficients to interpret the discriminant functions, as it was unnecessary to do so. Smart's dependent variables were principal components, which are uncorrelated, and for uncorrelated variables the interpretation from the 2 approaches is identical, since the coefficients and correlations are equal (Thorndike, 1976).

7.9.   THE CLASSIFICATION PROBLEM

The classification problem involves classifying subjects (entities in general) into the one of several groups which they most closely resemble on the basis of a set of measurements. We say that a subject most closely resembles group i if the vector of scores for that subject is closest to the vector of means (centroid) for group i. Geometrically, the subject is closest in a distance sense (Mahalanobis distance) to the centroid for that group. Recall that in Chapter 3 (on multiple regression) we used the Mahalanobis distance to measure outliers on the set of predictors, and that the distance for subject i is given as:

$$D_i^2 = (\mathbf{x}_i - \overline{\mathbf{x}})' \mathbf{S}^{-1} (\mathbf{x}_i - \overline{\mathbf{x}}),$$

where $\mathbf{x}_i$ is the vector of scores for subject i, $\overline{\mathbf{x}}$ is the vector of means, and $\mathbf{S}$ is the covariance matrix. It may helpful to review the section on Mahalanobis distance in Chapter 3, and in particular a worked out example of calculating it in Table 3.13 (p. 92).

Our discussion of classification is brief, and focuses on the two-group problem. For a thorough discussion see Johnson and Wichern (1982), and for a good, recent review of discriminant analysis see Huberty (1984).

Let us now consider several examples from different content areas where classifying subjects into groups is of practical interest:

1. A bank wants a reliable means, on the basis of a set of variables, to identify low risk vs. high risk credit customers.
2. A reading diagnostic specialist wishes a means of identifying in kindergarten those children who are likely to encounter reading difficulties in the early elementary grades from those not likely to have difficulty.
3. A special educator wants to classify handicapped children as either learning disabled, emotionally disturbed, or mentally retarded.
4. A Dean of a law school wants a means of identifying those likely to succeed in law school from those not likely to succeed.
5. A vocational guidance counselor, on the basis of a battery of interest variables, wishes to classify high school students into occupational groups (artists, lawyers, scientists, accountants, etc.) whose interests are similar.
6. A clinical psychologist or psychiatrist wishes to classify mental patients into one of several psychotic groups (schizophrenic, manic-depressive, catatonic, etc.).

The Two Group Situation

Let $\mathbf{x}' = (x_1, x_2, \ldots, x_p)$ denote the vector of measurements on the basis of which we wish to classify a subject into one of two groups, G_1 or G_2. Fisher's (1936) idea was to transform the multivariate problem into a univariate one, in the sense of finding the linear combination of the x's (a single composite variable) which will maximally discriminant the groups. This is, of course, the single discriminant function. It is assumed that the two populations are multivariate normal and have the same covariance matrix. Let $z = a_1 x_1 + a_2 x_2 + \ldots + a_p x_p$ denote the discriminant function, where $\mathbf{a}' = (a_1, a_2, \ldots, a_p)$ is the vector of coefficients. Let $\overline{\mathbf{x}}_1$ and $\overline{\mathbf{x}}_2$ denote the vectors of means for the subjects on the p variables in groups 1 and 2. The location of group 1 on the discriminant

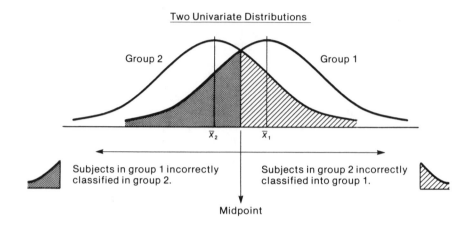

Two Univariate Distributions

Group 2   Group 1

$\bar{x}_2$ $\bar{x}_1$

Subjects in group 1 incorrectly   Subjects in group 2 incorrectly
classified in group 2.   classified into group 1.

Midpoint

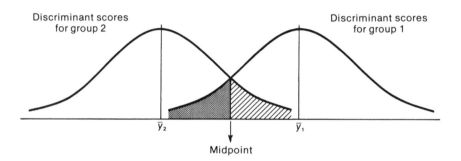

Discriminant scores   Discriminant scores
for group 2   for group 1

$\bar{y}_2$ $\bar{y}_1$

Midpoint

For this multivariate problem we have indicated much greater separation for the
groups than in the univariate example above. The amounts of incorrect classifications are indicated by the shaded and lined areas as in univariate example.

$\bar{y}_1$ and $\bar{y}_2$ are the means for the 2 groups on the discriminant function.

FIG. 7.3. Two Univariate Distributions and Two Discriminant Score Distributions
with Incorrectly Classified Cases Indicated.

function is then given by $\bar{y}_1 = \mathbf{a}'\bar{\mathbf{x}}_1$ and the location of group 2 by $\bar{y}_2 = \mathbf{a}'\bar{\mathbf{x}}_2$. The midpoint between the two groups on the discriminant function is then given by $m = (\bar{y}_1 + \bar{y}_2)/2$.

If we let z_i denote the score for the ith subject on the discriminant function, then the *decision rule* is as follows:

If $z_i \geq m$, then classify subject in group 1

If $z_i < m$, then classify subject in group 2

As we see in a following example, BMDP7M (stepwise discriminant analysis program) prints out the scores on the discriminant function for each subject and the means for the groups on the discriminant function (so that we can easily determine the midpoint m). Thus, applying the above decision rule, we are easily able to determine why the program classified a subject in a given group. In the above decision rule, we assume the group which has the higher mean is designated as group 1.

This midpoint rule makes intuitive sense, and is easiest to see for the single variable case. Suppose there two normal distributions with equal variances and means 55 (group 1) and 45. The midpoint is 50. If we consider classifying a subject with a score of 52, it makes sense to put him (her) in group 1. Why? Because the score puts the subject much closer to what is typical for group 1 (i.e., only 3 points away from the mean), whereas this score is nowhere near as typical for a subject from group 2 (7 points from the mean). On the other hand, a subject with a score of 48.5 is more appropriately placed in group 2 since his(her) score is closer to what is typical for group 2 (3.5 points from the mean) than what is typical for group 1 (6.5 points from the mean).

In Figure 7.3 we illustrate the percentages of subjects that would be misclassified in the univariate case and when using discriminant scores.

Example 2

We consider again the Pope (1980) data used in Chapter 6. Children in kindergarten were measured with various instruments to determine whether they could be classified as low risk or high risk with respect to having reading problems later on in school. The variables we considered here are word identification (WI), word comprehension (WC), and passage comprehension (PC). The group sizes are sharply unequal and the homogeneity of covariance matrices assumption here was not tenable at the .05 level, so that a quadratic rule may be more appropriate. But we are just using this example for illustrative purposes.

In Table 7.5 are the control lines for obtaining the classification results on BMDP7M (stepwise discriminant analysis program). Note that we have forced in all 3 variables. The hit rate, i.e., the number of correct classifications, is quite good, especially since 11 of the 12 high risk subjects have been correctly classified.

TABLE 7.5 BMDP7M Control Lines for Classifying Low & High Risk Subjects along with Classification Matrix, Mahalanobis D²'s and Group Probabilities

```
/PROBLEM TITLE IS 'OBTAINING MAHALANOBIS D SQUARES FOR PCPE DATA'.
/INPUT VARIABLES ARE 4. FORMAT IS STREAM.
/VARIABLE NAMES ARE GPID,WI,WC,PC. GROUPING IS GPID.
/GROUP CODES(1) ARE 1 TO 2.
 NAMES(1) ARE LOWRISK,HIGHRISK.
/DISCRIM LEVELS = 0,1,1,1.
 FORCE = 1.
/END
```

CLASSIFICATION MATRIX

GROUP	PERCENT CORRECT	NUMBER OF CASES CLASSIFIED INTO GROUP—	
		LOW RISK	HIGH RISK
LOWRISK	65.4	17	9
HIGH RISK	91.7	1	11
TOTAL	73.7	18	20

$$\text{Hit rate} = \frac{28}{38} \times 100 = 73.7\%$$

GROUP	LOWRISK	INCORRECT CLASSIFICATIONS	MAHALANOBIS D-SQUARE FROM AND POSTERIOR PROBABILITY FOR GROUP—	
			LOW RISK	HIGH RISK
1			6.8 0.932	12.1 0.068
2			6.5 0.984	14.8 0.016
3			2.8 0.860	6.4 0.140
4		HIGHRISK	1.7 0.436	1.2 0.564
5			3.2 0.961	9.6 0.039
6		HIGHRISK	2.4 0.251	0.2 0.749
7		HIGHRISK	3.5 0.345	2.2 0.655
8			0.8 0.688	2.4 0.312
9			1.4 0.893	5.6 0.107
10		HIGHRISK	6.3 0.256	4.2 0.744
11		HIGHRISK	2.5 0.427	1.9 0.573
12			2.3 0.926	7.3 0.074
13		HIGHRISK	3.4 0.345	2.2 0.655
14		HIGHRISK	1.7 0.321	0.2 0.679
15		HIGHRISK	3.3 0.230	0.9 0.770
16			2.4 0.793	5.0 0.207
17			13.5 0.986	22.0 0.014
18			4.6 0.878	8.6 0.122
19			8.8 0.917	13.6 0.083
20			1.0 0.576	1.6 0.424
21			1.8 0.791	4.4 0.209
22			1.2 0.668	2.6 0.332
23			1.5 0.834	4.7 0.166
24		HIGHRISK	3.6 0.291	0.8 0.799
25			2.1 0.826	5.3 0.174
26			2.2 0.947	8.0 0.053
GROUP	HIGHRISK		LOWRISK	HIGHRISK

CASE			LOWRISK	HIGHRISK
27			6.5 0.094	2.0 0.906
28			4.7 0.114	0.6 0.886
29			4.1 0.378	3.1 0.622
30			3.4 0.310	1.8 0.690
31			2.4 0.400	1.6 0.600
32			3.5 0.160	0.2 0.840
33			1.2 0.443	0.7 0.557
34			1.8 0.368	0.7 0.632
35			5.6 0.216	3.0 0.784
36		LOW RISK	0.4 0.570	0.9 0.430
37			4.8 0.143	1.3 0.857
38			4.2 0.147	0.7 0.853

Case is classified in group for which it's probability is greater (> .5). Thus, for Case 1 the probability is overwhelming that this subject belongs to low risk group. Case 6 is a member of low risk group, but the probability is much greater (.749) that this individual belongs in the high risk group.

In Table 7.6 are given the means for the groups on the discriminant function (.46 for lowrisk and -1.01 for high risk), along with the scores for the subjects on the discriminant function (these are listed under CAN.V—an abbreviation for canonical variate). The histogram for the discriminant scores shows that we have a fairly good separation, although there are several (9) mis-classifications of low risk subjects being classified as high risk.

Assessing the Accuracy of the Maximized Hit Rates

The classification procedure is set up to maximize the hit rates, i.e., the number of correct classifications. This is analagous to the maximization procedure in multiple regression, where the regression equation was designed to maximize predictive power. We saw how misleading the prediction on the derivation sample could be. There is the same need here to obtain a more realistic estimate of the hit rate through use of an "external" classification analysis. That is, an analysis is needed in which the data to be classified is *not* used in constructing the classification function. There are two ways of accomplishing this:

1.   We can use the *jackknife* procedure of Lachenbruch (1967). Here, each subject is classified based on a classification statistic derived from the remaining $(n - 1)$ subjects. This is the procedure of choice for small or moderate sample sizes and is obtained by specifying JACKKNIFE in the DISCRIMINANT paragraph in BMDP7M.
2.   If the sample size is large, then we can randomly split the sample and cross validate. That is, we compute the classification function on one sample and then check it's hit rate on the other random sample. This provides a good check on the external validity of the classification function. BMDP7M is set up nicely to do this cross validation and we show the control lines in a later example.

Using Prior Probabilities

Ordinarily we would assume that any given subject has a priori an equal probability of being in any of the groups to which we wish to classify. And the packages have equal prior probabilities as the default option. Different a priori group probabilities can have a substantial effect on the classification function, as we will show shortly. The pertinent question is, "How often are we justified in using unequal a priori probabilities for group membership?" If indeed, based on content knowledge, one can be confident that the different sample sizes result *because* of differences in population sizes, then prior probabilities are justified. However, several researchers have urged caution in using anything but equal priors (Lindeman, Merenda, & Gold, 1980; Tatsuoka, 1971).

In Table 7.7 we present the control lines for the classification with the Pope data with prior probabilities. All that we needed to add was PRIOR $= .684,.316$.

TABLE 7.6
Means for Groups on Discriminant Function, Scores for Cases on
Discriminant Function & Histogram for Discriminant Scores

GROUP	MEAN COORDINATES		SYMBOL FOR CASES	SYMEDL FOR MEAN
LOW RISK	① 0.46	0.00	L	1
HIGH RISK	-1.01	0.00	H	2

GROUP CASE	LOWRISK CAN.V	CASE	CAN.V	CASE	CAN.V
			②		
1	1.50	11	-0.47	21	0.63
2	2.53	12	1.44	22	0.20
3	0.96	13	-0.71	23	0.83
4	-0.44	14	-0.78	24	-1.21
5	1.91	15	-1.09	25	0.79
6	-1.01	16	0.64	26	1.68
7	-0.71	17	2.60		
8	0.27	18	1.07		
9	1.17	19	1.36		
10	-1.00	20	-0.06		

GROUP HIGHRISK

CASE	CAN.V		CASE	CAN.V
27	-1.81		37	-1.49
28	-1.66		38	-1.47
29	-0.81			
30	-0.82			
31	-0.55			
32	-1.40			
33	-0.43			
34	-0.64			
35	-1.15			
36	-0.08			

Histogram for Discriminant Function Scores

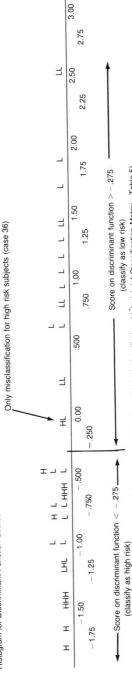

① These are the means for the groups on the discriminant function.

② The scores listed under CAN.V (for canonical variate) these are the scores for the subjects on the discriminant function.

TABLE 7.7. BMDP7M Control Lines for Classification with Prior Probabilities and Jackknifed Mahalanobis Distances

```
/PROBLEM TITLE IS 'OBTAINING MAHALANGBIS C SQUARES FOR POPE DATA.'
/INPUT VARIABLES ARE 4. FORMAT IS STREAM./
/VARIABLE NAMES ARE GPID,WI,WC,PC. GROUPING IS GPID.
/GROUP CODES(1) ARE 1 TO 2.
 NAMES(1) ARE LOWRISK,HIGHRISK, PRIOR = .684,316.
/DISCRIM LEVELS = 0,1,1,1.
 FORCE = 1.
/END
```

CLASSIFICATION MATRIX

GROUP	PERCENT CORRECT	NUMBER OF CASES CLASSIFIED INTO GROUP	
		LOWRISK	HIGHRISK
LOWRISK	84.6	22	4
HIGHRISK	58.3	5	7 ①
TOTAL	76.3	27	11

INCORRECT CLASSIFICATIONS

JACKNIFED MAHALANOBIS D-SQUARE FROM AND POSTERIOR PROBABILITY FOR GROUP—

GROUP	LOW RISK ②	INCORRECT	LOWRISK		HIGHRISK	
CASE						
1			9.0	0.932	14.2	0.068
2			8.4	0.989	17.5	0.011
3			3.2	0.847	6.6	0.153
4		HIGHRISK	1.9	0.411	1.2	0.589
5			3.7	0.963	10.2	0.037
6		HIGHRISK	2.7	0.223	0.2	0.777
7		HIGHRISK	4.1	0.284	2.3	0.716
8			0.8	0.675	2.3	0.325
9			1.5	0.887	45.7	0.113
10		HIGHRISK	8.1	0.151	4.6	0.849
11		HIGHRISK	2.9	0.384	1.9	0.618
12			2.5	0.923	7.5	0.077
13		HIGHRISK	4.0	0.286	2.2	0.714
14		HIGHRISK	1.9	0.300	0.2	0.700
15		HIGHRISK	3.9	0.186	0.9	0.814
16			2.7	0.773	5.1	0.227
17			23.3	0.996	34.2	0.004
18			5.6	0.864	9.3	0.136
19			12.4	0.912	17.1	0.088
20			1.1	0.560	1.5	0.440
21			2.0	0.774	4.4	0.226
22			1.3	0.650	2.5	0.350
23			1.7	0.823	4.7	0.177
24		HIGHRISK	4.2	0.156	0.9	0.844
25			2.4	0.811	5.3	0.189
26			2.5	0.946	8.2	0.054

GROUP	HIGHRISK		LOWRISK		HIGHRISK	
CASE						
27			6.6	0.108	2.4	0.892
28			4.6	0.123	0.7	0.877
29			4.2	0.471	4.0	0.529
30			3.4	0.357	2.2	0.643
31			2.4	0.449	2.0	0.551
332			3.5	0.168	0.3	0.832
33			1.2	0.464	0.9	0.536
34			1.7	0.388	0.8	0.612
35			5.8	0.276	3.9	0.724
36		LOWRISK	0.4	0.593	1.1	0.407
37			4.8	0.161	1.5	0.839
38			4.2	0.159	0.8	0.841

①Although the hit rate has increased slightly by inserting prior probabilities (cf. Table 7.5), the number of misclassifications of highrisk has increased substantially.

②These jackknifed distances obtained from separate run, by inserting JACK, in the DISCRIM paragraph.

TABLE 7.8
Randomly Splitting the Grades and College Groups of National Merit
Data and Cross Validating the Classification Function

```
/PROBLEM TITLE IS 'MERIT SCHOLARS-GRADES VS COLLEGE—CROSS VALD CLASSIFICATION FUNCTION'.
/INPUT VARIABLES = 4. FORMAT IS STREAM.
/VARIABLE NAMES ARE GPID,CONVEN,ENTERP,ARTISTIC.GROUPING IS GPID.
/TRANSFORM IF(RNDU(1235783) LE. 5) THEN GPID = GPID + 2.
/GROUP CODE(S) ARE 1 TO 4. NAMES(1) ARE GRAD,COLL,NEWGRAD,NEWCOLL. USE = 1 TO 2.
/ DISCRIM LEVELS ARE 0,1,1,1. FORCE = 1.
/END
```

It is the TRANSFORM paragraph that we split the cases in each of the
grades and college groups into two random subgroups. The random number
routine (RNDU) which generates numbers on the interval from 0 to 1 is
accessed. If the number generated is < .5, then the case in GRAD becomes
a member of a validation sample for GRAD. That is, this case goes in group 3
(NEWGRAD), since it's GPID = GPID + 2 = 1 + 2 = 3. If the number
generated for a case in GRAD is > .5, then the group identification for that
case remains as 1, and this case is a member of the derivation sample for
GRAD. The same type of thing is done in splitting the COLL cases into
derivation and validation subsamples. The USE = 1 to 2. in the GROUP
paragraph indicates that *only* the cases in groups 1 and 2 will be used in
deriving the classification function, which will then be tested on groups 3
and 4 (the validation subsamples).

CLASSIFICATION MATRIX

GROUP	PERCENT CORRECT	NUMBER OF CASES CLASSIFIED INTO GROUP-	
		GRAD	COLL
GRADE	62.5	30	18
COLL	68.8	10	22
NEWGRAD	0.0	24	18
NEWCOLL	0.0	17	26
TOTAL	65.0	81	84

The number of hit drops from 65% for the derivation sample (52 of 80) to 58.8%
for the validation sample (50 of 85). While this may not seem like a large
drop, it is large enough to cause the number of hits in validation sample to
dip to the chance level. To show this we employ the Huberty one-tailed z
statistic:

$$z = \frac{(o - e)\sqrt{N}}{\sqrt{e(N - e)}} = \frac{(50 - 42.5)\sqrt{85}}{\sqrt{42.5(85 - 42.5)}} = 1.62$$

which is not significant at the .05 level, since the critical value = 1.64. (o is
total number of hits and e is number of hits expected by chance.)

in the GROUP paragraph. The priors we used were simply the proportional group sizes, i.e., 26/38 = .684 and 12/38 = .316. We also present in Table 7.7 the jackknifed distances. The reader should compare these with the ordinary distances given in Table 7.5.

Example 3—National Merit Data

We consider a second example to illustrate randomly splitting the sample and cross validating the classification function with BMDP7M.. We use part of the data from the National Merit scholars example used earlier in this chapter. The national merit scholars whose parents had an eighth grade education or less are compared against the scholars both of whose parents had at least one college degree on the conventional, enterprising, and artistic variables. The control lines for running the analysis are given in Table 7.8, along with considerable annotation. The data is given in the Appendix for this chapter. The classification matrix, giving the number of hits in the derivation sample and the validation sample, is also presented in Table 7.8.

7.10. LINEAR VS. QUADRATIC CLASSIFICATION RULE

There is a more complicated quadratic classification rule available. However, the following comments should be kept in mind before using it. Johnson and Wichern (1982) indicate, "The quadratic . . . rules are appropriate if normality appears to hold but the assumption of equal covariance matrices is seriously violated. However, the assumption of normality seems to be more critical for quadratic rules than linear rules" (p. 504). And Huberty (1984) states, "The stability of results yielded by a linear rule is greater than results yielded by a quadratic rule when small samples are used and when the normality condition is not met" (p. 165).

7.11. CHARACTERISTICS OF A GOOD CLASSIFICATION PROCEDURE

One obvious characteristic of a good classification procedure is that the hit rate be high, i.e., we should have mainly correct classifications. But another important consideration, sometimes lost sight of, is the cost of misclassification (financial or otherwise). The cost of misclassifying a subject from group A in group B may be greater than misclassifying a subject from group B in group A. We give three examples to illustrate:

1. A medical researcher wishes classify subjects as low risk or high risk in terms of developing cancer on the basis of family history, personal health habits, and environmental factors. Here, saying a subject is low risk when

in fact he is high risk is more serious than classifying a subject as high risk when he is low risk.

2. A bank wishes to classify low and high risk credit customers. Certainly, for the bank, misclassifying high risk customers as low risk is going to be more costly than misclassifying low risk as high risk customers.

3. This example was illustrated previously, i.e., of identifying low risk vs. high risk kindergarten children, with respect to possible reading problems in the early elementary grades. Once again, misclassifying a high risk child as low risk is more serious than misclassifying a low risk child as high risk. In the former case, the child who needs help (intervention) doesn't receive it.

The Multivariate Normality Assumption

Recall that linear discriminant analysis is based on the assumption of multivariate normality, and that quadratic rules are also sensitive to a violation of this assumption. Thus, in situations where multivariate normality is particularily suspect, for example when using some discrete dichotomous variables, an alternative classification procedure is desirable. Logistic regression (Press & Wilson, 1978) is a good choice here; it is available on SPSSX (in the Loglinear procedure) and in the BMDP package.

7.12.   SUMMARY OF MAJOR POINTS

1.   Discriminant analysis is used for two purposes: (a) for describing major differences among groups, and (b) for classifying subjects into groups on the basis of a battery of measurements.

2.   The major differences among the groups are revealed through the use of uncorrelated linear combinations of the original variables, i.e., the discriminant functions. Since the discriminant functions are uncorrelated, they yield an additive partitioning of the between association.

3.   Use the discriminant function-variable correlations to name the discriminant functions and the standardized coefficients to determine which of the variables are redundant.

4.   About 20 subjects per variable are needed for reliable results, i.e., to have confidence that the variables selected for interpreting the discriminant functions would again show up in an independent sample from the same population.

5.   Stepwise discriminant analysis should be used with caution.

6.   For the classification problem, it is assumed that the two populations are multivariate normal and have the same covariance matrix.

7.   The hit rate is the number of correct classifications, and is an optimistic value, since we are using a mathematical maximization procedure. To obtain a

more realistic estimate of how good the classification function is use the jackknife procedure for small or moderate samples, and randomly split the sample and cross validate with large samples. The use of BMDP7M for cross validation was illustrated.

8.   If the covariance matrices are unequal, then a quadratic classification procedure should be considered.

9.   There is evidence that linear classification is more reliable when small samples are used and normality does not hold.

10.   The cost of misclassifying must be considered in judging the worth of a classification rule. Of procedures A and B, with the same overall hit rate, A would be considered better if it resulted in less "costly" misclassifications.

APPENDIX
NATIONAL MERIT DATA
USED FOR CROSS VALIDATION
OF CLASSIFICATION FUNCTION IN TABLE 7.8

CASE NO. LABEL	2 CONVEN	3 ENTERP	4 ARTISTIC
1	0	0	4
2	3	3	0
3	0	0	1
4	3	3	4
5	1	3	6
6	4	3	3
7	3	0	0
8	0	3	8
9	11	3	6
10	0	5	12
11	6	0	1
12	2	4	10
13	12	9	10
14	4	5	2
15	0	6	9
16	2	7	14
17	0	4	0
18	2	0	0
19	0	0	5
20	0	1	0
21	1	2	0
22	1	1	1
23	1	3	0
24	0	0	4
25	2	0	3
26	1	2	5
27	2	2	7
28	1	3	2
29	4	3	6
30	2	0	0
31	2	0	4
32	1	0	1
33	4	3	0
34	4	1	1
35	0	0	0
36	0	3	4
37	3	7	10
38	2	1	0
39	0	4	10
40	4	1	1
41	0	0	0
42	4	2	0

APPENDIX (*Continued*)
NATIONAL MERIT DATA
USED FOR CROSS VALIDATION
OF CLASSIFICATION FUNCTION IN TABLE 7.8

CASE NO. LABEL	2 CONVEN	3 ENTERP	4 ARTISTIC
43	4	3	8
44	7	8	8
45	1	2	1
46	0	1	5
47	6	9	14
48	0	1	8
49	0	6	5
50	2	0	4
51	0	0	4
52	13	11	11
53	1	2	7
54	4	4	9
55	2	3	8
56	1	0	5
57	6	4	3
58	0	1	0
59	3	0	8
60	0	1	13
61	1	4	4
62	2	0	5
63	1	0	5
64	2	0	0
65	2	3	8
66	8	2	1
67	1	0	0
68	1	1	3
69	1	0	0
70	2	9	2
71	5	7	14
72	3	1	1
73	1	1	6
74	4	4	0
75	1	1	0
76	1	0	1
77	14	11	14
78	5	4	12
79	5	4	5
80	4	3	6
81	2	1	4
82	2	3	2
83	1	1	0
84	10	4	3

APPENDIX (*Continued*)
NATIONAL MERIT DATA
USED FOR CROSS VALIDATION
OF CLASSIFICATION FUNCTION IN TABLE 7.8

CASE NO. LABEL	2 CONVEN	3 ENTERP	4 ARTISTIC
85	1	1	5
86	0	7	8
87	1	4	4
88	8	5	4
89	3	1	6
90	4	2	3
91	0	2	5
92	0	0	2
93	0	0	3
94	0	0	8
95	2	2	0
96	1	12	4
97	4	4	0
98	2	1	1
99	2	3	2
100	1	3	1
101	0	0	4
102	3	12	13
103	1	1	0
104	0	3	5
105	2	3	3
106	11	8	1
107	1	3	8
108	7	8	7
109	0	1	4
110	0	0	1
111	0	5	2
112	0	0	0
113	0	2	10
114	1	1	2
115	0	0	1
116	0	2	0
117	0	1	5
118	0	0	8
119	1	4	4
120	2	1	7
121	0	3	0
122	0	1	0
123	1	1	0
124	0	3	13
125	1	1	10
126	1	4	11

APPENDIX (Continued)
NATIONAL MERIT DATA
USED FOR CROSS VALIDATION
OF CLASSIFICATION FUNCTION IN TABLE 7.8

CASE NO. LABEL	2 CONVEN	3 ENTERP	4 ARTISTIC
127	0	1	8
128	2	3	8
129	4	2	3
130	0	0	3
131	1	5	5
132	1	2	10
133	0	2	8
134	5	5	10
135	1	9	10
136	2	1	6
137	0	0	0
138	0	0	8
139	0	4	2
140	6	9	11
141	2	5	7
142	0	0	4
143	3	2	2
144	0	5	12
145	2	1	13
146	1	1	1
147	0	0	7
148	2	5	6
149	0	2	8
150	0	3	8
151	0	0	2
152	3	10	14
153	5	6	9
154	1	5	8
155	3	5	9
156	0	4	3
157	0	2	4
158	3	9	7
159	2	5	2
160	1	5	0
161	0	0	0
162	0	0	10
163	3	0	8
164	0	0	0
165	0	0	0

Note: The first 90 cases are for the GRAD data and the last 75 cases are the COLL data.

EXERCISES FOR CHAPTER 7—DISCRIMINANT ANALYSIS

1.   Run a discriminant analysis on the data from Exercise 1 in Chapter 5 using SPSSX   MANOVA.   Use   the   following   PRINT   subcommand
PRINT = ERROR(SSCP) SIGNIF(HYPOTH) DISCRIM(RAW)/
     ERROR(SSCP) is used to obtain the error sums of square and cross products matrix, i.e., the **W** matrix. SIGNIF(HYPOTH) is used to obtain the hypothesis SSCP, i.e., the **B** matrix here, while DISCRIM(RAW) is used to obtain the raw discriminant function coefficients.
     a) How many discriminant functions are there?
     b) Which of the discriminant functions are significant at the .05 level?
     c) Show how the chi-square values for the residual test procedure are obtained, using the eigenvalues on the printout.
     d) Recall that $\mathbf{a}'$ was used to denote the vector of raw discriminant coefficients. By plugging the coefficients into $\mathbf{a}'\mathbf{Ba}/\mathbf{a}'\mathbf{Wa}$ show that the value is equal to the largest eigenvalue of $\mathbf{BW}^{-1}$ given on the printout.

2.   Plot the groups for the McNeil-Karr study (Table 7.3) in the discriminant plane. Which groups show the largest visual separation.

3.   (a) Given the results of the Smart study, which of the 4 multivariate test statistics do you think would be most powerful?
     b) From the results of the Stevens study, which of the 4 multivariate test statistics would be most powerful?

4.   Press and Wilson (1978) examined population change data for the 50 states. The percent change in population from the 1960 census to the 1970 census for each state was coded as 0 or 1, according to whether the change was below or above the median change for all states. This is the grouping variable. The following demographic variables are to be used to explain the population changes: (1) per capita income (in $1,000), (2) percent birth rate, (3) presence or absence of a coastline and (4) percent death rate.
     a) Run the discriminant analysis, forcing in all predictors, to see how well the states can be classified (as below or above the median). What is the hit rate?
     b) Run the jackknife classification. Does the hit rate drop off appreciably?

Data for Exercise 4

State	Population change	Income	Births	Coast	Deaths
Arkansas	0	2.878	1.8	0	1.1
Colorado	1	3.855	1.9	0	.8
Delaware	1	4.524	1.9	1	.9
Georgia	1	3.354	2.1	1	.9
Idaho	0	3.290	1.9	0	.8
Iowa	0	3.751	1.7	0	1.0
Mississippi	0	2.626	2.2	1	1.0
New Jersey	1	4.701	1.6	1	.9
Vermont	1	3.468	1.8	0	1.0
Washington	1	4.053	1.8	1	.9
Kentucky	0	3.112	1.9	0	1.0
Louisiana	1	3.090	2.7	1	1.3
Minnesota	1	3.859	1.8	0	.9
New Hampshire	1	3.737	1.7	1	1.0
North Dakota	0	3.086	1.9	0	.9
Ohio	0	4.020	1.9	0	1.0
Oklahoma	0	3.387	1.7	0	1.0
Rhode Island	0	3.959	1.7	1	1.0
South Carolina	0	2.990	2.0	1	.9
West Virginia	0	3.061	1.7	0	1.2
Connecticut	1	4.917	1.6	1	.8
Maine	0	3.302	1.8	1	1.1
Maryland	1	4.309	1.5	1	.8
Massachusetts	0	4.340	1.7	1	1.0
Michigan	1	4.180	1.9	0	.9
Missouri	0	3.781	1.8	0	1.1
Oregon	1	3.719	1.7	1	.9
Pennsylvania	0	3.971	1.6	1	1.1
Texas	1	3.606	2.0	1	.8
Utah	1	3.227	2.6	0	.7
Alabama	0	2.948	2.0	1	1.0
Alaska	1	4.644	2.5	1	1.0
Arizona	1	3.665	2.1	0	.9
California	1	4.493	1.8	1	.8
Florida	1	3.738	1.7	1	1.1
Nevada	1	4.563	1.8	0	.8
New York	0	4.712	1.7	1	1.0
South Dakota	0	3.123	1.7	0	2.4
Wisconsin	1	3.812	1.7	0	.9
Wyoming	0	3.815	1.9	0	.9
Hawaii	1	4.623	2.2	1	.5
Illinois	0	4.507	1.8	0	1.0
Indiana	1	.3.772	1.9	0	.9
Kansas	0	3.853	1.6	0	1.0

Data for Exercise 4 (*Continued*)

State	Population change	Income	Births	Coast	Deaths
Montana	0	3.500	1.8	0	.9
Nebraska	0	3.789	1.8	0	1.1
New Mexico	0	3.077	2.2	0	.7
North Carolina	1	3.252	1.9	1	.9
Tennessee	0	3.119	1.9	0	1.0
Virginia	1	3.712	1.8	1	.8

8 Factorial Analysis of Variance

8.1. INTRODUCTION

In this chapter we consider the effect of two or more independent or classification variables (e.g., sex, social class, treatments) on a set of dependent variables. Four schematic two-way designs, where just the classification variables are shown are given below:

	Treatments		
	1	2	3
Male			
Female			

	Teaching Methods		
	1	2	3
Urban			
Suburban			
Rural			

	Drugs			
	1	2	3	4
Schizop.				
Depressives				

	Stimulus Complexity		
	Easy	Aver.	Hard
Intell.			
Average			
Super.			

We indicate what the advantages of a factorial design are over a one-way design. We also remind the reader what an interaction means, and distinguish between the two types of interaction (ordinal and disordinal). The univariate, equal cell size (balanced design) situation is discussed first. Then we tackle the much more difficult disproportional (non-orthogonal or unbalanced) case. Three different ways of handling the unequal n case are considered, it is indicated why we feel one of these methods is generally superior. We then discuss a multivariate factorial design, and finally the interpretation of a three-way interaction. The control lines for running the various analyses is given, and selected printout from both SPSSX MANOVA and from BMDP4V are discussed.

8.2.   ADVANTAGES OF A TWO-WAY DESIGN

1.   A two-way design enables us to examine the *joint* effect of the independent variables on the dependent variable(s). We cannot get this information by running two separate one-way analyses, one for each of the independent variables. If one of the independent variables is treatments and the other some individual difference characteristic (sex, I.Q., locus of control, age, etc.), then a significant interaction tells us that the superiority of one treatment over another is *moderated* by the individual difference characteristic. (An interaction means that the effect one independent variable has on a dependent variable is not the same for all levels of the other independent variable). This moderating effect can take two forms:

a) The degree of superiority changes, but one subgroup always does better than another. To illustrate this, consider the following ability by teaching methods design:

	Methods of Teaching		
	T_1	T_2	T_3
High Ability	85	80	76
Low Ability	60	63	68

The superiority of the high ability students changes from 25 for T_1 to only 8 for T_3, but high ability students always do better than low ability students. Since the order of superiority is maintained, this is called an *ordinal* interaction.

b) The superiority reverses, i.e., one treatment is best with one group, but another treatment is better for a different group. A study by Daniels and Stevens (1976) provides an illustration of this more dramatic type of interaction, called a disordinal interaction. On a group of college undergraduates, they considered two types of instruction: (1) a traditional, teacher controlled (lecture) type and (2) a contract for grade plan. The subjects were classified as internally or externally controlled, using Rotter's scale. An internal orientation means that those subjects perceive positive events occur as a consequence of their actions (i.e., they are in control), while external subjects feel that positive and/or negative events occur more because of powerful others, or due to chance or fate. The design and the means for the subjects on an achievement posttest in psychology are given below:

		Instruction	
		Contract for Grade	*Teacher Controlled*
Locus of control	Internal	50.52	38.01
	External	36.33	46.22

The moderator variable in this case is locus of control, and it has a substantial effect on the efficacy of an instructional method. When the subject's locus of control is matched to the teaching method (internals with contract for grade and externals with teacher controlled) they do quite well in terms of achievement; where there is a mismatch achievement suffers.

This study also illustrates how a one-way design can lead to quite misleading results. Suppose Daniels and Stevens had just considered the two methods, ignoring locus of control. The means for achievement for the contract for grade plan and for teacher controlled are 43.42 and 42.11, nowhere near significance. The conclusion would have been that teaching methods don't make a difference. The factorial study shows, however, that methods definitely do make a difference, a quite positive difference if subject locus of control is matched to teaching methods, and an undesirable effect if there is a mismatch.

The general area of matching treatments to individual difference characteristics of subjects is an interesting and important one, and is called *aptitude-treatment interaction* research. A thorough and critical analysis of many studies in this area is covered in the excellent text *Aptitudes and Instructional Methods* by Cronbach and Snow (1977).

2.   A second advantage of factorial designs is that they can lead to more powerful tests by reducing error (within cell) variance. If performance on the dependent variable is related to the individual difference characteristic (the blocking variable), then the reduction can be substantial. We consider a hypothetical sex $\times$ treatment design to illustrate

	T_1		T_2	
Males	18, 19, 21 20, 22	(2.5)	17, 16, 16 18, 15	(1.3)
Females	11, 12, 11 13, 14	(1.7)	9, 9, 11 8, 7	(2.2)

Notice that *within* each cell there is very little variability. The within cell variances quantify this, and are given in parentheses. The pooled within cell error term for the factorial analysis is quite small, i.e., 1.925. On the other hand, if this had been considered as a two-group design, the variability is considerably greater, as evidenced by the within *group* (treatment) variances for T_1 and T_2 of 18.766 and 17.6, and a pooled error term for the t test of 18.18.

8.3. UNIVARIATE FACTORIAL ANALYSIS

Equal Cell *n* (Orthogonal) Case

When there are an equal number of subjects in each cell in a factorial design, then the sum of squares for the different effects (main and interactions) are uncorrelated (orthogonal). This is important in terms of interpreting results, since significance for one effect implies nothing about significance on another. This helps for a clean and clear interpretation of results. It puts us in the same nice situation we had with uncorrelated planned comparisons, which we discussed in Chapter 5.

Overall and Spiegel (1969), in a classic paper on analyzing factorial designs, discuss three basic methods of analysis:

Method 1: Adjust each effect for all other effects in the design to obtain it's unique contribution (regression approach).

Method 2: Estimate the main effects ignoring the interaction, but estimate the interaction effect adjusting for the main effects (experimental method).

Method 3: Based on theory and/or previous research, establish an ordering for the effects, and then adjust each effect only for those effects preceding it in the ordering (hierarchical approach).

For equal cell size designs all three of the above methods yield the same results, i.e., the same F *tests.* Therefore, it will not make any difference, in terms of the conclusions a researcher draws, as to which of these methods is used on one of the packages. *For unequal cell sizes, however, these methods can yield quite different results,* and this is what we consider shortly. First, however, we consider an example with equal cell size to show two things: (1) that the methods do indeed yield the same results, and (2) to demonstrate, using dummy coding for the effects, that the effects are uncorrelated.

Example—Two Way Equal Cell n

Consider the following 2 × 3 factorial data set:

		B		
		1	2	3
A	1	3, 5, 6	2, 4, 8	11, 7, 8
	2	9, 14, 5	6, 7, 7	9, 8, 10

In Table 8.1 we give the control lines for running the analysis on SPSSX MANOVA. In the MANOVA command we indicate the factors after the keyword

TABLE 8.1
Control Lines for Two-Way Univariate ANOVA on SPSSX with Sequential and Unique Sum of Square F Ratios

```
TITLE 'TWO WAY UNIVARIATE EQUAL N'
DATA LIST FREE/FACA FACB DEP
LIST

BEGIN DATA

1.00    1.00    3.00
1.00    1.00    5.00
1.00    1.00    6.00
1.00    2.00    2.00
1.00    2.00    4.00
1.00    2.00    8.00
1.00    3.00    11.00
1.00    3.00    7.00
1.00    3.00    8.00
2.00    1.00    9.00
2.00    1.00    14.00
2.00    1.00    5.00
2.00    2.00    6.00
2.00    2.00    7.00
2.00    2.00    7.00
2.00    3.00    9.00
2.00    3.00    8.00
2.00    3.00    10.00

END DATA

MANOVA DEP BY FACA(1,2) FACB(1,3)/
   DESIGN/
```

TESTS OF SIGNIFICANCE FOR DEP USING SEQUENTIAL SUMS OF SQUARES

SOURCE OF VARIATION	SUM OF SQUARES	DF	MEAN SQUARE	F	SIG. OF F
WITHIN CELLS	75.33333	12	6.27778		
CONSTANT	924.50000	1	924.50000	147.26549	.000
FACA	24.50000	1	24.50000	3.90265	.072
FACB	30.33333	2	15.16667	2.41593	.131
FACA BY FACB	14.33333	2	7.16667	1.14159	.352

TESTS OF SIGNIFICANCE FOR DEP USING UNIQUE SUM OF SQUARES

SOURCE OF VARIATION	SUM OF SQUARES	DF	MEAN SQUARE	F	SIG. OF F
WITHIN CELLS	75.33333	12	6.27778		
CONSTANT	924.50000	1	924.50000	147.26549	.000
FACA	24.50000	1	24.50000	3.90265	.072
FACB	30.33333	2	15.16667	2.41593	.131
FACA BY FACB	14.33333	2	7.16667	1.14159	.352

BY, with the beginning level for each factor first in parentheses and then the last level for the factor. The DESIGN subcommand lists the effects we wish to test for significance. In this case the program *assumes* a full factorial model by default, and therefore it is not necessary to list the effects.

Method 3, the hierarchical approach, is the *default* method of analysis for SPSSX MANOVA. This means that a given effect is adjusted for all effects to it's left in the ordering. The effects here would go in in the following order: FACA, FACB, FACA BY FACB. Thus, the A main effect is not adjusted for anything. The B main effect is adjusted for the A main effect, and the interaction is adjusted for both main effects.

We also ran this problem using Method 1, the regression approach, to obtain the unique contribution of each effect, adjusting for all other effects. Note, however, that the F ratios for both methods are identical (cf. Table 8.1). Why? Because the effects are uncorrelated for equal cell size, and therefore no adjustment takes place. Thus, the F for an effect "adjusted" is the same as an effect unadjusted.

To show that the effects are indeed uncorrelated we have dummy coded the effects in Table 8.2 and ran the problem as a regression analysis. The coding scheme is explained there. Predictor A1 represents the A main effect, predictors B1 and B2 represent the B main effect, and predictors A1B1 and A1B2 represent the interaction. We are using all these predictors to explain variation on y. Note that the correlations between predictors representing *different* effects are all 0. This means that those effects are accounting for distinct parts of the variation on y, or that we have an orthogonal partitioning of the y variation.

In Table 8.3 we present the stepwise regression results for the example with the effects entered as the predictors. There we explain how the sum of squares obtained for each effect is exactly the same as was obtained when the problem was run as a traditional ANOVA in Table 8.1.

Example—Two Way Disproportional Cell Size

The data for our disproportional cell size example is given in Table 8.4, along with the dummy coding for the effects, and the correlation matrix for the effects. Here there definitely are correlations among the effects. For example, the correlations between A1 (representing the A main effect) and B1 and B2 (representing the B main effect) are $-.163$ and $-.275$. This contrasts with the equal cell n case where the correlations among the effects were all 0 (Table 8.2). Thus, for disproportional cell sizes the sources of variation are confounded (mixed together). To determine how much unique variation on y a given effect accounts for we must adjust or partial out how much of that variation is explainable because of the effect's correlations with the other effects in the design. Recall that in Chapter 5 the same procedure was employed to determine the unique amount of between variation a given planned comparison accounts for out of a set of correlated planned comparisons.

TABLE 8.2
Regression Analysis of Two-Way Equal n ANOVA with Effects
Dummy Coded & Correlation Matrix for the Effects

/PROBLEM TITLE IS 'EFFECTS DUMMY CODED FOR 2 WAY—EQUAL N—FOR REGRESSION'.
/INPUT VARIABLES ARE 6. FORMAT IS STREAM.
/VARIABLE NAMES ARE A1,B1,B2,A1B1,A1B2,Y,
/PRINT CORR. DATA.
/REGRESS DEPENDENT IS Y. LEVELS ARE 1,2,2,3,3.
  FORCE = 3.
/END

Y	AI ①	B1	B2	A1B1	A1B2
3.000	1.000	1.000	0.0000	1.000	0.0000
5.000	1.000	1.000	0.0000	1.000	0.0000
6.000	1.000	1.000	0.0000	1.000	0.0000
2.000	1.000	0.0000	1.000	0.0000	1.000
4.000	1.000	0.0000	1.000	0.0000	1.000
8.000	1.000	0.0000	1.000	0.0000	1.000
11.00	1.000	−1.000	−1.000	−1.000	−1.000
7.000	1.000	−1.000	−1.000	−1.000	−1.000
8.000	1.000	−1.000	−1.000	−1.000	−1.000
9.000	−1.000	1.000	0.0000	−1.000	0.0000
14.00	−1.000	1.000	0.0000	−1.000	0.0000
5.000	−1.000	1.000	0.0000	−1.000	0.0000
6.000	−1.000	0.0000	1.000	0.0000	−1.000
7.000	−1.000	0.0000	1.000	0.0000	−1.000
7.000	−1.000	0.0000	1.000	0.0000	−1.000
9.000	−1.000	−1.000	−1.000	1.000	1.000
8.000	−1.000	−1.000	−1.000	1.000	1.000
10.00	−1.000	−1.000	−1.000	1.000	1.000

CORRELATION MATRIX

	A MAIN EFFECT	B MAIN EFFECT		AB INTERACTION		
	A1	B1	B2	A1B1	A2B2	Y
A1	1.0000					
B1	0.0000	1.0000				
B2	0.0000	0.5000	1.0000			
A1B1	0.0000	−0.0000	0.0000	1.0000		
A1B2	② 0.0000	−0.0000	−0.0000	0.5000	1.0000	
Y	−0.4118	−0.2642	−0.4563	−0.3122	−0.1201	1.0000

①The S's in the first level of B are coded a 1's on the first dummy variable (A1 here), with the S's for all other levels of B, except the last, coded as 0's. THe S's inthe last level of B are coded as −1's. Similarly, the S's on the second level of B are coded as 1's on the second dummy variable (B2 here), with the S's for all other levels of B, except the last, coded as 0's. Again, the S's in the last level of B are coded as −1.'s. To obtain the elements for the interaction dummy variables, ie., A1B1 and A1B2, multiply the corresponding elements of the dummy variables comprising the interaction variable. Thus, to obtain the elements of A1B1 multiply the elements of A1 by the elements of B1.

②Note that the correlations between variables representing *different* effects are all 0. The only non-zero correlations are for the two variables that jointly represent the B main effect (B1 and B2), and for the two variables (A1B1 and A1B2) that jointly represent the AB interaction effect.

TABLE 8.3
Stepwise Regression Results for Two-Way Equal n ANOVA with the
Effects Entered as the Predictors

STEP NO. 1		A1			
VARIABLE ENTERED					
ANALYSIS OF VARIANCE		SUM OF SQUARES	DF	MEAN SQUARE	F RATIO
REGRESSION		24.499954	1	24.49995	3.27
RESIDUAL		120.00003	16	7.500002	

STEP NO.	2	B2			
VARIABLE ENTERED					
ANALYSIS OF VARIANCE		SUM OF SQUARES	DF	MEAN SQUARE	F RATIO
REGRESSION		54.583191	2	27.29160	4.55
RESIDUAL		89.916794	15	8.994452	

STEP NO.	3				
VARIABLE ENTERED		B1			
ANALYSIS OF VARIANCE		SUM OF SQUARES	DF	MEAN SQUARE	F RATIO
REGRESSION		54.833206	3	18.27773	2.85
RESIDUAL		89.666779	14	6.404770	

STEP NO.	4				
VARIABLE ENTERED		A1B1			
ANALYSIS OF VARIANCE		SUM OF SQUARES	DF	MEAN SQUARE	F RATIO
REGRESSION		68.916504	4	17.22913	2.98
RESIDUAL		75.683481	13	5.814114	

STEP NO.	5				
VARIABLE ENTERED		A1B2			
ANALYSIS OF VARIANCE		SUM OF SQUARES	DF	MEAN SQUARE	F RATIO
REGRESSION		69.166489	5	13.83330	2.20
RESIDUAL		75.333496	12	6.277791	

Note that the sum of squares (*SS*) for regression for A1, representing the A main effect, is the same as the *SS* for FACA in Table 8.1. Also, the *additional SS* for B1 and B2, representing the B main effect, is $54.833 - 24.5 = 30.333$, the same as SS for FACB in Table 8.1. Finally, the additional SS for A1B1 and A1B2, representing the AB interaction, is $69.166 - 54.833 = 14.333$, the same as SS for FACA by FACB in Table 8.1

TABLE 8.4
Control Lines for Two-Way Disproportional Cell n ANOVA on SPSSX
with the Sequential and Unique Sum of Squares F Ratios

```
TITLE 'TWO WAY UNIVARIATE ANOVA UNEQUAL N'
DATA LIST FREE/ FACA FACB DEF
LIST
BEGIN DATA
   1.00        1.00        3.00
   1.00        1.00        5.00
   1.00        1.00        6.00
   1.00        2.00        2.00
   1.00        2.00        4.00
   1.00        2.00        8.00
   1.00        3.00       11.00
   1.00        3.00        7.00
   1.00        3.00        8.00
   1.00        3.00        6.00
   1.00        3.00        9.00
   2.00        1.00        9.00
   2.00        1.00       14.00
   2.00        1.00        5.00
   2.00        1.00       11.00
   2.00        2.00        6.00
   2.00        2.00        7.00
   2.00        2.00        7.00
   2.00        2.00        8.00
   2.00        2.00       10.00
   2.00        2.00        5.00
   2.00        2.00        6.00
   2.00        3.00        9.00
   2.00        3.00        8.00
   2.00        3.00       10.00
END DATA
MANOVA DEP BY FACA(1,2) FACB(1,3)/
```
① `METHOD = SSTYPE(UNIQUE)/`
② `DESIGN/`

TESTS FOR SIGNIFICANCE FOR DEP USING UNIQUE SUMS OF SQUARES

SOURCE OF VARIATION	SUM OF SQUARES	F		SIG. OF F
WITHIN CELLS	98.88333			
CONSTANT	1176.15503	225.99305		.000
FACA	42.38523	8.14414	③	.010
FACB	30.35239	2.91604		.079
FACA BY FACB	16.77800	1.61191		.226

TESTS OF SIGNIFICANCE FOR DEP USING SEQUENTIAL SUMS OF SQUARES

SOURCE OF VARIATION	SUM OF SQUARES	F		SIG. OF F
WITHIN CELLS	98.8333			
CONSTANT	1354.24000	260.21129		.000
FACA	23.22104	4.46182	③	.048
FACB	38.87763	3.73508		.043
FACA BY FACB	16.77800	1.61191		.226

①To obtain the unique contribution of each effect this method subcommand is inserted.

②By default a full factorial design is assumed by the program; thus it is not necessary to list each effect.

③Note that the F ratios for the interation effect are the same, however, the F ratios for the main effects are quite different.

TABLE 8.5
Dummy Coding of the Effects for the Disproportional Cell n ANOVA
and Correlation Matrix for the Effects

DESIGN
B

A	3, 5, 6	2, 4, 8	11, 7, 8, 6, 9
	9, 14, 5, 11	6, 7, 7, 8, 10, 5, 6	9, 8, 10

A1	B1	B2	A1B1	A1B2	Y
1.00	1.00	.00	1.00	.00	3.00
1.00	1.00	.00	1.00	.00	5.00
1.00	1.00	.00	1.00	.00	6.00
1.00	.00	1.00	.00	1.00	2.00
1.00	.00	1.00	.00	1.00	4.00
1.00	.00	1.00	.00	1.00	8.00
1.00	−1.00	−1.00	−1.00	−1.00	11.00
1.00	−1.00	−1.00	−1.00	−1.00	7.00
1.00	−1.00	−1.00	−1.00	−1.00	8.00
1.00	−1.00	−1.00	−1.00	−1.00	6.00
1.00	−1.00	−1.00	−1.00	−1.00	9.00
−1.00	1.00	.00	−1.00	.00	9.00
−1.00	1.00	.00	−1.00	.00	14.00
−1.00	1.00	.00	−1.00	.00	5.00
−1.00	1.00	.00	−1.00	.00	11.00
−1.00	.00	1.00	.00	−1.00	6.00
−1.00	.00	1.00	.00	−1.00	7.00
−1.00	.00	1.00	.00	−1.00	7.00
−1.00	.00	1.00	.00	−1.00	8.00
−1.00	.00	1.00	.00	−1.00	10.00
−1.00	.00	1.00	.00	−1.00	5.00
−1.00	.00	1.00	.00	−1.00	6.00
−1.00	−1.00	−1.00	1.00	1.00	9.00
−1.00	−1.00	−1.00	1.00	1.00	8.00
−1.00	−1.00	−1.00	1.00	1.00	10.00

FOR A MAIN EFFECT	FOR B MAIN EFFECT	FOR AB INTERACTION EFFECT			

CORRELATION:

	Al	B1	B2	A1B1	A1B2	Y
A1	1.000	−.163	−.275	−.072	.063	−.361
B1	−.163	1.000	.495	.059	.112	−.148
B2	−.275	.495	1.000	.139	−.088	−.350
A1B1	−0.72	0.59	1.39	1.000	.458	−332
A1B2	.063	.112	−.088	.468	1.000	−.089
Y	−.361	−.148	−.350	−.332	−.089	1.000

The correlations between variables representing different effects are boxed in. Contrast with the situation for equal cell size, as presented in Table 8.2.

In Table 8.5 we present the control lines for running the disproportional cell size example, along with Method 1 (unique sum of squares) results and Method 3 (hierarchical or called sequential on the printout) results. The F ratios for the interaction effect are the same, but the F ratios for the main effects are quite different. For example, if we had used the default option (Method 3) we would have declared a significant B main effect at the .05 level, but with Method 1 (unique decomposition) the B main effect is not significant at the .05 level. Therefore, with unequal n designs the method used can clearly make a difference in terms of the conclusions reached in the study. This raises the question of which of the three methods should be used for disproportional cell size factorial designs.

Which Method Should be Used?

Overall and Spiegel (1969) recommended Method 2 as generally being most appropriate. We do not agree, feeling that Method 2 would rarely be the method of choice, since it estimates the main effects ignoring the interaction. Carlson and Timm's comment (1974) is appropriate here: "We find it hard to believe that a researcher would consciously design a factorial experiment and then ignore the factorial nature of the data in testing the main effects" (p. 156).

We feel that Method 1, where we are obtaining the unique contribution of each effect, is generally more appropriate. This is what Carlson and Timm (1974) recommend, and what Myers (1979) recommends for experimental studies (random assignment involved), or as he put it, "whenever variations in cell frequencies can reasonably be assumed due to chance."

Where an a priori ordering of the effects can be established (Overall and Spiegel, 1969, give a nice psychiatric example), Method 3 makes sense. This is analogous to establishing an a priori ordering of the predictors in multiple regression. Pedhazur (1982) gives the following example. There is a 2×2 design in which one of the classification variables is race (black and white) and the other classification variable is education (high school and college). The dependent variable is income. In this case one can argue that race affects one's level of education, but obviously not vice versa. Thus, it makes sense to enter race first to determine it's effect on income, then to enter education to determine how much it adds in predicting income. Finally, the race $\times$ education interaction is entered.

8.4.   FACTORIAL MULTIVARIATE ANALYSIS OF VARIANCE

Here we are considering the effect of two or more independent variables on a set of dependent variables. To illustrate factorial MANOVA we use an example from Barcikowski (1983). Sixth grade students were classified as being of high,

TABLE 8.6
Control Lines for Factorial MANOVA on SPSSX Using Unique Sum
of Squares Decomposition

TITLE 'TWO WAY DISPROP CELL SIZE MANOVA'
DATA LIST FREE/ APTITUDE METHOD ATTIT ACHIEV
LIST

BEGIN DATA

1.00	1.00	15.00	11.0
1.00	1.00	9.00	7.00
1.00	2.00	19.00	11.00
1.00	2.00	12.00	9.00
1.00	2.00	12.00	6.00
1.00	3.00	14.00	13.00
1.00	3.00	9.00	9.00
1.00	3.00	14.00	15.00
1.00	4.00	19.00	14.00
1.00	4.00	7.00	8.00
1.00	4.00	6.00	6.00
1.00	5.00	14.00	16.00
1.00	5.00	14.00	8.00
1.00	5.00	18.00	16.00
2.00	1.00	18.00	13.00
2.00	1.00	8.00	11.00
2.00	1.00	6.00	6.00
2.00	2.00	25.00	24.00
2.00	2.00	24.00	23.00
2.00	2.00	26.00	19.00
2.00	3.00	29.00	23.00
2.00	3.00	28.00	26.00
2.00	4.00	11.00	14.00
2.00	4.00	14.00	10.00
2.00	4.00	8.00	7.00
2.00	5.00	18.00	17.00
2.00	5.00	11.00	13.00
3.00	1.00	11.00	9.00
3.00	1.00	16.00	15.00
3.00	2.00	13.00	11.00
3.00	2.00	10.00	11.00
3.00	3.00	17.00	10.00
3.00	3.00	7.00	9.00
3.00	3.00	7.00	9.00
3.00	4.00	15.00	9.00
3.00	4.00	13.00	13.00
3.00	4.00	7.00	7.00
3.00	5.00	17.00	12.00
3.00	5.00	13.00	15.00
3.00	5.00	9.00	12.00

END DATA
MANOVA ATTIT ACHIEV BY APTITUDE(1,3) METHOD(1,5)/
    PRINT = CELLINFO(MEANS,COV,COR)/
    METHOD = SSTYPE(UNIQUE)/
    DESIGN = APTITUDE, METHOD,APTITUDE BY METHOD/

average, or low aptitude, and then within each of these aptitudes were randomly assigned to one of 5 methods of teaching social studies. The dependent variables were measures of attitude and achievement. The data below resulted:

Method of Instruction

	1	2	3	4	5
	15, 11	19, 11	14, 13	19, 14	14, 16
High	9, 7	12, 9	9, 9	7, 8	14, 8
	12, 6	14, 15	6, 6	18, 16
Average	18, 13	25, 24	29, 23	11, 14	18, 17
	8, 11	24, 23	28, 26	14, 10	11, 13
	6, 6	26, 19		8, 7
Low	11, 9	13, 11	17, 10	15, 9	17, 12
	16, 15	10, 11	7, 9	13, 13	13, 15
			7, 9	7, 7	9, 12

Of the 45 subjects who started the study, 5 were lost for various reasons. This resulted in a disproportional factorial design. To obtain the unique contribution of each effect, the unique sum of squares decomposition was run on SPSSX MANOVA. The control lines for doing so are given in Table 8.6. The results of the multivariate and univariate tests of the effects are presented in Table 8.7. All of the multivariate effects are significant at the .05 level. We use the F's associated with Wilks to illustrate (aptitude by method: $F = 2.19$, $p < .018$; method: $F = 2.46$, $p < .025$, and aptitude: $F = 5.92$, $p < .001$). Since the interaction is significant, we focus our interpretation on it. The univariate tests for this effect on attitude and achievement are also both significant at the .05 level. Use of simple effects revealed that it was the attitude and achievement of the average aptitude subjects under methods 2 and 3 that were responsible for the interaction.

8.5. WEIGHTING OF THE CELL MEANS

In experimental studies that wind up with unequal cell sizes, it is reasonable to assume equal population sizes, and equal cell weighting is appropriate in estimating the grand mean. However, when sampling from intact groups (sex, age, race, SES, religions) in nonexperimental studies, the populations may well differ in size, and the sizes of the samples may reflect the different population sizes. In such cases equally weighting the subgroup means will not provide an unbiased estimate of the combined (grand) mean, whereas weighting the means will produce an unbiased estimate. *The BMDP4V program is specifically set up to provide either equal or unequal weighting of the cell means.* There are situations where one may wish to use both weighted and unweighted cell means in a single factorial design, i.e., in a semi-experimental design. In such designs one of the

TABLE 8.7
Results of Multivariate and Univariate Tests for Main Effects and Interaction for Factorial MANOVA Example

EFFECT .. APTITUDE BY METHOD

MULTIVARIATE TESTS OF SIGNIFICANCE (S = 2, M = 2 1/2, N = 11)

TEST NAME	VALUE	APPROX. F	HYPOTH. F	ERROR DF	SIG. OF F
PILLAIS	.75744	1.90496	16.00	50.00	.042
HOTELLINGS	1.72683	2.48232	16.00	46.00	.008
WILKS	.33341	2.19557	16.00	48.00	.018
ROYS	.60802				

UNIVARIATE F-TESTS WITH (8,25) D. F.

VARIABLE	HYPOTH. SS	ERROR SS	HYPOTH. MS	ERROR MS	F	SIG. OF F
ATT IT	503.32072	460.66667	62.91509	18.42667	3.41436	.009
ACHIEV	343.11228	237.16667	42.8904	9.485667	4.52098	.002

EFFECT .. METHOD

MULTIVARIATE TESTS OF SIGNIFICANCE (S = 2, M = 1/2, N = 11)

TEST NAME	VALUE	APPROX. F	HYPOTH. DF	ERROR DF	SIG. OF F
PILLAIS	.53430	2.27837	8.00	50.00	.037
HOTELLINGS	.91570	2.63264	8.00	46.00	.018
WILKS	.50269	2.46254	8.00	48.00	.025
ROYS	.45256				

UNIVARIATE F-TESTS WITH (4,25) D. F.

VARIABLE	HYPOTH. SS	ERROR SS	HYPOTH. MS	ERRORS MS	F	SIG. OF F
ATTIT	237.90643	460.66667	59.47661	18.42667	3.22775	.029
ACHIEV	189.88095	237.16667	47.47024	9.48667	5.00389	.004

EFFECT .. APTITUDE

MULTIVARIATE TESTS OF SIGNIFICANCE (S = 2, M = $-1/2$, N = 11)

TEST NAME	VALUE	APPROX. F	HYPOTH. DF	ERROR DF	SIG. OF F
PILLAIS	.57396	5.03102	4.00	50.00	.002
HOTELLINGS	1.17920	6.78038	4.00	46.00	.000
WILKS	.44855	6.91734	4.00	48.00	.001
ROYS	.53161				

UNIVARIATE F-TESTS WITH (2,25) D. F.

VARIABLE	HYPOTH. SS	ERROR SS	HYPOTH. MS	ERROR MS	F	SIG. OF F
ATTIT	256.50817	460.66667	128.25408	18.42667	6.96024	.004
ACHIEV	267.55842	237.16667	133. 7921	9.48667	14.10181	.000

TABLE 8.8
BMDP4V Control Lines for Factorial MANOVA with Multivariate and Univariate Tests for Effects

```
/PROBLEM TITLE IS ' 3 × 5 FACTORIAL MANOVA—APTITUDE × METHOD
/INPUT VARIABLES = 4. FORMAT IS STREAM.
/VARIABLE NAMES ARE APTITUDE,METHOD.
/BETWEEN FACTORS ARE APTITUDE,METHOD.
CODES(1) ARE 1 TO 3.
NAMES(1) ARE HIGH,AVER,LOW.
CODES(2) ARE 1 TO 5.
NAMES(2) ARE M1,M2,M3,M4,M5.
/WEIGHTS BETWEEN ARE EQUAL.
/END
DATA.
/END.
/ANALYSIS PROC = FACTORIAL
```

EFFECT	VARIATE	STATISTIC		F	DF		P
A: APTITUDE							
	ALL						
		① { LRATIO =	0.448555	5.92	4.	48.00	
		TRACE =	1.17920				
		TZSG = 29.4799					
		CHISQ =	3.60			15.344	0.0006
		MXROOT =	0.531611				0.0005
	ATTITUDE						0.0005
		SS =	256.508	6.96	2.	25	0.0040
		MS =	128.254	②			
	ACHIEV						
		SS =	267.558	14.10	2.	25	0.0001
		MS = 133.779					
M: METHOD							
	ALL						
		LRATIO =	0.502691	2.46	8.	48.00	0.0254
		TRACE =	0.915701				
		TZSQ =	22.8925				
		CHISQ =	10.08		21.081	0.0215	
		MXROOT =	0.452558				0.0287
	ATTITUDE						0.0289
		SS =	237.906				
		MS =	59.4766	3.23	4.	25	
	ACHIEV						
		SS =	189.881	5.00	4.	25	0.0042
		MS =	47.4702				
AM							
	ALL						
		LRATIO =	0.333408	2.20	16.	48.00	0.0184
		TRACE =	1.72683				
		TZSQ =	43.1708				
		CHISQ =	13.03			26.978	0.0111
		MXROOT = 0.608021					0.0454
	ATTITUDE						
		SS =	503.321	3.41	8.	25	.0087
		MS =	62.9151				
	ACHIEV						
		SS =	343.112	4.52	8.	25	0.0017
		MS = 42.8890					
ERROR							
	ATTITUDE						
		SS =	460.66667				
		MS =	18.426667				
	ACHIEV						
		SS =	237.16667				
		MS = 9.4866667					

①LRATIO—Wilk's Λ, TRACE—Hotellings, MXROOT—Roy's (largest root)
②These are the univariate tests for the dependent variables.

factors is an attribute factor (sex, SES, race, etc.) and the other factor is treatments. Suppose for a given situation it is reasonable to assume there are twice as many middle SES in a population as lower SES, and that two treatments are involved. Forty lower SES are sampled and randomly assigned to treatments, and 80 middle SES are selected and assigned to treatments. Schematically then, the setup of the weighted and unweighted means is:

		T_1	T_2	Unweighted Means
SES	Lower	$n_{11} = 20$	$n_{12} = 20$	$(\mu_{11} + \mu_{12})/2$
	Middle	$n_{21} = 40$	$n_{22} = 40$	$(\mu_{21} + \mu_{22})/2$
Weighted Means		$\dfrac{n_{11}\mu_{11} + n_{21}\mu_{21}}{n_{11} + n_{21}}$	$\dfrac{n_{12}\mu_{12} + n_{22}\mu_{22}}{n_{12} + n_{22}}$	

We illustrate the set up of the BMDP4V program for cell mean weighting with the previous aptitude by methods example. The control lines for equal cell mean weighting are given in Table 8.8. Notice that the weighting is requested in the following paragraph:

/WEIGHTS BETWEEN ARE EQUAL.

If we wished to use weighted means for the test of treatment main effect, and unweighted means for the test of the aptitude main effect, as in the above example, then we would make an additional run requesting weighted cell means:

/WEIGHTS BETWEEN ARE SIZES.

Then we would use the test from the weighted cell mean run for the treatment main effect, and use the test from the unweighted cell mean run for the aptitude main effect.

8.6.   THREE-WAY MANOVA

This section is included to show how to set up the control lines for running a three-way MANOVA, and to indicate a procedure for interpreting a three way interaction. We take the previous aptitude by method example and add sex as an additional factor. Then assuming we will use the same two dependent variables, the *only* change that is required in the control lines presented in Table 8.6 is that the MANOVA command becomes:

MANOVA ATTIT ACHIEV BY APTITUDE(1,3) METHOD(1,5) SEX(1,2)

We wish to focus our attention on the interpretation of a three-way interaction, if it were significant in such a design. First, what does a significant three-way interaction mean for a single variable? If the 3 factors are denoted by A, B, and C, then *a significant ABC interaction implies that the two-way interaction profiles for the different levels of the third factor are different.* A nonsignificant three-way interaction means that the two-way profiles are the same, i.e., the differences can be attributed to sampling error.

Example

Consider a sex (A) by treatments (B) by race (C) design. Suppose that the two way design (collapsed on race) looked like this:

	Treatments	
	1	2
Males	60	50
Females	40	42

This profile reveals a significant sex main effect and a significant ordinal interaction. But it does not tell the whole story. Let us examine the profiles for blacks and whites separately (we assume equal n per cell):

	Whites				*Blacks*	
	T_1	T_2			T_1	T_2
M	65	50		M	55	50
F	40	47		F	40	37

We see that for whites there clearly is an ordinal interaction, whereas for blacks there is no interaction effect. The two profiles are distinctly different. The point is, race further moderates the sex by treatments interaction.

In the context of aptitude-treatment interaction (ATI) research, Cronbach (1975) had an interesting way of characterizing higher order interactions:

> When ATI's are present, a general statement about a treatment effect is misleading because the effect will come or go depending on the kind of person treated . . . An ATI result can be taken as a general conclusion only if it is not in turn moderated by further variables. If Aptitude × Treatment × Sex interact, for example, then the Aptitude × Treatment effect does not tell the story. Once we attend to interactions, we enter a hall of mirrors that extends to infinity. (p. 119)

Thus, to examine the nature of a significant three-way multivariate interaction, one might first determine which of the individual variables are significant (by examining the univariate F's). Then look at the two-way profiles to see how they differ for those variables that are significant.

EXERCISES—CHAPTER 8

1.) Consider the following 2 × 4 equal cell size MANOVA data set (2 dependent variables):

B

6, 10	13, 16	9, 11	21, 19
7, 8	11, 15	8, 8	18, 15
9, 9	17, 18	14, 9	16, 13
11, 8	10, 12	4, 12	11, 10
7, 6	11, 13	10, 8	9, 8
10, 5	14, 10	11, 13	8, 15

A (to the left of the table, spanning both row groups)

a)   Run the factorial MANOVA on SPSSX using the default option.

b)   Which of the multivariate tests for the 3 different effects is(are) significant at the .05 level?

c)   For the effect(s) which show multivariate significance, which of the individual variables (at .025 level) are contributing to the multivariate significance?

d)   Run the above data set on SPSSX using METHOD = SSTYPE(UNIQUE). Are the results different? Explain.

2.)   An investigator has the following 2 × 4 MANOVA data set for 2 dependent variables:

B

6, 10	13, 16	9, 11	21, 19
7, 8	11, 15	8, 8	18, 15
	17, 18	14, 9	16, 13
		13, 11	
11, 8	10, 12	14, 12	11, 10
7, 6	11, 13	10, 8	9, 8
10, 5	14, 10	11, 13	8, 15
6, 12			17, 12
9, 7			13, 14
11, 14			

A (to the left of the table, spanning both row groups)

2.)   a) Run   the   factorial   MANOVA   on   SPSSX   using METHOD = SSTYPE(UNIQUE).

b)   Which of the multivariate tests for the 3 effects is(are) significant at the .05 level?

c)   For the effect(s) that show multivariate significance, which of the individual variables is(are) contributing to the multivariate significance at the .025 level?

d)   Is the homogeneity of the covariance matrices assumption for the cells tenable at the .05 level?

e)   Run the factorial MANOVA on the data set using the default option of SPSSX.

Are the F ratios different? Explain.

f)   Dummy code group (cell) membership and run as a regression analysis, in the process obtaining the correlations among the effects, as illustrated in Tables 9.2 and 9.5.

3.)   Consider the following hypothetical data for a sex $\times$ age $\times$ treatment factorial MANOVA on two personality measures:

TREATMENTS

	AGE	1		2	3
MALES	14	8,19 9,16 4,20 3,21	5,18 7,25 4,17	2,23 3,27 8,20	6,16 9,12 13,24 5,20
	17	9,22 11,15 8,14		4,30 7,25 8,28 13,23	5,15 5,16 9,23 8,27
FEMALES	14	10,17 12,18 8,14 7,22		8,26 2,29 10,23 7,17	3,21 7,17 4,15 9,22 12,23
	17	9,13 6,18 12,20	5,19 8,15 11,1	5,14 11,13 4,21 8,18	10,14 15,18 9,19

a) Run the three way MANOVA on SPSSX using METHOD = SSTYPE(UNIQUE).

b) Which of the multivariate effects are significant at the .025 level? What is the overall α for the set of multivariate tests?

c) Is the homogeneity of covariance matrices assumption tenable at the .05 level?

d) For the multivariate effects that are significant, which of the individual variables are significant at the .01 level? Interpret the results.

9

Analysis of Covariance

9.1 INTRODUCTION

Analysis of covariance is a statistical technique that combines regression analysis and analysis of variance. It can be quite helpful in nonrandomized studies in drawing more accurate conclusions. However, precautions have to be taken, or analysis of covariance (ANCOVA) can be misleading in some cases. In this chapter we indicate what the purposes of covariance are, when it is most effective, when the interpretation of results from covariance is "cleanest," and when covariance should not be used. We start with the simplest case, one dependent variable and one covariate, with which many readers may be somewhat familiar. Then we consider one dependent variable and several covariates, where our previous study of multiple regression is helpful. Finally, multivariate analysis of covariance is considered, where there are several dependent variables and several covariates. We show how to run a multivariate analysis of covariance on SPSSX, and explain the proper order of interpretation of the printout. An extension of the Tukey post hoc procedure, the Bryant-Paulson, is also illustrated.

Examples of Univariate and Multivariate Analysis of Covariance

What is a covariate? A potential covariate is any variable that is significantly correlated with the dependent variable. That is, we assume a *linear* relationship between the covariate (x) and the dependent variable (y). Consider now two typical univariate ANCOVAs with one covariate. In a two-group pretest–posttest design, then the pretest is often used as a covariate, since how the subjects score before treatments is generally correlated with how they score after treatments. Or, suppose three groups are compared on some measure of achievement. In this situation I. Q. is often used as a covariate, since I. Q. is usually at least moderately correlated with achievement.

The reader should recall that the null hypothesis being tested in ANCOVA is that the adjusted population means are equal. Since a linear relationship is assumed between the covariate and the dependent variable, the means are adjusted in a linear fashion. We consider this in detail shortly in this chapter. Thus, in interpreting printout, for either univariate or multivariate analysis of covariance (MANCOVA), it is the adjusted means that need to be examined. It is important to note that SPSSX and BMDP do not automatically provide the adjusted means; they must be requested.

Now consider two situations where MANCOVA would be appropriate. A counselor wishes to examine the effect of two different counseling approaches on several personality variables. The subjects are pretested on these variables and then posttested two months later. The pretest scores are the covariates and the posttest scores are the dependent variables. Secondly, a teacher educator wishes to determine the relative efficacy of two different methods of teaching 12th grade mathematics. He uses three subtest scores of achievement on a posttest as the dependent variables. A plausible set of covariates here would be grade in math 11, an I. Q. measure, and say, attitude toward education. The null hypothesis that is tested in MANCOVA is that the adjusted population mean vectors are equal. Recall that the null hypothesis for MANOVA was that the population mean vectors are equal.

Before we proceed further, there are four excellent references for further study of covariance: an elementary introduction (Huck, Cormier, & Bounds, 1974), two good classic review articles (Cochran, 1957, Elashoff, 1969), and especially a very comprehensive and thorough text by Huitema (1980).

9.2 PURPOSES OF COVARIANCE

ANCOVA is linked to the following two basic objectives in experimental design:

1. elimination of systematic bias
2. reduction of within group or error variance

The best way of dealing with systematic bias (e.g., intact groups that differ systematically on several variables) is through random assignment of subjects to groups, thus equating the groups on all variables within sampling error. If random assignment is not possible, however, then covariance can be helpful in reducing bias.

Within group variability, which is primarily due to individual differences among the subjects, can be dealt with in several ways: sample selection (subjects who are more homogeneous will vary less on the criterion measure), factorial designs (blocking), repeated measures analysis, and analysis of covariance. Precisely how covariance reduces error is considered soon. Since analysis of covariance is linked to both of the basic objectives of experimental design, it certainly is a useful tool if properly used and interpreted.

In an experimental study (random assignment of subjects to groups) the main purpose of covariance is to reduce error variance, since there will be no systematic bias. However, if only a small number of subjects (say ≤ 10) can be assigned to each group, then chance differences are more possible and covariance is useful in adjusting the posttest means for the chance differences.

In a nonexperimental study the main purpose of covariance is to adjust the posttest means for initial differences among the groups which are very likely with intact groups. It should be emphasized, however, that even the use of several covariates does *not* equate intact groups, i.e., does not eliminate bias. Nevertheless, the use of 2 or 3 appropriate covariates can make for a much fairer comparison.

We now give two examples to illustrate how initial differences (systematic bias) on a key variable between treatment groups can confound the interpretation of results. Suppose an experimental psychologist wished to determine the effect of 3 methods of extinction on some kind of learned response. There are 3 intact groups to which the methods are applied, and it is found that the average number of trials to extinguish the response is least for method 2. Now, it may be that method 2 is more effective, or it may be that the subjects in method 2 didn't have the response as thoroughly ingrained as the subjects in the other two groups. In the latter case, the response would be easier to extinguish, and it wouldn't be clear whether it was the method that made the difference or the fact that the response was easier to extinguish that made method 2 look better. The effects of the two are confounded or mixed together. What is needed here is a measure of degree of learning at the start of the extinction trials (covariate). Then, if there are initial differences between the groups, the posttest means will be adjusted to take this into account. That is, covariance will adjust the posttest means to what they would be if all groups had started out *equally* on the covariate.

As another example, suppose we are comparing the effect of 4 stress situations on blood pressure, and find that situation 3 was significantly more stressful than the other 3 situations. However, we note that the blood pressure of the subjects in group 3 under minimal stress is greater than for subjects in the other groups. Then as in the previous example, it isn't clear that situaton 3 is necessarily most stressful. We need to determine whether the blood pressure for group 3 would still be higher if the means for all 4 groups were adjusted, assuming equal average blood pressure initially.

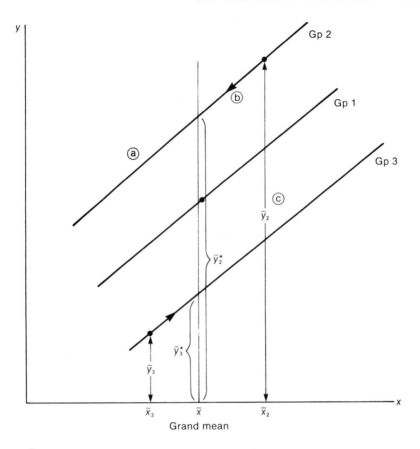

ⓐ positive correlation assumed between x and y

ⓑ The arrows on the regression lines indicate that the adjusted
means can be obtained by sliding the mean up (down) the
regression line until it hits the line for the grand mean.

ⓒ $\bar{y}_2$ is actual mean for Gp 2 and $\bar{y}_2^*$ represents the adjusted mean.

FIG. 9.1. Regression lines and adjusted means for three-group Analysis of Covariance.

Adjustment of Posttest Means

Basically, analysis of covariance adjusts the posttest means to what they would be if all groups had started out equally on the covariate, i.e., at the grand mean. This is illustrated graphically in Figure 9.1 for a hypothetical 3 group case. Since in Figure 9.1 a positive correlation is assumed between the covariate and dependent variable, this means higher x scores are associated with higher y scores. Thus, the mean for group 3 is adjusted upward since covariance estimates that

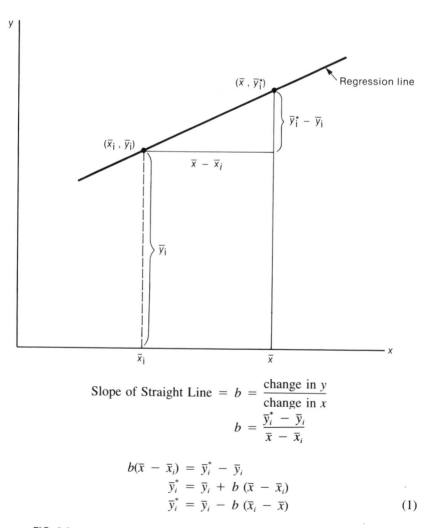

$$\text{Slope of Straight Line} = b = \frac{\text{change in } y}{\text{change in } x}$$

$$b = \frac{\bar{y}_i^* - \bar{y}_i}{\bar{x} - \bar{x}_i}$$

$$b(\bar{x} - \bar{x}_i) = \bar{y}_i^* - \bar{y}_i$$
$$\bar{y}_i^* = \bar{y}_i + b(\bar{x} - \bar{x}_i)$$
$$\bar{y}_i^* = \bar{y}_i - b(\bar{x}_i - \bar{x}) \tag{1}$$

FIG. 9.2. Deriving the general equation for the adjusted means in covariance.

if group 3 had scored higher on the average on x it would have scored higher on the average on y. Furthermore, since a linear relationship is assumed, the adjustment is made along the regression line for group 3.

In Figure 9.1 we didn't depict the original and adjusted means for group 1 since the mean for group 1 on the covariate is quite close to the grand mean, and therefore the original and adjusted means will differ by very little.

In Figure 9.2, assuming equal slopes (cf. 9.4) we derive the general equation for the adjusted means in ANCOVA for one covariate. The general equation follows from the basic definition for the slope of a straight line and some basic algebra.

Reduction of Error Variance

Consider a teaching methods study where the dependent variable is chemistry achievement and the covariate is I. Q. Then, within each teaching method there will be considerable variability on chemistry achievement due to individual differences among the students in terms of ability, background, attitude, etc. A sizable portion of this within-variability, however, is due to differences in I. Q. That is, chemistry achievement scores differ partly because the students differ in I. Q. If we can statistically remove this part of the within-variability, a smaller error term results, and hence a more powerful test. We denote the correlation between I. Q. and chemistry achievement by r_{xy}. Recall that the square of a correlation can be interpreted as "variance accounted for." Thus, for example, if $r_{xy} = .71$, then $(.71)^2 = .50$ or 50% of the within variability on chemistry achievement can be accounted for by variability on I. Q.

We denote the within-variability on chemistry achievement by MS_w, i.e., the usual error term for ANOVA. Now, symbolically the part of MS_w that is accounted for by I. Q. is $MS_w r_{xy}^2$. Thus, the within-variability that is left, after the portion due to the covariate is removed, is

$$MS_w - MS_w r_{xy}^2 = MS_w (1 - r_{xy}^2),$$

and this becomes our new error term for analysis of covariance, which we denote by MS_w^*. Technically, there is an additional factor involved, i.e.,

$$MS_w^* = MS_w (1 - r_{xy}^2) \{1 + 1/(f_e - 2)\} \tag{2}$$

where f_e is error degrees of freedom. However, the effect of this additional factor is slight as long as $N \geq 50$.

To show how much of a difference a covariate can make in increasing the sensitivity of an experiment, we consider a hypothetical study. An investigator runs a one-way ANOVA (3 groups and 20 subjects per group), and obtains $F = 200/100 = 2$, which is not significant, since the critical value at .05 is 3.18. He had pretested the subjects, but didn't use the pretest as a covariate since the groups didn't differ significantly on the pretest. (even though the correlation between pretest and posttest was .71). This is a common mistake made by some researchers who are unaware of the other purpose of covariance, that of reducing error variance. The analysis is redone by another investigator using ANCOVA. Using the equation that we just derived for the new error term for ANCOVA he finds:

$$MS_w{}^* \approx 100\ (1\ -\ (.71)^2)\ =\ 50$$

Thus, the error term for ANCOVA is only half as large as the error term for ANOVA. It is also necessary to obtain a new MS_b for ANCOVA, call it $MS_b{}^*$. Since the formula for $MS_b{}^*$ is complicated, we do not pursue it. Let us assume the investigator obtains the following F ratio for covariance analysis:

$$F^*\ =\ 190/\ 50\ =\ 3.8$$

This is significant at the .05 level. Therefore, the use of covariance can make the difference between not finding significance and finding significance. Finally, we wish to note that $MS_b{}^*$ can be smaller or larger than MS_b, although in a randomized study the expected values of the two are equal.

9.3.   CHOICE OF COVARIATES

In general, any variables which theoretically should correlate with the dependent variable, or variables which have been shown to correlate on similar types of subjects, should be considered as possible covariates. The ideal is to chose as covariates variables which of course are significantly correlated with the dependent variable *and* which have low correlations among themselves. If two covariates are highly correlated (say .80), then they are removing much of the *same* error variance from y; x_2 will not have much incremental validity. On the other hand, if two covariates (x_1 and x_2) have a low correlation (say .20), then they are removing relatively distinct pieces of the error variance from y, and we will obtain a much greater total error reduction. This is illustrated below graphically using Venn diagrams, where the circle represents error variance on y.

x_1 and x_2 Low correl.

x_1 and x_2 High correl.

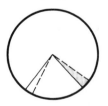

Solid lines—part of variance on y that x_1 accounts for.

Dashed lines—part of variance on y that x_2 accounts for.

The shaded portion in each case represents the incremental validity of x_2, ie., the part of error variance on y it removes that x_1 did not.

If the dependent variable is achievement in some content area, then one should always consider the possibility of at least 3 covariates:

1. a measure of ability in that specific content area
2. a measure of general ability (I. Q. measure)
3. one or two relevant noncognitive measures (e.g., attitude toward education, study habits, etc.)

An example of the above was given earlier, where we considered the effect of two different teaching methods on 12th grade mathematics achievement. We indicated that a plausible set of covariates would be grade in math 11 (a previous measure of ability in mathematics), an I. Q. measure, and attitude toward education (a noncognitive measure).

In studies with small or relatively small group sizes, it is particularly imperative to consider the use of 2 or 3 covariates. Why? Because for small or medium effect sizes, which are *very common* in social science research, power will be poor for small group size. Thus, one should attempt to reduce the error variance as much as possible to obtain a more sensitive (powerful) test.

Huitema (1980, p. 161) has recommended limiting the number of covariates to the extent that the ratio

$$\frac{C + (J - 1)}{N} < .10, \tag{3}$$

where C is the number of covariates, J is the number of groups, and N is total sample size. Thus, if we had a 3-group problem with a total of 60 subjects, then $(C + 2)/60 < .10$ or $C < 4$. We should use less than 4 covariates. If the above ratio is $> .10$, then the estimates of the adjusted means are likely to be unstable. That is, if the study were cross-validated, it could be expected that the equation used to estimate the adjusted means in the original study will yield very different estimates for another sample from the same population.

Importance of Covariate Being Measured Before Treatments

To avoid confounding (mixing together) of the treatment effect with a change on the covariate, one should use only pretest or other information gathered before treatments begin as covariates. If a covariate is used which is measured after treatments and that variable was affected by treatments, then the change on the covariate may be correlated with change on the dependent variable. Thus, when the covariate adjustment is made, you will remove part of the treatment effect.

9.4   ASSUMPTIONS IN ANALYSIS OF COVARIANCE

Analysis of covariance rests on the same assumptions as analysis of variance plus three additional assumptions regarding the regression part of the covariance analysis. That is, ANCOVA also assumes:

1. a linear relationship between the dependent variable and the covariate(s).
2. homogeneity of the regression slopes (for one covariate), i.e., that the slope of the regression line is the same in each group. For two covariates the assumption is parallelism of the regression planes, and for more than two covariates the assumption is homogeneity of the regression hyperplanes.
3. the covariate is measured without error.

Since covariance partly rests on the same assumptions as ANOVA, any violations that are serious in ANOVA (like the independence assumption) are also serious in ANCOVA. Violation of *all 3* of the remaining assumptions of covariance are also serious. For example, if the relationship between the covariate and the dependent variable is curvilinear, then the adjustment of the means will be improper. In this case, two possible courses of action are

1. Seek a transformation of the data which is linear.

This is possible if the relationship between the covariate and the dependent variable is monotonic

2. Fit a polynomial ANCOVA model to the data.

There is always measurement error for the variables that are typically used as covariates in social science research. And measurement error causes problems in both randomized and non-randomized designs, but is more serious in non-randomized designs. As Huitema (1980) notes, "In the case of randomized designs, . . . the power of the ANCOVA is reduced relative to what it would be if no error were present, but treatment effects are not biased. With other designs the effects of measurement error in *x* (covariate) are likely to be serious" (p. 299).

When measurement error is present on the covariate, then treatment effects can be seriously biased in non-randomized designs. In Fig. 9.3 we illustrate the effect measurement error can have when comparing two *different* populations with analysis of covariance. In the hypothetical example, with no measurement error we would conclude group 1 is superior to group 2, whereas with considerable measurement error the opposite conclusion is drawn: This example shows that if the covariate means are not equal, then the difference between the adjusted means is partly a function of the reliability of the covariate. Now, this problem

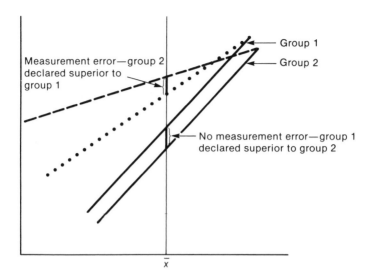

——— Regression lines for the groups with no measurement error
• • • Regression line for group 1 with considerable measurement error
— — Regression line for group 2 with considerable measurement error

FIG. 9.3. Effect of Measurement Error on Covariance Results When Comparing Subjects from Two Different Populations.

would not be of particular concern if we had a very reliable covariate like I. Q. or other cognitive variables from a good standardized test. If, on the other hand, the covariate is a noncognitive variable, or a variable derived from a nonstandardized instrument (which might well be of questionable reliability), then concern would definitely be justified.

A violation of the homogeneity of regression slopes can also yield misleading results if covariance is used. To illustrate this, we present in Figure 9.4 the situation where the assumption is met and two situations where the assumption is violated. Notice that with homogeneous slopes the estimated superiority of group 1 at the grand mean is an accurate estimate of group 1's superiority for all levels of the covariate, since the lines are parallel. On the other hand, for Case 1 of heterogeneous slopes, the superiority of group 1 (as estimated by covariance) is *not* an accurate estimate of group 1's superiority for other values of the covariate. For $x = a$, group 1 is only slightly better than group 2, while for $x = b$, the superiority of group 1 is seriously underestimated by covariance. The point is *when the slopes are unequal there is a covariate by treatment*

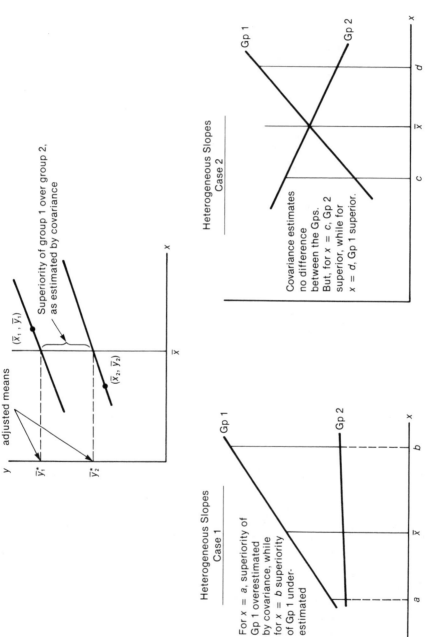

FIG. 9.4. Effect of Heterogeneous Slopes on Interpretation in ANCOVA

interaction. That is, how much better group 1 is depends on which value of the covariate we specify.

For Case 2 of heterogeneous slopes, use of covariance would be totally misleading. Covariance estimates no difference between the groups, while for $x = c$, group 2 is quite superior to group 1. For $x = d$, group 1 is superior to group 2. We will indicate, later in the chapter, in detail how the assumption of equal slopes is tested on SPSSX.

9.5   USE OF COVARIANCE WITH INTACT GROUPS

Analysis of covariance can be useful with intact groups; however, one must be aware of the limitations and be careful in interpreting results. First, as mentioned earlier, even the use of several covariates will not equate intact groups, and this should always be kept in mind.

Secondly, in some cases although covariance is possible, it may not be meaningful. Elashoff (1969) gives the following example. Teaching methods A and B are being compared. The class using A is composed of high ability students, whereas the class using B is composed of low ability students. A covariance analysis can be done on the posttest achievement scores holding ability constant, i.e., as if *A* and *B* had been used on classes of equal and average ability. But, as Elashoff notes, "It may make no sense to think about comparing methods A and B for students of average ability, perhaps each has been designed specifically for the ability level it was used with, or neither method will, in the future, be used for students of average ability."

Third, if measurement error is present on the covariate (which typically is the case in social science research), then treatment effects can be seriously biased (cf. Figure 9.3).

9.6   ERROR REDUCTION AND ADJUSTMENT OF POSTTEST MEANS FOR SEVERAL COVARIATES

What is the rationale for using several covariates? First, the use of several covariates will result in greater error reduction than can be obtained with just one covariate. The error reduction will be substantially greater if the covariates have relatively low intercorrelations amongst themselves (say $< .40$). Secondly, with several covariates we can make a better adjustment for initial differences between intact groups.

For one covariate the amount of error reduction was governed primarily by the magnitude of the correlation between the covariate and the dependent variable (cf. Equation 2). For several covariates the amount of error reduction is determined by the magnitude of the multiple correlation between the dependent variable and the set of covariates (predictors). This is why we indicated earlier it is desirable to have covariates with low intercorrelations amongst themselves, for then the multiple correlation will be larger, and we will achieve greater error reduction. Also, since R^2 has a variance accounted for interpretation, we can speak of the percentage of *within* variability on the dependent variable that is accounted for by the set of covariates.

Recall that the equation for the adjusted posttest mean for one covariate was given by:

$$\bar{y}_i{}^* = \bar{y}_i - b(\bar{x}_i - \bar{x}),$$

where b is the estimated common regression slope.

With several covariates $(x_1, x_2, \ldots, x_k)$ we are simply regressing y on the set of x's, and the adjusted equation becomes an extension of the above:

$$\bar{y}_j{}^* = \bar{y}_j - b_1 (\bar{x}_{1j} - \bar{x}_1) - b_2 (\bar{x}_{2j} - \bar{x}_2) - \ldots - b_k (\bar{x}_{kj} - \bar{x}_k), \quad (4)$$

where the b_i are the regression coefficients, $\bar{x}_{1j}$ is the mean for the covariate 1 in group j, $\bar{x}_{2j}$ is the mean for covariate 2 in group j, etc. and the $\bar{x}_i$ are the grand means for the covariates. We will illustrate the use of this equation on a sample MANCOVA problem.

9.7   MANCOVA—SEVERAL DEPENDENT VARIABLES AND SEVERAL COVARIATES

In MANCOVA we are assuming there is a significant relationship between the set of dependent variables and the set of covariates, or that there is a significant regression of the y's on the x's. This is tested through the use of Wilk's Λ. We are also assuming, for more than two covariates, homogeneity of the regression hyperplanes. The null hypothesis that is being tested in MANCOVA is that the adjusted population mean vectors are equal:

$$H_0 : \boldsymbol{\mu}_{1_{adj}} = \boldsymbol{\mu}_{2_{adj}} = \boldsymbol{\mu}_{3_{adj}} = \ldots = \boldsymbol{\mu}_{J_{adj}}$$

In testing the null hypothesis in MANCOVA adjusted $\mathbf{W}$ and $\mathbf{T}$ matrices are needed; we denote these by $\mathbf{W}^*$ and $\mathbf{T}^*$. In MANOVA recall that the null hypothesis was tested using Wilk's Λ. Thus, we have:

	MANOVA	MANCOVA
Test Statistic	$\Lambda = \dfrac{|\mathbf{W}|}{|\mathbf{T}|}$	$\Lambda^* = \dfrac{|\mathbf{W}^*|}{|\mathbf{T}^*|}$

The calculation of **W*** and **T*** involves considerable matrix algebra, which we wish to avoid. For the reader who is interested in the details, however, Finn (1974) has a nice worked out example.

In examining the printout from the statistical packages it is important to *first* make two checks to determine whether covariance is appropriate:

1. Check to see that there is a significant relationship between the dependent variables and the covariates.
2. Check to determine that the homogeneity of the regression hyperplanes is satisfied.

If either of these is not satisfied, then covariance is not appropriate. In particular, if (2) is not met, then one should consider using the Johnson-Neyman technique, which determines a region of nonsignificance, i.e., a set of x values for which the groups do not differ, and hence for values of x outside this region one group is superior to the other. The Johnson-Neyman technique is excellently described in Huitema (1980), where he shows specifically how to calculate the region of nonsignificance for one covariate, the effect of measurement error on the procedure, and other issues. For further extended discussion on the Johnson-Neyman technique see Rogosa (1977, 1980).

Incidentally, if the homogeneity of regression slopes is rejected for several groups, it does not automatically follow that the slopes for all groups differ. In this case one might follow up the overall test with additional homogeneity tests on all combinations of pairs of slopes. Often, the slopes will be homogeneous for many of the groups. In this case one can apply ANCOVA to the groups that have homogeneous slopes, and apply the Johnson-Neyman technique to the groups with heterogeneous slopes. Unfortunately, at present, none of the three major statistical packages (BMDP, SPSSX, SAS) has the Johnson-Neyman technique.

9.8   TESTING THE ASSUMPTION OF HOMOGENEOUS REGRESSION HYPERPLANES ON SPSSX

Neither SPSSX or BMDP automatically provide the test of the homogeneity of the regression hyperplanes. Recall that for one covariate, this is the assumption of equal regression slopes in the groups, and that for two covariates it is the assumption of parallel regression planes. In order to setup the control lines to test this assumption, it is necessary to understand what a violation of the assumption means. As we indicated earlier (and displayed in Figure 9.4), a violation means there is a covariate by treatment interaction. Evidence that the assumption is met means the interaction is not significant.

Thus, what is done on SPSSX is to set up an effect involving the interaction (for one covariate), and then testing whether this effect is significant. If the effect is significant, this means the assumption is *not* tenable. This is one of those cases where we don't want significance, for then the assumption is tenable and covariance is appropriate.

If there is more than one covariate, then there is an interaction effect for each covariate. We lump the effects together and then test whether the combined interactions are significant. Before we give two examples, we note that BY is the keyword used by SPSSX to denote an interaction and + is used to lump effects together.

Example 1—Two dependent variables and one covariate

We call the grouping variable TREATS, and denote the dependent variables by $Y1$ and $Y2$, and the covariate by $X1$. Then the control lines are

```
ANALYSIS = Y1,Y2/
DESIGN = X1,TREATS,X1 BY TREATS/
```

Example 2—Three dependent variables and two covariates

We denote the dependent variables by $Y1$, $Y2$, and $Y3$ and the covariates by $X1$ and $X2$. Then the control lines are

```
ANALYSIS = Y1,Y2,Y3/
DESIGN = X1 + X2,TREATS,X1 BY TREATS + X2 BY TREATS/
```

These two control lines will be imbedded among many others in running a multivariate MANCOVA on SPSSX, as the reader will see in the computer examples we consider next. With the above two examples, and the computer examples, the reader should be able to generalize the set up of the control lines for testing homogeneity of regression hyperplanes for any combination of dependent variables and covariates.

9.9   COMPUTER EXAMPLES

We now consider two examples to illustrate (1) how to setup the control lines to run multivariate analysis of covariance on SPSSX and (2) how to interpret the output, including that which checks whether covariance is appropriate. The first example uses artificial data and is simpler, having just two dependent variables and one covariate, while the second example uses data from an actual study and is more complex, involving 4 dependent variables and 4 covariates.

Example 3

This example has two groups, with 15 subjects in group 1 and 14 subjects in group 2. There are two dependent variables (denoted by POSTCOMP and POSTHIOR in the SPSSX control lines and on the printout) and one covariate (denoted by PRECOMP). The control lines for running the MANCOVA analysis

TABLE 9.1
SPSSX MANOVA Control Lines for Example 3:
Two Dependent Variables and One Covariate

```
TITLE MANCOVA CHAP 9'
DATA LIST FREE/GPID PRECOMP POSTCOMP POSTHIOR
LIST
BEGIN DATA
    1.00        15.00        17.00        3.00
    1.00        10.00         6.00        3.00
    1.00        13.00        13.00        1.00
    1.00        14.00        14.00        8.00
    1.00        12.00        12.00        3.00
    1.00        10.00         9.00        9.00
    1.00        12.00        12.00        3.00
    1.00         8.00         9.00       12.00
    1.00        12.00        15.00        3.00
    1.00         8.00        10.00        8.00
    1.00        12.00        13.00        1.00
    1.00         7.00        11.00       10.00
    1.00        12.00        16.00        1.00
    1.00         9.00        12.00        2.00
    1.00        12.00        14.00        8.00
    2.00         9.00         9.00        3.00
    2.00        13.00        19.00        5.00
    2.00        13.00        16.00       11.00
    2.00         6.00         7.00       18.00
    2.00        10.00        11.00       15.00
    2.00         6.00         9.00        9.00
    2.00        16.00        20.00        8.00
    2.00         9.00        15.00        6.00
    2.00        10.00         8.00        9.00
    2.00         8.00        10.00        3.00
    2.00        13.00        16.00       12.00
    2.00        12.00        17.00       20.00
    2.00        11.00        18.00       12.00
    2.00        14.00        18.00       16.00
END DATA
MANOVA PRECOMP POSTCOMP POSTHIOR BY GPID(1,2)/
ANALYSIS = POSTCOMP POSTHIOR WITH PRECOMP/          ①
PRINT = PMEANS/                                     ②
DESIGN/
ANALYSIS = POSTCOMP POSTHIOR/                        ③
DESIGN = PRECOMP,GPID,PRECOMP BY GPID/
```

①The keyword WITH precedes the covariates in SPSSX.

②This PRINT subcommand is necessary in order to obtain the adjusted means. These are what we are testing for significance in covariance. Starting with release 2.1, it is necessary to use the following to get adjusted means
PRINT = PARAMETERS(ESTIM) PMEANS.

③These ANALYSIS and DESIGN subcommands are required for testing the homogeneity of the regression slopes; see Example 1 of this chapter.

are given in Table 9.1, along with annotation. In Table 9.2 are the two tests for determining whether covariance is appropriate. First, there should be a significant linear relationship between the dependent variables and the covariate. Saying there is a significant linear relationship is equivalent to a significant regression of the dependent variables on the covariate. The multivariate tests for this, given under "EFFECT . . WITHIN CELLS REGRESSION," is significant at the .05 level. The other crucial assumption is that of equality of the regression slopes. Recall that a violation of this assumption implies a covariate by group interaction. Since BY is the keyword for interaction in SPSSX we test this assumption by testing whether "EFFECT . . PRECOMP BY GPID" is significant. As Table 9.2 shows, this effect is not significant at the .05 level. In Figure 9.5 we present the scatter plots for POSTCOMP, along with the slopes and the regression lines for each group.

The previous results indicate that covariance is appropriate. The multivariate null hypothesis tested in covariance is that the adjusted population mean vectors are equal, i.e.,

$$H_0 : \begin{pmatrix} \mu_{11}^* \\ \mu_{21}^* \end{pmatrix} = \begin{pmatrix} \mu_{12}^* \\ \mu_{22}^* \end{pmatrix}$$

The multivariate tests in Table 9.3 show that we reject H_0 at the .05 level and hence conclude that the groups differ on the set of two adjusted means. The univariate ANCOVA followup F's indicate that both variables are contributing to the overall multivariate significance. In Table 9.3 we also show how the adjusted means on the printout would be obtained.

Can we have confidence in the reliability of the adjusted means? According to Huitema's inequality we need $[C + (J - 1)]/N < .10$. Since here $J = 2$ and $N = 29$, we obtain $(C + 1)/ 29 < .10$ or $C < 1.9$. Thus, we should use less than 2 covariates for reliable results, and we have just used 1 covariate.

Example 4

Next we consider a social psychological study by Novince (1977) which examined the effect of behavioral rehearsal, and behavioral rehearsal plus cognitive restructuring (combination treatment) on reducing anxiety and facilitating social skills for female college freshmen. There was also a control group (group 2), with 11 subjects in each group. The subjects were pretested and posttested on 4 measures, thus the pretests were the covariates.

In Table 9.4 we present the control lines for running the MANCOVA, along with annotation explaining what the various subcommands are doing. The least obvious part of the setup is obtaining the test for the homogeneity of the regression hyperplanes. Tables 9.5, 9.6, and 9.7 present selected output from the MANCOVA run on SPSSX. Table 9.5 contains descriptive information, i.e., means on the covariates (pretests) and on the dependent variables (posttests). Table 9.6

TABLE 9.2

Multivariate Test for Relationship between Dependent Variables and Covariate and Test of Equality of Regression Slopes

EFFECT .. WITHIN CELLS REGRESSION

MULTIVARIATE TESTS OF SIGNIFICANCE (S = 1, M = 0, N = 11 1/2)

TEST NAME	VALUE	APPROX. F	HYPOTH. DF	ERRO DF	SIG. OF F
PILLAIS	.64521	22.73198	2.00	25.00	.000
HOTELLINGS	1.81856	22.73196	2.00	25.00	.000
① WILKS	.35479	22.73196	2.00	25.00	.000
ROYS	.64521				

UNIVARIATE F-TESTS WITH (1,26) D. F.

VARIABLE	SQ. MUL. R.	MUL. R	ADJ. R-SQ.	HYPOTH. MS.	ERROR MS	F	SIG. OF F
POSTCOMP	.63788	.79867	② .62395	247.97979	5.41451	45.79909	.000
POTHIOR	.01791	.13383	.00000	10.20072	21.51151	.47420	.497

EFFECT .. PRECOMP BY GPID

MULTIVARIATE TESTS OF SIGNIFICANCE (S = 1, M = 0, N = 11)

TEST NAME	VALUE	APPROX. F	HYPOTH. DF	ERROR DF	SIG. OF F
PILLAIS	.13699	1.90481	2.00	24.00	.171
HOTELLINGS	.15873	1.90481	2.00	24.00	.171
③ WILKS	.86301	1.90481	2.00	24.00	.171
ROYS	.13699				

UNIVARIATE F-TESTS WITH (1,25) D. F.

VARIABLE	HYPOTH. SS	ERROR SS	HYPOTH. MS	ERROR MS	F	SIG. OF F
POSTCOMP	3.69207	132.08528	8.69207	5.28341	1.64516	.211
POSTHIOR	47.94379	511.35549	47.94379	20.45422	2.34396	.138

①This multivariate test indicates there is a significant relationship between the 2 dependent variables and the covariate at the .05 level.

②These univariate results indicate that only POSTCOMP has a significant and strong linear relationship with the covariate. Note also that the multiple correlation (MUL. R) is actually a simple correlation here since there is only one predictor (covariate).

③This indicates that the assumption of equal regression slopes is tenable at .05 level, since .171 > .05.

TABLE 9.3
The Multivariate and Univariate Covariance Results and the Adjusted Means

EFFECT .. GPID

MULTIVARIATE TESTS OF SIGNIFICANCE (S = 1, M = 0, N = 11 1/2)

TEST NAME	VALUE	APPROX. F	HYPOTH. DF	ERROR DF	SIG. OF F
PILLAIS	.35108	6.76281	2.00	25.00	.004
HOTELLINGS	.54102	6.76281	2.00	25.00	.004
WILKS	.64892	6.76281	2.00	25.00	.004
ROYS	.35108				

①

UNIVARIATE F-TESTS WITH (1,26) D. F.

VARIABLE	HYPOTH. SS	ERROR SS	HYPOTH. MS	ERROR MS	F	SIG. OF F
POSTCOMP	28.49860	140.77735	28.49860	5.41451	5.26337	.030
POSTHIOR	211.69023	559.29928	211.59023	21.51151	9.83614	.004

②

ADJUSTED AND ESTIMATED MEANS

VARIABLE .. POSTCOMP

FACTOR	CODE	OBS. MEAN	ADJ. MEAN
GPID	1	12.20000	12.00555
GPID	2	13.78571	13.99406

④

VARIABLE .. POSTHIOR

FACTOR	CODE	OBS. MEAN	ADJ. MEAN
GPID	1	5.00000	5.03944
GPID	2	10.50000	10.45774

VARIABLE .. PRECOMP

FACTOR	CODE	OBS. MEAN
GPID	1	11.06667
GPID	2	10.71429

REGRESSION ANALYSIS

DEPENDENT VARIABLE .. POSTCOMP

COVARIATE

PRECOMP   1.1430650341

DEPENDENT VARIABLE .. POSTHIOR   ③

COVARIATE

PRECOMP   -.2318346046

① This is the main result, indicating that the adjusted population mean vectors are different at the .05 level, since .004 < .05. Thus, the groups differ on the set of 2 dependent variables.

② These are the F's that would result if a *separate* analysis of covariance was done on each dependent variable. The probabilities show that both variables are significant at the .05 level, and thus both are contributing to overall multivariate significance.

③ These are the regression coefficients used in obtaining the adjusted means.

④ Recall that the equation for the adjusted means is given by $\bar{y}_i^* = \bar{y}_i - b(\bar{x}_i - \bar{x}_.)$, where b is regression coefficient and $\bar{x}_i$ and $\bar{x}_.$ are group and grand means for the covariate. Thus, here we have $\bar{y}_i^* = 12.2 - 1.143(11.067 - 10.89) = 12.008$.

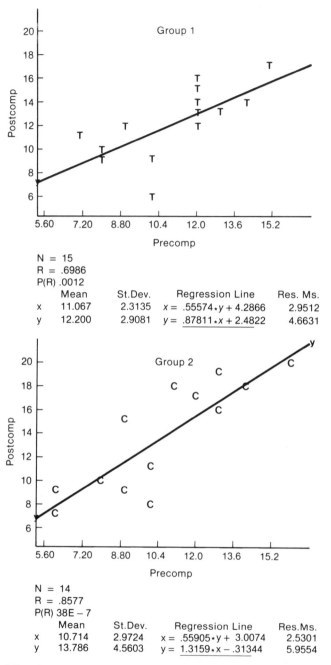

N = 15
R = .6986
P(R) .0012

	Mean	St.Dev.	Regression Line	Res. Ms.
x	11.067	2.3135	$x = .55574*y + 4.2866$	2.9512
y	12.200	2.9081	$y = .87811*x + 2.4822$	4.6631

N = 14
R = .8577
P(R) 38E − 7

	Mean	St.Dev.	Regression Line	Res.Ms.
x	10.714	2.9724	$x = .55905*y + 3.0074$	2.5301
y	13.786	4.5603	$y = 1.3159*x − .31344$	5.9554

The fact that the univariate test for POSTCOMP in Table 9.2 is not significant ($F = 1.645$, $p < .211$) means that the differences in slopes here (.878 and 1.316) are simply due to sampling error, i.e., the homogeneity of slopes assumption is tenable for this variable.

FIG. 9.5. Scatter Plots and Regression Lines for Postcomp vs Covariate in Two Groups

TABLE 9.4
SPSSX MANOVA Control Lines for Example 4: Four Dependent
Variables and Four Covariates

```
        TITLE 'MANCOVA NOVINCE DATA SELF REPORT VARIABES '.
        DATA LIST FREE/ TREATS AVOID NEGEVAL, SOCINT,SRINV,PREAVOID,
            PRENEG,PRESOCI,PRESR
        LIST
        BEGIN DATA
①       DATA LINES

        END DATA
        MANOVA AVOID,NEGEVAL,SOCINT,SRINV,PREAVOID,PRENEG,PRESCOI,
            PRESR BY TREATS(3,1)/
②       ANALYSIS = AVOID,NEGEVAL,SOCINT,SRINV WITH PREAVOID,PRENEG,
        PRESOCI,PRESR/
        PRINT = PMEANS/
        DESIGN/
      ┌ ANALYSIS = AVOID,NEGEVAL,SOCINT,SRINV/
③     ┤ DESIGN = PREAVOID + PREGNEG + PRESOCI + PRESR,TREATS,PREAVOID BY TREATS +
      │ PRENEG BY TREATS + PRESOCI BY TREATS + PRESR BY TREATS/
④     └ ANALYSIS = PREAVOID,PRENEG,PRESOCI,PRESR/
```

①The data is given in the Appendix at the end of this chapter.

②Recall that the keyword WITH precedes the covariates in SPSSX.

③These ANALYSIS and DESIGN subcommands are required for testing the homogeneity of the regression hyperplanes . The third effect in the DESIGN subcommand, i.e., PREAVOID BY TREATS + PRENEG BY TREATS + PRESOCI BY TREATS + PRESR BY TREATS, is testing whether the assumption of homogeneity of the regression hyperplanes is tenable. Recall that a violation of this assumption implies a covariate by treatment interaction. The keyword BY denotes an interaction and + is used for lumping effects together. We lump the 4 covariate by treatment interactions together here since we wish to know whether the covariates as a set violate the assumption.

④This subcommand is used for testing whether the groups differ on the set of covariates. Output from this analysis is needed in applying the Bryant-Paulson post hoc procedure for locating significant pairwise differences (cf. Table 9.8). For example, in a randomized study with several covariates, this analysis will yield the Hotelling-Lawley trace (called Hotelling's on the SPSSX output).

TABLE 9.5
Means on Posttests and Pretests for MANCOVA Problem, Example 4

ADJUSTED AND ESTIMATED MEANS

VARIABLE .. AVOID

FACTOR	CODE	OBS. MEAN	ADJ. MEAN
TREATS	1	116.98090	120.63733
TREATS	2	105.90909	110.17788
TREATS	3	132.27273	124.27570

TABLE 9.5
Means on Posttests and Pretests for MANCOVA Problem, Example 4

VARIABLE .. NEGEVAL

FACTOR	CODE	OBS. MEAN	ADJ. MEAN
TREATS	1	108.81818	112.37373
TREATS	2	94.36364	97.37026
TREATS	3	131.00000	124.43783

VARIABLE .. SRINV

FACTOR	CODE	OBS. MEAN	ADJ. MEAN
TREATS	1	150.18182	147.98037
TREATS	2	164.81818	161.24915
TREATS	3	127.45455	133.22502

VARIABLE .. SOCINT

FACTOR	CODE	OBS. MEAN	ADJ. MEAN
TREATS	1	102.36364	103.08738
TREATS	2	73.72727	76.11871
TREATS	3	111.27273	108.15755

VARIABLE .. PREVOID

FACTOR	CODE	OBS. MEAN
TREATS	1	104.00000
TREATS	2	103.27273
TREATS	3	113.63635

VARIABLE .. PRENEG

FACTOR	CODE	OBS. MEAN
TREATS	1	93.90909
TREATS	2	95.00000
TREATS	3	109.18182

VARIABLE .. PRESR

FACTOR	CODE	OBS. MEAN
TREATS	1	165.63636
TREATS	2	167.90909
TREATS	3	150.18182

VARIABLE .. PRESOCI

FACTOR	CODE	OBS.MEAN
TREATS	1	79.18182
TREATS	2	73.81818
TREATS	3	80.54545

TABLE 9.6
Multivariate Tests for Relationship between Dependent Variables and Covariates and Test for Parallelism of Regression Hyperplanes

EFFECT .. WITHIN CELLS REGRESSION

MULTIVARIATE TESTS OF SIGNIFICANCE (S = 4, M = -1/2, N = 10 1/2)

TEST NAME	VALUE	APPROX. F	HYPOTH. DF	ERROR DF	SIG. OF F
PILLAIS	1.40810	3.53124	16.00	104.00	.000
HOTELLINGS	4.19499	5.63702	16.00	86.00	.000
WILKS	.10599	4.80699 ①	16.00	70.90	.000
ROYS	.75381				

UNIVARIATE F-TESTS WITH (4,26) D. F.

VARIABLE	SQ. MUL. R	MUL. R	ADJ. R-SQ.	HYPOTH. MS	ERROR MS	F	SIG. OF F
AVOID	.73261	.8592	.69147	1538.84966	86.40774	17.80916	.000
NEGEVAL	.31079 ②	.55748	.20476	649.97439	225.16478	2.93107	.040
SOCINT	.49984	.70699	.42289	682.64351	105.090981	6.49581	.001
SRINV	.34026	.58332	.23876	905.43502	270.08692	3.35238	.024

EFFECT .. PREAVOID BY TREATS + PRENEG BY TREATS + PRESOCI BY TREATS + PRESR BY TREATS

MULTIVARIATE TESTS OF SIGNIFICANCE (S = 4, M = 1 1/2, N = 6 1/2)

TEST NAME	VALUE	APPROX. F	HYPOTH. DF	ERROR DF	SIG. OF F
PILLAIS	.91410	.66649	32.00	72.00	.897
HOTELLINGS	1.45615	.61431	32.00	54.00	.929
WILKS	.31997	.64392 ③	32.00	56.91	.910
ROYS	.42725				

① This multivariate test indicates that there is a significant relationship between the set of dependent and the set of covariates at the .05 level.

② These are for the multiple regression of each dependent variable separately on the set of 4 covariates. The .7326 for AVOID indicates that 73.26% of the within variability on this variable is accounted for by 4 covariates.

③ This indicates that the assumption of homogeneity of the regression hyperplanes is quite tenable here at the .05 level, since $F = .644, p < .910$.

TABLE 9.7

The Multivariate and Univariate Covariance Results and Regression Coefficients for the Avoidance Variable

EFFECT .. TREATS

MULTIVARIATE TESTS OF SIGNIFICANCE (S = 2, M = 1/2, N = 10 1/2)

TEST NAME	VALUE	APPROX. F	HYPOTH. DF	ERROR DF	SIG. OF F
PILLAIS	.84045	4.34886	8.00	48.00	.001
HOTELLINGS	2.76168	7.59463	8.00	44.00	.000
WILKS	.24352	① 5.90209	8.00	46.00	.000
ROYS	.72456				

UNIVARIATE F-TESTS WITH (2,26) D. F.

VARIABLE	HYPOTH. SS	ERROR SS	HYPOTH. MS	ERROR MS	F	SIG. OF F
AVOID	1047.45440	2246.60137	523.72720	86.40774	6.0611	.007
NEGEVAL	3433.94023	5854.28426	1716.90712	225.16478	② 7.62539	.002
SOCINT	5926.54223	2732.33503	2963.27112	105.08981	28.19751	.000
SRINV	3598.22806	7022.25991	1799.11403	270.08692	6.66124	.005

REGRESSION ANALYSIS FOR WITHIN CELLS ERROR TEAM (CONT.)

DEPENDENT VARIABLE .. AVOID

COVARIATE	B	BETA	STD. ERR	T-VALUE	SIG. OF T
PREAVOID	③ .5732142081	.6324648697	.10787	5.31371	.000
PRENEG	.2425192713	.2316063103	.12117	2.00224	.056
PRESOCI	.0041195162	.0042867469	.11024	.03737	.970
PRESR	-.1611494246	-2.088419383	.08515	-1.89245	.070

①This is the main result, indicating that the adjusted population mean vectors are significantly different at the .05 level ($F = 5.902$, $p < .000$). That is, the groups differ on the *set* of posttest means, after appropriate adjustments have been made for initial differences.

②These are the *F*'s that would result if a *separate* analysis of covariance was done on each dependent variable. The probabilities indicate that all variables are significant at the .05 level; thus, all of the variables are contributing to the overall multivariate significance.

③These are the regression coefficients that are used in obtaining the adjusted means for AVOID.

contains output for determining whether covariance is appropriate for this data. First, in Table 9.6 is the multivariate test for significant association between the dependent variables and the covariates (or significant regression of y's on x's). The multivariate $F = 4.807$ (corresponding to Wilk's Λ), which is significant beyond the .001 level. Now we make the second check to determine whether covariance is appropriate, i.e., is the assumption of homogeneous regression hyperplanes tenable. The multivariate test for this assumption is under

"EFFECT . . . PREAVOID BY TREATS + ... + PRESR BY TREATS"

Since the multivariate $F = .644$ (corresponding to Wilk's Λ), the assumption is quite tenable. Recall that a violation of this assumption implies a covariate by treatment interaction, and that is why we lump together the covariate by treatment interaction effects for each covariate. We then test to see whether this effect is significant.

The main result for the multivariate analysis of covariance, i.e., the multi-variate test to determine whether the adjusted population mean vectors are significantly different, is at the top of Table 9.7. The multivariate $F = 5.902$ (corresponding to Wilk's Λ) is significant beyond the .001 level. The univariate analyses of covariance at the bottom of Table 9.7 indicate that all of the variables are contributing to the overall multivariate significance at $\alpha = .05$.

Some other comments on the output in Tables 9.5 through 9.7. We already indicated there is a significant relationship between the set of dependent variables and the set of covariates. The univariate F's in Table 9.6 indicate additionally that the regression of each dependent variable on the set of covariates is also significant at the .05 level. Also, the "SQ. MUL. R" are the squared multiple correlations for each dependent variable regressed *separately* on the 4 covariates. Thus, the first squared multiple correlation for AVOID of .7326 indicates that above 73% of within group variability on AVOID is accounted for by the 4 covariates.

Recall that the equation for the adjusted mean for a variable when several covariates are involved is obtained through multiple regression and is given by

$$\bar{y}_j^* = \bar{y}_j - b_1 (\bar{x}_{1j} - \bar{x}_1) - b_2 (\bar{x}_{2j} - \bar{x}_2) - \ldots - b_k (\bar{x}_{kj} - \bar{x}_k)$$

To illustrate the application of this equation, we show how the adjusted mean on AVOID in group 1 of 120.637 is obtained. To obtain the adjusted mean the means for all 4 covariates in group 1 are required; these are given in the bottom half of Table 9.5. We also need the grand means for the covariates $(\bar{x}_i)$, which are obtained by simply taking the average (since the group sizes are equal) of the means for each variable over the groups. Thus, the grand mean for PREA-VOID is

$(104 + 103.273 + 113.636)/3 = 106.97$

Finally, we need the regression coefficients (b_i) for regressing AVOID on the 4 covariates. These are boxed in on Table 9.7. Therefore, the adjusted mean for AVOID in group 1 is given by:

$$\bar{y}_1^* = 116.91 - .5732 (104 - 106.97) - .2425 (93.91 - 99.36)$$

$$- .0041 (79.18 - 77.85) + .1612 (165.64 - 161.24) = 120.637$$

The one concern we have about this study involves the stability of the adjusted means, since sample size ($N = 33$) does not justify using 4 covariates (cf. Equation 3).

9.10   BRYANT-PAULSON SIMULTANEOUS TEST PROCEDURE

Since the covariate(s) used in social science research are essentially always random, it is important that this information be incorporated into any post hoc procedure following ANCOVA. This is *not* the case for the Tukey procedure, and hence it is not appropriate as a followup technique following ANCOVA. The Bryant-Paulson (1976) procedure was derived under the assumption that the covariate is a random variable and hence is appropriate in ANCOVA. It is a generalization of the Tukey technique. Which particular Bryant-Paulson (BP) statistic we use to determine whether a pair of means are significantly different depends on whether the study is a randomized or non-randomized design and on how many covariates there are (one or several). In Table 9.8 we have the test statistic for each of the 4 cases. Note that if the group sizes are unequal, then the harmonic mean is employed.

We now illustrate use of the Bryant-Paulson procedure on the computer example. Since this was a randomized study with four covariates, the appropriate statistic from Table 9.8 is

$$BP = \frac{\bar{Y}_i^* - \bar{Y}_j^*}{\sqrt{MS_W^* \left[1 + \frac{1}{(J-1)} TR(\mathbf{B}_x \mathbf{W}_x^{-1})\right]/n}}$$

Is there a significant difference between the adjusted means on avoidance for groups 1 and 2 at the .95 simultaneous level?

Table 9.6 under
ERROR MS
$$BP = \frac{120.64 \overset{\text{Table 9.5(top)}}{\longleftarrow} 110.18}{\sqrt{86.41[1 + 1/2(.307)]/11}} \quad \text{HOTELLING-LAWLEY trace for set of covariate}$$

$$BP = \frac{10.46}{\sqrt{86.41(1.15)/11}} = 3.49$$

TABLE 9.8
Bryant-Paulson Statistics for Detecting Significant Pairwise
Differences in Covariance Analysis for One and for Several
Covariates①

One Covariate	*Many Covariates②*

RANDOMIZED STUDY

$$\frac{\bar{Y}_i^* - \bar{Y}_j^*}{\sqrt{MW_W^*[1 + MS_{B_x}/SS_{W_x}]/n}}$$

$$\frac{\bar{Y}_i^* - \bar{Y}_j^*}{\sqrt{MS_W^*\,[1 + \dfrac{1}{(J-1)} TR(\mathbf{B}_x\mathbf{W}_x^{-1})]/n}}$$

WHERE

$\bar{Y}_i^*$ IS THE ADJUSTED MEAN FOR GROUP i

MS_{B_x} IS THE MEAN BETWEEN SQUARE ON THE COVARIATE

SS_{W_x} IS THE SUM OF SQUARES WITHIN ON THE COVARIATE

MS_W^* IS THE ERROR TERM FOR COVARIANCE

n ISTHE COMMON GROUP SIZE. IF UNEQUAL n, USE THE HARMONIC MEAN.

$\mathbf{B}_x$ IS THE BETWEEN SSCP MATRIX

$\mathbf{W}_x$ IS THE WITHIN SSCP MATRIX

TR $(\mathbf{B}_x\mathbf{W}_x^{-1})$ IS THE HOTELLING-LAWLEY TRACE.

THIS IS GIVEN ON THE SPSS MANOVA PRINTOUT.

NON-RANDOMIZED STUDY

$$\frac{\bar{Y}_i^* - \bar{Y}_j^*}{\sqrt{MS_W^*\{2/n + [(\bar{X}_i - \bar{X}_j)^2/SS_{W_x}]\}/2}}$$

$$(\bar{Y}_i^* - \bar{Y}_j^*) \Big/ \sqrt{\frac{MS_W^*[(2/n) + \mathbf{d}'\,\mathbf{W}_x^{-1}\mathbf{d}]}{2}}$$

WHERE $\bar{X}_i$ IS THE MEAN FOR THE COVARIATE IN GROUP i. NOTE THAT THE ERROR TERM MUST BE COMPUTED *SEPARATELY* FOR EACH PAIRWISE COMPARISON.

$\mathbf{d}'$ IS THE ROW VECTOR OF DIFFERENCES BETWEEN THE ith and jth GROUPS ON THE COVARIATES.

①THE BRYANT-PAULSON STATISTICS WERE DERIVED UNDER THE ASSUMPTION THAT THE COVARIATES ARE RANDOM VARIABLES, WHICH IS ALMOST ALWAYS THE CASE IN PRACTICE.

②DEGREES OF FREEDOM FOR ERROR IS $N - J - C$, WHERE C IS THE NUMBER OF COVARIATES.

We have not presented the Hotelling-Lawley trace as part of the selected output for the second computer example. It is the part of the output related to the last ANALYSIS subcommand in Table 4 comparing the groups on the set of covariates. Now, having computed the value of the test statistic, we need the critical value. The critical values are given in Table G in the back of this volume. Table G is entered at $\alpha = .05$, with $df_e = N - J - C = 33 - 3 - 4 = 26$, and for 4 covariates. The table only extends to 3 covariates, but the value of 3 will be a good approximation. The critical values for $df_e = 24$ with 3 covariates is 3.76, and the critical value for $df_e = 30$ is 3.67. Interpolating, we find the critical values $= 3.73$. Since the value of the BP statistics is 3.49, there is not a significant difference.

9.11   SUMMARY OF MAJOR POINTS

1.   In analysis of covariance a linear relationship is assumed between the dependent variable(s) and the covariate(s).

2.   Analysis of covariance is directly related to the two basic objectives in experimental design of (a) eliminating systematic bias and (b) reduction of error variance. While ANCOVA does not eliminate bias, it can reduce bias. This is particularly useful in nonexperimental studies comparing intact groups. The bias is reduced by adjusting the posttest means to what they would be if all groups had started out equally on the covariate(s), i.e., at the grand means(s).

3.   The main reason for using ANCOVA in an experimental study (random assignment of subjects to groups) is to reduce error variance, yielding a more powerful test. When using several covariates, greater error reduction will occur when the covariates have low intercorrelations amongst themselves.

4.   Limit the number of covariates (C) so that

$$\frac{C + (J - 1)}{N} < .10$$

where J is the number of groups and N is total sample size, so that stable estimates of the adjusted means are obtained.

5.   Measurement error on the covariate causes loss of power in randomized designs, and can lead to seriously biased treatment effects in non-randomized designs. Thus, if one has a covariate of low reliability or of questionable reliability, then true score ANCOVA should be contemplated.

6.   In examining printout from the statistical packages, first make two checks to determine whether covariance is appropriate, i.e., (1) check that there is a significant relationship between the dependent variables and the covariates, and (2) check that the homogeneity of regression hyperplanes assumption is tenable. If either of these is not satisfied, then covariance is not appropriate. In particular, if (2) is not satisfied, then the Johnson-Neyman technique should be used.

7.   Use the Bryant-Paulson procedure for determining where there are significant pairwise differences. This technique assumes the covariates are random variables, almost always the case in social science research, and with it one can maintain the overall α level at .05 or .01.

EXERCISES FOR ANCOVA—CHAPTER 9

1.   Scandura (1984) examined the effects of a leadership training treatment on employee work outcomes of job satisfaction (HOPPOCKA), leadership relations (LMXA), performance ratings (ERSA), and actual performance—quantity (QUANAFT) and quality of work (QUALAFT). Thus, there were 5 dependent variables. The names in parentheses are the names used for the variables that appear on selected printout we present here. Since previous research had indicated that the characteristics of the work performed—motivating potential (MPS), work load (OL1), and job problems (DTT)—are related to these work outcomes, these three variables were used as covariates. Of 100 subjects, 35 were randomly assigned to the leadership treatment condition and 65 to the control group. During the 26 weeks of the study, 11 subjects dropped out, about an equal number from each group. Scandura ran the two-group multivariate analysis of covariance on SPSSX.

   a) Show the control lines for running the MANCOVA on SPSSX such that the adjusted means and the test for homogeneity of the regression hyperplanes are also obtained. Assume free format for the variables.

   b) On pages 323–325 we present selected printout from Scandura's run. From the printout determine whether analysis of covariance is appropriate.

   c) If covariance is appropriate, then determine whether the multivariate test is significant at the .05 level.

   d) If the multivariate test is significant, then which of the individual variables, at the .01 level, are contributing to the multivariate significance?

   e) What are the adjusted means for the significant variable(s) found in (d)? Did the treatment group do better than the control (assume higher is better)?

2.   Consider the following data from a two-group MANCOVA with two dependent variables (Y1 and Y2) and one covariate (X):

GPS	X	Y1	Y2
1.00	12.00	13.00	3.00
1.00	10.00	6.00	5.00
1.00	11.00	17.00	2.00
1.00	14.00	14.00	8.00
1.00	13.00	12.00	6.00
1.00	10.00	6.00	8.00
1.00	8.00	12.00	3.00
1.00	8.00	6.00	12.00
1.00	12.00	12.00	7.00
1.00	10.00	12.00	8.00
1.00	12.00	13.00	2.00
1.00	7.00	14.00	10.00
1.00	12.00	16.00	1.00
1.00	9.00	9.00	2.00
1.00	12.00	14.00	10.00
2.00	9.00	7.00	3.00

GPS	X	Y1	Y2
2.00	16.00	13.00	5.00
2.00	11.00	14.00	5.00
2.00	8.00	13.00	18.00
2.00	10.00	11.00	12.00
2.00	7.00	15.00	9.00
2.00	16.00	17.00	4.00
2.00	9.00	9.00	6.00
2.00	10.00	8.00	4.00
2.00	8.00	10.00	1.00
2.00	16.00	16.00	3.00
2.00	12.00	12.00	17.00
2.00	15.00	14.00	4.00
2.00	12.00	18.00	11.00

Run the MANCOVA on SPSSX. Is MANCOVA appropriate? Explain. If it is appropriate, then are the adjusted mean vectors significantly different at the .05 level?

3. Consider a three-group study (randomized) with 24 subjects per group. The correlation between the covariate and the dependent variable is .25, which is statistically significant at the .05 level. Is covariance going to be very useful in this study? Explain.

4. For the Novince example, determine whether there are any significant differences on SOCINT at the .95 simultaneous confidence level using the Bryant Paulson procedure.

5. Suppose we were comparing two different teaching methods and that the covariate was I.Q. The homogeneity of regression slopes is tested and rejected, implying a covariate by treatment interaction. Relate this to what we would have found had we blocked on I.Q. and run a factorial design (I.Q. by methods) on achievement.

6. As part of a study by Benton et al. (1984), three tasks were employed to ascertain differences between good and poor undergraduate writers on recall and manipulaton of information: an ordered letters task, an iconic memory task and a letter reordering task. In the following table are means and standard deviations for the percentage of correct letters recalled on the three dependent variables. There were 15 subjects in each group.

Task	Good writers		Poor writers	
	M	SD	M	SD
Ordered letters	57.79	12.96	49.71	21.79
Iconic memory	49.78	14.59	45.63	13.09
Letter reordering	71.00	4.80	63.18	7.03

The following is from their results section (p. 824):

The data were then analyzed via a multivariate analysis of covariance using the background variables (English usage ACT subtest, composite ACT, and grade point average) as covariates, writing ability as the independent variable, and task scores (correct recall in the ordered letters task, correct recall in the iconic memory task, and correct recall in the letter reordering task) as the dependent variables. The global test was significant, $F(3, 23) = 5.43, p < .001$. To control for experimentwise Type I error rate at .05, each of the three univariate analyses was conducted at a per comparison rate of .017. No significant difference was observed between groups on the ordered letters task, univariate $F(1, 25) = 1.92, p > .10$. Similarly, no significant difference was observed between groups on the iconic memory task, univariate $F < 1$.

However, good writers obtained significantly higher scores on the letter reordering task than the poor writers, univariate $F(1, 25) = 15.02, p < .001$.

a) From what is said above, can we be confident that covariance is appropriate here?

b) The "global" multivariate test referred to above is not identified as to whether it is Wilk's Λ, Roy's largest root, etc. Would it make a difference as to which multivariate test was employed in this case?

c) Benton et al. talk about controlling the experimentwise error rate at .05 by conducting each test at the .017 level of significance. Which post hoc procedure that we discussed in Chapter 4 are they employing here?

d) Are there a sufficient number of subjects for us to have confidence in the reliability of the adjusted means?

APPENDIX—CHAPTER 9
Novince Data for Multivariate Analysis of Covariance Example (Table 9.4)

TREATS	AVOID	NEGEVAL	SOCINT	SRINV	PREAVOID	PRENEG	PRESOCI	PRESR
1.00	91.00	81.00	108.00	157.00	70.00	102.00	61.00	184.00
1.00	107.00	132.00	88.00	150.00	121.00	71.00	66.00	165.00
1.00	121.00	97.00	90.00	151.00	89.00	76.00	67.00	154.00
1.00	86.00	88.00	119.00	154.00	80.00	85.00	102.00	208.00
1.00	137.00	119.00	114.00	135.00	123.00	117.00	106.00	130.00
1.00	138.00	132.00	110.00	165.00	112.00	106.00	95.00	180.00
1.00	133.00	116.00	102.00	124.00	126.00	97.00	52.00	139.00
1.00	127.00	101.00	105.00	163.00	121.00	85.00	94.00	180.00
1.00	114.00	138.00	86.00	168.00	80.00	105.00	70.00	176.00
1.00	118.00	121.00	108.00	136.00	101.00	113.00	80.00	142.00
1.00	114.00	72.00	96.00	149.00	112.00	76.00	78.00	164.00
2.00	107.00	88.00	64.00	135.00	116.00	97.00	91.00	164.00
2.00	76.00	95.00	68.00	157.00	77.00	64.00	73.00	142.00
2.00	116.00	87.00	84.00	165.00	111.00	86.00	79.00	198.00
2.00	126.00	112.00	93.00	155.00	121.00	106.00	71.00	153.00
2.00	104.00	107.00	62.00	181.00	105.00	113.00	68.00	172.00
2.00	96.00	84.00	56.00	193.00	97.00	92.00	62.00	164.00
2.00	127.00	88.00	82.00	153.00	132.00	104.00	70.00	170.00
2.00	99.00	101.00	66.00	146.00	98.00	81.00	66.00	166.00
2.00	94.00	87.00	54.00	196.00	85.00	96.00	58.00	178.00
2.00	92.00	80.00	84.00	177.00	82.00	88.00	77.00	198.00
2.00	128.00	109.00	98.00	155.00	112.00	118.00	97.00	142.00
3.00	121.00	134.00	111.00	112.00	96.00	96.00	85.00	162.00
3.00	140.00	130.00	104.00	102.00	120.00	110.00	58.00	146.00
3.00	148.00	123.00	116.00	123.00	130.00	111.00	111.00	125.00
3.00	147.00	155.00	137.00	111.00	145.00	118.00	91.00	175.00
3.00	139.00	124.00	116.00	129.00	122.00	105.00	95.00	155.00
3.00	121.00	123.00	107.00	148.00	119.00	122.00	97.00	149.00
3.00	141.00	155.00	124.00	108.00	104.00	139.00	81.00	134.00
3.00	143.00	131.00	122.00	141.00	121.00	108.00	93.00	127.00
3.00	120.00	123.00	88.00	148.00	80.00	77.00	44.00	157.00
3.00	140.00	140.00	107.00	108.00	121.00	121.00	82.00	124.00
3.00	95.00	103.00	92.00	172.00	92.00	94.00	49.00	198.00

EFFECT .. WITHIN CELLS REGRESSION

MULTIVARIATE TESTS OF SIGNIFICANCE (S = 3, M = 1/2, N = 36)

TEST NAME	VALUE	APPROX. F	HYPOTH. DF	ERROR DF	SIG. OF F
PILLAIS	.32175	1.82605	15.00	228.00	.032
HOTELLINGS	.29799	1.92804	15.00	218.00	.022
WILKS	.69999	1.88208	15.00	204.68	.027
ROYS	.23303				

UNIVARIATE F-TESTS WITH (3,78) D.F.

VARIABLE	SQ. MUL. R	MUL. R	ADJ. R-SQ.	HYPOTH. MS	ERROR MS	F	SIG. OF F
HOPPOCKA	.05146	.22684	.01497	16.04757	11.37763	1.41045	.246
LNXA	.07412	.27225	.03851	33.51239	16.10126	2.08135	.109
ERSA	.13167	.36287	.09827	156.04864	39.58010	3.94260	.011
QUANAFT	.05930	.24351	.02312	.01169	.00713	1.63889	.187
QUALAFT	.14992	.38719	.11722	.00975	.00213	4.58530	.005

REGRESSION ANALYSIS FOR WITHIN CELLS ERROR TEAM

EFFECT .. MPS BY TRIMT2 + OLI BY TRIMT2 + DTT BY TRIMT2

MULTIVARIATE TESTS OF SIGNIFICANCE (S = 3, M = 1/2, N = 34 1/2)

	VALUE	APPROX. F	HYPOTH. DF	ERROR DF	SIG. OF F
PILLAIS	.18417	.95491	15.00	219.00	.504
HOTELLINGS	.20597	.95662	15.00	209.00	.503
WILKS	.82318	.95619	15.00	196.40	.503
ROYS	.13308				

UNIVARIATE F-TESTS WITH (3,75) D. F.

VARIABLE	HYPOTH. SS	ERROR SS	HYPOTH. MS	ERROR MS	F	SIG. OF F
HOPPOCKA	22.41809	865.03704	7.47270	11.53383	.64789	.587
LMXA	21.18137	1234.71668	7.06046	16.46289	.42887	.733
ERSA	249.38711	2837.86037	83.12904	37.83814	2.19696	.095
QUANAFT	.00503	.55127	.00168	.00735	.22812	.877
QUALAFT	.00263	.16315	.00088	.00218	.40343	.751

EFFECT .. TRTMT2

MULTIVARIATE TESTS OF SIGNIFICANCE (S = 1, M = 1 1/2, N = 34 1/2)

TEST NAME	VALUE	APPROX. F	HYPOTH. DF	ERROR DF	SIG. OF F
PILLAIS	.15824	2.66941	5.00	71.00	.029
HOTELLINGS	.18799	2.66941	5.00	71.00	.029
WILKS	.84176	2.66941	5.00	71.00	.029
ROYS	.15824				

UNIVARIATE F-TESTS WITH (1,75) D. F.

VARIABLE	HYPOTH. SS	ERROR SS	F	SIG. OF F
HOPPOCKA	32.81297	865.03704	2.84493	.096
LMXA	.20963	1234.71668	.01273	.910
ERSA	87.59018	2837.86037	2.31486	.132
QUANAFT	.80222	.55127	11.18658	.001
QUALAFT	.00254	.16315	1.16651	.284

ADJUSTED AND ESTIMATED MEANS VARIABLE .. HOPPOCKA

FACTOR	CODE	OBS. MEAN	ADJ. MEAN
TRTMT2	LMX TREA	19.23077	19.31360
TRTMT2	CONTROL	17.98246	17.94467

ADJUSTED AND ESTIMATED MEANS (CONT.)

VARIABLE .. LMXA

FACTOR	CODE	OBS. MEAN	ADJ. MEAN
TRTMT2	LMX TREA	19.03846	19.23177
TRTMT2	CONTROL	19.21053	19.12235

ADJUSTED AND ESTIMATED MEAN (CONT.)

VARIABLE .. ERSA

FACTOR	CODE	OBS. MEAN	ADJ. MEAN
TRMTMT2	LMX TREA	34.34615	34.76489
TRTMT2	CONTROL	32.71930	32.52830

ADJUSTED AND ESTIMATED MEANS (CONT.)

VARIABLE .. QUANAFT

FACTOR	CODE	OBS. MEAN	ADJ. MEAN
TRTMT2	LMX TREA	.38846	.39188
TRMTMT2	CONTROL	.32491	.32335

ADJUSTED AND ESTIMATED MEANS (CONT.)

VARIABL E.. QUALAFT

FACTOR	CODE	OBS. MEAN	ADJ. MEAN
TRTMT2	LMX TREA	.05577	.05330
TRTMT2	CONTROL	.06421	.06534

10 Stepdown Analysis

10.1 INTRODUCTION

In this chapter we consider a type of analysis that is similar to stepwise regression analysis (Chapter 3). The stepdown analysis is similar in that in both analyses we are interested in how much a variable "adds." In regression analysis the question is, "How much does a predictor add to predicting the dependent variable above and beyond the previous predictors in the regression equation?" The corresponding question in stepdown analysis is, "How much does a given dependent variable add to discriminating the groups, above and beyond the previous dependent variables for a given a priori ordering?" *Since the stepdown analysis requires an a priori ordering of the dependent variables, there must be some theoretical rationale or empirical evidence to dictate a given ordering.* If there is such a rationale, then the stepdown analysis determines whether the groups differ on the first dependent variable in the ordering. The stepdown F for the first variable is the same as the univariate F. For the second dependent variable in the ordering, the analysis determines whether the groups differ on this variable with the first dependent variable used as a covariate in adjusting the effects for variable 2. The stepdown F for the third dependent variable in the ordering indicates whether the groups differ on this variable after its' effects have been adjusted for variables 1 and 2, i.e., with variables 1 and 2 used as covariates, etc. Since the stepdown analysis is just a series of analyses of covariance, the reader should examine section 9.2 on purposes of covariance before going any farther in this chapter.

326

10.2 FOUR APPROPRIATE SITUATIONS FOR STEPDOWN ANALYSIS

To make the foregoing discussion more concrete we consider an example. Let the independent variable be three different teaching methods, and the three dependent variables be the three subtest scores on a common achievement test covering the three lowest levels in Bloom's taxonomy, i.e., knowledge, comprehension, and application. An assumption of the taxonomy is that learning at a lower level is a necessary but not sufficient condition for learning at a higher level. Because of this, there is a theoretical rationale for ordering the variables as given above. The analysis will determine whether methods are differentially affecting learning at the most basic level, i.e., knowledge. At this point the analysis is the same as doing a univariate ANOVA on the single dependent variable knowledge. Next, the stepdown analysis will indicate whether the effect has extended itself to the next higher level, i.e., comprehension, with the differences at the knowledge level eliminated. The stepdown F for comprehension is *identical* to what one would obtain if a univariate analysis of covariance was done with comprehension as the dependent variable and knowledge as the covariate. Finally, the analysis will show whether methods have had a significant effect on application, with the differences at the two lower levels eliminated. The stepdown F for the analysis variable is the *same one* that would be obtained if a univariate analysis of covariance was done with analysis as the dependent variable and knowledge and comprehension as the covariates. Thus, the stepdown analysis not only gives an indication of how comprehensive the effect of the independent variable is, but also details which aspects of a grossly defined variable (such as achievement) have been differentially affected.

A second example is provided by Kohlberg's theory of moral development. Kohlberg describes six stages of moral development, ranging from premoral to the formulation of self accepted moral principles, and argues that attainment of a higher stage should depend on attainment of the preceding stages. Let us assume that tests are available for determining which stage a given individual has attained. Suppose we were interested in determining the extent to which lower, middle, and upper class adults differ with respect to moral development. With Kohlberg's hierarchial theory we have a rationale for ordering from premoral as the first dependent variable on up to self-accepted principles as the last dependent variable in the ordering. The stepdown analysis will then tell us whether the social classes differ on premoral level of development, then whether the social classes differ on the next level of moral development with the differences at the premoral level eliminated, etc. In other words, the analysis will tell us where there are differences among the classes with respect to moral development and how far up the ladder of moral development those differences extend.

As a third example where the stepdown analysis would be particularly appropriate, suppose an investigator wishes to determine whether some conceptually newer measures (among a set of dependent variables) are adding anything beyond what the older, more proven variables contribute, in relation to some independent variable. The above case provides an empirical rationale for ordering the newer measures last, in order for them to demonstrate their incremental importance to the effect under investigation. Thus, in the previous example, the stepdown F for the first new conceptual measure in the ordering would indicate the importance of that variable, with the effects of the more proven variables eliminated. The utility of this approach in terms of providing evidence on variables which are redundant is clear.

A fourth instance in which the stepdown F's are particularly valuable is in the analysis of repeated measures designs, where time provides a natural logical ordering for the measures.

10.3 CONTROLLING ON OVERALL TYPE I ERROR

The stepdown analysis can control very effectively and in a precise way against type I error. To show how Type I error can be controlled for the stepdown analysis, it is necessary to note that *if H_0 is true (i.e., the population mean vectors are equal), then the stepdown F's are statistically independent* (Roy & Bargmann, 1958). How then is the overall α level set for the stepdown Fs for a set of p variables? Each variable is assigned an α level, the ith variable being assigned α_i. Thus, $(1 - \alpha_1)$ is the probability of no type I error for variable 1, $(1 - \alpha_2)$ is the probability of no type I error for variable 2, etc. Now, since the tests are statistically independent, these probabilities can be multiplied. Therefore, the probability of *no* type I errors for *all* p tests is $(1 - \alpha_1) \cdot (1 - \alpha_2)$ $\ldots (1 - \alpha_p)$. Using the symbol π, which denotes "product of," this expression can be written more concisely as $\prod_{i=1}^{p} (1 - \alpha_i)$. Finally, our overall α level is:

$$\text{overall } \alpha = 1 - \prod_{i=1}^{p} (1 - \alpha_i),$$

This is the probability of *at least one* stepdown F exceeding its critical value when H_0 is true.

Since we have one exact estimate of the probability of overall type I error, when employing the stepdown Fs it is unnecessary to perform the overall multivariate significance test. We may adopt the rule that the multivariate null hypothesis will be rejected if at least one of the stepdown F's is significant.

Recall that one of the primary reasons for the multivariate test with correlated dependent variables was the difficulty of accurately estimating overall type I error. As Bock and Haggard noted (1968), "Because all variables have been obtained from the same subjects, they are correlated in some arbitrary and unknown manner, and the separate F tests are not statistically independent. No exact probability that at least one of them will exceed some critical value on the null hypothesis can be calculated" (p. 102).

10.4   STEPDOWN *F*'S FOR TWO GROUPS

To obtain the stepdown F's for the two-group case the pooled within variance matrix $\mathbf{S}$ must be factored. That is, the the square root or Cholesky factor of $\mathbf{S}$ must be found. What this means is that $\mathbf{S}$ is expressed as a product of a lower triangular matrix (all 0's above the main diagonal) and an upper triangular matrix (all 0's below the main diagonal). For 3 variables, it would look as follows:

$$
\overset{\mathbf{S}}{\begin{bmatrix} s_1^2 & s_{12} & s_{13} \\ s_{21} & s_2^2 & s_{23} \\ s_{31} & s_{32} & s_3^2 \end{bmatrix}} = \overset{\mathbf{R}}{\begin{bmatrix} t_{11} & 0 & 0 \\ t_{21} & t_{22} & 0 \\ t_{31} & t_{32} & t_{33} \end{bmatrix}} \overset{\mathbf{R'}}{\begin{bmatrix} t_{11} & t_{12} & t_{13} \\ 0 & t_{22} & t_{23} \\ 0 & 0 & t_{33} \end{bmatrix}}
$$

Now, for two groups the stepdown analysis yields a nice *additive breakdown* of Hotelling's T^2. The first term in the sum (which is an F ratio) gives the contribution of variable 1 to group discrimination, the second term (which is the stepdown F for the second variable in the ordering) the contribution of variable 2 to group discrimination, etc. To at least partially show how this additive breakdown is achieved, recall that Hotelling's T^2 can be written as:

$$T^2 = n_1 n_2/(n_1 + n_2) \, \mathbf{d'} \, \mathbf{S}^{-1} \, \mathbf{d}, \text{ where}$$

$\mathbf{d}$ is the vector of mean differences on the variables for the two groups. Since factoring the covariance matrix $\mathbf{S}$ means writing it as $\mathbf{S} = \mathbf{R} \, \mathbf{R'}$, it can be shown that T^2 may then be re-written as

$$T^2 = n_1 n_2/(n_1 + n_2) \, (\mathbf{R}^{-1} \, \mathbf{d})' \, (\mathbf{R}^{-1}\mathbf{d})$$

But $\underset{(p \times p)}{\mathbf{R}^{-1}} \underset{(p \times 1)}{\mathbf{d}}$ is just a column vector and the transpose of this column vector is a row vector which we denote by $\mathbf{w'} = (w_1, w_2, \ldots, w_p)$. Thus, $T^2 = n_1 n_2/(n_1 + n_2) \, \mathbf{w'} \, \mathbf{w}$. But $\mathbf{w'} \, \mathbf{w} = w_1^2 + w_2^2 + \ldots w_p^2$.
Therefore, we get the following additive breakdown of T^2:

$$T^2 = \frac{n_1 n_2}{n_1 + n_2} w_1^2 + \frac{n_1 n_2}{n_1 + n_2} w_2^2 + \ldots + \frac{n_1 n_2}{n_1 + n_2} w_p^2$$

$$T^2 = \quad F_1 \quad + \quad F_2 \quad + \ldots + \quad F_p$$

univariate F for first variable in the ordering	stepdown F for second variable in ordering	stepdown F for last variable in the ordering

We now consider an example to illustrate numerically the breakdown of T^2. In this example we just give the factors $\mathbf{R}$ and $\mathbf{R}'$ of $\mathbf{S}$ without showing the details, as most of our readers are probably not interested in the details. Those who are interested, however, can find the details in Finn (1974).

Example

Suppose there are two groups of subjects ($n_1 = 50$ and $n_2 = 43$) measured on 3 variables. The vector of differences on the means (**d**) and the pooled within covariance matrix **S** are as follows:

$$\mathbf{d}' = (3.7, 2.1, 2.3), \quad \mathbf{S} = \begin{bmatrix} 38.10 & 14.59 & 1.63 \\ 14.59 & 31.26 & 2.05 \\ 1.63 & 2.05 & 16.72 \end{bmatrix}$$

$$\mathbf{S} = \begin{bmatrix} 6.173 & 0 & 0 \\ 2.634 & 5.067 & 0 \\ .264 & .282 & 4.071 \end{bmatrix} \begin{bmatrix} 6.173 & 2.364 & .264 \\ 0 & 5.067 & .282 \\ 0 & 0 & 4.071 \end{bmatrix}$$

Now, to obtain the additive breakdown for T^2 we need $\mathbf{R}^{-1}\mathbf{d}$. This is:

$$\mathbf{R}^{-1}\mathbf{d} = \begin{bmatrix} .162 & 0 & 0 \\ -.076 & .197 & 0 \\ -.005 & -.014 & .25 \end{bmatrix} \begin{bmatrix} 3.7 \\ 2.1 \\ 2.3 \end{bmatrix} = \begin{bmatrix} .60 \\ .133 \\ .527 \end{bmatrix} = \mathbf{w}$$

We have not shown the details but $\mathbf{R}^{-1}$ is the inverse of $\mathbf{R}$. The reader may check this by multiplying the two matrices. The product is indeed the identity matrix (within rounding error). Thus,

$$T^2 = \frac{50\,(43)}{93}\,(.60,\ .133,\ .527)\begin{pmatrix} .60 \\ .133 \\ .527 \end{pmatrix}$$

$$T^2 = 25.904\,(.36 + .018 + .278)$$

$$T^2 = \quad 9.325 \quad + \quad .466 \quad + \quad 7.201$$

| contribution of variable 1 | contribution of variable 2 with effects of variable 1 removed | contribution of variable 3 to group discrimination *above and beyond* what the first 2 variables contribute |

Each of the above numbers is just the value for the stepdown F (F^*) for the corresponding variable. Now, suppose we had set the probability of a type I error at .05 for the first variable and at .025 for the other two variables. Then, the probability of at least one type I error is $1 - (1 - .05)\,(1 - .025)$ $(1 - .025) = 1 - .903 = .097$. Thus there is about a 10% chance of falsely concluding that at least one of the variables contributes to group discrimination, when in fact it does not. What is our decision for each of the variables?

F_1^*
.05; 1, 91
$= 9.325$, (crit. val $= 3.95$) reject and conclude variable 1 significantly contributes to group discrimination

F_2^*
.025; 1, 90
$= .466 < 1$, so this can't be significant

F_3^*
.025; 1, 89
$= 7.201$, (crit. val $= 5.22$) reject and conclude variable 3 makes a significant contribution to group discrimination above and beyond what first 2 criterion variables do.

Notice that the degrees of freedom for error decreases by one for each successive stepdown F, just as we lose one degree of freedom for each covariate used in analysis of covariance. The general formula for degrees of freedom for error (df_{w*}) for the ith stepdown F then is $df_{w*} = df_w - (i - 1)$, where $df_w = N - k$, i.e., ordinary formula for df in a one-way univariate analysis of variance. Thus df_{w*} for the 3rd variable above is $df_{w*} = 91 - (3 - 1) = 89$.

10.5   COMPARISON OF INTERPRETATION OF STEPDOWN *F*'S VS. UNIVARIATE *F*'S

To illustrate the difference in interpretation when using univariate F's following a significant multivariate F vs. the use of stepdown F's, we consider an example. A different set of four variables which Novince (1977) analyzed in her study are presented in Table 10.1, along with the control lines for obtaining the step-down F's on SPSSX MANOVA.

The control lines are of exactly the same form as were used in obtaining a one-way MANOVA in Chapter 5. The only difference is that the last line

TABLE 10.1
Control Lines and Data for Stepdown Analysis on
SPSSX MANOVA for Novince Data

TITLE 'STEPDOWN ANALYSIS-NOVINCE DATA'
DATA LIST FREE/ JRANX JRNEGEVA JRGLOA JRSOCSKL TREATS
LIST

BEGIN DATA

2.00	2.50	2.50	3.50	1.00
1.50	2.00	1.50	4.50	1.00
2.00	3.00	2.50	3.50	1.00
2.50	4.00	3.00	3.50	1.00
1.00	2.00	1.00	5.00	1.00
1.50	3.50	2.50	4.00	1.00
4.00	3.00	3.00	4.00	1.00
3.00	4.00	3.50	4.00	1.00
3.50	3.50	3.50	2.50	1.00
1.00	1.00	1.00	4.00	1.00
1.00	2.50	2.00	4.50	1.00
1.50	3.50	2.50	4.00	2.00
1.00	4.50	2.50	4.50	2.00
3.00	3.00	3.00	4.00	2.00
4.50	4.50	4.50	3.50	2.00
1.50	4.50	3.50	3.50	2.00
2.50	4.00	3.00	4.00	2.00
3.00	4.00	3.50	3.00	2.00
4.00	5.00	5.00	1.00	2.00
3.50	3.00	3.50	3.50	2.00
1.50	1.50	1.50	4.50	2.00
3.00	4.00	3.50	3.00	2.00
1.00	2.00	1.00	4.00	3.00
1.00	2.00	1.50	4.50	3.00
1.50	1.00	1.00	3.50	3.00
2.00	2.50	2.00	4.00	3.00
2.00	3.00	2.50	4.50	3.00
2.50	3.00	2.50	4.00	3.00
2.00	2.50	2.50	4.00	3.00
1.00	1.00	1.00	5.00	3.00
1.00	1.50	1.50	5.00	3.00
1.50	1.50	1.50	5.00	3.00
2.00	3.50	2.50	4.00	3.00

END DATA

MANOVA JRANX TO JRSOCSKL BY TREATS(1,3)/
    PRINT = CELLINFO(MEANS,COV,COR)
    HOMOGENEITY(COCHRAN,BOXM)
    SIGNIF(STEPDOWN)/

Note: The last statement, i.e., SIGNIF(STEPDOWN)/ is required to obtain the stepdown F's.

TABLE 10.2
Multivariate Tests, Univariate *F*'s and Stepdown *F*'s for Novince Data

EFFECT .. TREATS

MULTIVARIATE TESTS OF SIGNIFICANCE (S = 2, M = 1/2, N = 12 1/2)

TEST NAME	VALUE	APPROX. F	HYPOTH. DF	ERROR DF	SIG. OF F
PILLAIS	.42619	1.89561	8.00	56.00	.079
HOTELLINGS	.69664	2.26408	8.00	52.00	.037
WILKS	.58362	2.08566	8.00	54.00	.053
ROYS	.40178				

UNIVARIATE F-TESTS WITH (2,30) D. F.

VARIABLE	HYPOTH. SS	ERROR SS	HYPOTH. MS	ERROR MS	F	SIG. OF F
JRANX	6.01515	26.86364	3.00758	.89545	3.35871	.048
JRNEGEVA	14.86364	25.36364	7.43182	.84545	8.79032	.001
JRGLOA	12.56061	21.40909	6.28030	.71364	8.80042	.001
JRSOCSKL	3.68182	16.54545	1.84091	.55152	3.33791	.049

ROY-BARGMAN STEPDOWN F - TESTS

VARIABLE	HYPOTH. MS	ERROR MS	STEP-DOWN F	HYPOTH. DF	ERROR DF	SIG. OF F
JRANX	3.00758	.89545	3.35871	2	30	.048
JRNEGEVA	2.99776	.66964	4.47666	2	29	.020
JRGLOA	.05601	.06520	.85899	2	28	.434
JRSOCSKL	.03462	.32567	.10631	2	27	.900

SIGNIF(STEPDOWN)/ is included to obtain the stepdown *F*'s. In Table 10.2 we present the multivariate tests, along with the univariate *F*'s and the stepdown *F*'s. Even though, as mentioned earlier in this chapter, it is *not* necessary to examine the multivariate tests when using stepdown *F*'s, it was done here for illustrative purposes. This is one of those somewhat infrequent situations where the multivariate tests would not agree in a decision at the .05 level. In this case 96% of between variation was concentrated in the first discriminant function, in which case the Pillai trace is known to be least powerful (Olson, 1976).

Using the univariate *F*'s for interpretation, we would conclude that each of the variables is significant at the .05 level, since all the exact probabilities are $< .05$. That is, when each variable is considered separately, not taking into account how it is correlated with the others, it significantly separates the groups.

However, if we were able to establish a logical ordering of the criterion measures and thus use the stepdown *F*'s, then it is clear that *only the first two* variables make a significant contribution (assuming the nominal levels had been set at .05 for the first variable and .025 for the other 3 variables). Variables 3 and 4 are redundant, i.e., given 1 and 2, they do not make a significant contribution to group discrimination above and beyond what the first 2 variables do.

10.6   STEPDOWN F'S FOR k GROUPS-EFFECT OF WITHIN AND BETWEEN CORRELATIONS

For more than two groups two matrices must be factored, and obtaining the stepdown F's becomes more complicated (Finn, 1974). We will not worry about the details, but instead concentrate on two factors (the within and between correlations), which will determine how much a step-down F for a given variable will differ from the univariate F for that variable.

The within group correlation for variables x and y can be thought of as the weighted average of the individual group correlations. (This is not exactly technically correct, but will yield a value quite close to the actual value and it is easier to understand conceptually.) Consider the data from Exercise 1 in Chapter 5, and in particular variables y_1 and y_2. Suppose we computed r_{y1y2} for subjects in group 1 only, then r_{y1y2} for subjects in group 2 only, and finally r_{r1y2} for subjects in group 3 only. These correlations are .637, .201, and .754 respectively, as the reader should check.

$$r_{y1y2(w)} = \frac{n_1 \cdot r_{(1)} + n_2 \cdot r_{(2)} + n_3 \cdot r_{(3)}}{N}$$

$$= \frac{11(.637) + 8(.201) + 10(.754)}{29} = .56$$

In this case we have taken the weighted average, since the groups sizes were unequal. Now, the actual within (error) correlation is .61, which is quite close to the .56 we obtained.

How does one obtain the between correlation for x and y? The formula for $r_{xy(B)}$ is identical in form to the formula used for obtaining the simple Pearson correlation between two variables. That formula is:

$$r = \frac{\sum_i (x_i - \bar{x})(y_i - \bar{y})}{\sqrt{\sum_i (x_i - \bar{x})^2 \sum_i (y_i - \bar{y})^2}}$$

The formula for $r_{xy(B)}$ is obtained by replacing x_i and y_i by $\bar{x}_i$ and $\bar{y}_i$ (group means) and by replacing $\bar{x}$ and $\bar{y}$ by the grand means of $\bar{\bar{x}}$ and $\bar{\bar{y}}$. Also, for the between correlation the summation is over *groups*, not individuals. The formula is:

$$r_{xy(B)} = \frac{\sum (\bar{x}_i - \bar{\bar{x}})(\bar{y}_i - \bar{\bar{y}})}{\sqrt{\sum(\bar{x}_i - \bar{\bar{x}})^2 \sum(\bar{y}_i - \bar{\bar{y}})^2}}$$

Now that we have introduced the within and between correlations, and keeping in mind that stepdown analysis is just a series of analyses of covariance, the following from Bock and Haggard (1968, p. 129) is important:

The results of an analysis of covariance depend on the extent to which the correlation of the concomitant and the dependent variables is concentrated in the errors (i.e., within group correlation) or in the effects of the experimental conditions (between correlation). If the concomitant variable is correlated appreciably with the errors, but little or not at all with the effects, the analysis of covariance increases the power of the statistical tests to detect differences. . . . If the concomitant variable is correlated with the experimental effects as much or more than with the errors, the analysis of covariance will show that the effect observed in the dependent variable can be largely accounted for by the concomitant variable (covariate). (p. 129)

Thus, the stepdown F's can differ considerably from the univariate F's and in *either* direction. If a given dependent variable in the ordering is correlated more within groups with the previous variables in the ordering than between groups, then the stepdown F for that variable will be larger than the univariate F, since more within-variability will be removed from the variable by the covariates (i.e., previous dependent variables) than between-groups variability. If, on the other hand, the dependent variable is correlated strongly between groups with the previous dependent variables in the ordering, then we would expect its stepdown F to be considerably smaller than the univariate F. In this case the mean sum of squares between for the variable is markedly reduced, i.e., its effect in discriminating the groups is strongly tied to the previous dependent variables or can be accounted for by them.

Specific illustrations of each of the above situations are provided by two examples from Morrison (1967, p. 127 and p. 154, #3). Our focus is on the first two dependent variables in the ordering for each problem. For the first problem those variables were called information and similarities, while for the second problem they were simply called variable A and variable B. For each pair of variables, the correlation was high (.762 and .657). In the first case, however, the correlation was concentrated in the experimental condition (between correlation), while in the second it was concentrated in the errors (within-group correlation). A comparison of the univariate and stepdown F's shows this very clearly: For similarities (2nd variable in ordering) the univariate $F = 12.04$, while the stepdown $F = 1.37$. Thus, most of the between-association for the similarities variable can be accounted for by its high correlation with the first variable in the ordering, i.e., information. On the other hand, for the other situation the univariate $F = 6.4$ for variable B (2nd variable in ordering), while the stepdown $F = 24.03$! The reason for this striking result is that variable B and variable A (first variable in ordering) are highly correlated *within* groups, and thus most of the error variance for variable B can be accounted for by variance on variable A. Thus, the error variance for B in the stepdown F is much smaller than the error variance for B in the univariate F. The much smaller error coupled with the fact that A and B had a lower correlation across the groups resulted in a much larger stepdown F for B.

10.7 SUMMARY

One could routinely always printout the stepdown F's. This can be dangerous however to users who may try to interpret these when not appropriate. In those cases (probably most cases) where a logical ordering can't be established, one should either not attempt to interpret the stepdown F's or do so very cautiously.

Some investigators may try several different orderings of the dependent variables in order to gather additional information. Although this may prove useful for future studies, it should be kept in mind that the different orderings are *not* independent. Although for a single ordering the overall α can be exactly estimated, for several orderings the probability of spurious results is unknown.

It is important to distinguish between the stepdown analysis, where a single a priori ordering of the dependent variables enables one to exactly estimate the probability of at least one false rejection, and so called stepwise procedures (as previously described in the multiple regression chapter) or as in the *BMDP7M* and *SPSSX* outputs discussed in the k group MANOVA chapter. In these latter stepwise procedures the variable which is the best discriminator among the groups is entered first, then the procedure finds the next best discriminator, etc. In such a procedure, especially with small or moderate sample sizes, there is a substantial hazard of capitalization on chance. That is, the variables which happen to have the highest correlations with the criterion (in multiple regression) or happen to be the best discriminators in the *particular* sample are those that are chosen. Very often, however, in another independent sample (from the population) some or many of the same variables may not be the best.

Thus, the stepdown analysis approach possesses two distinct advantages over such stepwise procedures: (1) It rests on a solid theoretical and/or empirical foundation—necessary to order the variables, and (2) the probability of one or more false rejections can be exactly estimated—statistically very desirable. The stepwise procedure, on the other hand, is likely to produce results that will not replicate and are therefore of dubious scientific value.

11

Principal Components

11.1 INTRODUCTION

Consider the following two common classes of research situations:

1. Exploratory regression analysis: An experimenter has gathered a moderate to large number of predictors (say 15 to 40) to predict some dependent variable.

2. Scale development: An investigator has assembled a set of items (say 20 to 50) designed to measure some construct (e.g., attitude toward education, anxiety, sociability). Here we will think of the items as the variables.

In both of these situations the number of simple correlations among the variables is very large, and it is quite difficult to summarize by inspection precisely what the pattern of correlations represents. For example, with 30 variables there are 435 simple correlations! Some means is needed for determining if there are a small number of underlying constructs which might account for the main sources of variation in such a complex set of correlations.

Furthermore, if there are 30 variables (whether predictors or items), we are undoubtedly not measuring 30 different constructs; hence, it makes sense to find some variable reduction scheme that will indicate how the variables cluster or hang together. Now, if sample size is not large enough (how large N needs to be is discussed in 11.7), then we need to resort to a logical clustering (grouping) based on theoretical and/or substantive grounds. On the other hand, with adequate sample size an empirical approach is preferable. Two basic empirical approaches are (1) principal components analysis and (2) factor analysis. In both approaches linear combinations of the original variables (the factors) are derived, and often a small number of these account for most of the variation or the pattern of correlations. In factor analysis a mathematical model is set up, and the factors can only be estimated, whereas in components analysis we are simply transforming the original variables into the new set of linear combinations (the principal components).

Both methods often yield similar results. We prefer to discuss principal components for several reasons:

1. It is a psychometrically sound procedure.
2. It is simpler mathematically, relatively speaking, than factor analysis. And a main theme in this text is to keep the mathematics as simple as possible.
3. The factor indeterminancy issue associated with common factor analysis (Steiger, 1979) is a troublesome feature.
4. A thorough discussion of factor analysis would require hundreds of pages, and there are other good sources on the subject (Gorsuch, 1983).

Recall that for discriminant analysis uncorrelated linear combinations of the original variables were used to additively partition the association between the classification variable and the set of dependent variables. Here we will be again using uncorrelated linear combinations of the original variables (the principal components), but this time to additively partition the variance for a set of variables.

11.2 THE NATURE OF PRINCIPAL COMPONENTS

If we have a single group of subjects measured on a set of variables, then principal components partitions the total variance (i.e., the sum of the variances for the original variables) by first finding the linear combination of the variables which accounts for the maximum account of variance:

$$y_1 = a_{11} x_1 + a_{12} x_2 + \ldots + a_{1p} x_p$$

y_1 is called the first principal component, and if the coefficients are scaled such that $\mathbf{a}_1' \, \mathbf{a}_1 = 1$, [where $\mathbf{a}_1' = (a_{11}, a_{12}, \ldots, a_{1p})$] then the variance of y_1 is equal to the *largest* eigenvalue of the sample covariance matrix. (Morrison, 1967, p. 224). The coefficients of the principal component are the elements of the eigenvector corresponding to the largest eigenvalue.

Then the procedure finds a second linear combination, *uncorrelated* with the first component, such that it accounts for the next largest amount of variance (after the variance attributable to the first component has been removed) in the system. This second component y_2 is

$$y_2 = a_{21} x_1 + a_{22} x_2 + \ldots a_{2p} x_p$$

and the coefficients are scaled so that $\mathbf{a}_2' \, \mathbf{a}_2 = 1$, as for the first component. The fact that the two components are constructed to be uncorrelated means that the Pearson correlation between y_1 and y_2 is 0. The coefficients of the second component are simply the elements of the eigenvector associated with the second largest eigenvalue of the covariance matrix, and the sample variance of y_2 is equal to the second largest eigenvalue.

The third principal component is constructed to be uncorrelated with the first two, and accounts for the third largest amount of variance in the system, etc. Principal components analysis is therefore still another example of a mathematical maximation procedure, where each successive component accounts for the maximum amount of the variance that is left.

Thus, through the use of principal components a set of correlated variables is transformed into a set of uncorrelated variables (the components). The hope is that a much smaller number of these components will acount for most of the variance in the original set of variables, and of course that we can meaningfully interpret the components. By most of the variance we mean about 75% or more, and often this can be accomplished with five or less components.

The components are interpreted by using the component-variable correlations (called *factor loadings*) which are largest in absolute magnitude. For example, if the first component loaded high and positive on variables 1, 3, 5, and 6, then we would interpret that component by attempting to determine what those four variables have in common. The component procedure has empirically clustered the four variables, and the job of the psychologist is to give a name to the construct that underlies variability and thus identify the component substantively.

In the above example we assumed that the loadings were all in the same direction (all positive). Of course, it is possible to have a mixture of high positive and negative loadings on a particular component. In this case we have what is called a *bipolar* factor. For example, in components analyses of I.Q. tests, the second component may be a bipolar factor constrasting verbal abilities against spatial-perceptual abilities.

Social science researchers would be used to extracting components from a correlation matrix. The reason for this standardization is that scales for tests used in educational, sociological, and psychological research are usually arbitrary. If, however, the scales are reasonably commensurable, performing a components analysis on the *covariance* matrix is preferrable for statistical reasons. (Morrison, 1967, p. 222). The components obtained from the correlation and covariance matrices are, in general, *not* the same. The option of doing the components analysis on either the correlation or covariance matrix is available on BMDP4M and SPSSX.

A precaution that researchers contemplating a components analysis with a small sample size (certainly any n around 100) should take, especially if most of the elements in the sample correlation matrix are small, is to apply Bartlett's sphericity test (Cooley & Lohnes, 1971, p. 103). This procedure tests the null hypothesis that the variables in the *population* correlation matrix are uncorrelated. If one fails to reject with this test, then there is no reason to do the components analysis since the variables are already uncorrelated. The sphericity test is available on both the BMDP and SPSSX packages.

11.3 THREE USES FOR COMPONENTS
AS A VARIABLE REDUCING SCHEME

We now consider three cases in which the use of components as a variable reducing scheme can be very valuable.

1. The first use has already been mentioned, and that is to determine empirically how many dimensions (underlying constructs) account for most of the variance on an instrument (scale). The original variables in this case are the items on the scale.

2. In a multiple regression context, if the number of predictors is large relative to the number of subjects, then we may wish to use principal components on the predictors to reduce markedly the number of predictors. If so, then the N/variable ratio increases considerably and the possibility of the regression equation holding up under cross-validation is much better (cf. Herzberg, 1969). We show later in the chapter (example 3) how to do this on the BMDP package.

The use of principal components on the predictors is also one way of attacking the multicollinearity problem (correlated predictors). Furthermore, since the new predictors (i.e., the components) are uncorrelated, the order in which they enter the regression equation makes no difference in terms of how much variance in the dependent variable they will account for.

3. In the chapter on k group MANOVA we indicated several reasons (reliability consideration, robustness, etc.) which generally mitigate against the use of a large number of criterion variables. Therefore, if there is initially a large number of potential criterion variables, it probably would be wise to perform a principal components analysis on them in an attempt to work with a smaller set of new criterion variables. We show later in the chapter (in Example 4) how to do this on the BMDP package. It must be recognized, however, that the components are *artificial* variables and are not necessarily going to be interpretable. Nevertheless, there are techniques for improving their interpretability, and we discuss these later.

11.4 CRITERIA FOR DECIDING ON HOW MANY COMPONENTS
TO RETAIN

There are four methods that can be used in deciding how many components to retain:

1.   Probably the most widely used criterion is that of Kaiser (1960): Retain only those components whose eigenvalues are greater than 1. Unless something else is specified, this is the rule that is used by SPSSX and BMDP4M. Although generally using this rule will result in retention of only the most important factors, blind use could lead to retaining factors which may have no practical significance (in terms of % of variance accounted for).

Studies by Cattell and Jaspers (1967), Browne (1968), and Linn (1968) have evaluated the accuracy of the eigenvalue > 1 criterion. In all three studies the authors determined how often the criterion would identify the correct number of factors from matrices with a known number of factors. The number of variables in the studies ranged from 10 to 40. Generally the criterion was accurate to fairly accurate, with gross overestimation occurring only with a large number of variables (40) *and* low communalities. (around .40). The criterion is more accurate when the number of variables is small (10 to 15) or moderate (20 to 30) and the communalities are high ($> .70$). The communality of a variable is the amount of variance on a variable accounted for by the set of factors. We see how it is computed later in this chapter.

2.   A graphical method called the *scree test* has been proposed by Cattell (1966). In this method the magnitude of the eigenvalues (vertical axis) are plotted against their ordinal numbers (whether it was the first eigenvalue, the second, etc.). Generally what happens is that the magnitude of successive eigenvalues drops off sharply (steep descent) and then tends to level off. The recommendation is to retain all eigenvalues (and hence components) in the sharp descent *before* the first one on the line where they start to level off. In one of our examples we illustrate this test. This method will generally retain components which account for large or fairly large and distinct amounts of variances (e.g., 31%, 20%, 13%, and 9%). Here, however, blind use might lead to not retaining factors which, although they account for a smaller amount of variance, might be practically significant. For example, if the first eigenvalue at the break point accounted for 8.3% of variance and then the next three eigenvalues accounted for 7.1%, 6%, and 5.2%, then 5% or more might well be considered significant in some contexts, and retaining the first and dropping the next three seems somewhat arbitrary. The scree plot is available on SPSSX (in FACTOR program) and in the SAS package. Several studies have investigated the accuracy of the scree test. Tucker, Koopman, and Linn (1969) found it gave the correct number of factors in 12 of 18 cases. Linn (1968) found it to yield the correct number of factors in 7 of 10 cases, while Cattell and Jaspers (1967) found it to be correct in 6 of 8 cases.

A more recent, extensive study on the number of factors problem (Hakstian, Rogers, & Cattell, 1982) adds some additional information. They note that for $N > 250$ and a mean communality $\geq .60$, either the Kaiser or Scree rules will yield an accurate estimate for the number of true factors. They add that such an estimate will be just that much more credible if the Q/P ratio is $< .30$ (P is the number of variables and Q is the number of factors). With mean communality

.30 or $Q/P > .3$, the Kaiser rule is less accurate and the Scree rule much less accurate.

3.   There is a statistical significance test for the number of factors to retain which was developed by Lawley (1940). However, as with all statistical tests, it is influenced by sample size, and large sample size may lead to the retention of too many factors.

4.   Retain as many factors as will account for a specified amount of total variance. Generally one would want to account for at least 70% of the total variance, although in some cases the investigator may not be satisfied unless 80 to 85% of the variance is accounted for. This method could lead to the retention of factors which are essentially variable specific, i.e., load highly on only a single variable.

So what criterion should be used in deciding how many factors to retain? *Since the Kaiser criterion has been shown to be quite accurate when the number of variables is < 30 and the communalities are > .70, or when N > 250 and the mean communality is ≥ .60, we would use it under these circumstances.* For other situations use of the scree test with an $N > 200$ will probably not lead us too far astray, provided that most of the communalities are reasonably large.

In all of the above we have assumed that we will retain only so many components, which will hopefully account for a sizable amount of the total variance, and simply discard the rest of the information, i.e., not worry about the 20 or 30% of the variance that is not accounted for. However, it seems to us that in some cases the following suggestion of Morrison (1967) has merit, "Frequently it is better to summarize the complex in terms of the first components with large and markedly distinct variances and include as highly specific and unique variates those responses which are generally independent in the system. Such unique responses could probably be represented by high loadings in the later components but only in the presence of considerable noise from the other unrelated variates" (p. 228).

In other words, if we did a components analysis on say 20 variables and only the first 4 components accounted for large and distinct amounts of variance, then we should summarize the complex of 20 variables in terms of the 4 components *and* those particular variables which had high correlations (loadings) with the latter components. In this way more of the total information in the complex is retained although some parsimony is sacrificed.

11.5   INCREASING THE INTERPRETABILITY OF COMPONENTS BY ROTATION

Although principal components are fine for summarizing most of the variance in a large set of variables with a small number of components, often the components are not easily interpretable. The components are artificial variates designed to maximize variance accounted for, not designed for interpretability.

To aid in interpreting, there are various so called rigid rotations that are available. They are rigid in the sense that the orthogonality (uncorrelatedness) of the components is maintained for the rotated factors. We discuss two such rotations:

1.   Quartimax—Here the idea is to clean up the variables. That is, the rotation is done so that each variable loads mainly on one factor. Then that variable can be considered to be a relatively pure measure of the factor. The problem with this approach is that most of the variables tend to load on a single factor (producing the so called "g" factor in analyses of I.Q. tests), making interpretation of the factor difficult.

2.   Varimax—Kaiser (1960) took a different tact. He designed a rotation to clean up the factors. That is, with his rotation each factor tends to load high on a smaller number of variables and low or very low on the other variables. This will generally make interpretation of the resulting factors easier. The Varimax rotation is the *default* option in the SPSSX and BMDP packages.

It should be mentioned that when the Varimax rotation is done the *maximum variance property* of the original components *is destroyed*. The rotation essentially reallocates the loadings. Thus, the first rotated factor will no longer *necessarily* account for the maximum amount of variance. The amount of variance accounted for by each rotated factor has to be recalculated. We show this in our examples. Even though this is true, and somewhat unfortunate, we feel it is more important to be able to interpret the factors.

11.6   WHAT LOADINGS SHOULD BE USED FOR INTERPRETATION?

Recall that a loading is simply the Pearson correlation between the variable and the factor (linear combination of the variables). Now, certainly any loading which is going to be used to interpret a factor should be statistically significant at a minimum. The formula for the standard error of a correlation coefficient is given in elementary statistics books as $1/\sqrt{N-1}$ and one might think it could be used to determine which loadings are significant. But in components analysis (where we are maximizing again) and in rotating there is considerable opportunity for capitalization on chance. This is especially true for small or moderate sample sizes, or even for fairly large sample size (200 or 300) if the number of variables being factored is large (say 40 or 50). Because of this capitalization on chance, the formula for the standard error of correlation can *seriously underestimate* the actual amount of error in the factor loadings.

A study by Cliff and Hamburger (1967) showed that the standard errors of factor loadings for orthogonally rotated solutions in all cases were considerably greater (150 to 200% in most cases) than the standard error for an ordinary correlation. Thus, a rough check as to whether a loading is statistically significant can be obtained by *doubling* the standard error, i.e., doubling the critical value required for significance for an ordinary correlation. This kind of statistical check is most crucial when sample size is small or small relative to the number of variables being factor analyzed. When sample size is quite large (say 1,000), or large relative to the number of variables ($N = 500$ for 20 variables), then significance is ensured. It may be that doubling the standard error in general is too conservative since for the case where a statistical check is more crucial ($N = 100$), the errors were generally less than one and a half times greater. However, since Cliff and Hamburger (1967, p. 438) suggest that the sampling error might be greater in situations that aren't as clean as the one they analyzed, it probably is advisable to be conservative until more evidence becomes available.

Given the Cliff and Hamburger results, we feel it is time that investigators stopped blindly using the rule of interpreting factors with loadings greater than $|.30|$, and take sample size into account. Also, since in checking to determine which loadings are significant many statistical tests will be done, it is advisable to set the α level more stringently for each test. This is done in order to control on overall α, i.e., the probability of at least one false rejection. We would recommend testing each loading for significance at $\alpha = .01$ (two-tailed test). To aid the reader in this task we present in Table 11.1 the critical values for a simple correlation at $\alpha = .01$ (two-tailed test) for sample size ranging from 50 to 1,000. Remember that the critical values in Table 11.1 should be doubled, and it is the doubled value that is used as the critical value for testing the significance of a loading. To illustrate the use of Table 11.1, suppose a factor analysis had been run with 140 subjects. Then only loadings $> 2(.217) = .434$ in absolute value would be declared statistically significant. If sample size in this example had been 160, then interpolation between 140 and 180 will give a very good approximation to the critical value.

Once one is confident that the loadings being used for interpretation are significant (because of a significance test or because of large sample size), then the question becomes which loadings are large enough to be practically significant. For example, a loading of .20 could well be significant with large sample size, but this indicates only 4% shared variance between the variable and the

TABLE 11.1
Critical Values for a Correlation Coefficient at $\alpha = .01$ for a Two-
Tailed Test

n	C. V.	n	C. V.	n	C. V.
50	.361	180	.192	400	.129
80	.286	200	.182	600	.105
100	.256	250	.163	800	.091
140	.217	300	.149	1000	.081

factor. It would seem that one would want in general a variable to share *at least* 15% of its variance with the construct (factor) it is going to be used to help name. This means only using loadings which are about .40 or greater for interpretation purposes. To interpret what the variables with high loadings have in common, i.e., to name the factor (construct), a substantive specialist is needed.

11.7 SAMPLE SIZE AND RELIABLE FACTORS

In terms of the sample size required for reliable factors, Gorsuch (1983) has stated, "*A present suggested absolute minimum ratio is five individuals per variable, but not less than 100 individuals for any analysis.* . . . The suggested minimum applies only when the expected communalities are high and there are many variables per expected factor" (p. 332, italics added).

Let us relate this to our earlier mentioned use of components analysis to determine the number of dimensions underlying an instrument (scale). Remember that the items are the variables, so that if a components analysis is done on a 40 or 50 item scale over 200 subjects will be needed for a reliable factor structure. Factor analyses done on 30 or 40 item scales with N's around 100 should be treated with considerable caution, since the results are unlikely to replicate.

The usefulness of components analysis in reducing the number of predictors in multiple regression makes good sense for several reasons (which we detail later on in Example 3), *provided* that adequate sample size is used to obtain reliable factors. Thus 20 predictors for $N = 150$ is not adequate sample size for a reliable regression equation; however, it is adequate to obtain reliable components. Very often ≤ 5 components will account for most of the variance, and these become our new predictors. Our new N/k ratio will then be at least 30/1, which will yield a reliable regression equation (Burkett, 1964).

11.8 FOUR COMPUTER EXAMPLES

We now consider four examples to illustrate the use of components analysis and the varimax rotation in practice. The first two involve two popular personality scales: the California Psychological Inventory and the Personality Research Form. Example 1 shows how to input a correlation matrix using the SPSSX FACTOR program, while Example 2 illustrates correlation matrix input for the BMDP4M factor program. Example 3 shows how to do a components analysis on a set of predictors and then pass the new predictors (the factor scores) to the BMDP2R regression program. Example 4 illustrates a components analysis and varimax rotation on a set of dependent variables and then passing the factor scores to the BMDP3D program for a two-group MANOVA.

Example 1—California Psychological Inventory (CPI)

The first example is a components analysis of the California Psychological Inventory followed by a varimax rotation. The data was collected on 180 college freshmen (90 males and 90 females) by Smith (1975). He was interested in gathering evidence to support the uniqueness of death anxiety as a construct. Thus, he wanted to determine to what extent death anxiety could be predicted from general anxiety, other personality variables (hence the use of the CPI), and situational variables related to death (recent loss of a love one, recent experiences with a deathly situation, etc.). In this use of multiple regression Smith was hoping for a *small* R^2, i.e., he wanted only a small amount of the variance in death anxiety scores to be accounted for by the other variables.

Table 11.2 presents the SPSSX control lines for the factor analysis, along with annotation explaining what several of the commands mean. The correlation

TABLE 11.2
SPSSX Factor Analysis Control Lines for
Components Analysis and Varimax Rotation
on CPI

```
    TITLE ' COMPONENTS ANALYSIS AND VARIMAX ROTATION ON CPI '
①  INPUT PROGRAM
    N OF CASES 100
    NUMERIC DO CS SY SP SA WB RE SO SC TA GI CM AC AI IE PY FX FE
    INPUT MATRIX FREE
    END INPUT PROGRAM
②  FACTOR READ=CORRELATION TRIANGLE/
        VARIABLES=DO TO FE/
③       PRINT=DEFAULT CORRELATION/
④       PLOT=EIGEN/
    BEGIN DATA
    1.0
    .467 1.0
    .681 .600 1.0
      ETC.
    .099 .061 −.069 −.158 −.097 −.038 .275 .159 .215 .032 .091 .139
    .071 .033 −.031 −.145 −.344 1.0
    END DATA
```

① When inputting a matrix, such as correlation matrix here, in SPSSX we must use the NUMERIC command for the variable names, and we also must enclose the NUMERIC and INPUT MATRIX commands in an INPUT PROGRAM—END INPUT PROGRAM structure. (see *SPSSX Advanced Statistics Guide*, 1985, pp. 444–445)

② The READ subcommand has to placed right after the FACTOR command. The TRIANGLE part of the subcommand tells the program we are reading in a lower triangular matrix, i.e., the bottom half of the correlation matrix.

③ In this PRINT subcommand we obtain the correlation matrix for variables by specifying CORRELATION, and obtain the eigenvalues, communalities, factor pattern and rotated factor pattern by specifying DEFAULT.

④ This PLOT subcommand is used to obtain the scree test.

TABLE 11.3
Intercorrelations of the California Psychological Inventory Scales for 180 College Students (90 Male and 90 Female)

Scale	DO	CS	SY	SP	SA	WB	RE	SO	SC	TO	GI	CM	AC	AI	IE	PY	FX	FE
DO	1.000																	
CS	.467	1.000																
SY	.681	.600	1.000															
SP	.447	.585	.643	1.000														
SA	.610	.466	.673	.612	1.000													
WB	.236	.324	.339	.357	.077	1.000												
RE	.401	.346	.344	.081	.056	.518	1.000											
SO	.214	.179	.242	.003	-.029	.517	.632	1.000										
SC	-.062	.105	-.001	-.130	-.352	.619	.476	.544	1.000									
TO	.227	.465	.295	.330	.004	.698	.502	.517	.575	1.000								
GI	.238	.392	.367	.178	.023	.542	.381	.367	.697	.501	1.000							
CM	.189	.146	.227	.159	.117	.336	.380	.384	.084	.192	-.001	1.000						
AC	.401	.374	.479	.296	.154	.676	.567	.589	.633	.588	.610	.307	1.000					
AI	.075	.400	.140	.289	-.027	.513	.369	.280	.464	.720	.359	.175	.465	1.000				
IE	.314	.590	.451	.457	.192	.671	.500	.442	.456	.716	.460	.333	.616	.688	1.000			
PY	.167	.337	.239	.336	.011	.463	.217	.182	.410	.502	.397	-.060	.393	.519	.466	1.000		
FX	.148	.203	-.028	.236	.037	.051	-.155	-.300	-.043	.218	.079	-.149	-.120	.444	.199	.276	1.000	
FE	.099	.061	-.069	-.158	-.097	-.038	.275	.159	.215	.032	.091	.139	.071	.033	-.031	-.145	-.344	1.000

TABLE 11.4
Eigenvalues, Communalities, and Scree Plot for CPI from SPSSX Factor Analysis
Program

FINAL STATISTICS:

VARIABLE	COMMUNALITY	FACTOR	① EIGENVALUE	PCT OF VAR	CUM PCT
DO	.66861	1	6.67907	37.1	37.1
CS	.61861	2	2.93494	16.3	53.4
SY	.83160	3	2.11392	11.7	65.2
SP	.72899	4	1.11592	6.2	② 71.4
SA	.80185				
WB	.69772				
RE	.66676				
SO	.69190				
SC	.89418				
TA	③ .77198				
GI	.77148				
CM	.78142				
AC	.74630				
AI	.77480				
IE	.78641				
PY	.58322				
FX	.69176				
FE	.33627				

```
6.679 +    *
      I                        SCREE PLOT
      I
      I
      I
      I
      I
      I
      I
      I
      I
      I
      I
      I
      I
      I
      I
2.935 +     *
      I
2.114 +      *
      I                  BREAK POINT
      I
      I
1.116 +    *
 .978 +      *
      I
 .571 +        *   *
 .426 +            *   *
 .211 +                  *   *   *   *   *
 .000 + ---+---+---+---+---+---+---+---+---+---+---+---+---+---+---+---*---*---*
         1   2   3   4   5   6   7   8   9  10  11  12  13  14  15 16 17 18
```

①The eigenvalue indicates the amount of variance accounted for by each factor.

②Since the Kaiser criterion is the default option, only factors with eigenvalues > 1 are retained. The 4 factors account for 71.4% of the total variance.

③Since 15 of the 18 communalities are either > .70 or very close to .70, the Kaiser criterion will be accurate here in identifying the true number of factors.

matrix for the CPI variables is given in Table 11.3. Table 11.4 presents part of the printout from SPSSX. The printout indicates that the first component (factor) accounted for 37.1% of the total variance. This is arrived at by dividing the eigenvalue for the first component (6.679), which tells how much variance that component accounts for, by the total variance (which for a correlation matrix is just the sum of the diagonal elements, or 18 here). The second component accounts for $2.935/18 \times 100 = 16.3\%$ of the variance, etc.

As to how many components to retain, Kaiser's rule of using only those components whose eigenvalues are greater than 1, would indicate that we should retain only the first four components (which is what has been done on the printout; remember Kaiser's rule is the default option for SPSSX). Thus, as the printout indicates, we account for 71.4% of the total variance. Cattell's scree test (cf. Table 11.4) would not agree with the Kaiser rule, since there are only three eigenvalues (associated with the first three factors) before the breaking point, the point where the steep descent stops and the eigenvalues start to level off. However, we interpret four factors, since the number of variables is less than 30 and most of the communalities are either greater than .70 or very close to .70 (15 of 18).

Table 11.5 gives the unrotated loadings and the varimax rotated loadings. From Table 11.1 the critical value for a significant loading is $2(.192) = .384$. Thus, this is an absolute minimum value for us to be confident that we are dealing with non-chance loadings. The original components are somewhat difficult to interpret, especially the first component, since 14 of the loadings are "significant." Therefore, we focus our interpretation on the rotated factors. The variables that we use in interpretation are boxed in on Table 11.5. The first rotated factor still has significant loadings on 11 variables, although since one of these (.386 for CS) is just barely significant, and is also substantially less than the other significant loadings (the next smallest is .597), we disregard it for interpretation purposes. Among the adjectives that characterize high scores on the other 10 variables, from the CPI manual, are: calm, patient, thorough, non-aggressive, conscientious, cooperative, modest, diligent, and organized. Thus, this first rotated factor appears to be a "conforming, mature, inward tendencies" dimension. That is, it reveals a low profile individual, who is conforming, industrious, thorough and nonaggressive.

The loadings that are significant on the second rotated factor, are also strong loadings (the smallest is .664): .794 for dominance, .664 for capacity for status, .878 for sociability, .748 for social presence and .875 for self acceptance. Adjectives, from the CPI manual, used to characterize high scores on these variables are: aggressive, ambitious, spontaneous, outspoken, self-centered, quick and enterprising. Thus, this factor appears to describe an "aggressive, outward tendencies" dimension. High scores on this dimension reveal a high profile individual who is aggressive, dynamic, and outspoken.

Factor 3 is somewhat dominated by the flexibility variable (loading $= -.814$),

TABLE 11.5
Unrotated Components Loadings and Varimax Rotated Loadings for California
Psychological Inventory

FACTOR MATRIX:

	FACTOR 1	FACTOR 2	FACTOR 3	FACTOR 4
DO	.50138	.55614	.29246	−.14969
CS	.64991	.43579	−.04968	−.06202
SY	.60979	.60143	.25638	−.17972
SP	.51249	.66550	−.13753	.06743
SA	.27041	.82105	.22488	−.06352
WB	.80595	−.19642	−.04812	.08525
RE	.67774	−.22010	.38890	.08805
SO	.61108	−.37498	.41038	.09723
SC	.60941	−.67660	−.06199	−.24732
TA	.81618	−.19838	−.22772	.12088
GI	.67347	−.20929	−.07448	−.51824
CM	.35560	−.01207	.43937	.67954
AC	.81977	−.15062	.18110	−.13710
AI	.67845	−.17075	−.45206	.28457
IE	.84604	.01749	−.14830	.21982
PY	.57314	−.04265	−.47150	−.17493
FX	.12880	.24623	−.76719	.16110
FE	.06827	−.27146	.49436	−.11630

ROTATED FACTOR MATRIX: ①

	FACTOR 1	FACTOR 2	FACTOR 3	FACTOR 4
DO	.14163	.79400	.12857	.03982
CS	.38642	.66435	−.16224	.04007
SY	.22573	.87857	.09161	.01933
SP	.17176	.74804	−.35729	.11079
SA	−.17010	.87575	−.04815	.06045
WB	.78875	.18571	.00605	.20268
RE	.59787	.21260	.40252	.31952
SO	.05350	.05621	.46943	.32275
SC	.86379	−.25241	.24986	−.14800
TA	.83224	.13884	−.16455	.18166
GI	.73890	.20992	.16605	−.39226
CM	.16277	.14699	.19767	.83322
AC	.75317	.32434	.26281	.06902
AI	.73196	.01485	−.42514	.24097
IE	.73722	.33508	−.19421	.30484
PY	.62886	.14622	−.34842	−.21207
FX	.14590	.05002	−.81464	−.06584
FE	.08839	−.05355	.56781	.05638

Legend: DO - Dominance, CS - Capacity for Status, SY - Sociability, SP - Social Presence, SA - Self Acceptance, WB - Sense of Well Being, RE -Responsibility, SO - Socialization, SC - Self-Control, TA - Tolerance, GI - Good Impression, CM - Communality, AC - Achievement via Conformance, AI - Achievement via Independence, IE - Intellectual Efficiency, PY - Psychological Mindedness, FX - Flexibility, FE - Femininity.

①To omit (blank out) small loading less than a given value (say .4) in SPSSX, use this subcommand:
FORMAT = SORT BLANK (.4)./

although we also consider the femininity variable for interpretation. Three other variables are also significant (RE, SO and Ai), although barely so. Also, since these variables were much more strongly associated with factor 1, we will not use them for interpretation of this factor. Low scores on flexibility, from the CPI manual, characterize an individual as cautious, guarded, mannerly, and overly deferential to authority. High scores on femininity reflect an individual who is patient, gentle, and as respectful and accepting of others. Factor three thus seems to be measuring a "demure inflexibility in intellectual and social matters."

Factor 4 is dominated by the communality variable, which is characterized in the CPI manual with adjectives like "dependable, tactful, reliable, and sincere."

Before proceeding to another example, there are a few additional points we wish to make. Nunnally (1978, pp. 433–436) has indicated, in an excellent discussion, several ways in which one can be fooled by factor analysis. One point he makes, which we wish to elaborate on, is that of ignoring the simple correlations among the variables after the factors have been derived. That is, not checking the correlations among the variables which have been used to define a factor, to see if there is communality among them in the simple sense. As Nunnally notes, in some cases variables used to define a factor may have simple correlations near 0.

For our example this is not the case. Examination of the simple correlations in Table 11.3 for the 10 variables used to define factor 1 shows that most of the correlations are in the moderate to fairly strong range. Also, the correlations among the 5 variables used to define factor 2 are also in the moderate to fairly strong range.

There is an additional interesting point concerning factor 2. The empirical clustering of the variables coincides almost exactly with the logical clustering of the variables given in the CPI manual. The only difference is that Wellbe is in the logical cluster but not in the empirical cluster (i.e., not on the factor).

Example 2—Personality Research Form

We now consider the interpretation of a principal components analysis and varimax rotation on the Personality Research Form for 231 undergraduate males from a study by Golding and Seidman (1974). The control lines for running the analysis on BMDP4M (factor analysis program) and the correlation matrix are presented in Table 11.6. The reader is reminded that the default options for BMDP4M are a components analysis, a varimax rotation and retention of only those factors whose eigenvalues are greater than 1 (the Kaiser criterion). In other words, all of these will be automatically done unless something else is specified by the user.

We are providing as input the correlation matrix. When the input is not the raw data, then the TYPE of input must be specified (see BMDP manual, 1983, p. 494). In Table 11.6 note that we have:

TABLE 11.6
Control Lines and Correlation Matrix for Components Analysis and
Varimax Rotation
of Personality Research Form on BMDP4M

```
/PROBLEM TITLE IS ' PRINCIPAL COMPONENTS AND VARIMAX ROTATION ON
  GOLDING AND SEIDMAN DATA - 15 SCALES ON PERSON. RES. FORM N=231.'
/INPUT VARIABLES ARE 15.
  TYPE IS CORR. SHAPE IS LOWER.
  FORMAT IS '(15F3.2)'.
/VARIABLE NAMES ARE ABASE,ACH,AGGRESS,AUTON,CHANGE,COGSTR,DEF,DOMIN,ENDUR,
  EXHIB,HARMAVOD,IMPULS,NUTUR,ORDER,PLAY.
/END
```

CORRELATION MATRIX

		1	2	3	4	5	6
ABASE	1	1.000					
ACH	2	0.010	1.000				
AGGRESS	3	−0.320	−0.080	1.000			
AUTON	4	0.130	0.030	0.040	1.000		
CHANGE	5	0.150	0.090	0.060	0.280	1.000	
COGSTR	6	−0.230	0.220	0.020	−0.170	−0.270	1.000
DEF	7	−0.420	0.060	0.570	0.040	−0.010	0.140
DOMIN	8	−0.220	0.370	0.250	0.080	0.170	−0.050
ENDUR	9	0.010	0.650	−0.110	0.090	0.030	0.200
EXHIB	10	−0.090	0.130	0.280	−0.070	0.150	−0.240
HARMAVOD	11	−0.220	−0.020	−0.010	−0.280	−0.330	0.450
IMPULS	12	0.140	−0.160	0.300	0.160	0.330	−0.460
NUTUR	13	0.330	0.300	−0.230	−0.240	0.030	−0.050
ORDER	14	−0.110	0.290	0.010	−0.130	−0.170	0.530
PLAY	15	0.050	−0.250	0.270	−0.020	0.120	−0.310

```
TYPE IS CORR. SHAPE IS LOWER.
FORMAT IS '(15F3.2)'./
```

TYPE is the paragraph name. CORR means we are feeding in a correlation
matrix. LOWER means we are just inputting the lower half of the correlation
matrix, i.e., the elements on the main diagonal and those below it. Recall that
15F3.2 indicates that the format F3.2 is being repeated 15 times. Also, each
row of the correlation matrix must begin on a *new* record (line, if one is using
a terminal, or new card if one is using cards). The format describes the longest
row; in this case 15F3.2, since we have 15 variables.

The first part of the printout appears in Table 11.7, and the output at the top
indicates that according to the Kaiser criterion only 4 factors will be retained
since there are only 4 eigenvalues > 1. Will the Kaiser criterion accurately
identify the true number of factors in this case? To answer this question it is
helpful to refer back to the Hakstian et al. (1982) study cited earlier. They note
that for $N > 250$ and a mean communality $\geq .60$, the Kaiser criterion is accurate.
The mean communality here is .623, as the reader may verify by referring to
Table 11.7 and computing the average. Although the N is not > 250, it is close

TABLE 11.6 (*continued*)

7	8	9	10	11	12	13	14	15
1.000								
0.320	1.000							
0.020	0.390	1.000						
0.100	0.520	0.080	1.000					
0.080	−0.210	−0.080	−0.220	1.000				
0.140	0.070	−0.230	0.340	−0.310	1.000			
−0.190	0.160	0.200	0.220	−0.040	0.040	1.000		
0.090	0.080	0.270	−0.110	0.220	−0.350	0.000	1.000	
−0.020	0.110	−0.270	0.430	−0.260	0.480	−0.100	−0.250	1.000

($N = 231$), and we feel the Kaiser rule will be quite accurate. To further support this claim, note that the Q/P ratio is here $4/15 = .267 < .30$, and Hakstian et al. indicate when this is the case the estimate of number of factors will be just that more credible.

To interpret the 4 factors, the sorted, rotated factor loadings in Table 11.8 are very useful. For these, all loadings $< |.25|$ are replaced by 0. Our annotation (footnote 2 in Table 11.8) is important. This sharpens the focus in terms of what are the salient loadings. Referring back to Table 11.1, we see that the critical value for a significant loading at the .01 level is $2(.17) = .34$. So, we certainly would not want to pay any attention to loadings less than .34 in absolute value. But we go even further than this, and limit our attention to loadings $> .50$ in absolute value. Admittedly, this is where things become a little more subjective. Those loadings $> .50$ are boxed in on Table 11.8.

The loadings on factor 1 imply a "unstructured, free spirit tendency." The loadings on factor 2 imply a "structured, hard driving tendency." The loadings on factor 3 indicate a "non-demeaning aggressive tendency," while the loadings on factor 4, which are somewhat dominated by the very high loading on autonomy, imply a "somewhat fearless tendency to act on one's own."

TABLE 11.7

Eigenvalues, Communalities and Unrotated Factor Loadings for Personality
Research Form Components Analysis

FACTOR	VARIANCE EXPLAINED	CUMULATIVE PROPORTION OF TOTAL VARIANCE
1	3.168359	0.211224
2	2.482114	0.376698
3	2.246351	0.526455
4	1.442163	0.622599
5	0.859129	0.679874
6	0.832561	0.735378
7	0.685947	0.781108
8	0.604735	0.821424
9	0.541110	0.857498
10	0.438190	0.886711
11	0.406026	0.913779
12	0.382601	0.939286
13	0.328260	0.961170
14	0.310785	0.981889
15	0.271670	1.000000

THE VARIANCE EXPLAINED BY EACH FACTOR IS THE EIGENVALUE FOR THAT FACTOR.

TOTAL VARIANCE IS DEFINED AS THE SUM OF THE DIAGONAL ELEMENTS OF THE
CORRELATION (COVARIANCE) MATRIX.

COMMUNALITIES OBTAINED FROM 4 FACTORS AFTER   1 ITERATIONS.
THE COMMUNALITY OF A VARIABLE IS ITS SQUARED MULTIPLE
CORRELATION (OR COVARIANCE) WITH THE FACTORS.

1	ABASE	0.5675
2	ACH	0.7159
3	AGGRESS	0.6710
4	AUTON	0.7011
5	CHANGE	0.4487
6	COGSTR	0.6241
7	DEF	0.6446
8	DOMIN	0.7020
9	ENDUR	0.7133
10	EXHIB	0.7243
11	HARMAVOD	0.5380
12	IMPULS	0.6029
13	NUTUR	0.6592
14	ORDER	0.4529
15	PLAY	0.5735

UNROTATED FACTOR LOADINGS (PATTERN)
FOR PRINCIPAL COMPONENTS

		FACTOR 1	FACTOR 2	FACTOR 3	FACTOR 4	
ABASE	1	0.185	−0.374	0.627	−0.018	①
ACH	2	−0.311	0.614	0.488	0.064	
AGGRESS	3	0.297	0.458	−0.611	0.025	
AUTON	4	0.273	0.047	0.131	0.779	
CHANGE	5	0.467	0.156	0.272	0.363	
COGSTR	6	−0.739	0.184	−0.210	−0.009	
DEF	7	0.035	0.543	−0.568	0.163	
DOMIN	8	0.180	0.809	0.112	−0.058	
ENDUR	9	−0.327	0.579	0.491	0.171	
EXHIB	10	0.489	0.533	0.056	−0.446	
HARMAVOD	11	−0.581	−0.114	−0.357	−0.246	
IMPULS	12	0.770	0.059	−0.063	−0.057	
NUTUR	13	−0.029	0.137	0.600	−0.529	
ORDER	14	−0.600	0.303	−0.027	0.005	
PLAY	15	0.663	0.021	−0.189	−0.312	

①Thus, the communality for a variable is just the sum of the squared loadings, since the factors, which are playing the role of predictors, are uncorrelated. Hence, $.5675 = (.185)^2 + (−.374)^2 + (.627)^2 + (−.018)^2$.

TABLE 11.8
Sorted, Varimax Rotated Loadings for Personality Research Form

SORTED ROTATED FACTOR LOADINGS (PATTERN)

		FACTOR 1	FACTOR 2	FACTOR 3	FACTOR 4
PLAY	15	0.732 ①	0.0	0.0	0.0
IMPULS	12	0.729	0.0	0.0	0.0
EXHIB	10	0.664	0.467	0.0	0.0
COGSTR	6	−0.658	0.0	0.0	−0.336
ORDER	14	−0.528	0.312	0.0	0.0
ACH	2	−0.263	0.798	0.0	0.0
ENDUR	9	−0.323	0.759	0.0	0.0
DOMIN	8	0.0	0.711	0.359	0.0
NUTUR	13	0.0	0.510	−0.502	−0.327
DEF	7	0.0	0.0	0.793	0.0
AGGRESS	3	0.292	0.0	0.765	0.0
ABASE	1	0.0	0.0	−0.713	0.0
AUTON	4	0.0	0.0	0.0	0.832
CHANGE	5	0.293	0.0	0.0	0.577
HARAVOID	11	−0.440	0.0	0.0	−0.536
VP		2.885	2.407	2.297	1.751

THE ABOVE FACTOR LOADING MATRIX HAS BEEN REARRANGED SO
THAT THE COLUMNS APPEAR IN DECREASING ORDER OF VARIANCE
EXPLAINED BY FACTORS. THE ROWS HAVE BEEN REARRANGED
SO THAT FOR EACH SUCCESSIVE FACTOR, LOADINGS GREATER
THAN 0.5000 APPEAR FIRST. *LOADINGS LESS THAN 0.2500*
HAVE BEEN REPLACED BY ZERO.   ②

①Boxed in entries are those used to interpret the factors. It would help if there were a statistical test, even a rough one, for determining when one loading on a given factor is significantly greater than another loading on the same factor. This would then provide a more solid basis for including one variable in the interpretation of a factor and excluding another, assuming both have exceeded the "critical value" we have discussed. This writer is not aware of such a test.

②This is a good idea, since for $N \leq 400$, loadings $< |.25|$ are probably chance loadings anyways. The critical value ($N = 400$) at $\alpha = .01$ (two tailed) from Table 11.1 is $2(.129) = .26$.

Example 3—Regression Analysis on Factor Scores

We mentioned earlier in this chapter that one of the uses of components analysis was in reducing the number of predictors in regression analysis. This makes good statistical and conceptual sense for several reasons. First, if there are a fairly large set of initial predictors (say 15), we are undoubtedly not measuring 15 different constructs, and hence it makes sense to determine what the main constructs are that we are measuring. Secondly, this is desirable from the viewpoint of scientific parsimony. Third, if we reduce from 15 initial predictors to say 4 new predictors (the components or rotated factor scores), our N/k ratio increases dramatically and this helps cross-validation prospects considerably. Fourth, our new predictors are uncorrelated, which means we have eliminated multicollinearity, which is a major factor in causing unstable regression equations. Fifth, since the new predictors are uncorrelated, we can talk about the unique contribution of each predictor in accounting for variance on y, i.e., there is an unambiguous interpretation of the importance of each predictor.

To illustrate the process of doing the components analysis on the predictors and then passing the factor scores to the BMDP2R regression program, we consider a situation with 10 predictors and 100 subjects. In this example our focus is not on interpreting the factors, but on linking the results of the factor analysis program with the regression program. To accomplish this we make use of an important feature of the BMDP package, the *SAVE file* feature. We also use the SAVE file in the next chapter, on canonical correlation.

With the SAVE file feature, data saved on Units 3 or 4 (for IBM operating systems) can be passed from program to program without any job control language (JCL). It is important to note that this is true if we are creating a *temporary* file, i.e., if we wish to pass data from one program to the next within one computer run. However, this is what we will be doing in the examples in this text. If, on the other hand, one wishes a permanent file, then the reader is referred to the manual.

Each BMDP file must be assigned a code name in the SAVE paragraph, and this code name must be specified each time the file is used as input. For the factor analysis program (BMDP4M) the scores for the original variables are first written on the file, and then the factor scores, which are named FACTOR1, FACTOR2, etc., appear. When NEW is specified, the BMDP file created is placed at the beginning of the system file; all BMDP files previously written on this system file are deleted.

One advantage of using files is that it simplifies the control language even further. For example, variable names, group names, etc., are stored on the file, and it is not necessary to repeat these when using the file as input to another program. This is shown in our example.

The control lines for our example, along with the correlation matrix for the predictors, appears in Table 11.9. Note that two runs are involved. The first run is to get the factor analysis. Then we would examine that output, interpret the factors and decide which (if any) of the original variables we may also want to retain for the regression analysis. The first two lines for each program are the *system lines,* which will vary from one computer installation to another. They have been included here simply to indicate that two different BMDP programs are being accessed in run 2. Note that in run 1 we make use of the USE command to "pick off" just the predictor variables, since it is these variables that we want to do the factor analysis on. We did this by stating:

USE = 2 to 11./

That is, the predictors were identified by their locations in the list of variable names. We could have also accomplished the same thing by stating:

USE = X1 TO X10./

i.e., by using the variable names.

TABLE 11.9

Control Lines for Components Analysis on Set of Predictors with BMDP4M and then Passing Factor Scores to BMDP2R Regression Program

```
            //   EXEC    BIMED,PROG = BMDP4M   ①
            //SYSIN   DD   *
            /PROBLEM TITLE IS ' COMPONENTS AND VARIMAX ON PREDICTORS '.
     R      /INPUT VARIABLES ARE 11.
     U        FORMAT IS STREAM.
     N      /VARIABLE NAMES ARE Y,X1,X2,X3,X4,X5,X6,X7,X8,X9,X10.
              USE = 2 TO 11.
R      1    /PRINT CASE=100. CORR.
            /SAVE UNIT=3. NEW. CODE IS FACSCO.
U           /END
                    DATA
N           //   EXEC    BIMED,PROG=BMDP2R
            //SYSIN   DD *
2           /PROBLEM TITLE IS ' MULTIPLE REGRESSION '.
            /INPUT UNIT =3. CODE IS FACSCO.
            /VARIABLE USE=FACTOR1,FACTOR2,X10,Y.   ②
            /REGRESSION DEPENDENT IS Y.
            /PRINT CORR.
            /END
```

CORRELATION MATRIX

	X1	X2	X3	X4	X5	X6	X7	X8	X9	X10
X1	1.000									
X2	0.166	1.000								
X3	−0.177	0.708	1.000							
X4	−0.240	0.432	0.526	1.000						
X5	−0.564	0.314	0.515	0.615	1.000					
X6	−0.165	0.433	0.522	0.325	0.447	1.000				
X7	−0.252	0.599	0.712	0.558	0.624	0.592	1.000			
X8	−0.450	0.244	0.453	0.392	0.566	0.340	0.503	1.000		
X9	0.585	−0.069	−0.279	−0.176	−0.395	−0.208	−0.295	−0.236	1.000	
X10	−0.011	0.232	0.270	0.206	0.203	0.193	0.417	0.160	−0.090	1.000

①The default options in the BMDP4M factor analysis program are a components analysis and varimax rotation, i.e., these are done automatically unless something else is specified.

②In RUN 2 we have passed the original variables and the factor scores on Unit 3 to the BMDP2R program, and have selected the factors which have eigenvalues > 1, along with variable X10 as our 3 predictors.

Table 11.10 presents the unrotated, rotated, and sorted, rotated loadings for the 10 predictors. Note first that only two factors were retained, which means that only the first two had eigenvalues > 1, since the default option is the Kaiser criterion. In particular, note that we retain predictor 10 as a separate variable for the regression analysis, since it is relatively independent of what the two factors are measuring. What we have done here relates directly to the comment mentioned earlier in this chapter from Morrison (1967), "Frequently it is better to summarize the complex in terms of the first components with large and markedly distinct variances and include as highly specific and unique variates

TABLE 11.10
Unrotated, Rotated and Sorted Rotated Loadings for Components Analysis on Set of 10 Predictors

UNROTATED FACTOR LOADINGS (PATTERN)
FOR PRINCIPAL COMPONENTS

		FACTOR 1	FACTOR 2
X1	2	-0.457	0.808
X2	3	0.628	0.599
X3	4	0.819	0.276
X4	5	0.708	0.071
X5	6	0.811	-0.289
X6	7	0.663	0.174
X7	8	0.872	0.186
X8	9	0.669	-0.244
X9	10	-0.457	0.574
X10	11	0.385	0.259
VP		4.439	1.697

THE VP FOR EACH FACTOR IS THE SUM OF THE SQUARES OF THE
ELEMENTS OF THE COLUMN OF THE FACTOR LOADING MATRIX
CORRESPONDING TO THAT FACTOR. THE VP IS THE VARIANCE
EXPLAINED BY THE FACTOR.

ROTATED FACTOR LOADINGS (PATTERN)

		FACTOR 1	FACTOR 2
X1	2	0.069	0.926
X2	3	0.854	0.149
X3	4	0.835	-0.225
X4	5	0.628	-0.334
X5	6	0.515	-0.691
X6	7	0.648	-0.224
X7	8	0.829	-0.330
X8	9	0.421	-0.575
X9	10	-0.061	0.731
X10	11	0.464	0.002
VP		3.594	2.542

THUS, THE PERCENT OF VARIANCE ACCOUNTED FOR BY THE FIRST TWO
PRINCIPAL COMPONENTS IS

$$\frac{4.439 + 1.697}{10} \times 100 = 61.37\%$$

SORTED ROTATED FACTOR LOADINGS (PATTERN)

		FACTOR 1	FACTOR 2
X2	3	0.854	0.0
X3	4	0.835	0.0
X7	8	0.829	-0.330
X6	7	0.646	0.0
X4	5	0.628	-0.334
X1	2	0.0	0.926
X9	10	0.0	0.731
X5	6	0.515	-0.691
X8	9	0.421	-0.575
X10	11 ①	0.464	0.0
VP		3.594	2.542

SINCE THESE ARE VARIMAX ROTATED LOADINGS, THE ROTATED FACTORS ARE STILL UNCORRELATED. NOTE THAT THE PERCENT OF VARIANCE ACCOUNTED FOR BY THESE TWO ROTATED FACTORS IS ALSO 61.37%. IN THE ROTATED SOLUTION, HOWEVER, THE VARIANCE IS SPREAD OUT MORE EVENLY AMONG THE FACTORS.

THE ABOVE FACTOR LOADING MATRIX HAS BEEN REARRANGED SO THAT THE COLUMNS APPEAR IN DECREASING ORDER OF VARIANCE EXPLAINED BY FACTORS. THE ROWS HAVE BEEN REARRANGED SO THAT FOR EACH SUCCESSIVE FACTOR, LOADINGS GREATER THAN 0.5000 APPEAR FIRST. LOADINGS LESS THAN 0.2500 HAVE BEEN REPLACED BY ZERO.

① HERE $N = 100$, THUS THE CRITICAL VALUE FOR A SIGNIFICANT LOADING IS $2(.256) = .512$. NOTE THAT X10 HAS CHANCE LOADINGS ON BOTH ROTATED FACTORS, THUS IT IS RELATIVELY INDEPENDENT OF WHAT THESE TWO FACTORS ARE MEASURING, AND WE WILL RETAIN IT AS A SEPARATE VARIABLE.

TABLE 11.11
Stepwise Regression Analysis Results on Rotated Factor Scores and Predictor 10

STEP NO.	1	
VARIABLE	ENTERED	12 FACTOR1

MULTIPLE R	0.5008
MULTIPLE R-SQUARE	0.2508
ADJUSTED R-SQUARE	0.2432
STD. ERROR OF EST.	1.4644

ANALYSIS OF VARIANCE

	SUM OF SQUARES	DF	MEAN SQUARE	F RATIO
REGRESSION	70.364395	1	70.36440	32.81
RESIDUAL	210.14500	98	2.144337	

VARIABLES IN EQUATION

VARIABLE	COEFFICIENT	STD. ERROR OF COEFF	STD REG COEFF	TOLERANCE	F TO REMOVE	LEVEL
(Y-INTERCEPT	3.06998)					
FACTOR1 12	−0.84306	0.1472	−0.501	1.00000	32.81	1

VARIABLES NOT IN EQUATION

VARIABLE		PARTIAL CORR.	TOLERANCE	F TO ENTER	LEVEL
FACTOR2	13	0.32456	1.00000	11.42	1
X10	11	−0.22744	0.78479	5.29	1

STEP NO.	2	
VARIABLE	ENTERED	13 FACTOR2

MULTIPLE R	0.5742
MULTIPLE R-SQUARE	0.3298
ADJUSTED R-SQUARE	0.3159
STD. ERROR OF EST.	1.3922

ANALYSIS OF VARIANCE

	SUM OF SQUARES	DF	MEAN SQUARE	F RATIO
REGRESSION	92.500366	2	46.25018	23.86
RESIDUAL	188.00903	97	1.938237	

| | VARIABLES IN EQUATION | | | | | | | VARIABLES NOT IN EQUATION | | | |
VARIABLE	COEFFICIENT	STD. ERROR OF COEFF	STD REG COEFF	TOLERANCE	F TO REMOVE	LEVEL		VARIABLE	PARTIAL CORR.	TOLERANCE	F TO ENTER	LEVEL
(Y-INTERCEPT	3.06998)											
FACTOR1 12	-0.84306	0.1399	-0.501	1.00000	36.30	1		X10 11	-0.24110	0.78479	5.92	1
FACTOR2 13	0.47286	0.1399	0.281	1.00000	11.42	1						

STEP NO. 3
VARIABLE ENTERED 11 X10

MULTIPLE R	0.6072
MULTIPLE R-SQUARE	0.3587
ADJUSTED R-SQUARE	0.3490
STD. ERROR OF EST.	1.3582

ANALYSIS OF VARIANCE

	SUM OF SQUARES	DF	MEAN SQUARE	F RATIO
REGRESSION	103.42923	3	34.47641	18.69
RESIDUAL	177.08017	96	1.844584	

| | VARIABLES IN EQUATION | | | | | | | VARIABLES NOT IN EQUATION | | | |
VARIABLE	COEFFICIENT	STD. ERROR OF COEFF	STD REG COEFF	TOLERANCE	F TO REMOVE	LEVEL		VARIABLE	PARTIAL CORR.	TOLERANCE	F TO ENTER	LEVEL
(Y-INTERCEPT	7.27170)											
FACTOR1 12	-0.66908	0.1541	-0.397	0.78479	18.86	1						
FACTOR2 13	0.47348	0.1365	0.281	1.00000	12.03	1						
X10 11	-0.04245	0.0174	-0.223	0.78479	5.92	1						

***** F-LEVELS(4.000. 3.900) OR TOLERANCE INSUFFICIENT FOR FURTHER STEPPING

those responses which are generally independent in the system" (p. 228). The unique variate being retained here is $X10$.

The stepwise regression analysis results on the rotated factor scores and predictor 10 appear in Table 11.11, and indicate that all 3 of these predictors are "significant" according to the default ENTER and REMOVE values of 4 and 3.9. Recall from the regression chapter that these F values are only rough guides as to the usefulness of the predictors, and not a great deal of confidence should be placed in them until they cross validate.

Example 4—Multivariate Analysis of Variance on Factor Scores

In Table 11.12 we illustrate a components analysis and varimax rotation on a hypothetical set of 15 dependent variables, and then passing the factor scores to the BMDP3D program for a two-group MANOVA. Since the components or varimax rotated factors are uncorrelated, someone might argue to just do 3 univariate tests, for in this case an exact estimate of overall α is available from $1 - (1 - .05)^3 = .145$. While an exact estimate is available, the multivariate approach covers a possibility which the univariate approach would miss, that is, the case where there are small nonsignificant differences on each of the variables, but cumulatively (with the multivariate test) there is a significant difference.

Also, with the addition of just a few control lines (we indicate what these

TABLE 11.12

Components Analysis on a Set of Dependent Variables and then Passing the Factor Scores to BMDP3D for Two-Group MANOVA

```
              //   EXEC    BIMED,PROG=BMDP4M  ①
              //SYSIN    DD    *
              /PROBLEM TITLE IS ' PRELIMINARY COMPONENTS ANALYSIS AND VARIMAX ROTATION'.
       R      /INPUT VARIABLES=16. FORMAT IS STREAM.
       U      /VARIABLE NAMES ARE GPID,Y1,Y2,Y3,Y4,Y5,Y6,Y7,Y8,Y9,Y10,Y11,Y12,Y13,Y14,Y15.
       N      USE=Y1 TO Y15.
       1      /SAVE UNIT=3. NEW. CODE=FACSCO.
  R           /END
                  DATA
  U           //   EXEC    BIMED,PROG=BMDP3D
              //SYSIN    DD    *
  N           /PROBLEM TITLE IS ' MANOVA ON FACTOR SCORES '.
              /INPUT UNIT=3. CODE=FACSCO.
  2           /VARIABLE GROUPING IS GPID.
              /TEST VARIABLES ARE FACTOR1,FACTOR2,FACTOR3. HOTELLING.  ②
              /END
```

①We are using the default options for the factor analysis program. One such default is that only factors corresponding to eigenvalues >1 are retained. Assume that in RUN 1 there were only 3 eigenvalues greater than 1, so that only 3 factors were retained. It is these 3 factors, which are named FACTOR1, FACTOR2 and FACTOR3, that are saved on UNIT 3 and passed to the BMDP3D program.

②Recall that HOTELLING is the keyword used to obtain the multivariate analysis.

are in the next section), one can obtain a good oblique rotation for correlated factors, which would then be passed to BMDP3D. Here the case for a multivariate analysis is even more compelling since an exact estimate of overall α is not available. Another case where some of the "variables" would be correlated is if we did a factor analysis and retained, say, 3 factors and 2 of the original variables which were relatively independent of the factors. Then there would be correlations between the original variables retained and between those variables and the factors.

11.9   OBLIQUE ROTATIONS—CORRELATED FACTORS

It can happen, of course, that not only are the components not interpretable, but even after a rigid rotation (such as varimax) the new factors still do not have a clean interpretation. This is a situation where the use of correlated factors may provide a better fit to reality. Now, many oblique rotations have been proposed (e.g., oblimax, quartimin, biquartimin, orthoblique [Kaiser-Harris], promax, max plane), which yield factors correlated to varying degrees. *The evidence, however, from many comparative studies of these oblique rotations suggests that the orthoblique and promax procedures generally give the best results.* Hakstian (1971), for example, rated the orthoblique procedure first, with promax right behind it. Orthoblique is available on BMDP4M and in the factor procedure on the SAS package. To obtain it for BMDP4M insert after the VARIABLE paragraph the following:

```
FACTOR METHOD IS LJIFFY./
ROTATE METHOD IS ORTHOB./
```

The control lines from BMDP4M for the Harris-Kaiser oblique analysis of the CPI are presented in Table 11.13, along with the sorted, rotated loadings and the oblique factor correlations. We leave as an exercise the interpretation of the oblique factors.

Promax is not available on BMDP or SPSSX, but it is available on the SAS package. We refer the reader to Gorsuch (1983) for a discussion of the Harris-Kaiser and Promax procedures.

11.10   THE COMMUNALITY ISSUE

In principal components analysis we simply transform the original variables into linear combinations of these variables, and often 3 or 4 of these combinations (i.e., the components) account for most of the total variance. Also, we used 1's in the diagonal of the correlation matrix. Factor analysis per se differs from components analysis in two ways: (1) The hypothetical factors that are derived can only be *estimated* from the original variables, whereas in components analysis, since the components are specific linear combinations, no estimate is involved, and (2) Numbers less than 1, called communalities, are put in the main diagonal of the correlation matrix in factor analysis. A relevant question is "Will different factors emerge if 1's are put in the main diagonal (as in components analysis), then will emerge if communalities (the squared multiple correlation of each variable with all the others is one of the most popular) are placed in the main diagonal? "The following quotes from three different sources give a pretty good sense of what might be expected in practice. Harman (1967) states, "As a saving grace, there is much evidence in the literature that for all but very small sets of variables, the resulting factorial solutions are little affected by the particular choice of communalities in the principal diagonal of the correlation matrix" (p. 83). Nunnally (1978) notes, "It is very safe to say that if there are as many as 20 variables in the analysis, as there are in nearly all exploratory factor analyses, then it does not matter what one puts in the diagonal spaces" (p. 418). Gorsuch (1983) takes a somewhat more conservative position, "If communalities are reasonably high (e.g., .7 and up), even unities are probably adequate communality estimates in a problem with more than 35 variables" (p. 108). A general, somewhat conservative conclusion from the above is that when the number of variables is moderately large (say > 30), and the analysis contains virtually no variables expected to have low communalities (e.g., .4), then practically any of the factor procedures will lead to the same interpretations. Differences can occur when the number of variables is fairly small (< 20), and some communalities are low.

11.11   A FEW CONCLUDING COMMENTS

We have focused on an internal criterion in evaluating the factor solution, i.e., how interpretable are the factors. However, an important external criterion is the reliability of the solution. If the sample size is large, then one should randomly split the sample to check the consistency (reliability) of the factor solution on both random samples. In checking to determine whether the same factors have appeared in both cases it is not sufficient to just examine the factor loadings. One needs to obtain the correlations between the factor scores for corresponding pairs of factors. If these correlations are high, then one may have confidence of factor stability.

Finally, there is the issue of "factor indeterminancy" when estimating factors as in the common factor model. This refers to the fact that the factors are not uniquely determined. The importance of this for the common factor model has been the subject of much hot debate in the literature. We tend to side with Steiger (1979), who states, "My opinion is that indeterminacy and related problems of the factor model counterbalance the model's theoretical advantages, and that the elevated status of the common factor model (relative to, say, components analysis) is largely undeserved" (p. 157).

11.12   SUMMARY OF MAJOR POINTS

1.   Principal components are uncorrelated, linear combinations of the original variables.

2.   When there are a large number of variables, say 30, the number of correlations is 435, and it is very difficult to summarize (by inspection) precisely what this pattern of correlations represents. Principal components analysis is a means of "boiling down" the main sources of variation in such a complex set of correlations, and often a small number of components will account for most of the variance.

3.   Three uses for components analysis as a variable reducing scheme were mentioned: (a) determining the number of dimensions underlying a test, (b) reducing the number of predictors, prior to a regression analysis, and (c) reducing the number of dependent variables, prior to a MANOVA.

4.   For reliable components, make sure that $N \geq 100$ and that there are at least 5 subjects per variable.

5.   The Kaiser rule will accurately determine the number of components to retain when the number of variables ≤ 30 and the communalities are $> .70$, *or* when $N > 250$ and the mean communality $\geq .60$. For other situations, when $N < 200$, a statistical test is advisable. For $N > 200$, use of the scree test will probably not lead us too far astray, provided most of the communalities are reasonably large.

6.   We suggest *doubling* the critical value for an ordinary correlation and using that, at the .01 level, to determine whether a loading is significant.

7.   For increasing the interpretability of factors, there are two basic types of rotations: (a) orthogonal—the rotated factors are still uncorrelated, and (b) oblique—the rotated factors are correlated.

8.   The best orthogonal rotation is varimax. There is some consensus in the literature that the Kaiser-Harris and Promax are the best oblique rotations. The Kaiser-Harris procedure is available on BMDP4M and Promax is available on the SAS package.

9.   With respect to using communality estimates in the main diagonal of the matrix being factor analyzed (rather than 1's), several sources suggest that when the number of variables > 30 and only a few variables have low communalities, then practically any of the factor procedures leads to the same conclusions. When the number of variables is < 20 and some of the communalities are low, then differences can occur.

10.   We showed how to use the BMDP package, and in particular the SAVE

FILE feature, to pass factor scores from the BMDP4M program to the regression and MANOVA programs.

EXERCISES—CHAPTER 11

1.   The notion of a linear combination of variables and how much variance that linear combination accounts for is fundamental not only in principal components analysis but also in other forms of multivariate analysis such as discriminant analysis and canonical correlation. We indicated in this chapter that the variances for the successive components are equal to eigenvalues of covariance (correlation) matrix. However, the variance for a linear combination is defined more fundamentally in terms of the variances and covariances of the variables which make up the composite. We denote the matrix of variances and covariances for a set of p variables as:

$$\mathbf{S} = \begin{bmatrix} s_1^2 & s_{12} & \cdots & s_{1p} \\ s_{21} & s_2^2 & \cdots & s_{2p} \\ \vdots & \vdots & & \vdots \\ s_{p1} & s_{p2} & & s_p^2 \end{bmatrix}$$

The variance of a linear combination is defined as:

$$\text{var}(a_{11} x_1 + a_{12} x_2 + \ldots + a_{1p} x_p) = \text{var}(\mathbf{a'x}) = \mathbf{a'Sa},$$

where $\mathbf{a'} = (a_{11}, a_{12}, \ldots, a_{1p})$.

a) Write out what the formula for the variance of a linear combination of 2 and 3 variables will be.

b) The covariance matrix $\mathbf{S}$ for a set of 3 variables was:

$$\mathbf{S} = \begin{bmatrix} 451.4 & 271.2 & 168.7 \\ & 171.7 & 103.3 \\ \text{symm} & & 66.7 \end{bmatrix}$$

and the first principal component of $\mathbf{S}$ was

$$y_1 = .81 x_1 + .50 x_2 + .31 x_3$$

What is the variance of y_1? (Ans. 681.9)

2.   Golding and Seidman (1974) measured 231 undergraduate males enrolled in an undergraduate psychology course on the *Strong Vocational Interest Blank*

for Men, and obtained the following correlation matrix on the 22 basic interest scales: public speaking, law/politics, business management, sales, merchandising, office practice, military activities, technical supervision, mathematics, science, mechanical, nature, agriculture, adventure, recreational leadership, medical service, social service, religious activities, teaching, music, art, and writing.

	1	2	3	4	5	6	7	8	9	10	11	12	13	14	15	16	17	18	19	20	21	22
1	1.0																					
2	.77	1.0																				
3	53	50	1.0																			
4	54	44	74	1.0																		
5	54	48	91	82	1.0																	
6	30	28	72	63	75	1.0																
7	16	20	28	19	26	31	1.0															
8	36	34	79	56	70	63	38	1.0														
9	−11	−05	08	02	05	20	03	14	1.0													
10	−10	−09	−03	−07	−08	02	15	05	50	10												
11	−02	−07	22	23	21	27	29	37	44	62	1.0											
12	14	−02	04	05	07	−03	23	11	−04	37	31	1.0										
13	09	−01	06	10	09	−03	24	11	−10	08	21	73	1.0									
14	21	18	15	15	14	−01	16	13	13	11	28	12	31	1.0								
15	16	21	22	22	22	23	29	18	03	−07	09	10	32	41	1.0							
16	23	24	09	12	12	05	19	08	08	41	24	33	05	12	10	1.0						
17	38	36	13	21	14	10	07	00	−19	−04	−07	23	09	−01	18	29	1.0					
18	32	17	18	22	17	27	17	13	−01	12	14	33	19	00	19	20	47	1.0				
19	37	23	29	35	28	30	15	20	−03	18	16	36	12	−02	12	22	51	41	1.0			
20	22	04	−01	05	06	−05	−22	−06	01	22	11	31	00	−05	−28	26	27	37	42	1.0		
21	19	−01	−06	04	05	−13	−15	−10	02	22	12	49	17	02	−22	23	26	25	34	73	1.0	
22	49	26	04	16	10	−08	−10	−06	−23	−04	−12	28	09	08	−02	15	42	31	42	57	62	1.0

Run a components analysis on this matrix. Also, do a varimax rotation, and compare the interpretations.

3. In which, if either, of the below cases would it be advisable to apply Bartlett's sphericity test before proceeding with a components analysis?

Case 1

1	.31	.45	.18	.56	.41	.50
	1	.27	.36	.04	.30	.21
		1	.63	.16	.41	.25
			1.	.28	.15	.32
				1	.46	.53
					1	.39
						1

125 subjects

Case 2

1	.29	.18	.04	.11	.15	111 subjects
	1	.07	.40	.12	.03	
		1	.23	.06	.13	
			1	$-.08$	$-.14$	
				1	.12	
					1	

The actual sphericity test statistic is:

$$\chi^2 = -(N - 1 - \frac{2p + 5}{6}) \ln |\mathbf{R}|, \text{ with } 1/2 \, p \, (p - 1) \, df$$

However, Lawley has shown that a good approximation to this statistic is:

$$\chi^2 = (N - 1 - \frac{2p + 5}{6}) \sum\sum r_{ij}^2,$$

where the sum extends only over the correlations (r_{ij}) above the main diagonal.

Use the Lawley approximation for the above two cases to determine whether you would reject the null hypothesis of uncorrelated variables in the population.

4.   Consider the following correlation matrix:

$$\mathbf{R} = \begin{bmatrix} 1 & .6579 & .0034 \\ & 1 & -.0738 \\ & & 1 \end{bmatrix}$$

A principal components analysis on this matrix produced the following factor structure, i.e., component-variable correlations:

	Principal Components		
	1	2	3
Variables			
1	.906	.112	.408
2	.912	$-.005$	$-.411$
3	$-.097$	.994	$-.048$

We denote the column of component-variable correlations for the first component by $\mathbf{h}_1$, for the second component by $\mathbf{h}_2$, and for the third component by $\mathbf{h}_3$. Show that the original correlation matrix $\mathbf{R}$ will be reproduced, within rounding error, by $\mathbf{h}_1\mathbf{h}_1' + \mathbf{h}_2\mathbf{h}_2' + \mathbf{h}_3\mathbf{h}_3'$. As you are doing this, observe what part of $\mathbf{R}$ the matrix $\mathbf{h}_1\mathbf{h}_1'$ reproduces, etc.

5.   Consider the following principal components solution on 5 variables and the corresponding varimax rotated solution. Only the first two components are given, since the eigenvalues corresponding to the remaining components were very small (< .3).

Variables	comp 1	comp 2	Varimax solution factor 1	factor 2
1	.581	.806	.016	.994
2	.767	−.545	.941	−.009
3	.672	.726	.137	.980
4	.932	−.104	.825	.447
5	.791	−.558	.968	−.006

a) Find the percent of variance accounted for by each principal component.
b) Find the percent of variance accounted for by each varimax rotated factor.
c) Compare the variance accounted for by component 1 (2) with variance accounted for by each corresponding rotated factor.
d) Compare the total percent of variance accounted for by the 2 components with the total percent of variance accounted for by the two rotated factors.

6.   Consider the following correlation matrix for the 12 variables on the General Aptitude Test Battery (GATB):

Correlation Matrix for General Aptitude Test Battery

Subtest	2	3	4	5	6	7	8	9	10	11	12
			General Aptitude Test Battery								
1. Names	.697	.360	.637	.586	.552	.496	.561	.338	.349	.390	.354
2. Arithmetic		.366	.580	.471	.760	.411	.501	.297	.247	.319	.325
3. 3 dimensions			.528	.554	.468	.580	.249	.276	.279	.358	.234
4. Vocabulary				.425	.616	.444	.465	.211	.209	.267	.283
5. Tools					.369	.531	.444	.292	.336	.361	.267
6. Math						.400	.407	.300	.234	.208	.311
7. Shapes							.387	.323	.401	.444	.428
8. Marking								.494	.540	.439	.422
9. Place									.773	.468	.453
10. Turn										.476	.482
11. ASMBL											.676
12. DASMBL											

a) Run the components analysis and varimax rotation on BMDP4M. How many components should we retain according to the Kaiser criterion?
b) How large of a sample size is necessary for reliable factors? Use the communalities from the printout in answering this question.

c) Interpret each of the components.

7. Bolton (1971) measured 159 deaf rehabilitation candidates on 10 communication skills, of which 6 were reception skills in unaided hearing, aided hearing,
speech reading, reading, manual signs and fingerspellings. The other four communication skills were expression skills: oral speech, writing, manual signs and
fingerspelling. Bolton did what is called a principal axis analysis, which is
identical to a components analysis, except that the factors are extracted from a
correlation matrix with communality estimates on the main diagonal rather than
1's, as in components analysis. He obtained the following correlation matrix
and varimax factor solution:

Correlation Matrix of Communication Variables for 159 Deaf Persons

	C_1	C_2	C_3	C_4	C_5	C_6	C_7	C_8	C_9	C_{10}	M	S
C_1	39										1.10	0.45
C_2	59	55									1.49	1.06
C_3	30	34	61								2.56	1.17
C_4	16	24	62	81							2.63	1.11
C_5	−02	−13	28	37	92						3.30	1.50
C_6	00	−05	42	51	90	94					2.90	1.44
C_7	39	61	70	59	05	20	71				2.14	1.31
C_8	17	29	57	88	30	46	60	78			2.42	1.04
C_9	−04	−14	28	33	93	86	04	28	92		3.25	1.49
C_{10}	−04	−08	42	50	87	94	17	45	90	94	2.89	1.41

Note—The italicized diagonal values are squared multiple correlations.

Varimax Factor Solution for 10 Communication Variables
for 159 Deaf Persons

		I	II
C_1	Hearing (Unaided)		49
C_2	Hearing (Aided)		66
C_3	Speech Reading	32	70
C_4	Reading	45	71
C_5	Manual Signs	94	
C_6	Fingerspelling	94	
C_7	Speech		86
C_8	Writing	38	72
C;9	Manual Signs	94	
C_{10}	Fingerspelling	96	
	Percent of Common Variance	53.8	39.3

Note—Factor loadings less than .30 are omitted.

a) Interpret the varimax factors. What does each of them represent?

b) Does the way the variables which defined factor 1 correspond to the way they are correlated. That is, is the empirical clustering of the variables by the principal axis technique consistent with the way those variables "go together" in the original correlation matrix?

8.   (a) Using BMDP4M, do a principal axis (factor) analysis on the Personality

TABLE 11.13

Control Lines from BMDP4M for Harris-Kaiser Oblique Solution of CPI along with Sorted, Rotated Loadings, and Factor Correlations

```
/PROBLEM TITLE IS ' CPI - OBLIQUE ROTATION- KAISER - HARRIS '.
/INPUT VARIABLES ARE 18. FORMAT IS STREAM. TYPE IS CORR. SHAPE IS LOWER.
/VARIABLE NAMES ARE DO,CS,SY,SP,SA,WB,RE,SO,SC,TA,GI,CM,AC,AI,IE,PY,FX,FE.
/FACTOR METHOD IS LJIFFY.      ⎫ ①
/ROTATE METHOD IS ORTHOB.      ⎭
/END
```

SORTED ROTATED FACTOR LOADINGS (PATTERN)

		FACTOR 1	FACTOR 2	FACTOR 3	FACTOR 4
AI	14	0.964	0.000	0.000	0.000
IE	15	0.741	0.000	0.000	0.000
TA	10	0.727	0.000	0.000	0.000
CM	12	0.541	0.000	-0.505	0.536
SY	3	0.000	0.883	0.000	0.000
SA	5	0.000	0.821	-0.288	0.000
DO	1	0.000	0.802	0.000	0.000
SP	4	0.289	0.641	0.000	0.000
CS	2	0.321	0.545	0.000	0.000
GI	11	-0.276	0.353	0.960	0.000
SC	9	0.000	0.000	0.847	0.000
FX	17	0.446	0.000	0.000	-0.679
SO	8	0.295	0.000	0.000	0.548
RE	7	0.371	0.000	0.000	0.485
WB	6	0.426	0.000	0.313	0.000
PY	16	0.286	0.000	0.390	-0.314
AC	13	0.000	0.348	0.469	0.000
FE	18	0.000	0.000	0.000	0.418

FACTOR CORRELATIONS FOR ROTATED FACTORS

			FACTOR 1	FACTOR 2	FACTOR 3	FACTOR 4
FACTOR	1		1.000			
FACTOR	2		0.481	1.000		
FACTOR	3	②	0.712	0.186	1.000	
FACTOR	4		0.183	0.159	0.477	1.000

①These are the two control lines that are needed to obtain the Harris-Kaiser oblique solution.

②Notice that oblique factors 1 and 3 are highly correlated (.712), and that factors 1 and 2 and factors 3 and 4 have moderate correlations.

Research Form correlation matrix in Table 11.6. Use the multiple correlation of each variable with all other variables as the communality estimates. To obtain this analysis simply add the following FACTOR paragraph immediately after the VARIABLE paragraph:

FACTOR METHOD = PFA./

PFA stands for principal factor analysis, and when this analysis is done the multiple correlations are automatically used as communality estimates.
b) Compare the sorted, rotated factor loadings for this analysis with the sorted, rotated loadings given in Table 11.8 (for components analysis). Do there appear to be any real differences in the factors that are emerging?

9.   Compare the rotated factors that emerged from the components analysis and varimax rotation of the CPI (Table 11.5) with the factors derived from the Harris-Kaiser oblique analysis of the CPI in Table 11.13.

12 Canonical Correlation

12.1 INTRODUCTION

In Chapter 3 we examined breaking down the association between two sets of variables using multivariate regression analysis. This is the appropriate technique if our interest is in prediction, and if we wish to focus our attention primarily on the individual variables (both predictors and dependent), rather than on linear combinations of the variables. *Canonical correlation* is another means of breaking down the association for two sets of variables, and *is appropriate if the wish is to parsimoniously describe the number and nature of mutually independent relationships existing between the two sets*. This is accomplished through the use of pairs of linear combinations which are uncorrelated. Since the combinations are uncorrelated, we will obtain a very nice additive partitioning of the total between association. Thus, there are several similarities between principal components analysis (discussed in the previous chapter). Both are variable reduction schemes that use uncorrelated linear combinations. In components analysis, generally the first few linear combinations (the components) account for most of the total variance in the original set of variables, while in canonical correlation the first few pairs of linear combinations (the so-called canonical variates) generally account for most of the between-association. Also, in interpreting the principal components we used the correlations between the original variables and the components. In canonical correlation the correlations between the original variables and the canonical variates will again be used to name the canonical variates.

One could consider doing canonical regression. However, as Darlington et al. (1973) have stated, investigators are generally not interested in predicting linear combinations of the dependent variables.

Let us now consider a couple of situations where canonical correlation would be useful. An investigator wishes to explore the relationship between a set of personality variables (say as measured by the Cattell 16 PF scale or by the California Psychological Inventory) and a battery of achievement test scores for a group of high school students. The first pair of canonical variates will tell us what type of personality profile (as revealed by the linear combination, and named by determining which of the original variables correlate most highly with this linear combination) is maximally associated with a given profile of achievement (as revealed by the linear combination for the achievement scores). The second pair of canonical variates will yield an uncorrelated personality profile that is associated with a different pattern of achievement, etc.

As a second example, consider the case where a single group of subjects is measured on the *same* set of variables at two different points in time. We wish to investigate the stability of the personality profiles of female college subjects from their freshmen to their senior years. Canonical correlation analysis will reveal which dimension of personality is most stable or reliable. This dimension would be named by determining which of the original variables correlate most highly with the canonical variates corresponding to the largest canonical correlation. Then the analysis will find an uncorrelated dimension of personality which is next most reliable. This dimension is named by determining which of the original variables have the highest correlations with the second pair of canonical variates, etc. This type of *multivariate reliability analysis* using canonical correlation has been in existence for some time. Merenda, Novack, and Bonaventure (1976) did such an analysis on the subtest scores of the California Test of Mental Maturity for a group of elementary school children.

12.2   THE NATURE OF CANONICAL CORRELATION

To focus more specifically what canonical correlation does, consider the following hypothetical situation. A researcher is interested in the relationship between "job success" and "academic achievement." He has two measures of job success: (1) the amount of money the individual is making, and (2) the status of the individual's position. He has four measures of academic achievement: (1) high school gpa, (2) college gpa, (3) number of degrees, and (4) ranking of the college where the last degree was obtained. We denote the first set of variables by x's and the second set of variables (academic achievement) by y's.

The canonical correlation procedure first finds two linear combinations (one from the job success measures and one from the academic achievement measures) which have the maximum possible Pearson correlation. That is,

$$u_1 = a_{11} x_1 + a_{12} x_2 \text{ and } v_1 = b_{11} y_1 + b_{12} y_2 + b_{13} y_3 + b_{14} y_4,$$

are found such that $r_{u_1 v_1}$ is maximum. Note that if this were done with data the a's and b's would be known numerical values and a single score for each subject on each linear composite could be obtained. These two sets of scores for the subjects are then correlated just as we would perform the calculations for the scores on two individual variables, say x and y. The maximized correlation for the scores on two linear composites ($r_{u_1 v_1}$) is called the largest canonical correlation, and we denote it by R_1.

Now, the procedure searches for a second pair of linear combinations, *uncorrelated* with the first pair, such that the Pearson correlation between this pair is the next largest possible. That is,

$$u_2 = a_{21} x_1 + a_{22} x_2 \text{ and } v_2 = b_{21} y_1 + b_{22} y_2 + b_{23} y_3 + b_{24} y_4,$$

are found such that $r_{u_2 v_2}$ is maximum. This correlation, because of the way the procedure is set up, will be less than $r_{u_1 v_1}$. For example, $r_{u_1 v_1}$ might be .73 and $r_{u_2 v_2}$ might be .51. We denote the second largest canonical correlation by R_2.

When we say that this second pair of canonical variates are uncorrelated with the first pair we mean that (1) the canonical variates *within* each set are uncorrelated, i.e., $r_{u_1 u_2} = r_{v_1 v_2} = 0$ and (2) the canonical variates are uncorrelated *across* sets, i.e., $r_{u_1 v_2} = r_{v_1 u_2} = 0$.

For this example there are just two possible canonical correlations and hence only two pairs of canonical variates. In general, if one has p variables in one set and q in the other set, the number of possible canonical correlations is min $(p,q) = m$ (cf. Tatsuoka, 1971, p. 186 as to the reason why). Therefore, for our example, there are only min $(2,4) = 2$ canonical correlations. To determine how many of the possible canonical correlations indicate statistically significant relationships a residual test procedure, identical in form to that for discriminant analysis, is used. Thus, canonical correlation is still another example of a mathematical maximization procedure (as were multiple regression and principal components), which partitions the total between association through the use of uncorrelated pairs of linear combinations.

12.3 SIGNIFICANCE TESTS

First, we determine whether there is *any* association between the two sets with the following test statistic:

$$V = -\{(N - 1.5) - (p + q)/2\} \sum_{i=1}^{m} \ln (1 - R_i^2)$$

where N is sample size, and R_i denotes the ith canonical correlation. V is approximately distributed as a χ^2 statistic with pq degrees of freedom. If this overall

TABLE 12.1

Number of roots found to differ from zero by the given tests under different conditions (Σ) and different Ns.

Condition	# of Significant Roots	N = 25				N = 50				N = 100				N = 200				N = 500			
		X^2_B	X^2_L	F	H	X^2_B	X^2_L	F	H	X^2_B	X^2_L	F	H	X^2_B	X^2_L	F	H	X^2_B	X^2_L	F	H
Σ_1	1	65	62	74	241	0	0	0	0	0	0	0	0	0	0	0	0	0	0	0	0
	2	567	538	569	549	45	39	45	20	0	0	0	0	0	0	0	0	0	0	0	0
	3	355	373	344	201	929	926	929	969	951	957	950	965	958	956	957	960	969	969	969	962
	4	12	15	12	4	24	32	24	16	47	49	48	34	36	38	37	40	30	30	30	38
	5 or more	1	2	1	0	2	3	2	0 ①	2	4	2	1	6	6	6	0	1	1	1	0
Σ_2	1	546	533	507	421	491	465	492	562	37	34	36	44	*				*			
	2	108	114	97	29	452	457	451	393	675	634	674	666	②							
	3	9	14	7	1	47	63	47	19	269	303	271	284								
	4	0	2	0	0	2	7	2	1	19	28	19	6								
	5 or more	0	0	0	0	0	0	0	0	0	1	0	0								
Σ_3	1	405	398	364	343	824	803	825	859	690	657	689	684	*				*			
	2	36	42	30	10	118	135	116	90	310	312	311	309								
	3	2	3	2	0	7	9	7	4	18	29	18	7								
	4	0	0	0	0	1	2	1	0	2	2	2	0								
	5 or more	0	0	0	0	0	1	0	0	0	0	0	0								

Σ_4	1	110	108	95	78	248	241	244	183	610	456	488	405	*					*	
	2	3	5	1	0	21	24	20	6	118	141	118	59							
	3	1	1	0	0	1	4	1	0	4	12	4	2							
	4	0	1	0	0	0	1	0	0	0	1	0	0						③
	5 or more	0	0	0	0	0	0	0	0	0	0	0	0							
Σ_5	1	99	99	71	63	153	150	154	124	366	351	365	326	631	592	631	619	*	
	2	3	3	3	0	15	16	14	2	46	60	47	26	185	208	186	158		
	3	0	0	0	0	0	2	0	0	2	2	2	0	16	31	16	1		
	4	0	0	0	0	0	0	0	0	0	1	0	0	0	1	0	0		
	5 or more	0	0	0	0	0	0	0	0	0	0	0	0	0	0	0	0		
Σ_6	1	48	48	38	47	42	42	42	42	56	52	56	45	*				*	
	2	2	2	2	0	1	1	1	0	1	4	1	1						
	3 or more	0	0	0	0	0	0	0	0	0	1	0	0						

X^2_B = Bartlett approximation   H = Harris test
X^2_L = Lawley approximation
*These conditions are not evaluated.

$\Sigma_1 = (\rho_1 = .9, \rho_2 = .8, \rho_3 = .7, \rho_4 = .7, \rho_5 = \rho_6 = 0)$
$\Sigma_2 = (\rho_1 = .7, \rho_2 = .5, \rho_3 = .3, \rho_4 = \rho_5 = \rho_6 = 0)$
$\Sigma_3 = (\rho_1 = .7, \rho_2 = .3, \rho_3 = .1, \rho_4 = \rho_5 = \rho_6 = 0)$
$\Sigma_4 = (\rho_1 = .3, \rho_2 = .25, \rho_3 = .2, \rho_4 = \rho_5 = \rho_6 = 0)$
$\Sigma_5 = (\rho_1 = .3, \rho_2 = .2, \rho_3 = .1, \rho_4 = \rho_5 = \rho_6 = 0)$
$\Sigma_6 = (\rho_1 = \rho_2 = \rho_3 = \rho_4 = \rho_5 = \rho_6 = 0)$

test is significant, then the largest canonical correlation is removed and the residual is tested for significance. If we denote the term in braces by k, then the first residual test statistic (V_1) is given by:

$$V_1 = -k \cdot \sum_{i=2}^{m} \ln (1 - R_i^2)$$

V_1 is distributed as a χ^2 with $(p - 1)(q - 1)$ degrees of freedom. If V_1 is not significant, then we conclude that only the largest canonical correlation is significant. If V_1 is significant, then we continue and examine the next residual (which has the two largest roots removed) V_2, where

$$V_2 = -k \cdot \sum_{i=3}^{m} \ln (1 - R_i^2)$$

V_2 is distributed as a χ^2 with $(p - 2)(q - 2)$ degrees of freedom. If V_2 is not significant, then we conclude that only the two largest canonical correlations are significant.

If V_2 is significant, examine the next residual, etc. In general then, when the residual after removing the first s canonical correlations is not significant, we conclude that only the first s canonical correlations are significant. The degrees of freedom for the ith residual is $(p - i)(q - i)$.

When we introduced canonical correlation it was indicated that the canonical variates additively partition the association. The reason they do is because the variates are uncorrelated both within and across sets. As an analogy, recall that when the predictors are uncorrelated in multiple regression, we obtain an additive partitioning of the variance on the dependent variable.

The sequential testing procedure has been criticized by Harris (1976). However, a Monte Carlo study by Mendoza, Markos, and Gonter (1978) has refuted Harris's criticism. Mendoza, et al. considered the case of a total of 12 variables, six variables in each set, and chose six population situations. The situations varied from three strong population canonical correlations (ρ_i), i.e.,.9, .8, and .7, to three weak population canonical correlations (.3, .2 and .1), to a null condition (all population canonical correlations = 0). The last condition was inserted to check on the accuracy of their generation procedure. One thousand sample matrices, varying in size from 25 to 100, were generated from each population, and the number of significant canonical correlations declared by Bartlett's test (the one we have described) and three other tests were recorded. Table 12.1 summarizes the results.

Notice first in Table 12.1 that with strong population canonical correlations (.9, .8 and .7) as small a sample size as 50 will detect these over 90% of the time (box labeled 1). For a more moderate population canonical correlation (.50) a sample size of 100 is needed to detect it about two thirds of the time (box labeled 2). A weak population canonical correlation (.30), which is probably *not* worth detecting since it would be of little practical value, requires a sample size of 200 to be detected about 60% of the time (box labeled 3). It is fortunate that the tests are conservative in detecting weaker canonical correlations, given the very tenuous nature of trying to accurately interpret the canonical variates associated with smaller canonical correlations (Barcikowski & Stevens, 1975), as we shall see in the next section.

12.4   INTERPRETING THE CANONICAL VARIATES

The two methods in use for interpreting the canonical variates are the same as were used for interpreting the discriminant functions:

1. Examine the standardized coefficients.
2. Examine the canonical variate–variable correlations.

For both of these methods it is the largest (in absolute value) coefficients or correlations that are used. We would now refer the reader back to the corresponding section in the chapter on discriminant analysis since all of the discussion there is relevant here and will not be repeated.

We add, however, some detail from the Barcikowski and Stevens (1975) Monte Carlo study on the stability of the coefficients and the correlations, since it was for canonical correlation. They sampled eight correlation matrices from the literature and found that *the number of subjects per variable necessary to achieve reliability in determining the most important variables for the two largest canonical correlations was very large, ranging from 42/1 to 68/1. This is a somewhat conservative estimate, and if we were just interpreting the largest canonical correlation, then a ratio of about 20/1 is sufficient for accurate interpretation.* However, it doesn't seem likely, in general, that in practice there will be just one significant canonical correlation. The association between two sets of variables is likely to be more complex than that.

To impress on the reader the danger of misinterpretation if the subject/variable ratio is not large, we consider the *second* largest canonical correlation for a 31 variable example from our study. Suppose we were to interpret the left canonical variate using the canonical variate–variable correlations for 400 subjects. This yields a subject/variable ratio of about 13 to 1, a ratio many readers might feel is large enough. However, the frequency rank table (i.e., a ranking of how often each variable was ranked from most to least important) which resulted is presented here:

Var.	Total number of times less than third	Rank 1 2 3	Population value
1	76	4 11 9	.43
2	43	34 7 16	.64
3	86	1 4 9	.10
4	74	6 12 8	.16
5	60	19 16 5	.07
6	92	2 4 2	.09
7	78	1 5 16	.34
8	64	11 13 12	.40
9	72	6 13 9	.27
10	55	16 15 14	.62

Variables 2 and 10 are clearly the most important. Yet, with an N of 400, about 50% of the time each of them is *not* identified as being one of the three most important variables for interpreting the canonical variate. Furthermore, variable 5 which is clearly not an important variable in the population, is identified 40% of the time as one of the three most important variables.

In view of the above reliability results, an investigator considering a canonical analysis on a fairly large number of variables (say 20 in one set and 15 in the other set) should consider doing a components analysis on *each* set to reduce the total number of variables dramatically. Then relate the two sets of components via canonical correlation. This should be done even if the investigator has 300 subjects, for this yields a subject/variable ratio less than 10 to 1 with the *original* set of variables. The practical implementation of this procedure, as will be seen in 12.7, can be accomplished efficiently with the BMDP package.

12.5   COMPUTER EXAMPLE USING BMDP6M

To illustrate how to run canonical correlation on BMDP6M and how to interpret the output, we consider data from a study by Lehrer and Schimoler (1975). This study examined the cognitive skills underlying an inductive problem solving method which has been used to develop critical reasoning skills for educable mentally retarded children. A total of 112 EMR's were given the Cognitive Abilities Test, which consists of four subtests measuring the following skills: oral vocabulary (CAT1), relational concepts (CAT2), multimental concepts (one that doesn't belong) CAT3, and quantitative concepts (CAT4). We relate these skills via canonical correlation to seven subtest scores from the Children's Analysis of Social Situations (CASS), a test which is a modification of the Test of Social Inference. The CASS was developed as means of assessing inductive reasoning processes. For the CASS, the children respond to a sample

TABLE 12.2
Correlation Matrix for Cognitive Ability Variables and Inductive
Reasoning Variables

CAT1	1.000									
CAT2	.662	1.000								
CAT3	.661	.697	1.000							
CAT4	.641	.730	.703	1.000						
CASS1	.131	−.112	.033	.040	1.000					
CASS2	.253	.031	.185	.149	.641	1.000				
CASS3	.332	.133	.197	.132	.574	.630	1.000			
CASS4	.381	.304	.304	.382	.312	.509	.583	1.000		
CASS5	.413	.313	.276	.382	.254	.491	.491	.731	1.000	
CASS6	.520	.485	.450	.466	.034	.117	.294	.595	.534	1.000
CASS7	.434	.392	.380	.390	.065	.100	.203	.328	.355	.508	1.000

picture and various pictorial stimuli at various levels: CASS1—labeling—identification of a relevant object; CASS2—detail—represents a further elaboration of an object; CASS3—low level inference—a guess concerning a picture based on obvious clues; CASS4—high level inference; CASS5—prediction—a statement concerning future outcomes of a situation; CASS6—low level generalization—a rule derived from the context of a picture but which is specific to the situation in that picture; and CASS7—high level inference—deriving a rule that extends beyond the specific situation.

In Table 12.2 we present the correlation matrix for the 11 variables, and in Table 12.3 give the control lines from BMDP6M for running the canonical correlation analysis, along with the significance tests.

Table 12.4 has the standardized coefficients and canonical variate-variable correlations that we use jointly to interpret the pair of canonical variates corresponding to the only significant canonical correlation. These coefficients and loadings are boxed in on Table 12.4. For the cognitive ability variables (CAT) note that all 4 variables have uniformly strong loadings, although the loading for CAT1 is extremely high (.953). Using the standardized coefficients we see that CAT2 through CAT4 are redundant, since their coefficients are considerably lower than that for CAT1. For the CASS variables the loadings on CASS4 through CASS7 are clearly the strongest and of uniform magnitude. Turning to the coefficients for those variables, we see that CASS4 and CASS5 are redundant, since they clearly have the smallest coefficients. Thus, the only significant linkage between the two sets of variables relates oral vocabulary (CAT1) to the children's ability to generalize in social situations, particularly low level generalization. We now consider two studies from the literature that used canonical correlation analysis.

TABLE 12.3

BMDP6M Control Lines for Canonical Correlation Analysis Relating
Cognitive Abilities Subtests to Subtests from Children's Analysis of
Social Situations

```
/PROBLEM TITLE IS 'CANONICAL CORRELATION— 4 VARS-SET 1 7 VARS-SET 2'.
① /INPUT VARIABLES ARE 11. TYPE IS CORR. SHAPE IS LOWER. FORMAT IS FREE.
② CASES = 112.
/VARIABLE NAMES ARE CAT1,CAT2,CAT3,CAT4,CASSI,
CASS2,CASS3,CASS4,CASS5,CASS6,CASS7.
③ /CANONICAL FIRST ARE CAT1,CAT2,CAT3,CAT4.
SECOND ARE CASS1,CASS2,CASS3,CASS4,CASS5,CASS6,CASS7.
/PRINT MATRICES ARE CORR,COEF,LOAD.
/END
```

①Here we are inputting a correlation matrix. We indicated in the Principal Components chapter how this is done on the BMDP package (cf. p. 352).

②The CASES = 112 is necessary in order to obtain the tests of significance.

③This CANONICAL paragraph indicates a canonical correlation analysis, with the variables following FIRST being those in the first set and the varibles following SECOND being those in the other set.

EIGENVALUE $\downarrow$ R_i^2	CANONICAL CORRELATION $\downarrow$ R_i	NUMBER OF EIGENVALUES	BARTLETT'S TEST FOR REMAINING EIGENVALUES		
			CHI-SQUARE	D.F.	TAIL PROBL.
0.38613	0.62139	1	④ 77.70	28	0.0000
0.11106	0.33325		26.46	18	0.0896
0.09549	0.30901	2	14.10	10	0.1684
0.03337	0.18269	3	3.56	4	0.4682

$$④ \quad V = -\{(N-1.5)-(p+q)/2\}\sum_{i=1}^{4} \ln(1-R_i^2) = -\{(112-1.5)-(4+7)/2\}(\ln(1)$$
$$-.386) + \ln(1-.111) + \ln(1-.0955) + \ln(1-.0334)) = 77.74$$
$$V_1 = -(105)\{\ln(.889) + \ln(.9045) + \ln(.9666)\}$$
$$= 26.50, \text{ with } (p-1)(q-1) = (4-1)(7-1) = 18df$$

12.6   TWO STUDIES THAT USED CANONICAL CORRELATION

Study 1: Relationship between Student Needs and Teacher Ratings

A study by Tetenbaum (1975) addressed the issue of the validity of student ratings of teachers. She noted that current instruments generally list several teaching behaviors and ask the student to rate the instructor on each of them. The assumption is made that all students focus on the same teaching behavior, and furthermore that when focusing on the same behavior, students perceive it in the same way. Tetenbaum noted that principles from social perception theory

TABLE 12.4
Standardized Coefficients and Canonical
Variate-Variable Loadings for Example 1

STANDARDIZED COEFFICIENTS FOR CANONICAL VARIABLES FOR FIRST SET OF VARIABLES

(THESE ARE THE COEFFICIENTS FOR THE STANDARDIZED VARIABLES—
MEAN ZERO, STANDARD DEVIATION ONE.)

		CNVRF1$_1$	CNVRF2$_2$	CNVRF3$_3$	CNVRF4$_4$
CAT1	1	0.634	−0.944	−0.032	−0.920
CAT2	2	0.167	1.161	−1.087	−0.355
CAT3	3	0.138	−0.573	−0.397	1.416
CAT4	4	0.184	0.509	1.529	0.037

CANONICAL VARIABLE LOADINGS

(CORRELATIONS OF CANONICAL VARIABLES WITH ORIGINAL VARIABLES)
FOR FIRST SET OF VARIABLES

		CNVRF1$_1$	CNVRF2$_2$	CNVRF3$_3$	CNVRF4$_4$
CAT1	1	0.953	−0.228	−0.034	−0.195
CAT2	2	0.817	0.508	−0.269	0.051
CAT3	3	0.803	−0.030	−0.101	0.587
CAT4	4	0.809	0.348	0.436	0.184

STANDARDIZED COEFFICIENTS FOR CANONICAL VARIABLES FOR SECOND SET OF VARIABLES

(THESE ARE THE COEFFICIENTS FOR THE STANDARDIZED VARIABLES—
MEAN ZERO, STANDARD DEVIATION ONE.)

		CNVRS1$_1$	CNVRS2$_2$	CNVRS3$_3$	CNVRS4$_4$
CASS1	5	−0.151	−0.349	0.857	−0.328
CASS2	6	0.244	−0.599	−0.007	1.050
CASS3	7	0.115	−0.496	−1.074	−0.701
CASS4	8	−0.096	0.628	0.670	0.482
CASS5	9	0.142	0.263	0.409	−1.173
CASS6	10	0.636	−0.153	−0.361	0.346
CASS7	11	0.368	0.039	−0.001	0.220

CANONICAL VARIABLE LOADINGS

(CORRELATIONS OF CANONICAL VARIABLES WITH ORIGINAL
VARIABLES)
FOR SECOND SET OF VARIABLES

		CNVRS1$_1$	CNVRS2$_2$	CNVRS3$_3$	CNVRS4$_4$
CASS1	5	0.123	−0.757	0.536	−0.178
CASS2	6	0.352	−0.700	0.364	0.130
CASS3	7	0.457	−0.615	−0.102	−.0376
CASS4	8	0.651	0.040	0.391	−0.074
CASS5	9	0.680	0.029	0.392	−0.470
CASS6	10	0.898	0.154	−0.033	0.023
CASS7	11	0.748	0.078	0.017	0.079

(Warr & Knapper, 1968) make both of the above assumptions questionable. She argued that the social psychological needs of the students would influence their ratings, stating, "It was reasoned that in the process of rating a teacher the student focuses on the need-related aspects of the perceptual situation and bases his judgement on those areas of the teachers performance most relevant to his own needs" (p. 418).

To assess student needs the *Personality Research Form* was administered to 405 graduate students. The entire scale was not administered because some of the needs were not relevant to an academic setting. The part administered was then factor analyzed and a four-factor solution was obtained. For each factor, the three subscales having the highest loadings ($>$ .50) were selected to represent that factor with the exception of one subscale (dominance) which had a high loading on more than one factor and one subscale (harm avoidance) which was not felt to be relevant to the classroom setting. The final instrument consisted of 12 scales, 3 scales representing each of the four obtained factors: Factor I: Cognitive Structure (CS), Impulsivity (IM), Order (OR); Factor II; Endurance (EN), Achievment (AC), Understanding (UN); Factor III: Affliation (AF), Autonomy (AU), Succorance (SU); Factor IV: Aggression (AG), Defendence (DE), Abasement (AB). These factors were named Need for Control, Need for Intellectual Striving, Need for Gregariousness-Defendence, and Need for Ascendancy respectively.

Student ratings of teachers were obtained on an instrument constructed by Tetenbaum, which consisted of 12 vignettes each describing a college classroom in which the teacher was engaged in a particular set of behaviors. The particular behaviors were designed to correspond to the four need factors, i.e., within the 12 vignettes there were 3 replications for each of the four teacher orientations. For example, in three teacher vignettes the orientation was aimed at meeting control needs. In these vignettes the teachers attempted to control the classroom environment by organizing and structuring all lessons and assignments so that the students would know what was expected of him; by stressing order, neatness, clarity and logic; and by encouraging delibration of thought and moderation of emotion.

Tetenbaum hypothesized that specific student needs (for example, control needs) would be related to teacher orientations which met those needs. The 12 need variables (set 1) were related to the 12 rating variables (set 2) via canonical correlation. Three significant canonical correlations were obtained: $R_1 = .486$, $R_2 = .389$ and $R_3 = .323$ ($p < .01$ in all cases). Tetenbaum chose to use the canonical variate–variable correlations to interpret the variates. These are presented in Table 12.5. Examining the underlined correlations for the first pair (i.e., for the largest canonical correlation), we see that it clearly reflects the congruence between the intellectual striving needs and ratings on the corresponding vignettes as well as the congruence between the ascendancy needs and ratings. The second pair of canonical variates (corresponding to the second largest

TABLE 12.5
Canonical Variate—Variable Correlations for Tetenbaum Study

First Pair		Second Pair		Third Pair		
Canonical Variables						
Needs	*Ratings*	*Needs*	*Ratings*	*Needs*	*Ratings*	
.111	.028	.614	.453	−.018	−.325	Control
−.099	−.051	−.785	.491	.078	−.397	
.065	.292	.774	.597	−.050	.059	
−.537	−.337	.210	.263	.439	.177	Intellectual Striving
−.477	−.294	.252	.125	.500	.102	
−.484	−.520	−.005	.154	.452	.497	
−.134	−.233	−.343	−.210	−.354	−.335	Gregarious
.270	−.141	.016	.114	.657	−.468	
−.271	−.072	−.155	−.175	−.414	−.579	
−.150	.395	.205	.265	.452	.211	Ascendancy
.535	.507	−.254	.034	.421	.361	
.333	.673	−.312	−.110	.289	.207	

*Correlations > |.3| are underlined.

canonical correlation) reflects the congruence between the control needs and ratings. Note that the correlation for implusivity is negative, since a low score on this variable would imply a high rating for a teacher who exhibits order and moderation of emotion.

The interpretation of the third pair of canonical variates is not as clean as it was for the first two pairs. Nevertheless, the correspondence between gregariousness–dependency needs and ratings is revealed, a correspondence that did *not* appear for the first two pairs. However, there are "high" loadings on other needs and ratings as well. The interested reader is referred to Tetenbaum's article for a discussion of why this may have happened.

In summary then, the correspondence that Tetenbaum hypothesized between student needs and ratings was clearly revealed by canonical correlation. Two of the need-rating correspondences were revealed by the first canonical correlation, a third correspondence (for control needs) was established by the second canonical correlation, and finally the gregariousness need-rating correspondence was revealed by the third canonical correlation.

Through the use of factor analysis, the author in this study was able to reduce the number of variables to 24 and achieve a fairly large subject/variable ratio (about 17/1). Based on our Monte Carlo results, one could interpret the largest canonical correlation with confidence, however, the second and third canonical correlations should be interpreted with some caution.

Study 2: Relationship between Expectancies and School Adjustment

A study by Gemunder (1979) investigated the relationship between generalized expectancies (set 1) and various measures of school adjustment (set 2) in 168 low socioeconomic class third and fourth graders. There were 86 boys and 82 girls in the sample. Measures used to assess the expectancies were the Intellectual Achievement Responsibility Questionnaire (IAR), the Children's Interpersonal Trust Scale, and the Paired Hands Test (Barnett & Zucker, 1975). The IAR assesses children's perceptions of causes for success or failure (in academic achievement situations) along an internal–external locus of control dimension. The generalized expectancy of internal control refers to the perception of events, whether positive or negative, as being a consequence of one's own actions and thereby under personal control. External control refers to the perception of events occurring because of luck, chance or because of powerful others. Since the developers of the IAR have argued that assessing responsibility for success can be independent of the way in which individuals interpret their failures, separate subtest scores from the IAR reflecting responsibility for success (failure) were included in this study.

The Interpersonal Trust Scale is an expectancy held by an individual or group that the word, promise, verbal or written statement of another individual or group, can be relied upon. The Paired Hands Test measures the others concept. The others concept refers to a person's general appraisal of people with whom he has little or no experience. The other's concept is an indicator of the manner in which an individual expects other people to react to and interact with him.

The first measure of school adjustment was the AML, which is a teacher rating scale of negative behaviors (acting out, moody, and learning problems) in the classroom. The second measure of school adjustment was a teacher rating scale to assess positive behavior, personal and social competence. Factor analysis of this scale has indicated that basically five dimensions are assessed: good student, gutsy (adaptive assertiveness), peer sociability, rules (ability to function within the constraints of the school environment), and frustration tolerance.

While the previous measures assessed how the teacher viewed the child, the final measure of school adjustment (from a Peer Rating Scale) determined how other children viewed the child, in both positive and negative ways. Thus, there were a total of 10 school adjustment variables (8 from the teachers ratings and 2 from the childrens ratings), and six expectancy variables (4 from the IAR, total score on the ITS and total score on the Paired Hands Test).

Since we have a total of 16 variables and 168 subjects, there is a subject/variable ratio of about 10 to 1. Now, recall that in order to accurately interpret the canonical variates a very large subject/variable ratio is needed; over 40 to 1 if interpreting the variables associated with the two largest canonical correlations, and about 20 to 1 if only interpreting the variates associated with the largest

TABLE 12.6
Varimax Rotated Factor Matrix of School Adjustment Measures

	Factor 1	Factor 2	Factor 3
Good Student	.385	.846	.105
Gutsy	.009	.620	.603
Peer sociability	.276	.020	.852
Rules	.884	.213	.179
Frustration tolerance	.762	.213	.405
Acting-out	.918	.239	.066
Moody-withdrawn	.637	.182	.547
Learning problems	.408	.779	−.082
Positive nominations	−.040	−.614	−.390
Negative nominations	.435	.422	.027
% of variance accounted for by each factor	31.9	24.6	17.6

Note: Factor 1 = "School maladjusted behavior"
      Factor 2 = "Learning problems—low popularity"
      Factor 3 = "Social isolation"

      Variables in boxes are those used in naming each factor.

canonical correlation. Therefore, it is important here to try to improve the 10 to 1 ratio. Hence, a factor analysis on the school adjustment measures (principal components followed by a varimax rotation) was done in order to explain variation in terms of a smaller number of constructs. Three rotated factors accounted for about 74% of the total variance. The rotated factor pattern, along with the names given the factors is presented in Table 12.6. Note that since the negative nominations variable did not load high on any factor (highest loading = .435), it was maintained as a separate variable.

The canonical correlation analysis on the total sample showed only one significant canonical correlation (R_1 = .528, p < .01). The standardized coefficients for the canonical variates along with the canonical variate–variable correlations are presented in Table 12.7. Examining first the correlations, we see that the responsibility for success due to ability and due to effort are outstandingly high for the expectancy set, while Factor 2 and negative nominations are high for the school adjustment set. Now, examining the standardized coefficients to see which of the above variables are redundant, given the others, we see that negative nomination is, since it's coefficient is only .334. The interpretation then of the canonical relationship is that students with learning problems

TABLE 12.7
Significant Canonical Correlation, Coefficients, and Components for
Each Canonical Variate for the Total Population

| Variables | Coefficients | | Correlation with |
	Raw	Standardized	Canonical Variate
Expectancy			
Responsibility for success due to ability	−.453	−.624	−.773
Responsibility for success due to effort	−.383	−.612	−.769
Responsibility for failure due to ability	.030	.042	−.287
Responsibility for failure due to effort	−.056	−.110	−.270
Children's Interpersonal Trust Scale	.002	.011	.057
Paired Hands Test	−.014	−.163	−.174
School Adjustment			
Factor 1 (maladjusted school behavior)	.377	.377	.500
Factor 2 (learning problems—low popularity)	.708	.709	.813
Factor 3 (social isolation)	.045	.044	.080
Negative Nominations	.019	.334	.693

Note: First canonical correlation = .528, $p < .001$; $N = 168$

(Factor 2) rate low on measures of internal responsibility for success (whether due to ability or effort). In other words, students with learning problems are externally controlled, and feel that their problems are due to chance, fate or whim, i.e., circumstances beyond the student's control.

To determine whether this relationship would differ for boys and girls, the sample was split and two separate analyses run. A relationship was not found for the boys, but a highly significant relationship was found for the girls. The results of the canonical correlation analysis for the girls is presented in Table 12.8. Using the boxed-in numbers to interpret the canonical relationship, we see that girls who are not having learning problems score high on responsibility for success due to ability and effort (internally controlled). That is, these girls feel that positive things happen to them (no learning problems) because of their ability and/or their effort, i.e., as a consequence of factors within their control.

How much confidence can we have that the canonical variates have been accurately interpreted? Since only the largest canonical correlation was significant, a subject/variable ratio of about 20 to 1 is sufficient for reliable results. Thus, the results from the analysis for the total sample can be interpreted with confidence (17/1 ratio). However, the results for females must be interpreted more tenuously since the ratio there is only about 8 to 1.

TABLE 12.8
Significant Canonical Correlation, Coefficients, and Components for
Each Canonical Variate for Females

Variables	Coefficients		Correlation with Canonical Variate
	Raw	Standardized	
Expectancy			
Responsibility for success due to ability	.387	.574	.739
Responsibility for success due to effort	.510	.692	.832
Responsibility for failure due to ability	− .015	− .020	.217
Responsibility for failure due to effort	− .016	− .033	.282
Children's Interpersonal Trust Scale	.002	.011	− .140
Paired Hands Test	.008	.101	.148
School Adjustment			
Factor 1 (maladjusted school behavior)	− .423	− .442	− .481
Factor 2 (learning problems-low popularity)	− .739	− .756	− .782
Factor 3 (social isolation)	.263	.252	− .042
Negative Nominations	− .024	− .361	− .573

Note: First canonical correlation $= .648$, $p < .0002$; $N = 81$

12.7 USING BMDP FOR CANONICAL CORRELATION ON TWO SETS OF FACTOR SCORES

As indicated previously, if there is a large or fairly large number of variables in each of two sets, it is desirable to do a factor analysis on each set of variables for two reasons:

1. To obtain a more parsimonious description of what each set of variables is really measuring.
2. To reduce the total number of variables that will appear in the eventual canonical correlation analysis so that a much larger subject/variable ratio is obtained, making for more reliable results.

It is important to note that the entire process of two separate component analyses (along with varimax rotations) and the canonical analysis relating the two sets of factor scores can be accomplished very efficiently and elegantly using the BMDP package. In a BMDP communication (June 1980) it is stated, "On IBM and similar systems Units 3 and 4 are scratch units that are available for you to write your data as a BMDP file to pass the data from problem to problem or from program to program."

The data we are passing from the factor analysis program to the canonical correlation program are the factor scores. The important feature about doing this on BMDP is that *no JCL* is needed to accomplish it. To pass the factor scores from program to program, we use the "SAVE FILE" feature of BMDP. Each BMDP file *must* be assigned a CODE name in the SAVE paragraph. The data saved includes both the raw scores on each of the original variables and the factor scores. The factor scores appear on the file *after* the data and are named FACTOR1, FACTOR2, etc.

In Table 12.9 we present the complete set of BMDP control lines for doing a components analysis (and varimax rotation—it is a default option) on each of the sets of variables, and then doing the canonical correlation analysis on the two sets of rotated factor scores. In the example there are 4 variables in set 1 and 6 variables in set 2. We chose a small number of variables for pedagogical purposes; obviously in practice with such a small number of variables a factor analysis would not be needed. Now, both of the components analyses can be done in just one pass through the computer by use of the control lines indicated in brackets by RUN 1 in Table 12.9.

All 10 variables are entered and then by virtue of the "USE" statement (① in Table 12.9) we select the first four variables (i.e., set 1) to perform the first components analysis. We retain only those components whose eigenvalues are greater than 1 (the default option). Suppose there were two such components. Using the SAVE paragraph (② in Table 12.9), we put the two factor scores on UNIT 3 and give the file the CODE name FIRST. Thus, the raw scores for all 10 original variables plus the two factor scores will be saved on UNIT 3.

Then we run the factor analysis program again on the other set of 6 variables. Suppose that again we retain only those components whose eigenvalues are greater than 1, and that there are 3 such components. Now, we use UNIT 4, giving it the CODE name SECOND, to save all the previous data (the scores on the original 10 variables, the two factor scores from set 1 *and* the three factor scores from set 2).

Now, using UNIT 4 as the input (③ in Table 12.9) to the canonical correlation program (BMDP6M) makes the setup of the control lines very simple and parsimonious. Since on UNIT 4 the factor scores for set 1 appear right after the original variables, they are variables 11 and 12. The factor scores for set 2 appear on UNIT 4 as the last three variables, i.e., variables 13, 14, and 15. Thus, for the canonical correlation analysis we wish to relate variables 11 and 12 to variables 13, 14, and 15. The control lines for accomplishing this are opposite ④ in Table 12.9.

As a further elaboration on the SAVE FILE feature, consider an investigator who is contemplating a canonical correlation analysis and who has 15 variables in set X and 20 variables in set Y. The components analysis and rotation is done on each set, as in the previous example, and 4 factors emerge from set X and 5 factors for set Y. On examining the output from the factor analysis for set X

TABLE 12.9

Biomedical (BMDP) Control Lines for Obtaining a Components Analysis and Varimax Rotation on Each of Two Sets of Variables and a Canonical Correlation Analysis Relating Two Sets of Rotated Factors

FOR ILLUSTRATIVE PURPOSES, CONSIDER 4 VARIABLES IN SET 1 AND 6 VARIABLES IN SET 2

```
//EXEC  BIMED,PROG = BMDP4M
//SYSIN DD *
/PROBLEM TITLE IS 'COMPONENTS WITH EIGENS > 1 & VARIMAX FOR SET 1'.
/INPUT VARIABLES = 10.
 FORMAT IS ' (5X,10(1X,F3.0))'.
/VARIABLES NAMES ARE V1,V2,V3,V4,V5,V6,V7,V8,V9,V10.
 USE = V1,V2,V3,V4.  ①
/SAVE NEW. UNIT = 3. CODE = FIRST.   ②
/END


    DATA LINES HERE
```

(RUN 1)

```
//EXEC  BIMED, PROG = BMDP4M
//SYSIN DD *
/PROBLEM TITLE IS ' COMPONENTS WITH EIGENS > 1 & VARIMAX FOR SET 2'.
/INPUT UNIT = 3. CODE = FIRST.
/VARIABLE USE = V5,V6,V7,V8,V9,V10.
/SAVE NEW. UNIT = 4. CODE = SECOND.
/END
```

(RUN 2)

```
//EXEC  BIMED,PROG = BMDP6M
//SYSIN DD *
/PROBLEM TITLE IS ' CANONICAL CORREL. ON ROTATED COMPS FROM SETS 1 & 2'.
 INPUT UNIT = 4. CODE = SECOND.     ③
/CANONICAL FIRST ARE 11,12.  ⎫
 SECOND ARE 13,14,15.        ⎬ ④
/END                         ⎭
```

NOTE: THE FOLLOWING IS THE WAY THE VARIABLES ARE ARRANGED ON UNIT 4 FOR THE CANONICAL CORRELATION ANALYSIS.

VARIABLES

1 V1	2 V2	3 V3	4 V4	5 V5
6 V6	7 V7	8 V8	9 V9	10 V10
11 FACTOR 1	12 FACTOR2	13 FACTOR 1	14 FACTOR 2	15 FACTOR 3

FACTORS FOR SET 1 (TWO EIGENVALUES > 1)   FACTORS FOR SET 2 (THREE EIGENVALUES > 1)

the investigator finds that the communalities for variables 2 and 7 are low. That is, these variables are relatively independent of what the four factors are measuring, and thus the investigator wishes to retain these original variables for the eventual canonical analysis. Similarly, the communality for variable 12 in set Y is low, and the investigator also wishes to retain this variable for the canonical analysis.

On UNIT 4 (the input unit for the canonical analysis) the original variables are the first 35 variables, the variables following these are subscripted 36 to 39 and are the factors from set X. Finally, the variables subscripted 40 to 44 are the factors for set Y. Thus, the two lines for the canonical correlation analysis here that correspond to those opposite ④ in Table 12.9 are:

CANONICAL FIRST ARE 2, 7, 36, 37, 38, 39.
SECOND ARE 27, 40, 41, 42, 43, 44./

12.8   THE REDUNDANCY INDEX OF STEWART
AND LOVE

In multiple regression the squared multiple correlation represents the proportion of criterion variance accounted for by the optimal linear combination of the predictors. In canonical correlation, however, a squared canonical correlation only tells us the amount of variance that the two canonical variates share, and does not necessarily indicate considerable variance overlap between the two sets of variables. The canonical variates are derived to maximize the correlation between them, and thus we can't necessarily expect each canonical variate will extract much variance from its set. For example, the third canonical variate from set X may be close to a last principal component, and thus extract negligible variance from set X. That is, it may not be an important factor for battery X. Stewart and Love (1968) realized that interpreting squared canonical correlations as indicating the amount of informational overlap between two batteries (sets of variables) was not appropriate, and developed their own index of redundancy.

The essence of the Stewart and Love idea is quite simple. First, determine how much variance in Y the first canonical variate (C_1) accounts for. How this is done will be indicated shortly. Then multiply the extracted variance (we denote this by VC_1) by the square of the canonical correlation between C_1 and the corresponding canonical variate (P_1) from set X. This product then gives the amount of variance in set Y that is predictable from the first canonical variate for set X. Next, the amount of variance in Y that the second canonical variate (C_2) for Y accounts for is determined, and is multiplied by the square of the canonical correlation between C_2 and the corresponding canonical variate (P_2) from set X. This product gives the amount of variance in set Y predictable from the second canonical variate for set X. This process is repeated for all possible canonical correlations. Then, the products are added (since the respective pairs of canonical variates are uncorrelated) to determine the redundancy in set Y, given set X, which we denote by $R_{Y/X}$. If the square of the ith canonical correlation is denoted by λ_i, then $R_{Y/X}$ is given by:

$$R_{Y/X} = \sum_{i=1}^{h} \lambda_i \, VC_i,$$

where h is the number of possible canonical correlations.

The amount of variance canonical variate i extracts from set Y is given by:

$$VC_i = \frac{\sum \text{squared canonical variate-variable correlations}}{q \ (\text{number of variables in set } Y)}$$

There is an important point we wish to make concerning the redundancy index. It is equal to the average squared multiple correlation for predicting the variables in one set from the variables in the other set. To illustrate, suppose we had 4 variables in set X and 3 variables in set Y, and we computed the multiple correlation for each y variable *separately* with the 4 predictors. Then, if these multiple correlations are squared and the sum of squares divided by 3, this number is equal to $R_{Y/X}$. This fact hints at a problem with the redundancy index, as Cramer and Nicewander (1979) have noted, "Moreover, the redundancy index is not multivariate in the strict sense because it is unaffected by the intercorrelations of the variables being predicted. The redundancy index is only multivariate in the sense that it involves several criterion variables." (p. 43)

This is saying we would obtain the same amount of variance accounted for with the redundancy index for three y variables which are highly correlated as we would for three y variables which have low intercorrelations (other factors being held constant). This is very undesirable in the same sense as it would be undesirable if in a multiple regression context the multiple correlation were unaffected by the magnitude of the intercorrelations among the predictors.

This defect can be eliminated by first orthogonalizing the y variables (e.g., obtaining a set of uncorrelated variables such as principal components or varimax rotated factors), and then computing the average squared multiple correlation between the uncorrelated y variables and the x variables. In this case we could of course compute the redundancy index, but it is unnecessary since it is equal to the average squared multiple correlation.

Cramer and Nicewander recommended using the *average squared canonical correlation* as the measure of variance accounted for. Thus, for example, if there were two canonical correlations, simply square each of them and then divide by 2.

12.9 PART AND PARTIAL CANONICAL CORRELATION

In beginning statistics the notions of part and partial correlation are introduced. A part correlation is the correlation between two variables x and y with a third variable z partialled out from either x or y. The partial correlation between x and y is the resulting correlation after z has been partialled out (held constant) from *both* x and y ($r_{xy \cdot z}$). Glass and Stanley (1970, p. 185) give a nice example for partial correlation and illustrate precisely what is meant by holding a third variable constant. Suppose a sample of 30 children, ranging in age (z) from 6 to 15 years, yields a correlation of .64 between reading performance (x) and visual perceptual ability (y), as evidenced by eye coordination, scanning speed, etc. This correlation may be entirely due to the fact that both reading performance and visual perceptual ability increase with age, i.e., both x and y are linearly related to age (z). For this example, this was precisely the case, i.e., $r_{ry \cdot z} = 0$. The important point here is that the partial correlation is an *estimate* of what r_{xy} would be for children of the same age. Statistically, the partial correlation has held age constant for us. If there were enough children readily available of the same age, we could compute r_{xy} on them to determine how good our estimate was.

In this section we are interested in considering the multivariate generalizations of part and partial correlation. Thus, we wish to estimate what the relationship is between set X and set Y with set Z partialled from either X or Y (part canonical correlation), or estimate the relationship between X and Y with Z partialled from both X and Y (partial canonical correlation). Cooley and Lohnes (1971, p. 205), in considering a study of how abilities, interests, and career plans change during high school, provided the following example of partial canonical correlation. They asked the question, "What is the relationship between grade 9 interests (such as physical science, social science, artistic, etc.—a total of 17 variables) and grade 12 abilities (such as social studies, math, music, law, etc.—a total of 38 variables) with grade 9 abilities controlled on ?" There was a relationship when the grade 9 abilities were partialled out, indicating there is variability on grade 9 interests (which is independent of grade 9 ability) which is related to variability (again independent of grade 9 abilities) in grade 12 abilities. Or, as Cooley and Lohnes put it, the abilities changed (from grade 9 to 12) in a manner consistent with grade 9 interests.

Of the major statistical packages we are discussing (as of Sept. 1985), only SAS (1982) does part and partial canonical correlation as a standard option.

12.10 ROTATION OF CANONICAL VARIATES

In the chapter on principal components it was stated that often the interpretation of the components can be difficult, and that a rotation (e.g., varimax) can be quite helpful in obtaining factors which tend to load high on only a small number of variables and therefore are considerably easier to interpret. In canonical correlation the same rotation idea can be employed to increase interpretability. The situation, however, is much more complex, since two sets of factors (the successive pairs of canonical variates) are being simultaneously rotated. Cliff and Krus (1976) have shown mathematically that such a procedure is sound, and the practical implementation of the procedure is possible in Multivariance (Finn, 1978). Cliff and Krus also demonstrate, through an example, how interpretation is made clearer through rotation.

When such a rotation is done the variance will be spread more evenly across the pairs of canonical variates, i.e., the maximization property is lost. Recall that this is what happened when the components were rotated. But we were willing to sacrifice this property for increased interpretability. Of course, only the canonical variates corresponding to *significant* canonical correlations should be rotated, in order to ensure that the rotated variates still correspond to significant association (Cliff & Krus, 1976).

12.11 OBTAINING MORE RELIABLE CANONICAL VARIATES

In concluding this chapter we mention five approaches that will increase the probability of accurately interpreting the canonical variates, i.e., the probability that the interpretation made in the given sample will hold up in another sample from the same population. The first two points have already been made, but are repeated as a means of summarizing:

1.   Have a very large (1,000 or more) number of subjects, or a large subject/variable ratio.
2.   If there is a large or fairly large number of variables in each set, then perform a components analysis on each set. Use only the components (or rotated factors) from each set which account for most of the variance in the canonical correlation analysis. In this way an investigator, rather than doing a canonical analysis on a total of, say, 35 variables with 300 subjects, may be able to account for most of the variance in each of the sets with a total of 10 components, and thus achieve a much more favorable subject/variable ratio (30/1). The components analysis approach is one means of attacking the multicollinearity problem, which makes accurate interpretation difficult.
3.   Ensure at least a moderate to large subject/variable ratio by judiciously selecting a priori a small number of variables for each of the two sets that will be related.
4.   Another way of dealing with multicollinearity is to use canonical ridge regression. With this approach the coefficients are biased, however, their variance will be much less, leading to more accurate interpretation. Monte Carlo studies (Anderson & Carney, 1974; Barcikowski & Stevens, 1978) of the effectiveness of ridge canonical show that it can yield more stable canonical variate coefficients and canonical variate–variable correlations. Barcikowski and Stevens examined 11 different correlation matrices which exhibited varying degrees of within and between multicollinearity. They found that in general ridge became more effective as the degree of multicollinearity increased. Secondly, ridge canonical was particularily effective with small subject/variable ratios. These are precisely the situations where the greater stability is deparately needed.
5.   Still another approach to more accurate interpretation of canonical variates

has been presented by Weinberg and Darlington (1976), who used biased coefficients of 0 and 1 to form the canonical variates. This approach makes interpretation of the most important variables, those receiving 1's in the canonical variates, relatively easy.

12.12   SUMMARY

Canonical correlation is a parsimonious way of breaking down the association between two sets of variables through the use of linear combinations. In this way, since the combinations are uncorrelated, we can describe the number and nature of independent relationships existing between two sets of variables. That canonical correlation does indeed give a parsimonious description of association can be seen by considering the case of 5 variables in set X and 10 variables in set Y. To obtain an overall picture of the association using simple correlations would be very difficult, since we would have to deal with 50 fragmented between-correlations. Canonical correlation, on the other hand, consolidates or channels all the association into five uncorrelated "big pieces," i.e., the canonical correlations.

There are two devices available for interpreting the canonical variates: (1) standardized coefficients, and (2) canonical variate–variable correlations. Both of these are quite unreliable unless the N/total number of variables ratio is very large; at least 42/1 if interpreting the largest two canonical correlations, and about 20/1 if interpreting only the largest canonical correlation. The correlations should be used for substantive interpretation of the canonical variates, i.e., for naming the constructs, while the coefficients are used for determining which of the variables are redundant.

Because of the probably unattainable large N required for reliable results (especially if there are a fairly large or large number of variables in each set), several suggestions were given for obtaining reliable results with the N available, or perhaps just a somewhat larger N. The first suggestion involved doing a components analysis and varimax rotation on each set of variables and then relating the comonents or rotated factors via canonical correlation. An efficient, practical implementation of this procedure, using the SAVE FILE feature of the BMDP package, was illustrated.

Some other means of obtaining more reliable canonical variates were:

1. Selecting a priori a small number of variables from each of the sets, and then relating these. This would be an option to consider if the N was not judged to be large enough to do a reliable components analysis. For example, if there were 20 variables in set X and 30 variables in set Y and $N = 120$.

2. The use of canonical ridge regression.

3. The use of the technique developed by Weinberg and Darlington.

Two studies from the literature that used canonical correlation were discussed in detail.

The redundancy index, for determining the variance overlap between two sets of variables, was considered. It was indicated that this index suffers from the defect of being unaffected by the intercorrelations of the variables being predicted. This is undesirable in the same sense as it would be undesirable if the multiple correlation were unaffected by the intercorrelations of the predictors.

Part and partial canonical correlation, i.e., the multivariate generalizations of part and partial correlation, were discussed. Here we have three sets of variables (X,Y,Z), and wish to examine the relationship between X and Y with Z partialled from only one set (part) or Z partialled from both sets (partial). An example showed how partial canonical correlation can be used to determine the relationship between grade 9 interests (X) and grade 12 abilities (Y) with grade 9 abilities (Z) controlled on.

Finally, in evaluating studies from the literature that have used canonical correlation, remember it just isn't the N in vacuum that is important. The N/total number of variables ratio, along with the degree of multicollinearity, must be examined to determine how much confidence can be placed in the results. Thus, not a great deal of confidence can be placed in the results of a study involving a total of 25 variables (say 10 in set X and 15 in set Y) based on 200 subjects. Even if a study had 400 subjects, but did the canonical analysis on a total of 60 variables, it is probably of little scientific value since the results are unlikely to replicate.

EXERCISES

1.   Name four features that canonical correlation and principal components analysis have in common.

2.   Suppose that a canonical correlation analysis on two sets of variables yielded r canonical correlations. Indicate schematically what the matrix of intercorrelations for the canonical variates would look like.

3.   In the Mendoza study discussed in this chapter each of the canonical correlations was tested for significance at the .05 level. Examine the numbers in Table 12.1 for the null condition, i.e., where all the population canonical correlations were 0. Do these numbers indicate that Mendoza's simulation procedure was operating properly?

4.   Consider the following selected output from BMDP6M. In the analysis grade point average required (GPREQ) and grade point average elective (GPAELEC) were set Y. These were related to high school general knowledge (HSGKT), I.Q. and educational motivation (EDMOTIV), i.e., set X ($N = 15$)

CORRELATIONS

		GPREQ	GPAELEC	HSGKT	I.Q.	FMDCTIV
		1	2	3	4	5
GPREQ	1	1.000				
GPAELEC	2	0.721	1.000			
HSGKT	3	0.752	0.606	1.000		
IQ	4	0.173	0.631	0.186	1.000	
EDMOTIV	5	0.395	0.502	0.554	0.106	1.000

EIGENVALUE	CANONICAL CORRELATION	NUMBER OF EIGENVALUES	CHI-SQUARE	D.F.	BARTLETT'S TEST FOR REMAINING EIGENVALUES TAIL PROB.
			20.78	6	0.0020
0.69217	0.83197	1	7.82	2	0.0201
0.50866	0.71321				

COEFFICIENTS FOR CANONICAL VARIABLES FOR FIRST SET OF VARIABLES

		CNVRF1	CNVRF2
		1	2
GPREQ	1	-0.892863	1.41311
GPAELEC	2	1.19035	-0.915916

CANONICAL VARIABLE LOADINGS

(CORRELATIONS OF CANONICAL VARIABLES WITH ORIGINAL VARIABLES)
FOR FIRST SET OF VARIABLES

		CNVRF1	CNVRF2
		1	2
GPREQ	1	0.565	0.825
GPAELEC	1	0.979	0.203

COEFFICIENTS FOR CANONICAL VARIABLES FOR SECOND SET OF VARIABLES

		CNVRS1	CNVRS2
		1	2
HSGKT	3	0.267448	1.08308
IQ	4	0.754959	-0.545159
EDMOTIV	5	0.351004	-0.333904

CANONICAL VARIABLE LOADINGS

(CORRELATIONS OF CANONICAL VARIABLES WITH ORIGINAL VARIABLES)
FOR SECOND SET OF VARIABLES

		CNVRS1	CNVRS2
		1	
HSGKT	3	0.602	0.797
IQ	4	0.842	-0.379
EDMOTIV	5	0.579	0.208

CANONICAL VARIABLE LOADINGS

CANON. VAR.	AVERAGE SQUARED LOADING FOR EACH CANONICAL VARIABLE (1ST SET)	AV. SQ. LOADING TIMES SQUARED CANON. CORREL. (1ST SET)	AVERAGE SQUARED LOADING FOR EACH CANONICAL VARIABLE (2ND SET)	AV. SQ. LOADING TIMES SQUARED CANON. CORREL. (2ND SET)	SQUARED CANON. CORREL.
1	0.63923	0.44246	0.46903	0.32465	0.69217
2	0.36077	0.18351	0.27395	0.13935	0.50866

THE AVERAGE SQUARED LOADING TIMES THE SQUARED CANONICAL CORRELATION IS THE AVERAGE SQUARED CORRELATION OF A VARIABLE IN ONE SET WITH THE CANONICAL VARIABLE FROM THE OTHER SET. IT IS SOMETIMES CALLED A REDUNDANCY INDEX.

NOTE: This example is for illustrative purposes only, since N is so small.

a) From examining the appropriate simple correlations, does it appear there is significant overall association between the two sets of variables?

b) Show how the χ^2 values of 20.78 and 7.82 were obtained.

c) Write out the canonical variates for set Y and for set X.

d) Indicate what the Pearson correlations are for *each pair* of canonical variates.

e) Using the canonical variate–variable correlations, how would you interpret the significant association corresponding to the largest canonical correlation? corresponding to the second largest canonical correlation?

f) What is the value of the redundancy index for set Y given set X? How would you interpret this value?

5.   Shin (1971) examined the relationship between creativity and achievement. He used Guilford's battery to obtain the following six creativity scores: ideational fluency, spontaneous flexibility, associational fluency, expressional fluency, and originality and elaboration. The Kropp test was used to obtain the following six achievement variables: knowledge, comprehension, application, analysis, synthesis, and evaluation. Data from 116 eleventh grade suburban high school students yielded this correlation matrix:

	IDEAFLU	FLEXIB	ASSOCFLU	EXPRFLU	ORIG	ELAB	KNOW	COMPRE	APPLIC	ANAL	SYNTH	EVAL
IDEAFLU	1.000											
FLEXIB	0.710	1.000										
ASSOCFLU	0.120	0.120	1.000									
EXPRFLU	0.340	0.450	0.430	1.000								
ORIG	0.270	0.330	0.240	0.330	1.000							
ELAU	0.210	0.110	0.420	0.460	0.320	1.000						
KNOW	0.130	0.270	0.210	0.390	0.270	0.380	1.000					
COMPRE	0.180	0.240	0.150	0.360	0.330	0.260	0.620	1.000				
APPLIC	0.080	0.140	0.090	0.250	0.130	0.230	0.440	0.660	1.000			
ANAL	0.100	0.160	0.090	0.250	0.120	0.280	0.580	0.660	0.640	1.000		
SYNTH	0.130	0.230	0.420	0.500	0.410	0.470	0.460	0.470	0.370	0.530	1.000	
EVAL	0.080	0.150	0.360	0.280	0.210	0.260	0.300	0.240	0.190	0.290	0.580	1.000

Examine the association between the creativity and achievement variables via canonical correlation, and from the printout answer the following questions:

a) How would you characterize the strength of the relationship between the two sets of variables from the simple correlations?

b) How many of the canonical correlations are significant at the .05 level?

c) Use the canonical variable loadings to interpret the canonical variates corresponding to the largest canonical correlation.

d) How large of an N is needed for reliable interpretation of the canonical variates in (c)?

e) Considering all the canonical correlations, what is the value of the redundancy index for the creativity variables given the achievement variables? Express in words what this number tells us.

f) Cramer and Nicewander (1979) have argued that the *average* squared canonical correlation should be used as the measure of association for two sets of variables, stating, "This index has a clear interpretation, being an arithmetic mean, and gives the proportion of variance of the average of the canonical variates of the y variables predictable from the x variables" (p. 53). Obtain the Cramer-Nicewander measure for the present problem, and compare it's magnitude to that obtained for the measure in (e). Explain the reason for the difference, and in particular, the direction of the difference.

6. Shanahan (1984) examined the nature of the reading-writing relationship through canonical correlation analysis. The following measures of writing ability (t unit, vocabulary diversity, episodes, categories, information units, spelling, phonemic accuracy and visual accuracy) were related to reading measures of vocabulary, word recognition, sentence comprehension and passage comprehension. Separate canonical correlation analyses were done for 256 second graders and 251 fifth graders.

Canonical Factor Structures for the Grade 2 and Grade 5 Samples:
Correlations of Reading and Writing Variables With Canonical Variables

| | Canonical variable | | | |
| | 2nd Grade | | 5th Grade | |
	Reading	Writing	Reading	Writing
Writing				
t-unit	.32	.41	.19	.25
Vocabulary diversity	.46	.59	.47	.60
Episodes	.25	.32	.20	.26
Categories	.37	.48	.33	.43
Information units	.36	.46	.24	.30
Spelling	.74	.95	.71	.92
Phonemic accuracy	.60	.77	.67	.86
Visual accuracy	.69	.89	.68	.88
Reading				
Comprehension	.81	.63	.79	.61
Cloze	.86	.66	.80	.62
Vocabulary	.65	.51	.89	.69
Phonics	.88	.68	.85	.66

a) How many canonical correlations will there by for each analysis?

b) Shanahan found that for second graders there were only two significant canonical correlations, and he only interpreted the largest one. Given his sample size, was he wise in doing this?

c) For fifth graders there was only one significant canonical correlation. Given his sample size. can we have confidence in the reliability of the results?

d) Shanahan presents the following canonical variate–variable correlations for the largest canonical correlation for both the second and fifth grade samples. If you have an appropriate content background, interpret the results and then compare your interpretation with his.

7.   Edwards (1984) collected data from 802 full time nursing faculty in 32 states on House's Leadership Behavior Scale and on Borrevak's Organizational Climate Questionnaire. Factor analysis of the leadership scale yielded these two factors: participatory/supportive leadership behavior (LBPS) and instrumental leadership behavior (LBI). Factor analysis of the organizational climate questionnaire produced the following three factors: organizational climate-intimacy, disengagement (OCID), organizational climate-consideration (OCC) and organizational climate-production emphasis (OCP). These three organizational climate factors were related via canonical correlation to the above two leadership behavior factors, education (ED) and faculty size (FSIZ). Missing data reduced the sample size for the canonical correlation to 662. The correlation matrix for the variables is

	OCC	OCID	OCP	LBPS	LBI	ED	FSIZ
OCC	1.000						
OCID	0.129	1.000					
OCP	0.429	0.070	1.000				
LBPS	0.895	0.104	0.402	1.000			
LBI	0.254	0.050	0.627	0.279	1.000		
ED	−0.036	0.021	−0.052	−0.043	−0.038	1.000	
FSIZ	−0.108	0.018	0.154	0.094	0.147	0.072	1.000

a) Run the canonical correlation on BMDP6M. How many significant canonical correlations are there at the .01 level?

b) Interpret the canonical variates corresponding to the significant canonical correlations.

c) Is sample size large enough to have confidence in the reliability of the results?

8.   Estabrook (1984) examined the relationship between the 11 subtests on the Wechsler Intelligence Scale for Children-Revised (WISC-R) and the 12 subtests on the Woodcock-Johnson Tests of Cognitive Ability for 152 learning disabled children. He seems to acknowledge sample size as a problem in his study, stating, "The primary limitation of this study is the size of the sample. . . . However, a more conservative criterion of $10(p + q) + 50$ (where p and q refer to the number of variables in each set) has been suggested by Thorndike." Is this really a conservative criterion according to the results of Barcikowski and Stevens (1975)?

13

Repeated Measures Analysis

13.1 INTRODUCTION

Recall that the two basic objectives in experimental design are the elimination of systematic bias and the reduction of error (within group or cell) variance. The main reason for within-group variability is individual differences among the subjects. Thus, even though the subjects receive the same treatment, their scores on the dependent variable can differ considerably because of differences on I.Q., motivation, SES, etc. One statistical way of reducing error variance is through analysis of covariance, which was discussed in Chapter 9. Another way of reducing error variance, which was mentioned earlier, is through blocking on a variable such as I.Q. Here the subjects are first blocked into more homogeneous subgroups, and then randomly assigned to treatments. For example, the subjects may be in blocks with only 9 point I.Q. ranges: 91–100, 101–110, 111–120, 121–130 and 131–140. The subjects within each block may score more similarily on the dependent variable, and the average scores for the subjects between blocks can be fairly large. But all of this variability between blocks is removed from the within-variability, yielding a much more sensitive (powerful) test. *In repeated measures designs*, blocking is carried to it's extreme. That is, *we are blocking on each subject. Thus, variability among the subjects due to individual differences is completely removed from the error term.* This makes these designs much more powerful than completely randomized designs, where different subjects are randomly assigned to the different treatments. Given the emphasis in this text on power, one should seriously consider the use of repeated measures designs where appropriate and practical. And there are many situations where such designs are appropriate. The simplest example of a repeated measures design the reader may have encountered in a beginning statistics course, i.e., the correlated or dependent samples t test. Here, the same subjects are pretested and posttested (measured repeatedly) on a dependent variable with an intervening treatment. The subjects are used as their own controls. Another class of repeated measures situations occurs when we are comparing the *same* subjects under several different treatments (drugs, stimulus displays of different complexity, etc.).

Repeated measures is also the natural design to use when the concern is with performance trends over time. For example, Bock (1975) presented an example comparing boys' and girls' performance on vocabulary over grades 8 through 11. Here we are also concerned with the mathematical form of the trend, i.e., whether it is linear, quadratic, cubic, etc.

Another distinct advantage of repeated measures designs, since the same subjects are being used repeatedly, is that far less subjects are required for the study. For example, if three treatments are involved in a completely randomized design, we may require 45 subjects (15 subjects per treatment). With a repeated measures design we would need only 15 subjects. This can be a very important practical advantage in many cases, since numerous subjects are not easy to come by in areas like counseling, school psychology, clinical psychology, and nursing.

In this chapter consideration is given to repeated measures designs of varying complexity. We start with the simplest design; a single group of subjects measured under various treatments (conditions), or at different points in time. Schematically, it would look like this:

	Treatments				
	1	2	3	· · · ·	k
1					
Subjects 2					
⋮					
n					

We then consider a one between and one within design. Many texts use the term "between" and "within" in referring to repeated measures factors. A between variable is simply a grouping or classification variable such as sex, age, social class. A within variable is one on which the subjects have been measured repeatedly (like time). Some authors even refer to repeated measures designs as within designs (Keppel, 1983). An example of a one between and one within design would be:

	Treatments		
	1	2	3
Males			
Females			

where the same males and females are measured under all three treatments.

Another example is given by Huck, Cormier, and Bounds (1974). We are interested in comparing the effect of three different teaching methods on achievement. But in addition, we wish to determine the residual effect of the methods on achievement, so we measure the subjects 6 weeks after the completion of the methods and 12 weeks later. Schematically the design is:

	Posttest	6 Weeks	12 Weeks
Teaching T_1			
Methods T_2			
T_3			

Here, teaching methods is the between variable and time is the within, or repeated measures factor.

There are three other names that are used for the one between and one within design by some authors: split plot, Lindquist Type I, and two-way ANOVA, with repeated measures on one factor.

We analyze a one between and one within design, where the within variable is trials, and do a trend analysis on trials.

Next, we consider a one between and two within repeated measures design, using the following example. There are two groups of subjects with two types of drugs administered at each of 3 doses. The study aims to estimate the relative potency of the drugs in inhibiting a response to a stimulus. Schematically, the design is:

		Drug 1			Drug 2		
Dose		1	2	3	1	2	3
Gp 1							
Gp 2							

Each subject is measured 6 times, for each dose of each drug. The two within variables are dose and drug.

For each of these designs we indicate the control lines for running both univariate and multivariate analyses on SPSSX MANOVA, and present and explain selected printout. We also present the control lines for running the single group repeated measures and the one between and two within design on BMDP4V, along with printout from BMDP4V.

Finally, we consider profile analysis, were two or more groups of subjects are compared on a battery of tests. The analysis determines whether the profiles for the groups are similar, i.e., parallel. If the profiles are parallel, then the analysis will determine whether they are coincident.

Although increased precision and economy of subjects are two distinct advantages of repeated measures designs, such designs also have potentially serious disadvantages, unless care is taken. When several treatments are involved, the order in which treatments are administered might make a difference in the subjects performance. Thus, it is important to counterbalance the order of treatments.

For two treatments this would involve randomly assigning half of the subjects to get treatment *A* first, and the other half to get treatment *B* first, which would look like this schematically:

Order of Administration

1	2
A	*B*
B	*A*

It is balanced since an equal number of subjects have received each treatment in each position.

For three treatments counterbalancing involves randomly assigning one third of the subjects to each of the following sequences:

Order of Administration
of Treatments

A	*B*	*C*
B	*C*	*A*
C	*A*	*B*

This is balanced since an equal number of subjects have received each treatment in each position. This type of design is called a Latin Square.

Also, it is important to allow sufficient time between treatments to minimize carryover effects, which certainly could occur if treatments were drugs. How much time is necessary is of course a substantive, not a statistical question. A nice discussion of these two problems is found in Keppel (1983) and Myers (1979).

13.2 SINGLE GROUP REPEATED MEASURES

Suppose we wish to study the effect of 4 drugs on reaction time to a series of tasks. Sufficient time is allowed to minimize the effect that one drug may have on the subject's response to the next drug. The following data is from Winer (1971):

S's	Drugs				Means
	1	2	3	4	
1	30	28	16	34	27
2	14	18	10	22	16
3	24	20	18	30	23
4	38	34	20	44	34
5	26	28	14	30	24.5
	26.4	25.6	15.6	32	24.9 (grand mean)

We will analyze this set of data in three different ways: (1) as a completely randomized design (pretending that there are different subjects for the different drugs), (2) as a univariate repeated measures analysis, and (3) as a multivariate repeated measures analysis. The purpose of including the completely randomized approach is to contrast the error variance that results against the markedly smaller error variance that results in the repeated measures approach. The multivariate approach to repeated measures analysis may be new to our readers, and a specific numerical example will help in understanding how some of the printout on the packages is arrived at.

Completely Randomized Analysis for the Drug Data

This simply involves doing a one-way ANOVA. Thus, we compute the sum of squares between (SS_b) and the sum of squares within (SS_w):

$$SS_b = n \sum_{j=1}^{4} (\bar{y}_j - \bar{y})^2 = 5[(26.4 - 24.9)^2 + (25.6 - 24.9)^2 + (15.6 - 24.9)^2$$
$$+ (32 - 24.9)^2]$$

$SS_b = 698.2$

$SS_w = (30 - 26.4)^2 + (14 - 26.4)^2 + \ldots + (26 - 26.4)^2 + \ldots +$
$\quad (34 - 32)^2 + (22 - 32)^2 + \ldots + (30 - 32)^2 = 793.6$

Thus, $MS_b = 698.2/3 = 232.73$ and $MS_w = 793.6/16 = 49.6$ and our $F = 232.73/49.6 = 4.7$, with 3 and 16 degrees of freedom. This is not significant at the .01 level, since the critical value is 5.29.

Univariate Repeated Measures Analysis for Drug Data

Note from the column of means for the drug of data that the subjects average responses to the 4 drugs differ considerably (ranging from 16 to 34). We quantify this variability through the so called sum of squares for blocks (SS_{bl}), where here we are blocking on the subjects. The error variability that was calculated above is split up into two parts, i.e., $SS_w = SS_{bl} + SS_{res}$, where SS_{res} stands for sum of squares residual. Denote the number of repeated measures by k.

Now we calculate the sum of squares for blocks:

$$SS_{bl} = k \sum_{i=1}^{5} (\bar{y}_i - \bar{y})^2$$

$$= 4[(27 - 24.9)^2 + (16 - 24.9)^2 + \ldots + (24.5 - 24.9)^2]$$

$$SS_{bl} = 680.8$$

Our error term for the repeated measures analysis is formed from $SS_{res} = SS_w - SS_{bl} = 793.6 - 680.8 = 112.8$. Note that the vast portion of the within variability is due to individual differences (680.8 out of 793.6), and that we have removed all of this from our error term for the repeated measures analysis. Now,

$$MS_{res} = SS_{res}/(n - 1)(k - 1) = 112.8/ 4(3) = 9.4$$

and $F = MS_b/MS_{res} = 232.73/ 9.4 = 24.76$, with $(k - 1) = 3$ and $(n - 1)(k - 1) = 12$ degrees of freedom. This is significant well beyond the .01 level, and is approximately 5 times as large as the F obtained under the completely randomized design.

13.3 THE MULTIVARIATE TEST STATISTIC FOR REPEATED MEASURES

Before we consider the multivariate approach, it is instructive to go back to the t test for correlated(dependent) samples. The subjects are pretested and post-tested, and difference (d_i) scores are formed:

S's	Pretest	Posttest	d_i
1	7	10	3
2	5	4	−1
3	6	8	2
. . . .			
n	3	7	4

The null hypothesis here is

$$H_0 : \mu_1 = \mu_2 \text{ or equivalently that } \mu_1 - \mu_2 = 0$$

The t test for determining the tenability of H_0 is

$$t = \frac{\bar{d}}{s_d/\sqrt{n}},$$

where $\bar{d}$ is the average difference score and s_d is the standard deviation for the difference scores. It is important to note that the analysis is done on the difference variable d_i.

In the multivariate case for repeated measures the test statistic for k repeated measures is formed from the (k − 1) *difference variables and their variances and covariances.* The transition here from univariate to multivariate parallels that for the two-group independent samples case

Independent Samples

$$t = \frac{(\bar{y}_1 - \bar{y}_2)^2}{s^2(1/n_1 + 1/n_2)}$$

$$t^2 = \frac{n_1 n_2}{n_1 + n_2} (\bar{y}_1 - \bar{y}_2) (s^2)^{-1} (\bar{y}_1 - \bar{y}_2)$$

In obtaining the multivariate statistic we replace the means by mean vectors and the pooled within-variance (s^2) by pooled within-covariance matrix.

$$T^2 = \frac{n_1 n_2}{n_1 + n_2} (\bar{y}_1 - \bar{y}_2)' \, \mathbf{S}^{-1} (\bar{y}_1 - \bar{y}_2)$$

S is the pooled within covariance matrix, i.e., the measure of error variability.

Dependent Samples

$$t^2 = \frac{\bar{d}^2}{s_d^2/n}$$

$$t^2 = n \bar{d} (s_d^2)^{-1} \bar{d}$$

To obtain the multivariate statistic we replace the mean difference by a vector of mean differences and the variance of difference scores by the matrix of variances and covariances on the (k − 1) created difference variables.

$$T^2 = n \, \mathbf{y}_d' \, \mathbf{S}_d^{-1} \, \mathbf{y}_d$$

$\mathbf{y}_d'$ is the row vector of mean difference on the (k − 1) difference variables, i.e. $\mathbf{y}_d' = (\bar{y}_1 - \bar{y}_2, \bar{y}_2 - \bar{y}_3, \ldots, \bar{y}_{k-1} - \bar{y}_k)$ and $\mathbf{S}_d$ is the matrix of variances and covariances on the (k − 1) difference variables, i.e., the measure of error variability.

We now calculate the above multivariate test statistic for dependent samples (repeated measures) on the drug data. This should help to clarify the somewhat abstract development thus far.

Multivariate Analysis of the Drug Data

The null hypothesis that we are testing for the drug data is that the drug population means are equal, or in symbols:

$$H_0 : \mu_1 = \mu_2 = \mu_3 = \mu_4$$

But this is equivalent to saying that $\mu_1 - \mu_2 = 0$, $\mu_2 - \mu_3 = 0$ and $\mu_3 - \mu_4 = 0$. (The reader is asked to show this in one of the exercises.) We create 3 difference variables on the adjacent repeated measures ($y_1 - y_2$, $y_2 - y_3$ and $y_3 - y_4$) and test H_0 by determining whether the means on all 3 of these difference variables are simultaneously 0. Below we display the scores on the difference variables:

$y_1 - y_2$	$y_2 - y_3$	$y_3 - y_4$	
2	12	-18	
-4	8	-12	
4	2	-12	
4	14	-24	Thus, the row vector of
-2	14	-16	mean differences here is

Means	.8	10	-16.4	$y_d' = (.8, 10, -16.4)$
Variances	13.2	26	24.8	

We need to create S_d, the matrix of variances and covariances on the difference variables. We already have the variances, but need to compute the covariances. The calculation for the covariance for the first two difference variables is given below, while calculation of the other two is left as an exercise.

$$S_{y1-y2,y2-y3} = \frac{(2 - .8)(12 - 10) + (-4 -.8)(8 - 10) + \ldots + (-2 - .8)(14 - 10)}{4} = -3$$

Recall that in computing the covariance for two variables the scores for the subjects are simply deviated about the means for the variables. The matrix of variances and covariances is

$$\begin{matrix} & y_1 - y_2 & y_2 - y_3 & y_3 - y_4 \\ S_d = & \begin{bmatrix} 13.2 & -3 & -8.953 \\ -3 & 26 & -19 \\ -8.953 & -19 & 24.8 \end{bmatrix} \end{matrix}$$

covariance for $(y_1 - y_2)$ & $(y_3 - y_4)$

covariance for $(y_2 - y_3)$ & $(y_3 - y_4)$

Therefore,

$$T^2 = 5(.8, 10, -16.4) \overset{S_d^{-1}}{\begin{bmatrix} .4555 & .381 & .450 \\ .381 & .4066 & .4436 \\ .450 & .4436 & .536 \end{bmatrix}} \overset{y_d}{\begin{pmatrix} .8 \\ 10 \\ -16.4 \end{pmatrix}}$$

$$T^2 = (-16.03, -14.52, -19.97) \begin{pmatrix} .8 \\ 10 \\ -16.4 \end{pmatrix} = 169.48$$

There is an exact F transformation of T^2, which is

$$F = \frac{n - k + 1}{(n - 1)(k - 1)} T^2, \text{ with } (k - 1) \text{ and } (n - k + 1) \text{ df}$$

Thus, $F = \dfrac{5 - 4 + 1}{4\,(3)} (169.48) = 28.25$, with 3 and 2 df

This is significant at the .05 level, exceeding the critical value of 19.16. The critical value is very large here, since the error degrees of freedom is extremely small (2). We conclude that the drugs are different in effectiveness.

13.4   MULTIVARIATE MATCHED PAIRS ANALYSIS

It was mentioned in Chapter 4 that often in comparing intact groups the subjects are matched or paired on variables known or suspected to be related to performance on the dependent variable(s). This is done so that if a significant difference is found, the investigator can be more confident it was the treatment(s) that "caused" the difference. In Chapter 4 we gave a univariate example, where kindergarteners were compared against non-kindergarteners on first-grade readiness, after they were matched on I.Q., SES, and number of children in the family.

Now consider a multivariate example, i.e., where there are several dependent variables. Kvet (1982) was interested in determining whether excusing elementary school children from regular classroom instruction for the study of instrumental music affected sixth-grade reading, language, and mathematics achievement. These were the three dependent variables. Instrumental and non-instrumental students from 4 public school districts were used in the study. We consider the analysis from just one of the districts. The instrumental and non-instrumental students were matched on the following variables: sex, race, I.Q., cummulative achievement in fifth grade, elementary school attended, sixth-grade classroom teacher, and instrumental music outside the school.

In Table 13.1 are the control lines for running the analysis on BMDP3D, along with some annotation explaining the setup. The data is given in the Appendix at the end of this chapter. Note that in the TRANSFORM paragraph we create the three difference variables (READIFF, LANGDIFF, and MATHDIFF); this is analogous to the creation of the difference variables in the multivariate approach to the single-group repeated measures analysis. Then in the TEST paragraph we determine whether the three difference variables (considered *jointly*) differ significantly from the **0** vector, i.e., whether the differences on all three variables are jointly 0. The keyword HOTELLING is used to obtain the multivariate test.

Again we obtain a T^2 value, like for the single sample multivariate repeated measures analysis, however, the exact F transformation is somewhat different:

$$F = \frac{N - p}{(N - 1)p}\, T^2, \text{ with } p \text{ and } (N - p)\ df$$

where N is the number of matched pairs and p is the number of difference variables.

TABLE 13.1
Control Lines for Multivariate Matched Pairs Analysis on BMDP3D
and Selected Output

/PROBLEM TITLE IS ' MATCHED PAIRS-INSTURM MUSIC VS NON'.
/INPUT VARIABLES ARE 6. FORMAT IS STREAM.
/VARIABLE NAMES ARE READ1,READ2,LANG1,LANG2,MATH1,MATH2,
READIFF,LANGDIFF,MATHDIFF.   ①
ADD IS 3.   ②
/TRANSFORM READIFF=READ1-READ2. LANGDIFF=LANG1 - LANG2.
MATHDIFF=MATH1-MATH2.
/TEST VARIABLES ARE 7 TO 9. HOTELLING.
/END

OUTPUT

HOTELLING T SQUARE		3.1253		
F VALUE	③	0.9115	P-VALUE	0.4604
DEGREES OF FREEDOM	3,	14.0		

DIFFERENCES ON SINGLE VARIABLES

READIFF   VARIABLE NUMBER   7

			MEAN	−0.7059
T STATISTIC	P-VALUE	DF	STD DEV	8.7304
			S.E.M.	2.1174
−0.33	0.7432	16	SAMPLE SIZE	17
			MAXIMUM	16.0000
			MINIMUM	−14.0000

LANGDIFF   VARIABLE NUMBER   8

			MEAN	1.7059
T STATISTIC	P-VALUE	DF	STD DEV	15.3654
			S.E.M.	3.7267
0.46	0.6533	16	SAMPLE SIZE	17
			MAXIMUM	28.0000
			MINIMUM	−30.0000

MATHDIFF   VARIABLE NUMBER   9

			MEAN	5.7647
T STATISTIC	P-VALUE	DF	STD DEV	14.7671
			S.E.M.	3.5815
1.61	0.1270	16	SAMPLE SIZE	17
			MAXIMUM	32.0000
			MINIMUM	−22.0000

---

①It is important to note that the difference variables, on which the analysis will be done, are included in the variable list.

②The ADD IS 3 tells the program that 3 variables (the difference variables) will be added by transformations.

③This is the multivariate test, comparing the matched groups on all 3 difference variables jointly, showing no significance at the .05 level.

The printout in Table 13.1 shows that the instrumental group does not differ from the non-instrumental group on the set of three difference variables ($F = .9115$, $p < .46$). Thus, the classroom time taken by the instrumental group did not adversely affect their achievement in these three basic academic areas.

To help the reader generalize the control lines for running other multivariate matched pairs analyses on BMDP3D, suppose there had been 5 achievement measures in the previous example (achievement in science and social studies also). Then the number of variables in the INPUT paragraph would be 10, and the VARIABLE through TEST paragraphs would be as follows:

```
/VARIABLE NAMES ARE READ1,READ2,LANG1,LANG2,MATH1,MATH2,SCIE1,
SCIE2,SOC1,SOC2,READDIFF,LANGDIFF,MATHDIFF,SCIEDIFF,SOCDIFF.
ADD IS 5.
/TRANSFORM READDIFF = READ1 − READ2. LANGDIFF = LANG1 − LANG2.
MATHDIFF = MATH1 − MATH2. SCIEDIFF = SCIE1 − SCIE2. SOCDIFF = SOC1 − SOC2.
/TEST VARIABLES ARE 11 TO 15. HOTELLING.
```

13.5   ASSUMPTIONS IN REPEATED MEASURES ANALYSIS

The three assumptions for a single-group univariate repeated measures analysis are:

1. independence of the observations
2. multivariate normality
3. sphericity (sometimes called circularity)[1]

The first two assumptions are also required for the multivariate approach, but the sphericity assumption is not necessary. The reader should recall from Chapter 6 that a violation of the independence assumption is very serious in independent samples ANOVA and MANOVA, and it is also serious here. Just as ANOVA and MANOVA are fairly robust against violation of multivariate normality, so that also carries over here.

What is the sphericity condition? Recall that in testing the null hypothesis for the previous numerical example, we transformed from the original 4 repeated measures to 3 new variables, which were then used jointly in the multivariate approach. In general, if there are k repeated measures, then we transform to $(k − 1)$ new variables. There are other choices for the $(k − 1)$ variables, than

[1]For many years it was thought that a stronger condition, called uniformity (compound symmetry) was necessary. The uniformity condition required that the population variances for all treatments be equal and also that all population covariances are equal. However, Huynh and Feldt (1970) and Rounet and Lepine (1970) showed that sphericity is an exact condition for the F test to be valid. Sphericity only requires that the variances of the differences for *all* pairs of repeated measures be equal.

the adjacent differences used in the drug example, which will yield the *same* multivariate test statistic. This follows from the invariance property of the multivariate statistic (Morrison, 1976, p. 145).

Suppose that the $(k - 1)$ new variates selected are orthogonal (uncorrelated) and are scaled such that the sum of squares of the coefficients for each variate is 1. Then we have what is called an *orthonormal* set of variates. If we the transformation matrix is denoted by C and the population covariance matrix for the original repeated measures by Σ, then the sphericity assumption says that the covariance matrix for the new (transformed) variables is a diagonal matrix, with equal variances on the diagonal:

$$
C' \, \Sigma \, C = \sigma^2 I =
\begin{array}{c}
\\
1 \\
2 \\
3 \\
\\
k - 1
\end{array}
\begin{array}{cccc}
\multicolumn{4}{c}{\text{Transformed Variables}} \\
1 \quad 2 \quad 3 \quad \cdots \quad k - 1 \\
\left[
\begin{array}{cccc}
\sigma^2 & 0 & 0 & 0 \\
0 & \sigma^2 & 0 & 0 \\
0 & 0 & \sigma^2 & \\
\multicolumn{4}{c}{\cdots\cdots\cdots\cdots} \\
0 & 0 & & \sigma^2
\end{array}
\right]
\end{array}
$$

Saying that the off diagonal elements are 0 means that the covariances for all transformed variables are 0, which implies that the correlations are 0.

Box (1954) showed that if the sphericity assumption is not met, then the F ratio is positively biased (we are rejecting falsely too often). In other words, we may set our α level at .05, but may be rejecting falsely 8% or 10% of the time. The extent to which the covariance matrix deviates from sphericity is reflected in a parameter called ϵ (Greenhouse & Geisser, 1959). We give the formula for $\hat{\epsilon}$ in one of the exercises. If sphericity is met, then $\epsilon = 1$, while for the worst possible violation the value of $\epsilon = 1/(k - 1)$, where k is the number of treatments. To adjust for the positive bias Greenhouse and Geisser suggested altering the degrees of freedom from

$(k - 1)$ and $(k - 1)(n - 1)$ to $[1/(k - 1)] \, (k - 1) = 1$

and $[1/(k - 1)] \, (k - 1)(n - 1) = n - 1$

Doing this makes the test *very* conservative, since adjustment is made for the worst possible case, and we don't recommend it. A more reasonable approach is to estimate ϵ. SPSSX (Version 4) and BMDP4V both print out $\hat{\epsilon}$. Then adjust the degrees of freedom from $(k - 1)$ and $(n - 1)(k - 1)$ to $\hat{\epsilon}(k - 1)$ and $\hat{\epsilon}(n - 1)(k - 1)$. Results from Collier, Baker, Mandeville, and Hayes (1967), Stoloff (1967), and Gary (1981) all show that this approach keeps the actual α close to the nominal α.

Bock (1975, pp. 459–460) presents a statistical test for checking sphericity, which is incorporated in the SPSSX MANOVA program. There is also another test for sphericity, due to Mauchley (Kirk, 1982, p. 259). However, based on the results of Monte Carlo studies (Keselman, Rogan, Mensoza, & Breen, 1980; Rogan, Keselman, & Mendoza, 1979), we don't recommend using either of these tests. The above studies showed that the tests are highly sensitive to departures from multivariate normality and from their respective null hypotheses.

Should We Use the Univariate or Multivariate Approach for Repeated Measures?

In terms of controlling on type I error, there is no real basis for preferring the multivariate approach, since use of the modified univariate test (i.e., multiplying the degrees of freedom by $\hat{\epsilon}$) yields an "honest" error rate. The choice then involves a question of power. Now, assumping sphericity, the univariate test is more powerful. When sphericity is violated, however, the situation is much more complex. Davidson (1972, p. 452) has stated, "when small but reliable effects are present with the effects being highly variable . . . the multivariate test is far more powerful than the univariate test." And O'Brien and Kaiser (1985), after mentioning several studies that compared the power of the multivariate and modified univariate tests, state, "Even though a limited number of situations have been investigated, this work found that no procedure is uniformly more powerful or even usually the most powerful." Thus, given an exploratory study, we agree with Barcikowski and Robey (1984) who recommend that *both* the univariate and multivariate tests be routinely used because they may differ in the treatment effects that they discern. In such a study half the experimentwise level of significance might be set for each test. Thus, if we wish our overall level of significance to be .05, simply do each test at the .025 level of significance.

13.6   COMPUTER ANALYSIS OF THE DRUG DATA

We now consider the univariate and multivariate repeated measures analysis of the drug data (that was worked out in numerical detail earlier in this chapter) on SPSSX MANOVA. The control lines for running the analysis are given in Table 13.2 and the means and standard deviations for the variables are given in Table 13.3. In Table 13.4 are given, in columns 2 through 4, the set of transformed variables which are tests for sphericity. The Bartlett test ($\chi^2 = .695$, $p < .874$) shows the variables are uncorrelated, and Hartley's F_{max} statistic indicates that these variables have equal variances at the .05 level. This is one of the tests of sphericity that we recommended against using earlier.

The multivariate test is given at the top of Table 13.5 and yields significance at the .05 level ($F = 28.41, p < .034$). Note that the F value, within rounding

TABLE 13.2
Control Lines for One Group Repeated Measures
on SPSSX

```
TITLE ' ONE GROUP REPEATED MEASURES- 4 DRUGS'
DATA LIST FREE/ Y1 Y2 Y3 Y4
LIST
BEGIN DATA
30 28 16 34
14 18 10 22
24 20 18 30
38 34 20 44
26 28 14 30
END DATA
MANOVA Y1 TO Y4/
```
①   `WSFACTOR = DRUG(4)/`
      `WSDESIGN = DRUG/`
②   `PRINT= TRANSFORM CELLINFO(MEANS) ERROR(COR) SIGNIF(AVERF)/`
③   `ANALYSIS(REPEATED)/`

---

①The WSFACTOR (within subject factor) and WSDESIGN (within subject design) subcommands are fundamental for running multivariate repeated analysis on SPSSX. In the WSFACTOR subcommand we specify which are repeated measures (i.e., within subjects) factors, and tell the program the number of levels, within the parentheses, for each of the factors. Here we just have one within factor and 4 levels, since there were 4 drugs given to the same subjects. The WSFACTOR *must* be the first subcommand following the MANOVA command.

The WSDESIGN, as the name indicates, specifies the design on the repeated measures. Here there is just the DRUG effect. If we had a factorial design on the repeated measures (say DRUG BY DOSE), then the WSDESIGN subcommand would be

WSDESIGN = DRUG,DOSE,DRUG BY DOSE/

②The ERROR(COR) yields Bartlett's test of sphericity. If this test is not significant, then the univariate approach is more desirable, especially for $N - k < 20$, since it tends to be more powerful. The SIGNIF(AVERF) is needed to obtain the univariate repeated measures test.

③This command tells the program to cycle throughout the within subjects effects.

error, agrees, with the F value calculated earlier ($F = 28.25$). The univariate test, at the bottom of Table 13.5, also shows significance at the .05 level ($F = 24.76$, $p < .000$).

In Table 13.6 we present the control lines for running the drug data on BMDP4V, and which yields the multivariate test, the univariate test *and* the adjusted univariate test. Although $\hat{\epsilon}$ differs somewhat from 1 ($\hat{\epsilon} = .60487$), the exact probabilities for the univariate and adjusted (modified) univariate tests differ by very little (.0000 and .0006 respectively).

If we had considered this an exploratory study, and adopted the position of Barcikowski and Rich (setting overall $\alpha = .05$, with $\alpha = .025$ for each test),

TABLE 13.3
Means and Standard Deviations for
Single Group   Repeated Measures

CELL MEANS AND STANDARD DEVIATIONS

VARIABLE .. Y1

	MEAN	STD. DEV.
FOR ENTIRE SAMPLE	26.40000	8.76356

VARIABLE .. Y2

	MEAN	STD. DEV.
FOR ENTIRE SAMPLE	25.60000	6.54217

VARIABLE .. Y3

	MEAN	STD. DEV.
FOR ENTIRE SAMPLE	15.60000	3.84708

VARIABLE .. Y4

	MEAN	STD. DEV.
FOR ENTIRE SAMPLE	32.00000	8.00000

then we would have rejected with the univariate test, but not with the multivariate test. That is, the univariate test is more powerful in this case. Note that since the adjusted univariate test was also significant well beyond the .05 level, we can be confident that significance was indeed due to the univariate approach being more powerful, and not due to a positive bias in the test statistic.

Further Comments on the Transformed Variables in Repeated Measures

We indicated earlier that the multivariate test statistic for repeated measures is based on the $(k - 1)$ transformed variables, not on the original k variables. SPSSX MANOVA creates a specific set of orthonormalized transformed variables on which the multivariate test is based, although the reader should recall that there are many different choices for the $(k - 1)$ transformed variables that yield the *same* multivariate test value. The specific set of orthonormal transformed variables for the drug data example was discussed in Table 13.4. The "univariate" tests following the multivariate test (cf. Table 13.5) are thus tests on the transformed variables, not on the original repeated measures.

If new names are not given to the transformed variables, then SPSSX uses the variable names given the original repeated measures; $Y1$, $Y2$, $Y3$ and $Y4$ for the drug data. These names are prefaced by an asterisk, indicating they denote transformed variables. Thus, although not displayed in Table 13.5, it would look like this for the drug effect:

TABLE 13.4
Transformation Matrix and Sphericity Test for Drug Data

ORTHONORMALIZED TRANSFORMATION MATRIX (TRANSPOSED)

		1	2	3 ①	4
Drugs	1	.50000	.70711	-.40825	-.28868
	2	.50000	.00000	.81650	-.28868
	3	.50000	.00000	.00000	.86603
	4	.50000	-.70711	-.40825	-.28868

WITHIN CELLS CORRELATIONS WITH STD. DEVS. ON DIAGONAL

	Y2	Y3	Y4
Y2	1.18322		
Y3	-.03408	2.86356	
Y4	-.49602	.18322	4.31277

STATISTICS FOR WITHIN CELLS CORRELATIONS

DETERMINANT = .72543
BARTLETT TEST OF SPHERICITY = .69547 WITH 3 D. F.
SIGNIFICANCE = .874

F(MAX) CRITERION = 13.28571 WITH (3.4) D. F.

$$F_{\max} = \frac{(4.31277)^2}{(1.18322)^2} = 13.2857$$

This is a chi-square statistic:

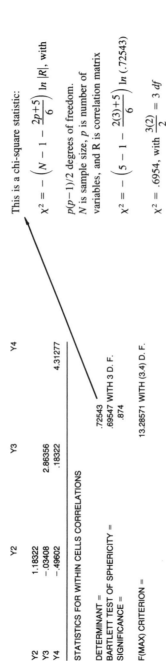

$$\chi^2 = -\left(N - 1 - \frac{2p+5}{6}\right)\ln|R|, \text{ with}$$

$p(p-1)/2$ degrees of freedom.
N is sample size, p is number of variables, and R is correlation matrix

$$\chi^2 = -\left(5 - 1 - \frac{2(3)+5}{6}\right)\ln(.72543)$$

$$\chi^2 = .6954, \text{ with } \frac{3(2)}{2} = 3 \; df$$

Critical value = 15.5 (at .05 level) ⇒ assumption of equal variances for 3 new vars is tenable. (We have squared the largest and smallest standard deviations in the above matrix.)

① The columns 2 through 4 give the contrast variates generated by the program for purpose of obtaining the multivariate test. The comparisons among the drugs generated by these contrasts may or may not be of interest to the researcher. Column 2 contrasts drug 1 vs drug 4, while column 3 contrasts drug 2 vs the average of drugs 1 and 4. Finally, column 4 contrasts drug 3 vs the average of drugs 1, 2, and 4.

The sphericity and $F_{\max}$ tests below jointly test whether the covariance matrix for the above set of transformed variables is (in columns 2–4) of the form

$$\begin{bmatrix} \sigma^2 & 0 & 0 \\ 0 & \sigma^2 & 0 \\ 0 & 0 & \sigma^2 \end{bmatrix}$$

The sphericity test determines whether the correlations are 0, which would imply that the covariances are 0.

TABLE 13.5
Multivariate and Univariate Tests of Significance for Drug Data

EFFECT .. DRUG

MULTIVARIATE TESTS OF SIGNIFICANCE (S = 1, M = 1/2, N = 0)

TEST NAME	VALUE	APPROX. F	HYPOTH. DF	ERROR DF	SIG. OF F
PILLAIS	.97707	28.41231	3.00	2.00	.034
HOTELLINGS	42.61846	28.41231	3.00	2.00	.034
WILKS	.02293	28.41231	3.00	2.00	.034
ROYS	.97707				

UNIVARIATE F-TESTS WITH (1.4) D. F. ①

VARIABLE	HYPOTH. SS	ERROR SS	HYPOTH. MS	ERROR MS	F	SIG. OF F
Y2	78.40000	5.60000	78.40000	1.40000	56.00000	.002
Y3	43.20000	32.80000	43.20000	8.20000	5.26829	.083
Y4	576.60000	74.40000	576.60000	18.60000	31.00000	.005

AVERAGED TESTS OF SIGNIFICANCE FOR Y USING SEQUENTIAL SUMS OF SQUARES

SOURCE OF VARIATION	SUM OF SQUARES	DF	MEAN SQUARE	F	SIG. OF F
WITHIN CELLS	112.80000	12	9.40000	②	
DRUG	698.20000	3	232.73333	24.75887	.000

①These are the tests of significance for the contrast variates referred to in Table 13.4. Y2 is significant at the .05 level, indicating that drug 1 is different in effectiveness from drug 4. Y3 is not significant at the .05 level, indicating drug 2 is not differentially effective from the average of drugs 1 and 4. Finally, Y4 is significant at the .05 level, indicating that drug 3 is different in effectiveness from the average of the other three drugs.

②This is the overall univariate test of significance.

Order of Variables for Analysis

Variates	Covariates	Not Used
*Y2		Y1
Y3		
Y4		

3 dependent Variables
  0 Covariates
  1 Variable not used

Note: "*" marks TRANSFORMED variables

In other words, $Y2*$, $Y3*$ and $Y4*$ actually stand for the following transformed variables (cf. Table 13.4):

$Y2^* = .70711\ Y1 - .70711\ Y4$

$Y3^* = .40825Y1 + .8165Y2 - .40825Y4$

$Y4^* = -.28868Y1 - .28868Y2 + .86603Y3 - .28868Y4$

Thus, it is these *contrasts on the repeated measures* that are being tested for significance.

As Norusis points out (1985, p. 263), the use of the original variable names prefaced by an asterisk can be very confusing, especially to the novice user. She therefore recommends renaming the transformed variables. We will do this in a few of our subsequent examples. In the drug example, however, there weren't any specific transformed variables we wished to specify a priori, but were simply interested in whether there was an overall difference. Thus, we let the program select the transformed variables. This is allright, provided the transformation matrix is examined to determine the nature of those transformed variables, so that if significance is found on some of the "univariate" followup F's we will know what specific contrasts among the repeated measures are contributing to the overall difference.

13.7 POST HOC PROCEDURES IN REPEATED MEASURES ANALYSIS

As in a one way independent samples ANOVA, if an overall difference is found, one would almost always want to determine which specific treatments or conditions differed. This entails a post hoc procedure. There are several reasons for preferring pairwise procedures: (1) they are easily interpreted, (2) they are quite meaningful, and (3) some of these procedures are fairly powerful. The Tukey procedure is appropriate in repeated measures designs, provided that the sphericity assumption is met. Recall that for the drug data the sphericity assumption was met (Table 13.5). We now apply the Tukey procedure, setting overall $\alpha = .05$, i.e., we take at most a 5% chance of one or more false rejections. Some readers may have encountered the Tukey procedure in an intermediate statistics course. The studentized range statistic (which we denote by q) is used in the procedure. If there are k samples and the total sample size is N, then any two means are declared significantly different at the .05 level if the following inequality holds:

$$|\bar{y}_i - \bar{y}_j| > q_{.05;k,N-k} \sqrt{\frac{MS_w}{n}},$$

where MS_w is the error term in a one-way ANOVA, and n is the common group size.

The modification of the Tukey for the one sample repeated measures is

$$|\bar{y}_i - \bar{y}_j| > q_{.05;k,(n-1)(k-1)} \sqrt{\frac{MS_{res}}{n}},$$

where $(n-1)(k-1)$ is the error degrees of freedom (replacing $N-k$, the error df for independent samples ANOVA), and MS_{res} is the error term for repeated measures, replacing MS_w (the error term for ANOVA).

Tukey Procedure Applied to the Drug Data

The drug means, from Table 13.3, are

	Drugs		
1	2	3	4
26.4	25.6	15.6	32

If we set overall $\alpha = .05$, then the appropriate studentized range value is $q_{.05;k,(n-1)(k-1)} = q_{.05;4,12} = 4.20$. The error term for the drug data, from Table 13.6 is 9.40, and the number of subjects is $n = 5$. Thus, two drugs will be declared significantly different if

$$|\bar{y}_i - \bar{y}_j| > 4.20 \sqrt{\frac{9.4}{5}} = 5.76$$

Reference to the means above shows that the following pairs of drugs differ: drugs 1 and 3, drugs 2 and 3, drugs 3 and 4, and drugs 2 and 4.

There are several other pairwise post hoc procedures which Maxwell (1980) discusses. One can employ the Tukey, but with separate error terms. The Roy-Bose intervals can be used. We recommended against the use of these in Chapter 4 because of their extreme conservativeness, and the same applies here. Still another approach is to use multiple *dependent* t tests, but employing the Bonferroni inequality to keep overall α under control. For example, if there are 5 treatments, then there will be 10 paired comparisons. If we wish overall α to equal .05, then we simply do each dependent t test at the .05/10 = .005 level of significance. In general, if there are k treatments, then to keep overall α at .05, do each test at the $.05/[k(k-1)/2]$ level of significance (since for k treatments there are $k(k-1)/2$ paired comparisons).

Maxwell (1980), using a Monte Carlo approach, has compared the following five pairwise post hoc procedures in terms of how well they control on overall α when the sphericity assumption is violated:

1. Tukey
2. Roy-Bose
3. Bonferroni (multiple dependent t tests)
4. Tukey, with separate error terms on $(n - 1)$ df
5. Tukey, with separate error term on $(n - 1)(k - 1)$ df

Results from Maxwell concerning the effect of violation of sphericity on type I error for 3, 4, and 5 treatments and for sample sizes of 8 and 15 are given in Table 13.7. This table shows, as expected, that the Roy-Bose approach is too conservative. It also shows that *the Bonferroni approach keeps the actual $\alpha <$*

TABLE 13.6
Control Lines for a Single Group Repeated Measures on BMDP4V and Selected Output

```
/PROBLEM TITLE IS 'SINGLE GROUP REPEATED MEASURES - 4 DRUGS'.
/INPUT VARIABLES=4. FORMAT IS STREAM.
/VARIABLE NAMES ARE REAC1,REAC2,REAC3,REAC4.
/WITHIN FACTOR IS DRUG.                            ①
  CODES ARE 1 TO 4. NAMES ARE DRUG1,DRUG2,DRUG3,DRUG4.
/WEIGHTS WITHIN ARE EQUAL.   ②
/END
  DATA
  /END
/ANALYSIS PROCEDURE IS FACTORIAL.   ③
```

WITHIN EFFECT: D: DRUG

EFFECT	VARIATE	STATISTIC		F		DF		P
D								
	DEP_VAR							
		TSQ=	170.474	④ 28.41		3,	2	0.0342
		WCP SS=	698.200					
		WCP MS=	232.733	24.76	⑤	3,	12	0.0000
		GREENHOUSE-GEISSER ADJ. DF		24.76	⑥	1.81,	7.26	0.0006
		HUYNH-FELDT ADJUSTED DF		24.76		3.00,	12.00	0.0000
ERROR								
	DEP_VAR							
		WCP SS=	112.80000					
		WCP MS=	9.4000000					
		GGI EPSILON=	0.60487	⑦				
		H-F EPSILON=	1.00000					

①In the WITHIN paragraph we simply name the within factor(s), and give names to the level of each factor.

②Since we have the option of equal or unequal cell weights, we must specify what we want.

③This ANALYSIS paragraph is required. For most applications the FACTORIAL procedure is appropriate. For other possibilities, consult the BMDP manual.

④This is the multivariate test—compare with SPSSX output Table 13.5.

⑤This is the univariate test—compare with SPSSX output Table 13.5 (at bottom).

⑥This is the adjusted F test, i.e., the test where the degrees of freedom are obtained by multiplying original degrees of freedom by the Greenhouse-Geisser epsilon parameter. Since epsilon = .60487 (see ⑦ above), the adjusted degrees of freedom are .60487 (3) and .60487 (12), or 1.81 and 7.26.

TABLE 13.7
Type I Error Rates for Various Pairwise Multiple Comparison
Procedures in Repeated Measures Analysis under Different
Violations of Sphericity Assumption

Type I Error Rates for $k=3$

		*		Method of Analysis			
n	ϵ		WSD	SCI	BON	SEP1	SEP2
15	1.00		.041	.026	.039	.046	.058
15	0.86		.043	.026	.036	.045	.058
15	0.74		.051	.025	.033	.040	.054
15	0.54		.073	.021	.033	.040	.045
8	1.00		.046	.035	.050	.065	.089
8	0.86		.048	.030	.042	.052	.082
8	0.74		.054	.028	.038	.050	.076
8	0.54		.078	.026	.036	.044	.064

min $\epsilon = 1/(3-1) = .50$

Type I Error Rates for $k=4$

			Method of Analysis			
n	ϵ	WSD	SCI	BON	SEP1	SEP2
15	1.00	.045	.019	.043	.056	.080
15	1.00	.044	.020	.044	.056	.083
15	0.53	.081	.014	.030	.042	.064
15	0.49	.087	.018	.036	.050	.073
8	1.00	.045	.010	.048	.070	.128
8	1.00	.048	.013	.048	.072	.126
8	0.53	.084	.011	.042	.061	.104
8	0.49	.095	.011	.032	.054	.108

min $\epsilon = 1/(4-1) = .333$

Type I Error Rates for $k=5$

			Method of Analysis			
n	ϵ	WSD	SCI	BON	SEP1	SEP2
15	1.000	.050	.007	.040	.065	.109
15	0.831	.061	.009	.044	.066	.108
15	0.752	.067	.008	.042	.060	.106
15	0.522	.081	.010	.038	.058	.092
8	1.000	.048	.003	.044	.071	.172
8	0.831	.058	.004	.044	.074	.162
8	0.752	.060	.002	.042	:072	.156
8	0.522	.076	.003	.044	.066	.137

*WSD - Tukey procedure, SCI—Roy-Bose, BON—Bonferroni, SEP1 - Tukey with separate
error term and $(n-1)df$, SEP 2 - Tukey with separate error term and $(n-1)(k-1)$df.

nominal α in all cases, even when there is a severe violation of the sphericity assumption. (e.g., for $k = 3$ the min $\epsilon = .50$, and one of the conditions modeled had $\epsilon = .54$). Because of this Maxwell recommended the Bonferroni approach for post hoc pairwise comparisons in repeated measures analysis if the sphericity assumption is violated. Maxwell also studied the power of the five approaches, and found the Tukey to be most powerful. Also, when $\epsilon > .70$ in Table 13.7 the deviation of actual α from nominal α is less than .02 for the Tukey procedure. This, coupled with the fact that the Tukey tends to be most powerful, would lead us to prefer the Tukey when $\epsilon > .70$. When $\epsilon < .70$, however, then we agree with Maxwell that the Bonferroni approach should be used.

13.8 ONE BETWEEN AND ONE WITHIN FACTOR—A TREND ANALYSIS

We now consider a slightly more complex design, i.e., one between (grouping) variable and one within (repeated measures) variable. We are not merely interested in whether there is a general within effect, but wish to determine the mathematical form of the effect; hence the trend analysis. For, as Bock (1975) has noted, "In many applications the existence of a general occasion (repeated measures) effect is a foregone conclusion and the overall test is not of interest. What is required is a more specific assessment of trend over occasions. For this orthogonal polynomials are suitable" (p. 452).

Before starting the analysis, some comments on what orthogonal polynomials are is in order. First, orthogonal is a mathematical way of saying uncorrelated. Now, the data may follow a proportional or a straight line relationship, in which case there is a linear trend (first degree polynomial). In other cases the relationship may be more complex or curvilinear, i.e., a curve may provide a better fit to the data. There may be one break point (or inflection point, as they are called in mathematics), in which case there is a quadratic relationship (second degree polynomial). A break point is a point where the scores for the subjects stop increasing (decreasing) and start decreasing (increasing). In a still more complex relationship there may be two break points, in which case there is a cubic relationship (third degree polynomial). We now give two examples of quadratic relationships and an example of a cubic relationship.

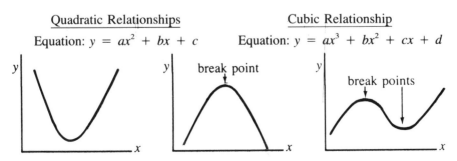

Quadratic Relationships

Equation: $y = ax^2 + bx + c$

Cubic Relationship

Equation: $y = ax^3 + bx^2 + cx + d$

break point

break points

The fact that the polynomials are uncorrelated means that the linear, quadratic, cubic, etc., components are partitioning distinct (different) parts of the variation in the data.

Example

We have three groups of subjects measured over four trials. The control lines for running the trend analysis on SPSSX MANOVA are given in Table 13.8. In Chapter 5 (in discussing planned comparisons) it was indicated that several different types of contrasts are available in the MANOVA program (Helmert, special, polynomial, etc.), and we also discussed the Helmert and special contrasts; here the polynomial contrasts are appropriate. Recall that the polynomial contrasts are built into the program, so that all we have to do is request them, which is what has been done in the CONTRAST subcommand.

TABLE 13.8
Control Lines for One Between & One
Within Repeated Measures on SPSSX with
Trend Analysis on Within Factor

```
      TITLE ' TREND ANALYSIS - 3 GROUPS AND 4 TRIALS '
      DATA LIST FREE/ Y1 Y2 Y3 Y4 GPID
      LIST
      BEGIN DATA
      9 8 8 5 1
      12 11 11 4 1
      15 18 13 10 1
      14 15 12 7 1
      20 11 12 9 2
      15 15 14 10 2
      12 19 18 7 2
      13 10 15 9 2
      8 7 6 6 3
      10 5 5 9 3
      8 7 7 8 3
      9 13 12 6 3
      END DATA
      MANOVA Y1 TO Y4 BY GPID(1,3)/
         WSFACTOR = TRIAL(4)/
 ①      CONTRAST(TRIAL) = POLYNOMIAL/
         WSDESIGN = TRIAL/
 ②      RENAME = MEAN,LINEAR,QUAD,CUBIC/
         PRINT = TRANSFORM CELLINFO(MEANS)
         ERROR(COR) SIGNIF(AVERF)/
         ANALYSIS(REPEATED)/
 ③      DESIGN = GPID/
```

①Used to obtain a trend analysis on the trial factor, that is, the program will test for linear, quadratic, and cubic trends.

②Here we are simply giving meaningful labels to our transformed variables.

③It is important to realize that with SPSSX MANOVA there is a design subcommand (WSDESIGN) for the within or repeated measures factor(s), and a *separate* DESIGN subcommand for the between (grouping) factor(s).

When *several groups are involved*, as in this example, *an additional assumption of the multivariate repeated measures analysis is homogeneity of the covariance matrices for the groups*. Small sample size here precludes the Box test to check the tenability of this assumption. Table 13.9 gives the means and standard deviations for the variables in the groups.

In Table 13.10 in the transformation matrix the four repeated measures are transformed into the three contrast variates of interest. The contrast variate in column 2 determines whether a linear trend is present, the contrast variate in column 3 whether a quadratic trend is present, and finally the variate in column 4 determines whether a cubic trend is present in the data. For those who are

TABLE 13.9
Means and Standard Deviations for One Between and One Within Repeated Measures

CELL MEANS AND STANDARD DEVIATIONS

VARIABLE .. Y1

FACTOR	CODE	MEAN	STD. DEV.
GPID	1	12.50000	2.64575
GPID	2	15.00000	3.55903
GPID	3	8.75000	.95743
FOR ENTIRE SAMPLE		12.08333	3.57919

VARIABLE .. Y2

FACTOR	CODE	MEAN	STD. DEV.
GPID	1	13.00000	4.39697
GPID	2	13.75000	4.11299
GPID	3	8.00000	3.46410
FOR ENTIRE SAMPLE		11.58333	4.50168

VARIABLE .. Y3

FACTOR	CODE	MEAN	STD. DEV.
GPID	1	11.00000	2.16025
GPID	2	14.75000	2.50000
GPID	3	7.50000	3.10913
FOR ENTIRE SAMPLE		11.08333	3.89541

VARIABLE .. Y4

FACTOR	CODE	MEAN	STD. DEV.
GPID	1	6.50000	2.64575
GPID	2	8.75000	1.25831
GPID	3	7.25000	1.50000
FOR ENTIRE SAMPLE		7.50000	1.97714

TABLE 13.10
Transformation Matrix and Group and Trial Trend Tests of Significance

ORTHONORMALIZED TRANSFORMATION MATRIX (TRANSPOSED)

	1	2	3	4
1	.50000	−.67082	.50000	−.22361
2	.50000	−.22361	−.50000	.67082
3	.50000	.22361	−.50000	−.67082
4	.50000	.67082	.50000	.22361
		Linear	Quadratic	Cubic

THESE ARE THE COEFFICIENTS FOR ORTHOGONAL POLYNOMIALS, ALTHOUGH THEY ARE SCALED
DIFFERENTLY SINCE THE VARIABLES ARE ORTHONORMALIZED (I.E., SUM OF SQUARED COEFFS = 1).
COMPARE, FOR EXAMPLE, MYERS, *FUNDAMENTALS OF EXPERIMENTAL DESIGN* (1979).

	GROUPS		COEFFICIENTS			
	4	LINEAR	−3	−1	1	3
		QUADRATIC	1	−1	−1	1
		CUBIC	−1	3	−3	1

SOURCE OF VARIATION	SUM OF SQUARES	DF	MEAN SQUARE	F	SIG. OF F
WITHIN CELLS	133.43750	9	14.82639		
CONSTANT	5355.18750	1	5355.18750	361.19297	.000
GPID	216.12500	2	108.06250	7.28852	.013

INDICATES SIGNIFICANT GP MAIN EFFECT AT .05 LEVEL.

EFFECT .. TRIAL

SIGNIFICANT LINEAR TREND (GPS LUMPED TOGETHER) OVER TRIALS.

UNIVARIATE F-TESTS WITH (1,9) D. F.

VARIABLE	HYPOTH. SS	ERROR SS	HYPOTH. MS	ERROR MS	F	SIG. OF F
LINEAR	121.83750	23.93750	121.83750	2.65972	45.80836	.000
QUAD	28.52083	122.93750	28.52083	13.65972	2.08795	.182
CUBIC	5.70417	20.43750	5.70417	2.27083	2.51193	.147

interested, Myers (1979) shows how the coefficients of the polynomials are derived. Results of the statistical tests in Table 13.10 show a significant group main effect and a significant linear trend (with the groups lumped together) over trials. However, the significant group × linear interaction effect ($F = 4.92$, $p < .036$) in Table 13.11 shows that the situation is more complex. We ignored the multivariate test for the group × trial interaction since it combines all three trends (linear, quadratic, and cubic) together, and use of it might cause a significant trend to be missed because it occurs mainly among error variation for the other trends. Besides, we are interested in specific trends, not a conglomeration of several different trends.

The *significant group × linear interaction implies that the nature of the linear relationship is different for the groups.* The plot of the groups in Table 13.11 shows that the interaction was caused by group 3. Note that groups 1 and 2 are

TABLE 13.11
Multivariate and Univariate Group × Trial Trend Analyses and Graph of Group × Linear Interaction

EFFECT .. GPID BY TRIAL

MULTIVARIATE TESTS OF SIGNIFICANCE (S = 2, M = 0, N = 2 1/2)

TEST NAME	VALUE	APPROX. F	HYPOTH. DF	ERROR DF	SIG. OF F
PILLAIS	.95217	2.42320	6.00	16.00	.074
HOTELLINGS	2.31380	2.31380	6.00	12.00	.102
WILKS	.24290	2.40102	6.00	14.00	.083

UNIVARIATE F-TESTS WITH (2,9) D. F.

INDICATES A SIGNIFICANT GP BY LINEAR INTERACTION, I.E., NATURE OF LINEAR RELATIONSHIP IS DIFFERENT FOR GROUPS.

VARIABLE	HYPOTH. SS	ERROR SS	HYPOTH. MS	ERROR MS	F	SIG. OF F
LINEAR	26.17500	23.93750	13.08750	2.65972	4.92063	.036
QUAC	19.29167	122.93750	9.64583	13.65972	.70615	.519
CUBIC	11.40833	20.43750	5.70417	2.27083	2.51193	.136

TRIALS

GPS	1	12.5	13	11.0	6.5
	2	15.0	13.75	14.75	8.75
	3	8.75	8.0	7.5	7.25

MEANS FOR VARIABLES (cf. Table 13.9)

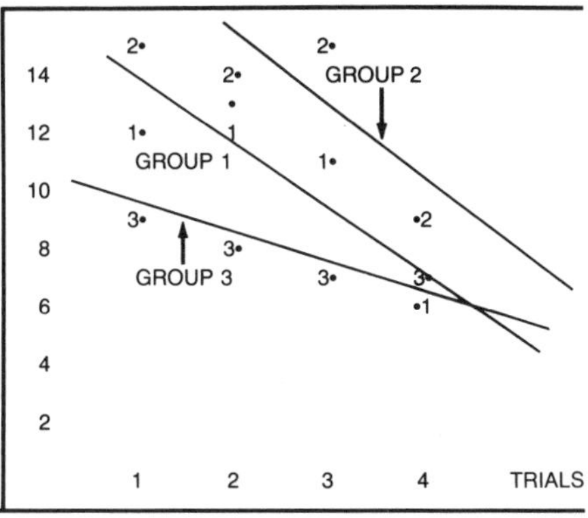

Graph (vertical axis 2–14, horizontal axis TRIALS 1 2 3 4):

GROUP 2, GROUP 1, GROUP 3 plotted as lines.

essentially parallel (implying no interaction for these groups), but that group 3 is not parallel to groups 1 and 2.

In concluding this example, the following from Myers (1979) is important, "Trend or orthogonal polynomial analyses should never be routinely applied whenever one or more independent variables are quantitative. . . . It is dangerous to identify statistical components freely with psychological processes. It is one thing to postulate a cubic component of A, to test for it, and to find it significant, thus substantiating the theory. It is another matter to assign psychological meaning to a significant component that has not been postulated on a priori grounds" (p. 456). The last part of this statement might refer to a situation where a single quadratic effect is significant out of, say, 10 different statistical tests on trend. This effect could well be spurious (type I error). This is just another illustration, in a different context, of the problem discussed in Chapter 1 of multiple statistical tests and the problem of spurious results. Here, instead of multiple t tests or multiple F tests from a factorial ANOVA, there are multiple tests for the different types of trend.

Now, suppose an investigator is in a part confirmatory and part exploratory study. He is conducting trend analyses on three different variables A, B, and C, and will be doing a total of 10 statistical tests. From previous research he is able to predict a linear trend on variable A, and from theoretical considerations he predicts a quadratic trend for variable C. He wishes to confirm these expectations; this is the confirmatory part of the study. He also wishes to determine if trends of any other nature are significant on variables A, B and C; this is the exploratory part of the study. A simple, but reasonable way, of maintaining control on overall type I error and yet having adequate power (at least for the predicted trends), would be to test each anticipated significant effect at the .05 level and test all other effects at the .005 level. Then, by the Bonferroni inequality, he is assured that

$$\text{overall } \alpha \leq .05 + .05 + 8(.005) = .14$$

13.9   ONE BETWEEN AND TWO WITHIN FACTORS

We consider both the univariate and multivariate analyses of a one between and two within repeated measures data set from Elashoff (1981). Two groups of subjects were given three different doses of two drugs. There are several different questions of interest in this study. Will the drugs be differentially effective for different groups? Is the effectiveness of the drugs dependent on dose level? Is the effectiveness of the drugs dependent on both dose level and on the group?

The control lines for obtaining the univariate and multivariate analyses for all effects on SPSSX MANOVA are given in Table 13.12. Since this is a fairly complex design, the schematic layout of it is given in Table 13.12. Note that each subject is measured 6 times, and these constitute the dependent variables, and furthermore that there is a crossed design on the dose and drug variables. Recall also, as in our first example, that SIGNIF(AVERF) is used in the PRINT subcommand to obtain the univariate tests. In Table 13.13 we present the means and standard deviations for the variables.

Regarding Table 13.14, it is again very important for the reader to get a feel for the transformed variables, through which the various effects in the design are tested. It is these transformed variables that are grouped and tested for significance by the program. In the previous problem the 4 repeated measures were transformed into variates measuring linear, quadratic, and cubic trends, and each of these was tested for significance. To obtain some insight into what the transformed variates in Table 13.14 are contrasting, it is essential to refer to the schematic layout of the design in Table 13.12. The contrast variate in

TABLE 13.12
Control Lines for One Between and Two Within
Repeated Measures on SPSSX

---

① TITLE ' REPEATED MEASURES - GPS(2) × DRUGS(2) × DOSE(3) '
DATA LIST FREE/ Y1 Y2 Y3 Y4 Y5 Y6 GPID
LIST
BEGIN DATA
19 22 28 16 26 22 1
11 19 30 12 18 28 1
20 24 24 24 22 29 1
21 25 25 15 10 26 1
18 24 29 19 26 28 1
17 23 28 15 23 22 1
20 23 23 26 21 28 1
14 20 29 25 29 29 1
16 20 24 30 34 36 2
26 26 26 24 30 32 2
22 27 23 33 36 45 2
16 18 29 27 26 34 2
19 21 20 22 22 21 2
20 25 25 29 29 33 2
21 22 23 27 26 35 2
17 20 22 23 26 28 2
END DATA
MANOVA Y1 TO Y6 BY GPID(1,2)/
②   WSFACTOR = DRUG(2),DOSE(3)/
    WSDESIGN = DRUG,DOSE,DRUG BY DOSE/
    PRINT = TRANSFORM HOMOGENEITY(BOXM) ERROR(COR)
    SIGNIF(AVERF) CELLINFO(MEANS)/
    ANALYSIS(REPEATED)/
③   DESIGN/

---

①Note that there are six measures for each subject. The design is given below schematically:

	Dose	Drug 1			Drug 2		
		D1	D2	D3	D1	D2	D3
		Y1	Y2	Y3	Y4	Y5	Y6

Gp 1 $\begin{cases} S_1 \\ S_2 \\ \vdots \\ S_8 \end{cases}$

Gp 2 $\begin{cases} S_9 \\ \vdots \\ S_{16} \end{cases}$

②We have a crossed design on the within variables, i.e., the repeated measures factors. Thus, we test each of the 3 effects for significance in the WSDESIGN subcommand.

③This DESIGN subcommand is for the between (grouping) variable.

TABLE 13.13
Means and Standard Deviations for One Between and Two
Within Repeated Measures

CELL MEANS AND STANDARD DEVIATIONS

VARIABLE .. Y1

FACTOR	CODE	MEAN	STD. DEV.
GPID	1	17.50000	3.42261
GPID	2	19.62500	3.42000
FOR ENTIRE SAMPLE		18.56250	3.48270

VARIABLE .. Y2

FACTOR	CODE	MEAN	STD. DEV.
GPID	1	22.50000	2.07020
GPID	2	22.37500	3.24863
FOR ENTIRE SAMPLE		22.43750	2.63233

VARIABLE .. Y3

FACTOR	CODE	MEAN	STD. DEV.
GPID	1	27.00000	2.61861
GPID	2	24.00000	2.72554
FOR ENTIRE SAMPLE		25.50000	3.01109

VARIABLE .. Y4

FACTOR	CODE	MEAN	STD. DEV.
GPID	1	19.00000	5.34522
GPID	2	26.87500	3.75832
FOR ENTIRE SAMPLE		22.93750	6.03842

VARIABLE .. Y5

FACTOR	CODE	MEAN	STD. DEV.
GPID	1	21.87500	5.89037
GPID	2	28.62500	4.62717
FOR ENTIRE SAMPLE		25.25000	6.19139

VARIABLE .. Y6

FACTOR	CODE	MEAN	STD. DEV.
GPID	1	26.50000	2.92770
GPID	2	33.00000	6.84523
FOR ENTIRE SAMPLE		29.75000	6.09371

TABLE 13.14
Transformation Matrix and Group and Group × Drug Tests of
Significance

ORTHONORMALIZED TRANSFORMATION MATRIX (TRANSPOSED)

	1	2	3	4	5	6
1	.40825	.40825	.50000	−.28868	.50000	−.28868
2	.40825	.40825	.00000	.57735	.00000	.57735
3	.40825	.40825	−.50000	−.28868	−.50000	−.28868
4	.40825	−.40825	.50000	−.28868	−.50000	.28868
5	.40825	−.40825	.00000	.57735	.00000	−.57735
6	.40825	−.40825	−.50000	−.28868	.50000	.28868

Contrast variate for testing the drug main effect. Contrast variates for testing the dose main effect. Contrast variates for testing the drug × dose interaction.

TESTS OF SIGNIFICANCE FOR Y1 USING SEQUENTIAL SUMS OF SQUARES

SOURCE OF VARIATION	SUM OF SQUARES	DF	MEAN SQUARE	F	SIG. OF F
WITHIN CELLS	532.97917	14	38.06994		
CONSTANT	55632.51042	1	55632.51042	1461.32381	.000
GPID	270.01042	1	270.01042	7.09248	.019

This indicates the group main effect is significant at .05 level.

TESTS OF SIGNIFICANCE FOR Y2 USING SEQUENTIAL SUMS OF SQUARES

SOURCE OF VARIATION	SUM OF SQUARES	DF	MEAN SQUARE	F	SIG. OF F
WITHIN CELLS	375.64583	14	26.83185		
DRUG	348.84375	1	348.84375	13.00111	.003
GPID BY DRUG	326.34375	1	326.34375	12.16255	.004

These indicate that both the drug main effect and the group × drug interaction are significant at the .05 level.

column 2 compares the first 3 repeated measures (corresponding to drug 1) against the last 3 repeated measures (corresponding to drug 2). Therefore, this variate is testing the drug main effect. The contrast variates in columns 3 and 4 *in combination* are testing the dose main effect. Why? First, there are 3 doses, thus only two degrees of freedom, and hence only two variates are needed. The variate in column 3 contrasts the first and fourth repeated measures (corresponding to dose level 1) against the third and sixth repeated measures (corresponding to dose level 3). The contrast variate in column 4 is orthogonal to the variate in column 3, and "soaks up" the remaining variation due to dose level. Notice that this variate does include dose level 2.

Examination of the significance tests in Table 13.14 shows that the main effects for group and drug, as well as the group × drug interaction, are all significant at the .05 level. Let us examine what caused all this significance so far. We take the means from Table 13.13 and insert them into the design yielding:

	Drug					
	1			2		
Dose	1	2	3	1	2	3
Gp 1	17.5	22.5	27	19	21.88	26.5
Gp 2	19.63	22.38	24	26.88	28.63	33

Now, collapsing on dose, the group $\times$ drug design means are obtained:

		Drug	
		1	2
Group	1	22.33	22.46
	2	22.00	29.50

The mean in cell 11 (22.33) is simply the average of 17.5, 22.5, and 27,

TABLE 13.15
Multivariate and Univarate Tests for Dose Main Effect and Group $\times$ Dose Interaction Effect

EFFECT .. DOSE

MULTIVARIATE TESTS OF SIGNIFICANCE (S = 1, M = 0, N = 5 1/2)

TEST NAME	VALUE	APPROX. F	HYPOTH. DF	ERROR DF	SIG. OF F
PILLAIS	.79534	25.26075	2.00	13.00	.000
HOTELLINGS	3.88627	25.26075	2.00	13.00	.000
WILKS	.20466	25.26075	2.00	13.00	.000
ROYS	.79534				

EFFECT .. GPID BY DOSE

MULTIVARIATE TESTS OF SIGNIFICANCE (S = 1, M = 0, N = 5 1/2)

TEST NAME	VALUE	APPROX. F	HYPOTH. DF	ERROR DF	SIG. OF F
PILLAIS	.18262	1.45223	2.00	13.00	.270
HOTELLINGS	.22342	1.45223	2.00	13.00	.270
WILKS	.81738	1.45223	2.00	13.00	.270
ROYS	.18262				

Univariate Tests

AVERAGED TESTS OF SIGNIFICANCE FOR Y USING SEQUENTIAL SUMS OF SQUARES

SOURCE OF VARIATION	SUM OF SQUARES	DF	MEAN SQUARE	F	SIG. OF F
WITHIN CELLS	290.95833	28	10.39137		
DOSE	758.77083	2	379.38542	36.50967	.000 ①
GPID BY DOSE	42.27083	2	21.13542	2.03394	.150

①These univariate tests of the dose main effect and group $\times$ dose interaction indicate that only the dose main effect is significant at the .05 level.

The multivariate tests, given above, yield the same conclusions.

while the mean in cell 12 (22.46) is the average of 19, 21.88, and 26.5, etc. It is now apparent that the "outlier" cell mean of 29.5 is what caused all the significance. For some reason drug 2 was not as effective with group 2 in inhibiting the response. We have indicated previously, especially in connection with multiple regression, how influential an individual subject's score can be in affecting the results. This example shows the same type of thing, only now the outlier is a mean.

In Table 13.15 we present the multivariate and univariate tests for the dose main effect and group $\times$ dose interaction effects. As indicated there, both the univariate and multivariate tests show the dose main effect significant at the .05 level, while both show the interaction effect is not significant. Table 13.16 gives the multivariate and univariate tests for the drug $\times$ dose and group $\times$ drug $\times$ dose interactions. Both the univariate and multivariate tests show that neither interaction is significant at the .05 level.

In Table 13.17 we present the control lines for running the above problem

TABLE 13.16
Multivariate and Univariate Tests for Drug $\times$ Dose and Group $\times$
Drug $\times$ Dose Interaction

EFFECT .. GPID BY DRUG BY DOSE

MULTIVARIATE TESTS OF SIGNIFICANCE (S = 1, M = 0, N = 5 1/2)

TEST NAME	VALUE	APPROX. F	HYPOTH. DF	ERROR DF	SIG. OF F
PILLAIS	.14314	1.08583	2.00	13.00	.366
HOTELLINGS	.16705	1.08583	2.00	13.00	.366
WILKS	.85686	1.08583	2.00	13.00	.366
ROYS	.14314				

EFFECT .. DRUG BY DOSE

MULTIVARIATE TESTS OF SIGNIFICANCE (S = 1, M = 0, N = 5 1/2)

TEST NAME	VALUE	APPROX. F	HYPOTH. DF	ERROR DF	SIG. OF F
PILLAIS	.12604	.93739	2.00	13.00	.417
HOTELLINGS	.14421	.93739	2.00	13.00	.417
WILKS	.87396	.93739	2.00	13.00	.417
ROYS	.12604				

Univariate Tests

AVERAGED TESTS OF SIGNIFICANCE FOR Y USING SEQUENTIAL SUMS OF SQUARES

SOURCE OF VARIATION	SUM OF SQUARES	DF	MEAN SQUARE	F	SIG. OF F
WITHIN CELLS	247.79167	28	8.84970		
DRUG BY DOSE	12.06250	2	6.03125	.68152	.514
GPID BY DRUG BY DOSE	14.81250	2	7.40625	.83689	.444

Both the multivariate and univariate tests indicate that neither the drug $\times$ dose or group $\times$ drug $\times$ dose interaction effects are significant at the .05 level, since the probabilities are >.05.

TABLE 13.17
Control Lines for One Between and Two Within Repeated Measures
on BMDP4V and Selected Output

```
/PROBLEM TITLE IS 'ONE BETWEEN AND 2 WITHIN REPEATED MEASURES - GPS X
DRUGS X DOSES'.
/INPUT VARIABLES=7. FORMAT IS STREAM.
/VARIABLE NAMES ARE GPID,Y1,Y2,Y3,Y4,Y5,Y6.
/BETWEEN FACTOR=GPID. CODES=1,2.                    ①
NAMES ARE GP1,GP2.
/WITHIN FACTORS ARE DRUG,DOSE.
CODES(1)=1,2. NAMES(1)=DRUG1,DRUG2. CODES(2) = 1 TO 3. NAMES(2)=DOSE1,
DOSE2,DOSE3.
/WEIGHTS BETWEEN=EQUAL. WITHIN=EQUAL.     ②
/END

        DATA
/END
/ANALYSIS PROCEDURE IS FACTORIAL
```

WITHIN EFFECT: DBS: WITHIN CASE MEAN

EFFECT	VARIATE	STATISTIC		F	DF		P
OVALL: GRAND MEAN							
	DEP__VAR						
		SS=	55632.5				
		MS=	55632.5	1461.32	1,	14	0.0000
G: GPID							
	DEP__VAR						
		SS=	270.010				
		MS=	270.010	③ 7.09	1,	14	0.0185
ERROR							
	DEP__VAR						
		SS=	532.97917				
		MS=	38.069940				

WITHIN EFFECT: D: DRUG

EFFECT	VARIATE	STATISTIC		F	DF		P
D							
	DEP__VAR						
		SS=	348.844				
		MS=	348.844	③ 13.00	1,	14	0.0029
(D) X (G: GPID)							
	DEP__VAR						
		SS=	326.344				
		MS=	326.344	③ 12.16	1,	14	0.0036
ERROR							
	DEP__VAR						
		SS=	375.64583				
		MS=	26.831845				

①Here we have both a BETWEEN and a WITHIN paragraph, where we simply name each of the between and within factors, and give names to each level of each factor.

②Since we have the option of equal or unequal cell weights, we specify which we wish separately for the between and the within factors.

③Compare these results with the SPSSX output in Table 13.14.

TABLE 13.18
Dose Main Effect and Dose Interaction Effects for One Between and Two Within Design from BMDP4V

WITHIN EFFECT: A: DOSE

EFFECT	VARIATE	STATISTIC		F	DF		P
A							
	DEP__VAR						
		TSQ=	54.4078 ①	25.26	2,	13	0.0000
		WCP SS=	758.771				
		WCP MS=	379.385 ②	36.51	2,	28	0.0000
		GREENHOUSE-GEISSER ADJ. DF		36.51	1.76,	24.60	0.0000
		HUYNH-FELDT ADJUSTED DF		36.51	2.00,	28.00	0.0000
(A) X (G: GPID)							
	DEP__VAR						
		TSQ=	3.12789	1.45	2,	13	0.2696
		WCP SS=	42.2708				
		WCP MS=	21.1354	2.03	2,	28	0.1497
		GREENHOUSE-GEISSER ADJ. DF		2.03	1.76,	24.60	0.1565
		HUYNH-FELDT ADJUSTED DF		2.03	2.00,	28.00	0.1497
ERROR							
	DEP__VAR						
		WCP SS=	290.95833				
		WCP MS=	10.391369				
		GGI EPSILON=	0.87868				
		H-F EPSILON=	1.00000				

WITHIN EFFECT: DA

EFFECT	VARIATE	STATISTIC		F	DF		P
DA							
③	DEP__VAR						
		TSQ=	2.01900	0.94	2,	13	0.4166
		WCP SS=	12.0625				
		WCP MS=	6.03125	0.68	2,	28	0.5140
		GREENHOUSE-GEISSER ADJ. DF		0.68	1.46,	20.43	0.4724
		HUYNH-FELDT ADJUSTED DF		0.68	1.70,	23.84	0.4927
(DA) X (G: GPID)							
④	DEP__VAR						
		TSQ=	2.33871	1.09	2,	13	0.3664
		WCP SS=	14.8125				
		WCP MS=	7.40625	0.84	2,	28	0.4436
		GREENHOUSE-GEISSER ADJ. DF		0.84	1.46,	20.43	0.4134
		HUYNH-FELDT ADJUSTED DF		0.84	1.70,	23.84	0.4283
ERROR							
	DEP__VAR						
		WCP SS=	247.79167				
		WCP MS=	8.8497024				
		GGI EPSILON=	0.72973				
		H-F EPSILON=	0.85129				

①The first F for each effect is the multivarate test (TSQ is an abbreviation for Hotelling's T^2 from which the F statistic is derived). Thus, $F = 25.26$ is the multivariate test for the dose main effect, $F = 1.45$ is the multivariate test for the dose $\times$ group interaction, etc.

②The statistics for each effect labeled "GREENHOUSE-GEISSER ADJ DF" is the modified univariate test. Thus, the modified univariate test for dose main effects is $F = 36.51$, for dose $\times$ group interaction is $F = 2.03$, etc.

③Since D is the code for drug and A is a code for dose, this is drug $\times$ dose interaction.

④This is the drug $\times$ dose $\times$ group interaction effect.

on BMDP4V, and the tests of the group and drug main effects. Table 13.18 gives the univariate and multivariate tests for the dose effects.

Another One Between and Two Within Design

A researcher in child development is interested in observing three groups of children (ages 3, 4, and 5) in two situations at two different times (morning and afternoon) of the day. She is concerned with the extent of their social interaction, and will measure this by having two observers independently rate the amount of social interaction. The average of the two ratings will serve as the dependent variable. The age of the children is the grouping or between variable here. The two within variables are situation and time of the day. There are four scores for each child: social interaction in situation 1 in the morning, social interaction in situation 1 in the afternoon, social interaction in situation 2 in the morning, and social interaction in situation 2 in the afternoon. We denote the 4 scores by $Y1$, $Y2$, $Y3$ and $Y4$.

The control lines for running the analysis on SPSSX MANOVA, which will yield both the univariate and multivariate tests, are given below:

```
TITLE ' REPEATED MEASURES — AGE(3) × SIT(2) × TIME(2) '
DATA LIST FREE/ Y1 Y2 Y3 Y4 AGE
LIST
BEGIN DATA

    DATA LINES

END DATA
MANOVA Y1 TO Y4 BY AGE(1,3)/
   WSFACTOR = SIT(2),TIME(2)/
   WSDESIGN/
   PRINT = TRANSFORM HOMOGENEITY(BOXM) SIGNIF(AVERF) CELLINFO(MEANS)/
   ANALYSIS(REPEATED)/
   DESIGN/
```

13.10 PROFILE ANALYSIS

In profile analysis the interest is in comparing the performance of two or more groups on a battery of test scores (interest, achievement, personality). It is assumed that the tests are scaled similarily, or that they are commensurable. In profile analysis there are three questions to be asked of the data in the following order:

1. Are the profiles parallel? If the answer to this were yes for two groups, it would imply that one group scored uniformly better than the other on all variables.

2. If the profiles are parallel, then are they coincident? In other words, did the groups score the same on each variable?

3.   If the profiles are concident, then are the profiles level? In other words, are the means on all variables equal to the same constant.

Below we present *hypothetical* examples of parallel and nonparallel profiles: (the variables represent achievement in content areas)

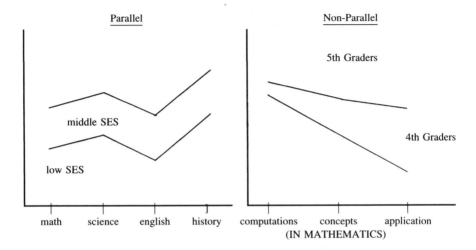

If the profiles are not parallel, then there is a group by variable interaction. That is, how much better one group does than another depends on the variable.

Why is it necessary that the tests be scaled similarly in order for the results of a profile analysis to be meaningfully interpreted? To illustrate, suppose we compared two groups on three variables, *A, B,* and *C,* two of which were on a 1 to 5 scale and the other on a 1 to 30 scale, i.e., not scaled similarily. Suppose the following graph resulted, suggesting nonparallel profiles:

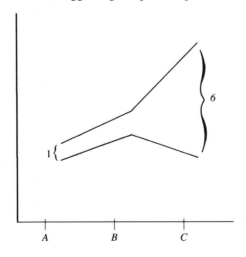

But the nonparallelism is a scaling artifact. The magnitude of superiority of group 1 for test A is 1/5, which is exactly the same order of speriority on test C, i.e., $6/30 = 1/5$. A way of dealing with this problem if the tests are scaled differently is to convert first to some type of standard score (e.g., z or T) before proceeding with the profile analysis.

We now consider the running and interpretation of a profile analysis on SPSSX MANOVA, using some data from Johnson and Wichern (1982).

Example

In a study of love and marriage, a sample of husbands and wives were asked to respond to the following questions:

1. What is the level of passionate love you feel for your partner?
2. What is the level of passionate love that your partner feels for you?
3. What is the level of companionate love that you feel for your partner?
4. What is the level of companionate love that your partner feels for you?

TABLE 13.19
Control Lines for Profile Analysis of Husband and Wife Ratings

```
TITLE ' PROFILE ANALYSIS ON HUSBAND AND WIFE RATINGS'
DATA LIST FREE/ SPOUSE PASSYOU PASSPART COMPYOU COMPPART
LIST
BEGIN DATA

      DATA LINES

END DATA
REPORT VARS=PASSYOU PASSPART COMPYOU COMPPART
   BREAK=SPOUSE/
   SUMMARY=MEAN/          ①
MANOVA PASSYOU TO COMPPART BY SPOUSE(1,2)
   TRANSFORM=REPEATED/
   RENAME=AVERAGE DIF2AND1 DIF3 AND2 DIF4AND3
   PRINT=TRANSFORM
   ANALYSIS=(DIF2AND1,DIF3AND2,DIF4AND3/ AVERAGE)   ②
   DESIGN
```

①The BREAK subcommand indicates what variable will define the subgroups (in this case husbands and wives). The SUMMARY subcommand tells the program what summary statistics we want printed for each subgroup; in this case we only want the means. See SPSSX User's Guide, 1983, Chap. 23.

②This subcommand defines two analyses. The first analysis, on the 3 difference variables before the / within the parentheses, answers questions 1 and 3 for the profile analysis. The second analysis, on the average variable, answers the question of coincident profiles. The general setup then of the ANALYSIS subcommand for k repeated measures in profile analysis would be

ANALYSIS=(DIF2AND1, DIF3AND2, . . . , DIFKANDK-1/ AVERAGE)/

For example, if k=7, then the ANALYSIS subcommand would be:

ANALYSIS=(DIF2AND1, DIF3AND2, DIF4AND3, DIF5AND4, DIF6AND5, DIF7AND6/ AVERAGE)/

The responses to all 4 questions were on a Likert type scale from 1 (none at all) to 5 (a tremendous amount). We wish to determine whether the profiles for the husbands and wives are parallel. There were 30 husbands and 30 wives that responded. The control lines for running the analysis on SPSSX are given in Table 13.19. The raw data is given in the appendix at the end of this chapter.

The test of parallelism appears in Table 13.20 and shows that parallelism is tenable at the .01 level, since the exact probability of .057 is greater than .01. Now, it is meaningful to proceed to the second question in profile analysis, and ask whether the profiles are coincident. The test for this is given in Table 13.21 and shows that the profiles can be considered coincident, i.e., the same. In other

TABLE 13.20
Test of Parallelism of Profiles for Husband and Wife Ratings

ORDER OF VARIABLES FOR ANALYSIS

	VARIATES	COVARIATES	NOT USED
	*DIF2AND1		AVERAGE
	*DIF3AND2		
	*DIF4AND3		

3 DEPENDENT VARIABLES
0 COVARIATES
1 VARIABLE NOT USED

NOTE.. "*" MARKS TRANSFORMED VARIABLES.

TRANSFORMATION MATRIX (TRANSPOSED)

	1	2	3	4
1	.25000	1.00000	.00000	.00000
2	.25000	−1.00000	1.00000	.00000
3	.25000	.00000	−1.00000	1.00000
4	.25000	.00000	.00000	−1.00000

EFFECT .. SPOUSE

MULTIVARIATE TESTS OF SIGNIFICANCE (S = 1, M = 1/2, N = 27)

TEST NAME	VALUE	APPROX. F	HYPOTH. DF	ERROR DF		SIG. OF F
PILLAIS	.12474	2.66027	3.00	56.00		.057
HOTELLINGS	.14251	2.66027	3.00	56.00	①	.057
WILKS	.87526	2.66027	3.00	56.00		.057
ROYS	.12474					

UNIVARIATE F-TESTS WITH (1,58) D. F.

VARIABLE	HYPOTH. SS	ERROR SS	HYPOTH. MS	ERROR MS	F	SIG. OF F
DIF2AND1	.81667	40.16667	.81667	.69253	1.17925	.282
DIF3AND2	.26667	50.46667	.26667	.87011	.30647	.582
DIF4AND3	.41667	4.56667	.41667	.07874	5.29197	.025

① This is the test of parallelism of the profiles, and indicates parallelism is tenable at the .01 level.

words, the differences for husbands and wives on the four variables can be considered due to sampling error. Finally, we ask whether husbands and wives scored the same on all 4 tests, i.e., the question of equal scale means. The test for equal scale means in Table 13.21 indicates this is not tenable. Reference to the univariate tests at the bottom of Table 13.21 shows that it is the difference in the way the subjects responded to scales 2 and 3 that was primarily responsible for the rejection of equal scale means. Note from the means at the top of Table 13.21 that the subjects scored somewhat higher on variable 3 than on variable 2.

Table 13.21
Test of Coincidence of the Profiles and Equal Scale Means

SPOUSE	PASSYOU	PASSPART	COMPYOU	COMPPART
1.00 MEAN	3.9000	3.9667	4.3333	4.4000
2.00 MEAN	3.8333	4.1333	4.6333	4.5333

ORDER OF VARIABLES FOR ANALYSIS

VARIATES	COVARIATES	NOT USED
*AVERAGE		DIF2AND1
		DIF3AND2
		DIF4AND3

TESTS OF SIGNIFICANCE FOR AVERAGE USING SEQUENTIAL SUMS OF SQUARES

SOURCE OF VARIATION	SUM OF SQUARES	DF	MEAN SQUARE	F		SIG. OF F
WITHIN CELLS	9.04167	58	.15589			
CONSTANT	1066.81667	1	1066.81667	6843.35853	①	.000
SPOUSE	.26667	1	.26667	1.71060		.196

EFFECT .. CONSTANT

MULTIVARIATE TESTS OF SIGNIFICANCE (S = 1, M = 1/2, N = 27)

TEST NAME	VALUE	APPROX. F	HYPOTH. DF	ERROR DF		SIG. OF F
PILLAIS	.30301	8.11513	3.00	56.00		.000
HOTELLINGS	.43474	8.11513	3.00	56.00		.000
WILKS	.69699	8.11513	3.00	56.00	②	.000
ROYS	.30301					

UNIVARIATE F-TESTS WITH (1,58) D. F.

VARIABLE	HYPOTH. SS	ERROR SS	HYPOTH. MS	ERROR MS	F	SIG. OF F
DIF2AND1	2.01667	40.16667	2.01667	.69253	2.91203	.093
DIF3AND2	11.26667	50.46667	11.26667	.87011	12.94848	.001
DIF4AND3	.01667	4.56667	.01667	.07874	.21168	.647

①This indicates the profiles are coincident at the .01 level, since .196 > .01.

②This test indicates that equal scale means is not tenable at the .01 level, since .000 < .01.

13.11   TWO BETWEEN AND TWO WITHIN FACTORS

This is a very complex design, an example of which appears in Bock (1975, pp 483–484). The data was from a study by Morter, who was concerned about the comparability of the first and second responses on the form definiteness and form appropriateness variables of the Holtzman Inkblot procedure for a pre-adolescent group of subjects. The two between variables were grade level (4 and 7) and I.Q. (high and low); thus there was a crossed design on the subjects. The two within variables were form and time; thus there was also a crossed design on the measures. The schematic layout for the design is given at the bottom of Table 13.22, which also gives the control lines for running the analysis on SPSSX MANOVA, along with the data. It may be quite helpful for the reader to compare the control lines for this example with those for the one between and two within example in Table 13.12, as they are quite similar. The main difference here is that there is an additional between variable, hence an additional factor after the keyword BY in the MANOVA command and 3 between effects in the DESIGN subcommand. The reader is referred to Bock for an interpretation of the results.

13.12   PLANNED COMPARISONS IN REPEATED MEASURES DESIGNS

Planned comparisons can also be easily setup on SPSSX MANOVA for repeated measures designs, although the WSFACTOR (within subject factor) subcommand must be included to indicate that the contrasts are being done on a repeated measures variable. To illustrate, we consider the setup of Helmert contrasts on a single group repeated measures design with data again from Bock (1975). The study involves the effect of 3 drugs on the duration of sleep of 10 mental patients. The drugs were given orally on alternate evenings, and the hours of sleep were compared with an intervening control night. Each of the drugs was tested a number of times with each patient. Thus, there are 4 levels for treatment, the control condition and the 3 drugs. The first drug (level 2) was of a different type from the remaining two, which were of a similar type. Therefore, Helmert contrasts were appropriate. The control lines for running the contrasts, along with the significance tests for the contrasts, are given in Table 13.23.

13.13   MULTIVARIATE REPEATED MEASURES ANALYSIS AND OTHER DESIGNS

Multivariate repeated measures analysis comprises a class of situations where a group(s) of subjects have been measured on several qualitatively distinct variables at each of several points in time, or for each of several treatments, or under

TABLE 13.22
Control Lines for Two Between and Two Within
Repeated Measures on SPSSX MANOVA

```
TITLE ' TWO BETWEEN(GRADE X I. Q.) & TWO WITHIN(FORM X TIME) REP. MEAS'
DATA LIST FREE/ FD1 FD2 FA1 FA2 GRADE IQ
LIST
BEGIN DATA
```

2.00	1.00	.00	2.00	1.00	1.00
−7.00	−2.00	−2.00	−5.00	1.00	1.00
−3.00	−1.00	−3.00	−1.00	1.00	1.00
1.00	1.00	.00	−3.00	1.00	1.00
1.00	−1.00	−4.00	−2.00	1.00	1.00
−7.00	1.00	−4.00	−3.00	1.00	1.00
.00	−4.00	−9.00	−7.00	1.00	2.00
−1.00	−9.00	−9.00	−4.00	1.00	2.00
−6.00	−6.00	3.00	−4.00	1.00	2.00
−2.00	−4.00	−4.00	−5.00	1.00	2.00
−2.00	−1.00	−3.00	−3.00	1.00	2.00
−9.00	−9.00	−3.00	1.00	1.00	2.00
3.00	4.00	2.00	−3.00	2.00	1.00
−1.00	−1.00	−3.00	−3.00	2.00	1.00
2.00	2.00	2.00	.00	2.00	1.00
2.00	.00	−2.00	.00	2.00	1.00
.00	−1.00	2.00	2.00	2.00	1.00
3.00	3.00	−4.00	−2.00	2.00	1.00
−1.00	2.00	2.00	−1.00	2.00	1.00
−3.00	−2.00	3.00	−2.00	2.00	1.00
−3.00	−2.00	5.00	2.00	2.00	2.00
2.00	3.00	−2.00	−3.00	2.00	2.00
2.00	4.00	1.00	3.00	2.00	2.00
3.00	2.00	−5.00	−5.00	2.00	2.00
−4.00	−3.00	−3.00	−3.00	2.00	2.00
6.00	4.00	−9.00	−9.00	2.00	2.00
2.00	1.00	−3.00	.00	2.00	2.00
−1.00	−4.00	−2.00	.00	2.00	2.00
−2.00	−1.00	2.00	−2.00	2.00	2.00
−2.00	−4.00	−1.00	.00	2.00	2.00

```
END DATA
```
① `MANOVA FD1 TO FA2 BY GRADE(1,2) IQ(1,2)`
    `WSFACTOR=FORM(2), TIME(2)`
② `WSDESIGN=FORM,TIME,FORM BY TIME`
    `PRINT=TRANSFORM CELLINFO(MEANS) HOMOGENEITY(BOXM)`
    `ERROR(COR) SIGNIF(AVERF)`
② `DESIGN=GRADE, IQ,GRADE BY IQ`

①Below we give the experimental design schematically:

	FORM	FD		FA	
	Time	1	2	1	2
GRADE 4	HI IQ				
	LOW IQ				
GRADE 7	HI IQ				
	LOW IQ				

②Again, as for the examples in Tables 13.8 and 13.12, there is a within S's design subcommand for the repeated measures factors, and a separate DESIGN subcommand for the between (grouping) factors. If we assume a full factorial model, as would be true in exploratory research, then these subcommands can be abbreviated to WSDESIGN/ and DESIGN/.

TABLE 13.23
Control Lines for Helmert Contrasts in a Single Group Repeated
Measures Design and Tests of Significance

```
        TITLE ' HELMERT CONTRASTS FOR REPEATED MEASURES '
        DATA LIST FREE/ Y1 Y2 Y3 Y4
        LIST
        BEGIN DATA
         .60    1.30    2.50    2.10
        3.00    1.40    3.80    4.40
        4.70    4.50    5.80    4.70
        5.50    4.30    5.60    4.80
        6.20    6.10    6.10    6.70
        3.20    6.60    7.60    8.30
        2.50    6.20    8.00    8.20
        2.80    3.60    4.40    4.30
        1.10    1.10    5.70    5.80
        2.90    4.90    6.30    6.40

        END DATA
        MANOVA Y1 TO Y4
①      WSFACTOR=DRUGS(4)
        CONTRAST(DRUGS)=HELMERT
②      WSDESIGN=DRUGS
        RENAME=MEAN,HELMERT1,HELMERT2,HELMERT3
③      PRINT=CELLINFO(MEANS) TRANSFORM
        ANALYSIS(REPEATED)
```

ORTHONORMALIZED TRANSFORMATION MATRIX (TRANSPOSED)

	1	2	3	4
1	.50000	.86603	.00000	.00000
2	.50000	−.28868	.81650	.00000
3	.50000	−.28868	−.40825	.70711
4	.50000	−.28868	−.40825	−.70711

UNIVARIATE F-TESTS WITH (1,9) D. F.

VARIABLE	HYPOTH. SS	HYPOTH. MS	ERROR MS	F	SIG. OF F
HELMERT1	24.29999	24.29999	2.76889	8.77608	.016
HELMERT2	16.53750	16.53750	1.08639	15.22245	④ .004
HELMERT3	.00050	.00050	.18272	.00274	.959

①②Recall that the WSFACTOR (within subjects factor) and WSDESIGN (within subjects design) subcommands must be included to indicate a repeated measures design; compare Table 13.2.

③We rename the variates being tested for significance for ease of reading of the output.

④These results indicate that the first two Helmert contrasts, defined by columns 2 and 3 in the transformation matrix above, are significant at the .05 level.

several different conditions. This is a quite complex situation, although not an unusual one in practice, and is rarely discussed in applied statistics texts. Bock (1975, pp 505–505) discusses it briefly, and Barcikowski (1983) has a detailed computer example for both SPSSX and for the BMDP package (i.e., BMDP4V). Although we considered a variety of the most commonly used repeated measures designs, there are other designs (e.g., nested and Latin squares) that arise occasionally. These are covered thoroughly by Myers (1979).

There are two important additional points to be made regarding planned comparisons with repeated measures designs. First, SPSSX MANOVA requires that the comparisons (contrasts) are orthogonal for within subjects factors. If a non-orthogonal set of contrasts is input, then MANOVA will orthogonalize them (*SPSSX User's Guide*, 2nd Ed., 1986, p. 517).

Secondly, it is very important that separate error terms are used for testing each of the planned comparisons for significance. Boik (1981) has shown that for even a very slight deviation from sphericity ($\epsilon = .90$) that use of a pooled error term can result in a type I error rate quite different from what one has set (level of significance). For $\epsilon = .90$ Boik showed, if testing at $\alpha = .05$, that the actual α for single degree of freedom contrasts ranged from .012 to .097. In some cases the pooled error term will underestimate the amount of error while for other contrasts the error will be overestimated, resulting in a conservative test. Fortunately, in SPSSX MANOVA the error terms are separate errors terms for the contrasts (cf Table 13.23). As O'Brien and Kaiser (1985, p. 319) note, "The MANOVA approach handles sets of contrasts in such a way that each contrast in the set remains linked with just its specific error term. As a result, we avoid all problems associated with general(average) error terms."

13.14 SUMMARY OF MAJOR POINTS FOR REPEATED MEASURES ANALYSIS

1. Repeated measures designs are much more powerful than completely randomized designs, since the variability due to individual differences is removed from the error term, and individual differences are the major reason for error variance.

2. Two major advantages of repeated measures designs are increased precision (because of the smaller error term), and the fact that many less subjects are needed than in a completely randomized design. Two potential disadvantages are that the order of treatments may make a difference (this can be dealt with by counterbalancing) and carryover effects.

3. Either a univariate or a multivariate approach can be used for repeated measures analysis. The assumptions for a single group univariate repeated measures analysis are (1) independence of the observations, (2) multivariate normality and (3) sphericity (also called circularity). For the multivariate approach, the first two assumptions are still needed, but the sphericity assumption is not needed. The sphericity assumption is that the $(k - 1)$ transformed variables are uncorrelated and have equal variances. Although statistical tests of sphericity exist, they are not recommended.

4. Under a violation of sphericity the type I error rate for the univariate approach is inflated. However, a modified univariate approach (obtained by

multiplying each of the degrees of freedom by ê) yields an honest type I error rate.

5.   As both the modified univariate approach and the multivariate approach control the Type I error rate, the choice between them involves the issue of power of the tests. Since neither the modified univariate test or the multivariate is usually most powerful, it is recommended that both tests be used, since they may differ in the treatments effects they will discern.

6.   If the sphericity assumption is tenable, then the Tukey procedure is a good post hoc technique to use for locating pairwise differences. If the sphericity assumption is not met, then the Bonferroni approach should be used. That is, do multiple correlated t tests, but use the Bonferroni inequality to keep the overall α level under control.

7.   When several groups are involved, then an additional assumption is homogeneity of the covariance matrices for the groups. This can be checked with the Box test, and would be of most concern when the group sizes are sharply unequal, as was true in MANOVA.

8.   In profile analysis we are comparing two or more groups of subjects on a battery of tests. It is assumed that the tests are scaled similarly. If they are not, then the scores should first be converted to some type of standard score (z, T) before proceeding with the profile analysis. Nonparallel profiles means there is a group by variable interaction. That is, how much better one group does than another depends on the variable.

APPENDIX
DATA FOR MULTIVARIATE MATCHED PAIRS
ANALYSIS

Pair	Reading	Language	Mathematics
1	62, 67	72, 66	67, 35
2	95, 87	99, 96	82, 82
3	66, 66	96, 87	74, 63
4	87, 91	87, 82	98, 85
5	70, 74	69, 73	85, 63
6	96, 99	96, 76	74, 61
7	85, 99	99, 71	91, 60
8	54, 60	69, 80	66, 71
9	82, 83	69, 99	63, 66
10	69, 60	87, 80	69, 71
11	55, 61	52, 74	55, 67
12	87, 87	88, 99	95, 82
13	91, 99	99, 99	99, 87
14	78, 72	66, 76	52, 74
15	78, 62	79, 69	54, 65
16	72, 58	74, 69	59, 58
17	85, 99	99, 75	66, 61

RAW DATA FOR HUSBAND AND WIFE PROFILE ANALYSIS

	SPOUSE	PASSYOU	PASSPART	COMPYOU	COMPPART
	1.00	2.00	3.00	5.00	5.00
	1.00	5.00	5.00	4.00	4.00
	1.00	4.00	5.00	5.00	5.00
	1.00	4.00	3.00	4.00	4.00
	1.00	3.00	3.00	5.00	5.00
	1.00	3.00	3.00	4.00	5.00
	1.00	3.00	4.00	4.00	4.00
	1.00	4.00	4.00	5.00	5.00
	1.00	4.00	5.00	5.00	5.00
	1.00	4.00	4.00	3.00	3.00
	1.00	4.00	4.00	5.00	5.00
	1.00	5.00	5.00	4.00	4.00
	1.00	4.00	4.00	4.00	4.00
	1.00	4.00	3.00	5.00	5.00
Husbands	1.00	4.00	4.00	5.00	5.00
	1.00	3.00	3.00	4.00	5.00
	1.00	4.00	5.00	4.00	4.00
	1.00	5.00	5.00	5.00	5.00
	1.00	5.00	5.00	4.00	4.00
	1.00	4.00	4.00	4.00	4.00
	1.00	4.00	4.00	4.00	4.00
	1.00	4.00	4.00	4.00	4.00
	1.00	3.00	4.00	5.00	5.00
	1.00	5.00	3.00	5.00	5.00
	1.00	5.00	5.00	3.00	3.00
	1.00	3.00	3.00	4.00	4.00
	1.00	4.00	4.00	4.00	4.00
	1.00	3.00	3.00	5.00	5.00
	1.00	4.00	4.00	3.00	3.00
	1.00	4.00	4.00	5.00	5.00
	2.00	4.00	4.00	5.00	5.00
	2.00	4.00	5.00	5.00	5.00
	2.00	4.00	5.00	5.00	5.00
	2.00	4.00	5.00	5.00	5.00
	2.00	4.00	4.00	5.00	5.00
	2.00	3.00	3.00	4.00	4.00
	2.00	4.00	3.00	5.00	4.00
	2.00	3.00	4.00	5.00	5.00
	2.00	4.00	4.00	5.00	4.00
	2.00	3.00	4.00	4.00	4.00
	2.00	4.00	5.00	5.00	5.00
	2.00	5.00	5.00	5.00	5.00
Wives	2.00	4.00	4.00	5.00	5.00
	2.00	4.00	4.00	4.00	4.00
	2.00	4.00	4.00	5.00	5.00
	2.00	3.00	4.00	4.00	4.00
	2.00	5.00	5.00	5.00	5.00
	2.00	4.00	5.00	4.00	4.00
	2.00	3.00	4.00	4.00	4.00
	2.00	5.00	3.00	4.00	4.00
	2.00	5.00	3.00	4.00	4.00
	2.00	4.00	5.00	4.00	4.00
	2.00	2.00	5.00	5.00	5.00
	2.00	3.00	4.00	5.00	5.00
	2.00	4.00	3.00	5.00	5.00
	2.00	4.00	4.00	4.00	4.00
	2.00	4.00	4.00	5.00	5.00
	2.00	3.00	4.00	4.00	4.00
	2.00	4.00	4.00	5.00	4.00
	2.00	4.00	4.00	5.00	5.00

EXERCISES—REPEATED MEASURES

1. In the multivariate analysis of the drug data we stated that $H_0 : \mu_1 = \mu_2 = \mu_3 = \mu_4$ is equivalent to saying that $\mu_1 - \mu_2 = 0$ and $\mu_2 - \mu_3 = 0$ and $\mu_3 - \mu_4 = 0$. Show this is true.

2. Consider the following data set from a single sample repeated measures design with three repeated measures:

	Treatments		
S's	1	2	3
1	5	6	1
2	3	4	2
3	3	7	1
4	6	8	3
5	6	9	3
6	4	7	2
7	5	9	2

a) Do a univariate repeated measures analysis, using the procedure employed in the text. Do you reject at the .05 level?

b) Do a multivariate repeated measures analysis by hand (i.e., using a calculator) with the following difference variables: $y_1 - y_2$ and $y_2 - y_3$.

c) Run the data on SPSSX, obtaining both the univariate and multivariate results, to check the answers you obtained in (a) and (b).

d) Note the $(k - 1)$ transformed variables SPSSX uses in testing for the multivariate approach, and yet the same multivariate F is obtained. What point that we mentioned in the text does this illustrate?

e) Assume the sphericity assumption is tenable and employ the Tukey post hoc procedure at the .05 level to determine which pairs of treatments differ.

3. A school psychologist is testing the effectiveness of a stress management approach in reducing the state and trait anxiety for college students. The subjects are pretested and matched on these variables and then randomly assigned within each pair to either the stress management approach or to a control group. The following data are obtained:

	Stress Management		Control	
Pairs	*State*	*Trait*	*State*	*Trait*
1	41	38	46	35
2	48	41	47	50
3	34	33	39	36
4	31	40	28	38
5	26	23	35	19
6	37	31	40	30

| | Stress Management | | Control | |
Pairs	State	Trait	State	Trait
7	44	32	46	45
8	53	47	58	53
9	46	41	47	48
10	34	38	39	39
11	33	39	36	41
12	50	45	54	40

a) Test at the .05 level, using the multivariate matched pairs analysis, whether the stress management approach was successful.

b) Which of the variables are contributing to multivariate significance?

4.   Suppose that in the Elashoff drug example the two groups of subjects had been given the three different doses of two drugs under two different conditions. Then we would have a 1 between and three within design. What modifications in the control lines from Table 13.12 would be necessary to run this analysis?

5.   Show that the covariance for the difference variables $(y_1 - y_2)$ and $(y_3 - y_4)$ in the drug data example is -8.95, and that the covariance for $(y_2 - y_3)$ and $(y_3 - y_4)$ is -19.

6.   The extent of the departure from the sphericity assumption is measured by

$$\hat{\epsilon} = \frac{k^2 (\bar{s}_{ii} - \bar{s})^2}{(k - 1)(\sum\sum s_{ij}^2 - 2k\sum_i \bar{s}_i^2 + k^2 \bar{s}^2)}$$

where

$\bar{s}$ is the mean of all entries in the covariance matrix $\mathbf{S}$

$\bar{s}_{ii}$ is mean of entries on main diagonal of $\mathbf{S}$

$\bar{s}_i$ is mean of all entries in row i of $\mathbf{S}$

s_{ij} is ijth entry of $\mathbf{S}$

Find $\hat{\epsilon}$ for the following two covariance matrices:

(a) $\mathbf{S} = \begin{bmatrix} 76.8 & 53.2 & 29.2 & 69 \\ 53.2 & 42.8 & 15.8 & 47 \\ 29.2 & 15.8 & 14.8 & 27 \\ 69 & 47 & 27 & 64 \end{bmatrix}$ (answer $\hat{\epsilon} = .605$)

(b) $\mathbf{S} = \begin{bmatrix} 4 & 3 & 2 \\ 3 & 5 & 2 \\ 2 & 2 & 6 \end{bmatrix}$ (answer $\hat{\epsilon} = .83$)

From the magnitude of $\hat{\epsilon}$ in the above two cases, would you be concerned in either of above cases?

7. An equivalent way of stating the sphericity condition is to say that the variances of the difference variables for all pairs of treatments are equal. Thus, for three treatments, this would mean that

$$\sigma^2_{y_1-y_2} = \sigma^2_{y_1-y_3} = \sigma^2_{y_2-y_3}$$

where y_1, y_2 and y_3 represent the repeated measures for the three treatments.
The formula expressing the variance of a difference variable in terms of the variances of the original variables and the covariance is:

$$\sigma^2_{y_i-y_j} = \sigma^2_{y_i} + \sigma^2_{y_j} - 2\sigma_{y_iy_j}$$

The above condition for sphericity then implies this is constant for all pairs (i and j) of treatments. Show that if uniformity holds, then sphericity will hold.

8. Twelve subjects were randomly assigned to two treatments. The following recall scores on verbal material after 1, 2, 3, 4, and 5 days were obtained:

			Days		
GPID	Y1	Y2	Y3	Y4	Y5
1.00	26.00	24.00	18.00	11.00	10.00
'1.00	34.00	35.00	29.00	22.00	23.00
1.00	41.00	37.00	25.00	18.00	15.00
1.00	29.00	28.00	22.00	15.00	13.00
1.00	35.00	34.00	27.00	21.00	17.00
1.00	28.00	25.00	16.00	11.00	10.00
2.00	42.00	38.00	26.00	20.00	15.00
2.00	31.00	30.00	21.00	15.00	13.00
2.00	45.00	40.00	33.00	25.00	18.00
2.00	29.00	27.00	17.00	11.00	8.00
2.00	39.00	36.00	26.00	20.00	18.00
2.00	33.00	32.00	22.00	12.00	7.00

Run the trend analysis on SPSSX MANOVA. Is there a significant group effect at the .05 level? Are any of the univariate interactions (linear × group, quadratic × group, etc.) significant at the .05 level? Which of the trends are significant at the .05 level for the days main effect? Which of these trends are most pronounced?

9. Consider the following covariance matrix:

$$
\begin{array}{cc}
& \begin{array}{ccc} y_1 & y_2 & y_3 \end{array} \\
S = \begin{array}{c} y_1 \\ y_2 \\ y_3 \end{array} & \begin{bmatrix} 1.0 & .5 & 1.5 \\ .5 & 3.0 & 2.5 \\ 1.5 & 2.5 & 5.0 \end{bmatrix}
\end{array}
$$

Calculate the variances of the three difference variables: $y_1 - y_2$, $y_1 - y_3$ and $y_2 - y_3$. If the above represented the covariance matrix for a single group repeated measures design, what are the above results telling us concerning the sphericity condition? What do you think $\hat{\epsilon}$ will be equal to in this case?

10. For the multivariate matched pairs example in 13.4 the correlation matrix for the transformed(difference) variables is:

READIFF	LANGDIFF	MATHDIFF
1		
-.1475	1	
-.5220	.4726	1

This matrix is obtained by specifying CORR in the TEST paragraph.
a) Using information in the printout in Table 13.1, along with the above correlation matrix, find the covariance matrix for the difference variables.
b) Find the inverse of the covariance matrix for the difference variables. Incidentally, PROC MATRIX from the SAS package can be conveniently used for this purpose.
c) Using the inverse found in (b), along with appropriate printout given in Table 13.1, show that Hotelling's T^2 is indeed 3.125 as shown on the printout.
d) How was the $F = .9115$ given in Table 13.1 obtained?

11. Some marketing researchers are conducting a study to evaluate both consumer beliefs and the stability of those beliefs about the following 4 brands of toothpaste: Crest, Colgate, Ultra Brite, and Gleem. The beliefs to be assessed are (1) good taste, (2) cavity prevention, and (3) breath protection. They also wish to determine the extent to which the beliefs are moderated by sex and by age (20–35, 36–50, and 51 and up). The subjects will be asked their beliefs at two points in time separated by a two month interval.
a) Set up schematically the appropriate repeated measures design.
b) Show the control lines necessary for running this design on SPSSX MAN-OVA in order to obtain both the univariate and multivariate tests.

12. Consider the following two data sets for 10 subjects on three repeated measures.

	DATA SET 1			DATA SET 2		
1	49	53	91	52	50	71
2	53	49	111	56	46	91
3	63	65	65	66	62	45
4	37	33	35	40	30	15
5	39	39	59	42	36	39
6	43	51	87	46	48	67
7	43	47	25	46	44	5
8	49	45	47	52	42	27
9	65	65	105	68	62	85
10	59	53	75	62	50	55

a) Run data set 1 on BMDP4V. Is the adjusted univariate test significant at the .05 level? Is the multivariate test significant at the .05 level? Relate these results to what was discussed in the chapter.

b) Run data set 2 on BMDP4V. Is the adjusted univariate test significant at the .05 level? Is the multivariate test significant at the .05 level? Relate these results to what was discussed in the chapter.

APPENDIX:
Statistical Tables

TABLE A
Percentile Points for χ^2 Distribution

Probability

df	.99	.98	.95	.90	.80	.70	.50	.30	.20	.10	.05	.02	.01	.001
1	.03157	.03628	.00393	.0158	.0642	.148	.455	1.074	1.642	2.706	3.841	5.412	6.635	10.827
2	.0201	.0404	.103	.211	.446	.713	1.386	2.408	3.219	4.605	5.991	7.824	9.210	13.815
3	.115	.185	.352	.584	1.005	1.424	2.366	3.665	4.642	6.251	7.815	9.837	11.345	16.268
4	.297	.429	.711	1.064	1.649	2.195	3.357	4.878	5.989	7.779	9.488	11.668	13.277	18.465
5	.554	.752	1.145	1.610	2.343	3.000	4.351	6.064	7.289	9.236	11.070	13.388	15.086	20.517
6	.872	1.134	1.635	2.204	3.070	3.828	5.348	7.231	8.558	10.645	12.592	15.033	16.812	22.457
7	1.239	1.564	2.167	2.833	3.822	4.671	6.346	8.383	9.803	12.017	14.067	16.622	18.475	24.322
8	1.646	2.032	2.733	3.490	4.594	5.527	7.344	9.524	11.030	13.362	15.507	18.168	20.090	26.125
9	2.088	2.532	3.325	4.168	5.380	6.393	8.343	10.656	12.242	14.684	16.919	19.679	21.666	27.877
10	2.558	3.059	3.940	4.865	6.179	7.267	9.342	11.781	13.442	15.987	18.307	21.161	23.209	29.588
11	3.053	3.609	4.575	5.578	6.989	8.148	10.341	12.899	14.631	17.275	19.675	22.618	24.725	31.264
12	3.571	4.178	5.226	6.304	7.807	9.034	11.340	14.011	15.812	18.549	21.026	24.054	26.217	32.909
13	4.107	4.765	5.892	7.042	8.634	9.926	12.340	15.119	16.985	19.812	22.362	25.472	27.688	34.528
14	4.660	5.368	6.571	7.790	9.467	10.821	13.339	16.222	18.151	21.064	23.685	26.873	29.141	36.123
15	5.229	5.985	7.261	8.547	10.307	11.721	14.339	17.322	19.311	22.307	24.996	28.259	30.578	37.697
16	5.812	6.614	7.962	9.312	11.152	12.624	15.338	18.418	20.465	23.542	26.296	29.633	32.000	39.252
17	6.408	7.255	8.672	10.085	12.002	13.531	16.338	19.511	21.615	24.769	27.587	30.995	33.409	40.790
18	7.015	7.906	9.390	10.865	12.857	14.440	17.338	20.601	22.760	25.989	28.869	32.346	34.805	42.312
19	7.633	8.567	10.117	11.651	13.716	15.352	18.338	21.689	23.900	27.204	30.144	33.687	36.191	43.820
20	8.260	9.237	10.851	12.443	14.578	16.266	19.337	22.775	25.038	28.412	31.410	35.020	37.566	45.315

21	8.897	9.915	11.591	13.240	15.445	17.182	20.337	23.858	26.171	29.615	32.671	36.343	38.932	46.797
22	9.542	10.600	12.338	13.041	16.314	18.101	21.337	24.939	27.301	30.813	33.924	37.659	40.289	48.268
23	10.196	11.293	13.091	14.848	17.187	19.021	22.337	26.018	28.429	32.007	35.172	38.968	41.638	49.728
24	10.856	11.992	13.848	15.659	18.062	19.943	23.337	27.096	29.553	33.196	36.415	40.270	42.980	51.179
25	11.524	12.697	14.611	16.473	18.940	20.867	24.337	28.172	30.675	34.382	37.652	41.566	44.314	52.620
26	12.198	13.409	15.379	17.292	19.820	21.792	25.336	29.246	31.795	35.563	38.885	42.856	45.642	54.052
27	12.879	14.125	16.151	18.114	20.703	22.719	26.336	30.319	32.912	36.741	40.113	44.140	46.963	55.476
28	13.565	14.847	16.928	18.939	21.588	23.647	27.336	31.391	34.027	37.916	41.337	45.419	48.278	56.893
29	14.256	15.574	17.708	19.768	22.475	24.577	28.336	32.461	35.139	39.087	42.557	46.693	49.588	58.302
30	14.953	16.306	18.493	20.599	23.364	25.508	29.336	33.530	36.250	40.256	43.773	47.962	50.892	59.703

Note: For larger values of *df*, the expression $\sqrt{2\chi^2} - \sqrt{2df - 1}$ may be used as a normal deviate with unit variance, remembering that the probability for χ^2 corresponds with that of a single tail of the normal curve.

Source: Reproduced from E. F. Lindquist, *Design and Analysis of Experiments in Psychology and Education*, Houghton Mifflin, Boston, 1953, p. 29, with the permission of the publisher.

TABLE B
Critical Values for t

	Level of significance for one-tailed test					
	.10	.05	.025	.01	.005	.0005
	Level of significance for two-tailed test					
df	.20	.10	.05	.02	.01	.001
1	3.078	6.314	12.706	31.821	63.657	636.619
2	1.886	2.920	4.303	6.965	9.925	31.598
3	1.638	2.353	3.182	4.541	5.841	12.941
4	1.533	2.132	2.776	3.747	4.604	8.610
5	1.476	2.015	2.571	3.365	4.032	6.859
6	1.440	1.943	2.447	3.143	3.707	5.959
7	1.415	1.895	2.365	2.998	3.449	5.405
8	1.397	1.860	2.306	2.896	3.355	5.041
9	1.383	1.833	2.262	2.821	3.250	4.781
10	1.372	1.812	2.228	2.764	3.169	4.587
11	1.363	1.796	2.201	2.718	3.106	4.437
12	1.356	1.782	2.179	2.681	3.055	4.318
13	1.350	1.771	2.160	2.650	3.012	4.221
14	1.345	1.761	2.145	2.624	2.977	4.140
15	1.341	1.753	2.131	2.602	2.947	4.073
16	1.337	1.746	2.120	2.583	2.921	4.015
17	1.333	1.740	2.110	2.567	2.898	3.965
18	1.330	1.734	2.101	2.552	2.878	3.922
19	1.328	1.729	2.093	2.539	2.861	3.883
20	1.325	1.725	2.086	2.528	2.845	3.850
21	1.323	1.721	2.080	2.518	2.831	3.819
22	1.321	1.717	2.074	2.508	2.819	3.792
23	1.319	1.714	2.069	2.500	2.807	3.767
24	1.318	1.711	2.064	2.492	2.797	3.745
25	1.316	1.708	2.060	2.485	2.787	3.725
26	1.315	1.706	2.056	2.479	2.779	3.707
27	1.314	1.703	2.052	2.473	2.771	3.690
28	1.313	1.701	2.048	2.467	2.763	3.674
29	1.311	1.699	2.045	2.462	2.756	3.659
30	1.310	1.697	2.042	2.457	2.750	3.646
40	1.303	1.684	2.021	2.423	2.704	3.551
60	1.296	1.671	2.000	2.390	2.660	3.460
120	1.289	1.658	1.980	2.358	2.617	3.373
∞	1.282	1.645	1.960	2.326	2.576	3.291

TABLE C
Critical Values for *F*

		df *for Numerator*							
df *error*	α	*1*	*2*	*3*	*4*	*5*	*6*	*8*	*12*
1	.01	4052	4999	5403	5625	5764	5859	5981	6106
	.05	161.45	199.50	215.71	224.58	230.16	233.99	238.88	243.91
	.10	39.86	49.50	53.59	55.83	57.24	58.20	59.44	60.70
	.20	9.47	12.00	13.06	13.73	14.01	14.26	14.59	14.90
2	.01	98.49	99.00	99.17	99.25	99.30	99.33	99.36	99.42
	.05	18.51	19.00	19.16	19.25	19.30	19.33	19.37	19.41
	.10	8.53	9.00	9.16	9.24	9.29	9.33	9.37	9.41
	.20	3.56	4.00	4.16	4.24	4.28	4.32	4.36	4.40
3	.001	167.5	148.5	141.1	137.1	134.6	132.8	130.6	128.3
	.01	34.12	30.81	29.46	28.71	28.24	27.91	27.49	27.05
	.05	10.13	9.55	9.28	9.12	9.01	8.94	8.84	8.74
	.10	5.54	5.46	5.39	5.34	5.31	5.28	5.25	5.22
	.20	2.68	2.89	2.94	2.96	2.97	2.97	2.98	2.98
4	.001	74.14	61.25	56.18	53.44	51.71	50.53	49.00	47.41
	.01	21.20	18.00	16.69	15.98	15.52	15.21	14.80	14.37
	.05	7.71	6.94	6.59	6.39	6.26	6.16	6.04	5.91
	.10	4.54	4.32	4.19	4.11	4.05	4.01	3.95	3.90
	.20	2.35	2.47	2.48	2.48	2.48	2.47	2.47	2.46
5	.001	47.04	36.61	33.20	31.09	29.75	28.84	27.64	26.42
	.01	16.26	13.27	12.06	11.39	10.97	10.67	10.29	9.89
	.05	6.61	5.79	5.41	5.19	5.05	4.95	4.82	4.68
	.10	4.06	3.78	3.62	3.52	3.45	3.40	3.34	3.27
	.20	2.18	2.26	2.25	2.24	2.23	2.22	2.20	2.18
6	.001	35.51	27.00	23.70	21.90	20.81	20.03	19.03	17.99
	.01	13.74	10.92	9.78	9.15	8.75	8.47	8.10	7.72
	.05	5.99	5.14	4.76	4.53	4.39	4.28	4.15	4.00
	.10	3.78	3.46	3.29	3.18	3.11	3.05	2.98	2.90
	.20	2.07	2.13	2.11	2.09	2.08	2.06	2.04	2.02
7	.001	29.22	21.69	18.77	17.19	16.21	15.52	14.63	13.71
	.01	12.25	9.55	8.45	7.85	7.46	7.19	6.84	6.47
	.05	5.59	4.74	4.35	4.12	3.97	3.87	3.73	3.57
	.10	3.59	3.26	3.07	2.96	2.88	2.83	2.75	2.67
	.20	2.00	2.04	2.02	1.99	1.97	1.96	1.93	1.91
8	.001	25.42	18.49	15.83	14.39	13.49	12.86	12.04	11.19
	.01	11.26	8.65	7.59	7.01	6.63	6.37	6.03	5.67
	.05	5.32	4.46	4.07	3.84	3.69	3.58	3.44	3.28
	.10	3.46	3.11	2.92	2.81	2.73	2.67	2.59	2.50
	.20	1.95	1.98	1.95	1.92	1.90	1.88	1.86	1.83
9	.001	22.86	16.39	13.90	12.56	11.71	11.13	10.37	9.57
	.01	10.56	8.02	6.99	6.42	6.06	5.80	5.47	5.11
	.05	5.12	4.26	3.86	3.63	3.48	3.37	3.23	3.07
	.10	3.36	3.01	2.81	2.69	2.61	2.55	2.47	2.38
	.20	1.91	1.94	1.90	1.87	1.85	1.83	1.80	1.76

(cont.)

TABLE C (*Continued*)

		df *for Numerator*							
df *error*	α	*1*	*2*	*3*	*4*	*5*	*6*	*8*	*12*
10	.001	21.04	14.91	12.55	11.28	10.48	9.92	9.20	8.45
	.01	10.04	7.56	6.55	5.99	5.64	5.39	5.06	4.71
	.05	4.96	4.10	3.71	3.48	3.33	3.22	3.07	2.91
	.10	3.28	2.92	2.73	2.61	2.52	2.46	2.38	2.28
	.20	1.88	1.90	1.86	1.83	1.80	1.78	1.75	1.72
11	.001	19.69	13.81	11.56	10.35	9.58	9.05	8.35	7.63
	.01	9.65	7.20	6.22	5.67	5.32	5.07	4.74	4.40
	.05	4.84	3.98	3.59	3.36	3.20	3.09	2.95	2.79
	.10	3.23	2.86	2.66	2.54	2.45	2.39	2.30	2.21
	.20	1.86	1.87	1.83	1.80	1.77	1.75	1.72	1.68
12	.001	18.64	12.97	10.80	9.63	8.89	8.38	7.71	7.00
	.01	9.33	6.93	5.95	5.41	5.06	4.82	4.50	4.16
	.05	4.75	3.88	3.49	3.26	3.11	3.00	2.85	2.69
	.10	3.18	2.81	2.61	2.48	2.39	2.33	2.24	2.15
	.20	1.84	1.85	1.80	1.77	1.74	1.72	1.69	1.65
13	.001	17.81	12.31	10.21	9.07	8.35	7.86	7.21	6.52
	.01	9.07	6.70	5.74	5.20	4.86	4.62	4.30	3.96
	.05	4.67	3.80	3.41	3.18	3.02	2.92	2.77	2.60
	.10	3.14	2.76	2.56	2.43	2.35	2.28	2.20	2.10
	.20	1.82	1.83	1.78	1.75	1.72	1.69	1.66	1.62
14	.001	17.14	11.78	9.73	8.62	7.92	7.43	6.80	6.13
	.01	8.86	6.51	5.56	5.03	4.69	4.46	4.14	3.80
	.05	4.60	3.74	3.34	3.11	2.96	2.85	2.70	2.53
	.10	3.10	2.73	2.52	2.39	2.31	2.24	2.15	2.05
	.20	1.81	1.81	1.76	1.73	1.70	1.67	1.64	1.60
15	.001	16.59	11.34	9.34	8.25	7.57	7.09	6.47	5.81
	.01	8.68	6.36	5.42	4.89	4.56	4.32	4.00	3.67
	.05	4.54	3.68	3.29	3.06	2.90	2.79	2.64	2.48
	.10	3.07	2.70	2.49	2.36	2.27	2.21	2.12	2.02
	.20	1.80	1.79	1.75	1.71	1.68	1.66	1.62	1.58
16	.001	16.12	10.97	9.00	7.94	7.27	6.81	6.19	5.55
	.01	8.53	6.23	5.29	4.77	4.44	4.20	3.89	3.55
	.05	4.49	3.63	3.24	3.01	2.85	2.74	2.59	2.42
	.10	3.05	2.67	2.46	2.33	2.24	2.18	2.09	1.99
	.20	1.79	1.78	1.74	1.70	1.67	1.64	1.61	1.56
17	.001	15.72	10.66	8.73	7.68	7.02	6.56	5.96	5.32
	.01	8.40	6.11	5.18	4.67	4.34	4.10	3.79	3.45
	.05	4.45	3.59	3.20	2.96	2.81	2.70	2.55	2.38
	.10	3.03	2.64	2.44	2.31	2.22	2.15	2.06	1.96
	.20	1.78	1.77	1.72	1.68	1.65	1.63	1.59	1.55
18	.001	15.38	10.39	8.49	7.46	6.81	6.35	5.76	5.13
	.01	8.28	6.01	5.09	4.58	4.25	4.01	3.71	3.37
	.05	4.41	3.55	3.16	2.93	2.77	2.66	2.51	2.34
	.10	3.01	2.62	2.42	2.29	2.20	2.13	2.04	1.93
	.20	1.77	1.76	1.71	1.67	1.64	1.62	1.58	1.53

TABLE C (*Continued*)

df *error*	α	\multicolumn{8}{c}{df *for Numerator*}
		1	2	3	4	5	6	8	12
19	.001	15.08	10.16	8.28	7.26	6.61	6.18	5.59	4.97
	.01	8.18	5.93	5.01	4.50	4.17	3.94	3.63	3.30
	.05	4.38	3.52	3.13	2.90	2.74	2.63	2.48	2.31
	.10	2.99	2.61	2.40	2.27	2.18	2.11	2.02	1.91
	.20	1.76	1.75	1.70	1.66	1.63	1.61	1.57	1.52
20	.001	14.82	9.95	8.10	7.10	6.46	6.02	5.44	4.82
	.01	8.10	5.85	4.94	4.43	4.10	3.87	3.56	3.23
	.05	4.35	3.49	3.10	2.87	2.71	2.60	2.45	2.28
	.10	2.97	2.59	2.38	2.25	2.16	2.09	2.00	1.89
	.20	1.76	1.75	1.70	1.65	1.62	1.60	1.56	1.51
21	.001	14.59	9.77	7.94	6.95	6.32	5.88	5.31	4.70
	.01	8.02	5.78	4.87	4.37	4.04	3.81	3.51	3.17
	.05	4.32	3.47	3.07	2.84	2.68	2.57	2.42	2.25
	.10	2.96	2.57	2.36	2.23	2.14	2.08	1.98	1.88
	.20	1.75	1.74	1.69	1.65	1.61	1.59	1.55	1.50
22	.001	14.38	9.61	7.80	6.81	6.19	5.76	5.19	4.58
	.01	7.94	5.72	4.82	4.31	3.99	3.76	3.45	3.12
	.05	4.30	3.44	3.05	2.82	2.66	2.55	2.40	2.23
	.10	2.95	2.56	2.35	2.22	2.13	2.06	1.97	1.86
	.20	1.75	1.73	1.68	1.64	1.61	1.58	1.54	1.49
23	.001	14.19	9.47	7.67	6.69	6.08	5.65	5.09	4.48
	.01	7.88	5.66	4.76	4.26	3.94	3.71	3.41	3.07
	.05	4.28	3.42	3.03	2.80	2.64	2.53	2.38	2.20
	.10	2.94	2.55	2.34	2.21	2.11	2.05	1.95	1.84
	.20	1.74	1.73	1.68	1.63	1.60	1.57	1.53	1.49
24	.001	14.03	9.34	7.55	6.59	5.98	5.55	4.99	4.39
	.01	7.82	5.61	4.72	4.22	3.90	3.67	3.36	3.03
	.05	4.26	3.40	3.01	2.78	2.62	2.51	2.36	2.18
	.10	2.93	2.54	2.33	2.19	2.10	2.04	1.94	1.83
	.20	1.74	1.72	1.67	1.63	1.59	1.57	1.53	1.48
25	.001	13.88	9.22	7.45	6.49	5.88	5.46	4.91	4.31
	.01	7.77	5.57	4.68	4.18	3.86	3.63	3.32	2.99
	.05	4.24	3.38	2.99	2.76	2.60	2.49	2.34	2.16
	.10	2.92	2.53	2.32	2.18	2.09	2.02	1.93	1.82
	.20	1.73	1.72	1.66	1.62	1.59	1.56	1.52	1.47
26	.001	13.74	9.12	7.36	6.41	5.80	5.38	4.83	4.24
	.01	7.72	5.53	4.64	4.14	3.82	3.59	3.29	2.96
	.05	4.22	3.37	2.98	2.74	2.59	2.47	2.32	2.15
	.10	2.91	2.52	2.31	2.17	2.08	2.01	1.92	1.81
	.20	1.73	1.71	1.66	1.62	1.58	1.56	1.52	1.47
27	.001	13.61	9.02	7.27	6.33	5.73	5.31	4.76	4.17
	.01	7.68	5.49	4.60	4.11	3.78	3.56	3.26	2.93
	.05	4.21	3.35	2.96	2.73	2.57	2.46	2.30	2.13
	.10	2.90	2.51	2.30	2.17	2.07	2.00	1.91	1.80
	.20	1.73	1.71	1.66	1.61	1.58	1.55	1.51	1.46

(*cont.*)

TABLE C (Continued)

df error	α	1	2	3	4	5	6	8	12
				df *for Numerator*					
28	.001	13.50	8.93	7.19	6.25	5.66	5.24	4.69	4.11
	.01	7.64	5.45	4.57	4.07	3.75	3.53	3.23	2.90
	.05	4.20	3.34	2.95	2.71	2.56	2.44	2.29	2.12
	.10	2.89	2.50	2.29	2.16	2.06	2.00	1.90	1.79
	.20	1.72	1.71	1.65	1.61	1.57	1.55	1.51	1.46
29	.001	13.39	8.85	7.12	6.19	5.59	5.18	4.64	4.05
	.01	7.60	5.42	4.54	4.04	3.73	3.50	3.20	2.87
	.05	4.18	3.33	2.93	2.70	2.54	2.43	2.28	2.10
	.10	2.89	2.50	2.28	2.15	2.06	1.99	1.89	1.78
	.20	1.72	1.70	1.65	1.60	1.57	1.54	1.50	1.45
30	.001	13.29	8.77	7.05	6.12	5.53	5.12	4.58	4.00
	.01	7.56	5.39	4.51	4.02	3.70	3.47	3.17	2.84
	.05	4.17	3.32	2.92	2.69	2.53	2.42	2.27	2.09
	.10	2.88	2.49	2.28	2.14	2.05	1.98	1.88	1.77
	.20	1.72	1.70	1.64	1.60	1.57	1.54	1.50	1.45
40	.001	12.61	8.25	6.60	5.70	5.13	4.73	4.21	3.64
	.01	7.31	5.18	4.31	3.83	3.51	3.29	2.99	2.66
	.05	4.08	3.23	2.84	2.61	2.45	2.34	2.18	2.00
	.10	2.84	2.44	2.23	2.09	2.00	1.93	1.83	1.71
	.20	1.70	1.68	1.62	1.57	1.54	1.51	1.47	1.41
60	.001	11.97	7.76	6.17	5.31	4.76	4.37	3.87	3.31
	.01	7.08	4.98	4.13	3.65	3.34	3.12	2.82	2.50
	.05	4.00	3.15	2.76	2.52	2.37	2.25	2.10	1.92
	.10	2.79	2.39	2.18	2.04	1.95	1.87	1.77	1.66
	.20	1.68	1.65	1.59	1.55	1.51	1.48	1.44	1.38
120	.001	11.38	7.31	5.79	4.95	4.42	4.04	3.55	3.02
	.01	6.85	4.79	3.95	3.48	3.17	2.96	2.66	2.34
	.05	3.92	3.07	2.68	2.45	2.29	2.17	2.02	1.83
	.10	2.75	2.35	2.13	1.99	1.90	1.82	1.72	1.60
	.20	1.66	1.63	1.57	1.52	1.48	1.45	1.41	1.35
∞	.001	10.83	6.91	5.42	4.62	4.10	3.74	3.27	2.74
	.01	6.64	4.60	3.78	3.32	3.02	2.80	2.51	2.18
	.05	3.84	2.99	2.60	2.37	2.21	2.09	1.94	1.75
	.10	2.71	2.30	2.08	1.94	1.85	1.77	1.67	1.55
	.20	1.64	1.61	1.55	1.50	1.46	1.43	1.38	1.32

Source: Reproduced from E. F. Lindquist, *Design and Analysis of Experiments in Psychology and Education,* Houghton Mifflin, Boston, 1953, pp. 41–44, with the permission of the publisher.

TABLE D
Percentile Points of Studentized Range Statistic

90th Percentiles

number of groups

df error	2	3	4	5	6	7	8	9	10
1	8.929	13.44	16.36	18.49	20.15	21.51	22.64	23.62	24.48
2	4.130	5.733	6.773	7.538	8.139	8.633	9.049	9.409	9.725
3	3.328	4.467	5.199	5.738	6.162	6.511	6.806	7.062	7.287
4	3.015	3.976	4.586	5.035	5.388	5.679	5.926	6.139	6.327
5	2.850	3.717	4.264	4.664	4.979	5.238	5.458	5.648	5.816
6	2.748	3.559	4.065	4.435	4.726	4.966	5.168	5.344	5.499
7	2.680	3.451	3.931	4.280	4.555	4.780	4.972	5.137	5.283
8	2.630	3.374	3.834	4.169	4.431	4.646	4.829	4.987	5.126
9	2.592	3.316	3.761	4.084	4.337	4.545	4.721	4.873	5.007
10	2.563	3.270	3.704	4.018	4.264	4.465	4.636	4.783	4.913
11	2.540	3.234	3.658	3.965	4.205	4.401	4.568	4.711	4.838
12	2.521	3.204	3.621	3.922	4.156	4.349	4.511	4.652	4.776
13	2.505	3.179	3.589	3.885	4.116	4.305	4.464	4.602	4.724
14	2.491	3.158	3.563	3.854	4.081	4.267	4.424	4.560	4.680
15	2.479	3.140	3.540	3.828	4.052	4.235	4.390	4.524	4.641
16	2.469	3.124	3.520	3.804	4.026	4.207	4.360	4.492	4.608
17	2.460	3.110	3.503	3.784	4.004	4.183	4.334	4.464	4.579
18	2.452	3.098	3.488	3.767	3.984	4.161	4.311	4.440	4.554
19	2.445	3.087	3.474	3.751	3.966	4.142	4.290	4.418	4.531
20	2.439	3.078	3.462	3.736	3.950	4.124	4.271	4.398	4.510
24	2.420	3.047	3.423	3.692	3.900	4.070	4.213	4.336	4.445
30	2.400	3.017	3.386	3.648	3.851	4.016	4.155	4.275	4.381
40	2.381	2.988	3.349	3.605	3.803	3.963	4.099	4.215	4.317
60	2.363	2.959	3.312	3.562	3.755	3.911	4.042	4.155	4.254
120	2.344	2.930	3.276	3.520	3.707	3.859	3.987	4.096	4.191
∞	2.326	2.902	3.240	3.478	3.661	3.808	3.931	4.037	4.129

TABLE D (Continued)

95th Percentiles

df error	number of groups 2	3	4	5	6	7	8	9	10
1	17.97	26.98	32.82	37.08	40.41	43.12	45.40	47.36	49.07
2	6.085	8.331	9.798	10.88	11.74	12.44	13.03	13.54	13.99
3	4.501	5.910	6.825	7.502	8.037	8.478	8.853	9.177	9.462
4	3.927	5.040	5.757	6.287	6.707	7.053	7.347	7.602	7.826
5	3.635	4.602	5.218	5.673	6.033	6.330	6.582	6.802	6.995
6	3.461	4.339	4.896	5.305	5.628	5.895	6.122	6.319	6.493
7	3.344	4.165	4.681	5.060	5.359	5.606	5.815	5.998	6.158
8	3.261	4.041	4.529	4.886	5.167	5.399	5.597	5.767	5.918
9	3.199	3.949	4.415	4.756	5.024	5.244	5.432	5.595	5.739
10	3.151	3.877	4.327	4.654	4.912	5.124	5.305	5.461	5.599
11	3.113	3.820	4.256	4.574	4.823	5.028	5.202	5.353	5.487
12	3.082	3.773	4.199	4.508	4.751	4.950	5.119	5.265	5.395
13	3.055	3.735	4.151	4.453	4.690	4.885	5.049	5.192	5.318
14	3.033	3.702	4.111	4.407	4.639	4.829	4.990	5.131	5.254
15	3.014	3.674	4.076	4.367	4.595	4.782	4.940	5.077	5.198
16	2.998	3.649	4.046	4.333	4.557	4.741	4.897	5.031	5.150
17	2.984	3.628	4.020	4.303	4.524	4.705	4.858	4.991	5.108
18	2.971	3.609	3.997	4.277	4.495	4.673	4.824	4.956	5.071
19	2.960	3.593	3.977	4.253	4.469	4.645	4.794	4.924	5.038
20	2.950	3.578	3.958	4.232	4.445	4.620	4.768	4.896	5.008
24	2.919	3.532	3.901	4.166	4.373	4.541	4.684	4.807	4.915
30	2.888	3.486	3.845	4.102	4.302	4.464	4.602	4.720	4.824
40	2.858	3.442	3.791	4.039	4.232	4.389	4.521	4.635	4.735
60	2.829	3.399	3.737	3.977	4.163	4.314	4.441	4.550	4.646
120	2.800	3.356	3.685	3.917	4.096	4.241	4.363	4.468	4.560
∞	2.772	3.314	3.633	3.858	4.030	4.170	4.286	4.387	4.474

(cont.)

TABLE D (*Continued*)

97.5th Percentiles

number of groups

df error	2	3	4	5	6	7	8	9	10
1	35.99	54.00	65.69	74.22	80.87	86.29	90.85	94.77	98.20
2	8.776	11.94	14.01	15.54	16.75	17.74	18.58	19.31	19.95
3	5.907	7.661	8.808	9.660	10.34	10.89	11.37	11.78	12.14
4	4.943	6.244	7.088	7.716	8.213	8.625	8.976	9.279	9.548
5	4.474	5.558	6.257	6.775	7.186	7.527	7.816	8.068	8.291
6	4.199	5.158	5.772	6.226	6.586	6.884	7.138	7.359	7.554
7	4.018	4.897	5.455	5.868	6.194	6.464	6.695	6.895	7.072
8	3.892	4.714	5.233	5.616	5.919	6.169	6.382	6.568	6.732
9	3.797	4.578	5.069	5.430	5.715	5.950	6.151	6.325	6.479
10	3.725	4.474	4.943	5.287	5.558	5.782	5.972	6.138	6.285
11	3.667	4.391	4.843	5.173	5.433	5.648	5.831	5.989	6.130
12	3.620	4.325	4.762	5.081	5.332	5.540	5.716	5.869	6.004
13	3.582	4.269	4.694	5.004	5.248	5.449	5.620	5.769	5.900
14	3.550	4.222	4.638	4.940	5.178	5.374	5.540	5.684	5.811
15	3.522	4.182	4.589	4.885	5.118	5.309	5.471	5.612	5.737
16	3.498	4.148	4.548	4.838	5.066	5.253	5.412	5.550	5.672
17	3.477	4.118	4.512	4.797	5.020	5.204	5.361	5.496	5.615
18	3.458	4.092	4.480	4.761	4.981	5.162	5.315	5.448	5.565
19	3.442	4.068	4.451	4.728	4.945	5.123	5.275	5.405	5.521
20	3.427	4.047	4.426	4.700	4.914	5.089	5.238	5.368	5.481
24	3.381	3.983	4.347	4.610	4.816	4.984	5.126	5.250	5.358
30	3.337	3.919	4.271	4.523	4.720	4.881	5.017	5.134	5.238
40	3.294	3.858	4.197	4.439	4.627	4.780	4.910	5.022	5.120
60	3.251	3.798	4.124	4.356	4.536	4.682	4.806	4.912	5.006
120	3.210	3.739	4.053	4.276	4.447	4.587	4.704	4.805	4.894
∞	3.170	3.682	3.984	4.197	4.361	4.494	4.605	4.700	4.784

TABLE D (Continued)

99th Percentiles

number of groups

df error	2	3	4	5	6	7	8	9	10
1	90.03	135.0	164.3	185.6	202.2	215.8	227.2	237.0	245.6
2	14.04	19.02	22.29	24.72	26.63	28.20	29.53	30.68	31.69
3	8.261	10.62	12.17	13.33	14.24	15.00	15.64	16.20	16.69
4	6.512	8.120	9.173	9.958	10.58	11.10	11.55	11.93	12.27
5	5.702	6.976	7.804	8.421	8.913	9.321	9.669	9.972	10.24
6	5.243	6.331	7.033	7.556	7.973	8.318	8.613	8.869	9.097
7	4.949	5.919	6.543	7.005	7.373	7.679	7.939	8.166	8.368
8	4.746	5.635	6.204	6.625	6.960	7.237	7.474	7.681	7.863
9	4.596	5.428	5.957	6.348	6.658	6.915	7.134	7.325	7.495
10	4.482	5.270	5.769	6.136	6.428	6.669	6.875	7.055	7.213
11	4.392	5.146	5.621	5.970	6.247	6.476	6.672	6.842	6.992
12	4.320	5.046	5.502	5.836	6.101	6.321	6.507	6.670	6.814
13	4.260	4.964	5.404	5.727	5.981	6.192	6.372	6.528	6.667
14	4.210	4.895	5.322	5.634	5.881	6.085	6.258	6.409	6.543
15	4.168	4.836	5.252	5.556	5.796	5.994	6.162	6.309	6.439
16	4.131	4.786	5.192	5.489	5.722	5.915	6.079	6.222	6.349
17	4.099	4.742	5.140	5.430	5.659	5.847	6.007	6.147	6.270
18	4.071	4.703	5.094	5.379	5.603	5.788	5.944	6.081	6.201
19	4.046	4.670	5.054	5.334	5.554	5.735	5.889	6.022	6.141
20	4.024	4.639	5.018	5.294	5.510	5.688	5.839	5.970	6.087
24	3.956	4.546	4.907	5.168	5.374	5.542	5.685	5.809	5.919
30	3.889	4.455	4.799	5.048	5.242	5.401	5.536	5.653	5.756
40	3.825	4.367	4.696	4.931	5.114	5.265	5.392	5.502	5.599
60	3.762	4.282	4.595	4.818	4.991	5.133	5.253	5.356	5.447
120	3.702	4.200	4.497	4.709	4.872	5.005	5.118	5.214	5.299
∞	3.643	4.120	4.403	4.603	4.757	4.882	4.987	5.078	5.157

Reproduced from H. Harter, "Tables of Range and Studentized Range," *Annals of Mathematical Statistics*, 1960. Reprinted with permission.

TABLE E
Sample Size Needed in Three-Group MANOVA for Power = .70, .80
and .90 for α = .05 and α = .01

		Power =	α = .05			α = .01		
			.70	.80	.90	.70	.80	.90
Number of Variables		2	11	13	16	15	17	21
Effect Size		3	12	14	18	17	20	24
	$q^2=1.125$	4	14	16	19	19	22	26
Very Large	$d=1.5$	5	15	17	21	20	23	28
	$c=0.75$	6	16	18	22	22	25	29
		8	18	21	25	24	28	32
		10	20	23	27	27	30	35
		15	24	27	32	32	35	42
Large	$q^2=0.5$	2	21	26	33	31	36	44
	$d=1$	3	25	29	37	35	42	50
	$c=0.5$	4	27	33	42	38	44	54
		5	30	35	44	42	48	58
		6	32	38	48	44	52	62
		8	36	42	52	50	56	68
		10	39	46	56	54	62	74
		15	46	54	66	64	72	84
Moderate	$q^2=0.2813$	2	36	44	58	54	62	76
	$d=0.75$	3	42	52	64	60	70	86
	$c=0.375$	4	46	56	70	66	78	94
		5	50	60	76	72	82	100
		6	54	66	82	76	88	105
		8	60	72	90	84	98	120
		10	66	78	98	92	105	125
		15	78	92	115	110	125	145
Small	$q^2=0.125$	2	80	98	125	115	140	170
	$d=0.5$	3	92	115	145	135	155	190
	$c=0.25$	4	105	125	155	145	170	210
		5	110	135	170	155	185	220
		6	120	145	180	165	195	240
		8	135	160	200	185	220	260
		10	145	175	220	200	230	280
		15	170	210	250	240	270	320

(cont.)

TABLE E (*Continued*)
**Sample Size Needed for Four-Group MANOVA for Power = .70, .80
and .90 at α = .05 and α = .01**

		Power =	α = .05			α = .01		
			.70	.80	.90	.70	.80	.90
Number of Variables		2	12	14	17	17	19	23
Effect Size		3	14	16	20	19	22	26
	$q^2=1.125$	4	15	18	22	21	24	28
Very Large	$d=1.5$	5	16	19	23	23	26	30
	$c=0.4743$							
		6	18	21	25	24	27	32
		8	20	23	28	27	30	36
		10	22	25	30	29	33	39
		15	26	30	36	35	39	46
Large	$q^2=0.5$	2	24	29	37	34	40	50
	$d=1$	3	28	33	42	39	46	56
	$c=0.3162$	4	31	37	46	44	50	60
		5	34	40	50	48	54	64
		6	36	44	54	50	58	70
		8	42	48	60	56	64	76
		10	46	52	64	62	70	82
		15	54	62	76	72	82	96
Moderate	$q^2=0.2813$	2	42	50	64	60	70	86
	$d=0.75$	3	48	58	72	68	80	96
	$c=0.2372$	4	54	64	80	76	88	105
		5	58	70	86	82	94	115
		6	62	74	92	86	100	120
		8	70	84	105	96	115	135
		10	78	92	115	105	120	145
		15	92	110	130	125	145	170
Small	$q^2=0.125$	2	92	115	145	130	155	190
	$d=0.5$	3	105	130	165	150	175	220
	$c=0.1581$	4	120	145	180	165	195	240
		5	130	155	195	180	210	250
		6	140	165	210	190	220	270
		8	155	185	230	220	250	300
		10	170	200	250	240	270	320
		15	200	240	290	280	320	370

(*cont.*)

TABLE E (*Continued*)
Sample Size Needed for Five Group MANOVA for Power = .70, .80 and .90 at α = .05 and α = .01

		Power =	$\alpha = .05$			$\alpha = .01$		
			.70	*.80*	*.90*	*.70*	*.80*	*.90*
Number of Variables		2	13	15	19	18	20	25
Effect Size		3	15	17	21	20	23	28
	$q^2 = 1.125$	4	16	19	23	22	26	30
Very Large	$d = 1.5$	5	18	21	25	24	28	33
	$c = 0.3354$	6	19	22	27	26	30	35
		8	22	25	30	29	33	39
		10	24	27	33	32	36	42
		15	28	33	39	38	44	50
Large	$q^2 = 0.5$	2	26	32	40	37	44	54
	$d = 1$	3	31	37	46	44	50	60
	$c = 0.2236$	4	34	42	50	48	56	66
		5	37	44	54	52	60	70
		6	40	48	58	56	64	76
		8	46	54	66	62	70	84
		10	50	58	72	68	78	90
		15	60	70	84	80	90	110
Moderate	$q^2 = 0.2813$	2	46	56	70	66	76	92
	$d = 0.75$	3	54	64	80	74	86	105
	$c = 0.1677$	4	60	72	88	82	96	115
		5	64	78	96	90	105	125
		6	70	82	105	96	110	135
		8	78	92	115	110	125	145
		10	86	105	125	120	135	160
		15	105	120	145	140	160	185
Small	$q^2 = 0.125$	2	100	125	155	145	170	210
	$d = 0.5$	3	120	145	180	165	195	240
	$c = 0.1118$	4	130	160	195	185	210	260
		5	145	170	220	200	230	280
		6	155	185	230	220	250	300
		8	175	210	260	240	280	330
		10	190	230	280	260	300	360
		15	230	270	330	310	350	420

TABLE E (Continued)
**Sample Size Needed for Six-Group MANOVA for Power = .70, .80 and
.90 at α = .05 and α = .01**

			α = .05			α = .01		
	Power =		.70	.80	.90	.70	.80	.90
Number of Variables		2	14	16	20	19	22	26
Effect Size		3	16	18	23	22	25	29
	q^2=1.125	4	18	21	25	24	27	32
Very Large	d=1.5	5	19	22	27	26	30	35
	c=0.2535							
		6	21	24	29	28	32	37
		8	23	27	33	31	35	42
		10	25	30	36	34	39	46
		15	30	35	42	42	46	54
Large	q^2=0.5	2	28	34	44	40	46	56
	d=1	3	33	39	50	46	54	64
	c=0.1690	4	37	44	54	52	60	70
		5	40	48	60	56	64	76
		6	44	52	64	60	68	82
		8	50	58	70	68	76	90
		10	54	64	78	74	84	98
		15	64	76	90	88	98	115
Moderate	q^2=0.2813	2	50	60	76	70	82	98
	d=0.75	3	58	70	86	80	94	115
	c=0.1268	4	64	76	96	90	105	125
		5	70	84	105	98	115	135
		6	76	90	110	105	120	145
		8	86	100	125	120	135	160
		10	94	110	135	130	145	175
		15	115	135	160	155	175	210
Small	q^2=0.125	2	110	135	170	155	180	220
	d=0.5	3	130	155	190	180	210	250
	c=0.0845	4	145	170	220	200	230	280
		5	155	185	230	220	250	300
		6	170	200	250	230	270	320
		8	190	230	280	260	300	350
		10	210	250	300	290	330	390
		15	250	290	360	340	380	460

[1]There exists a variate i such that $1/\sigma^2 \sum_{j=1}^{J} (\mu_{ij} - \mu_{i.}) \geq q^2$, where $\mu_{i.}$ is the total mean and σ^2 is variance. There exists a variate s such that $1/\sigma_i|\mu_{ij_1} - \mu_{ij_2}| \geq d$, for two groups j_1 and j_2. There exists a variate s such that for *all* pairs of groups 1 and m we have $1/\sigma_i|\mu_{i1} - \mu_{im}| \geq c$.

[2]The entries in the body of the table are the sample size required for *each* group for the power indicated. For example, for power = .80 at α = .05 for a large effect size with 4 variables, we would need 33 subjects per group.

Critical Values for F_{max} Statistic

df for * each variance	$1-\alpha$	Number of Variances										
		2	3	4	5	6	7	8	9	10	11	12
2	.95	39.0	87.5	142	202	266	333	403	475	550	626	704
	.99	199	448	729	1036	1362	1705	2063	2432	2813	3204	3605
3	.95	154	27.8	39.2	50.7	62.0	72.9	83.5	93.9	104	114	124
	.99	47.5	85	120	151	184	216	249	281	310	337	361
4	.95	9.60	15.5	20.6	25.2	29.5	33.6	37.5	41.4	44.6	48.0	51.4
	.99	23.2	37.	49.	59.	69.	79.	89.	97.	106.	113.	120
5	.95	7.15	10.8	13.7	16.3	18.7	20.8	22.9	24.7	26.5	28.2	29.9
	.99	14.9	22.	28.	33.	38.	42.	46.	50.	54.	57	60
6	.95	5.82	8.38	10.4	12.1	13.7	15.0	16.3	17.5	18.6	19.7	20.7
	.99	11.1	15.5	19.1	22.	25.	27.	30.	32.	34.	36	37
7	.95	4.99	6.94	8.44	9.70	10.8	11.8	12.7	13.5	14.3	151	15.8
	.99	8.89	12.1	14.5	16.5	18.4	20.	22.	23.	24.	26	27
8	.95	4.43	6.00	7.18	8.12	9.03	9.78	10.5	11.1	11.7	12.2	12.7
	.99	7.50	9.9	11.7	13.2	14.5	15.8	16.9	17.9	18.9	19.8	21
9	.95	4.03	5.34	6.31	7.11	7.80	8.41	8.95	9.45	9.91	10.3	10.7
	.99	6.54	8.5	9.9	11.1	12.1	13.1	13.9	14.7	15.3	16.0	16.6
10	.95	3.72	4.85	5.67	6.34	6.92	7.42	7.87	8.28	8.66	9.01	9.34
	.99	5.85	7.4	8.6	9.6	10.4	11.1	11.8	12.4	12.9	13.4	13.9
12	.95	3.28	4.16	4.79	5.30	5.72	6.09	6.42	6.72	7.00	7.25	7.48
	.99	4.91	6.1	6.9	7.6	8.2	8.7	9.1	9.5	9.9	10.2	10.6
15	.95	2.86	3.54	4.01	4.37	4.68	4.95	5.19	5.40	5.59	5.77	5.93
	.99	4.07	4.9	5.5	6.0	6.4	6.7	7.1	7.3	7.5	7.8	8.0
20	.95	2.46	2.95	3.29	3.54	3.76	3.94	4.10	4.24	4.37	4.49	4.59
	.99	3.32	3.8	4.3	4.6	4.9	5.1	5.3	5.5	5.6	5.8	5.9
30	.95	2.07	2.40	2.61	2.78	2.91	3.02	3.12	3.21	3.29	3.36	3.39
	.99	2.63	3.0	3.3	3.4	3.6	3.7	3.8	3.9	4.0	4.1	4.2
60	.95	1.67	1.85	1.96	2.04	2.11	2.17	2.22	2.26	2.30	2.33	2.36
	.99	1.96	2.2	2.3	2.4	2.4	2.5	2.5	2.6	2.6	2.7	2.7

"Reproduced with permission of the trustees of Biometrika.

*Equal group size (n) is assumed in the table; hence $df = n - 1$. If group sizes are not equal, then use the harmonic mean (rounding off to the nearest integer) as the n.

TABLE G
Chi Square Values for Multivariate Normality Test with Three and Four Variables

n^a	20		21		22		23		24		25		26		27		28		29		30	
p	3	4	3	4	3	4	3	4	3	4	3	4	3	4	3	4	3	4	3	4	3	4
1	24^b	51	19	43	19	43	19	43	19	43	19	43	19	43	19	43	19	43	19	43	19	43
2	49	92	45	85	45	85	45	85	40	78	40	78	40	78	40	78	35	71	35	71	35	71
3	71	124	63	111	63	111	63	111	63	111	58	106	58	106	54	99	54	99	54	99	49	92
4	91	153	87	147	83	141	79	136	79	136	75	130	75	130	71	124	71	124	67	118	67	118
5	113	181	104	170	104	170	101	165	95	159	91	153	87	147	87	147	83	141	79	136	79	136
6	133	208	125	197	121	192	117	187	113	181	108	176	104	170	101	165	101	165	95	159	91	153
7	155	236	147	225	142	220	138	214	129	203	125	197	121	192	117	187	113	181	108	176	108	176
8	178	264	169	253	160	241	155	236	147	225	142	220	138	214	133	208	129	203	125	197	121	192
9	202	293	192	281	183	269	174	258	169	253	160	241	155	236	151	230	142	220	138	214	133	208
10	227	324	212	306	202	293	192	281	187	275	178	264	169	253	164	247	160	241	155	236	151	230
11	254	356	237	336	227	324	217	312	207	299	197	287	187	275	183	269	178	264	169	253	164	247
12	283	390	266	370	249	350	237	336	227	324	217	312	207	299	202	293	192	281	187	275	178	264
13	317	429	295	404	278	384	260	363	249	350	237	336	227	324	217	312	212	306	202	293	197	287
14	353	471	324	438	302	412	289	397	272	377	260	363	249	350	237	336	227	324	222	318	212	306
15	397	521	360	480	338	454	317	429	302	412	283	390	272	377	260	363	249	350	237	336	227	324
16	445	576	407	532	377	499	345	463	331	446	309	421	295	404	278	384	266	370	260	363	249	350
17	512	653	454	587	416	543	387	510	360	480	338	454	317	429	302	412	289	397	278	384	266	370
18	592	743	512	653	464	599	425	554	397	521	367	488	345	463	331	446	317	429	295	404	283	390
19	719	881	592	743	528	671	464	599	435	565	407	532	377	499	360	480	338	454	324	438	309	421
20	984	1167	719	881	608	761	544	689	496	635	445	576	416	543	387	510	367	488	345	463	331	446
21			984	1167	719	881	608	761	560	707	496	635	454	587	425	554	397	521	377	499	353	471
22					984	1167	719	881	625	778	560	707	512	653	464	599	435	565	407	532	387	510
23							984	1167	750	915	625	778	560	707	512	653	464	599	445	576	416	543
24									984	1167	750	915	625	778	576	725	528	671	480	617	445	576
25											984	1167	750	915	656	812	592	743	544	689	496	635
26													984	1167	750	915	656	812	593	743	544	689
27															984	1167	782	949	687	846	592	743
28																	984	1167	782	949	687	846
29																			984	1167	781	949
30																					1134	1328

(cont.)

Chi Square Values for Multivariate Normality Test with Five and Six Variables

n	20	20	21	21	22	22	23	23	24	24	25	25	26	26	27	27	28	28	29	29	30	30
p	5	6	5	6	5	6	5	6	5	6	5	6	5	6	5	6	5	6	5	6	5	6
1	85	126	75	113	75	113	75	113	75	113	75	113	75	113	75	113	75	113	75	113	75	113
2	142	198	133	186	133	186	133	186	124	175	124	175	124	175	124	175	115	164	115	164	115	164
3	183	246	168	229	168	229	168	229	168	229	161	220	161	220	152	209	152	209	152	209	142	209
4	219	290	212	281	205	272	198	264	198	264	190	255	190	255	183	246	183	246	176	237	176	237
5	254	329	241	315	241	315	234	307	227	298	219	290	212	281	212	281	205	272	198	264	198	264
6	287	368	274	353	267	345	260	337	254	329	247	322	241	315	234	307	234	307	227	298	219	290
7	320	405	307	390	300	383	293	375	280	360	274	353	267	345	260	337	254	329	247	322	247	322
8	353	442	340	427	326	413	320	405	307	390	300	383	293	375	287	368	280	360	274	353	267	345
9	387	480	373	465	359	450	346	435	340	427	326	413	320	405	313	398	300	383	293	375	287	368
10	421	519	401	496	387	480	373	465	366	457	353	442	340	427	333	420	326	413	320	405	313	398
11	458	560	435	535	421	519	407	504	394	488	380	474	366	457	359	450	353	442	340	427	333	420
12	497	604	474	578	451	552	435	535	421	519	407	504	394	488	387	480	373	465	366	457	353	442
13	541	652	513	621	490	595	466	569	451	552	435	535	421	519	407	504	401	496	387	480	380	473
14	587	703	550	662	522	631	505	612	482	587	466	569	451	552	435	535	421	519	414	512	401	496
15	643	763	597	713	569	682	541	652	522	631	497	604	482	587	466	569	451	552	435	535	421	519
16	704	829	654	776	618	736	578	692	560	672	532	641	513	621	490	595	474	578	466	569	451	552
17	788	917	717	843	668	790	630	750	597	713	569	682	541	652	522	631	505	612	490	595	474	578
18	885	1019	788	917	729	856	680	803	643	763	606	723	578	692	560	672	541	652	513	621	497	604
19	1036	1180	885	1019	807	938	729	856	692	816	654	776	618	736	597	713	569	682	550	662	532	641
20	1339	1503	1036	1180	905	1040	827	958	769	897	704	829	668	790	630	750	606	723	578	692	560	672
21			1339	1503	1036	1180	905	1040	846	978	769	897	717	843	680	803	643	763	618	736	587	703
22					1339	1503	1036	1180	924	1065	846	978	788	917	729	856	692	816	654	776	630	750
23							1339	1503	1073	1220	924	1065	846	978	788	917	729	856	704	829	668	790
24									1339	1503	1073	1220	924	1065	866	999	807	938	749	876	704	829
25											1339	1503	1073	1220	961	1100	885	1019	827	958	769	897
26													1339	1503	1073	1220	961	1100	885	1019	827	958
27															1339	1503	1110	1259	998	1140	885	1019
28																	1339	1503	1110	1259	998	1140
29																			1339	1503	1107	1259
30																					1509	1681

(cont.)

Chi Square Values for Multivariate Normality Test with Seven and Eight Variables

p	20 (7)	20 (8)	21 (7)	21 (8)	22 (7)	22 (8)	23 (7)	23 (8)	24 (7)	24 (8)	25 (7)	25 (8)	26 (7)	26 (8)	27 (7)	27 (8)	28 (7)	28 (8)	29 (7)	29 (8)	30 (7)	30 (8)
1	172	219	156	203	156	203	156	203	156	203	156	203	156	203	156	203	156	203	156	203	156	203
2	257	319	243	303	243	303	243	303	230	288	230	288	230	288	230	288	217	273	217	273	217	273
3	313	382	293	360	293	360	293	360	293	360	283	349	283	349	270	334	270	334	270	334	257	319
4	363	437	353	426	343	415	333	404	333	404	333	393	323	393	313	382	313	382	303	371	303	371
5	407	487	391	468	391	468	382	459	373	448	363	437	353	426	353	426	343	415	333	404	333	404
6	450	534	433	515	425	506	416	497	407	487	399	478	391	468	382	459	382	459	373	448	363	437
7	492	580	475	562	467	553	459	544	442	525	433	515	425	506	416	497	407	487	399	478	399	478
8	533	624	516	606	500	589	492	580	475	562	467	553	459	544	450	534	442	525	433	515	425	506
9	574	670	558	651	541	633	524	615	516	606	500	589	492	580	483	571	467	553	459	544	450	534
10	618	716	592	697	574	670	558	651	549	642	533	624	516	606	508	598	500	589	492	580	483	571
11	663	764	635	734	618	716	601	697	583	679	566	660	549	642	541	633	533	624	516	606	508	598
12	709	814	682	784	654	754	635	734	618	716	601	697	583	679	574	670	558	651	549	642	533	624
13	761	870	728	835	700	804	672	774	654	754	635	734	618	716	601	697	592	688	574	670	566	660
14	816	929	772	882	731	847	719	824	691	794	672	774	654	754	635	734	618	716	609	706	592	688
15	881	997	827	940	794	905	761	870	739	847	709	814	691	794	672	774	654	754	635	734	618	716
16	952	1073	895	1012	852	967	805	917	783	894	750	858	728	835	700	804	682	784	672	774	654	754
17	1046	1173	966	1088	909	1028	866	982	827	940	794	905	761	870	739	847	719	824	700	804	682	784
18	1156	1289	1046	1173	980	1103	923	1043	881	997	838	952	805	917	783	894	761	870	728	835	709	814
19	1332	1464	1156	1289	1068	1196	980	1103	937	1058	895	1012	852	967	827	940	794	905	772	882	750	858
20	1662	1817	1332	1464	1178	1313	1090	1220	1024	1149	952	1073	909	1028	866	982	838	952	805	917	783	894
21			1662	1817	1332	1464	1178	1313	1112	1243	1024	1149	966	1088	923	1043	881	997	852	967	816	929
22					1662	1817	1332	1464	1202	1336	1112	1243	1046	1173	980	1103	937	1058	895	1012	866	982
23							1662	1817	1368	1508	1202	1336	1112	1243	1046	1173	980	1103	952	1073	909	1028
24									1662	1817	1368	1508	1202	1336	1134	1266	1068	1196	1002	1126	952	1073
25											1662	1817	1368	1508	1242	1379	1156	1289	1090	1220	1024	1149
26													1662	1817	1368	1508	1242	1379	1156	1289	1090	1220
27															1662	1817	1407	1551	1284	1422	1156	1289
28																	1662	1817	1407	1551	1284	1422
29																			1662	1817	1407	1551
30																					1848	2009

[a] n is the group size.

[b] Decimal points omitted. In all cases the implied point is two places to the left of the right most digit, i.e., 24 means .24.

TABLE H
Critical Values for Bryant-Paulson Procedure

Error df	Number of Covariates (C)	α	2	3	4	5	6	7	8	10	12	16	20
3	1	.05	5.42	7.18	8.32	9.17	9.84	10.39	10.86	11.62	12.22	13.14	13.83
		.01	10.28	13.32	15.32	16.80	17.98	18.95	19.77	21.12	22.19	23.82	25.05
	2	.05	6.21	8.27	9.60	10.59	11.37	12.01	12.56	13.44	14.15	15.22	16.02
		.01	11.97	15.56	17.91	19.66	21.05	22.19	23.16	24.75	26.01	27.93	29.38
	3	.05	6.92	9.23	10.73	11.84	12.72	13.44	14.06	15.05	15.84	17.05	17.95
		.01	13.45	17.51	20.17	22.15	23.72	25.01	26.11	27.90	29.32	31.50	33.13
4	1	.05	4.51	5.84	6.69	7.32	7.82	8.23	8.58	9.15	9.61	10.30	10.82
		.01	7.68	9.64	10.93	11.89	12.65	13.28	13.82	14.70	15.40	16.48	17.29
	2	.05	5.04	6.54	7.51	8.23	8.80	9.26	9.66	10.31	10.83	11.61	12.21
		.01	8.69	10.95	12.43	13.54	14.41	15.14	15.76	16.77	17.58	18.81	19.74
	3	.05	5.51	7.18	8.25	9.05	9.67	10.19	10.63	11.35	11.92	12.79	13.45
		.01	9.59	12.11	13.77	15.00	15.98	16.79	17.47	18.60	19.50	20.87	21.91
5	1	.05	4.06	5.17	5.88	6.40	6.82	7.16	7.45	7.93	8.30	8.88	9.32
		.01	6.49	7.99	8.97	9.70	10.28	10.76	11.17	11.84	12.38	13.20	13.83
	2	.05	4.45	5.68	6.48	7.06	7.52	7.90	8.23	8.76	9.18	9.83	10.31
		.01	7.20	8.89	9.99	10.81	11.47	12.01	12.47	13.23	13.84	14.77	15.47
	3	.05	4.81	6.16	7.02	7.66	8.17	8.58	8.94	9.52	9.98	10.69	11.22
		.01	7.83	9.70	10.92	11.82	12.54	13.14	13.65	14.48	15.15	16.17	16.95
6	1	.05	3.79	4.78	5.40	5.86	6.23	6.53	6.78	7.20	7.53	8.04	8.43
		.01	5.83	7.08	7.88	8.48	8.96	9.36	9.70	10.25	10.70	11.38	11.90
	2	.05	4.10	5.18	5.87	6.37	6.77	7.10	7.38	7.84	8.21	8.77	9.20
		.01	6.36	7.75	8.64	9.31	9.85	10.29	10.66	11.28	11.77	12.54	13.11
	3	.05	4.38	5.55	6.30	6.84	7.28	7.64	7.94	8.44	8.83	9.44	9.90
		.01	6.85	8.36	9.34	10.07	10.65	11.13	11.54	12.22	12.75	13.59	14.21
7	1	.05	3.62	4.52	5.09	5.51	5.84	6.11	6.34	6.72	7.03	7.49	7.84
		.01	5.41	6.50	7.20	7.72	8.14	8.48	8.77	9.26	9.64	10.24	10.69
	2	.05	3.87	4.85	5.47	5.92	6.28	6.58	6.83	7.24	7.57	8.08	8.46
		.01	5.84	7.03	7.80	8.37	8.83	9.21	9.53	10.06	10.49	11.14	11.64
	3	.05	4.11	5.16	5.82	6.31	6.70	7.01	7.29	7.73	8.08	8.63	9.03
		.01	6.23	7.52	8.36	8.98	9.47	9.88	10.23	10.80	11.26	11.97	12.51
8	1	.05	3.49	4.34	4.87	5.26	5.57	5.82	6.03	6.39	6.67	7.10	7.43
		.01	5.12	6.11	6.74	7.20	7.58	7.88	8.15	8.58	8.92	9.46	9.87
	2	.05	3.70	4.61	5.19	5.61	5.94	6.21	6.44	6.82	7.12	7.59	7.94
		.01	5.48	6.54	7.23	7.74	8.14	8.48	8.76	9.23	9.61	10.19	10.63
	3	.05	3.91	4.88	5.49	5.93	6.29	6.58	6.83	7.23	7.55	8.05	8.42
		.01	5.81	6.95	7.69	8.23	8.67	9.03	9.33	9.84	10.24	10.87	11.34
10	1	.05	3.32	4.10	4.58	4.93	5.21	5.43	5.63	5.94	6.19	6.58	6.87
		.01	4.76	5.61	6.15	6.55	6.86	7.13	7.35	7.72	8.01	8.47	8.82
	2	.05	3.49	4.31	4.82	5.19	5.49	5.73	5.93	6.27	6.54	6.95	7.26
		.01	5.02	5.93	6.51	6.93	7.27	7.55	7.79	8.19	8.50	8.99	9.36
	3	.05	3.65	4.51	5.05	5.44	5.75	6.01	6.22	6.58	6.86	7.29	7.62
		.01	5.27	6.23	6.84	7.30	7.66	7.96	8.21	8.63	8.96	9.48	9.88

(cont.)

473

Error df	Number of Covariates (C)	α	2	3	4	5	6	7	8	10	12	16	20
							Number of Groups						
12	1	.05	3.22	3.95	4.40	4.73	4.98	5.19	5.37	5.67	5.90	6.26	6.53
		.01	4.54	5.31	5.79	6.15	6.43	6.67	6.87	7.20	7.46	7.87	8.18
	2	.05	3.35	4.12	4.59	4.93	5.20	5.43	5.62	5.92	6.17	6.55	6.83
		.01	4.74	5.56	6.07	6.45	6.75	7.00	7.21	7.56	7.84	8.27	8.60
	3	.05	3.48	4.28	4.78	5.14	5.42	5.65	5.85	6.17	6.43	6.82	7.12
		.01	4.94	5.80	6.34	6.74	7.05	7.31	7.54	7.90	8.20	8.65	9.00
14	1	.05	3.15	3.85	4.28	4.59	4.83	5.03	5.20	5.48	5.70	6.03	6.29
		.01	4.39	5.11	5.56	5.89	6.15	6.36	6.55	6.85	7.09	7.47	7.75
	2	.05	3.26	3.99	4.44	4.76	5.01	5.22	5.40	5.69	5.92	6.27	6.54
		.01	4.56	5.31	5.78	6.13	6.40	6.63	6.82	7.14	7.40	7.79	8.09
	3	.05	3.37	4.13	4.59	4.93	5.19	5.41	5.59	5.89	6.13	6.50	6.78
		.01	4.72	5.51	6.00	6.36	6.65	6.89	7.09	7.42	7.69	8.10	8.41
16	1	.05	3.10	3.77	4.19	4.49	4.72	4.91	5.07	5.34	5.55	5.87	6.12
		.01	4.28	4.96	5.39	5.70	5.95	6.15	6.32	6.60	6.83	7.18	7.45
	2	.05	3.19	3.90	4.32	4.63	4.88	5.07	5.24	5.52	5.74	6.07	6.33
		.01	4.42	5.14	5.58	5.90	6.16	6.37	6.55	6.85	7.08	7.45	7.73
	3	.05	3.29	4.01	4.46	4.78	5.03	5.23	5.41	5.69	5.92	6.27	6.53
		.01	4.56	5.30	5.76	6.10	6.37	6.59	6.77	7.08	7.33	7.71	8.00
18	1	.05	3.06	3.72	4.12	4.41	4.63	4.82	4.98	5.23	5.44	5.75	5.98
		.01	4.20	4.86	5.26	5.56	5.79	5.99	6.15	6.42	6.63	6.96	7.22
	2	.05	3.14	3.82	4.24	4.54	4.77	4.96	5.13	5.39	5.60	5.92	6.17
		.01	4.32	5.00	5.43	5.73	5.98	6.18	6.35	6.63	6.85	7.19	7.46
	3	.05	3.23	3.93	4.35	4.66	4.90	5.10	5.27	5.54	5.76	6.09	6.34
		.01	4.44	5.15	5.59	5.90	6.16	6.36	6.54	6.83	7.06	7.42	7.69
20	1	.05	3.03	3.67	4.07	4.35	4.57	4.75	4.90	5.15	5.35	5.65	5.88
		.01	4.14	4.77	5.17	5.45	5.68	5.86	6.02	6.27	6.48	6.80	7.04
	2	.05	3.10	3.77	4.17	4.46	4.69	4.88	5.03	5.29	5.49	5.81	6.04
		.01	4.25	4.90	5.31	5.60	5.84	6.03	6.19	6.46	6.67	7.00	7.25
	3	.05	3.18	3.86	4.28	4.57	4.81	5.00	5.16	5.42	5.63	5.96	6.20
		.01	4.35	5.03	5.45	5.75	5.99	6.19	6.36	6.63	6.85	7.19	7.45
24	1	.05	2.98	3.61	3.99	4.26	4.47	4.65	4.79	5.03	5.22	5.51	5.73
		.01	4.05	4.65	5.02	5.29	5.50	5.68	5.83	6.07	6.26	6.56	6.78
	2	.05	3.04	3.69	4.08	4.35	4.57	4.75	4.90	5.14	5.34	5.63	5.86
		.01	4.14	4.76	5.14	5.42	5.63	5.81	5.96	6.21	6.41	6.71	6.95
	3	.05	3.11	3.76	4.16	4.44	4.67	4.85	5.00	5.25	5.45	5.75	5.98
		.01	4.22	4.86	5.25	5.54	5.76	5.94	6.10	6.35	6.55	6.87	7.11
30	1	.05	2.94	3.55	3.91	4.18	4.38	4.54	4.69	4.91	5.09	5.37	5.58
		.01	3.96	4.54	4.89	5.14	5.34	5.50	5.64	5.87	6.05	6.32	6.53
	2	.05	2.99	3.61	3.98	4.25	4.46	4.62	4.77	5.00	5.18	5.46	5.68
		.01	4.03	4.62	4.98	5.24	5.44	5.61	5.75	5.98	6.16	6.44	6.66
	3	.05	3.04	3.67	4.05	4.32	4.53	4.70	4.85	5.08	5.27	5.56	5.78
		.01	4.10	4.70	5.06	5.33	5.54	5.71	5.85	6.08	6.27	6.56	6.78

(*cont.*)

TABLE H (Continued)

Error df	Number of Covariates (C)	α	Number of Groups 2	3	4	5	6	7	8	10	12	16	20
40	1	.05	2.89	3.49	3.84	4.09	4.29	4.45	4.58	4.80	4.97	5.23	5.43
		.01	3.88	4.43	4.76	5.00	5.19	5.34	5.47	5.68	5.85	6.10	6.30
	2	.05	2.93	3.53	3.89	4.15	4.34	4.50	4.64	4.86	5.04	5.30	5.50
		.01	3.93	4.48	4.82	5.07	5.26	5.41	5.54	5.76	5.93	6.19	6.38
	3	.05	2.97	3.57	3.94	4.20	4.40	4.56	4.70	4.92	5.10	5.37	5.57
		.01	3.98	4.54	4.88	5.13	5.32	5.48	5.61	5.83	6.00	6.27	6.47
60	1	.05	2.85	3.43	3.77	4.01	4.20	4.35	4.48	4.69	4.85	5.10	5.29
		.01	3.79	4.32	4.64	4.86	5.04	5.18	5.30	5.50	5.65	5.89	6.07
	2	.05	2.88	3.46	3.80	4.05	4.24	4.39	4.52	4.73	4.89	5.14	5.33
		.01	3.83	4.36	4.68	4.90	5.08	5.22	5.35	5.54	5.70	5.94	6.12
	3	.05	2.90	3.49	3.83	4.08	4.27	4.43	4.56	4.77	4.93	5.19	5.38
		.01	3.86	4.39	4.72	4.95	5.12	5.27	5.39	5.59	5.75	6.00	6.18
120	1	.05	2.81	3.37	3.70	3.93	4.11	4.26	4.38	4.58	4.73	4.97	5.15
		.01	3.72	4.22	4.52	4.73	4.89	5.03	5.14	5.32	5.47	5.69	5.85
	2	.05	2.82	3.38	3.72	3.95	4.13	4.28	4.40	4.60	4.75	4.99	5.17
		.01	3.73	4.24	4.54	4.75	4.91	5.05	5.16	5.35	5.49	5.71	5.88
	3	.05	2.84	3.40	3.73	3.97	4.15	4.30	4.42	4.62	4.77	5.01	5.19
		.01	3.75	4.25	4.55	4.77	4.94	5.07	5.18	5.37	5.51	5.74	5.90

Answer Section

ANSWERS FOR CHAPTER 2

1.

a) $\mathbf{A} + \mathbf{C} = \begin{bmatrix} 3 & 7 & 6 \\ 9 & 0 & 6 \end{bmatrix}$

(b) $\mathbf{A} + \mathbf{B}$ not meaningful - must be of the same dimension to add.

(c) $\mathbf{A}\,\mathbf{B} = \begin{bmatrix} 13 & 12 \\ 14 & 24 \end{bmatrix}$

(d) $\mathbf{A}\,\mathbf{C}$ not meaningful - number of rows of $\mathbf{C}$ is not equal to number of columns of $\mathbf{A}$.

e) $\mathbf{u}'\mathbf{D}\,\mathbf{u} = 70$

f) $\mathbf{u}'\,\mathbf{v} = 23$

g) $(\mathbf{A} + \mathbf{C})' = \begin{bmatrix} 3 & 9 \\ 7 & 0 \\ 6 & 6 \end{bmatrix}$

h) $3\,\mathbf{C} = \begin{bmatrix} 3 & 9 & 15 \\ 18 & 6 & 3 \end{bmatrix}$

i) $|\mathbf{D}| = 20$

j) $\mathbf{D}^{-1} = \dfrac{1}{20} \begin{bmatrix} 6 & -2 \\ -2 & 4 \end{bmatrix}$

k) $|\mathbf{E}| = 1 \begin{vmatrix} 3 & 1 \\ 1 & 10 \end{vmatrix} - (-1) \begin{vmatrix} -1 & 1 \\ 2 & 10 \end{vmatrix} + 2 \begin{vmatrix} -1 & 3 \\ 2 & 1 \end{vmatrix} = 3$

by expanding along the first row

The same answer (i.e., 3) should be obtained by expanding along *any* row or column.

l) $\mathbf{E}^{-1} = ?$ Matrix of cofactors $= \begin{bmatrix} 29 & 12 & -7 \\ 12 & 6 & -3 \\ -7 & -3 & 2 \end{bmatrix}$ $|\mathbf{E}| = 3$

Therefore, $\mathbf{E}^{-1} = \dfrac{1}{3} \begin{bmatrix} 29 & 12 & -7 \\ 12 & 6 & -3 \\ -7 & -3 & 2 \end{bmatrix}$

m) $\mathbf{u}' \, \mathbf{D}^{-1} \, \mathbf{u} = 30/20$

n) $\mathbf{B} \mathbf{A} = \begin{bmatrix} 8 & 0 & 11 \\ 7 & 6 & 7 \\ 18 & 4 & 23 \end{bmatrix}$

o) $\mathbf{X}' \, \mathbf{X} = \begin{bmatrix} 51 & 64 \\ 64 & 90 \end{bmatrix}$

2. $\begin{bmatrix} y_1 \\ y_2 \\ \vdots \\ y_N \end{bmatrix} = \begin{bmatrix} e_1 \\ e_2 \\ \vdots \\ e_N \end{bmatrix} + \begin{bmatrix} 1 & x_{11} & x_{12} & x_{13} \\ 1 & x_{21} & x_{22} & x_{23} \\ & \cdots \cdots \cdots & \\ 1 & x_{N1} & x_{N2} & x_{N3} \end{bmatrix} \begin{bmatrix} b_0 \\ b_1 \\ b_2 \\ b_3 \end{bmatrix}$

　　$\begin{array}{cccc} \mathbf{y} & \mathbf{e} & + & \mathbf{X} & \mathbf{b} \\ (N \times 1) & (N \times 1) & & (N \times 4) & (4 \times 1) \end{array}$

Single matrix equation is: $\mathbf{y} = \mathbf{e} + \mathbf{X} \mathbf{b}$

3. $\mathbf{S}$ (covariance matrix) $= \dfrac{1}{4} \begin{bmatrix} 26.8 & 24 & -14 \\ 24 & 24 & -14 \\ -14 & -14 & 52 \end{bmatrix}$

4.

a) $r_{12} = \dfrac{s_{12}}{s_1 s_2} \Rightarrow s_{12} = r_{12} \, s_1 s_2 = .80 \,(10)(7) = 56$

Therefore, $\mathbf{S} = \begin{bmatrix} 100 & 56 \\ 56 & 49 \end{bmatrix} \Rightarrow |\mathbf{S}| = 1{,}764$

b) $s_{12} = .20 \,(9)(6) = 10.8$

Therefore, $\mathbf{S} = \begin{bmatrix} 81 & 10.8 \\ 10.8 & 36 \end{bmatrix} \Rightarrow |\mathbf{S}| = 2799.36$

The fact that the generalized variance is larger for (b) might seem surprising, since the variances for both variables are larger for (a). However, the fact that the variables are highly correlated in (a) means that much of the variance in either variable can be accounted for by the other variable. This fact reduces the generalized variance for (a) considerably.

ANSWERS FOR CHAPTER 3

1. a) For $k = 1$ and $N = 2$ this means $E(R^2) = 1/1 = 1$. Why is the expected value for the correlation squared equal to 1? Because we have only 2 subjects and hence 2 points in the plane. And a straight line will fit these points perfectly.

   b) For $k = 2$ and $N = 3$ we have $E(R^2) = 2/2 = 1$. Here with 2 predictors and 3 subjects we have 3 points in 3 space. But a plane will fit these points perfectly.

3. BMDP2R Control Lines

```
/PROBLEM TITLE IS ' EXERCISE 3 FROM CHAPTER 3 '.
/INPUT VARIABLES ARE 8. FORMAT IS STREAM.
/VARIABLE NAMES ARE Y,X1,X2,X3,X4,X5,X6,X7.
/PRINT CORR. DATA.
/REGRESSION DEPENDENT IS Y.
LEVELS ARE 0,2,1,1,2,1,3,3.
FORCE = 1.
/END
```

2. a) If x_1 enters the equation first, it will account for $(.60)^2 \times 100$, or 36% of the variance on y.

   b) To determine how much variance on y predictor x_1 will account for if entered second we need to partial out x_2. Hence we compute the following semi partial correlation:

$$r_{y1.2(s)} = \frac{r_{y1} - r_{y2}\, r_{12}}{\sqrt{1 - r_{12}^2}}$$

$$= \frac{.60 - .50(.80)}{\sqrt{1 - (.8)^2}} = .33$$

$$r_{y1.2(s)}^2 = (.33)^2 = .1089$$

Thus, x_1 accounts for about 11% of the variance if entered second.

   c) Since x_1 and x_2 are strongly correlated (multicollinearity), when a predictor enters the equation influences greatly how much variance it will account for. Here when x_1 entered first it accounted for 36% of variance, while it only accounted for 11% when entered second.

7. a) We can not have much faith in the reliability of the regression equations. It was indicated in the chapter that generally about 15 subjects per predictor are needed for a reliable equation. Here, in the second case the N/k ratio is $114/16 = 7/1$, far short of what is needed. In the first case we have a double capitilization on chance, with preselection (picking the 6 out of 16) and then the capitilization due to the mathematical maximiation property for multiple regression.

b) *Herzberg Formula*

$$\hat{\rho}_c^2 = 1 - (113/97)(112/96)(115/114)(1 - .32)$$

$$\hat{\rho}_c^2 = 1 - .933 = .067$$

Thus, if the equation were cross validated on many other samples from the same population we could expect to account for only about 7% of the variance on social adjustment.

8. The admissions official would use semi parital correlations to partial out the contributions of x_1 and x_2 first, and then determine how much unique variance in success x_3 and x_4 account for. In terms of the packages, one could achieve this by *forcing* x_1 and x_2 into the equation and assigning x_3 and x_4 the same level value to see which enters the equation next.

An educated guess is that x_4 would probably have the greater incremental validity. Although x_4 has a smaller correlation with y (.46) than x_3 (.60), it is only weakly correlated with x_1 and x_2, whereas x_3 has strong correlations with x_1 and x_2 (.6 and .8). Thus, x_3 is quite redundant. Most of the variance in success that it accounts for is the same variance that x_1 and x_2 account for.

ANSWERS FOR CHAPTER 4

1. a) This is a three-way univariate ANOVA, with sex, socioeconomic status, and teaching method as the factors and Lankton algebra test score as the dependent variable.

b) This is a multivariate study, a two-group MANOVA with reading speed and reading comprehension as the dependent variables.

c) This is a multiple regression study, with success on the job as the dependent variable and high school gpa and the personality variables as the predictors.

d) This is a factor analytic study, where the items are the variables being analyzed.

e) This is a multivariate study, and a complex repeated measures design (to be discussed in Chapter 13). There is one between or classification variable (social class) and one within variable (grade) and the subjects are measured on 3 dependent variables (reading comprehension, math ability, and science ability) at 3 points in time.

3. Because there are more variables (the items are the variables) here than subjects, the covariance matrix S is singular and can't be inverted. Another way of thinking about this is that there are no degrees of freedom for error since $N - p - 1 = 45 - 50 - 1 = -6!$ The investigator must consider substantially reducing the number of variables for analysis by logically grouping items into subsets and using the subtest total scores as the dependent variables.

4. You should definitely not be impressed with these results. Since this is a 3-way design (call the factors A, B, and C) there are 7 statistical tests (7 effects — A, B, and C main effects, the AB, AC, and BC interactions and the three way interaction ABC) being done for each of the 5 dependent variables, making a total of 35 statistical tests that were done at the .05 level. The chance of 3 or 4 of these being type I errors is quite high. Yes, we could have more confidence if the significant effects had been hypothesized a priori. For then there would have been a empirical (theoretical) basis for expecting the effects to be "real," which we would then be empirically confirming. Since there are 5 correlated dependent variables, a 3-way multivariate analysis of variance would have been a better way statistically of analyzing the data.

6. The within matrices for groups 1 and 2 are respectively:

$$\mathbf{W}_1 = \begin{bmatrix} 9.2 & -8 \\ -8 & 22 \end{bmatrix} \quad \mathbf{W}_2 = \begin{bmatrix} 2 & -1 \\ -1 & 2 \end{bmatrix}$$

Therefore the pooled within SSCP matrix is:

$$\mathbf{W} = \mathbf{W}_1 + \mathbf{W}_2 = \begin{bmatrix} 9.2 & -8 \\ -8 & 22 \end{bmatrix} + \begin{bmatrix} 2 & -1 \\ -1 & 2 \end{bmatrix} = \begin{bmatrix} 11.2 & -9 \\ -9 & 24 \end{bmatrix}$$

b) The pooled within covariance matrix S is given by:

$$S = \frac{1}{N - k} \mathbf{W} = \frac{1}{9 - 2} \begin{bmatrix} 11.2 & -9 \\ -9 & 24 \end{bmatrix} = \begin{bmatrix} 1.87 & -1.5 \\ -1.5 & 4 \end{bmatrix}$$

1.87 is the variance for y_1 and 4 is the variance for y_2

-1.5 is the covariance for y_1 and y_2

c) Hotelling's T^2 is given by:

$$T^2 = \frac{n_1 n_2}{n_1 + n_2} (\bar{y}_1 - \bar{y}_2)' S^{-1} (\bar{y}_1 - \bar{y}_2),$$

where $\bar{y}_1$ and $\bar{y}_2$ are the vectors of means for groups 1 and 2 and S^{-1} is the inverse of the covariance matrix.

$$S^{-1} = \frac{1}{5.23}\begin{bmatrix} 4 & 1.50 \\ 1.5 & 1.87 \end{bmatrix} = \begin{bmatrix} .765 & .287 \\ .287 & .358 \end{bmatrix}$$

where 5.23 is the determinant of S.

Now, the means for y_1 and y_2 in group 1 are 2.6 and 5, while the means for y_1 and y_2 in group 2 are 5 and 7. Thus,

$$\bar{y}_1 - \bar{y}_2 = \begin{pmatrix} 2.6 \\ 5.0 \end{pmatrix} - \begin{pmatrix} 5 \\ 7 \end{pmatrix} = \begin{pmatrix} -2.4 \\ -2.0 \end{pmatrix}$$

Therefore,

$$T^2 = \frac{5(3)}{8}(-2.4, -2)\begin{bmatrix} .765 & .287 \\ .287 & .358 \end{bmatrix}\begin{pmatrix} -2.4 \\ -2.0 \end{pmatrix} = 16.11$$

d) The multivariate null hypothesis is that the population mean vectors are equal, i.e., $\mu_1 = \mu_2$.

e) To test the multivariate null hypothesis we use the exact F transformation of T^2:

$$F = \frac{n_1 + n_2 - p - 1}{(n_1 + n_2 - 2)p}T^2 = \frac{8 - 2 - 1}{6\,(2)}(16.11) = 6.71$$

The critical value at the .05 level is:

$$F_{.05;\ p,\ N-p-1} = F_{.05;\ 2,5} = 5.79$$

Since $6.71 > 5.79$ we reject the multivariate null hypothesis and conclude that the groups differ on the set of 2 variables.

8. a) $s_1^2 = 9$, $s_2^2 = 4$ and $r_{12} = .70$ (given)

Also, the row vector of mean differences $d' = (1, -.5)$.

To calculate T^2 we need the covariance matrix for the variables. We already have the variances, but need the covariance. But,

$$r_{12} = \frac{s_{12}}{s_1 s_2} \rightarrow s_{12} = r_{12}\,s_1 s_2 = (.70)(3)(2) = 4.2$$

Therefore,

$$S = \begin{bmatrix} 9 & 4.2 \\ 4.2 & 4 \end{bmatrix} \Rightarrow S^{-1} = \begin{bmatrix} .218 & -.229 \\ -.229 & .491 \end{bmatrix}$$

$$T^2 = \frac{(30)(30)}{60}(1, -.5)\begin{bmatrix} .218 & -.229 \\ -.229 & .491 \end{bmatrix}\begin{pmatrix} 1 \\ -.5 \end{pmatrix} = 8.565$$

$$F = \frac{60 - 3}{58\,(2)}(8.565) = 4.21$$

Critical value at .05 is 3.15; therefore the multivariate test is significant at the .05 level.

Univariate Tests

$$F_1 = t_1^2 = \frac{1^2}{9\left(\dfrac{1}{30} + \dfrac{1}{30}\right)} = 1/.6 = 1.66$$

$$F_2 = t_2^2 = \frac{(-.5)^2}{4\left(\dfrac{1}{30} + \dfrac{1}{30}\right)} = .25/.266 < 1$$

Critical value at .05 $= F_{.05;\ 1,58} = 4$; thus neither of the variables is significant in a univariate sense.

b) $r_{12} = .20 \Rightarrow s_{12} = .2\ (3)(2) = 1.2$

$$\mathbf{S} = \begin{bmatrix} 9 & 1.2 \\ 1.2 & 4 \end{bmatrix} \Rightarrow \mathbf{S}^{-1} = \begin{bmatrix} .116 & -.035 \\ -.035 & .260 \end{bmatrix}$$

$$T^2 = \frac{30(30)}{60}\ (1,\ -.5) \begin{bmatrix} .116 & -.035 \\ -.035 & .260 \end{bmatrix} \begin{pmatrix} 1 \\ -.5 \end{pmatrix} = 3.25$$

$$F = \frac{60 - 3}{58\ (2)}\ (3.25) = 1.597$$

Since 1.597 is less than the critical value of 3.15, the multivariate test is not significant.

The reason multivariate significance is not obtained here is that the generalized error variance against which significance is being tested is much greater here ($|\mathbf{S}| = 34.56$) than it was in part (a), where $|\mathbf{S}| = 18.36$.

11. Using Table 4.6 with $D^2 = .64$ (as a good approximation):

Variables	n	.64
3	25	.74
5	25	.68

Interpolating between the power values of .74 for 3 variables and .68 for 5 variables, we see that about 25 subjects per group will be needed for power $= .70$ for 4 variables.

14. a) The multivariate null hypothesis is rejected at the .05 level, since $F = 3.7488$, $p < .016$.

b) The value of Mahalanobis $D^2 = 5.144$, which is a very large multivariate effect size! Thus, it is not surprising that the multivariate null hypothesis was rejected. With an effect size this large, not many subjects per group are needed for excellent power.

c) Setting overall $\alpha = .05$, via the Bonferroni approach, means that each variable is tested for significance at the $.05/6 = .0083$ level of significance. From the printout then the following variables are significant:

Variable	F	prob.
Tone	13.97	.001
Rhythm	9.34	.006
Inton	13.86	.001
Artic	17.17	.000

ANSWERS FOR CHAPTER 5

1. a) The multivariate null hypothesis is that the population mean vectors for the 3 groups are equal, i.e., $\mu_1 = \mu_2 = \mu_3$. We do reject the multivariate null hypothesis at the .05 level since $F = 3.34$ (corresponding to Wilk's Λ), $p < .008$.

   b) Groups 1 and 2 are significantly different at the .05 level on the set of 3 variables since $F = 3.6567, p < .0369$. Also, groups 2 and 3 are significantly different since $F = 8.351, p < .002$.

   c) Variables $Y2$ and $Y3$ are significantly different at the .05 level for groups 1 and 2 since the univariate t's for these variables are respectively t(pooled) $= -3.42, p < .0033$ and t(pooled) $= -2.57, p < .0199$.

   All variables are significant at the .05 level for groups 2 and 3: t_{Y1}(pooled) $= 2.33, p < .0333, t_{Y2}$(pooled) $= 5.27, p < .0001$ and t_{Y3}(pooled) $= 4.41, p < .0004$.

   d) Variables $Y2$ and $Y3$ are still significantly different for groups 1 and 2 with the Tukey confidence intervals, since the intervals do not cover 0.

   Variables $Y2$ and $Y3$ are still significantly different for groups 2 and 3, but $Y1$ is not significantly different since it's interval does cover 0.

3. We could not place a great deal of confidence in these results, since from the Bonferroni Inequality the probability of *at least one* spurious significant result could be as high as $12 (.05) = .60$. Thus, most of these 4 significant results could be type I errors. The authors did not a priori hypothesize differences on the variables for which significance was found.

4. To show that the contrasts are orthogonal (since the group sizes are equal), it suffices to show that the sum of the products of the coefficients for each pair is 0:

1 & 2: $1(0) + (-.25)(1) + (-.25)(1) + (-.25)(-1) + (-.25)(-1) = 0$
1 & 3: $1(0) + (-.25)(1) + (-.25)(0) + (-.25)(0) + (-.25)(-1) = 0$
1 & 4: $1(0) + (-.25)(0) + (-.25)(0) + (-.25)(1) + (-.25)(-1) = 0$
2 & 3: $0(0) + 1(1) + 1(-1) + (-1)(0) + (-1)(0) = 0$
2 & 4: $0(0) + 1(0) + 1(0) + (-1)(1) + (-1)(-1) = 0$
3 & 4: $0(0) + 1(0) + (-1)(0) + 0(1) + 0(-1) = 0$

b) To show that the set of contrasts are not orthogonal we need merely show that at least one of the pairs of contrasts is not orthogonal:

1 & 2: $1(1) + (-.25)(-.50) + (-.25)(-.50) + (-.25)(0) + (-.25)(0)$
$\neq 0$

c) Control lines for contrast set in part (a):

```
TITLE ' SPECIAL CONTRASTS FOR EXERCISE 4 '
DATA LIST FREE/ GPS Y1 Y2 Y3 Y4
LIST
BEGIN DATA
     DATA LINES
END DATA
MANOVA Y1 TO Y4 BY GPS(1,5)/
   CONTRAST(GPS) = SPECIAL(1 1 1 1 1 1  -.25  -.25  -.25  -.25
   0 1 1  -1  -1 0 1  -1 0 0 0 0 0 1  -1)/
   PARTITION(GPS)/
   DESIGN = GPS(1),GPS(2),GPS(3),GPS(4)/
   PRINT = CELLINFO(MEANS)/
```

The control lines for the second contrast set in part (a) is exactly the same except for the CONTRAST subcommand which now is:

```
CONTRAST(GPS) = SPECIAL(1 1 1 1 1 1  -.25  -.25  -.25  -.25
1  -.5  -.5 0 0 1 0 0  -.5  -.5 0 1 1  -1  -1)/
```

7.

T_2		T_3	
y_1	y_2	y_1	y_2
4	8	7	6
5	6	8	7
6	7	10	8
		9	5
$\bar{y}_{12} = 5$	$\bar{y}_{22} = 7$	7	6
		$\bar{y}_{13} = 8.2$	$\bar{y}_{23} = 6.4$

Computation of W_2 *for* T_2

$ss_1 = (4-5)^2 + (6-5)^2 = 2$

$ss_2 = (8-7)^2 + (6-7)^2 = 2$

$ss_{12} = ss_{21} = (4-5)(8-7) + (5-5)(6-7) + (6-5)(7-7) = -1$

Therefore,

$$\mathbf{W}_2 = \begin{bmatrix} 2 & -1 \\ -1 & 2 \end{bmatrix}$$

Computation of $\mathbf{W}_3$ *for* T_3

$ss_1 = (7 - 8.2)^2 + (8 - 8.2)^2 + (10 - 8.2)^2 + (9 - 8.2)^2$
$\qquad + (7 - 8.2)^2$
$\qquad = 1.44 + .04 + 3.24 + .64 + 1.44 = 6.8$

$ss_2 = (6 - 6.4)^2 + (7 - 6.4)^2 + (8 - 6.4)^2 + (5 - 6.4)^2$
$\qquad + (6 - 6.4)^2$
$\qquad = .16 + .36 + 2.56 + 1.96 + .16 = 5.2$

$ss_{12} = ss_{21} = (7 - 8.2)(6 - 6.4) + (8 - 8.2)(7 - 6.4)$
$\qquad\qquad + (10 - 8.2)(8 - 6.4) + (9 - 8.2)(5 - 6.4)$
$\qquad\qquad + (7 - 8.2)(6 - 6.4)$
$\qquad = .48 + (-.12) + 2.88 + (-1.12) + .48 = 2.6$

Therefore,

$$\mathbf{W}_3 = \begin{bmatrix} 6.8 & 2.6 \\ 2.6 & 5.2 \end{bmatrix}$$

ANSWERS FOR CHAPTER 6

2. The actual type I error rate, using Table 6.2, is .42.

5. a) We would not be concerned here with respect to type I error (even though the test is significant), since the group sizes are equal and various studies have shown that for equal n the actual α is very close to the nominal α. If power was an issue, however, we could be concerned given the Holloway and Dunn results (Table 6.8).

   b) Here we would be concerned with respect to type I error since the test is significant and the group sizes are sharply unequal. Since the large variability is associated with the small group size, the multivariate test statistics will be too liberal.

   c) Here we probably need not be concerned with respect to type I error even though the test is significant. This is because of a somewhat cancelling out type effect. There is large variability associated with the largest group size (which produces a conservative test) but also large variability associated with one of the smallest group sizes (group 1), which would produce a liberal test.

7. The skewness and kurtosis values from the BMDPAM printout are:

	GROUP 1 (11)		GROUP 2 (8)		GROUP 3 (10)	
	skewness	kurtosis	skewness	kurtosis	skewness	kurtosis
$Y1$	.50	-1.29	.14	-1.65	.07	-1.77
$Y2$	$-.37$	-1.03	$-.40$	-1.22	$-.09$	-1.50
$Y3$	$-.29$	-1.43	.54	-1.34	$-.07$	-1.94

Critical value for skewness at .01 for group 1 is 1.54, for group 2 is 1.601 and for group 3 is 1.505. None of the values in above table exceed any of critical values in absolute value, hence there is no significant deviation on any of the variables due to skewness.

Recall that to use the critical values from Table 6.5 in testing for kurtosis we must first add 3 to each of the values from the BMDPAM printout. This yields:

	GROUP 1	GROUP 2	GROUP 3
$Y1$	1.71	1.35	1.23
$Y2$	1.97	1.78	1.50
$Y3$	1.57	1.66	1.06

Since the critical values for significant deviation due to leptokurtosis are all greater than 3, there clearly is no significant deviation of this type. The critical values for a significant deviation due to platykurtosis for groups 1, 2 and 3 respectively are 1.43, 1.31 and 1.39. If any of the values in above table are *less* than these critical values we have a significant deviation. There is no significant deviation for groups 1 and 2. We do, however, have significant deviations due to platykurtosis on variables $Y1$ and $Y3$ in group 3. The appropriate transformation (cf. Fig. 6.3) is $1/2 \log \dfrac{1 + x}{1 - x}$.

b) Test for homogeneity of covariance matrices assumption:

Box test $F = 1.00622, p < .440$

This test is not significant at .05 level. Since the group sizes were approximately equal, the multivariate test statistics are robust with respect to type I error, and the concern is with type II error.

ANSWERS FOR CHAPTER 7

1. a) The number of discriminant functions is $\min(k - 1, p) = \min(3 - 1, 3) = 2$

b) Only the first discriminant function is significant at the .05 level. The tests occur under DIMENSION REDUCTION ANALYSIS

ROOTS	F	SIG of F
1 to 2	3.34	.008
2 to 2	.184	.833

d) The vector of raw discriminant coefficients is

$$\mathbf{a}_1 = \begin{pmatrix} .47698 \\ -.77237 \\ -.83084 \end{pmatrix}$$

The **B** matrix, from the printout is:

$$\begin{bmatrix} 4.67798 & 8.71215 & 7.42010 \\ 8.71215 & 16.85415 & 14.27574 \\ 7.42010 & 14.27574 & 12.10131 \end{bmatrix}$$

Now, rounding off to 3 decimal places, we compute $\mathbf{a}_1' \mathbf{B} \mathbf{a}_1$

$$(.477, -.772, -.831) \begin{bmatrix} 4.678 & 8.712 & 7.420 \\ 8.712 & 16.854 & 14.276 \\ 7.420 & 14.276 & 12.101 \end{bmatrix} \begin{pmatrix} .477 \\ -.772 \\ -.831 \end{pmatrix}$$

$$\mathbf{a}_1' \mathbf{B} \mathbf{a}_1 = (-10.66, -20.719, -17.538) \begin{pmatrix} .477 \\ -.772 \\ -.831 \end{pmatrix} = 25.484$$

Now, rounding off the **W** matrix to 3 decimal places, we have

$$\mathbf{a}_1' \mathbf{W} \mathbf{a}_1 = (.477, -.772, -.831) \begin{bmatrix} 24.684 & 10.607 & 17.399 \\ 10.607 & 18.111 & 14.690 \\ 17.399 & 14.690 & 17.864 \end{bmatrix} \begin{pmatrix} .477 \\ -.772 \\ -.831 \end{pmatrix}$$

$$\mathbf{a}_1' \mathbf{W} \mathbf{a}_1 = (-10.873, -21.13, -17.886) \begin{pmatrix} .477 \\ -.772 \\ -.831 \end{pmatrix} = 25.989$$

Now, the largest eigenvalue is given by $\mathbf{a}_1' \mathbf{B} \mathbf{a}_1 / \mathbf{a}_1' \mathbf{W} \mathbf{a}_1$

$$\phi_1 = 25.484/25.989 = .98057$$

and this agrees with the value on the printout within rounding error.

3. a) Since there were 3 significant discriminant functions in the Smart study, the association is diffuse and the Pillai-Bartlett trace is most powerful (see 5.12).

b) In the Stevens study there was only 1 significant discriminant function (concentrated association), and in this case Roy's largest root has been shown to be most powerful (again see 5.12).

ANSWERS FOR CHAPTER 9

1. a) Control lines for Scandura MANCOVA on SPSSX MANOVA:

```
TITLE ' MANCOVA 2 GROUPS - 5 DEP VARS AND 3 COVARIATES '
DATA LIST FREE/ TRTMT2 HOPPOCKA LMXA ERSA QUANAFT QUALAFT MPS OLI
    DTT
LIST
BEGIN DATA
  DATA LINES
END DATA
MANOVA HOPPOCKA TO QUALAFT BY TRTMT2(1,2)/
  ANALYSIS = HOPPOCKA LMXA ERSA QUANAFT QUALAFT WITH MPS OLI DTT/
  PRINT = PMEANS/
  DESIGN/
  ANALYSIS = HOPPOCKA LMXA ERSA QUANAFT QUALAFT/
  DESIGN = MPS + OLI + DTT,TRTMT2, MPS BY TRTMT2 + OLI BY TRTMT2 + DTT
  BY TRTMT2/
```

b) To determine whether covariance is appropriate two things need to be checked:

1. Is there a significant relationship between the dependent variables and the set of covariates, or equivalently is there a significant regression of the dependent variables on the covariates?
2. Is the homogeneity of the regression hyperplanes satisfied?

Under EFFECT . . . WITHIN CELLS REGRESSION are the multivariate tests for determining whether the two sets of variables are related. The multivariate F corresponding to Wilk's Λ shows there is a significant relationship at the .05 level ($F = 1.88, p < .027$). The test for the homogeneity of the regression hyperplanes appears under EFFECT . . . MPS BY TRTMT2 + OLI BY TRTMT2 + DTT BY TRTMT2. This test is not significant at the .05 level ($F = .956, p < .503$), meaning that the assumption *is* satisfied. Thus, from the above two results we see that covariance is appropriate.

c) The multivariate test for determining the 2 adjusted population mean vectors are equal appears under EFFECT . . . TRTMT2 The tests, which are equivalent (since there are only 2 groups), show significance at the .05 level ($F = 2.669, p < .029$).

d) The univariate tests show that only QUANAFT is significant at the .01 level ($F = 11.186, p < .001$).

e) The adjusted means for QUANAFT are .392 (for treatment group) and .323 (for control group), with the treatment group doing better.

4. Are there any differences on the SOCINT variable in Novince study using the Bryant Paulson 95% simultaneous confidence level? The following test statistic is appropriate (cf. Table 9.8).

$$BP = \frac{\bar{Y}_i^* - \bar{Y}_j^*}{\sqrt{MS_w^* \left[1 + \frac{1}{(J-1)} Tr(\mathbf{B}_x \mathbf{W}_x^{-1})\right]/n}}$$

The adjusted means for the 3 groups for SOCINT are (Table 9.5):

TREAT 1: 103.087   TREAT 2: 76.119   TREAT 3: 108.158

The adjusted error term for SOCINT is 105.09 (Table 9.6), and recall that $Tr(\mathbf{B}_x \mathbf{W}_x^{-1}) = .307$. First we compare groups 1 and 2:

$$BP = \frac{103.087 - 76.119}{\sqrt{105.09 \left[1 + \frac{1}{2}(.307)\right]/11}}$$

$$= \frac{26.968}{\sqrt{105.09\ (1.15)/11}} = \frac{26.968}{3.3146} = 8.136$$

Recall from the Novince example (no. 4) that the critical value $= 3.73$. Thus, we reject and conclude that groups 1 and 2 differ on SOCINT. Also, since the difference between the adjusted means for groups 2 and 3 is even larger, that difference will also be significant. Now we test the difference for groups 1 and 3:

$$BP = \frac{103.087 - 108.158}{3.3146} = -1.53$$

Since this is less (in absolute value) than the critical value of 3.73 groups 1 and 3 are not different.

6. a) From what is said we can not be confident that covariance is appropriate. First, no test is given indicating that there is a significant relationship between the 3 dependent variables and the covariates. Secondly, the test for the homogeneity of the regression hyperplanes is not given.

b) It would not have made a difference as to which multivariate test was used, since for two groups they are equivalent.

c) The post hoc procedure they are employing is the one using the Bonferroni Inequality, where for p dependent variables, if one wishes the overall α at .05, then each variable is tested at the $.05/p$ level of significance.

d) According to Huitema's inequality there are not enough subjects to have confidence in the reliability of the adjusted means. Since there are $J = 2$ groups and $N = 30$ subjects total, the number of covariates C should be limited so that

$$\frac{C + (2-1)}{30} < .10 \Rightarrow C < 2$$

ANSWERS FOR CHAPTER 11

1. a) Denote the linear combination for 2 variables as

$$y = a_1 x_1 + a_2 x_2$$

$$\text{var}(y) = (a_1, a_2) \begin{bmatrix} s_1^2 & s_{12} \\ s_{12} & s_2^2 \end{bmatrix} \begin{pmatrix} a_1 \\ a_2 \end{pmatrix}$$

$$= a_1^2 s_1^2 + 2 a_1 a_2 s_{12} + a_2^2 s_2^2$$

Denote the linear combination for 3 variables as

$$y_1 = a_1 x_1 + a_2 x_2 + a_3 x_3$$

$$\text{var}(y_1) = (a_1, a_2, a_3) \begin{bmatrix} s_1^2 & s_{12} & s_{13} \\ s_{12} & s_2^2 & s_{23} \\ s_{13} & s_{23} & s_3^2 \end{bmatrix} \begin{pmatrix} a_1 \\ a_2 \\ a_3 \end{pmatrix}$$

After all the matrix multiplication and combining of like terms the following is obtained:

$$\text{var}(y_1) = a_1^2 s_1^2 + a_2^2 s_2^2 + a_3^2 s_3^2 + 2 a_1 a_2 s_{12}$$

$$+ 2 a_1 a_3 s_{13} + 2 a_2 a_3 s_{23}$$

(b)

$$S = \begin{bmatrix} 451.4 & 271.2 & 168.7 \\ 271.2 & 171.7 & 103.3 \\ 168.7 & 103.3 & 66.7 \end{bmatrix}$$

s_{12} ↙   ↓ s_{13} ↓ s_{23}

$y_1 = .81 x_1 + .50 x_2 + .31 x_3$

↓ a_1 ↓ a_2 ↓ a_3

Now, plugging into the above formula for variance:

$$\text{var}(y_1) = (.81)^2 (451.4) + (.5)^2 (171.7)$$

$$+ (.31)^2 (66.7)$$

$$+ 2(.81)(.5)\ (271.2)\ +\ 2(81)(.31)(168.7)$$
$$+ 2(.5)(.31)(103.3)$$
$$\text{var}(y_1)\ =\ 296.16\ +\ 42.925\ +\ 6.41\ +\ 84.72$$
$$+ 219.67\ +\ 32.023\ =\ 681.9$$

3. In Case 1 it is not necessary to apply Barltett's sphericity test since 8 of correlations are at least moderate ($>.40$) in size. In Case 2, on the other hand, only 1 of the 15 correlations is moderate (.40), and almost all the others are very small. Thus here Bartlett's sphericity test is advisable. Using the Lawley approximation, we have:

$$\chi^2 = \left\{ 110 - \frac{2(6) + 5}{6} \right\}$$
$$[(.29)^2 + (.18)^2 + (.04)^2 + \ldots + (-.14)^2 + (.12)^2]$$
$$\chi^2 = (107.1667)(.4467) = 47.87$$

The critical value at $\alpha = .01$ is 30.58 (df $= 1/2\ (6)(5) = 15$). We reject and therefore conclude that the variables are correlated in the population.

5. a) Variance accounted for by component 1 : 57.43%
   Variance accounted for by component 2 : 35.92%
   b) Variance accounted for by varimax factor 1 : 50.44%
   Variance accounted for by varimax factor 2 : 42.96%
   c) The variance accounted for by the varimax rotated factors is spread out more evenly than for the components.
   d) The total amount of variance accounted for by the 2 components (93.35%) is the same, within rounding error, as that accounted for by the two varimax rotated factors (93.4%).

7. The first varimax factor is a manual communication construct, while the second varimax factor is an oral communication construct.
   b) The empirical clustering of the variables which load very high on varimax factor 1 (C_5, C_6, C_9 and C_{10}) is consistent with how the variables correlate in the original correlation matrix. The simple correlations for each pair of the above 4 variables ranges from .86 to .94.

ANSWERS FOR CHAPTER 12

1. Four features that canonical correlation and principal components have in common:
   a) both are mathematical maximization procedures

b) both use uncorrelated linear combinations of the variables

c) both provide for an additive partitioning; in components analysis an additive partitioning of the total variance, and in canonical correlation an additive partitioning of the between association.

d) correlations between the original variables and the linear combinations are used in both procedures for interpretation purposes.

3. The numbers do indicate that Mendoza's simulation procedure was operating properly. Since he replicated 1,000 times and tested the canonical correlations for significance at the .05 level, we would expect (under the null condition of all population 0 canonical correlations) to conclude approximately 5% of the time (or 50 times) that 1 or more of the correlations are non-zero. Adding the columns of numbers for the null condition in Table 12.1 we obtain:

$N = 25$				$N = 50$				$N = 100$			
50	50	40	48	43	43	43	42	57	57	57	46

Note that the number of false rejections bounces right around the value of 50 that are expected.

5. a) The association between the 2 sets of variables is weak, since 17 of the 26 simple correlations are less than .30.

b) Only the largest canonical correlation is significant at the .05 level - from the printout:

Chi-Sq	df	prob
92.96	36	.0000
21.70	25	.6533

c) The following are the loadings from the printout:

CREATIVITY		ACHIEVEMENT	
Ideaflu	.227	Know	.669
Flexib	.412	Compre	.578
Assocflu	.629	Applic	.374
Exprflu	.796	Anal	.390
Orig	.686	Synth	.910
Elab	.703	Eval	.542

The canonical correlation basically links the ability to synthesis (the loading of .910 dominates the achievement loadings) to last 4 creativity variables, which have loadings of the same order of magnitude.

d) Since only the largest canonical correlation was significant, about 20 subjects per variable are needed for reliable results, i.e., about $20(12) = 240$ subjects. So, the above results, based on an N of 116, must be treated somewhat tenuously.

e) The redundancy index for the creativity variables given the achievement variables is obtained from the following values on the printout:

Av. Sq.
Loading times
Sqed Can Correl
(1st Set)

.17787
.00906
.00931
.00222
.00063
.00019
.19928

This indicates that about 20% of the variance on the set of creativity variables is accounted for by the set of achievement variables.

f) The squared canonical correlations are given on the printout, and yield the following value for the Cramer-Nicewander index:

$$\frac{.48148 + .10569 + .06623 + .01286 + .00468 + .00917}{6} = .112$$

This indicates that the "variance" overlap between the two sets of variables is only about 11%, and is more accurate than the redundancy index since that index ignores the correlations among the dependent variables. And there are several significant correlations among the creativity variables, eight in the weak to moderate range (.32 to .46) and one strong correlation (.71).

8. The criterion of $10(p+q) + 50$ is not a conservative one according to the results of Barcikowski and Stevens. This criterion would imply, for example, if $p = 10$ and $q = 20$, that $10(10 + 20) + 50 = 350$ subjects are needed for reliable results. From Barcikowski and Stevens, on the other hand, about $30(20) = 600$ subjects are needed for reliable results, and more than that would be required if interpreting more than 1 canonical correlation.

ANSWERS FOR CHAPTER 13

2 . a) Univariate repeated measures analysis:

S	Treats 1	2	3	Row Means
1	5	6	1	4.0
2	3	4	2	3.0
3	3	7	1	3.667
4	6	8	3	5.667
5	6	9	3	6.0
6	4	7	2	4.333
7	5	9	2	5.333
Col means	4.571	7.143	2.0	4.571 (grand mean)

$$SS_b = 7[(4.571 - 4.571)^2 + (7.143 - 4.571)^2 + (2 - 4.571)^2]$$

$$SS_b = 7[6.615 + 6.61] = 92.575$$

$$SS_w = (5 - 4.571)^2 + (3 - 4.571)^2 + \ldots + (5 - 4.571)^2$$

$$+ (6 - 7.143)^2 + (4 - 7.143)^2 + \ldots + (9 - 7.143)^2$$

$$+ (1 - 2)^2 + (2 - 2)^2 + \ldots + (2 - 2)^2$$

$$SS_w = 32.57$$

$$SS_{b1} = 3[(4 - 4.571)^2 + (3 - 4.571)^2 + \ldots + (5.333 - 4.571)^2]$$

$$SS_{b1} = 22.476$$

Therefore,

$$SS_{res} = SS_w - SS_{b1} = 32.57 - 22.476 = 10.094$$

$$MS_{res} = SS_{res} / (n - 1)(k - 1) = 10.094/(7 - 1)(3 - 1) = .841$$

$$MS_b = SS_b / (k - 1) = 92.575/2 = 46.288$$

$$F = 46.288/.841 = 55.039$$

Critical value $F_{.05;2,12} = 3.88$

Thus, the treatments are significantly different at .05 level.

b) Multivariate repeated measures analysis using the difference variables $y_1 - y_2$ and $y_2 - y_3$:

$y_1 - y_2$	$y_2 - y_3$
−1	5
−1	2
−4	6
−2	5
−3	6
−3	5
−4	7

	$y_1 - y_2$	$y_2 - y_3$
Means	−2.571	5.143
Variances	1.619	2.476

Calculation for the covariance of $(y_1 - y_2)$ and $(y_2 - y_3)$:

$$s_{y1-y2,y2-y3} = \frac{(-1 + 2.571)(5 - 5.143) + (-1 + 2.571)(2 - 5.143)}{6}$$
$$\frac{+ (-4 + 2.571)(6 - 5.143) + \ldots + (-4 + 2.571)(7 - 5.143)}{6}$$

$$= -9.429/6 = -1.571$$

Thus, the covariance matrix S for the difference variables is:

$$S = \begin{bmatrix} 1.619 & -1.571 \\ -1.571 & 2.476 \end{bmatrix}$$

We need the inverse of this covariance matrix:

$$S^{-1} = \frac{1}{1.541} \begin{bmatrix} 2.476 & 1.571 \\ 1.571 & 1.619 \end{bmatrix} = \begin{bmatrix} 1.607 & 1.019 \\ 1.019 & 1.051 \end{bmatrix}$$

$$T^2 = 7\,(-2.571, 5.143) \begin{bmatrix} 1.607 & 1.019 \\ 1.019 & 1.051 \end{bmatrix} \begin{pmatrix} -2.571 \\ 5.143 \end{pmatrix} = 80.298$$

$$F = \frac{n - k + 1}{(n - 1)(k - 1)} T^2 = \frac{7 - 3 + 1}{6\,(2)} (80.298) = 33.45$$

c) When the analysis is run on SPSSX MANOVA the following univariate and multivariate results are obtained:

Univariate—Under AVERAGED TESTS OF SIGNIFICANCE

	SUM OF SQUARES	F	SIG OF F
WITHIN CELLS	10.095		
TREAT	92.571	55.02	.000

Multivariate—F = 33.402

Both of these results agree, within rounding error, with those calculated in (a) and (b).

d) The transformed variables used by SPSSX (in columns 2 and 3 of the TRANSFORMATION MATRIX) are

$$.70711y_1 - .70711y_3 \text{ and } -.40825y_1 + .8165y_2 - .40825y_3$$

The point this illustrates is that there are other choices, than adjacent difference variables, which will yield the same multivariate test statistic. This is due to the invariance property of the Hotelling T^2 statistic.

e) A pair of means is significantly different at the .05 level with the Tukey procedure if:

$$|\bar{y}_i - \bar{y}_j| > q_{.05;\ k,\ (n-1)(k-1)} \sqrt{\frac{MS_{res}}{n}}$$

Here, $q_{.05;3,12} = 3.773$ and $MS_{res} = .84127$ (from printout).
Thus, a pairs of means will be significantly different if

$$|\bar{y}_i - \bar{y}_j| > 3.773 \sqrt{\frac{.84127}{7}} = 1.308$$

The means are $\bar{y}_1 = 4.571$, $\bar{y}_2 = 7.143$ and $\bar{y}_3 = 2.0$.
The differences between each pair of means exceeds 1.308 in absolute value and hence all pairs of treatments differ.

4. The design would look as follows:

		Condition 1						Condition 2				
		Drug 1			Drug 2			Drug 1			Drug 2	
Dose	1	2	3	'1	2	3	1	2	3	1	2	3
	s_1 y_1	y_2	y_3	y_4	y_5	y_6	y_7	y_8	y_9	y_{10}	y_{11}	y_{12}
	s_2											
Gp1												
	s_8											
	s_9	. . . . . .			. . . . . .			. . . . .			. . .	
	s_{10}											
Gp 2												
	s_{16}											

Note that each subject is measured 12 times, so that there are 12 variables. The SPSSX MANOVA control lines now are:

TITLE ' GROUP BY CONDITION BY DRUG BY DOSE '
DATA LIST FREE/Y1 Y2 Y3 Y4 Y5 Y6 Y7 Y8 Y9 Y10 Y11 Y12 GPID
LIST

```
BEGIN DATA
    DATA LINES
END DATA
MANOVA Y1 TO Y12 BY GPID(1,2)/
    WSFACTOR = COND(2),DRUG(2),DOSE(3)/
    WSDESIGN/
    PRINT = TRANSFORM HOMOGENEITY (BOXM) ERROR(COR) SINGIF(AVERF)
    CELLINFO(MEANS)/
    ANALYSIS(REPEATED)/
    DESIGN/
```

6. b)

$$S = \begin{bmatrix} 4 & 3 & 2 \\ 3 & 5 & 2 \\ 2 & 2 & 6 \end{bmatrix} \begin{matrix} \bar{s}_i \\ 3 \\ 3.33 \\ 3.33 \end{matrix}$$

Here,

$$k = 3, \bar{s} = 3.222, \bar{s}_{ii} = (4 + 5 + 6)/3 = 5$$

$$\sum\sum s_{ij}^2 = 4^2 + 3^2 + 2^2 + \ldots + 2^2 + 6^2 = 111$$

$$\hat{\epsilon} = \frac{9 (5 - 3.222)^2}{2[111 - 2(3) \{9 + 11.09 + 11.09\} + 9 (10.381)]}$$

$$\hat{\epsilon} = \frac{28.45}{2[111 - 187.08 + 93.43]} = .82$$

7. Show that uniformity implies sphericity. Uniformity means that all the variances are equal, i.e.,

$$\sigma_{y_1}^2 = \sigma_{y_2}^2 = \ldots = \sigma_{y_k}^2 = \sigma^2$$

Uniformity also means that all the covariances are equal, i.e.,

$$\sigma_{y_1 y_2} = \sigma_{y_1 y_3} = \ldots = \sigma_{y_{k-1} y_k} = \sigma_{com}$$

The variance of the difference variable for ith and jth treatments is:

$$\sigma_{y_i - y_j}^2 = \sigma_{y_i}^2 + \sigma_{y_j}^2 - 2 \sigma_{y_i y_j}$$

But, from above, if uniformity holds then $\sigma_{y_i}^2 = \sigma_{y_j}^2$ and also $\sigma_{y_i y_j} = \sigma_{com}$. Thus, the variance for every difference variable is the same (which is the sphericity condition), namely $2\sigma^2 - 2 \sigma_{com}$.

8. The group effect is not significant at the .05 level ($F = .327$, $p < .580$). Which of the trends are significant at the .05 level for the DAYS main effect? From the printout we have:
    EFFECT . . . DAYS

Univariate F tests

Variable	F	Sig of F
Linear	343.86	.000
Quad	.14	.714
Cubic	129.13	.000
Quart	9.27	.012

From the above, the linear, cubic, and quartic trends are significant at .05. However, from the F ratios clearly the linear and cubic trends are most pronounced.

Are any of the univariate interactions (linear by group, etc.) significant at the .05 level?

From the printout we have:

EFFECT . . . GPID BY DAYS

Univariate F tests

Variable	F	Sig of F
Linear	5.45	.042
Quad	.14	.714
Cubic	.206	.659
Quart	1.91	.196

Thus, only the linear by group interaction is significant at .05. This means the slope of the lines is different for the 2 groups.

11. The design schematically would look as follows:

		Time 1					Time 2		
	Cr	Col	Ub	Gl		Cr	Col	Ub	Gl
Brand									
Belief	1 2 3 4 5 6 7 8 9 10 11 12 13 14 15 16 17 18 19 20 21 22 23 24								
AGE									
20–35									

M 36–50

51 & ↑

20–35

F 36–50

51 & ↑

Note that each subject is measured 24 times. Thus, there are 24 variables for the analysis.

Control lines for SPSSX MANOVA (2 between and 3 within variables)

```
TITLE ' SEX BY AGE BY TIME BY BRAND BY BELIEF '
DATA LIST FREE/ Y1 Y2 Y3 Y4 Y5 Y6 Y7 Y8 Y9 Y10 Y11 Y12 Y13 Y14 Y15 Y16 Y17
    Y18 Y19 Y20 Y21 Y22 Y23 Y24 SEX AGE
LIST
BEGIN DATA
    DATA LINES
END DATA
MANOVA Y1 TO Y24 BY SEX(1,2) AGE(1,3)/
  WSFACTOR = TIME(2),BRAND(4),BELIEF(3)/
  WSDESIGN/
  PRINT = TRANSFORM HOMOGENEITY(BOXM) SIGNIF(AVERF) CELLINFO(MEANS)/
  ANALYSIS(REPEATED)/
  DESIGN/
```

References

Ambrose, S. (1985). *The development and experimental application of programmed materials for teaching clarinet performance skills in college woodwind techniques courses.* Unpublished doctoral dissertation, University of Cincinnati.

Anderson, D. A. and Carney, E. S. (1974). Ridge regression estimation procedures applied to canonical correlation analysis. Unpublished manuscript, Cornell University.

Anscombe, V. (1973) Graphs in statistical analysis. *American Statistician, 27,* 17–21.

Barcikowski, R. and Stevens, J. P. (1975) A Monte Carlo study of the stability of canonical correlations, canonical weights and canonical variate-variable correlations. *Multivariate Behavioral Research,* 10, 353–364.

Barcikowski, R. S. (1981) Statistical power with group mean as the unit of analysis. *Journal of Educational Statistics,* 6, 267–285.

Barcikowski, R. S. (1983) *Computer packages and research design: Annotated output from BMDP.* University Press of America.

Barcikowski, R. S. (1983) *Computer packages and research design, Volume 3: SPSS and SPSSX,* Washington, D.C.: University Press of America.

Barcikowski, R. S. and Robey, R. R. (1984) Decisions in a single group repeated measures analysis: Statistical tests and three computer packages, *The American Statistician,* 38, 248–250.

Barnett, D., & Zucker, K. (1975) The others-concept and friendly and cooperative behavior in children. *Psychology in the Schools, 12,* 495–501.

Barnett, V. and Lewis, T. (1978). *Outliers in statistical data.* New York: Wiley.

Belsley, D. A., Kuh, E., and Welsch, R. (1980). *Regression diagnostics: Identifying influential data and sources of collinearity.* New York: Wiley.

Benton, S., Kraft, R., Goover, J. and Plake, B. (1984) Cognitive capacity differences among writers. *Journal of Educational Psychology,* 76, 820–834.

Bird, K. D. (1975) Simultaneous contrast testing procedures for multivariate experiments. *Multivariate Behavioral Research,* 10, 343–351.

BMDP (1983) BMDP statistical software. Berkeley: University of California Press.

Bock, R. D. (1975) *Multivariate statistical methods in behavioral research.* New York: McGraw-Hill.

Bock, R. D. and Haggard, Ed. (1968) The use of multivariate analysis of variance in behavioral research. In D. K. Whitla (ed.), *Handbook of measurement and assessment in behavioral sciences.* Reading, Massachusetts: Addison Wesley.

Boik, R. J. (1981). A priori tests in repeated measures design: Effects of nonsphericity. *Psychometrika,* 46, 241–255.

Bolton, B. (1971) A factor analytical study of communication skills and nonverbal abilities of deaf rehabilitation clients. *Multivariate Behavioral Research,* 6, 485–501.

Box, G. E. P. (1954). Some theorems on quadratic forms applied in the study of analysis of variance problems: II. Effect of inequality of variance and of correlation between errors in the two-way classification. *Annals of Mathematical Statistics*, 25, 484–498.

Bradley, R., Caldwell, B. and Elardo, R. (1977) Home environment, social status and mental test performance. *Journal of Educational Psychology*, 69, 697–701.

Browne, M. W. (1968) A comparison of factor analytic techniques. *Psychometrika*. 33, 267–334.

Bryant, J. L. and Paulson, A. S. (1976) An extension of Tukey's method of multiple comparisons to experimental designs with random concomitant variables. *Biometrika*, 631-638.

Burket, G. R. (1964) A study of reduced rank models for multiple prediction. *Journal of Educational Psychology*, 69, 697–701.

Carlson, J. E. and Timm, N. H. (1974) Analysis of non-orthogonal fixed effects designs. *Psychological Bulletin*, 81, 563–570.

Cattell, R. B. (1966) The meaning and strategic use of factor analysis. In R. B. Cattell (ed.) *Handbook of multivariate experimental psychology*. Chicago, Rand McNally, 174–243.

Cattell, R. B. and Jaspers, J. A. (1967) A general plasmode for factor analytic exercises and research. *Multivariate Behavioral Research Monographs*.

Cliff, N. and Hamburger, C. D. (1967) The study of sampling errors in factor analysis by means of artificial experiments. *Psychological Bulletin*, 68, 430–445.

Cliff, N. and Krus. D. J. (1976) Interpretation of canonical analysis: Rotated vs unrotated solutions. *Psychometrika*. 41, 35–42.

Clifford, M. M. (1972) Effects of competition as a motivational technique in the classroom. *American Educational Research Journal*. 9, 123–134.

Cochran, W. G. (1957) Analysis of covariance: Its nature and uses. *Biometrics*. 13, 261–281.

Cohen, J. (1968) Multiple regression as a general data-analytic system. *Psychological Bulletin*. 70, 426–443.

Cohen, J. and Cohen, P. (1975) *Applied multiple regression/correlation analysis for the behavioral sciences*. Hillsdale, New Jersey: Lawrence Erlbaum.

Cohen, J. (1977). *Statistical power analysis for the behavioral sciences*. New York, New York: Academic Press.

Cohen, J. and Cohen, P. (1983) *Applied multiple regression/correlation analysis for the behavioral sciences*. Hillsdale, New Jersey: Lawrence Erlbaum and Associates.

Collier, R. O., Baker, F. B. (1967) Mandeville, C. K. and Hayes, T. F. Estimates of test size for several test procedures on conventional variance ratios in the repeated measures design, *Psychometrika*, 32, 339–353.

Comrey, A. L. (1985). A method for removing outliers to improve factor analytic results. *Multivariate Behavioral Research*, 20, 273–281.

Conover, W. J., Johnson, M. E., & Johnson, M. M. (1981) Composite study of tests for homogeneity of variances, with applications to the outer continental shelf bidding data. *Technometrics, 23*, 351–361.

Cook, R. D. and Weisberg, S. (1982). *Residuals and influence in regression*. New York: Chapman and Hall.

Cooley, W. W. and Lohnes, P. R. (1971) *Multivariate data analysis*. New York: Wiley.

Cramer, E. and Nicewander, W. A. (1979) Some symmetric, invariant measures of multivariate association. *Psychometrika*, 44, 43–54.

Crocker, L. and Benson, J. (1976) Achievement, guessing and risk-taking behavior under norm referenced and criterion referenced testing conditions. *American Educational Research Journal*. 13, 207–215.

Cronbach, L. J. (1975) Beyond the two disciplines of scientific psychology. *The American Psychologist*, 30, 116–127.

Cronbach, L. and Snow, R. (1977) Aptitudes and instructional methods. New York: Irvington Press.

Crowder, R. (1975) An investigation of the relationship between social I.Q. and vocational evaluation ratings with an adult trainable mental retardate work activity center population. Unpublished doctoral dissertation, University of Cincinnati.

D'Agostino, R. B. and Tietjen, G. L. (1971) Simulation probability points of b_2 in small samples. *Biometrika*, 58, 669–672.

D'Agostino, R. B. and Tietjen, G. L. (1973) Approaches to the null distribution of b_1. *Biometrika*, 60, 169–173.

Daniel, C. and Wood, F. S. (1971) *Fitting equations to data*. New York: Wiley.

Daniels, R. L. and Stevens, J. P. (1976) The interaction between the internal-external locus of control and two methods of college instruction. *American Educational Research Journal*, 13, 103–113.

Darlington, R. B., Weinberg, S. and Walberg, H. (1973) Canonical variate analysis and related techniques. *Review of Educational Research*, 43, 433–454.

Davidson, M. L. (1972) Univariate versus multivariate tests in repeated measures experiments. *Psychological Bulletin*, 77, 446–452.

Draper, N. R. and Smith, H. (1981). *Applied regression analysis*. New York: Wiley.

Dizney, H. and Gromen, L. (1967) Predictive validity and differential achievement on three MLA Comparative Foreign Language tests. *Educational and Psychological Measurement*, 27, 1127–1130.

Dunnett, C. W. (1980) Pairwise multiple comparisons in the homogeneous variance, unequal sample size cases. *Journal of the American Statistical Association*, 75, 789–795.

Edwards, D. S. (1984) *Analysis of faculty perceptions of deans' leadership behavior and organizational climate in baccalaureate schools of nursing*. Unpublished doctoral dissertation. University of Cincinnati.

Elashoff, J. D. (1969) Analysis of covariance: A delicate instrument. *American Educational Research Journal*, 6, 383–401.

Elashoff, J. D. (1981) Data for the panel session in software for repeated measures analysis of variance. *Proceedings of the Statistical Computing Section*, American Statistical Association.

Everitt, B. S. A Monte Carlo investigation of the robustness of Hotelling's one and two sample T^2 tests. *Journal of the American Statistical Association*, 1979, 74, 48–51.

Feshbach, S., Adelman, H. and Williamson, F. (1977) Prediction of reading and related academic problems. *Journal of Educational Psychology*, 69, 299–308.

Finn, J. (1974) *A general model for multivariate analysis*. New York: Holt, Rinehart and Winston.

Finn, J. (1978) Multivariance: Univariate and multivariate analysis of variance, covariance and regression. National Educational Resources, Chicago, Illinois.

Fisher, R. A. (1936) The use of multiple measurement in taxonomic problems. *Annals of Eugenics*, 7, 179–188.

Friedman, G., Lehrer, B., and Stevens, J. (1983) The effectiveness of self directed and lecture/discussion stress management approaches and the locus of control of teachers. *American Educational Research Journal*, 20, 563–580.

Gary, H. E. (1981) The effects of departures from circularity on type I error rates and power for randomized block factorial experimental designs. Unpublished doctoral dissertation, Baylor University.

Gemunder, C. (1979) The relationship of generalized expectancies to school achievement in low socioeconomic class students. Unpublished doctoral dissertation, University of Cincinnati.

Glassnapp, D. and Poggio, J. (1985). *Essentials of statistical analysis for the behavioral sciences*. Columbus, Ohio: Charles Merrill.

Glass, G. V. and Hopkins K. (1984) *Statistical methods in education and psychology*. Englewood Cliffs: Prentice-Hall.

Glass, G. C. and Stanley, J. C. (1970) *Statistical methods in education and psychology*. Englewood Cliffs, Prentice-Hall.

Gnanadesikan R. (1977) *Methods for statistical analysis of multivariate observations*. New York: Wiley.

Golding, S. and Seidman, E. (1974) Analysis of multitrait-multimethod matrices: A two step principal components procedure. *Multivariate Behavioral Research*, 9, 479–496.

Gorsuch, R. L. (1983) *Factor analysis*. Hillsdale, New Jersey: Lawrence Erlbaum.

Greenhouse, S. W. and Geisser, S. (1959) On methods in the analysis of profile data, *Psychometrika,* 24, 95–112.

Griesinger, W. (1977) Short term group counseling of parents of handicapped children. Unpublished doctoral dissertation, University of Cincinnati.

Guttman, L. (1941). Mathematical and tabulation techniques. Supplementary study B. In P. Horst (Ed.). *Prediction of personnel adjustment.* New York: Social Science Research Council.

Hakstian, A. R. (1971) A comparative evaluation of several prominent methods of oblique factor transformation. *Psychometrika,* 36, 175–193.

Hakstian, A. R., Roed, J. C. and Lind, J. C. (1979) Two sample T^2 procedures and the assumption of homogeneous covariance matrices. *Psychological Bulletin.* 86, 1255–1263.

Hakstian, A. R., Rogers, W. D. and Cattell, R. B. (1982) The behavior of numbers factors rules with simulated data. *Multivariate Behavioral Research.* 17, 193–219.

Harman, H. (1983) *Modern factor analysis.* University of Chicago Press.

Harris, R. J. (1976) The invalidity of partitioned U tests in canonical correlation and multivariate analysis of variance. *Multivariate Behavioral Research.* 11, 353–365.

Hays, W. L. (1981) *Statistics* (3rd edition). New York, Holt, Rinehart and Winston.

Hawkins, D. M. (1976) The subset problem in multivariate analysis of variance. *Journal of the Royal Statistical Society* 38, 132–139.

Herzberg, P. A. (1969) The parameters of cross validation. *Psychometrika,* Monograph supplement, No. 16.

Hoaglin, D., and Welsch, R. (1978). The hat matrix in regression and ANOVA. *American Statistician,* 32, 17–22.

Hoerl, A. E. and Kennard, W. (1970). Ridge regression: Biased estimation for non-orthogonal problems. *Techometrics.* 12, 55–67.

Hogg, R. V. (1979). Statistical robustness. One view of its use in application today. *American Statistician,* 33, 108–115.

Holland, J. L. (1966) *The psychology of vocational choice.* Waltham, Massachusetts: Blaisdell.

Holloway, L. N. and Dunn, O. J. (1967) The robustness of Hotelling's T^2. *Journal of the American Statistical Association,* 124–136.

Hopkins, J. W. and Clay, P. P. F. (1963) Some empirical distributions of bivariate T^2 and homoscedasticity criterion M under unequal variance and leptokurtosis. *Journal of the American Statistical Association,* 58, 1048–1053.

Hotelling, H. (1931) The generalization of Student's ratio. *Annals of Mathematical Statistics,* 360–378.

Huber, P. (1977) *Robust statistical procedures* (No. 27, Regional conference series in applied mathematics), Philadelphia, Pennsylvania: SIAM.

Huberty, C. J. (1975) The stability of three indices of relative variable contribution in discriminant analysis. *Journal of Experimental Education,* 59–64.

Huberty, C. J. (1984) Issues in the use and interpretation of discriminant analysis. *Psychological Bulletin,* 95, 156–171.

Huck, S., Cormier, W. and Bounds, W. (1974) *Reading statistics and research.* New York: Harper and Row.

Huitema, B. (1980) *The analysis of covariance and alternatives.* New York: Wiley.

Hummel, T. J. and Sligo, J. (1971) Empirical comparison of univariate and multivariate analysis of variance procedures. *Psychological Bulletin,* 76, 49–57.

Huynh, H. and Feldt, L. S. (1970) Conditions under which mean square ratios in repeated measurements designs have exact F distributions, *Journal of the American Statistical Association,* 65, 1582–1589.

Ito, K. (1962). A comparison of the powers of two MANOVA tests. *Biometrika,* 49, 455–462.

James, W. & Stein, C. (1961) Estimation with quadratic loss. In *Proceedings of the Fourth Berkeley Symposium on Mathematical statistics and Probability,* Vol. 1. Berkeley: University of California, 361–379.

Johnson, N. and Wichern, D. (1982) *Applied multivariate statistical analysis.* Englewood Cliffs,

New Jersey: Prentice-Hall.

Kaiser, H. F. (1960) The application of electronic computers to factor analysis. *Educational and Psychological Measurement,* 1960, 20, 141–151.

Keppel, G. (1983) *Design and Analysis: A researchers' handbook.* Englewood Cliffs, New Jersey: Prentice-Hall.

Kerlinger, F. and Pedhazur, E. (1973) *Multiple regression in behavioral research.* New York: Holt, Rinehart and Winston.

Keselman, H. J., Murray, R. and Rogan, J. (1976) Effect of very unequal group sizes on Tukey's multiple comparison test. *Educational and Psychological Measurement.*

Keselman, H. J., Rogan, J. C., Mendoza, J. L., & Breen, L. L. (1980) Testing the validity conditions of repeated measures F tests. *Psychological bulletin,* 87, 479–481.

Kirk, R. E. (1982) *Experimental design: Procedures for the behavioral sciences.* Belmont, California: Brooks-Cole.

Krasker, W. S. and R. E. Welsch. (1979). Estimation with quadratic loss. In *Proceedings of the Fourth Berkeley Symposium on Mathematical Statistics and Probability,* Vol. 1. Berkeley: University of California, 361–379.

Kvet, E. (1982) Excusing elementary students from regular classroom activities for the study of instrumental music: The effect on sixth grade reading, language and mathematics achievement. Unpublished doctoral dissertation, University of Cincinnati.

Lachenbruch, P. A. (1967) An almost unbiased method of obtaining confidence intervals for the probability of misclassification in discriminant analysis. *Biometrics,* 23, 639–645.

Lauter, J. (1978) Sample size requirements for the T^2 test of MANOVA (Tables for One-Way Classification). *Biometrical Journal,* 20, 389–406.

Lawley, D. N. (1940) The estimation of factor loadings by the method of maximum likelihood. *Proceedings of the Royal Society of Edinburgh.* 60: 64.

Lehrer, B., and Schimoler, G. (1975) Cognitive skills underlying an inductive problem-solving strategy. *Journal of Experimental Education.* 43, 13–21.

Lindeman, R. H., Merenda, P. F. and Gold, R. Z. (1980) *Introduction to bivariate and multivariate analysis.* Glenview, Illinois: Scott, Foresman.

Linn, R. L. (1968) A Monte Carlo approach to the number of factors problem. *Psychometrika.* 33, 37–71.

Lohnes, P. R. (1961) Test space and discriminant space classification models and related significance tests. *Educational and Psychological Measurement.* 21, 559–574.

Lord, R. and Novick, M. (1968) *Statistical theories of mental test scores.* Reading, Massachusetts: Addison-Wesley.

Mallows, C. L. (1973) Some comments on Cp. *Technometrics,* 15, 661–676.

Mardia, K. V. (1971) The effect of non-normality on some multivariate tests and robustness to non-normality in the linear model. *Biometrika.* 58, 105–121.

Maxwell, S. E. (1980) Pairwise multiple comparisons in repeated measures designs, *Journal of Educational Statistics,* 5, 269–287.

McNeil, K. and Karr, S. (1972) Brief report: Psycholinguistic performance as an indicator of modernization. *Multivariate Behavioral Research,* 7, 397–399.

Mendoza, J. L., Markos, V. H. and Gonter, R. (1978) A new perspective on sequential testing procedures in canonical analysis: A Monte Carlo evaluation. *Multivariate Behavioral Research.* 13, 371–382.

Meredith, W. (1964) Canonical correlation with fallible data. *Psychometrika.* 29, 55–65.

Merenda, P., Novack, H. and Bonaventura, E. (1976) Multivariate analysis of the California test of mental maturity, primary forms. *Psychological Reports.* 38, 487–493.

Meyer, P. (1965) *Introductory probability and statistical applications.* Addison-Wesley.

Miller, R. (1977) Developments in multiple comparisons, 1966–1976. *Journal of the American Statistical Association,* 72, 779–788.

Morris, J. D. (1982) Ridge regression and some alternative weighting techniques: A comment on

Darlington. *Psychological Bulletin,* 91, 203–210.

Morrison, D. F. (1976). *Multivariate statistical methods.* New York: McGraw-Hill.

Morrison, D. F. (1983) *Applied linear statistical methods.* Englewood Cliffs, New Jersey: Prentice-Hall.

Mosteller, F. and Tukey, J. W. (1977). *Data analysis and regression.* Reading, Massachusetts: Addison-Wesley.

Myers, J. L. (1979) *Fundamentals of experimental design.* Boston: Allyn and Bacon.

Nold, E. and Freedman, S. (1977) An analysis of readers' responses to essays, *Research in English Education.*

Novince, L. (1977) The contribution of cognitive restructuring to the effectiveness of behavior rehearsal in modifying social inhibition in females. Unpublished doctoral dissertation, University of Cincinnati.

Nunnally, J. (1978). *Psychometric Theory.* New York: McGraw-Hill.

O'Brien, R. and Kaiser, M. (1985) MANOVA method for analyzing repeated measures designs: An extensive primer. *Psychological Bulletin,* 316–333.

O'Grady, K. (1982) Measures of explained variation: Cautions and limitations. *Psychological Bulletin.* 92, 766–777.

Olson, C. L. (1974) Comparative robustness of six tests in multivariate analysis of variance. *Journal of the American Statistical Association,* 69, 894–908.

Olson, C. L. (1976) On choosing a test statistic in MANOVA. *Psychological Bulletin.* 83, 579–586.

Overall, J. E. and Spiegel, D. K. (1969). Concerning least squares analysis of experimental data. *Psychological Bulletin.* 72, 311–322.

Park, C. and Dudycha, A. (1974). A cross validation approach to sample size determination for regression models. *Journal of the American Statistical Association.* 69, 214–218.

Pedhazur, E. (1982) *Multiple regression in behavioral research* (second edition). New York: Holt, Rinehart and Winston.

Pillai, K. and Jayachandian, K. (1967) Power comparisons of tests of two multivariate hypotheses based on four criteria. *Biometrika,* 54, 195–210.

Plante, T. and Goldfarb, L. (1984) Concurrent validity for an activity vector analysis index of social adjustment. *Journal of Clinical Psychology,* 40, 1215–1218.

Pope, J., Lehrer, B. and Stevens, J. P. (1980) A multiphasic reading screening procedure. *Journal of Learning Disabilities.* 13,98–102.

Porebski, O. R. (1966) Discriminatory and canonical analysis of technical college data. *British Journal of Mathematical and Statistical Psychology.* 19, 215–236.

Press, S. J. and Wilson, S. (1978) Choosing between logistic regression and discriminant analysis. *Journal of the American Statistical Association,* 7, 699–705.

Pruzek, R. M. (1971) Methods and problems in the analysis of multivariate data. *Review of Educational Research.* 41, 163–190.

Rencher, A. C. and Larson, S. F. (1980) Bias in Wilk's Λ in stepwise discriminant analysis. *Technometrics.* 22, 349–356.

Rogan, J. C., Keselman, H. J. and Mendoza, J. L. (1979) Analysis of repeated measurements. *British Journal of Mathematical and Statistical Psychology.* 32, 269–286.

Rogosa, D. (1977) Some results for the Johnson-Neyman technique. Doctoral dissertation, Stanford University.

Rogosa, D. (1980) Comparing non-parallel regression lines. *Psychological Bulletin.*

Rosenthal, R. and Rosnow, R. (1984) *Essentials of behavioral research.* New York: McGraw-Hill.

Rouanet, H. and Lepine, D. (1970) Comparison between treatments in a repeated measures design: ANOVA and multivariate methods. *British Journal of Mathematical and Statistical Psychology,* 23, 147–163.

Roy, S. N. and Bose, R. C. (1953) Simultaneous confidence interval estimation. *Annals of Math-*

ematical Statistics. 24, 513–536.

Roy, J. and Bargmann, R. E. (1958) Tests of multiple independence and the associated confidence bounds. *Annals of Mathematical Statistics.* 29, 491–503.

Rummel, R. J. (1970) *Applied factor analysis.* Evanston: Northwestern University Press.

SAS Institute, Inc. (1985) *SAS user's guide: Statistics.* Cary, N.C.: SAS Institute, Inc.

Scandura, T. (1984) Multivariate analysis of covariance for a study of the effects of leadership training on work outcomes. Unpublished research paper, University of Cincinnati.

Schutz, W. (1977) Leaders of schools: FIRO theory applied to administrators. La Jolla, California: University Associates.

Shanahan, T. (1984) Nature of the reading-writing relation: An exploratory multivariate analysis. *Journal of Educational Psychology.* 76, 466–477.

Sharp, G. (1981) Acquisition of lecturing skills by university teaching assistants: Some effects of interest, topic relevance and viewing a model videotape. *American Educational Research Journal,* 18, 491–502.

Shin, S. H. (1971) Creativity, intelligence and achievement; A study of the relationship between creativity and intelligence, and their effects on achievement. Unpublished doctoral dissertation, University of Pittsburgh.

Skilbeck, W., Acosta, F., Yamamoto, J. and Evans, L. (1984) Self reported psychiatric symptoms among black, hispanic and white outpatients. *Journal of Clinical Psychology,* 40, 1184–1192.

Smart, J. C. (1976) Duties performed by department chairmen in Holland's model environments. *Journal of Educational Psychology.* 68, 194–204.

Smith, A. H. (1975) A multivariate study of factor analyzed predictors of death anxiety in college students. Unpublished doctoral dissertation, University of Cincinnati.

Smith, G. and Campbell, F. (1980). A critique of some ridge regression methods. *Journal of the American Statistical Association,* 75, 74–81.

SPSS, Inc. (1983) *SPSSX user's guide.* New York: McGraw-Hill.

Stevens, J. P. (1972) Four methods of analyzing between variation for the k group MANOVA problem. *Multivariate Behavioral Research.* 7, 499–522.

Stevens, J. P. (1979) Comment on Olson: Choosing a test statistic in multivariate analysis of variance. *Psychological Bulletin,* 86, 355–360.

Stevens, J. P. (1980) Power of the multivariate analysis of variance tests. *Psychological Bulletin.* 88, 728–737.

Steiger, J. H. (1979) Factor indeterminancy in the 1930's and the 1970's: Some interesting parallels. *Psychometrika,* 44, 157–167.

Stewart, D., & Love, W. (1968). A general canonical correlation index. *Psychological Bulletin,* 70, 160–163.

Stoloff, P. H. May, 1967. An empirical evaluation of the effects of violating the assumption of homogeneity of covariance for the repeated measures design of the analysis of variance. University of Maryland, Technical Report.

Tatsuoka, M. M. (1971) *Multivariate analysis: Techniques for educational and psychological research.* New York: Wiley.

Tatsuoka, M. M. (1973) Multivariate analysis in behavioral research. In F. Kerlinger (ed.) *Review of Research in Education.* Itasca, Illinois: F. F. Peacock.

Tetenbaum, T. (1975) The role of student needs and teacher orientations in student ratings of teachers. *American Educational Research Journal.* 12, 417–433.

Timm, N. H. (1975) *Multivariate analysis with applications in education and psychology.* Monterey, California: Brooks-Cole.

Tucker, L. R., Koopman, R. F., and Linn, R. L. (1969) Evaluation of factor analytic research procedures by means of simulated correlation matrices. *Psychometrika.* 34, 421–459.

Weinberg, S. L., & Darlington, R. B. (1976). Canonical analysis when the number of variables is large relative to sample size. *The Journal of Educational Statistics, 1,* 313–332.

Weisberg, S. (1985). *Applied linear regression.* New York: Wiley.

Wilk, H. B., Shapiro, S. S. and Chen, H. J. (1965) A comparative study of various tests of normality. *Journal of the American Statistical Association.* 63, 1343–1372.

Wilkinson, L. (1979). Tests of significance in stepwise regression. *Psychological Bulletin,* 86, 168–174.

Winer, B. J. (1971) *Statistical principles in experimental design* (2nd edition) New York: McGraw-Hill.

Yao, Y. (1965) An approximate degree of freedom solution to the multivariate Behrens-Fisher problem. *Biometrika,* 52, 139–147.

Zwick, R. (1985) Nonparametric one-way multivariate analysis of variance: A computational approach based on the Pillai-Bartlett trace. *Psychological Bulletin,* 97, 148–152.

Author Index

Subject Index